ROBERT MOSES
AND THE
MODERN CITY
THE
TRANSFORMATION
OF
NEW YORK

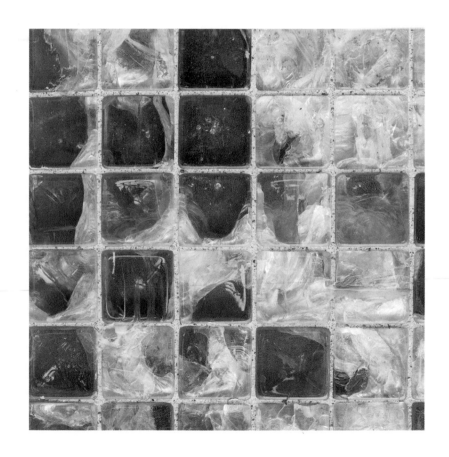

ROBERT MOSES AND THE MODERN CITY

THE TRANSFORMATION OF NEW YORK

EDITED BY
HILARY BALLON AND
KENNETH T. JACKSON

W. W. Norton & Company
NEW YORK · LONDON

The publication has been generously supported by the National Endowment for the Arts, the New York State Council on the Arts, Graham Foundation for Advanced Studies in the Fine Arts, and Furthermore: a program of the J.M. Kaplan Fund.

This book is published in conjunction with the three-part exhibition "Robert Moses and the Modern City":

"Remaking the Metropolis"
Museum of the City of New York
January 27 through May 6, 2007

"The Road to Recreation"
Queens Museum of Art
January 28 through May 13, 2007 and

"Slum Clearance and the Superblock Solution"
Miriam and Ira D. Wallach Art Gallery, Columbia University
January 30 through April 14, 2007

Managing editor: Sarah Elliston Weiner, Wallach Art Gallery
Photo editor: Jeanette E. Silverthorne, Wallach Art Gallery

Book design: Abigail Sturges
Production manager: Leeann Graham
Manufacturing: Colorprint Offset

Page 1. Astoria Pool, glass block, detail of the pool house, Astoria, Queens, 2005. Photograph by Andrew Moore

Pages 2–3. Highbridge Pool and water tower, Washington Heights, Manhattan, 2005. Photograph by Andrew Moore

Library of Congress Cataloging-in-Publication Data

Robert Moses and the modern city : the transformation of New York / edited by Hilary Ballon and Kenneth T. Jackson.
    p. cm.
    Includes bibliographical references and index.
    ISBN 13: 978-0-393-73206-1 (hardcover)
    ISBN 10: 0-393-73206-1 (hardcover)
    1. Moses, Robert, 1888-1981. 2. City planners–New York (State)–New York–History–20th century. 3. Municipal officials and employees–New York (State)–New York–History–20th century. 4. Public works–New York (State)–New York–History–20th century. 5. New York (State)–New York–History–20th century. I. Ballon, Hilary. II. Jackson, Kenneth T.

  NA9085.M68R64 2007
  711'.4092–dc22
                                    2006037123
  ISBN 13: 978-0-393-73206-1
  ISBN 13: 978-0-393-73243-6 (pbk)

W. W. Norton & Company, Inc.
500 Fifth Avenue, New York, N.Y. 10110
www.wwnorton.com

W. W. Norton & Company Ltd.
Castle House, 75/76 Wells Street, London W1T 3QT

0 9 8 7 6 5 4 3 2 1

CONTENTS

ACKNOWLEDGMENTS

This book is published in conjunction with "Robert Moses and the Modern City," a three-part exhibition, and, as exhibition curator, my first debt is to the co-organizing institutions. "The Road to Recreation" appears at the Queens Museum of Art, where Moses remains a palpable presence. He created Flushing Meadows–Corona Park, the site of the museum, and was responsible for the highways that now encircle it like a moat. The museum is housed in the New York City Pavilion, designed by Aymar Embury II, Moses's preferred architect, and built for the World's Fair of 1939, in which Moses played a leading role. The large-scale model of New York City that Moses had made for the World's Fair of 1964–65 is a major attraction of the permanent collection. Tom Finkelpearl, the director of the museum, Valerie Smith, David Dean, and Lauren Schloss, an outstanding team, have a keen interest in their historic landscape and in making it accessible to new generations of New Yorkers. With the assistance of Queens Borough President Helen Marshall and the New York City Council, the museum is supported in part by public funds from the New York City Department of Cultural Affairs, the New York City Department for the Aging, and the New York City Department of Youth and Community Development. Additional funding is provided by the New York State Legislature, the New York State Council on the Arts, New York Council on the Humanities, National Endowment for the Arts, the Institute for Museum and Library Services, generous corporate and foundation supporters, and members and friends.

The Museum of the City of New York is hosting "Remaking the Metropolis." I am grateful to the director, Susan Henshaw Jones for her commitment to this project and for the opportunity to work with Sarah Henry, Emerson Beyer, Susan Johnson, and Kate Louis. The exhibition is made possible by contributions from Susan and Roger Hertog, the Lily Auchincloss Foundation, Mr. Steven Roth, Studley Inc., The Durst Organization, Deban and Tom Flexner, Mr. David Rockefeller, the General Contractors Association of New York Inc., the Richard Ravitch Foundation, the New York Building Congress, and the New York Council for the Humanities, a state affiliate of the National Endowment for the Humanities. Any views, findings, conclusions or recommendations expressed in the exhibition do not necessarily represent those of the National Endowment for the Humanities.

"Slum Clearance and the Superblock Solution" is presented at the Miriam and Ira D. Wallach Art Gallery of Columbia University, my home base. I can not overstate my gratitude to Sarah Elliston Weiner for her work as both gallery director and managing editor of this volume, which involved preparing the writings of nineteen authors for publication. Her attention to detail, intelligence, and good judgment have improved every aspect of the book. The extensive illustration program was coordinated by Jeanette Silverthorne, who deftly resolved countless issues involved in collecting the more than two hundred images in these pages. We remain ever indebted to Miriam and Ira D. Wallach for their generous support of the gallery.

The book begins with a portfolio of photographs by Andrew Moore, commissioned for the exhibition. The impact of a structure is best understood over time. The purpose of the commission was to record how Moses's structures were faring in the living city. Andrew Moore embraced this challenge and over a period of two years enthusiastically wandered the five boroughs, aiming his sharp eye at sites built by Moses.

The historical reinterpretation of Moses took off with an essay in 1989 by Kenneth T. Jackson, master historian of New York City. His broad view of urban history and incisive formulation of key questions have sharpened my perspective and enriched this project in vital ways. In addition to co-editing this volume, we taught a seminar at Columbia where the students undertook fascinating research, and, with support from the Herbert H. Lehman Center for American History, we convened a planning symposium that allowed the essayists to vet their arguments and other scholars to share their related research.

My research was supported by a sabbatical in 2004–5 as a Mel and Lois Tukman Fellow at the Dorothy and Lewis B. Cullman Center for Scholars and Writers of the New York Public Library, where the director, Jean Strouse and a remarkable group of fellows created an ideal working environment. I spent a good portion of the year poring through the Robert Moses Papers in the Manuscripts and Archives Division. My thanks to the librarians and to Paul LeClerc, the president of this remarkable and essential New York institution.

I would like to acknowledge the assistance I received during research campaigns at a variety of institutions and archives and from individuals who assisted in various ways: Sony Onishi, John Mattera, and Steve Rizick at the New York City Department of Parks and Recreation; Laura Rosen at the MTA Bridges and Tunnels Special Archive; Janet Parks and Julie Tozer at Avery Architectural and Fine Arts Library, Drawings and Archives, Columbia University; Judith Johnson at the Archives of Lincoln Center for the Performing Arts; Katherine Drake and Dwidson Metayer at Pei Cobb Freed & Partners; Richard Lane of the Olnick Organization; Karen Hecht; and many other institutions that are lending materials for the exhibitions. James Becker was an exceptional research assistant. Kate Louis applied her talents to many aspects of this project and was nothing short of indispensable, and Marta Gutman, with whom I visited the pools and inspected construction drawings, has been an ongoing interlocutor. The strength of a collaborative book comes from the varied perspectives and expertise of the authors. I am grateful to the fine scholars who have enriched this volume.

Publication of the book is supported by grants from the National Endowment for the Arts, the New York State Council on the Arts, Furthermore: a program of the J. M. Kaplan Fund, and the Graham Foundation for Advanced Studies in the Fine Arts. Abigail Sturges skillfully designed the book. It has benefited from the unerring judgment, intelligence, and conviction of a remarkable editor at W. W. Norton, Nancy Green. Working with her is a privilege.

Finally, the three people impossible to thank. I have mined my husband's knowledge of urban finance and public policy and lured my children to join me on countless Moses expeditions. I dedicate my share of this book to Orin, Sophie, and Charles Kramer. — HB

ROBERT MOSES PROJECTS

A Portfolio of Photographs

ANDREW MOORE

SUNSET POOL
Sunset Park, Brooklyn

P-1. Entry pavilion on
the pool side, 2005

P-2. View from the entry
pavilion, 2005

FACING PAGE
P-3. Ceiling of the entry
pavilion, 2005

ASTORIA POOL
Astoria, Queens

P-4. Canopy above the filtration room, 2005

P-5. Entrance to the women's locker room, 2005

P-6. Diving pool, with the Triborough Bridge, 2005

BETSY HEAD POOL
Brownsville, Brooklyn

P-7. Pool and recreation center, 2005

FACING PAGE
P-8. Men's locker room, 2005

BETSY HEAD POOL

Brownsville, Brooklyn

P-9. Viewing stand and roof
structure, 2005

FOLLOWING PAGES
P-10. Pool and athletic field,
2005

CROTONA POOL

East Tremont, Bronx

P-11. Entrance, 2006

CROTONA POOL
East Tremont, Bronx

P-12. Women's locker room, 2005

FACING PAGE
P-13. Pool, 2005

CROTONA POOL
East Tremont, Bronx

P-14. Entry tower, 2006

P-15. Side view of the pool house, 2006

P-16. Window mullion in the form of a pelican, 2006

FACING PAGE
P-17. Entry pavilion brickwork, 2005

JACKIE ROBINSON
RECREATION CENTER
Harlem, Manhattan

P-18. Entrance, 2005

P-19. Capital, 2006

FACING PAGE
P-20. Lobby, 2005

JACKIE ROBINSON RECREATION CENTER

Harlem, Manhattan

P-21. Pool, 2005

FOLLOWING PAGES
P-22. Park on 145th Street,
2005

JACKIE ROBINSON PARK
Harlem, Manhattan

P-23. Band shell, 2006

McCARREN POOL

Greenpoint, Brooklyn

P-24. Entrance, 2006

P-25. Cornerstone, 2006

P-26. View of the entry pavilion from the pool, 2006

ORCHARD BEACH

Pelham Bay Park, Bronx

P-28. Arcade shop, 2005

FACING PAGE
P-29. Colonnade, 2005

ORCHARD BEACH
Pelham Bay Park, Bronx

P-30. Rear view of the main
structure, 2005

P-31. Entrance to the
women's locker room, 2005

FACING PAGE
P-32. Stairwell and niche,
2005

RIVERSIDE PARK
Manhattan

P-33. Athletic fields along the Henry Hudson River, 2006

P-34. Athletic fields, 2006

CROSS-BRONX EXPRESSWAY

P-35. View west from the Grand Concourse, 2006

P-36. View east at the Jerome Avenue overpass (day), 2006

P-37. View east at the Jerome Avenue overpass (night), 2006

MORNINGSIDE GARDENS

Morningside Heights, Manhattan

P-38. View west, 2005

FACING PAGE
P-39. View north, with General Grant
Houses in the background, 2005

LENOX TERRACE

Harlem, Manhattan

FACING PAGE
P-40. View of 132nd Street, 2006

P-41. Entrance of 40 West 135th Street, 2006

KIPS BAY PLAZA
Kips Bay, Manhattan

P-42. View west of the north building, 2005

FACING PAGE
P-43. Entrance of the north building, 2005

FOLLOWING PAGES
P-44. Facade detail, 2005

P-45. Lobby of the north building, 2005

WASHINGTON SQUARE VILLAGE

Greenwich Village, Manhattan

P-46. View north from Silver Towers, 2005

WASHINGTON SQUARE VILLAGE

Greenwich Village, Manhattan

P-47. Garden facade of the north building,
2006

SILVER TOWERS AND 110 BLEECKER STREET

Greenwich Village, Manhattan

P-48. View south from Bleecker Street along Wooster
Street, 2006

LINCOLN TOWERS

Manhattan

P-49. View north from 66th Street
and West End Avenue, 2006

P-50. View west from Amsterdam Avenue, 2006

CHATHAM GREEN

Civic Center, Manhattan

P-51. View west from Madison Street,
2005

CHATHAM TOWERS

Civic Center, Manhattan

P-52. View from Chatham
Square, 2005

Robert Moses, 1938.
Photograph by Fernand
Bourges, for *Fortune*
magazine

INTRODUCTION

HILARY BALLON AND KENNETH T. JACKSON

Robert Moses (1888–1981) had a greater impact on the physical character of New York City than any other individual, and given how the process of city building has changed since his time, it is unlikely anyone in the future will match him. Moses fits with New York's distinguished history of daring, large-scale public works: the Commissioner's plan of 1811 that devised Manhattan's grid, the Croton water supply system, the Brooklyn Bridge, the parks of Frederick Law Olmsted, the subway, and now a new water tunnel. They demonstrate the city's capacity to organize private and public actors in the face of collective dangers and to develop an infrastructure of shared resources to keep the city strong. Yet even in the context of this heroic city-building tradition, Moses is in a league of his own.

Moses's reign as building maestro in New York City extended from 1934, when Mayor Fiorello La Guardia appointed him the first city-wide commissioner of parks, to 1968, when the Triborough Bridge and Tunnel Authority merged with the MTA and Moses was ousted as chairman. During that thirty-four-year period, Moses's output was remarkable by every measure: the number of public works completed; the speed of their execution; their geographical scope across five boroughs; their exceptional quality; and, most especially, their range, including beaches, swimming pools, playgrounds, parks, and golf courses; bridges, parkways, and expressways; garages and a convention center. He also conceived and set into motion one of the largest slum clearance–urban renewal programs in the United States.

Moses's public works, now fifty or more years old, are so indispensable it is impossible to imagine New York without them: the Triborough, Whitestone, and Verrazano bridges; the Henry Hudson Parkway, Brooklyn-Queens Expressway, Cross-Bronx Expressway, to name a few. Other structures, less widely known, have welcomed successive waves of ethnic groups;

the pools, parks, and playgrounds are thriving points of entry into the civic realm. Indeed, few New Yorkers recognize the extent to which their city was shaped by Robert Moses. This book and the related three-part exhibition *Robert Moses and the Modern City*—at the Museum of the City of New York, the Queens Museum of Art, and the Miriam and Ira D. Wallach Art Gallery at Columbia University—recover this important chapter in city building. The book consists of seven essays by scholars with different types of expertise—urban history, architectural history, African-American history—and an extensive catalog of Moses's public works, built and unbuilt. It amplifies the exhibitions but does not mirror their organization or contents.

All this comes at a time when Moses's reputation is on an upswing. In the 1930s, the press and public admired Moses for turning federal aid into a magnificent public works program and renewing the city's shabby nineteenth-century recreational and road system. The positive view prevailed during the 1940s, when he organized the city for an enormous postwar building effort. But in the 1950s, Moses's standing sank as the city experienced the physical destruction and social displacement caused by three major postwar building programs: Interstate highways, urban renewal, and public housing. Moses's reputation reached a nadir with that of New York City in the 1970s, when Robert Caro's influential biography *The Power Broker: Robert Moses and the Fall of New York* was published. As the title indicates, the book links Moses to the city's decline.

Since the 1980s, Moses's reputation has been rising, propelled by a fear that New York can no longer execute ambitious projects because of a multilayered process of citizen and governmental review. A turning point was the defeat in 1985, after fourteen years of debate and litigation, of Westway, a federally funded project to replace the West Side Highway with an underground road and waterfront park development. In the twenty-first century, after a long period when the city's infrastructure has been ignored, the desire for governmental actors that can tame the bureaucracy and overcome the opposition is projected onto Moses, who, we imagine, would have capitalized on the opportunity to rebuild lower Manhattan after 9/11. He has become a symbolic figure in discourse about the future of the city, its capacity to think and build big.

This book brings to bear a new body of scholarly research in another round of historical revisionism. Although the contributors have divergent views of Moses, certain underlying themes and concerns emerge in these pages. They align Moses with national and municipal policies and demonstrate that he was symptomatic of his age. The intention is not to disavow his remarkable qualities, flatten his achievements, or diminish his failings, yet Moses looks different in a national context than he does in isolation. His building programs reflected federal priorities and required federal funds. By setting the Moses record against the opportunities and constraints of his time, it becomes possible to better calibrate his personal achievements.

Kenneth T. Jackson's opening essay puts Moses in a national context and argues that the net effect of his programs was to equip New York to function in the modern age. The impact of national policy is taken up in Owen Gutfreund's essay on road building. Gutfreund, an authority on the history of highways, contrasts Moses's landscaped parkways in the 1930s with the bleak expressways of the 1950s and relates the change in engineering standards, design qualities, and funding constraints to federal mandates. Hilary Ballon's essay on urban renewal likewise insists on the federal context of Moses's slum clearance efforts and describes his controversial revision of the federal procedures to make an ill-considered program work in New York's high-priced real estate market. Mapping Moses's public works onto national policies also clarifies the widely perceived divide in his career: the good Moses of the 1930s is associated with a faith in government's ability to act on the public behalf, and the bad Moses of the 1950s mirrors a loss of faith in government to act wisely, particularly in urban affairs where governmental programs, however well intended, had destructive consequences.

A thrust of the research presented here is to shift attention from Moses's unbridled power to his effectiveness within a system of constraints. As Robert Fishman indicates in his essay on citizen planning, Moses fashioned his image of superpower. He skillfully publicized his projects with press releases, stylish brochures, and a distribution list for memos sometimes half a page long. He pulled the levers of public opinion to create the impression of indefatigable energy, a perception reinforced by his pugnacious and arrogant personality. But as powerful as he was, Moses was not omnipotent. He fought other bureaucratic stakeholders inside government and alternatively threatened, manipulated, badgered, and appeased private-sector partners and federal and state officials to get his way. More often than is usually recognized, Moses had to trim projects to accommodate objectors. Fishman tells the story of Moses's defeat at Washington Square Park. Other unbuilt projects recorded in the book also testify to his limits. The outright failures were, however, unusual. More typically, Moses compromised in response to political, financial, community, and other pressures; thus the record of his set-

backs and concessions is wrapped up in the building history of the executed works; this fine-grained information is provided in the catalog entries.

Moses was a builder, and the overarching purpose of the book is to focus on what he built. His powerful personality tends to draw attention away from the structures themselves, but in the end, they are what shaped New York City and continue to sustain it. Moreover, his public works substantially expanded the public realm and set a standard of high-quality design that remains unmatched to this day. The exceptional distinction of Moses's public works of the 1930s were due to the trio of Aymar Embury II, architect; Gilmore D. Clarke, landscape architect; and Othmar Ammann, engineer. Although Ammann's genius as a bridge designer is well known, the important contribution of Embury and Clarke is here examined in depth for the first time. Moses believed that public architecture should be aligned with, and not ahead of, public taste. Embury and Clarke, both conservative designers, shared this view and adapted the great tradition of historical architecture and landscape design to ennoble the public sphere.

The rise of public-private partnerships and blurred boundaries of public space in our time set in sharp relief Moses's expansion of the public realm as well as his experimentation with public-private partnerships in the urban renewal work of the 1950s. Marta Gutman's essay on the eleven monumental outdoor swimming pools supervised by Embury and Clarke and opened in the summer of 1936 leaves no doubt that the pools constitute one of the finest bodies of American public architecture. Gutman analyzes the engineering of the pools as well as their social history, addressing in particular the charge that Moses promoted racial segregation at the pools. Martha Biondi, an authority on twentieth-century African-American history, also explores the impact of Moses's policies on minorities and looks into his presumed racism, particularly in the realm of housing, where she tracks his changing positions. Moses denounced the planning profession but planning is undeniably what he did. The essay by Joel Schwartz addresses Moses's relation to the planning tradition. Sadly, it is posthumously published. Underscoring Moses's debt to established planning theory, Schwartz sketches his ties to a discipline and mental outlook that favored large-scale, holistic urban thinking.

Moses grasped the city as a whole. Although he was oriented to the automobile, his preferred point of view for planning was from the sky, where people disappeared from sight and the city appeared as a physical tapestry of land masses, waterways, and structures. Moses used aerial photographs as a planning tool, a means that represented the strengths and weaknesses of his planning style. Aerial photos abetted his interest in the city as a whole. He did not see distinct neighborhoods, nor five separate boroughs, nor the kingdom of Manhattan. Moses saw New York City as a unit. His mission was to modernize the metropolis and keep it strong, and he dismissed as a necessary cost of progress the damage inflicted by public works on neighborhoods and people. The problem is that Moses felt himself uniquely able to interpret the public good. Putting his trust in experts, he doubted the capacity of democratic methods to arrive at the common good. What is the public good and how to achieve it in the context of city building? *Robert Moses and the Transformation of New York* offers new perspectives on these hard questions.

ROBERT MOSES AND THE RISE OF NEW YORK

THE POWER BROKER IN PERSPECTIVE

KENNETH T. JACKSON

Since World War II, America's northeastern and midwestern cities have been in both relative and absolute decline. Their once proud central business districts have typically slipped into retail and business irrelevance; their neighborhoods have lost their once dense networks of bakeries, shoe stores, and pharmacies; and their streets have too often become dispiriting collections of broken bottles, broken windows, and broken lives. After dark, pedestrians retreat from the empty sidewalks, public housing projects come under the sway of gangs and drug dealers, and merchants lower graffiti-covered metal gates. Too often, no one is at home. Newark, for example, had 439,000 residents in 1950; by 2000, that number had fallen to 272,000. In the same five decades, Buffalo fell from 580,000 to 292,000; Detroit from 1,850,000 to 951,000; Pittsburgh from 677,000 to 335,000; Philadelphia from 2,072,000 to 1,600,000; Boston from 801,000 to 589,000; and Cleveland from 915,000 to 478,000. The decline of Saint Louis was particularly astonishing. In 1950, that once resplendent Mississippi River city had 857,000 residents; by 2000, only 348,000 persons called it home.

To a large extent, the human exodus was fueled by a sharp decline in industrial employment. At midcentury, for example, Newark was a center of paint, jewelry, apparel, and leather manufacture. By the end of the twentieth century, those factories were forlorn and quiet; weeds and bushes were growing where hundreds and even thousands of laborers once earned a family wage. Similarly, Detroit in 1950 was the Motor City in fact as well as in name. All three great automakers made the Michigan metropolis their headquarters, and all focused their manufacturing operations in the dozens of plants in the metropolitan area. Meanwhile, Pittsburgh was so identified with the great blast furnaces along the Monongahela and Allegheny rivers that it

was everywhere known as the Steel City. But by 2000, the astonishing productivity of those cities was a thing of the past.

To an important degree, these changes affected all American cities, even those in the booming sunbelt, like Houston, San Diego, Dallas, and Jacksonville, if only because federal policies toward highways, income-tax deductions for mortgage interest payments, and the placement of public housing tended to follow a national pattern. In such places, the population rose because municipal boundaries were pushed out beyond the new subdivisions. But inner city neighborhoods suffered in those cities also. Thus, in Memphis, the total population grew from 396,000 in 1950 to 675,000 in 2000. But because the area encompassed by the city grew by about five times in those years, the absolute density of the community declined from 9,000 per square mile in 1950 to 2,000 per square mile in 2000, and many once thriving neighborhoods seemed deserted.

New York was part of this larger story. In 1950, it was the unchallenged center of American life, and its skyline was famous around the world. The city was a virtual United Nations in miniature, its citizens drawn from every continent and almost every nation. Its five boroughs were renowned for excellent public schools, pure and abundant water, spacious and well-kept parks, and matchless mass transit. New York was also the world's leading industrial city, and its many thousands of shops and factories produced most of the nation's women's clothes, one-fifth of its beer, most of its magazines and books, and many of its specialty goods. Its great harbor, protected from North Atlantic storms by the narrow opening between Brooklyn and Staten Island—later the site of one of Robert Moses's great bridges—was by many measures the largest and finest in the world. It was also the busiest port anywhere, and its hundreds of bustling docks and piers gave employment to tens of thousands of sailors, longshoremen, tugboat operators, maritime workers, and shipbuilders. Meanwhile, Wall Street was the heart of American finance, Madison Avenue of advertising, Seventh Avenue of fashion, Fifth Avenue of elegant shopping, and Broadway of entertainment.

But New York, imperial though it was, could not resist the larger national pressures toward dispersion, and post–World War II Gotham experienced the same malaise that gripped the other great cities of the Northeast and Midwest. Between 1950 and 1975, New York's population declined by almost a million persons, its factory employment plummeted by two-thirds, its public schools deteriorated, its infrastructure sagged, its parks fell victim to vandals, and its public transit system lost half of its riders. Around the huge city, crime rates rose, graffiti appeared on almost every surface, corporations moved their headquarters either to the suburbs or to the Sunbelt, the city fell toward bankruptcy, and President Gerald Ford famously told the beleaguered metropolis, "Drop dead."

The Bronx became the poster child of the depressed metropolis. So many landlords abandoned their apartment buildings that the city covered their windows with decals of lampshades and curtains to camouflage the offending residences. Whole blocks emptied of residents and habitable structures, and the results were compared unfavorably to bombed-out Dresden or Cologne in 1945. Just east of Crotona Park, in a neighborhood once enlivened by thousands of Jewish and Italian residents, Charlotte Street became an international symbol of abandonment and ruin. Popular perception associated shopping malls, corporate office parks, and suburban residential subdivisions with the future; cities seemed dangerous and decrepit, places where the problems of poverty, race, and crime came together in the perfect storm known as the South Bronx.

It was in this context that Robert A. Caro's *Power Broker: Robert Moses and the Fall of New York* appeared in 1974. Extraordinary in conception and execution, the book generated exceptional attention and won both the Pulitzer and Francis Parkman prizes as the best book of the year. It was a page-turner: persuasively argued, beautifully written, and thoroughly researched. It held that Moses was a brilliant and idealistic reformer who ultimately soured on politics and ruthlessly marshaled power to follow his own muse and become the greatest builder the United States had ever seen. Although *The Power Broker* is in many respects a monument to the awesome achievements of a dedicated public servant, its subtitle and overarching thesis suggest that the builder almost destroyed the city he was trying to save and that the desperation of Gotham in 1974 was partly the result of his misplaced priorities.

I posit a different hypothesis about Moses's impact upon New York. Unlike most cities in the Frost Belt (except perhaps Boston), New York has experienced a renaissance since 1975. In the space of three decades it changed from a poster child of urban despair to an international symbol of glamour, sophistication, success, competition, and safety. Meanwhile, its crime rate plummeted, public transit ridership increased by 50 percent, graffiti diminished, tourism exceeded forty million visitors per year, Broadway ticket sales set new records, and real estate prices—perhaps the ultimate barometer of urban health in a capitalist society—reached levels unequalled in any city in the history of the world. In the single decade of the 1990s, the official population of the five boroughs surged by 700,000.

The reasons for New York's impressive turnaround since its nadir in the 1970s are many and varied. Some credit Mayor Edward I. Koch's take-charge attitude following his election in 1977. Others credit mayors Rudolph Giuliani and Michael Bloomberg for restoring faith in the city's ability to handle its own problems. Still others point to the "broken-window theory" of crime prevention, the legalization of abortion in New York and adjacent states, the tripling of the prison population, the decline in the numbers of minority male teenagers, the passing of the crack epidemic, the growth of neighborhood-watch associations, or the surge in foreign immigration (legal and illegal).

Whatever the cause of the New York turnaround, it would not have been possible without Robert Moses. Had he not lived, or had he chosen to spend his productive years in isolation on a beach or a mountaintop, Gotham would have lacked the wherewithal to adjust to the demands of the modern world. Had the city not undertaken a massive program of public works between 1924 and 1970, had it not built an arterial highway system, and had it not relocated 200,000 people from old-law tenements to new public housing projects, New York would not have been able to claim in the 1990s that it was the capital of the twentieth century, the capital of capitalism, and the capital of the world.

Moses was such a complex figure and his accomplishments so diverse and numerous that it is necessary to break down his public career into a conceptual framework that allows us to see him in a larger national context. For the purposes of this discussion, let us consider the scope, price, and quality of the things he built; the nature of his vision; the question of his racism; the quality of his housing; and the issue of his financial honesty.

ROBERT MOSES IN THE NATIONAL CONTEXT

By any definition, Robert Moses had an exceptional life. Even a simple list of his various pools, beaches, playgrounds, parks, parkways, expressways, bridges, public housing projects, Title I efforts, and Mitchell-Lama developments—not to mention Lincoln Center, the United Nations, and two world's fairs—runs to many pages. As Caro noted, Moses was the greatest builder in American history.

But *The Power Broker* exaggerates Moses's influence on American life and makes him too much of an evil genius. For example, despite the many miles of roadway attributed to Moses, New York never became as hospitable to the motorcar as other American cities. In Caro's narrower context, we do not learn that Detroit voters chose the highway over public transportation in the 1920s or that the city of Cincinnati built a subway line in the 1930s and never opened it. Similarly, *The Power Broker* ignores Los Angeles's construction of nine hundred miles of highways and twenty-one thousand miles of paved streets in the twentieth century, both totals substantially eclipsing those of New York. The great builder simply was swimming with the tide of history. During most of his lifetime, the question was not whether to build highways or heavy rail systems; virtually everyone believed that the private car was the greatest invention since fire or the wheel. Public transportation seemed to be nothing more than a relic of the past. Thus, in a comparative sense, what is striking about the New York metropolitan region is not the number of its expressways, but rather their rarity; not the existence of traffic, but rather that congestion is actually less of a problem than it is in smaller cities like Atlanta, Houston, or Los Angeles; not the presence of a rubber-tire mentality, but rather that per-capita oil consumption in New York is easily the lowest in the United States.

Caro argues not only that Moses built roads on an unimaginable scale, but that he destroyed what was once the world's greatest public transit system and foreclosed possible future improvement by refusing to save space in the middle of his highways for rail lines. From the perspective of the 1970s, it no doubt seemed that the New York subways and buses were in crisis. Since that time, however, ridership has increased dramatically and the riding experience has become cleaner and safer. How that happened runs counter to Caro's thesis. Indeed, the explanation is exactly the opposite of the argument in *The Power Broker*. A century ago, when Moses was just beginning his career, fewer than 20 percent of the nation's transit riders were in the New York region; in 2006, between 35 and 40 percent of America's bus, subway, and commuter rail passengers are in the same area. Why has Gotham's public transit system survived when those of the rest of the nation have so often collapsed?

It is true that Moses took no action to save either the nickel fare or the subways. But those responsibilities were not his. Moreover, as most transit historians now agree, the nickel fare should have been abandoned in the 1920s, not the 1940s, when the infrastructure had deteriorated badly. Because the fare box could not pay for everyday operating costs, let alone new tracks or equipment, the subway system could not make the improvements that might have staved off the deterioration that plagued it after World War II. Finally, remember that Fiorello La Guardia, the sainted mayor of New York City between 1934 and 1945, was himself a vigorous advocate of the car who opposed rail transit and endorsed the ripping up of Manhattan trolley tracks.

Or consider the case of slum clearance and urban renewal. Moses was notoriously fond of bulldozers and ever anxious to clear away "slums" and to replace them with new buildings. Frequently remarking that you cannot make an omelet without breaking eggs, he felt confident that he was doing the right thing as he ran roughshod over neighborhoods that many residents felt were viable, safe, affordable, and friendly. As Moses responded early in 1968 to a question about the concentration of low-income people in a few neighborhoods, "There's only one answer. That is to tear down every building in the slums and put up new ones on less land, then bring the people back."

Moses did tear down slums in New York, and he never built enough new projects to rehouse their dispossessed residents. But in a comparative sense, he was not so quick to turn to the federal bulldozer as the leaders of Detroit, New Haven, and White Plains—and the complaints in other cities were as justified as those in Gotham. He was sustained and supported in his slum clearance efforts by the city's liberal establishment, which was perfectly willing to sacrifice working-class neighborhoods to luxury apartments, breathtaking medical and cultural centers, and expanded college campuses.

In the matter of public housing, Caro wrongly posits that the New York projects were disproportionately large (in fact, its 345 public housing developments in 2005 were not, on balance, as large as those in other cities) and that Moses cut corners in construction because he had such little regard for the poor. Rather, it was congressional legislation of 1937 that limited the amount of money that could be spent on individual units, essentially discriminating against Gotham, where land and construction costs were above average. Southern lawmakers were never eager to see Washington largesse lavished upon the nation's largest city, so they fought for, and won, stipulations that effectively tied Moses's hands.

It is of course true that New York had (and has) the largest stock of government-assisted units of any municipality in the United States. This might be expected in the nation's largest city. But Moses did not build as many apartments per capita as neighboring Newark, where Louis Danzig was as arrogant and iron-willed as Moses was. Nor were his projects as large as such Chicago behemoths as the Robert Taylor Homes.

In the national context, what made Moses unusual was his ability to marshal the resources necessary to see a project through from conception to completion. He built effective and talented teams of engineers and workers who were able to alter the physical environment with speed, efficiency, and attention to detail. The Bronx-Whitestone Bridge, for example, acclaimed by many as the most beautiful suspension bridge in the world when it opened on April 29, 1939, was finished *under* budget and three months *early*. It remains as impressive in the twenty-first century as it was before World War II. In contrast, the Tappan Zee Bridge, only twenty miles away, which Moses did not build, was over budget and behind schedule when it opened in 1956; and now in the first decade of the twenty-first century civil engineers are worried that without exceptional efforts the structure will collapse.

Moses's projects were unusual in their beauty, their structural integrity, and their durability. For example, Marta Gutman, in her essay on Moses and recreation, writes that it was not enough that he build a swimming pool or park; he wanted to build beautiful structures that could withstand both the test of time and the test of excited children. Not surprisingly, most of his projects merit our attention decades after his death because they continue to serve the people and the purposes for which they were first built. He gave his engineers, architects, and planners the resources and the direction to produce bridges, highways, buildings, and public facilities of high quality. And Moses prioritized ease of maintenance and inexpensive upkeep.

THE VISION OF ROBERT MOSES

What did the power broker intend to do with the public's money? What was his ultimate aim? Was the purpose of redevelopment to build strong neighborhoods with active sidewalks and healthy retail establishments, or was the metropolitan region essentially a traffic problem? Was it the task of reformers to move cars and people over long distances quickly and efficiently? Did

Moses realize that parkways would more likely allow breadwinners to drive to work than families to drive to the beach?

Just as it is often said that the power broker liked the public rather than individuals, so also did he see the metropolis as a whole rather than as a series of discrete neighborhoods, each with a particular feel and history and pattern. Indeed, as Robert Fishman reminds us, Moses asserted that urban agglomerations are created "by and for traffic." Jane Jacobs, author of the acclaimed *The Death and Life of Great American Cities*, published in 1961 as an antidote to Moses's vision, disagreed completely, arguing that visionaries should plan "by and for neighborhoods."

Moses's lifelong tendency to value big projects over human-scale initiatives is suggested by his 1969 plan for the Rockaway Peninsula on the extreme southeastern edge of Queens. Concerned that more than 35 percent of New York's 6,600 acres of slums were located in either Bedford-Stuyvesant or East New York, he proposed moving 160,000 tenants from those areas to the Rockaways and then rebuilding in Brooklyn, section by section. Imagine the hubris of moving 160,000 people, but Moses proposed just that at a luncheon of the city's Housing and Planning Council on May 8, 1969. Had he made the suggestion twenty or thirty years earlier, when he wielded greater power, it might have come to fruition.

The Power Broker suggests that Moses was a perceptive dreamer and a visionary, the kind of exceptional intellect who could see beyond the limitations and clutter of contemporary life to the possibilities and potential of a very different future environment. Examples include his plan for a parkway that would follow the route of the Brooklyn water supply, for a West Side improvement that would cover the oppressive railroad tracks and junk heaps along Manhattan's Hudson River shoreline, or for an arterial highway system fit for the world's greatest metropolis. In fact, none of those ideas was original to Moses; all were derivative of plans conceived and published by others long before he laid claim to them. What made him unusual was not the originality of his thought but the personal qualities that allowed him to build where others could only dream. Moses the visionary was second rate; Moses the builder was in a class by himself.

THE HONESTY AND INTEGRITY OF ROBERT MOSES

A recurring theme of *The Power Broker* is that New York's great builder was corrupt and only too willing to avert his eyes so that others might feed illegally at the public trough. Similarly, Caro suggests that Moses allowed investment bankers to overcharge for bonds, legislators to use inside information to speculate in real estate, and his own party givers to indulge in their expensive culinary and alcoholic tastes.

It is difficult to prove a negative—that Moses never acted nefariously or illegally. How could we be sure? Certainly, the history of cities, of builders, of politicians, and of organized labor suggests that powerful men have long been on the take and that opportunities for graft can overwhelm even upstanding and respectable individuals.

Robert Moses was born to wealth and privilege; educated at Yale, Oxford, and Columbia; and accustomed to the finer things of life. He had sufficient resources to do as he wished and even to refuse payment when he thought that working for free might enhance his power and prestige. That said, he died a relatively poor man. His estate in 1981 was valued at $50,000, less than that of many individuals who were born with nothing and worked for a salary all their lives. He never owned a fancy house or expensive automobile and was not known for his success as an investor. If he spent any time at all trying to engage in unseemly or illegal activity, this extraordinarily successful man was a dismal failure at it.

Rather, we should acknowledge that Robert Moses was a dedicated public servant in the best sense of that term. While he may not have built what we would have wanted, while he may not have listened to critics or to residents about to lose their homes, while he may not even have liked the cities he claimed to be serving, he nevertheless acted without the goal of gaining wealth from his actions. In this regard, Robert Caro captured the essence of the man: Moses was not interested in possessing women, owning real estate, or enjoying world travel. He sought power, influence, and importance.

ROBERT MOSES AS A RACIST

Racism has been such a persistent and ubiquitous phenomenon in North America during the past four centuries that no one should be surprised that Moses was a racist. It would have been surprising if he could have overcome his time, place, and circumstances and used his enormous power to lessen the burden on people of color in a white man's world. The important questions, however, are not whether Moses was prejudiced—no doubt he was—but whether that prejudice was something upon which he acted frequently. Did he go out of his way to discriminate against African-Americans? Did he violate the trust placed in him by public officials to weigh all his actions and projects against a standard of equality for all citizens?

The evidence does not support Caro's claims that racism was a defining aspect of Moses's character, or that his actions had a disproportionately negative effect upon African-Americans. When he first came to a position of great responsibility in the 1920s, prejudice based upon skin color was an established fact in the metropolitan region. In the middle of Harlem, for example, the most famous black neighborhood in all the world, restaurants, theaters, and stores routinely treated African-Americans as second-class citizens. But Moses did try to place swimming pools and park facilities within reach of black families and accessible by convenient public transportation. He did not build bridges too low to accommodate buses so that black families would stay away from Jones Beach, nor did he control the water temperature so as to discourage black patronage.

Moses had contempt for the poor and rarely expressed admiration for African-Americans. But he did have a consistent and powerful commitment to the public realm: to housing, highways, parks, and great engineering projects that were open to everyone. While Moses was in power, the word "public" had not yet become pejorative, and the power broker was willing to override private interests in order to enlarge the scope of public action. In the twenty-first century, when almost anything "public" is regarded as second-rate and when the city cannot afford to repair—let alone construct—grand edifices, that alone is a remarkable achievement.

I wish that Robert Moses had been in charge of the subways instead of the highways. I wish that he had been as concerned about equality for African-Americans as he was about the importance of open spaces and beaches. I wish that he had been as attentive to neighborhoods as he had been to highway interchanges and gigantic bridges. But he was what he was, and on balance he was a positive influence on the city. In fact, he made possible New York's ability to remain in the front rank of world cities into the twenty-first century. Had Moses never lived, America's greatest city might have deteriorated beyond the capabilities of anyone to return it to prosperity. As it is, the power broker built the infrastructure that secured New York's place among the greatest cities in the history of the world. Alexander Garvin has said it succinctly: "Nobody, not even Baron Haussmann in 19th-century Paris, has ever done more to improve a city."

Moses himself once said of the man who rebuilt the French capital in the 1850s and 1860s: "Baron Haussmann has been described as a talker, an ogre for work, despotic, insolvent, full of initiative and daring, and carrying not a straw for legality." Moses might have been describing himself. And so also Moses's conclusion about Haussmann: "Everything about him was on a grand scale, both good qualities and faults. His dictatorial talents enabled him to accomplish a vast amount of work in an incredibly short time, but they also made him many enemies, for he was in the habit of running roughshod over all opposition."[1] Baron Haussmann operated under the tutelage of Napoleon III. Moses also operated in a special time, when most people thought that government could and should do grand things for ordinary families. In the twenty-first century, circumstances have changed radically. Alan Altshuler and David Luberoff have even argued that the age of urban megaprojects has passed.[2] But whether or not another American power broker should emerge in the decades to come, Robert Moses will be remembered as a key actor in the rise of New York, not its fall.

NOTES

1. Moses, *Public Works*, xi. See Selected Bibliography for full citation.
2. Alan A. Altshuler and David Luberoff, *Mega-Projects: The Changing Politics of Urban Investment* (Washington, D.C.: Brookings Institution, 2003), 270.

EQUIPPING THE PUBLIC REALM

RETHINKING ROBERT MOSES AND RECREATION

MARTA GUTMAN

In the mid-1930s, New Yorkers watched an astonishing transformation unfold as Robert Moses, the new commissioner of parks, dug deeply into the pockets of the federal government and procured the financial resources needed to equip the city with new facilities for public recreation.[1] Within weeks of his appointment on January 19, 1934, tens of thousands of construction workers, supervised by hundreds of architects, landscape architects, and engineers at the Department of Parks, were hard at work. They made countless improvements across the five boroughs to parks, beaches, playgrounds, vacant lots, and other open spaces.[2] Writing in the *New Yorker* in 1936, Lewis Mumford lavished praise on this aspect of the Moses program for New York, singling out its effects on the tarnished crown jewel of the park system. In 1920, Central Park "might have been used for a movie background of a shell-torn battle area," the critic wrote. The "old park was arranged primarily for the eye, and it was always at its best on weekdays when there were not too many visitors. . . . The new park (Mr. Moses's park) is what the Germans call a *Volkspark*. It is a place where crowds of people can meet and mingle; the landscape is just a fringe of verdure around the faces and bodies of the crowd."[3]

My focus here is on the grand public swimming pools that were built under Moses's directive and infused with a social vision similar to that which Mumford discerned in the refurbished Central Park. Costing about $1 million each, eleven new pools opened—one each week and with great fanfare—during the hot summer of 1936.[4] Applauded as "oases in New York's heat wave," the pools, along with new wading pools and reconstructed beaches, could accommodate tens of thousands of people a day, offering a welcome respite from the sultry summer heat.[5]

These grand works of civic architecture immediately caught the public eye, presenting, as the editors of *Fortune* pointed out, a "conspicuous example of the social dividend" promised by the New Deal.[6] Brilliant, tempestuous, and arrogant, "Robert (Or-I'll-Resign) Moses" arrived at the Department of Parks flush with the success of having transformed 7,700 acres of swampy shoreline on Long Island into the public playground called Jones Beach.[7] The commissioner had no qualms about manipulating, even flouting, the conventions of democratic politics to bring to fruition an even grander program of public works for recreation in New York City—a program that Robert Caro argued helped launch Moses's lifelong search for power.[8]

I shall step back from relating the pool-building project to that facet of the Moses phenomenon and instead assess the democratizing effects of his remarkable vision for aquatic recreation. The decisions taken about social program, neighborhood location, and building design challenge the prevailing view of Moses as a high and mighty planner and a heavy-handed executor of slum clearance programs.[9] On the contrary, in the mid-1930s Moses called on planning strategies rooted in the reform urbanism of the Progressive Era to weave astonishing works of modern architecture into an existing infrastructure of parks, schools, and playgrounds; that is, to integrate monumental modern buildings into the fabric of everyday urban life. The extent of the building initiative—designed to encourage active recreation among adults, teenagers, and children—and its architectural quality were unique in the United States during the New Deal, although in keeping with and perhaps inspired by modernist experiments in Europe.[10] As Ken Worpole has shown, the magnificent open-air swimming pools that were built in European cities during the turbulent interwar years created "new spaces of public informality."[11] He makes a strong case that these remarkable works of modern architecture promoted democracy—albeit principally for white people—and helped to break down boundaries between working-class men and women by offering them the benefits of clean water, sunlight, and fresh air in gender-integrated settings.[12]

The Moses-era pools, each one open to the sun and fresh air, enhanced the city's public landscape in the manner that Worpole describes, becoming new public places that men and women could inhabit informally together and with their children. The new pool complexes also brought to working-class New Yorkers a range of modern recreational facilities previously reserved for wealthier classes. In spite of the commissioner's well-known disdain for ordinary people, access to public recreation underwent remarkable, if uneven, democratization in New York after Mayor Fiorello La Guardia appointed Moses head of the Department of Parks.[13] Frances Perkins, then the secretary of labor, is reported to have said, "He loves the public, but not as people. The public is   a great amorphous mass to him; it needs to be bathed, it needs to be aired, it needs recreation, but not for personal reasons just to make it a better public."[14] For these and other reasons, the commissioner used New Deal work-relief programs to New York's advantage, constructing facilities for swimming, handball, tennis, basketball, and other sorts of outdoor recreation, which were made available to the public at minimal or no charge. Under Moses, new open-air facilities for swimming and bathing, and additions to existing ones, dotted the landscape of the entire city, albeit to a greater degree in Manhattan than in the outer boroughs and to a lesser degree in African-American neighborhoods than in white ones. I will discuss the uneven distribution of this achievement, and its relation to race prejudice, after a review of how the Moses-made landscape came into being.

THE PARKS CZAR AND THE NEW DEAL

Known as the Parks Czar for insisting that the Department of Parks be consolidated into one agency, Moses orchestrated the largest urban park and playground construction program in the United States during the New Deal.[15] With one-third of the nation's entire work force unemployed when he took office in 1933, Franklin D. Roosevelt quickly put in place several work-relief programs, intending to put 3.5 million people back to work in two years' time. Prime among them was the Works Progress Administration (WPA), authorized by Roosevelt in 1935 to "carry on small useful projects designed to assure a maximum employment in all localities."[16] No city matched New York in dollars received from this program and in the scope of ensuing construction. La Guardia won for the nation's biggest city special status in the WPA administrative framework, and, propelled by Moses's iron will and administrative genius, the city proceeded to take in one-seventh of all expenditures made by the WPA in 1935 and 1936. Moses directed most of the funding to the Department of Parks, spending in the first two years some $113 million on parks and recreation alone.[17]

Across the city, physical evidence of the extent of the Moses endeavors quickly came into view, from the modest signs posted on construction sites announcing that WPA employees were at work to the new pools, zoos, playgrounds, and ball fields that seemed to appear almost overnight in public parks. Through scope—17 swimming pools, 11 bathhouses, 73 wading pools, 255 new playgrounds, the reconstruction of two zoos and three beaches, and one new beach pavilion—and grand architectural scale, the interventions made tangible the expectation that reemployment would pull the nation out of the Great Depression. The modernization of the New York park system, as was noted at the time, became a monument not only to Moses but to the Depression itself.[18] Of course, the federal government had more than one motive in offering handsome subsidies for constructing swimming pools and other facilities for public recreation. As other historians have pointed out, Harold Ickes, the secretary of the Department of the Interior and director of the rival Public Works Administration (PWA), endorsed the use of federal money to build recreation facilities and community-based institutions, seeing in them the potential to rejuvenate democracy. By contrast, Harry Hopkins, the director of the WPA, asserted that building more facilities for organized leisure would encourage mass consumption. The latter goal was taken by some economists to be a surer cure to the nation's economic problems than working toward full employment.[19]

Although mindful of these disputes about how best to jump-start the economy, Moses brought to the Department of Parks other convictions about the need for public works. Like other New Deal activists, Moses was nurtured on the Progressive Era ideal of paternalist reform. He believed recreation ought to be organized for the public good, especially for children, and he sought to stem the commercialization of recreation and entertainment, which he staunchly opposed. At the same time, Moses was also aware of changing patterns of leisure, and thus intent on modernizing the city's recreational landscape to include sites for active recreation that would appeal to adults as well as attract young people—to mix adult playgrounds, as it were, with abundant facilities for children's active play.[20]

Moses was not alone in discerning the need to modernize municipal amenities by making public recreation intergenerational rather than focused on children. By the time of the New Deal, as Phoebe Cutler has demonstrated, it was clear that the "genteel bucolic settings" of the pleasure park "could not fill all the recreation needs of the leisure-rich twentieth century."[21] In response to the sports boom, which accelerated in the 1920s, and mounting concerns about public health, reform organizations, most importantly the National Recreation Association (NRA), began to lobby for sites for adult recreation as well as for children's active play.[22] During the Great Depression, the group insisted that the predicament of enforced leisure, meaning massive unemployment, underscored the value of properly organized recreation for all ages. "Leisure for everyone," Joseph Lee, the president of the NRA, wrote in 1931, "is a new thing under the sun. It means the coming of something unheard of in all history—the opportunity for every man to live."[23]

The forty-hour workweek, written into federal law in the 1930s, and the repeal of Prohibition led to fretting among elites about the loss of moral compass among Americans, especially working-class men. They were perceived to have a disconcerting abundance of free time due to the collapse of the

E-2. River swimming, New York, n.d.

E-3. Interior of Battery Floating Bath, ca. 1898. Photograph by E. Stopff

economy. "The challenge of the new leisure," Jesse Steiner wrote in 1933, after Congress repealed Prohibition, "presents to America not only an opportunity but a problem of large-scale planning and social control."[24] Steiner, one of President Herbert Hoover's advisers, warned against the temptations embedded in saloons, movie theaters, and other amusements. He argued for a federally funded public works program—one that would alleviate unemployment, promote morality, and improve public health through financing projects in recreation.

MODERNIZING NEW YORK'S AQUATIC LANDSCAPE

In the 1930s, New York City's aquatic landscape begged for government intervention, and for more reasons than offered by Steiner. When Moses arrived at the Department of Parks, the city's parks, pools, and beaches were in deplorable condition, having been sullied for decades by poor maintenance and corrupt management. "I found a run-down park system, understaffed with old, inefficient personnel," Moses wrote in 1936.[25] The physical degradation extended to the shoreline, sorely compromised by haphazard development and grossly polluted boundary waters.[26] Each day millions of gallons of raw sewage poured into the water surrounding the city, Moses asserted—that is, before he took charge. As he explained with characteristic bravado, "A scientific analysis of the state of pollution of the waters around New York convinced me that the entire Hudson River front of the city and all the waters from Spuyten Duyvil to Mott Haven and from Hell Gate to the Narrows were not fit to bathe in and never would be again."[27]

New Yorkers still found free, or relatively inexpensive, places to swim. The tradition of river swimming, pervasive in the nineteenth century, had never completely died out, despite extensive water pollution (fig. E-2).[28] Prompted by concerns about personal cleanliness, especially among immi-

grants, the city opened in 1870 the first free-floating water bath, a large wood-frame structure suspended on pontoons with an open well for water. River water filled the floating pools, which were enthusiastically used by hundreds of people during the summer months, even though wooden slats scarcely filtered out decaying fish, other detritus, and menaces to public health. After the turn of the century, fifteen floating pools were moored at municipal recreation piers and at other docks along the waterfront, competing with industry for valuable space (fig. E-3). The pools, used by men and women separately, were by 1914 required by law to be watertight and filled with purified water.[29]

The pursuit of cleanliness also led middle-class reformers, starting in the 1880s, to press for the construction of public bathhouses. The Association for Improving the Condition of the Poor opened the first one, the People's Baths, on the Lower East Side in the early 1890s, and bona fide public facilities followed shortly thereafter, prompted by a new state law (1895) mandating their construction. Ornate Beaux-Arts buildings decorated with moralizing slogans—for example, "Cleanliness Next to Godliness" was emblazoned on the facade of the People's Baths—made the reform agenda palpable to working-class clients.[30] Inside the buildings, as Andrea Renner has shown, the bathing experience was standardized in factorylike interiors: men and women were offered twenty-minute showers in small stalls, located on opposite sides of each facility. The routine was never popular with working-class New Yorkers, and after 1904 swimming pools and gymnasia were added to municipal baths in the hope that these amenities would entice more people to use them.[31]

In the 1930s, Moses inherited the indoor swimming pools at the municipal bathhouses, which were showing signs of aging, and the three antiquated floating pools that also remained in service. He also took charge of public beaches in the Bronx and Brooklyn, which had been infringed upon by private interests. These facilities, too, were unsanitary and had been poorly maintained.[32] As for outdoor pools, the city had opened numerous wading pools for children in working-class neighborhoods during the Progressive Era but owned only two swimming pools: one at Betsy Head Park in Brownsville, Brooklyn, which was falling apart, and one in Faber Park on Staten Island, built in 1932.[33]

The construction of outdoor swimming pools had skyrocketed in the U. S. in the 1920s, but not in the nation's largest city.[34] This is not surprising as there was relatively little investment in any sort of public recreation during this period in New York, a point that Moses underscored after he took charge of the Department of Parks. Nonetheless, the lack of modernization offered to New York's aquatic landscape is startling when compared with public investment in swimming pools, wading pools, and bathing beaches in other North American cities.[35] The avid embrace of swimming resulted from the widespread thirst for sun, fresh air, health, and athletics that erupted internationally—and across social classes—in the interwar period.[36] The enthusiasm for outdoor exercise built on the fascination with youth culture and the idealized human body, both seen as indicators of modernity; the acceptance of swimming as a sport suitable for women; and the sense of swimming as a family sport.[37] The NRA in its publications especially emphasized this last

point and also noted that modern recreation facilities could produce revenue needed to stabilize municipal budgets. In 1929, the NRA publication *Playground and Recreation* singled out for praise the new sand beach, pool, and bathhouse in Wichita, Kansas (fig. E-4). "The commodious bath house, the expanse of water, and the many trees and shrubs combine to make this spot especially appealing," the editors wrote, approving the generous size of the pool and beach.[38] The journal also reported that 96,300 people used the pool during the preceding year and were charged ten cents for a swim and an additional five cents each for a towel and a bathing suit. In the end, the city garnered almost $3,000 in revenue from the facility.[39]

In Europe, governments of all political persuasions funded the building of exemplary swimming pools and bathhouses during the interwar years, responding to the cultural changes just mentioned and to concerns about public health (prevalent in countries devastated by World War I).[40] In fact, the extent of investment in recreational facilities in Europe created the sense in the U.S. that it lagged behind, that it needed to put money into infrastructure for recreation in order to keep up with its European competitors.[41] In addition to providing needed employment, the public works programs for recreation in European cities linked the state building of the 1920s and 1930s with social experimentation, radical architecture, and the intent to

E-4. Sand area, pool, and bathhouse, Wichita, Kansas, 1929

E-5. Pioneer Health Centre, London, 1935. Photograph by Eric Owen Williams

E-6. Great Hall, Strandbad Wannsee (Berlin), ca. 1930

improve the human body through athletic endeavor.[42]

High-quality modern design was common, especially in England, Switzerland, and other social democracies. Progressive city councils erected spectacular open-air swimming pools with modernist designs and, in contrast to policies in place at municipal bathhouses, allowed women and girls to swim in these pools and use the surrounding public areas at the same time as men and boys.[43] The benefits of swimming, sun, and fresh air were highlighted in other sorts of public projects. For example, in 1935, a sleek public health center, designed by Eric Owen Williams, opened in the working-class neighborhood of Peckham in South London (fig. E-5). Run by progressive doctors committed to preventive medicine, the philanthropic facility contained, in addition to medical offices, an Olympic-size swimming pool, a playground, a gymnasium, and a lounge with moveable glass panels that opened to let in fresh air.[44] Outside Berlin, Richard Ermisch and Martin Wagner expanded the public beach at Wannsee, making it the largest inland facility of this sort in Europe when completed in 1930 (fig. E-6). The new pavilion, lauded as an outstanding example of the New Objectivity, was an enormous two-story structure with four halls, roof terraces for sunbathing and sports, and a grand promenade along the water.[45]

Aware in all likelihood of at least some of these projects and with the success of Jones Beach not far behind him, Robert Moses launched an ambitious pool-building program in New York City during the New Deal, which he coordinated with beach improvements and the construction of modern sewage treatment plants. "Clean, healthful, and adequate bathing facilities were practically out of the reach," he wrote, "both geographically and financially, of millions of the city's inhabitants."[46] Although mindful of the need for an affordable program, Moses adopted the economic model promoted by the NRA and insisted that the pools be financially self-sustaining. He instituted admission fees: twenty cents for adults to swim and ten cents for children after 1:00 P.M. In the lean years of the Depression, even these modest charges elicited protest, leading the mayor to urge children to take a morning swim and save their parents a dime.[47] Nevertheless, as Davidson has argued, the modest fees do not seem to have prevented many people from using the new pools, given the numbers who flocked to them as soon as they opened. La Guardia and Moses faced tough choices in 1936 and 1937 as they struggled to augment the public realm with new social services, and the pool fees were one means used to stabilize the municipal budget.[48]

The site-selection strategy directly addressed geographic accessibility. On July 23, 1934, Moses announced that the parks department intended to build open-air swimming pools on twenty-three sites across the five boroughs. The press release, written by the commissioner, underscored that the decentralized pool-building program was intended to counter the deleterious effects of water pollution on the daily lives of New Yorkers. "It is one of the tragedies of New York life, and a monument to past indifference, waste, selfishness, and stupid planning that the magnificent natural boundary waters of the city have been in large measure destroyed for recreational purposes by haphazard industrial and commercial developments."[49] Moses substantiated the claim with a map showing the areas that were unfit for bathing and those that could be improved. Not surprisingly, he chose to build new open-air swimming pools near these places. He also explained that siting decisions would be directed toward crowded neighborhoods: "the problem therefore resolves itself into one of providing open-air swimming pools, properly located in the most congested sections."[50] Moses would continue to emphasize this point. Soon magnificent new open-air swimming pools arose in existing open spaces (mostly parks), with new construction, rather than slum clearance, used to relieve urban congestion . The press release concluded by stating that relief funds (the only resource available) would be used and that construction would begin at nine sites, all but one located in existing parks. Moses made it clear that the design process, relying on typical details and standard plans, had already started.[51]

In the end, the scope of the work was trimmed from twenty-three to ten new pools; one existing public pool was also fully renovated. When asked in 1936 to explain the rationale for site selection.[52] William H. Latham, the parks engineer and a member of Moses's inner circle, expanded on points the commissioner had made two years earlier. Latham stated that siting public pools was especially difficult in New York City, given scarcity of land and intensity of use, and that the choices had been determined by population density and available parkland, and also by the need to minimize land acquisition costs and meet the tight construction schedule. Although he did not mention politics, locating stellar works of public architecture in working-class, immigrant, or African-American neighborhoods had an added benefit—that of rewarding political constituencies important to Mayor La Guardia (and the New Deal political project overall).

Most of the new pools were built in parks in working-class neighborhoods, close to playgrounds or other existing recreational and civic facilities (figs. E-7–8). In Manhattan, four outdoor pools were built next to Progressive Era municipal bathhouses; one was erected next to a gymnasium from the Progressive Era; and brand-new bathhouses and large outdoor pools were added to Jefferson, Colonial, and Highbridge parks. In the Bronx, another large pool with bathhouse was constructed in Crotona Park, while the outdoor swimming pools in Faber Park and Brownsville were enlarged, the latter being fully rebuilt. Enormous new pools and bathhouses were added to McCarren Park in Brooklyn and Astoria Park in Queens and to underused sites along the waterfront that were being turned into grand new parks, thanks to the WPA. These sites were in Red Hook, Brooklyn, close to a parcel slated for public housing; in Tompkinsville, Staten Island; and Flushing Meadows in Queens (the site of the 1939

World's Fair).[53] The barge pools were also renovated and made into a modern bathhouse and two pools (fig. E-9).[54]

Why did Moses elect to build pools on existing public sites, adding facilities to the standing network of recreational space, rather than constructing an entirely new infrastructure for aquatic recreation (as, for example, was done for parkways and public housing)? The reasons historians have offered for this pragmatism include stiff competition for urban space and the need for economy and expediency, which prevailed in all WPA-funded projects (prompted by the concern that federal money would evaporate without warning).[55] Moses's resistance to pressure from private interests and his tough-minded realism have also been singled out. In fact, when Moses explained his methodology, he underscored the need for practicality, insisting that city planners focus on solving the actual problems of cities rather than trying to implement high-minded plans based on abstract aesthetic, social, or scientific objectives.[56] Although important, these points do not connect the New Deal site selection strategy to other dynamics that shaped urban development in the United States during the twentieth century. Many of the Moses-era pools were located in parks opened in response to the Small Parks Act of 1887 or on sites that were deemed in need of improvement by the Regional Plan.[57] The placement of WPA-funded public facilities on these sites reinforced the reform landscape put in place in New York starting in the late nineteenth century and emphasized the value of a specific kind of recreation: civic, not commercial; uplifting, not honky-tonk; public, not private.

This aspect of Moses's recreational project for New York shows that reform interventions created a physical armature, a spatial framework that guided the community building of the emerging welfare state. As I have

E-7. Hamilton Fish Park, before Moses's alterations, 1922.
Photograph by Ewing Galloway

E-8. Hamilton Fish Park, looking east, September 8, 1937.

E-9. Floating pool and bathhouse
in the Hudson River, 1938

shown to be the case in other cities, the linkage of new recreational facilities to existing infrastructure extended to the fine grain of community organization, again drawing on Progressive Era models.[58] In the early twentieth century, reformers proposed that small parks and playgrounds be located near public schools, settlement houses, and other reform outposts in working-class communities. The clustering of these facilities, which created nodes of civic amenities in ordinary neighborhoods, integrated social services into the fabric of everyday life. The planning ideal, referred to as the school-park plan, made sense to Moses, who promoted it in the annual reports of the Department of Parks (fig. E-10).[59] The model clearly influenced the siting strategy used for pools and bathhouses. The pools at Sunset, McCarren, Crotona, Colonial, Highbridge, and Jefferson parks were placed close to public schools and near playgrounds opened during the Progressive Era. Similarly, the outdoor pools built next to bathhouses and gymnasia in

Manhattan and Brooklyn complemented improvements dating from the Progressive Era. In Astoria Park, the pool, four times Olympic size, was aligned with a war memorial erected in the 1920s.

Of course, the master planner had more on his mind than patiently knitting New Deal public works into the reform landscape of another era. Moses admitted as much when he insisted that public pools be built in large public parks, not on isolated small plots. He also promised that pool construction result in no loss of playground space and that in almost every instance park extensions must replace play space turned over to swimming facilities.[60] The modifications to Jefferson Park in East Harlem reveal how these motives shaped park alterations (fig. E-11). Originally intended to provide a respite for Italian immigrants and playgrounds for their children, Jefferson Park in its pre-Moses layout respected the Progressive Era design paradigm for the reform park. Two oval lawns, dotted with play spaces for children, flanked a genteel promenade that opened onto a Beaux-Arts pavilion overlooking the East River. The park also included farm gardens for children, separate gymnasia for boys and girls, a kindergarten, and public baths.[61] By placing the new pool complex in the center of the park, Moses disrupted existing park uses and replaced space for promenading with the pool and other facilities for active recreation. When the new complex, equipped with athletic fields, bocce courts, playgrounds, and pools, opened on June 27, 1936, the astonishing work of public architecture made clear that the older model of the urban park was history.

SOUND VERNACULAR MODERNISM

Architecturally speaking, the spacious brick bathhouses that opened during the hot summer of 1936 belonged to the hard-edged modernist sensibility of the New Deal, not to the genteel decorum of the Beaux-Arts. Lewis

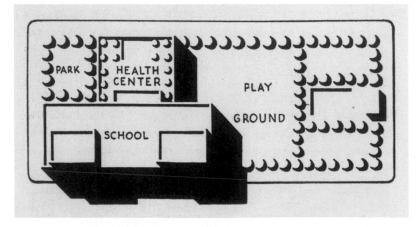

E-10. School-park-playground diagram, 1940

Mumford invented an apt phrase for the Moses-era pool buildings: "sound vernacular modern architecture." As he wrote, "the long brick buildings, with bands of windows that fill their bays form an excellent frame for the pools" and are well suited to the "children of the Machine Age."[62] The sense is that employees of the parks department, who were fed up with the fussiness of the Beaux-Arts park landscape, welcomed the new approach to design—the integration of active play, the use of hard surfaces and modern materials, and the grand scale—that arrived when Moses took over the department in 1934.[63] Moses reorganized the department by dividing it into design and construction divisions (similar to the New York City Housing Authority) and hired new, highly qualified professionals, some of whom had previously worked with him and for organizers of other park and pool projects (fig. E-12). In short order, the Moses team included the architects Aymar Embury II, John Matthews Hatton, Dwight James Baum, and Herbert Magoon; the landscape architects Francis Cormier and Gilmore D. Clarke; and the engineers W. Earle Andrews, Carl E. Shaw, and Latham, the parks engineer.[64]

Their mandate was to work fast, very fast. As with site selection, the fear that the federal subsidies for design and construction would quickly evaporate had consequences on what was built.[65] The "New Deal traits of utility, standardization, and austerity," Cutler has argued, affected the pools as much as any other work of architecture subsidized by the federal government in this period.[66] The Department of Parks was required to hire unemployed workers (not necessarily highly skilled in construction) and to use a limited palette of materials that met the fiscal parameters set by the government. These demands pulled the Moses team between two poles, as *Architectural Forum* pointed out: the desire to stretch New Deal dollars as far as possible and the intent to equip the new pools as fully as possible. Fortunately, "simple materials simply disposed" were used to great effect.[67] The end result was the extraordinary collection of public buildings that won Mumford's praise as sound examples of vernacular modernism.

Although capacious, Mumford's words hardly suggest the range of remarkable structures that WPA construction workers built across the five boroughs. With the federal government amenable to stylistic variety, low-slung mod-

E-11. Jefferson Park, 1927.
Fairchild Aerial Surveys, Inc.

E-12. Playland at Rye Beach, 1931

recreation, including baseball diamonds, handball courts, and playgrounds.

The Moses-era pool complexes celebrated swimming in the open air, turning the sport into a grand public spectacle. The complexes were enormous (much bigger than most European public pools), the largest of them allowing several thousand people to swim at one time; they offered the requisite variety of recreational amenities; and they were planned for year-round use—pools could become dance floors and changing rooms could become basketball courts, for example (fig. E-13).[69] The standard site plan, usually symmetrical, included grand bathhouses and almost always three in-ground pools: a large, often very large, reinforced-concrete pool for informal swimming and organized races; a smaller pool for diving; and a wading pool (outside the pool enclosure). The pools were also technically up to date, with modern filtration and aeration systems that were expressive elements in themselves. Great fountains sprayed water into the pools, and underwater lights made it possible for working people to swim at night. Generous paved areas, bleachers, and rooftop terraces offered places for sunbathing, informal socializing, and watching the ongoing pageantry, both inside and outside the pool precincts.[70] The likely objects of attention included divers plunging from astonishing, reinforced-concrete diving platforms, which were graced with one, two, and even at times three tiers of diving boards.

Respecting but not bound by strict definitions of modernism, Embury and his colleagues used brick, concrete, and prefabricated building materials to create monumental bathhouses that added to the sense of theatricality in the pool complexes. In accordance with the tenets of early modernist design, the structural bays of the steel-frame buildings were expressed on brick-clad elevations, and industrial sash and glass block were used to let light into locker rooms. Other design traditions were also freely incorporated, rather more so than in Europe where streamlined modernism prevailed in public

ernist buildings with a touch of classical detail were added to Jefferson, Highbridge, and Sunset parks; monumental structures with enormous central gateways, seemingly inspired by Roman imperial architecture, were built in McCarren, Crotona, Colonial, and Red Hook parks; and sleek modern bathhouses were erected in Astoria and Betsy Head parks.[68] These complexes met the New Deal ideal of providing leisure activities for all ages, while retaining some segregation of uses for convenience and safety. Just beyond the enclosed pool complexes, families could find more opportunities for active

E-13. Crotona Pool converted to use as a basketball court, ca. 1939

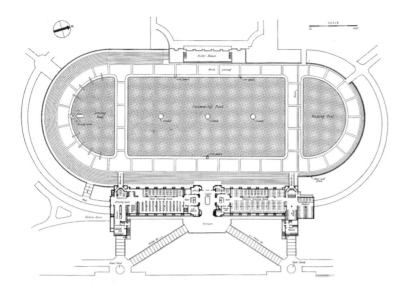

E-14. Plan of Astoria Pool, 1936

pool design.[71] All but one of the pool pavilions in New York was symmetrical and had monumental central entries. Decorative details ranged from historicizing to modernist: thin concrete lintels, stout columns, curved brick, streamlined corners, and column capitals that recalled different architectural traditions. Clocks, towers, arches, domes, fountains, and bleachers also added to the drama of the settings.

Standardized building plans helped to balance the WPA desire for grandeur with the mandate for efficiency, economy, and hygiene (also inherited from the Progressive Era).[72] The designers freely incorporated lessons from Beaux-Arts planning to give the buildings an urban presence and to create remarkable architectural processions that added to the sense of spectacle and underscored the importance of personal hygiene and sanitation (fig. E-14). Usually a bathhouse was built along or close to a city street and had a grand, central doorway that was on axis with a street or a major feature in the park landscape. The entryway was given a clear geometric configuration; was endowed with astonishing architectural features, such as a dome, grand arches, central column, and porticoes; and was open to the air, offering swimmers a breath of fresh air and a glimpse of the pool as they entered the sparkling, clean bathhouse. This structure formed at least one side of the pool enclosure and contained big, sanitary locker rooms for men and women, which opened directly onto the pool precinct. In keeping with the counsel of the American Public Health Association and other advisory groups, men and women (and boys and girls) were strictly separated from each other at the entrance to and within the bathhouse, meeting up again on the pool deck.[73] On either side of the building, as noted in *Architectural Forum*, "the interior layout presents a simple progression from admission booth through locker rooms, toilets, shower room (shower obligatory) and footbaths."[74] The footbaths were also obligatory, part of the measures taken to assure swimmers' personal cleanliness before they jumped into the pool.

A BETTER PUBLIC

As the swimming pools opened, one each week during July and August of 1936, they won praise in the local press for their grandeur, modernity, and accessibility—qualities that revealed the best face of the New Deal, the social dividend that FDR had promised to deliver during his 1932 election campaign. Again and again, Moses and his colleagues were lauded for putting ordinary people first; for celebrating them with remarkable, technically sophisticated public architecture; for democratizing access to recreation; and for using New Deal dollars to run play schools and day camps and to offer swimming lessons at the pool complexes.[75] The social objectives of these programs were evident to civic leaders, who praised them for expressing Moses's ideas about children and recreation: "Out of the gangs [and] into the playgrounds."[76] The architectural press also chimed in, suggesting that innovative design and breadth of social vision went hand in hand. "If you are thinking of designing a system of parks for your own city, you might well go to New York," *Architectural Forum* advised. "You will find America's only modern models for public beaches and public pools. You will find some extremely ingenious innovations in equipment. And above all you will find a constant and invaluable awareness that recreation must be for all the people, not only for the young, but equally for the adult."[77]

The crowds that thronged the pools and the pool openings only added to the aura of extraordinary success. Moses, a brilliant publicist, staged the events to great effect, drawing thousands of people. The celebrations rose to a crescendo when 75,000 attended the opening of McCarren Pool in Brooklyn at the end of July and concluded in the middle of August with 40,000 coming to the last opening of the season at the new park in Red Hook, Brooklyn. Like many others, it took place at night, to heighten the drama, and was attended by Moses, the mayor, and other politicians who listened to housewives, factory workers, shopkeepers, and children cheer at each mention of President Roosevelt's name. Moses explained to the crowd that the swimming pool was the first imprint in a much grander scheme that would cover about 50 acres when finished and bring a running track; football, baseball, and soccer fields; tennis and basketball courts; and playgrounds to the working-class community.[78] The films of this and other WPA pools and accounts of them in oral histories give some sense of their astonishing popularity and intensity of their use: by enthusiastic children learning to swim, by ebullient crowds watching swimming races and diving competitions, and by teenagers who courted on pool decks and played basketball, softball, and other sports in converted facilities during the off-season.[79]

The welcome was not uniform, however. According to the *New York Times*, generally a great fan of Moses, Italian-American residents of East Harlem tried to halt the construction of the Jefferson Pool; protesters marched at pool openings, disputing the WPA wage scale; the owners of private pools objected to competition from the government; and parents objected to admission fees.[80] The effects of ethnic and race prejudice also shaped the human experience of the Moses-made aquatic landscape, underscoring the persistence of ingrained social biases during the New Deal (even as some of them and other restrictive cultural practices were successfully challenged).[81]

For example, Charlotte Oppenheim, a young German-Jewish émigré who arrived in New York City in 1938, welcomed the cultural openness toward women swimming in public, selecting sites in the New York metropolitan area where young men and women felt comfortable swimming together, as she had done in Germany. Yet, Mrs. Oppenheim never swam in a public pool in the city, going instead to Jones Beach and the Rockaways. "That was where working people like us spent our weekends," she recalled, emphasizing that the beaches were affordable and offered welcome relief from the summer heat. Although aware of the notable quality of the architecture at Jones Beach, she preferred it for other reasons. "Jones Beach was a beach for everybody"—clean, safe, and "mixed," meaning that all areas of the beach were safe for women and open to Jews and other immigrants. That was not the case, though, for African-Americans. "They had their own beach," Mrs. Oppenheim said, implying that they swam elsewhere, perhaps on another area of this beach. She noted that Rockaway Beach was even more rigidly segregated than Jones Beach, where sections that remained privately owned were closed to Jews, blacks, and other groups.[82]

What about other migrants who arrived in New York during the Great Depression? Although Moses's siting decisions have been tarred with charges of race prejudice, the commissioner did not ignore the needs of the city's rapidly growing black community in the pool building campaign.[83] For example, his decision to expand Colonial Park along a rock outcrop in western Harlem turned an underused piece of land into a much-needed civic amenity.[84] The need for this sort of investment had been made clear the previous year when race riots exploded in Harlem and the lack of recreational facilities was cited as a contributing cause.[85] The park improvements included the construction of a grand new swimming pool, mall, music pavilion, playgrounds, and Embury's magnificent and fortresslike brick bathhouse. The pool opened even before the building was fully finished, in part because of the urgent social need, in part to counter charges of racial bias in the city's public works program. At the opening ceremony, La Guardia promised a cheering crowd of 25,000 Harlem residents that their community would receive equal treatment as long as he was mayor, and he offered the pool as evidence that the "knockers," who criticized his administration for treating Harlem unfairly, were wrong. Speaking after the mayor, Moses reported that the pool had been built by the people of Harlem and would be operated by them; he also urged the crowd to take care of the pool (advice that was offered at each opening).[86] The program featured the African-American performers Roland Hayes and Bill Robinson and celebrated black athletic achievement. Nonetheless, with the race riots in recent memory, the stern imagery of this building may have had more than one meaning to people at the festivities.

In Brooklyn, stories of race prejudice cloud the WPA achievements at Betsy Head Park in Brownsville. Christopher Legree, whose grandparents emigrated from the Deep South, was taught about the racist policies that restricted use of the Betsy Head Pool in the late 1930s and early 1940s. Exclusion based on race was in effect in other public swimming pools in the New York metropolitan area, as Martha Biondi has shown, with racial integration raising for whites the unwelcome "prospect of interracial intimacy"

as well as being associated with "racist ideas of unclean bodies."[87] Although Jewish members of the Brownsville community joined with African-Americans to support racial integration, it was an unwritten rule that African-Americans could swim in this Brooklyn pool only in the late afternoon, after white residents had vacated the premises—a rule that was enforced by employees at the Department of Parks, according to Mr. Legree. His recollection of segregation at the pool, confirmed by film footage from the late 1930s that shows a whites-only environment, is in accord with other memories that the park was strictly off-limits to blacks during the New Deal.[88] Moses himself recognized that the differential provision of recreational facilities in Brownsville was problematic. "Even at the present time, Betsy Head Park is hardly large enough to meet the needs of the neighborhood," he stated in 1941, acknowledging that the completion of Brownsville Houses, a public housing project, would exacerbate the problem. As Wendell Pritchett has pointed out, in communities like Brownsville blacks competed for recreational facilities that did not exist.[89]

Do these observations lend credence to claims, in *The Power Broker* and elsewhere, that Moses used public swimming pools, playgrounds, and other facilities for public recreation to physically underscore the power of white privilege? Some of Caro's most damning charges concern Jefferson Pool in East Harlem, largely an Italian-American neighborhood in the 1930s, where, he alleges, the Department of Parks, at Moses's insistence, hired white lifeguards to work at the pool. This practice, called flagging, was intended to dissuade blacks, who were moving into central Harlem, and Puerto Ricans, who were moving into blocks closer to the pool, from swimming in it; to signal to people of color that the facility was for whites only. Caro also asserts that this particular practice was coupled with an explicit directive, from Moses, to fill the pool with cold water, supposedly because blacks in particular disliked swimming in it.[90] Given that Caro's sources are not fully identified or dated, these charges cannot be confirmed. But photographs and unedited film footage from the mid- and late 1930s in the parks department archives show Jefferson Pool to be a white-only environment. Whether or not Moses condoned (or ordered) this policy, visual evidence and other accounts of extreme racial tension in East Harlem in this period lend credence to Caro's point about de facto racial segregation in this pool. Equally important, however, the water in all WPA pools in New York, including Jefferson Pool and Colonial Pool in Harlem, was *capable* of being heated. Although this amenity was unusual for outdoor pools in the 1930s, especially those intended only for summer use, it meant that black New Yorkers could swim in heated water, just like other residents.[91]

Oral histories and unedited film footage in the parks department archives shed light on this important issue of Moses, race, and swimming. The films show that in the main white and black New Yorkers swam in different pools, an unsurprising finding given the prevalence of ethnic enclaves and racial segregation in the city's neighborhoods in the 1930s and 1940s. Nevertheless, the films also show that on occasion black and white New Yorkers did swim in the same public pools, and with apparent indifference to each other: African-Americans used the predominantely white Highbridge and McCarren pools, and whites the predominantely black

Colonial Pool.[92] Oral histories also testify to racial integration, on occasion, at Colonial and McCarren pools.[93] In some pools, at least, the parks department staff tolerated black and white bodies coming in close contact with one another—rather extraordinary given prevailing social norms (at least among whites) in the 1930s and 1940s.[94]

In the end, and as Judith Davidson has argued persuasively, Moses did use public money to equip black neighborhoods with recreational facilities, especially when pressed by African-American protest. She points out that the number of recreational facilities increased in Harlem and other black neighborhoods during the New Deal and that the African-American community benefited from these resources, even though they may have been built to "deflect black hostility and resentment" of the La Guardia administration and to create physical "buffers" between black and immigrant neighborhoods.[95] Although the steps were limited, she argues that it is unlikely that this sort of provisioning of the public realm during the New Deal would have taken place without Moses—specifically without his masterful manipulation of federal funds. Davidson and other historians have also stated that, the egregious effects of racial segregation notwithstanding, blacks benefited from the commitment of public resources to recreation during the New Deal in other ways: that the Department of Parks hired African-Americans as park workers and that they tended to benefit more than whites from relief employment because they remained unemployed for longer periods of time (again due to the egregious effects of racial segregation in private sector).[96] This last benefit may have been an unintended consequence of New Deal public policy but was nonetheless important to the economy of New York's black community.

Any use of public recreation to inscribe racial boundaries justly deserves to be condemned. But examples of antidemocratic practices from the 1930s should not blind us to the considerable achievements of the New Deal pool-building project, including occasional tolerance of racial integration. The history of the WPA pools reveals that the contradictory ideals of democratic societies are embodied in public space and architecture, with the relations between civic architecture and the public changing as definitions of citizenship expand or contract.[97] Robert Moses invested in extraordinary public buildings and outdoor spaces that celebrated new ideals of leisure and made clear that providing recreational space is a responsibility of government. Adhering to the New Deal vision of active recreation for adults and children, Moses superimposed monumental modern buildings on existing infrastructure and underused sites. The siting decisions, especially, which were rooted in the reform urbanism of the Progressive Era, made new civic amenities accessible and helped to integrate them into the fabric of everyday urban life. The architectural choices made by Moses and his design team at the Department of Parks stood New Yorkers in good stead in the 1930s and have continued to do so, extending the public realm and in the long run aiding the democratization of recreation overall.

Today, most of the WPA pools remain open for public use and, despite signs of wear, are full of all sorts of New Yorkers: families with children; summer campers; African-Americans, Puerto Ricans, Dominicans, and many others who have arrived in the city on the successive waves of migration that continue to enrich the social and cultural fabric of the city. Much

as Moses envisioned in the 1930s, new immigrants and young people, especially, come to the pools year-round: to seek relief from the summer heat, to learn to swim, to play games on outdoor athletic fields and inside bathhouse changing rooms, which are still converted to gymnasiums after the pools are drained for the winter. This continuing success, based on forging a progressive relation between citizenship, public health, public space, and the human body, should be inspirational in our time, when the city's interest in developing and maintaining public amenities has waned and the spread of private indoor facilities supplants the New Deal goal of equipping the public realm with affordable outdoor recreation for all.[98]

NOTES

1. I extend special thanks to Hilary Ballon and Kenneth Jackson as well as to Mary Beth Betts, Martha Biondi, Ning de Coninck-Smith, Rachel Iannacone, Christopher Klemeck, Roy Kozlovsky, and Benjamin Marcus for materials and comments that have helped me to develop this essay and the catalog entries. I am deeply indebted to the following people who graciously helped me track down sources: John Krawchuk, Director of Historic Preservation; John Mattera, Park Librarian; Scott Sendrow, Park Historian; and Steven Rizick, Director of Document Services at the New York City Department of Parks and Recreation; and the librarians at the City College of New York, in particular to Judith Connorton and Nilda Sanchez at the Ruderman Architecture Library, and Sydney C. Van Nort, Archives and Special Collections at the Cohen Library. Special thanks go also to Charlotte Oppenheim and Christopher Legree for discussing pool uses with me, to Andrew S. Dolkart and Kate Louis for sharing research materials, and to Gene Sparling for wise editing, smart comments, and taking the time to pour over drawings in the parks department archives and help me to understand the mechanical systems of the WPA pools.

2. Moses, "Municipal Recreation," 22; Rosenzweig and Blackmar, *Park and the People*, 460; and Schwartz, "Moses, Robert," in Jackson, *Encyclopedia of New York City*, 774–75. See Selected Bibliography for full citations.

3. Mumford, "Skyline: Parks and Playgrounds," 168–69.

4. Each pool opening was announced in the *New York Times*: "Mayor Dedicates Big Harlem Pool," June 28, 1936; "$1,000,000 City Pool Opens Wednesday," June 21, 1936; "East Side Cheers as City Opens Pool," June 24, 1936; "Mayor Dedicates Big Harlem Pool," June 28, 1936; "Mayor Occupies Summer City Hall," July 3, 1936; "Mayor to Dedicate Swim Pool Tuesday," July 5, 1936; "Staten Island Pool Is Opened by Mayor,", July 8, 1936; "Pool Opens Tomorrow," July 13, 1936; "Mayor Opens Pool in Highbridge Park," July 15, 1936; "Mayor Opens Pool in Brooklyn Park," July 21, 1936; "5,000 in the Bronx at Pool Opening," July 25, 1936; "Pool Is Dedicated at M'carren Park," August 1, 1936; "New Swimming Pool Will Open Tomorrow," August 7, 1936; "City Pool Is Opened without Ceremonies," August 8, 1936; "25,000 at Opening of Harlem Pool," August 9, 1936; "40,000 at Opening of Red Hook Pool," August 18, 1936. Also see New York City Department of Parks, *Six Years of Park Progress*.

5. "Oases in New York's Heat Wave: The New Public Swimming Pools," *New York Times*, July 19, 1936. Also see Caro, *Power Broker*, 456; and Coplan, "Urban Waters," 66.

6. "Robert (or-I'll-Resign) Moses," 71–79ff.

7. Herring, "Robert Moses and His Parks," 27.

8. Caro, *Power Broker*, 478–83.

9. Ibid., 480. In no small measure, the reputation was welcomed, if not fabricated, by Moses. For example, see Moses, "What Happened to Haussmann," 57–66. For the need to rethink Moses, see Berman, *All That Is Solid*, 289–99; Krieg, *Robert Moses: Single-Minded Genius*; Lopate, "Rethinking Robert Moses," 42–48; and Zapatka, "In Progress's Own Image," 102–31. For the cultural legacy of his New Deal improvements, see Todd W. Bressi, "Parkway, Beach, and Promenade: Robert Moses's Regional Vision," *Places* 6, no. 2 (1990), 90–91; and Jeffrey A. Kroessler, "Robert Moses and the New Deal in Queens," in Krieg, *Robert Moses: Single-Minded Genius*, 101–8. For the New Deal overall, see Robert D. Leighninger, Jr., "Cultural Infrastructure: The Legacy of New Deal Public Space," *Journal of Architectural Education* 49, no. 4 (May 1996), 226–36.

10. I am grateful to Ning de Coninck-Smith, Christopher Klemeck, and Roy Kozlovsky for sharing insights on European pools. Also see Worpole, *Here Comes the Sun*, 113–28; and Stern, Gilmartin, and Mellins, *New York 1930*, 717. Although the Moses-era pools in New York City were publicized in the architectural press, newspapers, and popular journals during the 1930s, since then they have not received much attention from historians. In addition to the overview in Stern, see Caro, *Power Broker*, 456–57; Coplan, "Urban Waters," 66–70; and Cutler, *Public Landscape*, 23–25.

11. Worpole, *Here Comes the Sun*, 114, 115. For an overview of swimming pool history, see Van Leeuwen, *Springboard in the Pond*.

12. Worpole, *Here Comes the Sun*, 10, 115.

13. For democratization, see Davidson, "Federal Government and the Democratization of Public Recreational Sport," and Rosenzweig and Blackmar, *Park and the People*, 458, 460. Also see Irving, "Parks for Seven Million," 10.

14. Perkins, "Reminiscences," cited in Caro, *Power Broker*, 318. The interview was conducted by Dean Albertson from 1951 to 1955 in the Oral History Research Office at Columbia University and is available online at www.columbia.edu/cu/lweb/digital/collections/nny/perkinsf/index.html.

15. Blumberg, *New Deal and the Unemployed*, 127. On consolidation, see Cormier, "Some New York City Parks and Parkways," 124; Irving, "Parks for Seven Million," 10–11; and New York City Department of Parks, *Six Years of Park Progress*, 6. State law also permitted Moses to act as head of the state's park system and thus coordinate park, parkway, and highway developments.

16. Executive Order No. 7034, cited in Davidson, "Federal Government and Democratization of Recreational Sport," 158.

17. For the special status of the city, see ibid., 160. In effect, New York was treated as a forty-ninth state. For statistics, see Cutler, *Public Landscape*, 11; and Rosenzweig and Blackmar, *Park and the People*, 460. Also see Coplan, "Urban Waters," 66; and Garvin, *American City*, 37.

18. Irving, "Parks for Seven Million," 19. Moses complained about the expense of the WPA program, arguing that relief workers, whom the department was required to hire, were inefficient. Having to hire them doubled labor costs, in effect, because they took twice as long to achieve what well-trained construction workers would have accomplished in the same time (!). He conceded, though, that without federal subsidy, his improvement projects would never have come into being. For Moses and labor, see Blumberg, *New Deal and the Unemployed*, 136–38; Millett, *Works Progress Administration*, 61–65; and Rosenzweig and Blackmar, *Park and the People*, 327–41.

19. For the federalization of recreation, see Cutler, *Public Landscape*, 8; Leighninger, "Cultural Infrastructure," 228, 231; and Rosenzweig and Blackmar, *Park and the People*, 459. For an overview of social and recreation buildings funded by the PWA, see Short and Stanley-Brown, *Public Buildings*, 327–41.

20. Davidson, "Federal Government and Democratization of Recreational Sport," 180. For organized play in relation to park design, see Robin Bachin, *Building the South Side: Urban Space and Civic Culture in Chicago, 1890–1919* (Chicago: University of Chicago Press, 2004), 138–59; and Cranz, *Politics of Park Design*, 65–68. Regarding New York, see Hanmer, *Public Recreation*, 157–75. For changing concepts of childhood, see Viviana A. Zelizer, *Pricing the Priceless Child: The Changing Social Value of Children* (New York: Basic Books, 1985).

21. Cutler, Public Landscape, 9. Also see Cranz, *Politics of Park Design*, 101–6.

22. The National Recreation Association was formed to promote organized play for children on purpose-built playgrounds. The organization's attention to public health issues mounted after World War I, prompted by the return of soldiers from the battlefield and the growing recognition that their wounds were psychological as well as physical. See Richard F. Knapp, *Play for America: The National Recreation Association, 1906–1965* (Arlington, Va.: National Park and Recreation Association, 1979), 82. For the sports boom and debate about its timing, see Davidson, "Federal Government and Democratization of Recreational Sport," 290–91; Foster Rhea Dulles, *America Learns to Play* (New York: D. Appleton-Century, 1940), 349; Spears and Swanson, *History of Sport and Physical-Activity*, 201–2, 239; and John R. Tunis, "Changing Trends in Sport," *Harper's Magazine* 170 (December 1934), 75–86.

23. Joseph Lee, "Leisure," *Playground and Recreation* 25, no. 2 (May 1931), 57. For challenges of the new leisure, see Cranz, *Politics of Park Design*, 105–6.

24. Steiner, "Challenge of the New Leisure," 1–2; and Cutler, *Public Landscape*, 8–9. Cutler points out that the article by Steiner, who served on Hoover's Council for Research in Social Trends, popularized the council's conclusions.

25. Moses, "Municipal Recreation," 21. Also see Cormier, "Some New York City Parks and Parkways," 124; and Irving, "Parks for Seven Million," 10. The point is also emphasized by Caro, *Power Broker*, 331–36; and Davidson, "Federal Government and Democratization of Recreational Sport," 55, 76.

26. For water pollution, see John Duffy, *A History of Public Health in New York City* (New York: Russell Sage Foundation, 1974), 115–18, 364; and Hanmer, *Public Recreation*, 70. For the impact of the demand for public pools, see "City Held Wanting in Bathing Places," *New York Times*, July 19, 1936.

27. Irving, "Parks for Seven Million," 10–11; and New York City Department of Parks, *Six Years of Park Progress*, 19–20.

28. See Nasaw, *Children of the City*, 34, 35.

29. Buttenwieser, "Awash in New York City, 8–11; idem, "Awash in New York," 12–19; Corrine T. Field and Marilyn Thornton Williams, "Bathhouses," in Jackson, *Encyclopedia of New York City*, 87–88; and Williams, *Washing the Great Unwashed*, 18–20.

30. Andrea Renner, "A Nation That Bathes Together: The Structuring of Morality and Class in New York City's Progressive Era Public Baths" (master's thesis, University of Delaware, 2005), 21.

31. Ibid., 29–38. Also see Williams, *Washing the Great Unwashed*, 41–67; and sources cited in n. 29.

32. For barges, see "Antiquated Barges Become Floating Pools and Bathhouse, Madigan & Hyland, Engineers," *Architectural Record* 84 (December 1938), 57. For a photograph of the indoor pool at the 60th Street bathhouse, see "Branch Public Bath, West 60th Street, New York, N.Y., Werner &

Windolph, Architects," *American Architect and Building News* 90, pt. 1, no. 1600 (August 1906), 71. For the condition of beaches, see Herring, "Robert Moses and His Parks," 31.

33. New York City Department of Parks, *Six Years of Park Progress*, 20; Hanmer, *Public Recreation*, 171–73; and "Huge Park Program," *New York Times*, March 8, 1936.

34. Jesse Frederick Steiner, *Americans at Play: Recent Trends in Recreation and Leisure Time Activities* (New York: McGraw-Hill, 1933), 54. Steiner claimed there were 985 public swimming pools in the United States in 1930, an increase of 80 percent since 1923. He used figures published in the annual yearbook of *Playground and Recreation*, the NRA journal.

35. For 1929, see "Bathing Beaches," *Playground and Recreation* 23, no. 5 (1929), 297–305; "Outdoor Swimming Pools," ibid., 273–77; and "Wading Pools," ibid., 306–14.

36. I am grateful to Ning de Coninck-Smith for this insight. Also see Stern, Gilmartin, and Mellins, *New York 1930*, 717; Worpole, *Here Comes the Sun*, 14–15; and Gavin Weightman and Steve Humphries, The Making of Modern London, 1914–1939 (London: Sidgwick & Jackson, 1984), 160–64.

37. Spears and Swanson, *History of Sport*, 201–2.

38. "Outdoor Swimming Pools," 277.

39. Ibid., 276.

40. For Britain, see the discussion in Tim Benton, "The Biologist's Lens: The Pioneer Health Centre," *Architectural Design* 49, no. 10–11 (1979), 57, citing G. C. M. M'Gonigle and J. Kirby, *Poverty and Public Health* (London, 1936).

41. For example, see Eunice Barnard, "In Classroom and on Campus," *New York Times*, September 4, 1932; Victor H. Bernstein, "Group Play Grows," *New York Times*, August 30, 1932; Howard Bracher et al., "The World at Play," special issue, *Playground and Recreation* 25, no. 8 (November 1931). American awareness of European successes was heightened at the first meeting of the International Recreation Congress, held in Los Angeles in 1932. See Knapp, *Play for America*, 105; and Harry Lamport, "Los Angeles Plans for the International Congress," *Playground and Recreation* 25, no. 10 (January 1932), 581.

42. A fascinating study of interest in gymnastics in interwar Sweden is Jonas Frykman's "In Motion: Body and Modernity in Sweden between the World Wars," *Ethnologia Scandinavica* 22 (1992), 36–37. Also see his "On the Move" (1994). For the argument that cultural change involves change in bodily practice, see Norbert Elias, *The Civilizing Process: The History of Manners*, trans. Edmund Jephcott, vol. 1 (New York: Urizen, 1978; first pub. 1939); and Michel Foucault, *Discipline and Punish: The Birth of the Prison*, trans. Alan Sheridan (New York: Vintage Books, 1979).

43. Worpole, *Here Comes the Sun*, 114–15, 117; and Bruno Maurer, "From 'Public Baths' to 'Park Pools': Neues Bauen Open-Air Swimming Facilities in Switzerland," *Daidalos* 55 (March 1995), 72–79. These authors emphasize the importance of the shedding of sex segregation in the 1930s projects. Also see "Amburgo Rossa," *Abitare* 298 (July–August 1991), 156; "Frederiksberg Kommunes Nye Badeanstalt Ned Svømmehal," *Arkitekten* 47 (1931), 237–39; and KHR AS Arkitekter, "The Restoration of Østerbro Swimming Hall," *Arkitektur DK* 6 (2002), 360–67.

44. Benton, "Biologist's Lens," 56–59; Worpole, *Here Comes the Sun*, 25, 26, 59, 61; and Roy Kozlovsky, "Reconstruction through the Child: English Modernism and the Welfare State" (Ph.D. diss., Princeton University, forthcoming), chap. 2. The Peckham pool was published extensively in the architectural press in the 1930s. See "Health Centers: The Pioneer Health Centre, St. Mary's Road, Peckham, London," *Architectural Record* 77, no. 21 (June 1935), 437–44; "Neue Bauen von Sir Owen Williams, London," *Moderne Bauformen* 34 (November 1935), 565–69; and "The World's Largest Covered Bath, Designed by Sir Owen Williams," *Architectural Review* 76 (September 1934), 92–96. Williams also designed the magnificent Empire Pool at Wembley. See "The Empire Swimming Pool," *Architect's Journal* (August 2, 1934), 152–57; "Empire Swimming Pool and Sports Arena, Wembley, Sir E. Owen Williams, K.B.E., Engineer," *Builder*, November 3, 1933, 704; "The Empire Swimming Pool, Wembley; Engineer: Sir E. Owen Williams, K.B.E.," *Architect and Building News* 136 (1933), 125; and Roy Perlmutter and Robert Mark, "Engineer's Aesthetic vs. Architecture: The Design and Performance of the Empire Pool at Wembley," *Journal of the Society of Architectural Historians* 31, no. 1 (March 1972), 56–60.

45. See www.ghwk.de/engl/exhibit-garden/bath.htm. Also see Joachim G. Jacobs and Petra Hubinger, "Weltstadtbad in Preubens Arkadien: Das Berliner Standbad Wannsee und seine Aubgenanlagen," *Die Gartenkunst* 16, no. 2 (2004), 383–93. I am grateful to Christopher Klemeck for alerting me to this example. Although erected as a public project by a social democratic government, the site later became notorious as the place where the Nazis planned the final solution.

46. Moses, "Municipal Recreation," 22. Also see New York City Department of Parks, *Six Years of Park Progress*, 19–20.

47. "40,000 at Opening of Red Hook Pool." Also see "Huge Park Program"; "Moses Plans Park Sports Fees to Support Recreation Centers," *New York Times*, March 2, 1936.

48. Davidson, "Federal Government and Democratization of Recreational Sport," 194. Also see Sewell Chan, "New York Says Poor Must Pay for Recreation," *New York Times*, March 18, 2006.

49. Robert Moses, "Public Swimming Facilities in New York City," press release, New York City Department of Parks, July 23, 1934. I am very grateful to Kate Louis for bringing this document to my attention. Also see "23 Bathing Pools Planned by Moses," *New York Times*, July 23, 1934.

50. Moses, "Public Swimming Facilities."

51. Protest developed quickly from private pool operators, who complained about unfair competition from the government. See "Moses to Ignore Protests on Pools," *New York Times*, August 9, 1934; "Beach Park Plan Upheld by Moses," *New York Times*, November 22, 1934. Also various interest groups demanded that new pools be constructed on other sites, including in Central Park. See "Boys of West Side Ask for Park Pool," *New York Times*, August 31, 1935; "Swimming Pools" [editorial], *New York Times*, September 2, 1935.

52. Latham, "Swimming Pool Construction," 33. The following thirteen pools were announced in July 1934 but not built: in Manhattan, at Riverside Drive and 75th Street, Mt. Morris Park, and DeWitt Clinton Park; in the Bronx, at St. Mary's Park and Van Cortlandt Park; in Brooklyn, at Bushwick Park, Dyker Beach Park, and at Black and Euclid avenues; and in Queens, at St. Albans Park, Kissena Park, Chisholm Park, Jacob Riis Park, and Forest Park.

53. The city opened Astoria Park in 1913, pressed by a citizen's committee. Kroessler and Rappaport, *Historic Preservation in Queens*, 70. Also see Kroessler, "Robert Moses and the New Deal in Queens," 101–8.

54. "Antiquated Barges Become Floating Pools and Bathhouse," 57.

55. Cranz, *Politics of Park Design*, 119–21. Also see Latham, "Swimming Pool Construction," 33.

56. See Moses, "Mr. Moses Dissects," idem, "Parks, Parkways," 53, 56; idem, *Public Works*, 420–24; and "Robert Moses—Park Creator Extraordinary," 289–91. The title of the 1944 article is tinged with more than a hint of red-baiting.

57. For the Small Parks Act, see Iannacone, "Open Space for the Underclass." For the sites identified by the Regional Plan as in need of improvement, see Hanmer, *Public Recreation*, 167–86. For Moses's use of vacant land, see Caro, *Power Broker*, 374; and Davidson, "Federal Government and Democratization of Recreational Sport," 165.

58. Gutman, "What Kind of City." Also see Knapp, *Play for America*, 31, 59; and Iannacone, "Open Space for the Underclass," 157–58. On siting, see Henry V. Hubbard, "The Size and Distribution of Playgrounds and Similar Recreation Facilities in American Cities," *Landscape Architecture* 4, no. 4 (July 1914), 133–36; George F. Pentecost Jr., "City Gardens," *Architectural Record* 14, no. 1 (July 1903), 50–61; and ongoing discussion in *The Playground* (published by the NRA and precursor to *Playground and Recreation*).

59. Cranz, *Politics of Park Design*, 108, 120. Also see New York City Department of Parks, *Eighteen Years of Park Progress*, 26; and idem, *Six Years of Park Progress*, 49.

60. "Moses to Ignore Protests on Pools"; Moses, "Municipal Recreation," 22.

61. Iannacone, "Open Space for the Underclass," 155–58. The Library of Congress has photographs of the Progressive Era reform landscape of this park taken by Charles Downing Lay, the landscape architect of the City of New York. See Charles Downing Lay, "Park Design and the Preservation of the Park Idea," *Landscape Architecture* 11, no. 2 (January 1921), 76–83; idem, "Playground Design," *Landscape Architecture* 2, no. 2 (January 1912), 62–75.

62. Mumford, "Skyline: Parks and Playgrounds," 170.

63. I am grateful to Rachel Iannacone for this insight.

64. See "Astoria Pool Pavilion, John Matthews Hatton, Architect," *Architectural Forum* 67 (August 1937), 127–28; Moses, "Municipal Recreation," 28–31; and Stern, Gilmartin, and Mellins, *New York 1930*, 717. Also see Caro, *Power Broker*, 365; Cormier, "Some New York City Parks and Parkways," 124; and Rodgers, *Robert Moses*, 82–84.

65. Cutler, *Public Landscape*, 16.

66. Ibid., 15.

67. "Pattern for Parks," 512–13

68. C. W. Short, from the Public Works Administration, and R. Stanley-Brown, from Public Building Administration, made clear the openness of the federal government to stylistic variety in their introduction to a volume celebrating PWA accomplishments; see Short and Stanley-Brown, *Public Buildings*, 1–3.

69. "Pattern for Parks," 507. Also see James V. Mulholland, "The Multiple Uses of Recreation Facilities," *Playground and Recreation* 33, no. 1 (April 1939), 28–30; and "Park Pools Turned into Skating Rinks," *New York Times*, September 21, 1936.

70. Latham, "Swimming Pool Construction," 33–34.

71. For European parallels see, Worpole, *Here Comes the Sun*, 117, citing Charles Sprawson, *The Haunts of the Black Masseur* (London: 1992), 195. Also see van Leeuwen, *Springboard in the Pond*, 45.

72. Irving, "Parks for Seven Million," 10–11. Also see "Bath Houses," *Architectural Record* 89 (April 1941), 94–95. For playground design, the Moses design team adopted standards developed by the National Recreation Association.

73. *Swimming Pool Data and Reference Annual* (New York: 1935), 6, as cited in Marcus, "Last One In," 44.

74. "Pattern for Parks," 510.

75. For example, "City-Ridden Pupils to Get Gay Summer," *New York Times*, May 24, 1936; and Robbins, "Gay Days," 10, 17. For claims about beneficial effects of parks on children's safety and behavior, see New York City Department of Parks, *Six Years of Park Progress*, 17, 21.

76. Harry Schmidt, a civic leader on the Lower East Side, made this statement at the opening of the Hamilton Fish Pool on June 24, 1936. "East Side Cheers as City Opens Pool," *New York Times*, June 24, 1936.

77. "Pattern for Parks," 510.

78. "40,000 at Opening of Red Hook Pool." Also see "75,000 Hail Opening of Pool in Greenpoint," *Brooklyn Daily Eagle* (August 1, 1936), cited in Marcus, "Last One In," 34.

79. "Views of New York" (New York: New York City Department of Parks, 1938–1949), VHS tape 1, 4. The 16mm footage has been transferred to videotape and is available at the library of the New York City Department of Parks and Recreation. Also see Marcus, "Last One In," 60–67.

80. "Pattern for Parks," 510, and sources cited above, n. 47 and n. 51.

81. Worpole makes a similar point in *Here Comes the Sun*, 14–15.

82. Charlotte Woolf Oppenheim, interview with author, Berkeley, Calif., August 9, 2005. Also see Kaplan and Kaplan, *Between Ocean and City*, 132–33.

83. For accusations of Moses's race prejudice, see Caro, *Power Broker*, 491–93, 509–12, 513–14, 558–60; and Rosenzweig and Blackmar, *Park and the People*, 461. A refutation of Caro's charges regarding pool siting was offered by Kate Louis, Katherine Gressel, Peter Lederman, Diane Simonson, and Julia Werb in a seminar presentation entitled "Robert Moses and Racism: A Study of Public Pools" (Columbia University, May 3, 2006). Also see Davidson, "Federal Government and Democratization of Recreational Sport," 180–81, 292; Kaplan and Kaplan, *Between Ocean and City*, 88–89; and Kenneth T. Jackson, "Robert Moses and the Planned Environment: A Re-Evaluation," in Krieg, *Robert Moses: Single-Minded Genius*, 26–27. For a discussion of hope for the "democracy of play" in relation to race, see Hubbard, "Size and Distribution of Playgrounds," 140–41.

84. WPA Federal Writers' Project, *The WPA Guide to New York City: The Federal Writers' Guide to 1930s New York* (New York: Pantheon, 1982), 253–54. Also see "Harlem Gets News of Big Play Centre," *New York Times*, August 9, 1935.

85. For the Harlem riot, see Rosenzweig and Blackmar, *Park and the People*, 461; Davidson, "Federal Government and Democratization of Recreational Sport," 200; and Jackson, "Robert Moses and the Planned Environment," 26.

86. "25,000 at Opening of Harlem Pool," *New York Times*, August 9, 1936; and "New Swimming Pool Will Open Tomorrow," *New York Times*, August 7, 1936.

87. Biondi, *To Stand and Fight*, 83. For successful racial integration at a public pool in a northern city, see "Milwaukee's Lapham Pool," *Parks and Recreation* 24 (May 1941), 424–26.

88. Christopher Legree, conversation with author, Brooklyn, May 28, 2005. Also see Pritchett, *Brownsville, Brooklyn*, 57, 92.

89. Ibid., 55–56. The quote from Moses is cited by Pritchett.

90. Caro, *Power Broker*, 513–14. For a description of the "Italian" Harlem, see WPA Federal Writers' Project, *WPA Guide to New York City*, 269.

91. I examined the archived construction drawings for mechanical systems at two pools. At Jefferson Pool, water was heated by capturing heat generated by the diesel-driven pump that circulated pool water. Drawings of Colonial Pool show water-heating equipment clearly connected to the pool water circulating system. See the mechanical drawings of Jefferson Pool (ME-47 404PL, dated March 13, 1936; ME 47-400 PL, dated July 15, 1935) and of Colonial Pool (ME 14 425 PL, revised July 9, 1936, first issued May 27, 1936), on file in the Map Room at the Olmsted Center in Flushing Meadow Park, New York. I am indebted to John Mattera for discussing racial tension in East Harlem. Also see Marcus, "Last One In," 75.

92. "Views of New York," VHS tape 4.

93. John Purvis, interview by John Mattera, New York, March 24, 2006; Marcus, "Last One In," 41–42.

94. See Martha Biondi's essay, this volume, pp. 00.

95. Davidson, "Federal Government and Democratization of Recreational Sport," 181, 200.

96. Ibid., 292; and Blumberg, *New Deal and the Unemployed*, 291–93.

97. Bachin, *Building the South Side*, 9–12; Margaret Kohn, *Radical Space: Building the House of the People* (Ithaca, N.Y.: Cornell University Press, 2003), 3–12; and Mary P. Ryan, *Women in Public: Between Banners and Ballots, 1825–1880* (Baltimore: Johns Hopkins University Press, 1990), 5–14.

98. Also see Worpole, *Here Comes the Sun*, 125.

REBUILDING NEW YORK IN THE AUTO AGE

ROBERT MOSES AND HIS HIGHWAYS

OWEN D. GUTFREUND

When Robert Moses first came to power, in 1924, congestion was slowly strangling the great metropolis. Growing numbers of automobiles competed for scarce street space with streetcars, elevated trains, horse-drawn freight carts, and pedestrians. The city's street system, much of which had been planned and mapped more than a century earlier, could not handle all the traffic. By the time he lost power forty-four years later, Moses had supervised the construction of dozens of parkways, bridges, and expressways. His projects spanned all five boroughs and extended far into the northern and eastern suburbs, giving New York a coherent highway network to complement its comprehensive rail-based mass-transit system. The resultant balanced transport system, combining extensive subway and commuter rail lines with a far-flung web of major roads, enabled the city to grow and thrive in the auto age.

An assessment of Moses's impact, however, must take into account not only his impressive record of accomplishments but also the context of his times. Moses was the right person in the right place at the right time. He did not invent a vision of a new New York from whole cloth, but instead he deftly appropriated innovations and plans of others, adapting and combining them to suit his purposes and then readapting them as circumstances changed. He was a gifted opportunist and pragmatic administrator, able to shepherd public works projects through to completion at a breakneck pace by shrewdly accumulating institutional power and harnessing ever-shifting funding streams. These remarkable talents, in combination with good timing, enabled him to cast a larger-than-life shadow over New York City's history.

Moses started building roads in 1924, as soon as he took on his first public works project, Jones Beach State Park. In order to provide access to his lavish new recreational facility on the south shore of Long Island, he simultaneously began work on a network of parkways that would span the region. The first of these, the Southern State Parkway, opened in 1927, followed soon thereafter by the Wantagh State Parkway in 1929, as well as Ocean Parkway and the first major sections of the Northern State Parkway in 1930 (fig. E-15). Last among this first batch of Moses's Long Island parkways was the Meadowbrook State Parkway, which opened in 1934.[1]

Like most of his subsequent public works projects, these parkways were the product of Moses's blend of ambition and creative pragmatism. They were *parkways* for two main reasons. First, and probably foremost, Moses had not been put in charge of highways or roads, which were tightly controlled, in keeping with federal mandates, by the engineers at the State Highway Department and the federal Bureau of Public Roads.[2] But when he drafted the enabling statutes for the two new administrative positions that he assumed in 1924, the chairmanship of the State Council of Parks and of the Long Island State Park Commission, he shrewdly followed the precedent set by the Westchester Parks Commission the year before. His new posts could not officially encompass regular highway construction, so he ensured that they included the authority to build recreational routes and access roads within parks. He used this artfully created loophole to create ribbonlike parks with landscaped roads within them, i.e., parkways. Second, Moses had a successful model to follow. Just as he embarked on his public works career, the landscape architects Hermann Merkel and Gilmore Clarke completed the Bronx River Parkway, hailed as the first modern American parkway (fig. E-16). This pioneering project—proposed in 1906, under construction since 1916, and officially opened in 1923—was widely praised as a glimpse of a future where automobiles would enable the urban masses to drive through

E-15. Southern State Parkway, 1927

E-16. Bronx River Parkway, near Woodlawn Metro-North Railroad Station, 1922

the countryside and escape the overcrowded city.[3] Moses, ever the keen observer, saw that this type of project would garner the public and political support that had escaped his earlier civil service reform efforts. Building upon Clarke's innovative design and public acclaim, Moses assembled his own team of landscape architects and engineers (including Clarke himself, as a consultant) and built the web of parkways that would link his Jones Beach masterpiece to the rest of the metropolitan area. As would happen again and again in his career, Moses demonstrated that he was a consummate opportunist, adapting his activities to the spending priorities of the times, even while selectively borrowing the planning and design ideas innovated or advanced by others.

Moses next turned to what was to become one of his most celebrated accomplishments, the project known as the West Side Improvement, which encompassed the wholesale salvage and redesign of Manhattan's western shore. Others had long ago suggested that great cities should have great waterfront parkways, but it was Moses who got the job done along the Hudson River. In 1905, Daniel Burnham had included a shoreline parkway in his plans for San Francisco, as he did in his plan for Chicago in 1908. John Nolen had proposed a harborfront drive for San Diego.[4] Robert Moses was one of many who recognized that New York could also have a similarly scenic waterfront thoroughfare. The idea had first been publicly proposed by the city engineer Nelson Lewis in the Manhattan borough president's annual report for 1922 and was promptly taken up and advocated by the Regional Plan Association (RPA) when it was formed that same year.[5] Lewis, along with his son Harold, was later retained by the RPA to survey the area's transportation facilities and develop a scheme for weaving together the entire metropolitan area with a coherent net-

work of new highways. The resultant plan was eventually published in the landmark *Regional Plan of New York and Its Environs* of 1929 (fig. E-17). It laid out, conceptually, many of the routes that Moses would eventually build, including waterfront highways on the shores of Manhattan.[6] By the time they were completed, Moses had left his own imprint on the projects that he supervised, always adjusting and updating them according to the circumstances. In this respect, the West Side Improvement—which included the Henry Hudson Parkway, the expansion and relandscaping of Riverside Park, and the Henry Hudson Memorial Bridge—is a classic example of a Moses project. He was not the only one to imagine such a highway, and was almost certainly not the first, but in the end he was the person who took the idea, shaped it by applying the latest design principles and lessons learned from previous work, and carried it through to completion.

Fortuitously, in the mid 1930s, just as Moses's first parks and parkway projects on Long Island had earned him a reputation as a man who could get things done, the federal government initiated an unprecedented flood of funding for public works projects: the New Deal. Consequently, in 1933, Moses was put in charge of the state's Emergency Public Works Commission. He promptly used money from the generous new federal work-relief programs, together with the park funds that he already controlled, not only to transform Manhattan's west shore, as he had long imagined, but also to build a network of new bridges and parkways stretching from Manhattan through the Bronx and into suburban Westchester County. The Saw Mill Parkway opened in 1935, the Henry Hudson Memorial Bridge in 1936, the West Side Highway in 1937, the Henry Hudson Parkway in 1938, and the Hutchinson River Parkway in 1941. For the two Westchester parkways from this period

KEY PLAN
FOR
REGIONAL HIGHWAY ROUTES

SCALE IN MILES
0 2 4 6 8 10

LEGEND
Metropolitan Loop ——————
Other Routes ——————
Metropolitan By-Pass • • • • •

REGIONAL PLAN OF
NEW YORK AND ITS ENVIRONS
ENGINEERING DIVISION

MAY 1928

E-17. Regional highway routes, May 1928, published in the *Regional Plan of New York and Its Environs*, 1929

(the Saw Mill and the Hutchinson River), Moses was primarily responsible only for the portions that extended into New York City. His influence on the northern segments was more limited and derived from his close working relationship with Gilmore Clarke and also from his power as chair of the State Parks Council, which controlled all state funds used by the Westchester Parks Commission. Meanwhile, he continued work on Long Island parkways and bridges, including the Interborough Parkway (now the Jackie Robinson Parkway), which opened in 1934; the Grand Central Parkway, in 1936; the Marine Parkway and Bridge, in 1937; and the Bronx Whitestone Bridge, in 1939. The next year, 1940, was particularly busy, marking the openings of the Belt Parkway, the Cross Island Parkway, and the Long Island Expressway.

To finance these projects, Moses had to reach beyond parks money and New Deal work programs. Therefore, for all the new bridges and many of the new roadways, he installed toll booths and created special stand-alone government agencies to build, own, operate, and maintain the new facilities. As with his earlier appropriation of the innovations of the Bronx River Parkway, Moses's use of these special public benefit corporations was also patterned after a nearby pioneer that he had observed up close, the Port of New York Authority, run by Julius Cohen and Austin Tobin.[7] He recognized a legal structure similar to the Port Authority's would ensure that his new agencies would be flexible and durable tools to build his power, establish proprietary funding sources, and thereby expand his reach. Moses used the revenues gathered by these new toll-collecting agencies to obtain construction loans, pay for the initial planning stages of potential future projects, and eventually secure additional borrowing that funded subsequent projects. At first, he could take only an incremental approach to growing this toll-fed revenue machine. For example, the Henry Hudson Memorial Bridge was initially built as a single-decked span because lenders were uncertain if toll revenues would be sufficient to repay the cost of a more expensive structure. As soon as the first phase was opened and the toll receipts flowed in predictably, Moses could borrow the additional money needed to complete the second level of the bridge.

These new free-standing agencies seemed like a panacea to elected officials, who were seduced by the seemingly magical combination: major new public works projects, in the midst of the Great Depression, with little or no up-front outlay and no drain on public budgets for ongoing maintenance. Furthermore, the bonded debt of these agencies did not require approval via cumbersome and unpredictable ballot measures. Nor would the debt count toward state and municipal debt limits, which were already strained. Moreover, as Moses well knew from his earlier research and from his direct involvement in the creation of these agencies, they would have a life of their own, insulated from typical oversight and accountability measures.

The Triborough Bridge, of all Moses's toll roads and toll bridges, was by far the biggest revenue generator. Triborough, the keystone of Moses's otherwise fragmented highway network, was finished in 1936. Once opened to drivers, it quickly became the cash cow that sustained the growth of his rapidly expanding empire (fig. E-18). It was these toll revenues, collected by the Triborough Bridge Authority and the many other bridge and parkway authorities that he controlled, that enabled Moses to continue his building binge long after he had outgrown the limited funds available for parks and long after the expiration of the New Deal work programs. Not only was Moses's prized Triborough Bridge Authority based upon a structure innovated by others, the public benefit corporation, but the Triborough Bridge itself had also been conceived, initiated, and approved long before Moses got involved. Construction had been halted at the onset of the Depression only to be rescued later by Moses's opportunistic administrative and resource-gathering skills. Similarly, when the New York City Tunnel Authority ran out of money partway through the construction of the Queens Midtown Tunnel in 1938, Moses rescued the project, completed it by 1940, and took over the controlling agency, merging it with Triborough to form the Triborough Bridge and Tunnel Authority. He was in the right place at the right time, with the right skills, and he took every opportunity to make the most of the situation, expanding his power, his tools, and his mandate.

During this same period, Mayor Fiorello La Guardia put Moses in charge of the 1939 New York World's Fair. Among the fair's most famous and most popular exhibits were two that offered the public a view of the future similar to that which Moses was already building: General Motors' Futurama, designed by Norman Bel Geddes; and Democracity, the core exhibit within the fair's iconic Perisphere. Both depicted a far-flung futuristic city held together by bridges and highways, with no mass transit. Even before the fair, many Americans had shared this view of the future, but these immensely popular scale models created even more converts. Outside the fairgrounds,

E-18. Manhattan toll plaza, Triborough Bridge, ca. 1937. Photograph by Richard Averill Smith. Collection MTA Bridges and Tunnels Special Archive

E-19. Grand Central Parkway, January 3, 1938

E-20. Cross Island Parkway, July 10, 1940

E-21. Grand Central Parkway, with adjacent bike path, February 14, 1941

Robert Moses's empire was still at work, remaking the metropolitan area along these auto-centric lines, and the public seemed to embrace each new project as a step into the future. Subsequently, Moses has often been criticized for excluding mass-transit facilities from all his projects. And, in hindsight, it is easy to see that it would have been desirable to integrate mass transit into them. It is also apparent that his failure to do so kept poorer New Yorkers—many of whom were African-Americans—from using most of his new transport network. There is little evidence, however, that anyone at the time was effectively advocating a transit-based alternative to Moses's auto based metropolitan transport plans. Prompted by federal policies that encouraged the dispersal of the huddled masses across the open countryside, the vast majority of the public shared his opinion that the automobile was integral to an optimistic view of the future, and that rail-based transit was associated with the overcrowded and dysfunctional cities of the past. Robert Moses was simply the most visibly effective instrument of these government policies and the related cultural preferences.

As time passed, the design of Moses's road projects gradually changed. Initially, this was a result of the rapidly advancing state of the art of parkways. Later, it was a product of shifts in the sources of funding and road usage patterns. The design approach used on the Bronx River Parkway was simultaneously groundbreaking and flawed, hampered by terrible inadequacies that came to light as auto use increased and technological advances allowed for higher speeds. Through the 1930s and 1940s, Moses's design team implemented improvements, even while retaining many signature elements, such as overly wide rights-of-way with careful landscaping, roadway routes that were integrated into the existing topography, rustic-style wooden signs, and grade separations at crossings, often utilizing architecturally distinctive stone bridges (figs. E-19–21). The Meadowbrook Parkway (1934) was the first to divide traffic in opposite directions along the entire route, either by a center barrier or by splitting the parkway into two separate roadways, each with its own carefully arranged alignment. This latter approach was used increasingly, and landscaped medians of variable widths became a standard parkway feature nationwide. Also, while earlier designs had lanes that were only ten feet across, sometimes even narrower to get under bridges or around obstacles, the lanes were later more consistent and wider, first twelve feet and then fourteen. Design changes that built upon Clarke's earlier innovations increasingly allowed for higher speeds and greater traffic capacities. Acceleration and deceleration lanes were lengthened; cloverleaves were used more frequently and their diameter expanded. Roadway geometry also gradually improved, with even smoother transitions and even gentler curves, now carefully banked. Instead of two narrow lanes in each direction, later roadways typically provided three wide lanes plus a full-width shoulder, which was often known as a break-down lane. One cumulative impact of all these changes was that eventually, by the 1950s, Moses's projects lost their parkway aesthetic altogether.[8] This transition, however, was not solely because of the incremental design changes and the increased focus on safely raising speed limits and on boosting technical efficiency. It was also a consequence of changes in the institutional and financial foundations of Moses's road-building power.

As toll revenues rose on Moses's bridges and parkways, he grew less dependent on park funds. Also, as predicted at the World's Fair, Americans increasingly turned to automobiles for routine transportation, including commuting to and from new suburban homes. Furthermore, although his many parkways had made it easier for cars to get around the metropolitan area, they had done nothing for trucks, which carried ever-greater quantities of freight through the region each year. Not only did the physical limitations of the parkways—narrow roadways, low bridges, difficult entrances and exits—make truck use impractical, the rules of the parkways prohibited commercial traffic. Moses could no longer proceed under the unrealistic presumption that his roads were mainly for recreational excursions, and he no longer needed to pretend that his roads were actually parks in order to obtain funding. Accordingly, when he resumed building after the end of World War II, his highways placed diminished emphasis on carefully landscaped borders and medians and favored designs that were less scenic and more utilitarian, with wider lanes, longer sightlines, and broader shoulders. This change in emphasis led to changes in Moses's design staff. Whereas the earlier parkways had been overseen by landscape architects like Gilmore Clarke, aided by engineers, the later expressways were supervised by engineers who only occasionally brought in landscape architects to consult on minor matters. This shift in professional dominance, from landscape architects to engineers, was manifest both internally, within Moses staff, as well as externally. For example, while Clarke's consulting firm was still retained by Moses for frequent projects, these were more likely, as time passed, to be parks and not highways. For the latter, Moses engaged his favorite consulting engineering firms, such as Jack Madigan's Madigan-Hyland. At the same time, because of changes in funding sources, more and more of Moses's projects had to meet strict federally mandated technical design guidelines and also were required—by law—to closely involve engineers at the State Highway Department and the federal Bureau of Public Roads. In order to ease this bureaucratic process, Moses shrewdly ensured that the plans for his projects were always prepared and submitted by staff or consultants with the same background and training as the bureaucrats themselves.

Once federal Interstate Highway funds became available in enormous quantities after 1956, incremental design changes ceased and Moses entirely discarded the last vestiges of parkway design characteristics. For more than thirty years, he had been able to bypass the federally imposed structure of highway planning and financing. Starting with park money, later making the most of the New Deal and generating his own revenue sources by levying tolls, Moses was able to realize his earlier projects almost wholly independent of the State-Aid and Federal-Aid highway systems. In any case, these aid systems had excluded urban highways and prohibited tolls, except on bridges. Furthermore, the grants were tightly controlled by highway engineers in Albany and Washington. After the Federal-Aid Highway Act of 1944 added "urban extensions" to the grant-eligible highway system, however, and the amount of available federal aid ballooned starting in 1946, matched dollar for dollar by mandatory state contributions, Moses adapted his development approach so that some of his projects could qualify. The first of these was the Van Wyck Expressway, which was finished in 1950; the

E-22. Brooklyn-Queens Expressway, ca. 1960

Prospect Expressway followed in 1955. At the same time, he was not entirely finished building parkways. The Sprain Parkway, in Westchester County, running nearly parallel to the northernmost portions of the now almost obsolete Bronx River Parkway, was completed in 1953. Then, in 1956, when the Interstate Highway legislation raised the federal portion to 90 percent of construction costs, with enticing allotments for urban projects, Moses focused almost exclusively on qualifying projects.[9] Nevertheless, with this abundant new federal support came strict design standards and a ban on toll roads. In this environment, Moses's role changed as well. In many instances, his formal relation to these projects was as City Construction Coordinator. Yet, in some cases, he was able to construe new highways as approaches to bridges controlled by one or another of his authorities, and for these projects he had greater supervisory responsibilities. In all cases, he used his institutional and financial resources to expedite the projects, handling the inevitable political issues by drawing upon his extensive state and local influence, while also speeding the design processes by drawing on existing off-the-shelf plans prepared by staff engineers or external consulting engineers. Moses adapted, conforming to the new funding system and continuing to remake New York for the auto age, but now with an expressway aesthetic that was more efficient and safer than his earlier parkway efforts, and also markedly less scenic and attractive.

During the next ten years, Moses oversaw the completion of some of his biggest highways thus far, vital links in the city's modern transport system. They included portions of the New England Thruway, which opened to drivers in 1958; the Major Deegan Expressway, which was completed in 1961; the Cross-Bronx Expressway and the Whitestone Expressway, both finished in 1963; and the Staten Island Expressway, which opened to traffic in 1964, the same year that the last segments of the Brooklyn-Queens Expressway,

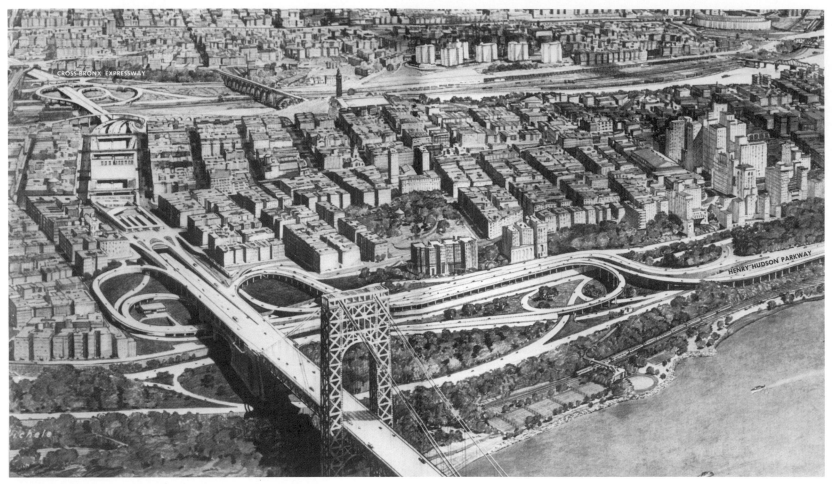

CROSS-BRONX EXPRESSWAY

HENRY HUDSON PARKWAY

E-23. Access roads in Manhattan to the George Washington Bridge, January 1955. Rendering by Julian Michele. Courtesy MTA Bridges and Tunnels Special Archive

including the Gowanus Expressway, were finalized (fig. E-22). Meanwhile, he continued to oversee the construction of additional toll bridges, completing the Throgs Neck Bridge in 1961 and linking the last of the five boroughs, Staten Island, to his metropolitan web in 1964 with an enormous suspension bridge across New York Harbor, the Verrazano-Narrows Bridge.

Despite his ever-expanding reach, Moses suffered a series of setbacks in the late 1950s and early 1960s that eventually led to his fall from power. Earlier, interspersed among his many high-profile successes were occasional defeats. Sometimes, he lost battles over the exact route of one of his roads or the exact boundaries of a new park. Most of the time, however, these failures were overshadowed by his more frequent and more visible successes— thanks to his active and well-oiled publicity operations. In the prewar era, there were only two exceptions to this pattern: his abysmal run for governor in 1934, the one and only time he campaigned for elected office, and his attempt to build a Brooklyn-Battery Bridge in 1939. This latter effort, which turned out to be a harbinger of his postwar public battles, demonstrated two

important constraints on Moses's vaunted ability to get things done. First, although his power was immense, even at its peak it was not absolute. He wanted a bridge while others wanted a tunnel, and in the end he lost the battle. Politically powerful opposition could thwart Robert Moses. Second, despite his generally high popular support, he could not afford to disregard the instances when his proposals met with well-organized public disapproval. Later, defeats like these became more frequent and ultimately brought about his downfall.

Moses's later proposals were so controversial that they resulted in high-profile defeats. One reason is that, while his earliest projects had been at the edges of the metropolitan region, as time passed they gradually moved inward to more-settled and highly developed areas. Consequently, these proposals would displace more people, were more likely to disrupt established neighborhoods and communities, and generally had the potential to do more damage to existing property and the surrounding urban fabric (fig. E-23). Second, the altered design aesthetic of his roads, together with the perceived need for more traffic lanes to accommodate ever-mounting traffic flows, meant that the later highways were much bigger and much uglier. Third, all across the nation, in city after city, urban Americans were beginning to resist the construction of additional expressways. Public sentiment no longer automatically lined up in nearly unanimous support of highway projects, as in earlier periods. Resistance grew. In New York, Moses had over the years displayed little sympathy for those who were displaced by his highways, nor had he demonstrated much willingness to listen to those who opposed his projects. On the contrary, his heavy-handed and imperious manner had tarnished his once-gleaming reputation. Moses himself fostered the growth of his own opposition.

For a few years, Moses was able to fight past this growing resistance. The Cross-Bronx Expressway and portions of the Brooklyn-Queens Expressway were controversial, but he completed them anyway. He was less successful, however, with a series of projects that would have entirely rearranged Manhattan's core, the very heart of New York City. He revived plans for two highways that had originally been proposed in the 1920s by the Regional Plan Association, large expressways crossing from the East River to the Hudson, one through Midtown and one through lower Manhattan. In an abstract and theoretical way, the two expressways seemed to make sense: connecting the Hudson River tunnels with the East River crossings and removing all the through traffic from the city streets. But, in practice, both of these projects promised to do immeasurable damage to their highly developed surroundings, displacing many thousands of residences and businesses, creating divisive barriers, and slicing up the center of the metropolis. At the same time, Moses was also advocating two other highly controversial projects: a huge bridge across Long Island Sound, from Oyster Bay to Westchester County, and a widening of the lower portions of Fifth Avenue, including an incursion through Washington Square Park. None of these came to fruition. Finally, Moses could push his transportation efforts no further. The city's appetite for his highways seemed to have reached its practical limit, even as his remarkable ability to adapt his activities to changing circumstances seemed to have similarly run out. Times had changed, and his projects had changed; the two were not aligned and instead were in conflict. He was no longer the right man, in the right place, at the right time.

In 1960, as Moses's ability to launch new projects waned, and amidst mounting political problems related to his housing activities, he was persuaded to relinquish some of his New York City government positions in exchange for a lucrative seven-year contract as head of the 1964 World's Fair. Then, starting in 1962, Governor Nelson Rockefeller gradually reclaimed power from Moses at the state level. Whereas his talents and resources had once made him indispensable, so much so that successive mayors and governors had concluded that they absolutely needed him, Moses gradually became dispensable. In 1968, Rockefeller delivered the final blow, merging the Triborough Bridge and Tunnel Authority into the newly formed Metropolitan Transportation Authority and removing Moses from power altogether.

Moses's highway-building efforts seemed to have been stopped at exactly the right moment. To be sure, without his remarkable talents, New York's adaptation to the auto age would probably have been less extensive, and consequently less successful, leaving the city ill-equipped for modern times. Nevertheless, if he had been allowed to proceed, completing his last proposed spate of massive new expressways, he might have pushed the city past the proverbial tipping point, destroying its center in favor of easing suburban and peripheral travel and thereby undermining the long-term sustainability of the city's core. Instead, America's dominant city of the nineteenth century survived to thrive in the twenty-first century. It is worth noting, however, that despite Moses's extraordinary effectiveness, New York City remains the least auto-dependent city in the United States, by far. Ultimately, it was the conjunction of Moses's roads with the region's world-class mass-transit system that sustained the metropolitan economy.

Despite his frequent and outspoken disdain for urban planners, Robert Moses was one of the most influential figures involved in the planning and construction of urban infrastructure in the twentieth century. He has been both celebrated for his accomplishments—the completion of public works on a scale unrivaled by any other public official in American history—and vilified for the manner in which he achieved them. He earned a national reputation such that he and his staff were sought after as consultants and expert advisers by many cities across the United States. Neither an architect nor an engineer—all of his projects were actually planned and designed by others—Moses built his reputation upon his remarkable effectiveness as an administrator, his opportunistic appropriation of others' visions, and his artful public relations efforts, including a consistent outpouring of press releases, illustrated brochures, and guided tours for reporters. His expansive reputation was also based on his remarkable ability to gather and sustain power, to take advantage of ever-changing funding streams, and, ultimately, to complete highly visible public works projects that others could only imagine.

NOTES

1. Names and completion dates for Moses's highway and bridge projects, as well as much of the biographical information, comes from three main sources: Caro, *Power Broker;* Gutfreund, "Robert Moses," in *American National Biography*; and Krieg, *Robert Moses: Single Minded Genius.*
2. Seely, *Building the American Highway System.*
3. On the Bronx River Parkway and the design details of early parkways, see Campanella, "American Curves," 40–43; and Davis, "Mount Vernon Memorial Highway," 20, 186–93.
4. Buttenwieser, *Manhattan, Water-Bound*, 155.
5. Gutfreund, "Path of Prosperity," 147–83.
6. Regional Plan Association, *Regional Plan of New York and Its Environs*, vol. 2, 299–301; Nelson P. Lewis, Chief Engineer for the New York City Board of Estimate, untitled city planning pamphlet (New York: 1915); and Manhattan Borough President, *1922 Annual Report*, 35.
7. For more on the Port Authority and its innovations, see Doig, *Empire on the Hudson*, 47–73.
8. The best treatment of parkway design characteristics, and their gradual evolution, is Davis, "Mount Vernon Memorial Highway," 29–210, 639–709.
9. For details on the federal aid highway system and its attendant constraints, see Gutfreund, *Twentieth-Century Sprawl*, 9–59.

ROBERT MOSES AND URBAN RENEWAL

THE TITLE I PROGRAM

HILARY BALLON

Robert Moses led the nation's largest slum clearance program in the 1950s. As in the 1930s, when he built a dazzling web of recreational facilities with New Deal dollars, so too his work in urban renewal was made possible by a federal program, Title I of the U.S. Housing Act of 1949. Title I provided deep federal subsidies for clearance of slum areas in order to stimulate their reconstruction by private developers.[1] Scores of cities, even in Alaska and Hawaii, joined the program. Although slow to take off, by 1960 Title I funding had set 838 projects in motion. Moses was the pacesetter and experimenter-in-chief.

As chairman of the Mayor's Committee on Slum Clearance, the entity through which he ran Title I from 1949 to 1960, Moses demonstrated his characteristic skill at capturing federal funds and expediting public works. He began planning early, in December 1948, and put in place enabling legislation so that when Title I became law, in July 1949, New York alone was primed for action. In January 1951, while other cities were still dumbstruck by the innovative legislation, Moses announced seven slum clearance projects, and he maintained that hectic pace to the end, as a tally of his work confirms. Moses obtained planning grants for thirty-two urban renewal projects, moved seventeen redevelopments into execution (another four were carried out by his successors) (fig. E-24). Due to his efforts, New York won more Title I aid than any other city. During his twelve-year reign over Title I, the city received $65.8 million; Chicago, the second biggest spender, received less than half that amount, $30.8 million.[2]

A productive record, yet it has long been considered a disaster, both for the city and for Moses, since Title I brought him down. In March 1960, when Moses was forced to resign as chairman of the Committee on Slum Clearance, his approach to urban renewal was publicly rejected and his reputation was in tatters. Mayor Robert Wagner disbanded the committee and installed a new system designed to correct Moses's errant ways: his secretive selection of sites and sponsors, privatization of relocation, and opposition to preservation. His antidemocratic methods and indifference to community values had incited a citizen planning movement that he did not comprehend and could not accommodate. "The democratic way is to allow the people of the community to have a voice in its projected use," a citizen wrote the general. "We urge you to schedule public hearings in which we may participate before you proceed. We cherish the right to participate in the planning of our community." To which the uncomprehending general replied, "It must be obvious that this [planning issue] cannot be settled by a mass meeting."[3] Moses trusted the wisdom of professional expertise over the local concerns of residents, and he put the interests of the city over those of a neighborhood.

Our historical distance and experience of a thriving, resurgent city inevitably cast the Title I work in a new light. When Robert Caro published *The Power Broker* in 1974, the city was failing, the wounds of large-scale clearance were fresh, and urban renewal was still under way. Caro highlighted the sponsor scandals and Moses's Olympian blindness to the misery he caused. What we see fifty years later is rather different: the Moses projects have been absorbed into the fabric of the city; problems that he identified, such as the vulnerable stake of the middle class in the city, remain a challenge; and solutions that he devised remain valid, in particular, the potential of art centers and universities to serve as engines of redevelopment. It is time to reassess Moses's urban renewal program and its impact on the growth of New York City.

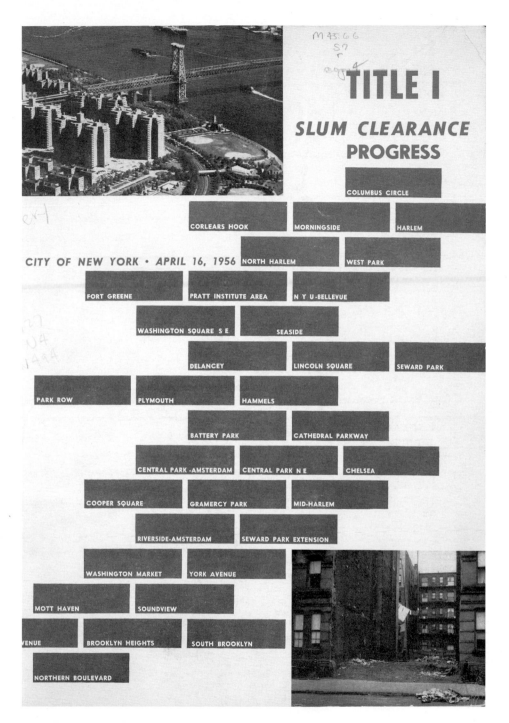

TITLE I

SLUM CLEARANCE PROGRESS

COLUMBUS CIRCLE

CORLEARS HOOK | MORNINGSIDE | HARLEM

CITY OF NEW YORK · APRIL 16, 1956 | NORTH HARLEM | WEST PARK

FORT GREENE | PRATT INSTITUTE AREA | N Y U -BELLEVUE

WASHINGTON SQUARE S E. | SEASIDE

DELANCEY | LINCOLN SQUARE | SEWARD PARK

PARK ROW | PLYMOUTH | HAMMELS

BATTERY PARK | CATHEDRAL PARKWAY

CENTRAL PARK -AMSTERDAM | CENTRAL PARK N E | CHELSEA

COOPER SQUARE | GRAMERCY PARK | MID-HARLEM

RIVERSIDE-AMSTERDAM | SEWARD PARK EXTENSION

WASHINGTON MARKET | YORK AVENUE

MOTT HAVEN | SOUNDVIEW

VENUE | BROOKLYN HEIGHTS | SOUTH BROOKLYN

NORTHERN BOULEVARD

E-24. Brochure cover showing 35 slum clearance projects, some under way and others in planning but never built, 1956

This reappraisal is built on two main points. First, the New York Title I work should be understood in relation to Moses's attempt to negotiate between public and private claims on land use. The dominant Moses narrative plays up the myth of his unbounded power; in this story line, the Title I work demonstrates his gross abuse of power. Of course, Moses fostered the idea of his omnipotence to intimidate rivals, even as he battled the myriad forces—political, bureaucratic, financial, democratic, journalistic—that hedged his power. This essay makes a point of reinserting his Title I work into the context of a national program in order to underscore the constraints Moses faced as well as his aggressive responses, particularly to federal rules that failed, in his view, to acknowledge the unique demands of building in New York City. Moreover, the national policy framework more sharply defines the basic job Moses faced: managing the difficult and ill-defined partnership between the federal government, the city, and private developers in urban renewal.

"The federal bulldozer" was Martin Anderson's moniker for Title I in his 1964 critique of the program. True, the funding was mostly federal, but in other respects urban renewal was a local program.[4] The U.S. Housing Act of 1949 gave responsibility for planning to local authorities, who structured their own urban renewal programs and determined the sites, plans, mixture of uses, developers, and methods of execution and relocation—albeit subject to federal approval. The local authority was also reliant on private investors to buy the land and redevelop it. The blinding effect of Moses—his larger-than-life persona, autocratic methods, astounding productivity, and publicity machine—obscures all but his role as decision maker, yet in truth he functioned as an intermediary between the government and private investors. He had to induce reluctant developers to enter the risky business of urban renewal while restraining counterproductive federal actions that undermined Title I. Moses may have had the personality of a commanding general, but in reality he was a middleman, negotiating between public and private interests in land use.

Throughout his life, Moses was devoted to both the public realm and the private market, two values that were at times in conflict. Indeed, the arc of his career and his evolving approach to public works take on greater meaning when seen in light of this historical American dilemma: how to balance private property rights and the public good. The intractable problem of the slums—a city killer—posed the conflict between public and private control of land in an acute form. Slums were the dark side of the private property regime: the cost of city services exceeded tax revenues, yet slumlords extracted profits from impoverished residents. As Moses saw it, he was on "a middle course between the leftwingers who want government to do everything . . . and the old-fashioned tycoons who still demand that the State give away its basic, legally inalienable, national resources."[5] His work on Title I can be seen as a culminating chapter of a career-long attempt to shape the processes of the market through planning.

The second major claim of this essay can be put simply: Moses had a coherent and intelligent plan. Whereas the standard view holds that he was subservient to real estate interests and proceeded opportunistically without a larger purpose, I argue that Moses had a strategic vision. His aim was to strengthen the center city in an age of decentralization, suburban drift, and urban decay. Toward this end, he pursued a three-part strategy: build housing for the middle class, expand higher education, and promote the city's cultural preeminence. Admittedly, this redevelopment agenda did not benefit all alike. The losers were those displaced from tenement districts: the poor, Puerto Ricans and blacks, and small-business owners, often banished to other slums. The beneficiaries were middle- and upper-class residents; universities, college students, and an economy propelled by brainpower; and cultural institutions, suburbanites, and tourists who saw New York as a cultural magnet.

What stands behind the Title I work is an idea of New York as an irresistible center of gravity. "I am not much of an evangelist," Moses allowed, "but I share the latent American idealism which lurks under the hairiest chest and the hardest crust."[6] The lurking idealism in that most pragmatic of men stemmed from a driving faith in the city. He said:

> For youth of any age, aware, observant, impressionable, the city is endlessly fascinating, and that is why so many families gravitate to population centers, why suburbs continue to be suburbs and satellites, why the vast hinterland may talk against the big town, deprecate and deplore it, minimize its attractions, but somehow can't keep away from it, why our domestic critics carp, groan, crock, vent their spleen but are unable to tear themselves away . . . why, in spite of analogies with Babylon and Babel, traffic and other congestion, it will never be dispersed, decentralized and abandoned.[7]

It is unfamiliar to hear Moses speak in this lyrical mode, but his remarks convey something that was part and parcel of the expediter, master builder, and power broker: a commitment to the survival of New York City, which motivated his urban renewal work.

THE FRAMEWORK OF TITLE I

In retrospect, Title I seems a reckless assault on the urban fabric, both its physical and social order, but the willingness to shred and reshape the city at midcentury grew out of a broad consensus on the slum problem. It had been forged during the previous thirty to forty years and had become as widely accepted as our regnant street-centered model is today. Precisely because a countertheory of urbanism is now supreme and it is difficult to fathom how what we see as misguided was once idealized, we should begin by recouping the convictions that shaped national policy and Moses's actions.

The three elements of Title I—large-scale clearance, replanning, and private redevelopment—emerged from a long-established view of the slum problem. According to that view, improvement of slum conditions required large-scale operations. The slums were a "cancer" endangering the future of the city, which if not excised would spread and destroy it. Rehabilitation of individual buildings or clearance of a single block was not enough to change the character of a neighborhood. Indeed, as a Title I manual explained, "Patching up hopelessly worn-out buildings on a temporary or minimum basis presents the possible result of slum preservation rather than slum clearance."[8] To achieve areawide change, the solution was to aggregate large properties, clear them, and rebuild on a large scale.

A second, related conviction concerned the configuration of the built environment. Urbanists and housing reformers as varied as Frederick Law Olmsted, Jacob Riis, Lewis Mumford, and Le Corbusier agreed on one thing: the traditional pattern of street-oriented, gridiron urbanism created unhealthy living conditions. It produced damaging population density and high land coverage that deprived people of basic human needs: open space, light, and air. Disinclined to attribute these problems to property relations and economic forces, American urbanists put their faith in changing the physical order of the city. Create a tabula rasa, enlarge the dimension of the grid by merging several blocks into one, and replace street walls with freestanding towers on superblocks. This reform recipe had been promoted by modern architects since the 1920s and ultimately was rendered official doctrine by Title I. A Title I manual summed it up: "Bad housing is only one manifestation of slum conditions and fixing up substandard houses will neither cure nor even seriously alter the factors that make slums—unwise mixture of residential and commercial uses of land, overcrowding and bad planning of the land, lack of recreational facilities, frozen patterns of street layouts and traffic congestion."[9] Comprehensive replanning was needed.

The third premise of Title I was that housing construction and redevelopment were private-market activities. An exception was made in the circumscribed field of low-income housing, which did not interest the private sector, but even in that area there was considerable resistance to government intervention. In order to appease the home-building industry and allies opposed to public housing, the sponsors of the U.S. Housing Act of 1949 choked funding for low-income housing while more generously subsidizing private redevelopment of slums. Acknowledging the anxiety about government intervention in the field of housing, Moses positioned Title I work as a middle path between the free hand of the market, which on its own would not cure the slums (slumlords made money), and a federal takeover of housing. "The size of New York's problem can be measured by the 9,000 acres of recognized slums which cannot be eradicated by ordinary private, speculative building. . . . [But] obviously, private capital must be brought into the picture on a large scale if we hope to escape a tremendously enlarged public housing program with all the implications which go with it."[10] As in other areas of federal policy, the idea of public subsidy was more readily accepted when the beneficiaries were not only the poor.

Although reflecting a consensus view of the slum problem. Title I came without a road map. Moses truthfully stated at the beginning of each slum clearance plan that the field of urban renewal was "new, untried and experimental" and that progress was therefore likely to be "slow and cumbersome." Title I proposed an unfamiliar model of public-private partnership. Such partnerships, now the norm in urban redevelopment, have become sophisticated instruments for shifting public responsibilities to private management, but Title I launched the first wide-scale use of this model of development. At that time, there was virtually no empirical experience to call upon in defining public and private roles, only the knowledge that previous efforts to interest private capital in the slum problem had largely failed.

Moses's approach to Title I was informed by his efforts in the 1940s to involve private capital in slum clearance. In 1942, New York State passed the Redevelopment Companies Law, an important step in expanding the powers of eminent domain and the definition of a public purpose to facilitate slum clearance. Taking advantage of the powers granted by this law, Moses assisted the Metropolitan Life Insurance Company in assembling the sites for three slum clearance–redevelopment projects in Manhattan: Stuyvesant Town, Riverton Houses, and Peter Cooper Village. The Redevelopment Companies Law solved the problem of site assemblage but did not provide sufficient incentives to motivate private investors; Met Life stood alone. In an effort to appease Met Life and to attract other private investment, Moses sweetened the terms of the deal. The state law as amended in 1943 retained rent controls but relieved private sponsors of rehousing obligations and extended tax exemptions. Moreover, Moses acquiesced to housing segregation in order to accommodate prevailing market conditions. The development of Stuyvesant Town embroiled Met Life in damaging controversies over tenant relocation, racial segregation, and rent controls—more reasons for private investors to avoid the messy business of slum clearance.[11]

Despite the Met Life experience, Moses remained committed to private slum clearance, and this bias shaped his attitude to the postwar program of the New York City Housing Authority. In 1946, it advanced a plan to build moderate-income units on undeveloped sites, where land costs were lower than those on developed sites. Although Moses was seen to dictate NYCHA policy and site selection, he initially opposed what was called the "no-cash subsidy program" for two reasons: he regarded the construction of middle-class housing as a private-sector activity, and he favored redevelopment in inner-city slums over construction on undeveloped land.[12] Moses ultimately backed the program, which had Mayor William O'Dwyer's support, but he disapproved of the approach. In drawing the line between public and private action, Moses firmly believed that the private sector could adequately meet the housing needs of the middle class. Put in the context of housing programs in the 1940s, in particular the failure of state laws to induce private investment and the expansion of NYCHA into middle-class housing, Moses's Title I work can be seen as a more aggressive effort to enlist private capital in urban redevelopment.

The essence of Title I was a land subsidy known as the write-down. The cost to the city of assembling and clearing a redevelopment site was greater than the market value of the cleared land. The federal government covered two-thirds of the loss or write-down, with the city absorbing the other third. It was expected that the city would recoup this loss through higher tax revenues as the value of the redeveloped property rose over time. The explicit purpose of the program was to stimulate private investors to build market-rate housing in slum areas. But while the Title I write-down discounted the cost of land, it did not diminish other expenses—construction, debt service, and taxes—that raised housing costs beyond the reach of the middle class. Congress had assumed that lowering the cost of land would be sufficient to decrease the cost of housing, but as Jeanne Lowe put it in her groundbreaking early study of Title I, "Congress was unsophisticated in its housing economics."[13] In an expensive city like New York, the framework of Title I yielded luxury housing. To obtain moderate-priced housing, government would need to provide other subsidies.

THE MOSES RULES

As king of Title I, Moses had more concentrated power over the physical development of New York than any man had ever had or is ever likely to have again. Slum clearance involved all aspects of urbanism—not just roads and recreation, the domain Moses had commanded in the 1930s; not just housing, which was added to his portfolio in the 1940s; but every aspect of city growth—site selection, streets, circulation, sanitation, community facilities, social use, and design. Renewal projects were crafted by the Mayor's

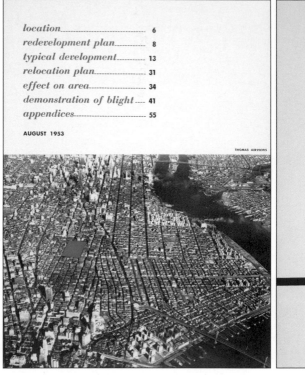

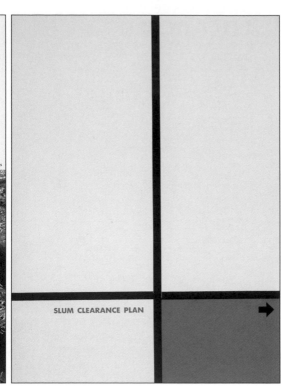

E-25. Pages from *Washington Square Southeast: Slum Clearance Plan under Title I of the Housing Act of 1949*, August 1953

Committee on Slum Clearance, which included leaders of relevant municipal departments: the New York City Housing Authority, City Planning Commission, Board of Estimate, Department of Buildings, Comptroller, and Corporation Counsel. But it was a committee in name only.[14]

Concentrating power in a redevelopment czar was not unusual. Most cities with robust Title I programs had powerful leaders: Louis Danzig in Newark, Edward Logue in New Haven and then Boston, Edmund Bacon in Philadelphia. Conversely, where power was dispersed, redevelopment often lagged, as in Boston until Logue arrived. Redevelopment intersected most parts of city government; to cut through the thicket of bureaucratic obstacles and compel coordinated action required concentrated power and fierce leaders like Moses and Logue.

But while wielding giant power at home, the redevelopment czars had relatively little power with the federal government. In a local context, Moses looked like Goliath; in dealings with the federal government, he sometimes came closer to David. Moses challenged federal rules that he thought obstructed the Title I program in three particular areas: sponsor selection, appraisal standards, and clearance procedures. The nitty-gritty information about operational intricacies presented here explains how Moses made a rough-hewn federal program work in a real estate market as expensive as Manhattan's.

RULE 1: Prenegotiated Sales. The federal guidelines neatly divided the public and private parts of the redevelopment process in prescribing the fol-

lowing sequence of events. The city selects a renewal site, buys it, relocates tenants, and demolishes the buildings; then and only then does the city sell the vacant land to a redeveloper who subsequently takes over. Moses upended the sequence so that city and sponsor interacted before the sale; selection of sponsor and site coincided at the outset of the process and preceded the city's acquisition of the site. In the federal model, competitive land auctions established fair market values on which the write-down was based; the higher the sale price, the smaller the write-down. In New York, the land auction was a ceremonial occasion with one party bidding on a prenegotiated sale. In theory, the auctions were open to other bidders, as Moses would inform prospective sponsors, but in practice, the advanced state of planning and customized terms at auction precluded other parties—only one groom comes to the altar.

Moses argued that cities could not afford to purchase and clear a multi-acre site only to discover afterward that no one would buy it. "If you are looking for private capital, you can't in a City like this persuade elected officers, the press and public to condemn and clear slums first and then look around for sponsors. You must snare them first," Moses explained to the Urban Renewal Agency. "Is there anyone dumb enough to think any Committee on Slum Clearance could persuade the governing body of New York (the Board of Estimate), with its shortage of capital funds, to condemn 50 odd acres of congested land in the center of Manhattan, like the Lincoln Square area, put out the tenants and raze the buildings, in the hope that in a year or so spon-

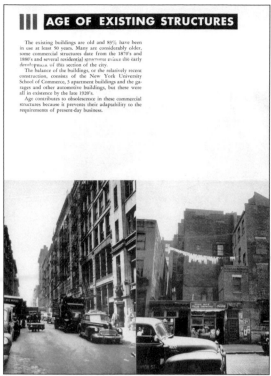

DEMONSTRATION
OF BLIGHT

I   *land use*
II   *condition of existing structures*
III *age of existing structures*
IV *land coverage*
V   *existing zoning*
VI *commercial obsolescence*
VII *residential obsolescence & tenant data*

41

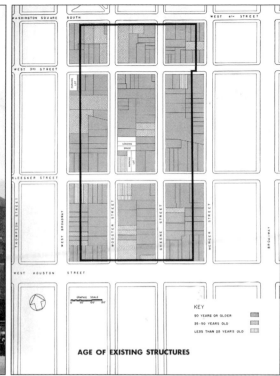

III AGE OF EXISTING STRUCTURES

The existing buildings are old and 85% have been in use at least 50 years. Many are considerably older, some commercial structures date from the 1870's and 1880's and several residential structures evince the early development of this section of the city.

The balance of the buildings, or the relatively recent construction, consists of the New York University School of Commerce, 3 apartment buildings and the garages and other automotive buildings, but these were all in existence by the late 1920's.

Age contributes to obsolescence in these commercial structures because it prevents their adaptability to the requirements of present-day business.

AGE OF EXISTING STRUCTURES

KEY
50 YEARS OR OLDER
25-50 YEARS OLD
LESS THAN 25 YEARS OLD

---

sors of music, education, housing and what not would turn up eager to pay any old price to bail the City out?"[15]

Detroit and Newark learned this lesson the hard way. In Detroit, officials spent several years planning the redevelopment of the Gratiot area before testing the interest of the private sector. There were no bidders at the first auction, in 1952, and only two bidders at a second auction, in 1953. The land was sold and cleared, but when the buyer's renewal scheme proved unacceptable, the city canceled the sale and was stuck for a time with a desolate site.[16] After a similar experience, the Newark Housing Authority, the local redevelopment agency, changed procedures and gave precedence to developers. "We took an awful chance in the North Ward . . . by guessing at what redevelopers wanted," an official reflected. "Then we had to go around peddling vacant land. Now we let redevelopers tell us where they want to build." The new rule: "find a redeveloper first, and then see what interests him."[17] As Harold Kaplan explains in his study of the Newark Title I program, site feasibility forced the city to bypass the hard-core slums. The Title I requirement to attract private capital dictated a quest for the "right blight" with investment potential. In due course, the federal government accepted the procedure of prenegotiated sale, which became standard operating practice.

Site feasibility involved more than site selection; it included the development of a business plan to make the deal economically feasible for the investor. The Slum Clearance Committee was conceived as "a negotiating group of city officials," the corporation counsel explained, with Moses as the negotiator.[18] Upon matching a sponsor with a site, he shaped a viable deal, determining the land resale price, the number of dwelling units in residential projects, and tax abatements, if any. Thus, by the time a project was introduced to the public, it was a fully packaged deal.

Moses presented the redevelopment projects to the public in stunning brochures designed by Richard C. Guthridge. Their bold graphics, potent images, detailed plans, construction schedules, and financial calculations made untested experiments in urbanism look like irrefutable, routine projects (fig. E-25). The brochures constructed a powerful visual argument and demonstrated Moses's sophisticated use of images, charts, and other visual material to shape perceptions. "I don't want the texts to be long," Moses instructed his staffer. "It's the schedules themselves, the plans and pictures that count with the statement that we mean business, that the procedure will be entirely fair and orderly and that hardships will be, so far as humanly possible, avoided."[19] The brochures also demonstrated Moses's commitment to professional expertise. The materials were prepared by Skidmore, Owings & Merrill (SOM), whom Moses appointed as coordinating architects for the Title I program, and by two reputable real estate firms, Charles F. Noyes Company and Wood, Dolson Company. Deaf to the citizen's voice, Moses relied on experts in real estate and finance, architecture and engineering to translate the public good into specific renewal plans.

The brochures were organized in three parts: the redevelopment plan, demonstration of slum conditions, and appendices. The redevelopment plan was cast in terms of square-foot and dollar calculations rather than social vision. It included a site plan, aerial rendering of the redevelopment, apartment layouts, business plan, and relocation schedule. The demonstration of slum conditions made the case that the area in question was, indeed, a slum. Title I did not define a slum or blighted area; it left the determination to the federal administrator.[20] For a definition of slum, one had to refer to the U.S. Housing Act of 1937: "The term 'slum' means any area where dwellings predominate which, by reason of dilapidation, overcrowding, faulty arrangement or design, lack of ventilation, light or sanitation facilities, or any combination of these factors, are detrimental to safety, health or morals."[21] Following these indicators, Moses presented data on the existing structures: their age, condition, heating and sanitary facilities; land coverage; population density; and tenant data, including family size and income.[22] The appendices preemptively addressed controversial matters with supporting evidence: acquisition and resale appraisals to rebut federal questions about the write-down, and letters from city officials about tenant relocation.

The brochures were submitted to the Board of Estimate and City Planning Commission for public hearings and approvals, then to the federal administrator, the Federal Housing and Home Finance Agency, a division of the Urban Renewal Administration, for federal review and approval. "Be sure to mention the fact that the City Planning Commission will ultimately have an opportunity to report on the Title I project," Moses instructed a staffer editing a brochure. "I want this in the booklet so no one will be able to say that they will not, in the end, be consulted before final action is taken."[23] To Moses, public input was accomplished through such gestures. The degree to which he controlled the hearings has been overstated, however. Of the first set of seven plans, all published in January 1951, Moses dropped or revised four, as he learned how to tailor more successful projects.[24] During the public review process, projects were often delayed and modified to accommodate critics; for example, the City Planning Commission rejected the enlargement of West Broadway when it approved the Washington Square Southeast Title I. Still, Moses had an overwhelming rate of success, which was primarily due to the buy-in of the city's political and business leadership in the renewal program rather than to his puppetlike control of the Board of Estimate and City Planning Commission.

RULE 2: Appraisals Based on Future Use, Not Market Value. The writedown, the key to Title I, was a soft number. It was the difference between the acquisition price, which could be firmly established, and the resale price, which was based on guesswork. The write-down raised many questions. How, for example, would the city fund its one-third share of the write-down? "Can this be done by some special type of City-wide assessment based upon the theory that the amortization and interest will be met as the new buildings go up and become taxable?" Moses queried Spargo, his numbers man. "We certainly have to have some theory in mind to guide us in determining how far down we can write these values. . . . I know how difficult it is to spell things out of the Federal rules, but it is time we got down to essentials."[25]

Moses developed an unarticulated theory of the write-down: quasi-public institutions serving the common good should not pay market value for land.

Values should be based on the prospective use of the land. The concept of use value, now accepted, was a contentious part of Moses's Title I plans and sparked skirmishes with the federal government.

New York University (NYU) agreed to pay $5 per square foot for the property on Washington Square South where the university library now stands. The city approved the deal, which covered the three-block area extending to Mercer Street, about a third of the Washington Square Southeast renewal area, but federal officials challenged the price. A private developer had entered a bid of $10.50 per square foot for the land directly to the south (where Washington Square Village was later built). Land valuations should be the same on adjoining land: this was the position of the federal administrator James Follin, regional director of the Division of Slum Clearance and Urban Redevelopment of the Housing and Home Finance Agency. Moses and NYU countered that the lower bid properly reflected the public purpose of the university.

The chancellor of NYU, Henry Heald, was well versed in the civic arguments for slum clearance. As president of the Illinois Institute of Technology in the 1940s, he had pioneered in this domain, taking advantage of state laws to acquire and clear a slum area where he launched the construction of IIT's iconic campus, designed by Mies van der Rohe. Upon arriving at NYU in 1952, Heald responded enthusiastically to an overture from Moses. When Moses conveyed his dismay with NYU's previous leader, because of his silent response to vocal critics, Heald offered reassurance: "You need have no fear about my backing out of the program because there is some opposition to it. I learned long ago that no slum clearance project could ever be 100% popular."[26] When the federal government rejected the low NYU appraisal, Heald mounted a vigorous case for use value. He argued that, first, the university should not "be penalized because the area in which it is located is ideal for redevelopment"; second, New York City had a stake in the quality and scope of the service provided by NYU; and third, NYU would raise surrounding property values. "In many projects it is in the best interests of the public to include areas for institutional or public use which by their very nature will produce no direct dollar income. Such inclusion is justified where the institutional or public use serves a broad public purpose and where such a use, by adding an increment of value to the adjacent area, provides greater security for the private investment." Ultimately, Heald acknowledged, "there is no formula by which a fair value price can be arrived at for land for education use." Lacking an exact formula, Moses and NYU agreed on a 50 percent discount.[27]

Eventually, Moses and NYU prevailed, but the federal government mounted a similar challenge to the appraisal of the Lincoln Center site, which was lower than that of the adjacent housing site. Differentiated valuations benefited about a dozen quasi-public institutions, which paid land prices well below market value because they served a public purpose. Although the framework of Title I dictated a real estate orientation, Moses did not narrowly pursue the bottom line. His position was consistent with his career-long view of public works as an engine of economic development: a civic investment in public infrastructure will drive up property values and ultimately make economic sense.

RULE 3: Sponsor Relocation and Clearance. Federal guidelines defined tenant relocation and clearance as municipal responsibilities; this phase of work was supposed to precede the land sale. Moses rewrote these rules: he sold redevelopment sites before relocation and clearance and required the sponsor to handle these operations. The federal model assumed that the city would better manage the challenge. Moses believed that if the city ran relocation, political pressures would produce interminable delays. He was correct: after the city took control of relocation in 1960, it slowed to a snail's pace. Efficiency was Moses's critical concern. Conceiving of relocation as a practical and technical challenge, not a social problem, he envisioned relocation and clearance as an incremental process to be flexibly coordinated with the phasing of construction rather than as a stage precedent to construction.[28] Phasing allowed for the gradual displacement of site residents, but it also subjected them to abuses, and Moses's system afforded no protection to tenants awaiting eviction.

As a result of Moses's hand's-off approach, relocation procedures varied from project to project, depending upon the sponsor's standards. There were bad sponsors, the most notorious being the team at Manhattantown. In 1954, a Senate investigation threw a national spotlight on this Upper West Side project, located between Central Park West and Amsterdam Avenue from 97th to 100th Street. The sponsors had acquired the renewal site in 1951; three years later, there was no new construction, and only a fraction of the site had been cleared. Meanwhile, the sponsors were making money as old-fashioned slumlords and collecting rent on condemned tenements while letting them rot. Moses subsequently imposed a municipal monitor, but he fiercely defended both private relocation and the right of Title I sponsors to collect rents before demolition.

There were also conscientious sponsors, like Lincoln Center for the Performing Arts and Fordham University. They hired a reputable relocation firm, Braislin, Porter & Wheelock, which staffed an on-site relocation office and maintenance department. Communicating with owners and tenants in Spanish as well as English, the firm brought buildings into code compliance, maintained apartments during the waiting period, and actively assisted in the search for new housing. They paid brokers for listings and landlords for painting replacement apartments. The on-site office housed representatives of the New York City Housing Authority, who assisted in the search for public housing, and the New York City Bureau of Real Estate, the municipal body that monitored relocation.

Herbert Greenwald, a national Title I developer, also tried to handle relocation in a responsible manner (fig. E-26). He had come to the rescue in Detroit, where he bought the Gratiot area, and rescued the Pratt Institute project from a defaulting sponsor. Greenwald updated Moses on his progress in 1957:

> Our relocation experience leads us to believe that the method of the Slum Clearance Commission, which has come in for so much criticism of late is overly much maligned. A sponsor willing and able to carry out his contract can do a good relocation job and possibly even a better job than City authorities. If the atmosphere of suspicion and bickering were not in the background, we might have proceeded more slowly in our relocation program. Despite our speed, no one suffered grievous injury. In the end,

E-26. Herbert Greenwald, May 27, 1957. Photograph by Hedrich-Blessing. Courtesy Chicago History Museum, neg. HB20465

bidders might be more eager for a project if an atmosphere of confidence were restored and a sponsor allowed to work in a more orderly fashion.[29]

Greenwald indicated another factor complicating relocation. After Title I's slow start in the early 1950s, all parties—the federal government, Moses, the press, and the public—demanded results. The pressure was to clear and build quickly, but responsible relocation attempting to address individual needs moved at a slower pace.

Even at its best, relocation was hobbled by structural forces with brutal consequences: underfunding of relocation and a severe shortage of affordable housing. Title I provided meager support for relocation expenses. Commercial property owners and tenants received no compensation under the 1949 legislation. (The Housing Act of 1956 permitted relocation payments up to $2,000 to businesses.) Residential property owners received $500; Lincoln Center and Fordham added bonuses for self-relocators ($275 to $500, depending on the apartment size); by comparison, NYCHA grants were $100. Most important, there was inadequate replacement housing: a 1960 study put the shortage at 430,000 units.[30] The demand for low-income units was aggravated by the postwar influx of Puerto Ricans and southern blacks, by the cumulative effects of clearance necessitated by public housing and arterial highways as well as Title I, and by the incommensurate growth of the public housing program.[31] Tenants displaced by Title I clearance could not afford the on-site replacement housing, which was intended for higher income residents. Nor could they typically afford to remain in the gentrified neighborhood. In theory, the best option was public housing, but it was in short supply, with waiting lists in the tens of thousands. In a relocation analysis of the first five hundred evicted families, Lincoln Center documented trends that generally characterized the Title I diaspora in New York City: 70 percent moved outside the neighborhood (broadly defined in this case as the Upper West Side); the average rent of the displaced rose from $51.82 to $65.26; and only 11.4 percent moved into public housing.[32]

PAIRING UP WITH PUBLIC HOUSING

One response to the demand for low-income housing was to use a Title I site for that purpose. Moses pursued this strategy in the Washington Square South plan, which dedicated seven of forty acres to a New York City Housing Authority project, named Houston Houses on the plan (fig. E-27). As Joel Schwartz established, the lending community opposed this integrated approach.[33] So did the federal administrator who reminded Moses that Title I was intended for redevelopment by private enterprise: "It would not appear that the use of sites cleared under the Title I program exclusively or to a predominant degree for redevelopment in public housing would be consistent with this general policy."[34] Moses never again included public housing in a Title I project. He did not, however, abandon the idea of mixing incomes.

Morningside Gardens (the Morningside-Manhattanville Title I) introduced a new approach, which coordinated the Title I project with a neighboring public housing project. The expectation was that tenants displaced from the Title I site could be locally rehoused in the NYCHA project. In his report "Essential Postwar Improvements" of April 1946, Moses called for the coordinated construction of public and moderate-income housing:

> There is, beyond question by the toughest individualist, a large part of our population which will have no decent lodgings, much less homes, unless government provides them on a frankly uneconomical basis, if dollars are the only measurement. . . . Those helped by the government should not be segregated, nor should they monopolize whole neighborhoods. This is why redevelopment, limited dividend and speculative building, with all the services that go with them, should go on step by step and block by block with public housing for the lowest income groups. Postponing one or another is a dangerous business. They must be timed to go together.[35]

It would seem that Moses had contradicted this position in the 1940s when, as the city construction coordinator, he was associated with a housing program that rebuilt much of the Lower East Side as public housing. Nevertheless, in the 1950s, when he controlled site selection for Title I, he located twelve of his seventeen executed projects beside public housing. Only in two cases, Morningside and Manhattantown, were the Title I apartments built in tandem with new NYCHA projects, the General Grant Houses and Frederick Douglass Houses respectively (fig. E-28). In the other instances, Moses chose Title I sites adjacent to preexisting NYCHA projects (fig. E-29).[36]

Coordination proved difficult: NYCHA and Title I were pulled in different directions by divergent constituencies, locational strategies, and funding constraints. Moses was obliged to target more expensive, developed land for clearance, whereas the federal public housing program (Title III of the U.S. Housing Act of 1949) put limits on land costs that obstructed this approach.[37] The pairing of Title I and NYCHA projects offered various benefits, including the formation of mixed-income neighborhoods, but the coordinated projects did not come close to solving the relocation problem, as the numbers revealed: only 18 percent of the tenants displaced by the two Morningside slum clearance projects (the Title I cooperative, Morningside Gardens, and the NYCHA project, General Grant Houses) moved into public housing elsewhere in the city.[38] Moses did not reckon with the hard truth: public housing was no haven for Title I evictees.

Moses blamed NYCHA's tough eligibility standards, which ruled out single-parent families, noncitizens, and the unemployed. In 1959, he again suggested a coordinated Title I–public housing program with phased construction to deal with relocation. NYCHA would first build a low-income project on the site of the Polo Grounds (involving no evictions) to provide housing for those displaced from two proposed clearance sites in Harlem. William Reid, the chairman of the NYCHA, would not prioritize Title I evictees and reminded Moses that only 12 percent of tenants of Title I sites were relocated to NYCHA projects, attributing the low figure to the bonuses and finder's fees offered by Title I sponsors, which ostensibly made alternative housing more attractive. Moses's reply to Reid gives some sense of the intragovernment battles he fought and, as in this case, lost: "We had hoped for a better position and assurance which would make most of the tenants eligible. . . . It would be helpful if your staff, in reviewing applications for relocation to public housing projects, would be more liberal and flexible in qualifying our site occupants."[39]

Slum clearance affected black New Yorkers more profoundly than others. Some Title I projects were located in integrated neighborhoods, such as Manhattantown, and the result of redevelopment was to resegregate those areas, with the expensive new housing generally pricing out minority residents. The discrimination in the housing market and the limited options available to blacks landed them in other slums, but Moses did not recognize this problem. "What type of housing is referred to by the term new slum?" Moses was asked in a questionnaire sent to him in 1957 by Whitney North Seymour, the president of the Municipal Art Society. Your letter "makes no sense to me," Moses answered. "I don't know who invented the term 'new slums' or what it means, and don't propose to be hornswoggled into any such silly controversy. When by the way, did the members of your Society stop beating their wives?"[40] The problem of the new slums and the racialized impact of clearance did not deter Moses. On the contrary, New York's thousands of slum acres reinforced his conviction of the need to bulldoze and build.

Moses compartmentalized the problems that he attacked and accepted what Scott Greer felicitously called the "cage of constraints" surrounding Title I policy.[41] That cage allowed Moses to ignore the secondary effects of Title I clearance: a housing crisis, resegregation and discrimination, and shrinking central-city housing options. He failed to acknowledge that slum clearance begat slums. His ability to see the city as an organic unity and the wide scope of his operations put Moses in the unique position to advance integrated solutions. The tragedy is that instead he declared limited objectives to rationalize the social damage he caused.

THE TITLE I DEVELOPERS AND FEDERAL ROADBLOCKS

As a group, the New York Title I developers were suspect, tainted by their secretive selection. There was no transparent bidding process or established procedure to submit redevelopment proposals. Moses not only decided what the city needed and where; he also anointed the Title I sponsors with limited vetting. Construction delays and cases of malfeasance compounded the problem. Manhattantown became emblematic, shaping the view of sponsors as slumlords, political cronies, and cheats who profiteered from a state-sponsored land rush. Putting the program in historical perspective, William Zeckendorf described the write-down as "a variant of the land subsidies through which our early railroads were built."[42] But in the early years of Title I, before regulations were loosened, there was no land rush. Absorbed by colorful sponsor scandals, the press missed an important and unexpected story: at the outset, Title I failed to attract private capital.[43] Moses certainly chose some bad sponsors, but the main problem was the risky business of slum clearance, not the sponsor selection process.

Moses was disheartened to find that relatively few developers were interested in slum real estate. In January 1950, he acknowledged that "for vari-ous reasons those representing large reservoirs of private capital in banks, insurance companies, real estate and building enterprises have been hesitant to take a lively interest in slum clearance." His report ends with an entreaty to investors: the "Committee recommends at this time that further steps be taken to invite a larger interest in this slum clearance and redevelopment program. We hope that additional private investment groups will come forward."[44] Moses had encountered such resistance in the 1940s, and now discovered that the write-down did not sufficiently change the financial equation for investors.

Several discouraging factors were at work. First, slums were a real estate profit center. A 1957 study by the Council for Better Housing acknowledged that "favorable yields on the existing properties provide little incentive for redevelopment. It is more profitable to keep structures in their present conditions at a 67 percent return than to demolish them to erect new structures earning a smaller return."[45]

Second, the pioneer redevelopers could not obtain financing. Banks would not fund the risky business of urban renewal without federal mortgage insurance, and the Federal Housing Administration (FHA) adopted the same risk-averse attitude as banks. As the administrator of the Housing and Home Finance Agency explained, the FHA was not "permitted to insure houses in slum areas because a slum was regarded as beyond redemption."[46] Thirty lending institutions reportedly refused to finance the NYU-Bellevue project.

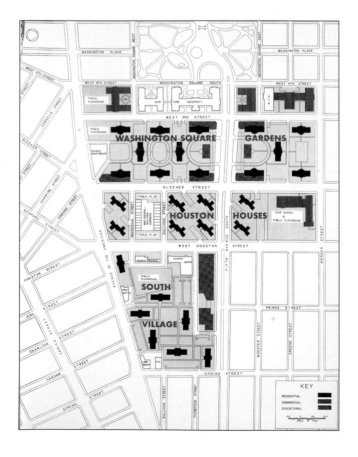

E-27. Composite site plan of Washington Square South and South Village Title I redevelopments, January 1951. Houston Houses was planned as a public housing project.

E-28. Brochure cover showing aerial view of Morningside Gardens (bottom) and General Grant Houses, public housing project (top), 1957. Courtesy MTA Bridges and Tunnels Special Archive

Morningside-Manhattanville

Morningside Gardens
General Grant Houses

Manhattantown

Park West Village
Frederick Douglas Houses

Columbus Circle & Lincoln Square

Columbus Circle Appartments
Lincoln Tower & Princess Gardens
Amsterdam Houses

Penn Station South

Penn Station South Houses
Chelsea Houses

Washington Square

Washington Square Village
Silver Towers

Harlem

Lenox Terrace
Delano Village
Abraham Lincoln Houses

NYU-Bellevue

Kips Bay Plaza

Corlears Hook, Park Row
Park Row Extension, & Seward Park

East River Cooperative Houses
Vladeck Houses& Baruch Houses
Chatham Green & Chatham Towers
Governor Alfred E. Smith Houses
Seward Houses
LaGuardia and Rutgers Houses

E-29. Map of Manhattan, showing Title I projects executed by Robert Moses, with adjacent low-income housing of the New York City Housing Authority.
Map by James Conlon

The FHA had been established to support housing construction but, following banker's logic, undermined the goals of urban renewal. Federal policy was at odds with itself. As Zeckendorf noted, "The FHA, while freely funneling funds to the suburbs, treated proposals to build in slum areas with about as much enthusiasm as your maiden aunt getting an invitation to a strip tease show."[47]

Moses complained incessantly to his federal contacts and lobbied Senator Robert A. Taft to amend the 1949 law, recommending mortgages of up to 90 percent of construction costs, without limitation on the basis of room or apartment count.[48] Moses got the first part of the request, the 90 percent mortgage, when Congress amended the housing law in 1954 and authorized the FHA to insure urban renewal projects, based on the value of the completed redevelopment. The first government-insured mortgage for a Title I project anywhere in the nation was issued to Delano Village (the North Harlem Title I) in 1955.[49] The primary reason for the Title I standstill during its first five years was the policy of the FHA, not wayward sponsors. Once mortgage insurance was available, projects came to life.

But FHA insurance came with restrictions disadvantageous to city builders. The FHA set a maximum base cost of $8,400 per room; an additional $1,000 per room was allowed in areas of high construction costs, such as New York City, but only in apartments of four or more rooms. In order for city developers to qualify for FHA mortgages, they were compelled to reduce costs and build cut-rate housing. Moreover, a room had to meet an idiosyncratic FHA definition—balconies but not bathrooms were defined as rooms—that created an incentive to build balconies and penalized bathrooms. I. M. Pei, who was involved in several Title I projects, predicted that as a result apartments in Alaska would begin sprouting balconies; certainly they sprouted all over New York. At Kips Bay Plaza, Pei persuaded the FHA to count the alcovelike projection of the structural wall as balcony space, although it was inaccessible, and in this way his design complied with FHA price ceilings.[50]

The FHA was only one part of the problem. Title I entangled developers in a web of bureaucratic rules, red tape, and government oversight that caused expensive delays and timing problems. Standard developments did not impose these restrictions. And in New York, sponsors faced the additional burden of managing relocation. Given the financial risks, public scrutiny, and unproven market appeal of redeveloped slums, the early sponsors were often less motivated by business sense—there were safer investments elsewhere—than by commitment to an urban future. The pioneering sponsors included Herbert Greenwald, who worked with Mies van der Rohe; Abraham Kazan and Shirley Boden, leaders of the union-sponsored cooperative housing movement; Robert S. Olnick, who at the start of his career sponsored the Harlem Title I and provided Harlem with its first apartment buildings with doormen, at Lenox Terrace (fig. E-30); and, most important, William Zeckendorf, whose large-scale imagination and dazzling ambition made him a fine match for Moses (fig. E-31).

Having previously collaborated on the United Nations, Zeckendorf and Moses partnered again in connection with the Fort Greene Title I, announced in December 1952. This project provided Long Island University (LIU) with seven and a half acres to build a proper campus surrounding its outpost in a converted theater on Flatbush Avenue in Brooklyn, where it served ex-G.I.s and a local student population.[51] Zeckendorf was president of the university's board of trustees and donated the funds ($500,000) for the land purchase. The site met several of Moses's criteria: it was beside a public housing project (Fort Greene Houses), a park (Fort Greene Park), and Brooklyn Hospital, and could buttress an already significant investment in public resources. Still, Zeckendorf's association with LIU, a fledgling university founded in 1926, had to have been a major consideration in the selection of this site for Title I funding.

Zeckendorf's role in this early project was limited to financial support; his first venture as a Title I developer came a year later, in 1953, in the Southwest Washington project, which was followed by intensive Title I work between 1956 and 1958. As Zeckendorf explained in his spellbinding autobiography, his firm Webb & Knapp studied possibilities in about thirty cities and submitted proposals in half that number to reap a harvest of eight projects nationwide.[52] He entered New York in a big way in 1957, as sponsor of three projects. By this time, Moses had given up on small-time, inexperienced developers and favored veterans on whom he could rely to get the job done. Zeckendorf rescued the notorious Manhattantown and the NYU-Bellevue projects, paying the back taxes; he was rewarded with the sponsorship of the Lincoln Square housing, which required Moses to break a contract with the novice developer whom he had originally designated. In addition to deep experience with Title I, Zeckendorf brought his brilliant architect, I. M. Pei, who set a high design standard at Kips Bay Plaza, as the NYU-Bellevue venture was renamed. Alas, Zeckendorf overreached. To avoid bankruptcy, he sold his three New York City Title I housing projects to Alcoa in 1962 (bankruptcy happened anyway in 1965), which became an important institutional participant in urban renewal. With significant projects in Hyde Park, Chicago; Society Hill, Philadelphia; Southwest Washington; and New York City, among other places, Zeckendorf's Title I work was unparalleled and remains an untold chapter in the history of postwar American urbanism.

THE STRATEGY: HOW TO SAVE THE CITY

Moses proudly assumed an antivisionary stance: "I recommend you file the 'Master Plan of Land Use' and forget it." Contemptuous of "long-haired planners" who promoted wholesale change yet had no idea how to get things done, he saw himself as an administrator "driving persistently at limited objectives and reaching them. . . . There it is," Moses proclaimed in mocking self-debasement, "you can't expect anything better from moles who are blind, crawl short distances under the earth, and have only the most limited objectives."[53] In principle, he opposed master planning, but in practice he made and executed plans. The question is, what if any idea of the city informed those plans?

E-30. Doormen at the Americana, Lenox Terrace,
10 West 135th Street, ca. 1958. Photograph by Cecil Layne

E-31. Caricature of William Zeckendorf, by Paul Davis, 1961. The original caption reads: "The Sand Hog, or Badger (Zeckendorfus barbarus): A burrowing animal, fully webbed and napped except for the sharp claws used in operating its famous game called 'urban renewal.' In this process the resourceful little creature, equipped with such clever devices as ground leases, accelerated depreciation allowances, mortgage pyramids, and mergers—yet rarely a penny of its own money—can level a city faster than you can say 'Robert Moses.' Reproduces by subdividing. Approach of its bulldozing claws into hitherto unharmed areas marked by sudden appearance of white X's on windows and shutting off of heat unless taken to court, where it knows everyone anyway. Makes grunting noise that sounds like 'Title One! Title One!' abhors high ceilings, thick walls, and decorative architecture. Naturalists believe it instinctively builds drab buildings the way the beaver builds leaky dams."

The prevailing view of Moses is that he had no overarching urban public purpose. Caro portrays an empty soul crazed by power who, by the 1950s, had lost the public mission of his early years. Stressing Moses's "real estate project approach to community building," Jeanne Lowe sees Moses as servile to the market imperatives of Title I, a point echoed by Joel Schwartz. "Moses actually had in mind purposeful reclamations for mixed-uses, but under the studied indifference of investors adopted the opportunist approach. The resulting Title I's," Schwartz concluded, "had no central purpose other than to improve isolated areas, fill the city's write-down quotas, and preserve the prerogatives of the construction coordinator."[54] Granted, Moses was opportunistic; it does not follow that he lacked a guiding vision.

Indeed, a survey of his urban renewal projects indicates that his opportunism served well-defined goals.

Moses shaped Title I to reinforce the role of the central city and to keep New York the thriving center of a spreading metropolitan region and a magnet for suburbanites, the U.S., and the world. He pursued three objectives. Objective one was to recapture the middle class, which had chosen the suburb over the city, by building modern, affordable housing. Objective two was to establish New York as a center of higher education by making land available for university expansion. Objective three was to elevate the national and international stature of New York with magnetic world-class institutions: Lincoln Center for the Performing Arts, the Coliseum, and the United Nations. (The United Nations did not involve Title I clearance and thus is not discussed here, but it was part of this strategic vision.) Moses concentrated the Title I program in Manhattan: of the seventeen executed projects, thirteen were in Manhattan, two in Brooklyn, two in Queens. Manhattan represented the ideal ground for Title I: slums were extensive, land values inflated, and real estate interest high. But unlike other cities, which used Title I to lure banks and department stores and office buildings back into ailing downtowns, New York under Moses avoided commercial land uses. The only exception was the Coliseum, New York's first purpose-built convention center, which had a showcase role and fit with Moses's desire to put New York on display.

Economic critiques of urban renewal serve to highlight the opposing values that motivated Moses. In his penetrating study of 1965, Scott Greer concluded that the total costs of renewal were not reflected in the increased advantages of enterprises' returning to the central business district.[55] According to his economic reasoning, he saw no inherent benefit in a strong center city, whereas Moses had an a priori commitment to the city. Nationwide, Greer noted, few careful demand studies were made before urban renewal project sites were cleared. By the 1960s, Chester Rapkin and other urban sociologists were studying the economic opportunities in the region and the demand for inner-city, middle-income housing, but Moses did not collect such data. He molded renewal projects more on faith in the city than on empirical proof that middle-class families would come back from the suburbs and that universities and the arts were key to an urban future.

Moses warned that New York would become a polarized city of rich and poor unless it took aggressive steps to provide for the middle class. His first objective was to build affordable housing for teachers, nurses, garment workers, municipal employees—the broad middle class. New York City had a strong tradition of union-sponsored cooperative housing going back to 1926. Although Moses had no sympathy for the movement's ideology, his pragmatism led him into a productive alliance with the cooperators; through Title I, he launched the biggest expansion of union-backed cooperatives in the city's history: eight Title I housing cooperatives in all.

Moses found a partner in Abraham Kazan, a union leader focused on housing issues. In 1951, Kazan established the United Housing Foundation (UHF) to capitalize on Title I, and under his leadership the UHF sponsored three Title I cooperative projects: the East River Houses at Corlears Hook; Seward Park Houses, also on the Lower East Side; and Penn Station South.

The UHF was also slated to sponsor the Cooper Square Title I, which was canceled after Moses's reign ended. (It went on to sponsor the Jamaica Race Track development and Co-op City.) In each case, the UHF worked with a sponsoring labor union. Louis Pink, another UHF leader, sponsored Kingsview in Brooklyn, part of the Fort Greene Title I; and Shirley F. Boden, who got his start with Kazan, was involved with three Title I cooperatives. Boden structured the housing cooperative at Morningside Gardens, which was sponsored by a consortium of Morningside academic and religious institutions. He then established the Middle Income Housing Corporation, which sponsored Chatham Green and Chatham Towers (Park Row and Park Row Extension Title I) with the backing of city and state credit unions. Located near the heart of city government, these apartment buildings were intended to provide municipal workers with apartments they could afford to own. The last of the Title I cooperatives, Princess Gardens, a single building in the Lincoln Square development, rejected the ideology of cooperativism but retained the financial structure as a way of reducing housing costs.

The disappointing truth about Title I was that it naturally resulted in luxury housing unless market forces were restrained, or other subsidies provided, or both, as with the cooperatives. The cooperatives contained costs by three means: equity down payments at the start of the project allowed advantageous long-term mortgages and reduced financing costs; speculative profits were eliminated; and, thanks to Moses's advocacy, tax abatements were provided. After an initial down payment of roughly $700 per room, owners paid modest monthly charges of about $20 per room.[56] The tax abatements alone saved purchasers a meaningful amount: $3 to $4 per room per month, or $149 to $192 a year on a four-room apartment.[57] The city comptroller Lawrence Gerosa opposed the tax abatements, arguing that they undercut the Title I goal of growing the city's tax revenues. The comptroller's recommendations, Moses responded, "would ultimately make not only Manhattan but all of New York City a home for the very rich and the very poor, with no place for the real 'forgotten man' with middle income who can support himself if rents are reasonable."[58]

The cooperatives gave Moses a mechanism to control real estate market forces while populating the city with middle-class home owners. At the opening of the Seward Park Houses in October 1958, he paid tribute to the cooperators, "substantial and reliable people who have a real stake in the City . . . and ask only that City and Federal agencies help them get started. They don't want the City to be their landlord; they want to pay their way." With cooperatives, we shall "rebuild the City for those who want to stay and for those who, in increasing numbers, want to come back to town from the suburbs."[59]

The second objective of Moses's Title I program was to support higher education. He directed projects to benefit private universities—New York University and NYU Medical Center, Long Island University, Pratt Institute, Fordham University, and the Juilliard School—as well as the academic institutions on Morningside Heights. Yeshiva University and the Cooper Union were slated to participate in two canceled projects, Riverside-Amsterdam and Cooper Square respectively. The transfer of land to universities was a response to the postwar explosion of college enrollments. With the public

sector funding the expansion of the city colleges and the establishment of the state university system in 1948, Moses used Title I to support private universities, or what he preferred to call quasi-public institutions because they served the public interest.

Title I provided private universities with tools that they otherwise would not possess: eminent domain, land assemblage, and discounted land. Through Title I, NYU was able to shift its center of operations from the Bronx to Washington Square and complete its takeover of the south side of the square. As the development evolved and the sponsor of the private housing opted out, NYU acquired the entire renewal site, stretching from Washington Square to Houston Street. Fordham University was an invisible presence in Manhattan, with dispersed classrooms complementing the main Bronx campus. Moses provided a two-block site at Lincoln Square for a full-fledged campus. The Lincoln Square Title I also accommodated a new building for the Juilliard School, which expanded its curriculum and profile in a monumental new structure. (A high school of performing arts was added to the project after Moses's retirement.) Moses did not originate the idea of using slum clearance on behalf of universities; Henry Heald had previously done this in Chicago. But recognizing a good idea, Moses translated it into a large-scale building program and urban mission.

The third objective was to enhance the stature of the city with new institutions that would draw national and international attention. Both the Coliseum and Lincoln Center were publicized as proof of American urban progress; the former was a magnet for trade, the latter a beacon of cultural achievement. Lincoln Center, probably the most influential Title I project in the nation, demonstrates Moses's originality in execution, not in conception. When Fiorello La Guardia first conceived of a performing arts center, in 1938, he asked Moses to study the idea. Moses dismissed it, unable to imagine a project involving "so much expense, so much cooperation among quasi public and private interests and such complexities in the establishment of the operating corporation." He correctly gauged the future challenges that Lincoln Center would face, but he would reverse the position that he staked out in 1938.[60] Moses came to embrace La Guardia's vision as he witnessed the inability of the Metropolitan Opera and the Philharmonic-Symphony Orchestra to cope with the real estate challenges of New York City and recognized cultural institutions as a source of urban prestige and international renown.

Determined to assist the Metropolitan Opera in its thirty-year quest for a new home, Moses offered the organization two Title I sites, Columbus Circle and Washington Square, before the parties agreed on Lincoln Square. The forty-five-acre project, the city's largest Title I project, included land for Fordham, housing, and a commercial theater complex to be developed by Roger Stevens. When the federal government balked at the large write-down, Moses dropped the commercial complex, the part with the highest tax ratables. John D. Rockefeller III and the exploratory committee that he chaired were ultimately responsible for the high quality of Lincoln Center for the Performing Arts, which expanded from the opera and symphony to embrace five additional cultural entities plus a park with band shell, but Moses played an essential role in its realization.

Moses grasped the appetite for culture in the postwar period, a trend diagnosed by Alvin Toffler in his book *The Culture Consumers*, which appeared in 1964. The public marketing of Lincoln Center was part of its mission, with outreach to suburban audiences and school programs built in from the start. Historically, the opera and symphony were hermetic, and their elite donor circles provided limited financial support; by contrast, Lincoln Center launched a broad-based capital campaign, appealing to a wide public. Lincoln Center illustrated what Toffler described as an organizational revolution in the culture industry, a revolution fundamentally connected to the urban strategy that Moses devised, based on centralization, monumental architecture, and urban prominence.

SUPERBLOCK SOLUTIONS

"I am inclined to think of it in terms of people rather than buildings," the *New York Times* editor Lester Markel wrote in explaining why he objected to Moses's approach to slum clearance. For Moses, the slums were like war-torn Dresden—dead structures to be demolished before new life could flourish. They were a physical, not a social, problem, to be cured by replanning and new building. "The big unresolved question seems to me to be this," Markel continued. "What do you do with the inhabitants of a slum area when you clear up that area for purposes other than low-income housing?"[61] These social matters fell outside Moses's shuttered view of the slum problem, but planning did not; planning was at the heart of the problem as he understood it. Replot the streets, replace the site plan, build anew, and the reformatted, upgraded city would generate a better life.

Yet, despite this environmental premise, Moses did not attach importance to urban and architectural design in his planning process. He determined land use and produced preliminary site plans, then turned the project over to the sponsor without imposing design standards. Moses conceived of design decisions as a matter of private choice, outside the sphere of government control.

The categorization of design as a private preference is unsurprising. Although buildings and site plans establish the physical framework of urban life and have long-lasting effects, design was, and still is, rarely considered a domain of public policy. Even so, given Moses's conception of urban renewal as a building program, his lack of interest in design was a serious blind spot. For all his overreaching power, when it came to physical form and urban design, Moses did not go far enough. He relinquished control of these fundamental aspects of renewal to the sponsor.

The planning process began with the land-use plan, which fixed the allocation and distribution of uses on a renewal site and wholly reflected Moses's decision making. Mixing tax-exempt and full tax-paying uses, he aimed for a net tax gain without adhering to a formula in balancing these uses. Although nonresidential uses came under attack on the grounds that slum clearance money should be used only for housing, the Housing Act of 1949 imposed no land-use restrictions if the site had been a residential slum.[62]

Next came the site plan, which involved a collaboration between the sponsor's architect and SOM, representing Moses. Although various architects were involved in this work, site plans followed the same pattern. High-rise apartment buildings floated on a superblock, the towers set back from the street but usually aligned with the city grid. To bring apartment living into the automotive age, sites contained several surface parking lots and sometimes an underground garage.[63] To compensate for the closure of streets within the superblock, the bounding cross streets were enlarged to accommodate the displaced traffic. These extra-wide streets are, indeed, good for cars but further separate the projects from the surrounding fabric. Moses and his planners placed a premium on open space and reduced land coverage: renewal dramatically decreased land coverage from 80 to 90 percent in the slums to 30 percent in the redevelopments (fig. E-32). But despite its amplitude, the open space was fragmented by scattered buildings and parking lots, and landscaping was an afterthought. The promise of reduced land coverage all too often resulted in surface parking.

A banal but significant feature of the housing projects was the one-story commercial strip fronting on the avenue. The strips maintained the traditional building line and the commercial vernacular of the street while providing modern commercial space. Gone were the mom-and-pop shops of tenement buildings; the new commercial space could be flexibly sized to accommodate the larger retail operations demanded by national chains and postwar consumer trends. One of Harlem's first large supermarkets, if not the first, opened in the retail space at Lenox Terrace. Unlike the NYCHA projects, which excluded shops, the commercial-residential mix in Title I projects was an asset.[64]

The site plans often included new public facilities—a playground or school—or incorporated existing community facilities. Lenox Terrace is the best example of a flexible site plan; it wrapped the new structures around a preexisting play center (the Children's Aid Society and its playground), and integrated a church (formerly a theater), public bath, and power substation in the superblock (fig. E-33). The success of this approach reinforced Moses's effort to site Title I projects near existing community structures in order to shore up the public infrastructure.

Site planning was managed by SOM, a firm Moses had first hired in 1939, when it was newly formed, to work on the World's Fair and had used ever since. As Nathaniel Owings explained, the Moses connection helped the firm grow and "gave SOM a niche in the tight hierarchy which controlled architectural, planning, engineering and construction jobs in New York City."[65] By 1949, when Moses hired SOM to coordinate planning for the Slum Clearance Committee, there was no more distinguished corporate firm in the city. The urban renewal point men at SOM were Robert Cutler, one of the founding partners in the New York office; Kenneth Young; and Major General George J. Nold, an engineer with exceptional experience in managing large-scale projects. As director of the Joint Construction Agency, European Command, Nold headed the building program for all American fighting forces in Europe from 1953 to 1955, whereupon he joined SOM.[66] That Moses enlisted the military's top engineer to oversee the reconstruction of New York indicates his approach to renewal as a technical, engineering, and management problem.

IV LAND COVERAGE

The only land in the redevelopment site which is not solidly built up is in streets, sidewalks, two small parking lots and one off-street truck-loading space. The adjacent map indicates that the coverage within lot lines is virtually 100%. So little ground area is devoted to small, inadequate and isolated airshafts and light courts as to be negligible. In this respect no distinction can be made between commercial or residential properties.

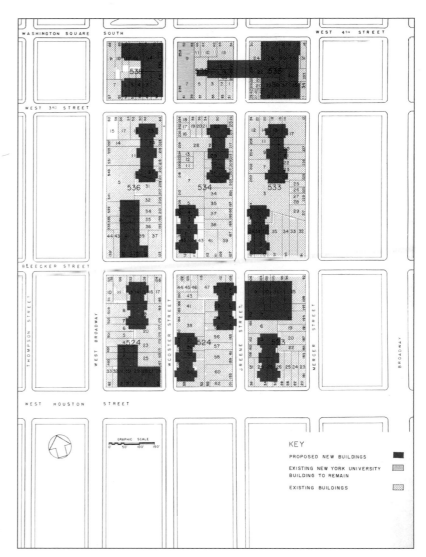

E-32. Existing buildings and proposed new buildings showing reduction in land coverage, 1953

SOM did more than act as project manager; the firm worked with the sponsor's architects, approved all designs, and at times submitted its own plans (their site plans in the Harlem and North Harlem Title I brochures are notably uninspired). It is clear that Moses expected SOM to guide planning from an early stage, as when he instructed Cutler to "see what sort of attractive plan of the Riverside-Amsterdam area can be figured out with the City Planning Commission and Yeshiva University."[67] SOM, however, did not respond creatively to the urban design opportunity that Moses offered. Ultimately, Moses is accountable for the mediocre site plans that his committee issued, which he might have more fully controlled. Nevertheless, he was not schooled in urban design nor were most redevelopment czars. (The exception was in Philadelphia, where the urban designer Edmund Bacon shaped urban renewal and achieved significant refinement in design.) Moses hired distinguished professionals from whom he expected excellence

and outstanding performance. He had done as much in the 1930s: the talents of his top designers—the architect Aymar Embury II, the landscape architect Gilmore D. Clarke, and the engineer Othmar Ammann—can be seen in the high-quality designs of pools, recreational landscapes, and bridges from that period.

The failure of the Title I work to meet the same high standards has several causes. One was a lack of creative urban thinking: the architectural profession was not prepared to handle the great challenge of urban renewal.[68] The modernist paradigm of superblock urbanism was the default response, and Title I bluntly exposed its inattention to neighborhood scale and other social inadequacies. Procedural and programmatic issues also undermined design: a federal approval process that obstructed design improvements, Moses's deferral to private developers, and the bottom-line orientation of redevelopment. A letter from Cutler to Moses in 1959 captures SOM's complacent

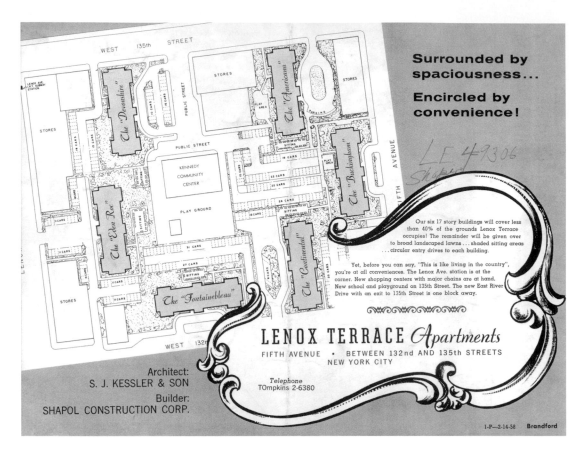

E-33. Site plan of Lenox Terrace Apartments (Harlem Title I), from rental brochure, 1958

posture.[69] The inflexibility of the federal approval process blocked design improvements. The site plans and corresponding aerial views published in the slum clearance brochures were schematic and recorded an early stage of planning, but under certain circumstances those plans were binding. After approval by the Urban Renewal Administration and a grant of FHA mortgage insurance, any subsequent change in the site plan required new approvals. The case of Herbert Greenwald and the Pratt Institute Title I illustrates how the FHA obstructed design improvements.

Greenwald inherited a mediocre plan when he took over the housing portion of the Pratt Institute Title I project. For the Brooklyn block bounded by Myrtle and Willoughby avenues (Area B), S. J. Kessler and Sons made a typical site plan of parking lots and apartment slabs (fig. E-34). But, as Greenwald explained to Moses, "We felt that it was an anachronism to place automobiles between buildings . . . [and] much preferred the complete segregation of automobiles from people and green areas." Greenwald pursued an alternate plan for the project called Willoughby Walk with the consulting architects, SOM, and arrived at an agreement on what he regarded as a superior scheme. Greenwald provided Moses with an account of his failed effort to improve the design:

We then approached the FHA and were flatly rejected. Several alternate plans were devised for the benefit of the FHA Land Planner, and in April 1958, a compromise plan was submitted to SOM which received their approval. At this juncture we went to see Mr. Lebwohl [the director of the Committee on Slum Clearance] and apprise him of our desire to execute the plans . . . and to enlist his support. To his credit . . . he went to the FHA with our people; that he made several telephone calls apprising the Land Planner and the Director at FHA that the SCC, SOM and the sponsor were in unanimous accord that the new site plan should be used. All this was to no avail.

As a final step, I discussed with the Director of FHA the possibility that I might appeal his decision to Washington. I was then told that if I insisted upon my plan, which would mean a reprocessing of the commitments (I was willing to pay for this), the jobs would be stopped and that no commitment would be available to me for Building # 3. With this immovable force, there could be no further argument. In order not to postpone the occupancy of the buildings, we reluctantly retreated to the original site plan.

We are disheartened that we were compelled to produce an inferior situation when an excellent alternative was available. We fought long and hard. SOM fought for us, Mr. Lebwohl was on our side, but the FHA controls the purse strings and I reluctantly yielded. . . . I can only promise you, in the Quadrangles we will have *ab initio* a site plan we believe in before we go to FHA for any commitments.[70]

Greenwald was forced to build Willoughby Walk as Kessler had planned it. He set Mies van der Rohe to work on the Quadrangles, his other part of the Pratt Institute renewal project, but Greenwald died in 1959—en route to New York to discuss Title I business, his plane crashed in the East River—which ended Mies's involvement and changed the course of this project as well as the Battery Park Title I, for which he was also the sponsor.

Design was also defeated by other government rules. "Don't touch it," Gordon Bunshaft of SOM warned Pei about Title I. "That's not for architects. That's for lawyers."[71] The busiest Title I architect in New York was S. J. Kessler and Sons, a firm headed by Melvin E. Kessler, an entrepreneurial figure who specialized in apartment buildings but whose real talent was mastery of the regulatory apparatus. He began his career at the New York State Housing Division; in private practice, he worked for the NYCHA, in 1946 built the first FHA-insured apartments in Scarsdale, and was quick to see Title I as a business opportunity. The Kessler firm was the housing planner on six Moses projects and, presumably on Moses's recommendation, was hired as the housing architect by sponsors of seven Title I projects.[72] Even Zeckendorf retained Kessler as a consultant to advise Pei on compliance with Title I/FHA rules.

Moses broke down the wall dividing public and private phases of redevelopment in order to negotiate financial plans, but he did not insert design into this conversation. Nothing was written into the ground rules to advance architecture. The rare cases of good design that survived both this process and the stringent economics of slum redevelopment represented an exceptional commitment on the sponsor's part and his patronage of a talented architect. There were five quality designs: Zeckendorf's Kips Bay Plaza, designed by Pei; the three towers for NYU (originally University Village, now called Silver Towers, and 110 Bleecker Street), also designed by Pei; Shirley Boden's neighboring cooperative projects, Chatham Green and Chatham Towers, both by Kelly and Gruzen; and Lincoln Center.

Nevertheless, there were limits to individual efforts. Absent public control, there was no mechanism to regulate how the parts of a renewal project related to one another or how a project related to the bounding streets. Each sponsor was left to operate as if on a self-contained island. Lincoln Center demonstrates the best and worst of this system. Under the enlightened leadership of John D. Rockefeller III, Lincoln Center set high design standards and worked with internationally acclaimed architects. The plan created a cross axis to link up with Fordham, but Fordham turned inward, declining the invitation to extend the axis into its campus. More troubling, the Slum Clearance Committee did not consider how the superblock related to the environs. Lincoln Center is built on a platform that closes off Damrosch Park to the potential community of users residing across the street in the Amsterdam Houses, and ignores Amsterdam Avenue and the side streets. (At present, Lincoln Center is attempting to address some of the problems of the original urban design and animate 65th Street with a design by Diller Scofidio + Renfro.)

Once title was transferred to the sponsor, Moses drew a sharp line and claimed no right to intervene. "We have no control over [the selection of architects] and want none" was his policy position.[73] It was not that he was undiscerning or indifferent. Moses personally had conservative taste and held that the design of public works should meet conventional standards of beauty. For the preliminary designs of the project at Washington Square, he chose Eggers and Higgins, the successor firm of John Russell Pope known for its mastery of historical styles, as the Jefferson Memorial in Washington, D.C., and NYU's Georgian-style law school exemplify. When NYU unveiled Max Abramovitz's modern design for a student center, Moses complained to the university's chancellor:

> You will remember that all the brochures and other publications and sketches published and circulated with respect to the Title I project promised Georgian architecture. There is genuine, not merely woozy sentiment on this subject, not only in the

E-34. Perspective of Pratt Institute Title I, with the Quadrangles (left), Pratt Institute (center), and Willoughby Walk (right), July 1953. Collection MTA Bridges and Tunnels Special Archive

neighborhood but throughout the City. . . . We develop enough support . . . only if we meet reasonable demands and expectations for the maintenance of the traditional Colonial or Georgian architecture which we have promised. While we cannot control what you do on the plot west of the area you acquired in connection with the Title I redevelopment [where Abramovitz's student center was located], I must make it clear to you that we shall have to use our full power in connection with the land incorporated in the Title I redevelopment to compel adherence to the Colonial or Georgian plan. [In public works,] I have to be something of a traditionalist.[74]

Moses's concern about community standards was legitimate; NYU eventually built misguided modern buildings on Washington Square.

It should be noted, however, that Eggers and Higgins did not offer a Georgian or Colonial design, but an overscaled superblock scheme. Their site plan demonstrates the extent to which the modernist agenda of superblock urbanism had been absorbed by the profession, including its most conservative wing. Despite his being a self-proclaimed traditionalist, Moses's urban renewal projects were a fulfillment of the modernist urban paradigm, not as interpreted by creative designers but in the vernacular of the professional mainstream. They delivered light and air and open space in a dense, high-rise setting. It was a model that privileged the experience of the apartment dweller rather than the experience of the pedestrian in the street. Perhaps that is why, according to my thoroughly unscientific, anecdotal evidence, these projects seem well appreciated by their residents.[75]

Notwithstanding the design failures of Title I, most of these projects are flourishing. This is a tribute in part to the gentrifying effects of the renewal projects on their environs and to the strength of New York City today. But the Moses-Title I template also had certain regenerative features that have fostered the reintegration of these superblocks in the urban fabric. The commercial strips on the streets have maintained street life, in contrast to the scenario at the housing enclaves built by the NYCHA. A size comparison of Title I projects across the country remains to be done, but my working hypothesis is that those in New York were relatively small: the Southwest Washington Title I encompassed 427 acres; New York's biggest slum clearance project, Lincoln Square, covered 45 acres; the average size of the Title I projects in Manhattan was 16 acres; Corlears Hook and Washington Square South were each 14.5 acres. The modest size of Moses's projects combined with the commanding authority of the city's great grid limited the deadening effects of superblock urbanism. Moreover, Moses embraced density, which is now recognized as a precondition of the city's diversity, vitality, and mass-transit system. Yet his Title I program notably failed to integrate buildings at varied scales and to combine rehabilitation with selective clearance, as in I. M. Pei's work at Society Hill, Philadelphia. Indeed, the rehabilitation issue brings us to the end of this story and exposes the outdated conceptual framework in which Moses was stuck.

THE END OF BULLDOZER CLEARANCE

As criticism of Title I mounted across the nation, Moses took heart from his star lineup of New York City sponsors. He welcomed the prospect of congressional hearings in the city in 1959. "The more I think of it, the more the picture of a parade of witnesses including [those from] the top universit[ies], labor cooperative[s, and] all other reputable sponsors appeals to me—the sponsors of Lincoln Square for instance including the Performing Arts, Fordham, Red Cross, etc., Long Island University, New York University, Pratt Institute, the needle and building trades cooperatives, Morningside Gardens headed by David Rockefeller and including [President] Dwight D. Eisenhower as Honorary Chairman."[76] Nevertheless, city leaders were moving urban renewal in a different direction. Moses was forced to resign in March 1960, and Mayor Wagner overhauled the urban renewal apparatus, establishing a central relocation bureau and the Housing and Redevelopment Board to manage Title I work under new procedures. According to Moses's tally, during his reign over Title I, 314 acres were cleared and 28,400 apartments were built. This compares to 30,680 public housing dwelling units built in Manhattan alone during the period from 1947 to 1959.[77] Moses's effort was prodigious, but in the face of the great structural forces reorganizing the metropolitan region and in a city as large as New York, the overall impact of Title I was small.

In 1956, the City Planning Commission hatched an alternative renewal program based on spot clearance and rehabilitation. James Felt, its chairman, obtained federal funding for a study of the Upper West Side based on the premise that conservation could rescue a declining neighborhood to avoid demolition. The 1949 housing law had funded only advanced planning and clearance; an amendment in 1954 authorized funding for rehabilitation and conservation to broaden the range of renewal strategies. (The 1954 amendment replaced the term *urban redevelopment* with *urban renewal* to signal the new approach.) Moses adamantly opposed rehabilitation. Trapped in a mind-set formed in the 1930s, he saw slums as a spreading cancer, and clearance and superblock urbanism as the only effective cure. His imaginative capacity failed him when a more modest approach to renewal took hold; he did not fathom how small-scale measures could transform a neighborhood and have large-scale effects.

Felt is an interesting counterpoint to Moses. His business was real estate; he had been involved in early clearance projects—his real estate company had assembled the land for Peter Cooper Village and Stuyvesant Town—and had run relocation programs. But Felt had a more nuanced view of the slums than Moses had. In 1939, he distinguished three stages of decay: areas in need of clearance, areas where complete rehabilitation was appropriate, and "twilight zones" requiring strict code enforcement. But this dissenting view went underground in the 1940s, as demands for bold action swayed public policy.[78]

The West Side Urban Renewal Study was published in 1958.[79] The plan covered a larger territory than typical of Moses's renewal plans: a seventy-four-acre, twenty-block area from 87th to 97th Street and from Central Park West to Amsterdam Avenue. While worried about "creeping blight," Felt's study looked at the city through a new lens that revealed the social fabric of the Upper West Side. It praised the positive role of block-improvement associations and community groups, and endorsed racial integration as a goal. Under the banner of "self-preservation" and incremental change, the West Side Renewal Plan overthrew the superblock model and pursued selective inter-

E-35. West Side Renewal Plan, new and rehabilitated buildings with public walk through block, 1958

vention with the existing gridiron street pattern left intact (fig. E-35). A fine-grained analysis sorted out high-rent elevator buildings in good shape, structurally sound old-law tenements and run-down brownstones in need of remodeling, and structures to be demolished. Instead of the speedy, military-style implementation that Moses favored, Felt called for slow, "judicious phasing." The West Side Plan signaled a complete paradigm change from clearing to pruning: "Renewal can be more like pruning a tree," Felt explained, "resulting in a healthier and more fruitful organism."[80] Pictures of street tree plantings, community fix-ups, and streetscapes with buildings at different scales indicated the new, small-bore approach to the city.[81]

Wielding the watchword of reformers, the West Side Plan called for a "comprehensive" approach to renewal, including more open space, school improvements, and expanded community services. In practice, Moses integrated these elements in his Title I projects, but he rhetorically denounced the idea of comprehensive planning and its collaborative, all-inclusive approach; his pragmatism led him to segment issues into containable, circumscribed tasks. Moses's strength and weakness were one and the same: the pursuit of limited objectives. Moreover, in looking at tenement blocks, Moses did not see the self-healing powers that Jane Jacobs extolled in *The Death and Life of Great American Cities*, published in 1961 in response to urban renewal. He saw the destructive forces of real estate speculation that profited from slums and a need for sweeping government action.

Some of the problems with Title I, which recurred across the country, flowed from the law, its real estate orientation, and built-in assumptions about

clearance. Other problems flowed from Moses's management of the program and his abstracted, bird's-eye-view of the city. Yet, to a surprising degree, he managed to stretch the framework of Title I in order to provide middle-class housing, expand higher education, and create a world-class performing arts center. He developed innovative strategies of urban renewal that remain effective engines of economic redevelopment, and he tackled serious problems, in particular the lack of affordable housing, which persists in Manhattan where the high cost of housing is squeezing out the middle class.

In response to constraints on his maneuverability and scope of action, Moses tactically pursued limited objectives. This approach was the precondition of his prolific record of public works, but it also rationalized his willful disregard of collateral effects and refusal to pursue comprehensive solutions. Moses failed to go far enough in asserting public control over relocation and over the planning and design process; these two major shortcomings of New York's Title I program were not due to his overreaching but to his reticence to assert public control over the private sector.

To a generation of post-Moses urbanists, his concentrated power made him a public danger. Yet, exaggerating his power and disregarding the constraints that he faced—from federal policy and local politics, lending institutions, and citizen groups—reinforces the myth of omnipotence that Moses shaped and distracts from the clash of public and private interests in urban space and land markets that he embodied. His Title I work crystallizes the persistent challenge of directing market forces to serve public goals and of promoting a public good that transcends local interests.

NOTES

1. While my view of Moses was primarily formed through archival work, I drew on the rich literature from the 1960s on the national Title I program. Three outstanding books in particular deserve to be better known: Jeanne R. Lowe, *Cities in a Race with Time: Progress and Poverty in America's Renewing Cities* (1967), the sole book to address design issues; Charles Abrams, *The City Is the Frontier* (1965); and Scott A. Greer, *Urban Renewal and American Cities: The Dilemma of Democratic Intervention* (1965). The Title I program is spottily discussed in Robert Caro's *Power Broker* (1974), which highlights Manhattantown and Lincoln Center, sponsor scandals, and relocation problems. The most important book on Title I is Joel Schwartz's *New York Approach: Robert Moses, Urban Liberals, and Redevelopment of the Inner City* (1993), which established the deep bed of support for Moses's renewal agenda. I am in awe of the book's archival depth, which allowed Schwartz to track decision making with astounding texture. In contrast to his close-up view of political dynamics, my essay considers renewal as urbanism, by which I mean urban design and physical and social planning.

    Throughout this essay I refer to *urban renewal* because it has passed into common usage, but technically the correct term to describe Moses's work is *redevelopment*. The 1949 law referred to urban redevelopment; as amended in 1954, the law adopted the term urban renewal to indicate a broader range of planning options, including rehabilitation as well as clearance.

2. The key source on the legislation is Mark I. Gelfand's *Nation of Cities: The Federal Government and Urban America, 1933–1965* (1975). Moses followed the congressional debate over federal housing policy and advised the senators who took the lead on the issue: New York's Robert Wagner; Mr. Republican, the Ohio senator Robert A. Taft; and the Louisiana senator Allen Ellender. Hearings in 1943 opened a legislative battle that divided on the scope of federal intervention, more specifically the degree to which the government should be involved in housing construction. In 1945, the senators introduced a housing bill; it failed to pass in 1946 and again in 1948, but Moses discerned the shape of compromise legislation and began to plan in anticipation of its passage.

    Moses described the preparatory measures in the two reports of the Committee on Slum Clearance: *Preliminary Report on Initial New York City Projects under Title I of the Housing Act of 1949*, July 14, 1949; and *Second Report to Mayor William O'Dwyer from the Mayor's Committee on Slum Clearance by Private Capital*, January 23, 1950.

    Of the 32 projects for which Moses obtained planning grants, 26 resulted in published plans; and at the time of Moses's resignation, in 1960, the following 6 projects were in the stage of advanced planning: Cooper Square, Seward Park Extension, Delancey Street, Mid-Harlem, Division Street, and Bellevue South.

    For national data, see U.S. Housing and Home Finance Agency, Urban Renewal Administration, *Urban Renewal Project Directory* (Washington, D.C.: 1960), cited in Kaplan, *Urban Renewal Politics*, 3. Also see the compilation of national data on urban renewal in Anderson, *Federal Bulldozer*, appendix A.

3. Dunbar McLaurin, letter to Moses on the development of the Polo Grounds, August 26, 1957, and Moses's reply, August 29, 1957, New York Public Library, Manuscripts and Archives Division, Robert Moses Papers, Box 116, File: Committee on Slum Clearance 1957. This archive is hereafter abbreviated as Moses Papers. The archive is uncataloged and only roughly organized by the positions that Moses held, for example, Slum Clearance Committee, Construction Coordinator, Parks Department. Each box contains numerous unnumbered files; I have provided the name exactly as it appears on each file.

4. Anderson, *Federal Bulldozer*.

5. "The Critics Build Nothing," an address by Robert Moses at a luncheon meeting of the New York Building Congress, November 10, 1959, Moses Papers, Box 117, File: Housing File 1/1/59–12/31/59, Library Corr. Folder 4 of 6.

6. Moses, "Practical vs. Theoretical Planning," *Public Works*, 477.

7. Remarks of Robert Moses at the Annual Teachers' Institute of the Archdiocese of New York, March 5, 1959, Moses Papers, Box. 117, File: Housing File 1/1/59–12/31/59, Library corr. Folder 4 of 6.

8. Division of Slum Clearance and Urban Redevelopment, Housing and Home Finance Agency, *The Relationship between Slum Clearance and Urban Redevelopment and Low-Rent Housing* (Washington, D.C.: 1950), 13.

9. Ibid.

10. This statement appeared at the beginning of every plan published by the Mayor's Committee on Slum Clearance.

11. On the Redevelopment Companies Law of 1942, the 1943 amendment that liberalized the private sector obligations, and the Metropolitan Life Insurance Company's developments, see Schwartz, *New York Approach*, 82–83, and chap. 4.

12. In NYCHA's no-cash subsidy program, rents averaged $74 to 75, the level required to cover operating expenses; in subsidized low-income projects, rents averaged $37 to $38.

13. Lowe, *Cities in a Race with Time*, 184.

14. Moses made decisions, assisted by indispensable and long-time deputies: George Spargo, an engineer turned financial analyst; Harry Taylor, and later William Lebwohl, both lawyers who served as staff director. George Spargo was assistant to the director, who began working for Moses in the 1930s after serving in the Queens borough president's office. Like his boss, Spargo wore multiple hats: in the parks department, Triborough Bridge and Tunnel Authority, Office of the City Construction Coordinator, and on the Slum Clearance Committee. Moses lent him to Mayor O'Dwyer, whom Spargo served as deputy mayor. In 1938, when Spargo was an executive officer at the parks department, he was known the Accelerator. Moses commended his ability in financing Triborough bonds. In 1959, Spargo became embroiled in a controversy over a conflict of interest when it was revealed that he was the director of a bank making mortgage loans to slum clearance sponsors; see Wayne Phillips, "Spargo Is Dropped from Slum Agency," *New York Times*, January 29, 1960. Lebwohl, the director of the Slum Clearance Committee, was a lawyer at the Triborough Bridge and Tunnel Authority.

15. Remarks of Robert Moses at the conference of the Federal Housing and Home Finance Agency, Region I, April 17, 1958, Moses Papers, Box 117, File 1: Committee on Slum Clearance 1958.

16. On the Gratiot area urban renewal, see Roger Montgomery, "Improving the Design Process in Urban Renewal," in Wilson, *Urban Renewal*, 459–66; and Waldheim, *CASE: Hilberseimer/Mies van der Rohe*.

17. Kaplan, *Urban Renewal in Politics*, 24.

18. John P. McGrath [Corporation Counsel, 1947–51], letter to the editor, *New York Times*, July 27, 1959.

19. Robert Moses, memorandum to William S. Lebwohl, December 3, 1956, Moses Papers, Box 116, File: Robert Moses's Library Corr. From Housing File Folder 1 of 3.

20. The law offered the following definition: "'Urban renewal area' means a slum area or a blighted, deteriorated, or deteriorating area in the locality involved which the Administrator approves as appropriate for an urban renewal project." U.S. Housing Act of 1949 as amended through August 1955, Title I, Section 110. The original language was even broader; it defined a redevelopment area as "an area which is appropriate for development or redevelopment and within which a project area is located."

21. U.S Housing Act of 1937, Section 2.3.

22. The relocation surveys were completed by Frederick E. Marx, associated with Wood, Dolson, then later as vice president of Helmsley-Spear. On Marx's work for the Slum Clearance Committee, see Peter Kihss, "Slum Aide Hints Job Favoritism," *New York Times*, July 18, 1959.

23. Robert Moses, memorandum to Harry Taylor, December 11, 1950, Moses Papers, Box 90.

24. The next 13 plans, published between September 1951 and August 1957, were all executed. But the last 6 plans, published between November 1958 and June 1959, ran into trouble. Moses quickly withdrew one plan (Gramercy), and two were executed (Park Row Extension and Soundview, a Mitchell-Lama project), and the fate of 3 projects (Riverside-Amsterdam, Battery Park, and Cadman Plaza) was determined by Moses's successors.

25. Robert Moses, memorandum to George Spargo, September 5, 1950, Moses Papers, Box. 90.

26. Henry Heald, letter to Moses, December 6, 1952, NYU Archives, Box 12, Folder 5. This folder contains other relevant correspondence between Heald and the Slum Clearance Committee.

27. Henry Heald, memorandum to James Follin, April 3, 1954, NYU Archives, Box 12, Folder 7.

28. See Moses's letter to J. Anthony Panuch, the special adviser to Mayor Wagner on housing and urban renewal, commenting on the desirability of a central city agency for tenant relocation, October 16, 1959, Moses Papers, Box 117, File: Housing File 1/1/59–12/31/59.

29. Herbert Greenwald, letter to Moses, December 26, 1957, Moses Papers, Box 117, File: Committee on Slum Clearance 1958.

30. Panuch, *Building a Better New York*, 35.

31. The Committee on Slum Clearance quantified "concurrent government displacement activities" estimated as of April 30, 1956: New York City Housing Authority (public housing), 20,853; Committee on Slum Clearance (Title I), 15,385; Bureau of Real Estate (schools, parks, playgrounds, hospitals, traffic arteries), 14,897; State-Federal Arterial Road Program, 10,320. Mayor's Committee on Slum Clearance, *Comprehensive Relocation Plan. Park Row NYR3. Title I Urban Renewal Project* (New York: [1956]), 7.

32. Braislin, Porter & Wheelock, Inc., *The First 500 Families: A Relocation Analysis*, mimeographed report, [1960]. I consulted a copy in the Fordham University Archives, Box P-M-15, Folder LCPA, Subcommittee 1958; another copy can be found in the Lincoln Center Corporate Archives. On studies of relocation in other cities, see Wilson, *Urban Renewal*, part 4, "Relocation and Community Life," 291–404.

33. Schwartz, *New York Approach*, 143.

34. N. S. Keith [Director, Slum Clearance and Urban Redevelopment], letter to Moses, February 27, 1950, Moses Papers, Box 90.

35. Moses Papers, Box 90. For another endorsement of this policy, see Robert Moses, letter to Helen Harris [Executive Director], October 21, 1958, Moses Papers, Box 117, File: Committee on Slum Clearance 1958.

36. This strategy, which is at odds with the prevailing view of Moses, has rarely been noticed; an exception is Joshua Benjamin Freeman, *Working-Class New York: Life and Labor since World War II* (New York: New Press, 2000), 114. The twelve Title I projects with the neighboring NYCHA project are as follows.

Title I	Housing	Adjacent Public Housing
Corlears Hook	East River Coop. Houses	Vladeck & Baruch Houses
Columbus Circle	Columbus Circle Apts.	Amsterdam Houses
Harlem	Lenox Terrace	Abraham Lincoln Houses
Lincoln Square	Lincoln Towers and	Amsterdam Houses
	Princess Gardens	
Manhattantown	Park West Village	Frederick Douglass Houses
Morningside	Morningside Gardens	General Grant Houses
Park Row	Catham Green	Governor Alfred E. Smith Houses
Park Row Ext.	Chatham Towers	Governor Alfred E. Smith Houses
Penn Station South	Penn Station South	Chelsea Houses
Seward Park	Seward Houses	La Guardia and Rutgers Houses
Fort Greene	University Towers and Kingsview	Walt Whitman & Ingersoll Houses
Hammel	Dayton Towers	Hammel Houses

37. Schwartz, *New York Approach*, 172. Title III limited property acquisition to 25 percent of total project costs.

38. John T. Metzger, "Rebuilding Harlem: Public Housing and Urban Renewal, 1920–1960," *Planning Perspectives* 9 (1994), 276. Abraham Kazan described the resistance of the NYCHA to rehouse tenants dislocated from the United Housing Foundation sites; see "The Reminiscences of Abraham Kazan," 1968, 425, in the Oral History Collection of Columbia University.

39. Robert Moses, letter to William Reid, September 2, 1959; Reid, letter to Moses, December 4, 1959; Moses, letter to Reid, December 9, 1959, Moses Papers, Box 118, File: Housing File 1/1/59–12/31/59, Robert Moses—Library corres. Folder 6 of 6. There was generally a sizable gap between the preclearance estimate of tenants eligible for public housing and the actual number that relocated to public housing. Moses attributed the gap to two factors: an estimated 20 percent of eligible familiar either rejected units offered or did not apply for public housing, and 4 percent proved to be ineligible at the time of processing their applications. Moses also argued that Title I relocation was comparable to that of the NYCHA. See Mayor's Committee on Slum Clearance, *Comprehensive Relocation Plan. Park Row*, 13–14, 28–31.

40. Whitney North Seymour, letter to Moses, January 3, 1957, and Moses's reply, January 7, 1957. Moses Papers, Box 116, File: Committee on Slum Clearance 1957.

41. Greer, *Urban Renewal and American Cities*, 125.

42. Zeckendorf, *Autobiography*, 202.

43. Several writers on urban renewal have called attention to the low investor interest in Title I; see Anderson, *Federal Bulldozer*, chap. 7; and Lowe, *Cities in a Race with Time*, chap. 4.

44. *Second Report to Mayor William O'Dwyer from the Mayor's Committee on Slum Clearance by Private Capital* (January 23, 1950), n.p.

45. City-Wide Council for Better Housing, *New York City's Slum Clearance Committee: A Critical Study* (New York: 1957), 24.

46. "Big Slum Project Insured by F.H.A.," *New York Times*, September 30, 1955.

47. Zeckendorf, *Autobiography*, 203.

48. Robert Moses, letter to Robert A. Taft, November 28, 1952, Moses Papers, Box 90.

49. "Big Slum Project Insured by F.H.A."

50. "Pei's Apartments Round the Corner," *Architectural Forum* 11, no. 5 (August 1961), 106–14.

51. Zeckendorf, *Autobiography*, 227.

52. Ibid., esp. chap. 16 and 17.

53. Robert Moses, "Commissioner Moses Dissects the 'Long-Haired Planners'," *New York Times Magazine* (June 25, 1944), 38.

54. Lowe, *Cities in a Race with Time*, 48; and Schwartz, *New York Approach*, 301.

55. Greer, *Urban Renewal and American Cities*, 157–59.

56. At Corlears Hook, the down payment was $625 per room and monthly maintenance was $17 a room. At Morningside Gardens, the down payment was $750 per room, monthly maintenance, $21.

57. Stephen G. Thompson, "Co-op Housing: N.Y.C. vs. U.S.A.," *Architectural Forum* 111, no. 1 (July 1959), 133.

58. Robert Moses, letter to Mayor Robert Wagner, May 24, 1956, in response to the *Report to the Board of Estimate on Title I Slum Clearance Projects and Tax Exempt Housing*, Lawrence Gerosa, Comptroller (May 9, 1956), Moses Papers, Box 116, File: 1956 Robert Moses' Library Correspondence from Housing File Folder 3 of 3.

59. Remarks by Moses at Seward Park, October 11, 1958, Moses Papers, Box 117, File: Committee on Slum Clearance 1958.

60. *Report to the Mayor from the Park Commissioner on the Proposed Municipal Music Art Center* (September 20, 1938), brochure. A manuscript copy of the letter from Moses to Mayor La Guardia of the same date is in the Moses Papers, Box 97.

61. Lester Markel, letter to Moses, March 4, 1958, Moses Papers, Box 117, File: Committee on Slum Clearance 1958.

62. Amendments in 1954 and 1959 increasingly liberalized the restrictions on nonresidential uses.

63. An amendment to the zoning law adopted on June 21, 1950, required new dwellings to provide garage or parking space for cars of occupants. In A and B districts (most of the Title I sites), parking spaces had to be provided for 20 percent of the dwelling units. See New York City Planning Commission, *Planning Progress 1940–50* (New York: 1951), 24.

64. On the absence of stores in public housing and the resultant problems, see Charles Grutzner, "Shopping Scarce in City Projects," *New York Times*, June 16, 1957.

65. Nathaniel Alexander Owings, *The Spaces In Between: An Architect's Journey* (Boston: Houghton Mifflin, 1973), 77.

66. Nold was consulting engineer to SOM from 1955 to 1962, when he died.

67. Robert Moses, letter to Robert Cutler, June 5, 1959, Moses Papers, Box 118, File: Committee on Slum Clearance 1959.

68. On the demise of CIAM and the related establishment of an urban design program at Harvard, see Eric Mumford, "The Emergence of Urban Design in the Breakup of CIAM," *Harvard Design Magazine* 24 (spring–summer 2006), 10–20. This special issue, on the origins and evolutions of "urban design" 1956–2006, contains other relevant articles on the state of urban design in the 1950s. Also see idem, *The CIAM Discourse on Urbanism, 1958–1960* (Cambridge, Mass.: MIT Press, 2000).

69. Robert Cutler, letter to Moses, September 17, 1959, Moses Papers, Box 118, File: Committee on Slum Clearance 1959. I should like to acknowledge a potential bias in my sources. It may be that the SOM archives would afford a different perspective on their role as consultants. My initial queries did not turn up relevant material but continued research is needed.

70. Herbert Greenwald, letter to Moses, October 2, 1958, Moses Papers, Box 117, File: Committee on Slum Clearance 1958.

71. Cited by Cannell, *I. M. Pei*, 143.

72. The Kessler firm was the housing planner on the following projects: Manhattantown, NYU-Bellevue, Lincoln Square, Battery Park, Gramercy Park, and Riverside-Amsterdam. Kessler designed the following buildings: Lenox Terrace (Harlem Title I); Park West (Manhattantown Title I); Willoughby Walk (Pratt Title I); the two projects in Rockaway, Seaside and Hammels; Kips Bay, with I.M. Pei (NYU-Bellevue); and Washington Square Village, with Paul Lester Wiener (Washington Square Southeast). Kessler, together with his father and brother, had a 5-percent ownership interest in the corrupt Manhattanville project. This combined with his dominant role in Title I cast suspicion on the firm, and in July 1959 Mayor Wagner barred him from obtaining additional Title I work. "New York's Title I Controversy Spotlights Architect Kessler—A Combination of Know-How and Know-Who," *Architectural Forum* 3, no. 2 (August 1959), 13–15; and Wayne Phillips, "Barred Designer Has 2 Slum Jobs," *New York Times*, November 2 1959.

73. "Statement by Robert Moses, Chairman as to Architectural Services of the Kessler Firm," July 2, 1959, Moses Papers, Box 118.

74. Robert Moses, letter to Henry Heald, September 2, 1955, Moses Papers, Box 116, File: Housing Correspondence for Mr. Moses's Library Project Jan. 1, 1955 to Dec. 31, 1955.

75. When asked to recommend an architect, Moses offered these respectable suggestions: SOM; Eggers and Higgins; McKim, Mead & White; Harrison & Abramovitz; Voorhees, Walker; Kelly and Gruzen; Chapman, Evans & Delehanty; and Brown, Guenther and Booss. Memo, November 30, 1959, Moses Papers, Box 117, File: Housing File 1/1/59–12/31/59.

76. Robert Moses, letter to Congressman Charles Buckley, July 27, 1959, Moses Papers, Box 118, File: Housing File 1/1/59–12/31/59; Robert Moses—Library corres. Folder 6 of 6.

77. Metzger, "Rebuilding Harlem," 283, note 3.

78. James Felt, "The Problem of the Old Law Tenement: An Address before the New York Metropolitan Association of Real Estate Boards at the Hotel Commodore, N.Y.," brochure, January 11, 1939, 7.

79. James Felt, New York City Department of City Planning, *A Report on the West Side Urban Renewal Study to Mayor Robert F. Wagner and the Board of Estimate of the City of New York, and to the Urban Renewal Administration* (New York: [1958]), 8. The study was prepared by the following team of consultants: Donald Monson, general consultant; Elizabeth Kempton, community organization consultant; Brown & Guenther, architectural consultant (Moses also used this firm); Chester Rapkin, economic consultant.

80. Ibid., 85.

81. In some respects, the West Side plan vindicated Moses's point of view. In a supporting study of the real estate market in the renewal area, Chester Rapkin, a planner at the University of Pennsylvania, confirmed Moses's view that rehabilitation was not financially sound for tenement owners: rehabilitation costs ran high and resulted in less rental income if rehabilitated properties met higher occupancy standards. Sustained government intervention and subsidy were needed for the middle class, while the demand for luxury and moderate-income apartment houses would grow. Rapkin, *Real Estate Market*.

ROBERT MOSES, RACE, AND THE LIMITS OF AN ACTIVIST STATE

MARTHA BIONDI

In a stunning coincidence, on August 1, 1943, the Harlem Riot began and the *New York Times* published an essay by Robert Moses in which the parks commissioner denounced civil rights laws, praised the leadership of Booker T. Washington, and proudly described—in detail—his successful effort to sabotage a civil rights amendment to the 1938 New York State constitution.[1] This conjuncture—the essay and the uprising—discloses a surprising and dramatic collision between traditional Jim Crow thinking and the new mood of fast-growing migrant black neighborhoods. How could Moses, the quintessential modernist and activist city builder, espouse such myopic ideas? Moreover, he was a northern New Dealer, and a Jew writing just as a black-Jewish alliance to fight religious and racial bigotry in New York was about to commence.

"There are stories of unrest among our colored citizens," he wrote, no doubt referring to the wave of racial violence that swept the nation that year, most lethally in Detroit, where a riot in June led to thirty-four deaths, seven hundred injured, and six thousand federal troops occupying the city. Detroit catapulted urban racial conditions into the national spotlight. In New York, the mayor and other officials scrambled to interpret the unrest and devise schemes to prevent a riot. Robert Moses, however, chose this volatile moment to explain why the government should not take the lead in securing racial justice. "We have, it is true, a Negro problem," Moses announced, although he cautioned against following those "Negro leaders who accept nothing but complete social equality" and offered praise for those "following in the footsteps of Booker T. Washington." Washington, who died in 1915, symbolized a strategy for black advancement that Moses favored: ethnic self-help and evolutionary development, better known as accommodationism. The dreaded alternative was "social equality" between blacks and whites, which in the Jim Crow mind-set was an unnatural state of affairs that antidiscrimination laws might forcibly and disastrously impose. (Think Reconstruction.) Of course, "social equality" was also Jim Crow code for interracial marriage—indeed, for a whole range of intimate social interactions, of which, as we shall see, racially mixed swimming pools were a leading example.[2]

Robert Moses tried mightily to ensure that a legislative civil rights movement would not happen in New York. Arguably his most significant racial intervention in New York was his extraordinary effort to nullify a proposed civil rights amendment to the state constitution. In 1938, delegates to the constitutional convention proposed a pioneering clause that would authorize the state to aggressively combat discrimination in *private* housing, education, and employment—areas not covered under the Fourteenth Amendment to the U.S. Constitution. The clause read: "No person shall be denied the equal protection of the laws of this state or any subdivision thereof. No person shall, because of race, color, creed or religion, be subjected to any discrimination by any other person or by any firm, corporation, or institution, or by the state or an agency or subdivision of the state." Moses persuaded the delegate-sponsors to insert the phrase "in his civil rights" after the word "discrimination," a change, he hoped, that would make "the whole thing meaningless," since prevailing case law defined "civil rights" rather narrowly.[3] Moses boasted of his handiwork in the *New York Times Magazine*. "You cannot legislate tolerance by constitutional amendment or statute," he wrote. "It is difficult enough to attempt to carry out guarantees of equal protection by the government. It is impossible . . . as applied to private persons, firms, corporations and institutions."[4] The consequences of Moses's actions were far-reaching but not as restrictive to antidiscrimination legislation as he had hoped.[5]

Not long before Moses's essay appeared in the *Times*, he had been in the headlines as the leading supporter of the Metropolitan Life Insurance Company's decision to exclude African-Americans from its new housing project, Stuyvesant Town. Instead of using this unprecedented joint public-private housing venture as an opportunity to encourage integration, which many city and civic leaders were urging him to do, Moses clung to the traditional rationale that racial integration was a risky investment and would deter private capital from urban redevelopment. Not surprisingly, the city's decision to enter into such a deal had sparked an outpouring of criticism, and Moses used the essay to lash out at his critics. "Unfortunately, housing reform attracts crackpots and irresponsible enthusiasts . . . and sensible projects must run the gamut of hysterical attacks and insane criticism from perfectionists, day dreamers, and fanatics of a dozen breeds." Clearly unnerved by popular scrutiny and criticism of his plans, the parks commissioner assailed "long-haired critics, fanatics and demagogues who refuse to recognize the difference between public and private enterprise."[6]

This portrait of Moses may not come as a great surprise to readers of Robert Caro's *Power Broker*, which characterizes him as indifferent and often hostile to the needs of black New Yorkers. There are various anecdotes, for example, describing Moses's personal aversion to black and white children swimming together. Yet, in many ways, *The Power Broker* underplays his extraordinary constitutional and legislative interventions in promoting racial segregation in New York. Caro omits the epic story of Stuyvesant Town, the Moses-aided, whites-only housing project that launched the fair housing movement in the United States. Perhaps for Caro, writing in the aftermath of the southern civil rights movement and the many media evocations of the liberal north, it seemed compelling to personalize the origins of race-based policy decisions in New York City. In this view, part of Moses's abuse of power was his ability to project his personal biases onto the metropolitan landscape.[7]

But none of this was unique to New York City or to Robert Moses. Swimming pools became particular hot spots in the civil rights struggle in both the North and the South, as whites deployed all manner of tactics, including violence, to forestall sharing their bathing water with bodies of color. The owner of Palisades Park in New Jersey called in police officers to physically eject youthful members of the newly formed Congress of Racial Equality (CORE) who were conducting "stand-ins" to protest the park's whites-only pool policy. Echoing the shifting rationales of Moses and other defenders of segregation in the postwar era, the owner defended his policy in overtly racialist terms as a prudent business practice and in anticommunist terms, labeling the protest a communist plot.[8] In 1957, the legendary civil rights activist Robert F. Williams led the National Association for the Advancement of Colored People (NAACP) branch in Monroe, North Carolina, in an effort to get the city to open the public swimming pool to black children for one or two days a week. The protests followed the drowning deaths of several black children in dangerous, isolated swimming holes. But city officials balked, saying they would have to drain and refill the pool every time the black children used it.[9]

Nor was Robert Moses's defense of restricted housing anomalous. Indeed, his career exemplifies a central tragedy of modern American liberalism—that it emerged during the era of Jim Crow. Southern segregationists and their northern allies shaped New Deal legislation, making many benefits and programs racially exclusionary, if not explicitly in every instance, certainly in both intent and effect. From social security to mortgage insurance, blacks and whites benefited unequally from the liberal state.[10] Scholars of housing, especially Kenneth T. Jackson, Douglass Massey, and Nancy Denton, have shown the central role that race has played in shaping building, home sales, rentals, and mortgage lending throughout the United States.[11] Residential segregation was produced by a dense web of public and private actors, most notably the Home Owners' Loan Corporation and the Federal Housing Administration, which kept racial maps of cities and redlined mixed or black areas. Thus, the federal government itself, not just private banks and builders, was a major force in the decline of inner cities and the spread of all-white suburbs across the nation as the twentieth century unfolded. These housing policies generated a powerful ideology according to which the presence of black people lowered property values and thus fueled considerable white violence as African-Americans sought new homes and neighborhoods. Robert C. Weaver, a longtime housing advocate and the secretary of housing and urban development during the Johnson administration, argued that such violence went hand in hand with public policy. As long as racially restrictive covenants were embraced by the respectable classes, he believed, the lower classes would deploy their own tactics for preserving neighborhood "racial purity."[12] This was the professional culture that shaped Robert Moses. A critical demand that civil rights leaders were making just as the deal for Stuyvesant Town was signed, and just as the black migration out of the South was at its peak, was for modern urban liberalism to reject the historic conflation between race and residence, and to insist upon, as they often put it, "democratic living."

This is what the Stuyvesant Town struggle was all about. It began in June 1943, when the City of New York and the Metropolitan Life Insurance Company signed a contract to create the largest urban redevelopment housing project in the United States (fig. E-36). It would provide thousands of modern, spacious, low-rent apartments exclusively to young veterans and their families. But the deal sparked a firestorm of controversy when it became clear that Frederick Ecker, the president of Met Life, was determined to restrict occupancy to whites only. "Negroes and whites don't mix," he said on the eve of the Board of Estimate's favorable vote; "if we brought them into the development it would be to the detriment of the city, too, because it would depress all the surrounding property." The battle for Stuyvesant Town, as it came to be known, launched the modern fair housing movement in the United States. Yet Met Life never surrendered, going all the way to the United States Supreme Court to defend its "right" to discriminate, a right that Robert Moses had handed them on a silver legislative platter.[13]

In 1943, the parks commissioner engineered an amendment to the 1942 Redevelopment Companies Act specifically to ensure that Met Life would be free to bar blacks from Stuyvesant Town. "If control of selection of tenants" is "to be supervised by public officials," he insisted, "it will be impossible to get insurance companies and banks to help us clear sub-standard, rundown, and cancerous areas in the heart of the city." Moses strongly urged Ecker not to give in to Mayor Fiorello La Guardia's last-minute attempt to

E-36. Stuyvesant Town (foreground) and
Peter Cooper Village, ca. 1950.
Photograph by Thomas Airviews. Collection MTA
Bridges and Tunnels Special Archive

add language to the contract signaling nondiscriminatory tenant selection. The law and contract authorized an unprecedented transfer of state resources to a for-profit private venture, including a twenty-five-year tax exemption estimated at $53 million, the ceding of public streets, and the condemnation of private property, which involved the forced removal of ten thousand residents.[14]

Activists endeavored to desegregate Stuyvesant Town through a variety of tactics: lawsuits, legislation, and eventually direct action, by subletting to black families. A broad popular mobilization finally pressured the city council to integrate the complex; but the judicial branch consistently upheld Stuyvesant Town's right to discriminate in tenant selection. Moses's interventions—both in his narrowing of the antidiscrimination amendment to the 1938 state constitution and in his deletion of public oversight of tenant selection from the Redevelopment Companies Law—were instrumental in the court's reasoning. In June 1947, just as occupancy of Stuyvesant Town was about to begin, three African-American veterans sued Met Life. The named plaintiff was Joseph R. Dorsey, a former army captain, social worker, and resident of a condemned tenement in Harlem. The NAACP, the American Jewish Congress, and the American Civil Liberties Union brought the suit, which was argued by Thurgood Marshall, Will Maslow, and Charles Abrams. Maslow headed the American Jewish Congress's Committee on Law and Social Action and drafted many of the antidiscrimination laws passed in New York State after the war. He argued that government assistance to

Stuyvesant Town qualified as state action under the equal protection clauses of the U.S. and state constitutions. The tax exemption, use of eminent domain, and government-determined rent and profit ceilings, all made possible under a public law that had deemed Stuyvesant Town a "superior public use," qualified as "state action."[15]

In July 1947, Justice Felix C. Benvenga of the State Supreme Court ruled in favor of Stuyvesant Town. "Housing is not a civil right," he wrote in a ruling that showed the effects of Moses's action at the 1938 constitutional convention. In addition, because there was no "established civil right where the question of private housing accommodations were concerned," he refused to enjoin the discriminatory tenant selection process. The *People's Voice*, a Harlem weekly, expressed incredulity that "a property which in effect is a township" could be deemed beyond state control. "With its money and power," the newspaper warned, "Metropolitan is crystallizing patterns of segregation and condemning thousands of Negroes to a secondary citizenship status for generations to come." Since the Redevelopment Companies Law had already been copied in eleven other states, such foreboding was based on real and rapid legal and social changes. Leo Miller, a white resident of Stuyvesant Town, who fought in the Battle of the Bulge, where "the courage and sharp shooting of a Negro machine-gunner saved my life," asked, "Can anyone of us who live in Stuyvesant Town say he may not be my neighbor? I can't." Another white veteran and his wife said, "we don't want our children growing up as part of a privileged group and believing from their experiences that Negroes are a people apart. And we don't think our taxes should be used to support an unnatural division of people."[16]

The attorneys appealed *Dorsey v. Stuyvesant Town* to the state's highest court. In July 1949, in a four-to-three decision, the New York State Court of Appeals affirmed that there was no state role in the operation of Stuyvesant Town. Judge Bruce Bromley, whose opinion galvanized an NAACP campaign for his defeat at the polls in November, concluded that Stuyvesant Town's selection of tenants did not constitute state action. According to the court, the state action extended only to Met Life's clearing of the site, but its activities as a landlord were private.[17] Judge Stanley H. Fuld in his dissent reached the opposite conclusion: "Stuyvesant is in no sense an ordinary private landlord. Its title bespeaks its character. With buildings covering many city blocks, housing a population of twenty-five thousand persons, Stuyvesant is a 'Town' in more than name. Its very being depended upon constitutional amendment, statutory enactment and city contract. The exercise of a number of governmental functions was absolutely prerequisite to its existence. As a geographic entity, Stuyvesant Town was created by the City's exercise of its eminent domain and street-closing powers and by its act of transferring such condemned land and public property to respondents."

Also critical to the decision was Bromley's finding that the state legislature "deliberately and intentionally refrained from imposing any restriction upon a redevelopment company in its choice of tenants." The handiwork of Robert Moses had succeeded. The judge reasoned that the many efforts of Moses and other city officials either to expressly permit or fail to stop the well-known discriminatory intent of Ecker amounted to a kind of immunity for the state:

> The matter of the exclusion of Negroes from the development arose in connection with the approval by the Governor of the 1943 amendments to the Redevelopment Companies Law and in contract negotiations between Metropolitan and the city. Commissioner Robert Moses, active in the plan, stated publicly to the Governor and the board of estimate that if any requirement was imposed which deprived the landlord of the right to select its tenants, no private venture would go into the business. Certainly the general impression was created—which Metropolitan did nothing to dispel—that Stuyvesant Town would not rent to Negroes. . . . In the board of estimate at least three votes were cast against approval of the contract on the ground that exclusion on racial grounds would be practiced. The contract was finally approved without any provision regarding discrimination in the selection of tenants. It may be noted in passing that thereafter the New York City Council passed legislation withholding tax exemption from any subsequent redevelopment company unless it gave assurance that no discrimination would be practiced in its rental policies. This provision, however, expressly excluded from its operation any project "hitherto agreed upon or contracted for.[18]

In striking contrast, Judge Fuld found that governmental approval of a discriminatory contract itself constituted impermissible state action. "Especially in two items . . . the city contract sanctioning the very discrimination complained of and the city legislation actually ratifying that discriminatory conduct, do I find most clearly that 'state action' which the Federal Constitution interdicts."[19] Robert Moses's imprint on the ruling is striking; the case illustrates the profound impact that an appointed official could have

on formulating New York State law. But there were many more contradictions. Moses was the quintessential state activist—he used public authority to literally rebuild the city—yet the government somehow became useless when the challenge was promoting racial reform.

Change at Stuyvesant Town came at a snail's pace. For the next twenty years, the city did virtually nothing to enforce the 1951 law barring discrimination in publicly aided housing projects. In 1960, there were 47 black tenants out of a total tenant population of 22,405, or 0.2 percent. In 1968, the city's Commission on Human Rights initiated a complaint against Met Life because the numbers of black tenants in its three large housing projects—Stuyvesant Town, Peter Cooper Village, and the enormous Parkchester in the Bronx—were extremely low. In Parkchester, 0.1 percent of tenants were black. Peter Cooper housed ten black families in its 2,495 apartments. In many respects, Stuyvesant Town was an ominous harbinger of the mass dislocation and of the race and class bias in Title I of the 1949 Housing Act. It set the pattern for postwar urban redevelopment: the transfer of prized urban space to the white professional class under the reformist rubric of slum clearance. But there was a positive outgrowth to Stuyvesant Town. It mobilized a national fair housing movement. Formed in 1949, the New York State Committee against Discrimination in Housing helped to win passage in 1950 of a law barring racial discrimination in any housing constructed under Title I; it also helped to gain passage of a state law in 1963 barring discrimination in private housing. This group spawned the National Committee against Discrimination in Housing, which campaigned for fair housing laws across the country, culminating in the passage of the federal Fair Housing Act in 1968.[20]

Robert Moses himself seems to have been somewhat chastened by the growing civil rights upsurge in the city and by the resulting shifts in public opinion. He began to engage in historical revisionism. In his book *Robert Moses: Builder of Democracy* (1952), Cleveland Rodgers said that "the long and bitter conflict over admitting Negroes as tenants to Stuyvesant Town came as a surprise to Moses." Ecker becomes the sole culprit. According to Rodgers, "Moses' conclusion about the case is that while Mr. Ecker is an 'exceedingly able, experienced, shrewd, hard-boiled, conservative gentleman,' he has some poor advisers; that he should take more Negro tenants in both Stuyvesant Town and Peter Cooper Village (which does not have partial tax exemption), and that the company management 'needs more of the milk of human kindness' and 'to keep abreast of the times.'"[21]

Some of that milk could have been used to assuage the turmoil and disruption of peoples' lives that accompanied many of Robert Moses's projects, most famously those authorized under Title I of the 1949 Housing Act. Once again, critics discovered a special deal, an exception to the rules, engineered by Moses behind the scenes. This time it was an exception to the Housing Act's requirement of government supervision of tenant relocation: only in New York City was an arrangement created whereby the private developer would oversee relocation. Coincidentally, a leading critic of this ad hoc relocation process, Elinor Black, happened to be married to Algernon Black, the leader of the New York State Committee against Discrimination in Housing. As a member of the Women's City Club, she helped to conduct a study of the effects of "slum clearance" on an upper Manhattan site and concluded that neither Moses, as head of the Slum Clearance Committee, nor the private developer were properly relocating tenants. In fact, they were not in possession of information about where people had gone, even though the law required this. Elinor Black found that this unsupervised relocation was worsening slum conditions and overcrowding in nearby neighborhoods—hardly the "slum clearance" that the public had authorized. The Women's City Club also reported that Title I had disproportionately uprooted poor and working-class blacks and Puerto Ricans, populations that faced considerable discrimination in finding new housing. A *New York Times* study in 1954 confirmed that Moses had failed to oversee the relocation, as required by law.[22]

Suspicion that urban redevelopment was exacerbating racial segregation was confirmed four years later when the press revealed that Moses's slum clearance committee was asking for racial identification on relocation forms—an unlawful act. If, as this practice suggested, residents of comparatively heterogeneous "slums" were being relocated to neighborhoods or housing projects along racial lines, then residential segregation in the city was getting worse. The city council, which a year earlier had passed a landmark law banning discrimination in private rental housing, quickly condemned the practice, and Moses's committee released a statement that it would desist. Still, the episode indicates the continuing power of racial classification in determining residential patterns, especially for a population with little control over the matter. According to the veteran African-American journalist Ted Poston, Title I and the forcible demographic transfer it provoked—a process that black New Yorkers called "Negro Removal"—was a cause of the Harlem riot of 1964.[23]

Ironically, as a direct result of discrimination at Stuyvesant Town, Moses became a builder of housing for middle-income African-Americans. As a defense against litigation, he urged Ecker to build projects in black communities to show that he was also undertaking "model housing for colored folks." In 1944, Met Life announced the construction of the Riverton Houses in Harlem, an affordable, middle-income development "for Negroes" (fig. E-37). Thus, this project did not signal a change of heart or constitute support for integrated living. Yet, despite Ecker's pledge that Riverton would be segregated and exclude whites, Harlemites knew that it would be subject to a new municipal antidiscrimination law—albeit one that had purposely exempted Stuyvesant Town. Because Harlem was a neighborhood of extreme overcrowding, residents welcomed the prospect of more than 1,200 modern apartments. When Riverton opened in 1947, Met Life judged the 50,000 applicants for the 1,232 units according to their "desirability," a category that African-Americans allegedly had not been able to fill downtown. The Riverton became a fashionable residence, home to, for example, future mayor David N. Dinkins and the future court of appeals judge Fritz W. Alexander.[24]

The success of Riverton made an impression on Robert Moses, who was determined that New York would take the lead in building Title I projects and, therefore, in attracting federal dollars. Riverton likely taught him a lesson about the unmet housing needs of middle-class African-Americans, thus giving him the confidence to imagine an eager constituency for a slum clearance project uptown. Shortly after passage of the Housing Act, Moses proposed the construction of Lenox Terrace, to be located between 132nd and 135th streets and between Fifth Avenue and Lenox Avenue, now Malcolm X

E-37. Lenox Terrace under construction (center), Abraham Lincoln Houses (cross-shaped towers at right), and Riverton Houses (double-cross slabs), early 1958. Fairchild Aerial Surveys, Inc.

Boulevard, but it suffered many delays and did not open until 1958. The builder encountered difficulty in acquiring financing for this Harlem property; but Moses interceded and convinced the Bank of Savings and New York Savings Bank to make the loan—an example of what determined leadership could accomplish.[25] Ten years later, Lenox Terrace had become a highly sought-after uptown address; its residents were a cosmopolitan cross section of Harlem, including politicians, musicians, actors, and activists; nurses, teachers, and social workers.[26]

Moses's public works not only housed people and provided recreation and roadways, they also created tens of thousands of good jobs. The distribution of these jobs further illustrates how the liberal state disproportionately benefited whites, although African-Americans would increasingly demand equal access to public works employment. Two examples, both of which prompted the involvement of civil rights leaders, demonstrate the point. The first concerns the Brooklyn-Battery Tunnel. While black workers had long been employed in tunnel building, they were typically assigned to the most dangerous and lowest paying positions. When several black workers complained of discrimination in pay and promotion at the Brooklyn-Battery Tunnel, a project under Moses's supervision, they were met, according to an NAACP attorney, "by a reign of terror." The men took their case to the newly created State Commission against Discrimination, but Moses refused to intervene or address their grievances. Two workers later won small settlements, but according to Ed Cross, a tunnel worker who led the fight for equality, he and several other African-American workers were blacklisted from tunnel building for the next several years in retaliation for having testified before the commission.[27]

The second example is the 1964 World's Fair, an enormous undertaking that entailed years of planning and major construction at its site in Flushing

Meadows Park in Queens. Moses left his Slum Clearance Committee post in order to oversee construction of the fair. Building the fair in the park had the same advantage that building Rochdale Village on the site of the old Jamaica Race Track did (see pp. 00): no one lived there, so no difficult and messy tenant relocation was needed.[28] Nonetheless, Moses was once again charged with racial bias, this time regarding his labor force. Congressman Adam Clayton Powell Jr. complained in 1962 that there were no African-Americans among the sixty-four executives planning the fair. As we have seen, Moses did not respond well to criticism. In a public speech, he assailed "professional integrationists who charge us with color bias because we don't appoint Negro vice-presidents as such, and seek to compel us to dictate and police the employment and administrative practices of every exhibitor and concessionaire, foreign and domestic, at the fair."[29]

Like many employers, Moses clearly had not interpreted the 1945 Law against Discrimination to mean that businesses actually had to hire black people.[30] Note his use of the phrase "as such," which suggests opposition to black inclusion as a goal in itself, which was of course the logic of civil rights enforcement. He used the phrase in a similar fashion in his book *Working for the People* (1956) in describing his opposition to the proportional-representation method of electing the New York City Council. Civil rights advocates had applauded its ability to produce a more ethnically, racially, and religiously representative body, but Moses, echoing other critics, argued that "proportional representation is the architect of communism and disorder. Its twin objectives are to enfranchise minorities as such and to kill big parties."[31] Clearly, we are supposed to see the first objective as problematic. But even Moses himself could not turn back the tide of the civil rights movement. A month after Powell's protest, Moses hired an African-American, Dr. George H. Bennett, for the international division of the world's fair; moreover, the Urban League announced that it had reached an agreement with the commissioner "insuring equal access to all jobs connected with the exhibit." The league credited community groups, which had threatened to picket the fair and lobby the White House, with the victory.[32]

It is troubling that the man who built so much of the New York metropolitan area's infrastructure was influenced by the long arm of Jim Crow in shaping national racial ideology and practices. Many of Robert Moses's most admired creations have racist overtones. The beautiful Jones Beach State Park he built in the 1930s today has more than twenty-three thousand parking spaces and still no easy access by public transportation. Robert Caro's view that Moses intended to discourage nonwhite attendance, although based on anecdotal evidence, gains credence from the very well-documented history of racial discrimination and exclusion that surrounded so many of Moses's undertakings.[33] But the built environment of New York City is not forever bound by Moses's vision. Certainly, his parkways, expressways, bridges, and tunnels are traversed by the most diverse population in the world—some of whom might be on their way to Jones Beach. And his numerous housing developments have become increasingly multiracial.

Robert Moses fashioned a city, a region, a state that all future New Yorkers will use, regardless of his original intent. Moreover, some of his projects that were sharply criticized for uprooting and destroying communities of color—especially the Sheridan Expressway in the Bronx and the Gowanus Expressway in Brooklyn—are now targets for reform by vibrant diverse communities. In the Bronx, the goal is to demolish an ill-conceived, underused expressway; in Brooklyn, the goal is to move the Gowanus underground.[34] Indeed, an important and enduring lesson of the Moses era is that popular participation and oversight of urban governance cannot be thwarted by back-room deals or elite fiats, at least not for long, and not forever.

NOTES

1. Moses, "What's the Matter with New York?" 8.
2. Ibid., 9.
3. Moses's addition remains in the New York State constitution.
4. Moses, "What's the Matter with New York?" 9.
5. For example, in 1945 the state enacted the Law against Discrimination, which barred discrimination by private employers and labor unions, and it explicitly defined employment as a "civil right" under the 1938 state constitution. Moses was a vocal opponent of this historic first state fair-employment law in the country. Biondi, *To Stand and Fight*, 18–19.
6. Moses, "What's the Matter with New York?" 11.
7. Caro, *Power Broker*, 510–14.
8. Biondi, *To Stand and Fight*, 82–84.
9. Timothy B. Tyson, *Radio Free Dixie: Robert F. Williams and the Roots of Black Power* (Chapel Hill: University of North Carolina Press, 1999), 83–84.
10. A recent book on this subject is Ira Katznelson's *When Affirmative Action Was White: An Untold History of Racial Inequality in Twentieth-Century America* (New York: Norton, 2005).
11. Kenneth T. Jackson, *Crabgrass Frontier: The Suburbanization of the United States* (New York: Oxford University Press, 1985); and Douglas S. Massey and Nancy Denton, *American Apartheid: Segregation and the Making of the Underclass* (Cambridge, Mass.: Harvard University Press, 1993).
12. Biondi, *To Stand and Fight*, 113.
13. Ibid., 122–23.
14. Ibid., 122.
15. Ibid., 124.
16. Ibid., 128.
17. *Dorsey v. Stuyvesant Town Corp.*, 299 N.Y. 512; 87 N.E.2d 541; 1949 N.Y. LEXIS 961; 14 A.L.R.2d 133
18. Ibid.
19. Ibid.
20. Biondi, *To Stand and Fight*, 135.
21. Rodgers, *Robert Moses*, 215–16.
22. Caro, *Power Broker*, 970–76; "City Lags in Help to Slum Tenants," *New York Times*, April 2, 1954.
23. *New York Times*, June 18, 1958; and Biondi, *To Stand and Fight*, 226. The earlier destruction of the predominantly black San Juan Hill neighborhood in order to build the Abraham Lincoln Houses near Lincoln Center also produced race-based tenant relocation. See Elizabeth Hinton, "Bomb Blast in San Juan Hill: the Destruction of Manhattan's Other 'Black Belt,' 1900–1948," (bachelor's thesis, New York University, 2005).
24. Biondi, *To Stand and Fight*, 123–24.
25. "Luxury Housing Opens in Harlem," *New York Times*, October 17, 1958; "Builder to Start Harlem Project," *New York Times*, March 25, 1957.
26. Ernest Dunbar, "The View from Lenox Terrace," *New York Times*, March 3, 1968. Peter Eisenstadt has noted Moses's leadership in the construction of Rochdale Village, a racially integrated housing cooperative in South Jamaica, Queens, which opened in 1963. He argues that Moses's views on race had not really changed, but that he had come to believe that resisting fair housing laws was no longer worth the effort. Eisenstadt, "Rochdale Village and the Fate of Integrated Housing in New York City" (2006), unpublished paper.
27. Biondi, *To Stand and Fight*, 102–4; and Caro, *Power Broker*, 736.
28. Caro, *Power Broker*, 1062; and Eisenstadt, "Rochdale Village."
29. "Powell Inquiry Set on Negroes at Fair," *New York Times*, March 12, 1962.
30. Biondi, *To Stand and Fight*, 99–104.
31. Moses, *Working for the People*, 17.
32. *New York Times*, April 21, 1962.
33. Caro, *Power Broker*, 318–19.
34. Omar Freilla, "Burying Robert Moses's Legacy in New York City," in Robert D. Bullard, Glenn S. Johnson, and Angel O. Torres, eds., *Highway Robbery: Transportation Racism and New Routes to Equity* (Cambridge, Mass.: South End Press, 2004), 75–98.

REVOLT OF THE URBS

ROBERT MOSES AND HIS CRITICS

ROBERT FISHMAN

In the end, Robert Moses was a gift to his critics, but, for most of his career, his critics were a gift to him. As political scientist Raymond Moley observed, Moses "utterly destroyed the old concept that a public administrator must avoid controversy."[1] In fact, Moses needed his critics because they had a vital role to play in the self-created drama of the man the *Daily News* called "Big Bob the Builder."[2] Moley's uncontroversial public administrators of the past had by preference worked behind the scenes, patiently assembling broad coalitions to support the long-term infrastructure projects—water, sewers, docks, bridges, subways—that had transformed New York. Moses by preference always "went public," turning every project into a ritual combat in which he personified progress, efficiency, rationality, and a disinterested zeal for the public good. His opponents, by contrast, were cast as "selfish and shortsighted"[3] or, as he once put it, "partisans, enthusiasts, crackpots, fanatics, or other horned cattle."[4]

In the course of his career, Moses perfected his own version of the master politician's art of rhetorical jujitsu: turning the force of an attack back on the attacker. This political theater emerged fully developed in Moses's first great joust with his critics, the battle to run the Southern State Parkway in Long Island through the elite estates of Wheatley Hills in the 1920s. A prudent civil servant would have worked to enlist the area's wealthy landowners in the park project and gratefully accepted whatever land they chose to donate or sell. Moses, by contrast, boldly threatened to appropriate whatever land *he* wanted. When the estate owners protested, they were greeted with a headline in the *New York Times*: "A Few Rich Golfers Accused of Blocking Plan for State Park."[5] After that, the impassioned protests of "abuse of power" from critics like W. Kingsland Macy only reinforced the negative image that Moses had thrust on them and burnished his own reputation for advancing the public good.[6]

Moses was thus able to combine the high-minded idealism of a public servant with the insults and innuendos of a Tammany politician. But Macy and the other "rich golfers" were only the first in a series of critics who found themselves unwilling players in the drama written by Big Bob the Builder. The estate owners were followed by the townships that controlled the Long Island waterfront that Moses wanted for Jones Beach; they were snobs, reactionaries, and profiteers standing in the way of healthy recreation for the people. Then came the gift that kept on giving: the New York City politicians whose graft, ignorance, and laziness had stalled the great Triborough Bridge project, wasted the people's resources, and deprived the city of the key transportation link that it needed. In this fight, Moses was able to defeat even the greatest master of political jujitsu at the national level, Franklin D. Roosevelt. When in 1934 Roosevelt attempted through his secretary of the interior, Harold Ickes, to remove Moses from the Triborough Bridge Authority[7]—"the President has a feeling of dislike of him that I haven't seen him express with respect to any other person," Ickes wrote in his diary — Moses responded by casting FDR as yet another politician attempting to interfere for selfish ends with the People's Administrator. With the support of Mayor Fiorello H. La Guardia, Moses forced Ickes and Roosevelt to back down.[8]

Moses even used his critics' frequent charges of bullying and disrespect for the law to his own advantage. James Scheuer, a housing activist and later a congressman, asserted, "I cannot think of a public servant whose talent for colorful vituperation has been so frequently exercised since Catiline berat-

E-38. Washington Square Park and environs, llooking north, 1925. Fairchild Aerial Surveys, Inc.

ed the Roman Senate 2,000 years ago.'"[9] But far from moderating his "colorful vituperation," Moses flaunted his bullying. He claimed with great effect to be a bully for the people, and his many critics counted as testimony to his effectiveness in getting things done. One astute observer even compared Moses to Baron Eugène Haussmann, who had transformed nineteenth-century Paris under the authoritarian government of Louis-Napoléon. Haussmann's "dictatorial talents enabled him to accomplish a vast amount of work in an incredibly short time, but they also made him many enemies, for he was in the habit of riding rough-shod over all opposition." That observer was Robert Moses himself.[10]

The drama of Big Bob the Builder required the audience's continuing belief that Moses, like Haussmann, was engaged in a series of great works as necessary for the greatness and even the survival of twentieth-century New York as Haussmann's boulevards and sewers had been for nineteenth-century Paris. As long as that belief remained strong, even devastating criticism could be marginalized. In 1951 and in 1954, for example, the Women's City Club of New York produced two stunningly documented reports on the human consequences of forced relocation, especially on poor black households, for the Manhattantown urban renewal project on the Upper West Side. But these reports did not challenge the basic logic of slum clearance and radical rebuilding that made such relocations inevitable. The reports in the end argued only for more efficient relocation, i.e., more resources for the man who supervised relocation, Robert Moses.[11]

As his critics eventually realized, Moses could be challenged only by a fundamental critique of the urban doctrines that he represented. Moses by his own choice *personified* those doctrines, and thus opened for scrutiny the

nexus of planning power and doctrine that in other cities and at the national level was carefully concealed among a score of anonymous bureaucracies. (With perhaps greater wisdom, Moses's great rival in the New York region, Austin Tobin, always masked his power behind the institutional facade of the Port Authority of New York and New Jersey, which he headed).[12] The ultimate story of Moses and his critics was how the critics rewrote the drama of Big Bob the Builder, casting him as the principal villain in their own production of "The People versus the Planner."

This rewriting was a long process, and the final script was not produced until the appearance of Robert Caro's biography in 1974. But for me, the key incident was one that Caro omits completely from his book: the battle of Washington Square, the long-running controversy, from 1952 to 1958, over Moses's attempt to push a highway through Washington Square Park (fig. E-38). Lower Fifth Avenue stopped at the park, with only a carriageway used mostly as a bus turnaround continuing to the narrow streets to the south. Moses sought to expand the carriageway into a four-lane arterial that would continue as Fifth Avenue South past his Southeast Washington Square urban renewal project, cutting through what is now Soho and ultimately linking up with his cherished elevated Lower Manhattan Expressway at Broome Street.

Today, we are shocked that a parks commissioner could have proposed an act that Lewis Mumford rightly called "civic vandalism . . . [that would have] cut the Square into two unrelated halves . . . endangered pedestrians and children and reduced, by many hundred square feet, an inadequate—and therefore doubly precious—recreation space."[13] Moses could hardly have been surprised, when word of his plan leaked out in 1952, that a small but impassioned group of Greenwich Village mothers whose children depended on the park went to the city's Board of Estimate to win a temporary reprieve. As a *New York Times* headline announced in May 1952, "Villagers Defeat New Traffic Plan/Project that Would Put New Roads in Washington Sq. Park Upset by Women."[14]

This "upset" was part of Moses's modus operandi with his critics. A local group was provoked into raising objections, and then their objections were relentlessly criticized and marginalized by Moses and his allies. The Washington Square Committee, as the women called themselves, would join the Long Island golfers and the Tammany politicians as one more manifestation of Moses's superior wisdom and concern for the greater good of all New Yorkers. But in the unique setting of Greenwich Village, Moses's jujitsu was finally turned against him.

The women's effort to save their park became a rallying point for a full-scale critique of the Moses approach, drawing in such figures as Mumford, William H. Whyte, Charles Abrams, and, above all, one of the park mothers, Jane Jacobs. It was in defense of Washington Square that these and other activists first brought to the fore the issues that now define American urbanism: the primacy of diverse neighborhoods as the real essence of the city; the privileging of the pedestrian and mass transit over the automobile; the meaning and importance of public space; the value of the traditional streetscape over the towers-in-the-park of urban renewal; and the wisdom of the citizen over and against the top-down expertise of the planner. As Charles Abrams said in a remarkable 1958 speech titled "Washington Square and the Revolt of the Urbs," which anticipated not only Jacobs's work but virtually all subsequent urban theory, "It is no surprise that, at long last, rebellion is brewing in America, that the American city is the battleground for the preservation of diversity, and that Greenwich Village should be its Bunker Hill. . . . In the battle of Washington Square, even Moses is yielding, and when Moses yields, God must be near at hand."[15]

Like so many other decisive battles, the battle of Washington Square was fought over terrain that was seemingly marginal to the main conflict. In Moses's highway master plan of 1955 for the New York region, the *Joint Study of Arterial Facilities*,[16] Fifth Avenue South is a minor connection compared to such megaprojects as the Cross-Bronx and the (never-built) Cross-Brooklyn expressways, the Narrows bridge, and his plans for gargantuan elevated Lower Manhattan and Mid-Manhattan expressways. Yet, there is a deeper appropriateness that Moses wound up being bogged down in Greenwich Village. The very scope of his 1955 map implied that only the regional scale mattered, and that only an administrator with the power and vision to see the region as a whole could transform New York into a modern metropolitan area. But ever since escaping the relentless order of the 1811 Commissioner's grid, the Village had exemplified the importance of unique neighborhood character in the larger metropolis—what Jane Jacobs would celebrate as "close-grained diversity."[17] In taking on Greenwich Village, Moses had found his Opposite.

The regional vision that Moses was attempting to impose in the 1950s had undergone significant changes since the 1920s era of the Long Island parkways and Jones Beach. Then, he had viewed the automobile and the highway as a means for the middle class to escape the city for its unspoiled hinterlands.

In the 1930s, his work on the Triborough Bridge led him toward a more radically modernist view of automobile transportation and of the city in general. Like so many self-proclaimed hardheaded realists, Moses was increasingly captivated by a vision—the vision of a city of towers-in-parks and expressways—that derived ultimately from Le Corbusier's Ville Contemporaine (1922) and Plan Voisin for Paris (1925) and the CIAM (Congrès internationaux d'architecture moderne) Athens Charter (1933). As specified by Le Corbusier's disciple (and later dean of the Harvard Graduate School of Design) José Luis Sert in *Can Our Cities Survive?* (1942), this doctrine held that the typical urban fabric of New York City was fundamentally obsolete, its narrow streets and dense dwellings a failing relic of the horse-and-buggy era. Like Sert, Moses rejected the solution put forward by Lewis Mumford and Rexford Tugwell to deconcentrate the central city and move population and industry to "New Towns" spread throughout the region.

Moses, again following the CIAM vision, proclaimed instead that "our big cities must be rebuilt, not abandoned."[18] Even he never proposed the complete demolition of New York's urban fabric, but he did envision massive slum clearances that would open up whole districts for the modernist landscape of towers-in-the-park and wide express highways that would save New York as a great city. This landscape first began to take shape in the low-rent housing projects built after the Housing Act of 1937, and Moses himself promoted its first definitive version, the highrise towers-in-the-park for the middle class of Stuyvesant Town (1947), sited on the East River adjacent to the FDR Drive.[19]

Postwar national politics created the dizzying prospect that the federal government might be the chief funding source for the large-scale urban transformation that Moses envisioned. The Housing Act of 1949 had the federal government assuming all the capital costs for low-rent projects as well as deeply subsidizing the acquisition of expensive urban land by eminent domain for middle-class Title I projects. When the Interstate Highway System was proposed by the Eisenhower administration, Moses became the principal spokesman of the U.S. Conference of Mayors in urging that the interstates "must go right through cities and not around them."[20] To secure urban support for passage of the bill, Congress agreed with Moses, which meant that his megaprojects like the Lower and Mid-Manhattan expressways would now be eligible for 90 percent federal funding. Although President Harry Truman had earlier rejected the idea of coordinating urban slum clearance and highway projects at the federal level, Moses's position as both chair of the Mayor's Slum Clearance Committee and Construction Coordinator gave him exactly those combined powers to rebuild New York as the world's great modernist city.[21]

With such sweeping visions, Moses might have overlooked the small patch of green called Washington Square Park. But the way this patch interrupted the flow of traffic seems to have offended him. As early as 1935, he proposed widening the streets around the park for improved traffic flow, but opposition from New York University students and faculty deterred him.[22] By the early 1950s, however, he had identified twelve acres of industrial lofts and aging apartments south of the square as a "blighted" area to be demolished for a middle-class Title I project. As modernist urbanism recommend-

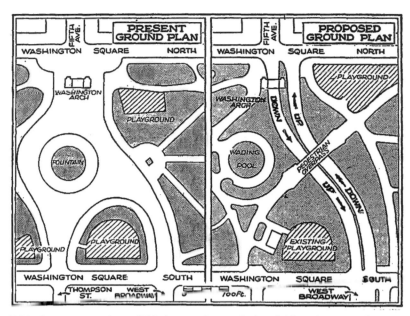

E-39. Comparative plans of Washington Square Park with Moses's proposed alterations at right, 1955

E-40. Hulan Jack's revised proposal of roadway, 1957

ed, he intended to coordinate slum clearance and new towers with a new highway. He would cut a four-lane highway straight through the park, continuing through the "blight" and "industrial slums" we now call Soho to link up with the projected Lower Manhattan Expressway (figs. E-39, 41).[23]

But this "civic vandalism," as Mumford called it, never happened, and the critic who did the most to stop it was not Mumford, Jane Jacobs, or any other famous author, but a now-forgotten local activist named Shirley Hayes. An aspiring actress who gave up her career to be the mother of four children, she personified the Village's unique "social capital."[24] For more than six years, she defied Moses to keep her Washington Square Park Committee active and united, and yet her name does not even appear in the index to Caro's 1,250-page book.

Moreover, Hayes's contributions were more than organizational. A week after her initial success at the Board of Estimate in May 1952, she put forward the demand that would define the controversy and lead eventually to her improbable victory. After several other groups had suggested smaller and less obtrusive roadways, Hayes proclaimed that the goal of the committee was not to negotiate with Moses for a *better* road but to ban *all* traffic through Washington Square and to resist any attempt to widen the roads around the square.[25] This simple demand had deep significance, because it implicitly elevated the needs of this single neighborhood—a safe place for children to play, a lively place for adults to congregate—over the increased traffic flow that Moses saw as imperative for the city as a whole. "Cities are created by and for traffic,"[26] he proclaimed in his version of Le Corbusier's motto "The city that achieves speed achieves success."[27] Hayes and her allies would define urban success in very different terms.

Jane Jacobs had a vivid memory of the only time she saw Moses in person: when, to justify the road through Washington Square, he appeared

before a meeting of the city's Board of Estimate that Hayes, Jacobs, and other activists had made necessary. "He stood up there gripping the railing, and he was furious at the effrontery of this [opposition] and I guess he could already see that his plan was in danger. Because he was saying 'There is nobody against this—NOBODY, NOBODY, NOBODY, but a bunch of, a bunch of MOTHERS!' And then he stomped out."[28]

Urbanist Marshall Berman has rightly emphasized women's perspective in Jacobs's work, and it was precisely the ability of this "bunch of mothers" to see what was best for their children and for their neighborhood that gave them the critical faculty to challenge conventional planning wisdom.[29] Moses was clearly unaware that he was now facing not just the local protesters he was used to pushing aside but the mother of all citizen activist groups. This group could mobilize every form of influence from intellectuals ruminating on the meaning of the city to hardball politicians and backroom operators. As Hayes and her allies well understood, Moses as parks commissioner and the compliant traffic commissioner T. T. Wiley could not simply implement the road plan. That required the approval of the Board of Estimate, the powerful body composed of Mayor Robert Wagner Jr., two members elected citywide, and the five borough presidents. Packing these meetings with energized protesters became the committee's principal form of political theater, with the "performances" spilling out into numerous protest meetings held throughout the Village and, of course, in the park itself.

The success of these protests depended to a significant degree upon the activist role of the first-in-the-nation alternative neighborhood newspaper, the *Village Voice*. The *Voice* began publication in 1955, and its editor, Dan Wolf, immediately took up the cause of saving the park.[30] The *New York Times* would cover the story with competence and objectivity, always giving the protesters' side as well as Moses's. But the *Voice* opened its columns and editorial pages to Hayes and her colleagues, not only to publicize rallies but to engage the larger issues raised by the controversy. *Voice* readers found, in articles sandwiched between ads for Dizzy Gillespie at the Village Vanguard, Sonny Rollins at the Five Spot, and Brecht and Ionesco at off-Broadway theaters, the *intellectual* opposition to Moses that would transform American urbanism.

Dan Wolf himself initiated this opposition with an editorial in the paper's third issue that tried to define the special role of the park in the neighborhood. Although he does not use the term *public space*, his editorial is perhaps the earliest insertion of that key concept into the Washington Square debate and into the larger debate on American urbanism. The editorial is also notable for the way that he ties the idea of public space to the parallel ideals of community, identity, and diversity. "It is our view," Wolf begins, "that any serious tampering with Washington Square Park will mark the true beginning of the end of Greenwich Village as a *community*. . . . Greenwich Village will become another characterless place." As he goes on to explain, "Washington Square Park is a symbol of unity in diversity. Within a block of the Arch are luxury apartments, cold-water flats, nineteenth-century mansions, a university, and a nest of small businesses. It brings together Villagers of enormously varied tastes and backgrounds. At best, it helps people to appreciate the wonderful complexity of New York. At worst, it reminds them of the distance they have to cover in their relations with other people."[31]

A subsequent Wolf editorial brought into focus what would be another great theme both for this protest and for the development of American urbanism: citizen participation. Wolf was reacting against a statement made by Moses's trusted aide Stuart Constable to the *World Telegram and Sun*: "I don't care how those people [in Greenwich Village] feel. They can't agree on what should be done. They're a nuisance. They're an awful bunch of artists down there." Wolf replied, "Not only do we applaud Mr. Constable's outspokenness in this matter, but we feel he is right when he says that Villagers are a nuisance. Anyone who joins in community action to preserve local traditions and resources is always a terrible nuisance to The Authorities. We hope there are thousands of nuisances like that within a stone's throw of this office."[32]

Wolf backed the force of his rhetoric by opening the *Voice* to extended statements by sympathetic writers and planners who reinforced the radical idea that Moses, in fact, did not embody Progress and asserted that the local "nuisances" had a far better idea of the larger urban common good than he did. The best examples of these once-radical challenges came in a panel discussion at the New School that the Joint Emergency Committee to Close Washington Square Park to Traffic—an umbrella group that united Hayes's organization with other sympathetic groups—organized in June 1958. The panelists included the anthropologist Margaret Mead, the journalist and urbanist William H. Whyte, and Charles Abrams, the housing activist and chair of the New York State Commission against Discrimination, whose talk was reprinted in full by the paper.

Whyte introduced the then-novel theme that the towers-in-the-park middle-class housing planned for Washington Square South did not embody progress or the salvation of the city. The projects were, he pointed out, "planned by people who don't like cities, and in far too many cases they are

not design[ed] for people at all. If you've seen one urban redevelopment project you've seen almost all. No hint of tradition, nothing native in the architecture is allowed to interrupt their vast redundancy . . . no sense of intimacy or of things being on a human scale." The solution, he told the "packed audience," was to "raise hell!"[33]

It was Charles Abrams, who raised the most effective hell that evening, with his "Washington Square and the Revolt of the Urbs." Abrams was the "anti-Moses," a professor of planning at Columbia University who moved in the same privileged circles as Moses, but who used his influence to fight racial discrimination and to preserve urban diversity.[34] His book *Forbidden Neighbors* (1955) remains the locus classicus for the whole fair-housing movement in cities and suburbs, and his "Revolt of the Urbs" is for me the locus classicus for all subsequent critiques of Moses. In fewer than two thousand words, he sounded all the themes that authors from Mumford to Jacobs to Caro would use to radically reinterpret Moses and his works.

Abrams began with the ringing proclamation of "the revolt of the urbs" as "the revolt of urban people against the destruction of their values; of the pedestrian against the automobile; the community against the project; the home against the soulless multiple dwelling; the neighborhood against the wrecking crew; of human diversity against substandard standardization."[35] The talk is perhaps most remarkable for its brilliant melding of a planning critique with a larger social vision. He ties the Village's "rediscovery of what is good in our cities" to a larger stand against the "heedless destruction that has been the theme of the slide-rule era 1935–1958": "The old city could have been made more livable but was subordinated in national concern for the new suburb. Instead of improving the city, the motif of the past 23 years has been to flee it and hem it in. In the process, the city became the residuum to which the poorer people were relegated . . . and federal aid was geared toward clearance, not restoration, and to elimination, not discovery." Yet, this discovery was being made, in spite of Robert Moses, by a new group of citizens, the "urbs," who were learning to value place as we would now put it—"community roots, a new social interaction . . . local schools, parks, and playgrounds"—and to fight the "reckless destruction of their good existing buildings." His conclusion would resound in a thousand other threatened neighborhoods: "Greenwich Village is sound. It needs no broad highways, no great projects, no straightening out of streets. Its values must be rediscovered, and built upon, not destroyed."

Just as Abrams and Whyte were broadening their criticism of Moses to encompass the whole philosophy of urbanism that he personified, the four-year battle over the road through the park was coming to a climax. Moses used his control over the process to alternate long delays with abruptly scheduled key votes in the City Planning Commission and the Board of Estimate, testing his opponents' patience and their ability to respond quickly. Far from compromising, he now insisted that the road be *widened* to 48 feet, but run through the park in a trench below grade, crossed only by a few pedestrian bridges. Moses nevertheless seemed to acquiesce when the Manhattan borough president, Hulan Jack, the highest ranking black elected official in the city, proposed a 36-foot-wide "compromise" roadway (fig. E-40). By May 1957, Jack's compromise appeared to have won over "respon-

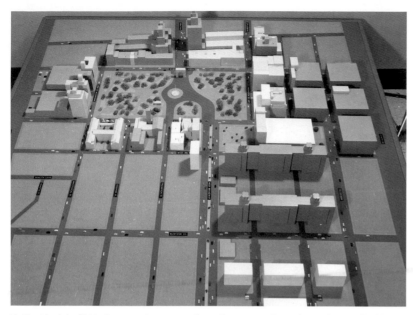

E-41. Model of Washington Square Park, with existing through road, NYU buildings south of square, and Washington Square Southeast Title I at right, April 1961

around the park "with the park corners rounded to permit free flow of traffic."[44] But if Moses really expected the neighborhood to reverse itself, he was completely mistaken. As Jane Jacobs pointed out, the "mess" never materialized, as cars found alternate routes and people found alternate means of transportation.[45] Dan Wolf at the *Voice* drew this lesson: "Rarely has there been such a clear demonstration of the superior predictive judgment of a community over that of the 'official' city experts. . . . Perhaps the greatest significance of the Washington Square fight is the proof that when the common sense and good judgment of citizens in a community are focused on the thorny problems of complicated urban life, they may contribute profoundly to their solutions."[46] Long before becoming Big Bob the Builder, Robert Moses had concluded his doctoral thesis on the British civil service, written at Columbia in 1914, with an admiring reference to Woodrow Wilson's contrast between the statesmanship of the expert civil servant versus the mob rule of the masses.[47] Not only did the Washington Square controversy produce a powerful critique of the doctrines of urban renewal that Moses had sought to implement for more than twenty years, but it generated a powerful critique of the ideal of expertise on which he had based his whole career.

The *New York Times* celebrated the closing of Washington Square, with caution. An editorial asserted that "Washington Square was unique, a place that merited exemption from 'progress,'" and concluded, "This is one neighborhood that is to be allowed to stand still."[48] But if the *Times* was implying that other neighborhoods should not seek to share the same exemption, then it too was proved wrong. Washington Square may have been unique, but the Washington Square model for stopping highways proved remarkably reproducible, both in New York City and nationwide. Four years later, the neighborhoods in the path of the Lower Manhattan Expressway employed this model—a solid bloc of energized citizens who then impel their local representatives to forceful opposition—to stop this key link in Moses's vision of arterial highways that "go right through cities." Backed by more than six hundred of his constituents in Little Italy, the assemblyman Louis DeSalvio told the Board of Estimate in December 1962, "except for one old man, I have been unable to find anyone of technical competence who is truly for this so-called expressway, and this old man is a cantankerous, stubborn old man . . . [and] the time has come for the stubborn old man to realize that too many of his technicians' dreams turn out to be nightmares for the City."[49]

Moses was certainly not alone in his continuing support for the Lower Manhattan Expressway—the project was not definitively stopped until 1969[50]—but he was indeed increasingly isolated among urbanists, as writers involved in the battle of Washington Square brought the key themes of the debate to a national audience. In the midst of his efforts to prevent Moses's "civic vandalism," Lewis Mumford published perhaps his greatest single essay in his long career, "The Highway and the City" (1958). "The fatal mistake we have been making is to sacrifice every other form of transportation to the motorcar," Mumford proclaimed. "Today, the highway engineers have no excuse for invading the city with their regional and transcontinental trunk systems." Instead, he called for a *balanced* system of transportation: the revival of mass transit in cities, and the recognition that for "urban space,

sible" public opinion and even several Village groups.[36] But the compromise was destroyed by Moses himself when, in November 1957, he sent Jack a condescending "Dear Hulan" letter in which he instructed the borough president that only a 48-foot road would do.[37]

If Moses thought he could now get all that he wanted, he was very much surprised by the effectiveness of the "bunch of mothers" who outmaneuvered him at the supposed height of his influence. Hayes and the Village activist Raymond S. Rubinow had formed a Joint Emergency Committee that not only succeeded in keeping the Village united behind the demand to ban all traffic but managed to secure thirty thousand signatures on a petition to close the park to traffic.[38] The joint committee then succeeded in out-brokering the power broker by putting pressure on the boss of the city's Democratic machine, Carmine De Sapio. This "last of the bosses" lived in the Village, and his power base was thus vulnerable to the Village Independent Democrats, like the young Ed Koch, who were mobilizing against him. To defend himself, De Sapio threw his support to the mothers.[39] He appeared before a "raucous" Board of Estimate meeting on September 18, 1958, and, as the *Voice* put it, "made an impassioned plea for human values."[40] Jack then withdrew his road proposal and instead supported an "experimental" closing of the park to traffic.[41] On November 1, 1958, the Village celebrated its victory as De Sapio held one end of a ceremonial ribbon and Jane Jacobs's daughter, Mary, representing the children symbolically reclaiming their park, held the other that closed the park to traffic.[42]

Moses's defeat was not yet complete. A year before the closing, he had predicted that such a move would "result in a traffic mess as bad as anywhere in the city" and reflected that "letting this mess develop might be the best way to educate the public under the democratic process."[43] When the road through the park was closed, Moses demanded to widen the streets

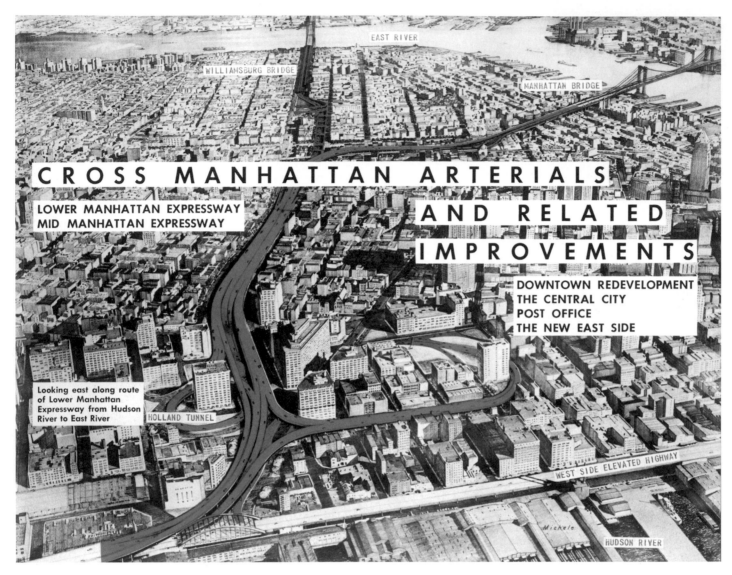

CROSS MANHATTAN ARTERIALS AND RELATED IMPROVEMENTS

LOWER MANHATTAN EXPRESSWAY
MID MANHATTAN EXPRESSWAY

DOWNTOWN REDEVELOPMENT
THE CENTRAL CITY
POST OFFICE
THE NEW EAST SIDE

Looking east along route
of Lower Manhattan
Expressway from Hudson
River to East River

EAST RIVER

WILLIAMSBURG BRIDGE

MANHATTAN BRIDGE

HOLLAND TUNNEL

WEST SIDE ELEVATED HIGHWAY

Michele

HUDSON RIVER

E-42. Brochure cover showing Lower Manhattan Expressway (proposed), looking east from above the West Side Highway, ca. 1959. Rendering by Julian Michele. Courtesy MTA Bridges and Tunnels Special Archive

short distances, and high densities" the pedestrian must be at the center of transportation planning.[51]

The work that truly brought the battle of Washington Square into the heart of planning theory was Jane Jacobs's *Death and Life of Great American Cities* (1961). Compared to Shirley Hayes, Jacobs had been more a foot soldier than a leader in the actual battle, collecting petitions from her neighbors and speaking out at local rallies and the Board of Estimate. (Her first mention in the *New York Times* referred to her as Mrs. James Jacobs.[52]) Although *Death and Life* presented a national perspective on urban issues, it was dedicated to her family and to New York City. The struggle to save the unique built environment of the Village and its park was the leitmotif that ran through almost every chapter. Mumford once defined the city as a place where significant conversations could take place.[53] One way of measuring Jacobs's achievement is to say that *Death and Life* is the distillation of all those conversations that the fight with Moses generated. Jacobs turned the Village

experience into a coherent philosophy of urbanism that had the power to displace even the great CIAM manifestos of Sert and Le Corbusier.

William H. Whyte had asserted that the towers-in-the-park projects were failures. It was Jacobs who demonstrated in detail why they failed and why the "obsolete" streets and sidewalks of the Village provided a much more complex urban environment. Dan Wolf had perceived the unique value of public space for a community. Jacobs broadened his insights by taking the issue of public space out of the parks and squares and onto every sidewalk in the city. Charles Abrams recognized that "the values [of Greenwich Village] must be rediscovered and built upon, not destroyed." It was Jacobs who fully accomplished this rediscovery, analyzing the way every element of the "obsolete" Greenwich Village streetscape—from the "eyes on the street" to the stores on the sidewalk to the narrow roads and mixture of workplaces and residences—fostered the "close-grained diversity" that is the essence of urbanism.

Above all, Jacobs vindicated Shirley Hayes's original intuition that saving the park for her children and her neighbors' children was somehow more important than all Moses's megahighways. Where Moses had asserted that "cities are created by and for traffic," Jacobs asserted that they are created by and for neighborhoods, for the intense sociability, diversity, and complexity that only a pedestrian-oriented, densely built city can generate. In one great book, Jacobs completed the "transvaluation of urban values" that a true critique of Moses demanded.

It would be deeply satisfying to end this essay with the observation that Robert Moses fully merits the obloquy that has become the conventional response whenever his name is mentioned. But perhaps he deserves a brief attempt at the fairness that he so seldom accorded to others. We today can only rejoice that he was stopped before he bisected Washington Square Park and, even more, before he bisected Manhattan Island with his two mega-expressways (fig. E-42). But Lewis Mumford, writing in 1959, demanded with impeccable consistency that, once the expressways were stopped, the Narrows bridge, which threatened to displace more than eight thousand people on the Brooklyn side alone, should be stopped also.[54] Today we can hardly imagine the region functioning at all without the Verrazano-Narrows Bridge, the Cross-Bronx Expressway, and so many other Moses works. Greenwich Village may not have needed new roads, but the New York region certainly did.

Moses was the last of the driven men who strove with obsessive tenacity to connect New York City to its hinterland and to the nation. His auto obsession was an echo of the canal, bridge, rail, and subway obsessions that in their times successively dominated the city. Precisely because he was stopped by his critics before he could fully implement his single-minded autopia, Moses inadvertently left the New York region with the potential for Mumford's ideal of a balanced system of transportation. New York has thrived since Moses's time in large part by repairing and renewing the already existing rail and subway infrastructure to bring them into balance with his roads. Such balance required the keen attention to urban diversity and complexity that Moses's critics brought to urban theory. As the metropolitan region outgrows its aging infrastructure and bold new initiatives are called for, a place must be found for Moses as well as for his critics.

NOTES

1. Raymond Moley, foreword to Moses, *Public Works*, xi.
2. Ibid., 292.
3. Ibid., 294.
4. Moses, "Plan and Performance," 128.
5. *New York Times*, January 8, 1925; Caro, *Power Broker*, chap. 11.
6. "Macy Says Moses Abuses his Power," *New York Times*, September 14, 1925.
7. Quoted in Moses, *Public Works*, 174. This strange memoir with extensive documentation is notable for Moses's willingness to quote at length the comments of his critics.
8. Moses, *La Guardia*, 15.
9. "Housing Expert Replies to Moses," New York Times, November 12, 1959.
10. Moses, *Public Works*, xi.
11. Black, *Manhattantown Two Years Later*, 32–34; and Women's City Club of New York, *Tenant Relocation at West Park: A Report Based on Field Interviews* (New York: The Club, 1954).
12. Doig, *Empire on the Hudson*, 374–90.
13. Mumford, "The Skyway's the Limit" (1959), in *Highway and the City*, 226.
14. Sanka Knox, "Villagers Defeat New Traffic Plan," *New York Times*, May 28, 1952.
15. Charles Abrams, "Washington Square and the Revolt of the Urbs," *Village Voice*, July 2, 1958.

16. At this point, Moses and the Port Authority were operating in tandem.
17. Jacobs, *Death and Life of Great American Cities*, 14.
18. Moses, *Working for the People*, 88.
19. Moses, *Public Works*, 430–33.
20. Ibid., 293.
21. Joel Schwartz's *New York Approach, Robert Moses, Urban Liberals, and Redevelopment of the Inner City* (1993) remains the best analysis of Moses's powers and supporters during this period.
22. "Protests at Park Plans," *New York Times*, April 12, 1935.
23. "Slum Project Assailed," *New York Times*, January 23, 1954.
24. Douglas Martin, "Shirley Hayes, 89; Won Victory over Road," *New York Times*, May 11, 2002.
25. "Traffic Ban Is Aim in Washington Sq.," *New York Times*, June 4, 1952.
26. Moses, *Public Works*, 308.
27. Le Corbusier, *The City of To-morrow and Its Planning*, trans. from *Urbanisme*, pub'd. 1928 (New York: Payson and Clark, 1929), 114.
28. Jane Jacobs, interview with James Howard Kunstler, Toronto, September 6, 2000, www.kunstler.com/mags_jacobs2.htm.
29. Berman, *All That Is Solid Melts into Air*, chap. 5. Berman's pages on Robert Moses and the Expressway World (290–311) remain the most trenchant cultural critique of Moses.
30. Kevin McAuliffe, *The Great American Newspaper: The Rise and Fall of the Village Voice* (New York: Scribner, 1978), 91–97.
31. Dan Wolf, "The Park," *Village Voice*, November 9, 1955.
32. Dan Wolf, "Those People Down There," *Village Voice*, May 30, 1956.
33. William H. Whyte, Jr., quoted in "Projects Assailed as 'Dull Utopias' at Packed Meeting," *Village Voice*, July 2, 1958.
34. A. Scott Henderson, *Housing and the Democratic Ideal: The Life and Thought of Charles Abrams* (New York: Columbia University Press, 2000).
35. Abrams, "Washington Square."
36. "Road Through Square Likely," *Village Voice*, May 1, 1957.
37. Murray Illson, "Moses Fights Jack on Roadway Plan," *New York Times*, November 2, 1957.
38. Charles G. Bennett, "Showdown Looms in Washington Sq.," *New York Times*, September 16, 1958. For Rubinow, see Robert McG. Thomas, Jr., "Raymond S. Rubinow, Master of Civic Causes," *New York Times*, April 8, 1996.
39. Clayton Knowles, "Hearing Date Set on Village Road," *New York Times*, September 12, 1958.
40. Dan Wolf, "Villagers Win Major Victory," *Village Voice*, September 24, 1958.
41. Charles, G. Bennett, "Washington Sq. Traffic to Halt while Road Issue Is Decided," *New York Times*, October 24, 1958.
42. Mary Perot Nichols, "City Closed Square Saturday," *Village Voice*, November 5, 1958; "Symbolic Ribbon Ties Off Sq. as Hundreds Celebrate Ban on Traffic," *New York Times*, November 2, 1958.
43. Joseph C. Ingraham, "Moses Says Jack Reneges on Road," *New York Times*, December 24, 1957.
44. "Moses' Road Plan for Park Revived," *New York Times*, September 24, 1959.
45. Jacobs, *Death and Life of Great American Cities*, chap. 18.
46. Dan Wolf, "One Month Later," *Village Voice*, November 26, 1958.
47. Moses, *Civil Service of Great Britain*, 134.
48. "Washington Square," *New York Times*, April 11, 1959.
49. Louis DeSalvio, quoted in Moses, *Public Works*, 307–8. Strangely enough, Moses quotes DeSalvio's polemic at length, perhaps only so that he can then denounce DeSalvio's "personal denunciation, billingsgate and libel." Old habits die hard.
50. Maynard T. Robison, "Rebuilding Lower Manhattan" (Ph.D. diss., City University of New York, 1976), chap. 5.
51. Mumford, *Highway and the City*, 247, 249, 254.
52. "De Sapio Supports Study," *New York Times*, December 20, 1957. In addition to De Sapio and Jacobs, Victor Gruen also spoke out against the road at this meeting.
53. Mumford, *City in History*, 117.
54. Mumford, "The Skyway's the Limit," 227–29.

ROBERT MOSES AND CITY PLANNING

JOEL SCHWARTZ

Joel Schwartz died before he could complete his essay for this volume. We include this unfinished draft, however, as a tribute to his scholarship on Robert Moses and in grateful recognition of the generous spirit of this kind and decent man. KJ

Robert Moses was not fond of city planning. This judgment rests largely on Moses's relentless attacks on "the long-haired planners" and his ridicule of their collectivist vision. It also stems from three episodes that evidenced Moses's intolerance of what planning meant. First, he dismissed Rexford Tugwell's cherished "greenbelts" in the late 1930s, which forced the New Dealer to withdraw as chairman of the city planning commission. Second, the aggrandizement of the Federal Title I program, a kingdom over public works after World War II, was unprecedented in the city's history. And third was the dustup with Jane Jacobs over megaliths and an expressway that threatened Greenwich Village. Never mind that Tugwell once called Moses the "second or third best thing that ever happened" to New York; that other cities, like Chicago, Cleveland, and Detroit, suffered greater depredations to their neighborhoods from Title I clearance; or that Ms. Jacobs's wrath was more justly aimed at anti-urbanists, like Le Corbusier. The condemnation is chiseled in stone: Robert Moses's hubris, his hijacking of city planning into a vehicle for personal power, destroyed whatever contribution the discipline might have made to the public good and led to, according to Robert Caro, the fall of New York.

The problem with this judgment is that it takes city planning as a tangible ideal, when it was more often a receding goal, unreachable in most American cities and certainly beyond the grasp of New York. Jon A. Peterson in his book *The Birth of City Planning in the United States: 1840–1917* (2003) has emphasized comprehensive planning's far-reaching, multifaceted approach to the large city and its problems: transportation, central business districts, housing and health, neighborhood refinements—all taken together. This was the ideal of the "master plan" as it took form in the years before World War I. But for New York the opportunity for master planning was an opportunity that had come and gone. Merchants along Fifth, Sixth, and Seventh avenues launched the idea of zoning to protect the Ladies' Mile from obnoxious garment workers. And Dual Subway Contracts put into permanent form the commercial and business concentration in Manhattan as well as linear cities strung along transit routes in the outer boroughs and surrounding counties. Between these two developments, major planning questions within New York had been put to rest.

PLANNING IN THE 1920s

In the decade after World War I, city planning was torn between mundane pretense and ambitious endeavors in master planning. The creation of vast rail and transit grids trumped major planning issues. The holistic approach had lost ground to narrow specialties like traffic control, sewerage, or tenement reform, when it was not ensnared by zoning and subdivisions. Hundreds of communities took up zoning; in most this amounted to a reactionary zeal to "protect" home grounds against the "invasions" of gas stations, oil tanks, and apartments.

There was, of course, the sustained effort by the Regional Plan Association of New York and Its Environs (RPNY), sponsored by the Russell Sage Foundation. RPNY was most notable for its forecasts of continued centripetal growth as Manhattan and Brooklyn spun out their manufacturing plants and port facilities to cheap zones on the periphery. RPNY's rail expert, William R. Wilgus, and its chief theoretician, Thomas Adams, called for rationalization of the region's transport and "reconcentration" of urban densities along outlying rail junctions. RPNY gave the intellectual imprimatur to the most important of metropolitan visions (the latest version of the city-efficient): the land near Wall Street was too valuable for the tenements that sat on it; the Lower East Side deserved clearance and gentrification; and the working class needed to be shifted to the outer boroughs. To reclaim the evacuated portions of the Lower East Side, Clarence A. Perry called for the rebuilding of the evacuated portions of lower Manhattan into svelte pieds-à-terre built as "neighborhood units." Harland Bartholomew saw six-lane boulevards as the means to smooth commercial traffic, promote abutting real estate, and cordon neighborhoods into natural zones. Local boosters, encouraged by the RPNY, pushed for city-busting highways. One can almost hear their refrain, "We need to destroy the Lower East Side in order to save it."

Far more grandiose were the plans of a small, clamorous group, the Regional Planning Association of America, led by Clarence Stein, Benton MacKaye, and Lewis Mumford, which came to represent comprehensive planning's shining image. They admired British reformer Ebenezer Howard's idea for "garden cities," tightly controlled places of thirty thousand people surrounded by agricultural greenbelts. Guided by technocrats who understood mankind's "dominion of the earth," the RPAA wanted government to transform "sterile villages" in the Hudson and Mohawk valleys into a series of urban diadems linked by "townless highways" and "giant power," energy of the St. Lawrence, Niagara, and Black rivers to drive light-metals plants or Ford Motor–type assembly-line facilities. From this distance, the RPAA's vision seems typical of the hubris that took hold between the wars, the faith in big research by government, universities, and foundations that spawned high-brow committees to comment on recent social trends, national resources, even Professor Alfred Kinsey's collection of twenty thousand sexual histories. These all aimed at achieving the totalist view of American life as an objectified, quantified mechanism. Within that perspective, Moses was a creature of his time.

Moses started out a sterling candidate for the planning cause. At Oxford, he studied public administration, admired the steeliness of the English civil service, and came under the sway of British socialists like Graham Wallas, who coined the term "Great Society" to capture the hopes for a purposeful public sphere. Moses returned to America enamored of this viewpoint and worked for the good-government crowd in New York City. Through family connections, Moses gained notice of Alfred E. Smith, then New York State Assembly leader, who admired the bright, young Columbia Ph.D., made him secretary of his Reconstruction Commission, a position that meant working with the executive budget, the gubernatorial cabinet, the New York Port Authority, state power development, and public housing. Nearly all these plans were swept away by the Warren Harding presidential landslide in 1920; but when Smith again became governor in 1922, he brought Moses back with a renewed agenda. Moses became the architect of the state's comprehensive park system, the coordinator of regional highways, and chief advocate of the state power authority.

Giving Moses the parks portfolio, Governor Smith expected his protégé to draw together the development of parks across the state. In a series of reports, Moses gave him that much and more. He called upon Albany in 1924 to take a "unified and comprehensive" approach (which became his mantra), enact a state council on parks, and provide for an executive secretary (assuredly him) "to insure the continuance of unified state park plan-

ning." There was no time to be lost. Burgeoning cities, from New York to Buffalo, needed protected watersheds for their aqueducts and hydropower; and, just as important, recreation grounds for families, children, and seniors. (In this respect, Moses shared the reformers' concept of the city as an archipelago of settlement areas, each with its own youth program.) For Gotham and its suburbs, Moses sketched a "Grand Circuit" drive, the equivalent of the "townless highway," from the Bronx River Parkway reaching past Peekskill and circling Bear Mountain State Park, then back again via the Palisades Interstate Parkway.

In his first report of the State Council in 1925, Moses embellished upon the necessity of state-wide planning. Recreation grounds, like the Catskills Forest Preserve and Allegany State Park, flanked the zone of urban growth that spread along the Hudson and Mohawk valleys. Further concentration of commerce, industry, and people within this corridor, accompanied by the continued emptying of the agricultural countryside, gave the State Council both the opportunity and duty to acquire acreage for recreation. Moses even brought the State Council to the verge of city planning, when it called for the coordination of park and parkway plans between city and state officials. It also recommended that New York City purchase the Brooklyn waterfront at Gerritsen Basin and Dyker Beach, and "the remaining wooded areas of Queens and Richmond"—greenbelts by another name. These proposals represented a toe placed into the waters of city planning, but a telling one.

HOUSING AND RECREATION

One common theme of the Moses story is that he muscled his way to control city planning by the late 1930s. But planning New York–style was Moses's turf from the start. The city had no planning apparatus until Mayor Fiorello H. La Guardia appointed an advisory committee in 1934, the same year that he made Moses parks commissioner with a five-borough ("unified and comprehensive") authority. In the minds of La Guardia and civic leaders, New York was potentially a galaxy of recreation areas; and this goal, so vital to civic leaders, gave the parks commissioner a mandate to create a far-reaching strategy for parks, parkland, and parkways, which enabled him to retain the moral high ground.

But the many parks and parklands that dominated the process of comprehensive planning more accurately undermined it. At the NYCHA, policies for slum clearance hinged on the fact that the site had a long relationship with a social settlement—and adequate recreation space. As one site-picker put it, they featured "self-contained" stands of slum housing preferably ten blocks in length, "with suitable provision for social life and recreation."

This site opportunism, in the midst of the Great Depression, made it probable that any Moses plan, any plan, would captivate civic leaders. In the summer of 1938, Moses made no secret of his dismay at the dilatory, uncoordinated approach of the NYCHA toward creating a programmatic message for New York State voters on the Housing Amendment—and a coherent housing program for the city. He urged Mayor La Guardia to revamp the NYCHA by placing it in the hands of seasoned housing administrators or, as he clearly preferred, a single housing czar. Soon after the passage of the Housing

Amendment, Article XVIII of the State Constitution, in November, 1938, Moses unveiled his own plan, calling for a combined, massive housing program of ten low-rent projects and five subsidized limited-dividends with a price tag of $200 million. As far as he was concerned, he was the only one who understood what Article XVIII heralded: the power of eminent domain to create superblocks and appurtenances for nearby parks. He shrewdly located clearance projects near parks, taking advantage of his control over recreation in the city. Moses made clear to civic leaders that housing without recreation, streets, and related improvements would be a joke. He accused the NYCHA chairman Alfred Rheinstein of shopping around for cheap land without having a definite program. Moses recommended instead that the NYCHA concentrate on a few plots where something could be accomplished for the entire neighborhood

Of course, Moses also shopped around for park sites and for locations for public housing. His criteria for the latter typically were: a large enough acreage, close to parkland or playground (or better yet, defined by it) and close to industrial properties but not compromised by them (or ruled out altogether as not slum clearance), not crossed by a major thoroughfare that would endanger the project's coherence, the right kind of low-assessed valuations, and convenience to mass transit. Along with all this, Moses wanted to segregate the races. All his criteria were neighborhood-specific; they had virtually nothing to do with city-wide or regional concerns, other than to maintain racial boundaries.

Moses's attitude toward picking housing sites was summed up in a memo written on October 2, 1942. "I have been looking at Astoria for many years—knew it when it was still quite a flourishing place with fine big houses facing Hell Gate and the East River. Then smaller houses and apartments of various kinds were built. Then came our Triborough Bridge, the folding up of the ferry and the decay of the community. Today there is an opportunity to acquire a large tract at low cost, to build a bulkhead out into the river with a park and esplanade along the waterfront, to wipe out some pretty poor buildings, a few fairly good ones, and to build on native land. There can be a really first-rate housing plan here with small ground coverage and three- or at the most four-story buildings. If there is such a thing as drawing people out of certain poor neighborhoods to better ones, it can be done here."

This opportunistic approach to construction projects put Moses on a collision course with the City Planning Commission. During 1939 and 1940, under the chairmanship of Rexford G. Tugwell, the Planning Commission revealed a series of initiatives for slum clearance sites, schools, highways, parkland, and open space in New York's master plan. But many of the key features seemed less than masterful. The January 3, 1940, map adhered to the simplest criteria, which amounted to proximity to recreation space, transportation, and industrial employment. With the Queensbridge Houses in mind, the commission saw an opportunity for more people to live closer to their work, especially the very poor, who needed to save on carfare; and given that their work was generally harder and less rewarding, they needed leisure time and a place for recreation. In effect, the Planning Commission saw the city as static, with neighborhoods that needed refurbishment for a stable population. There would be no grand shift of population; working-class New York would remain where it was, with no forecast of any major

reallocation of the city's population beyond the old observations of the RPNY. The declining industrial sector north of Canal Street deserved recycling as a residential area. The map of highways and expressways would "make it possible to drive speedily from any section of the city to any other on continuous modern highways free of traffic lights."

The Master Plan on Land Use, revealed in fall 1940, featured what was dubbed as "greenbelts" and captured the imagination of the city and the ire of Robert Moses. One of his team, George Spargo, quickly concluded, "This is 98% ivory tower." The plan purported to envision the city's 1938 pattern of land use as it gradually gave way to a first stage in 1965 and a second stage in 1990. Acreage set aside for residences would shrink from 100,000 in 1938 to 91,000 fifty years later. Land needed for commerce and industry would increase from 18,000 to 30,000. But the most dramatic transformation would occur in the outer boroughs, where some 51,000 acres of vacant space would be collapsed to little more than a thousand; and the area devoted to parks, large "open institutions," and cemeteries would nearly triple from 29,000 to over 76,000 acres—equivalent to sixty-five Central Parks. The Planning Commission never spelled out its expectations for the use of such expansive greenbelts; nor for that matter what their relation was to the working class in the projects near the industries along the East River. What, after all, was the meaning of greenbelts—which Ebenezer Howard deemed as forests and agricultural land—in New York City, other than parkland?

The Planning Commission never described how these greenbelts would be realized, through eminent domain (enlarged to encompass whole reservations rather than circumscribed park sites) or through zoning. Or perhaps tax delinquency might be encouraged or even taxation of unearned increments. Moses warned Mayor La Guardia on December 4, 1940, that the Master Plan for parkways and land use was "more than an innocent diversion," that once these projects were on the map, property owners would know the city's official intent. The impact on values, assessments, and likely improvements were all thrown into the bargain. At the December 11, 1940, hearings, Moses pounced on the specter of tax delinquency and municipal bankruptcy.

Tugwell was unsuccessful against Moses's large projects because he was not an infighter and did not have much allegiance to a revitalized New York. He preferred the greenbelt approach because it meshed with the suburban trend and did not raise the challenge of dealing with central city slums. Greenbelts would involve less eminent domain than the proscriptions on property involved in indicative planning of a powerful kind, not to mention the differential taxation of unearned increments.

TITLE I

The Title I program involved the use of federal subsidies to write down the cost of slum clearance. Moses never spelled out any visionary sense of how the redevelopment would transform New York. In 1942, he told Paul Windels that at least one substantial park or playground area should be included in each large project. This veritable cliché was grasped by Al Smith, who told Governor Herbert Lehman that the project for the Lower East Side should, of course, include recreation space, wide streets, and "everything else that goes with proper slum clearance." In late 1942, Moses wrote to Frederick H. Ecker, the Metropolitan Life chief who was scanning the city for another insurance-company housing project. A member of the City Planning Commission and constituting its subcommittee-of-one on housing, Moses had been studying Queens. He alerted Ecker to the possible use of two racetrack sites for a Met Life development related to incidental streets, recreational and other improvements. Although there were two likely sites in southern Queens and a third on the Queens-Nassau border, Ecker focused on the Lower East Side, which he considered having the additional value of anchoring population in Manhattan.

Hardly a community failed to thrust ideas on Moses, the construction coordinator. The list included Chelsea, the Lower East Side, Cooper Square, Delancey Street, Washington Square, Bloomingdale, and Morningside Heights. All featured standard, American Institute of Architects–approved plans with bulldozer clearance on a superblock scale, a high-rise apartment on a large plaza, and an underground garage or interior parking lot. All assumed widespread tenant dislocations to squatter camps in New Jersey (in the case of Washington Square), makeshift rooming houses (Manhattantown), or public housing sites under construction or in blueprint (Morningside Heights). The final version of Delancey Street, sponsored by a local settlement, called for leveling an enormous superblock near a cross-Manhattan expressway. Redevelopments proposed by the city's planners, in fact, included cross-Manhattan expressways at 125th Street, 97th Street, 47th Street, 34th Street, and Houston Street, none of which ever materialized.

Opportunism rather than grand commercial visions drove Moses's Title I projects. And he refused to go along with many gargantuan ideas, either because plans went far beyond the city's overall needs or because they were too taxing on the infrastructure. Moses rejected both the Columbia University plan for the redevelopment and clearance of nearly all of Morningside Heights to 125th Street and the NYU-Bellevue plan for a similar reach along First Avenue. And famously, Moses denied Walter O'Malley's plans for a new domed stadium for the Brooklyn Dodgers on Flatbush Avenue. Moses concluded that the borough needed housing more than it needed a modern replacement for Ebbets Field.

ST. JANE AND THE DRAGON

Was Jane Jacobs a heroine or did she merely give an eloquent voice to Greenwich Village chauvinism, bolstered by reform Democratic politics, which combined into a selfish NIMBYism? Although Jacobs attacked the RPAA–Clarence Perry ethos and its contempt for urban dwellers and ordinary contact, her real concern was the preservation of politically functional districts and their reform Democratic clubs. She favored increased population density—beyond the planner's orthodoxy of twelve people per acre—to promote diversity. Her preference was at least 100 persons per acre—the Village had 125 to 200 per acre, but arranged in a variety of building styles and heights. Her interest in diversity, her allowance of factories and plants, for instance, was not tied to any economic or jobs strategy but to foster a varied "ambience"—a carnival atmosphere in the West Village, an array of

delights and attractions for the flâneur, the casual observer, and the middle-class café idler. Note that she applauded changes from factories to services and residences, never the reverse. She could abide woodwork factories, coffee bars, and offices, all compatible with residential streets, as long as they did not overwhelm them in scale. She supported blue-collar jobs only when they sustained the ambience of middle-class residential neighborhoods.

Considering Jacobs's blithe comments about "unslumming," the bootstrap improvement of incomes without an incomes policy, she was naïve and simplistic compared to Moses, who recognized that municipal policies must be the handmaiden to economic development, particularly in a post industrial economy. Moses had a responsibility to the entire city, the city of work and manufacturing. He was complicit in Title I's ravaging of thousands of blue-collar jobs across lower Manhattan and Brooklyn. But he was more of a mercantilist, whose economic policies were suffused with a kind of crony capitalism. At the very least, Moses was a handmaiden for the emergence of post-industrial New York, whose economy would see health and hospitals as the city's largest generator of wealth. In the end, Jacobs's recommendation for district control of planning and redevelopment (with soft mortgages) was a recipe for NIMBYism, for dog-in-the-manger Villagers and Upper West Siders.

What has been comprehensive planning's impact on New York? What kind of a city might it have been had Moses stuck to narrow interests? Would it have been appreciably different? If Moses had not intruded on the planning process, would the New York City Housing Authority have not built the phalanx of public housing that shadows the Lower East Side? One could argue that the City Planning Commission has done little more than engage in zoning reviews and, far more important, track the city's changing demography. But did the commission's zoning reviews appreciably alter the reality of central Manhattan's shift of office towers west of Sixth Avenue? Or overcome the NIMBYism that prevented gentrified towers from impinging on Chelsea, Hell's Kitchen, or even the svelte East Side? Did the Planning Commission anticipate vast changes that would foreclose on the Seventh Avenue garment district or recognize the social transformation of Flushing, Queens, into the city's third commercial hub, a cacophony of immigrants, languages, and human vitality that rejuvenated New York in spite of the Planning Commission's indifference to borough government? Was it planning that ushered in the prodigious growth of the city since 1980 and once again made New York into the storied town of eight million?

New York has been transformed by global forces quite beyond the reach of the planning commissioners' ability to understand, let alone anticipate. Probably, in this respect, the most important planning activities have been connected with the Board of Education and the laying out of schools and districts and the construction of CUNY's impressive system of community colleges. This seems a reminder of Friedrich Hayek's judgment of British central planning after World War II: to have a plan meant that all must get behind it, allow no dissidence or doubt as to its validity, maintain a totalist front toward its implementation, lest the whole scheme unravel. Exactly how could comprehensive planning be made an object for pluralist, cacophonous New York?

CATALOG OF
BUILT WORK AND PROJECTS IN NEW YORK CITY,
1934–1968

The wide scope of Moses's responsibilities allowed him to weigh in on most, if not all, large-scale construction in New York City between 1934, when he was appointed to his first city office, and 1968, when he retired. The following list of his official positions and dates of occupancy is taken from the 1981 edition of *Who's Who in America*, the last version that Moses composed before his death in 1981.

New York City Department of Parks, Commissioner, 1934–60
Triborough Bridge and Tunnel Authority, member, 1934–; chairman, 1936–68
Henry Hudson Parkway Authority and Marine Parkway Authority,
    merged into New York City Parkway Authority, sole member, 1934
City Planning Commission, member, 1942–60
Mayor's Emergency Committee on Housing, chairman, 1946
New York City Construction Coordinator, 1946–60
Mayor's Committee for Permanent World Capitol, chairman, 1946
Mayor's Committee on Slum Clearance, chairman, 1946–60
Coordinator of Arterial Projects, City of New York, 1960–66
New York World's Fair 1964–65 Corporation, president, 1960–67

This catalog does not aim to encompass all projects that passed Moses's various desks. Rather, it focuses on individual public works and unexecuted projects with which he was closely involved in New York City. (His work on Long Island and elsewhere in New York State is not covered.) Although calibrating the precise degree of his involvement is difficult in many cases, a distinction can be drawn between those projects that Moses initiated, shaped, planned, funded, staffed, and executed and those that intersected his administrative purview. This guiding principle explains why public housing is not included in the catalog. Although he exerted direct and indirect influence on the public housing program, he did not set policy, choose sites, commission architects, or determine occupancy regulations. Moses single-handedly devised the Title I program; he did not command the New York City Housing Authority in this way. The purpose in hewing to the outlined principle of selection is to begin to deconstruct the myth of his omnipotence, which he fostered through a mix of genuine power, force of personality, and an effective publicity machine. Moses operated in a complex governmental bureaucracy that imposed limits on his power. His success in disguising those limits is remarkable.

The catalog is organized by building type, and the sequence of each section follows an internal but hopefully transparent logic. The public pools are organized chronologically by date of opening to capture the momentum and response from one pool to the next. The Title I urban renewal projects are organized chronologically by date of plan publication to illuminate the evolution of Moses's thinking. The roads are large networks built incrementally over long periods of time; thus this section is organized geographically. The playgrounds are too numerous and repetitive in design to treat individually. The intriguing question is how Moses found so many playground sites in a developed city; consequently, his strategies of land acquisition frame the playground section. The entries highlight the physical character of the structures: site planning, engineering, architectural design, landscape, materials, and construction history.

The following scholars have mined archives and inspected building sites to produce this close-up look at Moses's program of public works.

Hilary Ballon
Ray Bromley
Peter Eisenstadt
David M. Foxe
Owen D. Gutfreund
Marta Gutman
Jennifer Hock
Rachel Iannacone

Julia Kite
Jeffrey A. Kroessler
Matthew Gordon Lasner
Kate Louis
Benjamin Luke Marcus
Blagovesta Momchedjikova
Laura Rosen

POOLS

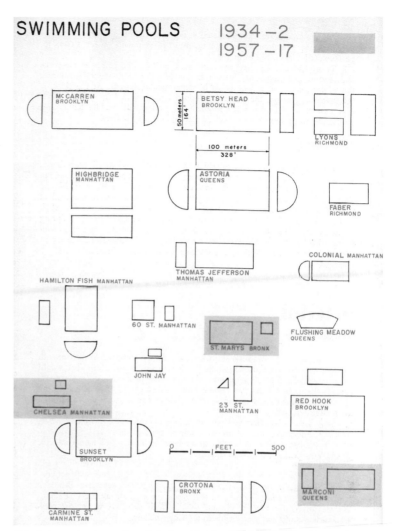

SWIMMING POOLS 1934–2 1957–17

C-1. Schematic plans of pools built and proposed (shaded) by Moses, January 1958

On June 24, 1936, thousands of cheering New Yorkers gathered on the Lower East Side to celebrate the opening of a new municipal swimming pool in Hamilton Fish Park, the first imprint of an ambitious public works project that over the summer would bring new swimming pools to all the city's five boroughs. Robert Moses, the commissioner of the Department of Parks, envisioned—and secured federal funding for—the pool-building project, the largest of its kind in the United States during the New Deal and one that offered work to thousands of unemployed New Yorkers. The modern facilities for aquatic recreation, which cost about $1 million each, usually consisted of a monumental brick bathhouse and three in-ground, reinforced-concrete pools, the largest for swimming and the smaller for wading and diving. Moses determined the pools would be open, at a modest charge, from 10:00 A.M. to 10:30 P.M. during the summer; but free to children under the age of fourteen on weekday mornings. Almost immediately, Mayor Fiorello La Guardia extended the hours to midnight as New Yorkers thronged the pools during the extraordinary heat wave that descended on the city in early July. According to the *New York Times*, the annual income from the ten new swimming complexes and the two already in place was estimated to be almost $950,000 and expected to meet all expenses of their operation.[1] Although the modest entry fees were controversial, the expecta-

tions for attendance were more than met: 1,650,000 people swam in the pools during the first summer.

Moses brilliantly staged the opening of each pool, and the city's newspapers readily cooperated, publicizing the dedication ceremonies as the pools opened one each week during the summer of 1936. The catalog entries below are organized to capture the sense of excitement that built over the summer, as thousands filled what were quickly acknowledged to be magnificent works of public architecture. "The city was deeply surprised when . . . Moses' version of municipal pools began to blossom out in the five boroughs," *Architectural Forum* reported in December 1936.[2] From the first, at Hamilton Fish Park, through to the last complex to open, in Red Hook Park near the Brooklyn docks, the architect Aymar Embury II, the landscape architect, Gilmore Clarke, and their col-

leagues in the Division of Design at the Department of Parks skillfully manipulated New Deal design parameters to create monumental settings that turned swimming into a grand public spectacle. After the first phase of construction was completed, the department added outdoor swimming pools to four Progressive Era bathhouses in Manhattan, renovated the remaining barge pools (in use since the beginning of the century), and turned the New York State Marine Amphitheatre, at the 1939 World's Fair grounds in Queens, into a bona fide public pool.

The reorganization of the Department of Parks into design and construction divisions in the winter of 1934 made it possible to realize this public works project in record time. Moses appointed a trusted colleague, William H. Latham, the parks engineer and supervisor of the Division of Design. Located in the

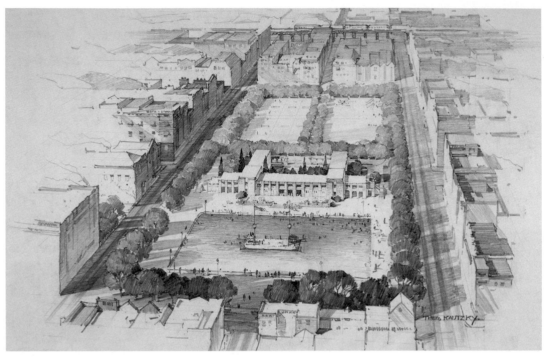

C-2. Model swimming pool, 1934. Rendering by Theo Kautzky

loudspeakers attached. The wading pool, typically 100 by 50 feet, was located outside the enclosed area, so that it could be used without charge.

Usually the three main pools were on axis with one another and the central entry of the bathhouse, which was almost always open to the air and equipped with a freestanding ticket kiosk. Many entryways were several stories high and embellished with columns, arches, domes, patterned brick, metal panels, and curved glass-block walls. In this area, men and women lined up separately (on a hot summer afternoon, the lines spilled onto local streets) and passed through turnstiles or elaborate entries (shallow apses, carved metal doors) to reach their respective locker rooms on either side of the bathhouse. The changing rooms and showers were arranged to facilitate the efficient movement of hundreds of people as they collected clean towels (included in the entry fee), changed their clothes, and took showers (equipped with individual controls). Street clothes, placed in wire baskets, were checked with pool attendants, who stored them on metal shelves; bathers received in exchange a numbered key on an elastic band (worn on wrist or ankle). Girls and women were given cubicles to change clothes and take showers; boys and men, assumed to need less privacy, used congregate showers and locker rooms.[7] Walls were covered with white tile to a height of eight feet; light came from fixed windows, made of glass block or industrial sash; and typically mechanical louvers provided ventilation. Structural systems were exposed in the locker rooms (the bathhouses were framed in steel or concrete); and tall ceilings, simple volumes, and moveable furniture made it possible to convert each one to a gymnasium during the off-season.

When asked to explain the basic principles of the Moses pools, Latham did not discuss architectural and social issues but rather emphasized the importance of economy, safety, sanitation, and modern materials and methods of construction, which, he boasted, "would do credit to a modern ocean liner."[8] Design standards were researched and used to calculate the human capacity of each pool (20 square feet per person for swimming; 50 square feet for diving) and bathhouse. These numbers were balanced with other factors to determine the size and quantity of each component, from diving boards to pool area. The Department of Parks used bathhouse capacity to estimate that the eleven pools altogether could accommodate 49,000 people in 1936. Diving pools were separated from swimming pools (to assure swimmer safety) and at least one dimension of the main pool was set at 55 yards, so races could be held at regulation distances. Latham

Arsenal in Central Park, the division was arranged into units by trade or profession, such as architecture, landscape architecture, and engineering.[3] Each unit reported to Latham, who along with the engineer W. Earle Andrews, also a member of Moses's inner circle, and other aides approved each stage of the design. Latham's office reviewed and stamped every drawing, from the initial site survey through construction details. After the topographical survey and schematic landscape design were accepted, architects led the team, working with engineers and landscape architects, to develop final designs. Although Embury, John Matthews Hatton, Stanley Brogren, and other special design consultants hired by Moses would be credited as lead designers, numerous other hands touched the drawings. The staff at the parks department grew in the mid-1930s to include almost 2,000 professionals and technicians, with most made eligible for work-relief by the Great Depression. The names of the draftsmen who signed the drawings on file in the Department of Parks suggest the diversity of this team. For Astoria and Jefferson pools, they include McMinn, Sanfillipo, Bernasniakoff, Raad, Homa, Paletta, Nelson, Coryll, De Piazza, Kiely, McGarr, Ahrens, Savarti, and Hautman.

Faced with a tight construction schedule and budget, the design staff adopted guidelines that allowed architectural innovation while meeting the need for speed and the strict federal requirements for economy in building materials, equipment, and labor.[4] Although no complex looked like another, taken as a whole the designs indicate the high value that Embury, Clarke, and their colleagues placed on geometric clarity in site planning, on prismatic monumental buildings, and on "simple materials simply disposed."[5] As aerial photographs make clear, the strong geometric imprint on park landscapes was achieved by using orthogonal geometry to coordinate architecture and landscape and by encompassing the pools with walls, fences, and other architectural features. Inside the enclosure, which served to assure swimmer safety as well as payment of fees, a large symmetrical brick bathhouse, often with an enormous shaded roof terrace, faced equally large reinforced-concrete swimming and diving pools. Surrounding the pools were concrete bleachers and more terraces to accommodate swimmers, their families, and the crowds who came to watch swimming races, diving competitions, and water ballets. A wide promenade encircled the diving and swimming pools, which were trimmed with broad, shallow gutters, called scum gutters in the 1930s.[6] Other standard features included streamlined railings and ladders, made of brass or bronze (as were exposed plumbing and mechanical fixtures); concrete diving platforms, some three tiers high; wood diving boards; and metal flagpoles, with

stressed that the pools were designed for maximum use, minimum maintenance expense, and simple operation; and that straightforward materials had been selected, for durability, safety, and ease of use by the unskilled laborers who built the facilities. In true New Deal style, he highlighted the social benefit of technical innovations: underwater lights for night swimming; underground access tunnels, so that filters, valves, lights, and other equipment could be adjusted or repaired without draining the pools or otherwise disturbing their operation; and what was called the "most modern" systems for sanitizing and circulating pool water. Vacuum cleaners were also provided at each pool.

Cleanliness was crucial to realizing Moses's vision: making public swimming sanitary had been a prime reason for the pool-building program.[9] Great care was taken in the design and detailing of the mechanical systems; for the men and women who worked for Moses, the success of these systems was as important as architectural grandeur. Every facility was furnished with clean city water (not polluted river water) and included a filter house, an up-to-date system for purifying pool water, and enormous underground tanks for storing it. A diesel or electric pump recirculated pool water every eight hours so that it could be filtered, treated with chemicals, and sterilized by a certified operator.[10] Pressurized injector jets, located at regular intervals along the walls and on small islands in the middle of the largest pools, ensured uniform distribution of purified water; valves and deflectors on the nozzles allowed the direction and flow of water to be adjusted. The equipment was designed to eliminate areas of stagnant water, which compromised cleanliness. Unusually for outdoor pools in the 1930s, the pool water could be regulated to a comfortable temperature by means of special heaters or through recycling the heat generated by the pump engines.[11] Each bathhouse was also equipped with a boiler, to heat the facility in the winter and to provide hot water for showers year-round. One can imagine that the many New Yorkers who lived in cold-water flats used these facilities for personal bathing, as well as to comply with the mandatory shower and footbaths. Shallow basins were placed so that bathers had to walk through them as they left the locker rooms: the first basin was filled with an acid disinfectant; the second with rinse water (to prevent the acid solution from neutralizing the chlorine in the main pools). Signs—and locker room attendants—also reminded swimmers to bathe before walking onto the pool deck.

Amenities such as footbaths, wire baskets, pressurized jets, and heated pool water set new standards for public outdoor swimming pools, as Moses and Latham were quick to point out.[12] Although their claims are filled with the usual bravado, certain architectural features stand out for integrating sanitarian ideals with inventive scenarios for human use. The design of the scum gutters and pool promenades, and the coordination of one with the other, is a case in point. In the Moses pools, the scum gutter's utilitarian function was transformed by the use of modern materials, intelligently deployed. At 7 inches deep and 18 inches wide, the gutters were wider and shallower than was usual for public pools so that they could be cleaned easily, swimmers would not trip on them, and sunlight would penetrate and kill bacteria in standing water (or so Latham claimed).[13] They were close to the edge of the pool deck, the promenade, and designed to be a generous shelf or step, as well as a drain. The surface—12-inch-square blue-green tiles—echoed the color of the pool water on a bright sunny day; sand was baked into the finish to create a nonskid surface; and the tile extended over the upper lip of the gutter to meet the pool promenade, as well as under the lower lip to the wall of the pool basin.[14] Children were enthusiastic users of scum gutters, which gave them a place to splash in the shallow water and hang onto the lower edge as they practiced kicking during swimming lessons. Lifeguards, dressed in standard black swimming suits and brilliant white hats, stood in the gutters and led these lessons, shouting instructions through megaphones.[15]

The pool promenade received similar attention. Typically located directly above the service tunnel, it was paved in oblong tiles, dark red in color (sometimes called quarry tiles), with a rough nonporous surface to prevent slipping and to facilitate cleaning. In the largest pools, the promenade was wider along the side of the pool closest to the bathhouse, creating what was known as a concrete beach. The scum gutter was retained along this edge, but the water depth was reduced to 6 inches and the basin sloped gradually toward the center of the pool. This was done to blur the edge of the pool and the edge of the water, as on a sand beach. Recollections of McCarren Pool indicate that swimmers perceived the widened promenade as intended, "almost like a beach, the shoreline just gradually going down." This design facilitated water play, especially among children learning to swim.[16]

Sixteen-millimeter films of the swimming pools, taken between 1938 and 1949, confirm the importance of technology and standardization to the Moses team. The films also document the accomplishments of the WPA program: the pools reinforced the reform landscape put in place in New York during the Progressive Era; constructed on existing open space, these new amenities helped to relieve congestion in working-class neighborhoods; the pools were racially integrated on occasion; and they were designed to be public places that men, women, and children could enjoy informally and together.[17] In the films, the ease of use, the delight in swimming, and the fascination with public spectacle are apparent. Not surprisingly, the films highlighted the pleasure of young users, showing that these sites met a defining objective of the Moses administration: getting children out of the streets and into playgrounds, and providing swimming pools and other clean, modern, and, above all, public facilities for play.[18] — MG

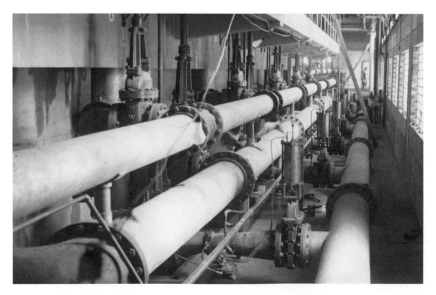

C-3. Water purifying system at Crotona Pool, 1936

HAMILTON FISH POOL AND BATHHOUSE

Originally Hamilton Fish Gymnasium, 1898–1900
Manhattan: Hamilton Fish Park, 127 Pitt Street,
    between Stanton and East Houston streets
New pools and renovated bathhouse opened June 24,
    1936; gymnasium/bathhouse designated a New
    York City landmark 1982; pool and bathhouse
    restored by John Ciardullo and Associates 1992
Figs. E-7–8, C-4

On a chilly June day, New York's first WPA swimming
pool opened in the heart of the Lower East Side, in
Hamilton Fish Park. Mayor La Guardia sold the first
admission ticket and, together with Commissioner
Robert Moses and Victor F. Ridder, Works Progress
Administrator, addressed 5,000 people. The spectators sat on tenement fire escapes and rooftops to
watch the festivities, which culminated with a performance by the Jones Beach water troupe. Standing
on a platform in front of the new diving pool, the
mayor announced that the facility "represents the last
word in engineering skill, in architectural skill and in
the science of building swimming pools." He asked
the audience to keep the rehabilitated park in fine
condition. "It is a gem of a spot and it's yours."[19]

The transformation of Hamilton Fish Park set the
stage for the modernization of other city parks during the New Deal. It figured prominently in Moses's
plans, being on the list of proposed sites issued in
1934; it was one of the first selected for construction, even though its playground had been praised
only five years earlier in the *Regional Plan* as
having a "good influence" on children.[20] After the
Small Parks Act of 1887, the parks department had
begun to open parks in crowded tenement districts.
Designed by the noted architectural firm of Carrère
and Hastings, Hamilton Fish Park opened in 1900;
it occupied two city blocks between East Houston,
Pitt, Sheriff, and Stanton streets. The small (about 4
acres), formally designed park, divided in half by
Willet Street, was soon equipped with playgrounds;
a baseball diamond; a wading pool; a brick and
stone gymnasium, also designed by Carrère and
Hastings; and two matching pavilions at the northwest and southwest corners of the park. Centered on
the Pitt Street side of the park, the gymnasium contained public showers and toilets as well as men's
and women's gyms.[21] The Moses team closed Willet
Street, renovated the pavilions, cleared most of the
land, and constructed new swimming and diving
pools. They were centered on the two-story, barrel-
vaulted entry to the renovated Beaux-Arts
gymnasium, which had been turned into a modern

C-4. Hamilton Fish Pool, ca. 1936

bathhouse, capable of serving 2,200 swimmers.
The refurbished park demonstrated the department's
interest in developing the landscape for inter
generational use, albeit in different parts of the
park: shade trees were planted near benches
installed for adults; a new wading pool was located
outside the pool enclosure, near a new playground
for small children. Other new playgrounds and
athletic fields were provided, intended for boys
and girls of various ages: playgrounds—with jungle
gyms, swings, slides, and seesaws—for younger
boys and girls, and a softball field for older boys.[22]

This complex was relatively modest in comparison
to the far grander ones that would open in a few
weeks' time. Nevertheless, in the press release
announcing this pool, the parks department proudly
promoted its capacity and technical features to indicate the ambition of the overall pool-building program. The main swimming pool (165 by 100 feet)
held 485,000 gallons of water, the diving pool
375,000. Fifty pounds of chlorine gas, 17 pounds of
ammonia gas, 60 pounds of alum sulphate, and 60
pounds of soda ash were used each day to purify pool
water. The department also announced that the bathhouse, like those to come, would be converted during

off-season into a gymnasium; the pools would be used
for paddle tennis, handball, volleyball, shuffleboard,
and ice-skating. Uniformed civil servants would staff
the facility.[23]

Although it was too cold to swim on opening day,
immigrant children soon filled the swimming pools,
thus meeting officials' expectations that the new center would keep them off the streets and out of the
disease-laden East River.[24] Stepping out of the locker
rooms (on the basement level in this facility) and onto
a broad terrace, swimmers faced the semicircular diving pool and rectangular swimming pool, enclosed by
a promenade, seats, and an iron fence. Part of a
monumental and formally ordered complex, the sleek,
stripped-down pool architecture of the 1930s stood in
sharp contrast to the historical detail of the original
buildings. The facilities encouraged active play
among boys and girls who mixed casually in the pool
enclosure. Film footage taken of this pool shows the
blue water, red terrace and promenade, metal pipe
rails, and shallow blue scum gutters sparkling in the
sunlight. Adding to the festive sense of the place were
swimming lessons, offered to children of all ages, and
diving and swimming exhibitions. — MG

THOMAS JEFFERSON POOL AND BATHHOUSE

Manhattan: Thomas Jefferson Park, First Avenue,
    East 111th to East 114th Street
Pools and bathhouse opened June 27, 1936; pool
    and recreation center renovated by Richard Dattner
    and Associates 1992
Figs. E-11, C-5

A few days after the opening of Hamilton Fish Pool, a brand-new recreation complex opened under sunny skies in Thomas Jefferson Park in East Harlem. It was equipped with a purpose-built, low-slung modern bathhouse as well as the requisite in-ground pools, playgrounds, and athletic fields. Boccie courts were provided in recognition of the park's locale in the heart of what was then known as Little Italy. As with other pools, the choice of site acknowledged the mayor's political debts; thus Moses, not surprisingly, included it on his 1934 list of proposed sites. At the opening ceremony, La Guardia reminded the crowd of 10,000 that in 1929 he had promised the community that, if elected mayor, he would improve Jefferson Park. He offered its startling transformation as evidence that he had kept his promise, describing it as the "last word in engineering, hygiene, and construc-

tion," clear proof that the "little knockers" who tried to halt the reconstruction of the park were wrong.[25]

Originally proposed in the 1890s, Jefferson Park, a small park of about 15 acres, opened in 1905, having been designed as a park-playground by Samuel Parsons.[26] It was envisioned as a place of respite for Italian immigrants, especially for neighborhood children who worked in factories. Reformers hoped that both children and adults would benefit from oval lawns and walkways for promenading and that children especially would enjoy the many sites offered for organized play: playgrounds, separate gymnasiums for boys and girls, a kindergarten, and a recreation pavilion. After 1911, farm gardens were introduced, with more than 1,000 small plots close to the edge of the East River. These amenities notwithstanding, the *Regional Plan* noted that far more children preferred to play on city streets than in Jefferson Park.[27] As often happened in the Progressive Era, other reform outposts and public institutions were constructed in the park and nearby, filling out the civic landscape of a neighborhood. Here, they included a public bath (in the park), branches of the New York Public Library and the Boys' Club, and a public school.

In 1936, Embury and his colleague the architect Stanley Brogren removed many outdated features

from Jefferson Park, turning it into the New Deal exemplar of active recreation for all ages. They integrated the new bathhouse and pool enclosure into the surrounding neighborhood, at the same time using the wall of tenements around three sides of the park to set off the brand-new amenity. Erected courtesy of New Deal work-relief programs, this facility showed how new construction—which highlighted the benefits of recreation and active play to immigrant families—could cure congestion. As the heat wave intensified in July 1936, reports in the Times picked up on this aspect of the design, emphasizing that this new pool (and the one at Hamilton Fish Park) offered "relief from the heat in the shadow of Manhattan's tenements."[28]

The new recreational complex sat on the western edge of Jefferson Park, sited so that the bathhouse was on axis with the old-fashioned recreation pavilion. Unlike the older building, which was surrounded by greenery, the bathhouse faced and engaged the street space of First Avenue; patrons could enter the paying part of the pool complex directly from the main thoroughfare. The entry courtyard was open to the air, with no archway covering the ticket kiosk or courtyard. Swimmers stepping up to pay fees could look into the pool enclosure and see on the main axis a flag pole, the tallest diving board, fountains spouting water in the main swimming pool (246 by 100 feet), and the older recreation pavilion outside the pool enclosure, with the East River beyond. A concrete colonnade made up of stout columns and deep lintels surrounded the entry courtyard on three sides; elegant lettering incised into the lintels identified the north pool house as being for women, the south for men. The two L-shaped buildings wrapped around the diving pool (100 by 51 feet) and part of the main swimming pool (246 by 100 feet); an iron fence and raised terrace, on the park side of the fence, completed the enclosure. Seated on the terrace, furnished with shade trees, spectators could observe activities in the pool and the park. As at Hamilton Fish Park, the wading pool was in the park proper.[29]

The steel-frame bathhouse, clad in brick and concrete, quickly won Lewis Mumford's praise as an example of sound vernacular modernism. "The long brick buildings, with bands of windows that fill their bays form an excellent frame for the pools," he wrote in the *New Yorker*, referring specifically to the bathhouse at Jefferson. But as much as he appreciated its gracious design, Mumford had no patience for the "weak festoons in brick" on the side elevations, one of several classicizing details that were likely intended to honor the historical figure for whom the

C-5. Thomas Jefferson Pool on opening day, June 27, 1937. Photograph by Max Ulrich

park had been named. He hoped that with "a little more doctrinaire narrowness something more completely consistent in detail as well as in the large would emerge" from the architects at the parks department.[30] In short order, his hopes would be met—with the startling works of swimming pool architecture that opened later in the summer, most of them located in the outer boroughs.

This pool soon had a reputation for being unwelcome to minority groups. Sources, some of whom even today insist on remaining anonymous, report that the pool was off-limits to African-Americans and Puerto Ricans in the middle of the twentieth century. East 106th Street is cited as the boundary that people of color crossed at grave personal risk. Robert Caro damningly offers events at Jefferson Pool as proof of Moses's unrelenting racism, claiming that the water was intentionally kept cold to discourage African-Americans and Puerto Ricans from using the pool. Supposedly, blacks in particular disliked swimming in cold water. Although Caro's allegation can be neither confirmed nor denied, my recent examination of drawings on file at the parks department reveals that the water in this pool could be heated. Its mechanical systems did not differ from others constructed by Moses in the mid-1930s.[31] — MG

C-6. Astoria Pool, with Hell's Gate Bridge, August 20, 1936

ASTORIA POOL AND PLAY CENTER

Queens: Astoria Park, 19th Street and 23rd Drive
Pools and bathhouse opened July 2, 1936; partially
   restored 1983 and 1997; complex designated a
   New York City landmark 2006
Figs. P-4–6, E-12, C-6

Astoria Pool, the third to open in the summer of 1936, was the grandest of the WPA pool projects in New York City and the first public pool in the city to meet Olympic specifications. Stunningly sited in Astoria Park along the East River, and with dramatic views of the Manhattan skyline, the Triborough Bridge, and Hellgate Railroad Bridge, this pool was reputed to have been Moses's favorite. Its proximity to the Triborough—and views of it—offer a reason for his interest in its grandeur. Astoria was one of the more congested neighborhoods in Queens, another reason that building a majestic swimming pool on this site figured early in the commissioner's plans. In the summer of 1934, Moses indicated that seven parks in Queens were under consideration as sites for new pools, including Astoria Park, one of two that would

come to fruition. By the fall, it had been determined that the main swimming pool would be at least Olympic size; the same was proposed for pools intended for Crotona Park and St. Albans Park (the latter was subsequently abandoned as a pool site).[32] The enormous scale of the complex in Astoria— 78,390 square feet of pool area, a main pool big enough for 3,000 people to swim at once, and a bathhouse capacity of 6,200—contributed to its high cost: $1.5 million. As built, the main swimming pool exceeded standard Olympic size by four times.

The aquatic complex is a prime example of the way in which the design guidelines adopted by the parks department allowed architectural innovation while satisfying the demand for standardization, economy, and speed during the New Deal. The pool was added to a municipal park that had opened in 1913 as the East River Park. A war memorial was erected in 1926, and the footprint extended in 1937 with the construction of a new playground under the approach to the Triborough Bridge. Centered on the war memorial and built on top of a dirt-bottom wading pool, the pool complex was set below the park embankment, with the entrance to the bathhouse facing uphill. The linear plan of the complex, stretched out along the shore and under the embankment, opened the pool to dramatic vistas on three sides. The symmetrical, reinforced-concrete-frame bathhouse extended along the length of the main pool (330 by 165 feet), which had semicircular diving and wading pools (165 feet in diameter) at either end; a fence separated the wading pool from the part of the pool enclosure that required a fee. Ten ranks of concrete bleachers surrounded the uphill side of the pools, including in front of the bathhouse. Seen from above, from either the Hellgate or Triborough Bridge, the enclosed pool complex looked like a Roman stadium made for the modern world.

The architect John Matthews Hatton, in charge of the bathhouse design, took advantage of the site in designing a sleek brick, concrete, and glass-block box that satisfied the demand for spectacle in WPA pools. As swimmers walked down the stairs, set diagonally in the hillside, they could see over the roof of the bathhouse the dramatic cantilevered concrete diving platform, three tiers high, with lower diving boards on either side; the Triborough Bridge gleamed in the background. The bathhouse roof was a multilevel terrace and promenade; oval ventilation towers, clad in curved brick, and stainless-steel sculptures of nude female athletes, the work of Emile Siebern, bracketed the entry below. From the entry, which was open to the air, swimmers stepping up to the ticket kiosk had striking views of three fountains in the middle of the swimming pool and giant concrete parasols on the far side of the complex. Each umbrella sat on a raised platform at either end of the terrace over the filter house. Hatton used glass block in the locker rooms and in large sections of the entryway walls—to the acclaim of the architectural press. The inset panels of glass block—sitting on a stepped concrete platform, flanked by streamlined brick piers, and topped by ventilating louvers—offered privacy and were easy to maintain.[33]

At the opening of the pool, La Guardia and Moses presided over a daylong celebration that included a parade, swimming races, and diving competitions. This was the first opening to extend into the evening. As the press release promised, "The pools are equipped with underwater floodlights and the skyscrapers of New York City across the water sparkling with lights in the fading twilight will offer a fitting setting for this modern noteworthy project."[34] The celebration culminated after sunset when the mayor switched on the pool's underwater lights to the astonishment and delight of 20,000 spectators. In response, Harry Hopkins, the Federal Works Progress

administrator, called the pool "the finest in the world."[35] The opening was timed so that the final trials for the U.S. Olympic swimming and diving teams, starting July 4th, could be held at the pool.[36]

The spectacle at Astoria Pool—some of it informal, some arranged by the parks department—continued through the New Deal. The parks department featured this pool in its film footage, showing children cavorting on the fountains in the middle of the swimming pool, lifeguards teaching them to swim, and families seeking respite from the heat under the giant sunshades. Mayor La Guardia, dressed in a gleaming white suit, is also shown, visiting citywide championship swimming races, sponsored by the department, and congratulating the winners. As trains rolled by on the Hellgate Bridge, girls raced; young boys dressed in zebra-stripe swim suits (known as "Aquazanies") performed trick dives off the high board followed by pairs of teenage boys and girls diving in tandem off the same board. The off-season program of team sports for boys and girls is also documented.[37] — MG

JOSEPH H. LYONS POOL

Originally Tompkinsville Pool
Staten Island: Pier 6 and Victory Boulevard
Pool and bathhouse opened July 7, 1936; pools and
    locker rooms reconstructed, new mechanical, filtration, and electrical systems installed 1984–86
Fig. C-7

A few days after the gala inauguration of Astoria Pool, 7,500 people gathered to celebrate the opening of the new swimming pool in Tompkinsville. Many observed from the roof terraces of the new bathhouse, which had been opened expressly for the event. Just before switching on the underwater pool lights, Mayor La Guardia told the cheering crowd that the Lyons Pool was one of many public projects—including high schools, playgrounds, and parks—demonstrating that his administration in dispensing WPA funds would "give Staten Island an even break with the other boroughs." The pool, especially, was "a monument" to a Progressive government that "would not and could not see unemployed men on the breadline." The mayor insisted that it would not have been finished but for the "splendid work" of the man standing next to him on the podium, the parks commissioner Robert Moses.[38] These festivities took place in the evening, as would almost all the other pool openings in July and August 1936.

In the summer of 1934, Moses announced his intention to build a public swimming pool on Staten Island, perhaps in the town of New Brighton. By the end of the year, the Department of Docks had granted the parks department permission to use a narrow swath of land along the waterfront in Tompkinsville, between the Staten Island Railroad and Victory Boulevard. Initially, the parcel was turned into a playground; subsequently, a pool and bathhouse were added.[39] The site created significant planning challenges for the design team and others on the parks department staff. The typical solution—a freestanding symmetrical building, with a central entry facing a large swimming pool—was impossible, given the small size of the parcel (3.17 acres) and its location between a railroad station and tracks on one side and major public streets on the others.

Aymar Embury, Dwight James Baum, and J. Weisberg turned to a compact layout, designing an L-shaped bathhouse that accommodated 2,800 swimmers. By setting the long arm of the brick building against the embankment of the railroad tracks, the architects opened the complex to the harbor and used the bathhouse to create two sides of the enclosure around the main pool (165 by 100 feet) and the

C-7. Joseph H. Lyons Pool, July 3, 1936. Photograph by Max Ulrich

HIGHBRIDGE POOL AND BATHHOUSE

Manhattan: Highbridge Park, Amsterdam Avenue,
 West 172nd to West 174th Street
Pools and bathhouse opened July 14, 1936;
 renovated in 1985, 1996, and 2001 including
 installation of new mechanical, filtration, and
 electrical systems
Fig. C-8 and pages 2–3

Highbridge, the fifth pool to open in 1936, figured early in Moses's plans and may have been the first site to be selected. In April 1934, the *New York Times* announced that two unused reservoirs had been offered to the parks department and would be turned into parks and playgrounds. Highbridge was one; Williamsbridge, south of Van Cortlandt Park in the Bronx, was the other. As the newspaper pointed out, the smaller reservoir, at Highbridge, could be converted easily and economically into a public swimming pool.[43]

Perched high above the city, Highbridge offered extraordinary views of the Harlem River valley, the High Bridge (built in 1848), and the stone water tower (1872) adjacent to the reservoir.[44] The bridge, tower, and reservoir were part of the system built to deliver water from Westchester to New York via the Croton Aqueduct, the city's first dependable water system, erected between 1837 and 1848. The property for the park was acquired gradually, starting in 1867 and continuing through the 1960s; most of the land was obtained through condemnation at the turn of the century. At Moses's request, the Department of Water Supply, Gas, and Electricity turned over the reservoir, the tower, and the immediate grounds (about 2.5 acres) to the parks department in the spring of 1934.[45]

The new pool, 228 by 166 feet, was initially expected to be ready that summer, but construction took more than two years to be completed.[46] The diving and swimming pools were placed at the site of the former reservoir because the 16-foot depth of the basin simplified excavation and reduced construction costs, and the area was expanded to accommodate both pools. At the dedication ceremonies on July 14, 1936, which were attended by the mayor, the commissioner, and other officials, swimming and diving champions performed.[47] Extraordinary views of the water tower and the vista beyond could be had from within the pool enclosure. Just outside it, the overlook sitting area allowed swimmers and other users of the park to come close to the tower and the edge of the cliff that plunged precipitously down to the Harlem River.

wading and diving pools (100 by 68 feet each); an elegant brick and concrete wall completed the enclosure.[40] Inside the building, women's and men's locker rooms were placed on either side of a circular, two-story entry hall, which was topped by a shallow saucer dome; glass block set into the drum allowed sunlight into the space. At one end of the bathhouse, a curved outdoor staircase, made of brick, swept swimmers up to a shaded roof terrace above the women's locker rooms; other stairs led to open-air bleachers above the men's locker rooms and the filter house. The use of standard WPA materials and design elements was especially inventive in this complex, as in the attenuated metal railings along the roof terraces, the reticulated brickwork, the curved brick columns, and the streamlined corners of the bathhouse. The chimney stack and boiler room were integral to the composition: clad in a brick box and decorated with thin concrete stripes, the chimney stack was high enough to be seen from the town center up the hill, signaling the location of the pool to pedestrians in town as well as to people arriving by train. Poolside, the chimney was set back from the promenade and flanked by curved glass-block panels that delivered light into the boiler room.[41]

Like all the Moses pools, the new pool at Tompkinsville immediately attracted crowds: the average daily attendance was 5,700 during the first summer.[42] — MG

C-8. Highbridge Pool and environs, September 8, 1937

The brick bathhouse, with a capacity of 4,880, was a grand work of public architecture, albeit relatively sober when compared to the exuberant bathhouses that opened later in the summer. Designed in a classical mode and with classicizing details, the Highbridge Bathhouse closely resembled that at Jefferson Pool. The bathhouse faced Amsterdam Avenue; the bowed entry portico, with two great concrete piers holding up a curved concrete lintel, was raised above grade and centered on West 173rd Street. The service entry, giving access to the underground tunnels wrapping around the diving and swimming pools, also faced Amsterdam Avenue. (Although skillfully integrated into the Amsterdam Avenue elevation, the more typical solution would have been to place this utilitarian section less conspicuously.)

Washington Heights, the area around Highbridge Pool, was largely a white neighborhood in the 1930s, inhabited by Jews and Irish-Americans. Nonetheless,

contemporaneous film footage from the parks department shows both whites and African-Americans swimming together in this pool, seemingly oblivious of each other and focused on the athletic activities.[48] Sadly, the tolerance of racial difference was short-lived; in subsequent years, the locker rooms at Highbridge became the scene of ugly battles between black and white teenagers.[49] — MG

SUNSET POOL

Brooklyn: Sunset Park, Seventh Avenue, 41st to 44th Street
Pool and bathhouse opened July 20, 1936; pools restored and filtration system updated 1984; playground expanded and modernized 1988
Figs. P-1–3, C-9

When Mayor Fiorello La Guardia, turned on the underwater lights at Sunset Park on July 20, 1936, he inaugurated the first WPA swimming pool in Brooklyn. The *New York Times* reported that hundreds of "vocally enthusiastic children" were in the audience of about 3,500 that evening. After the speeches were over, professional swimmers, both men and women, plunged into the pool to entertain the crowd. They had been employed by the parks department as part of the WPA work-relief program to perform at this and other opening ceremonies.[50]

Sunset Park, like many others where Moses proposed to add pools, was developed during the Progressive Era in an immigrant neighborhood, originally Polish, Norwegian, and Finnish, followed by Italians.[51] The city had begun to acquire land for a neighborhood park on the crest of a hill high above the Brooklyn docks in the 1890s. The site offered breathtaking vistas: to the west of New York Harbor, to the north of important enterprises of nineteenth-century reformers, namely Green-Wood Cemetery; Prospect Park lay beyond. During the first decade of the twentieth century, Sunset Park was expanded to almost 25 acres and was developed to include a pond, a Beaux-Arts pavilion, a carousel, and even a golf course (most of these structures were removed when the park was modernized during the New Deal).[52]

Herbert Magoon, the architect at Jones Beach, was in charge of the design of the new center for aquatic recreation in Sunset Park (which opened only four days before his pool complex at Crotona Park in the Bronx). In Brooklyn, as in the Bronx, the new pool was integrated into the neighborhood: across the street from a public school and near tenements and other buildings. The one-story brick bathhouse, centered on the eastern edge of the park, could accommodate as many as 4,850 swimmers at one time. The two-story entry—a spacious cylindrical rotunda, topped by a shallow dome—was centered on the main swimming pool (256 by 165 feet) and was bracketed by a semicircular diving pool on one end and a wading pool on the other (165 feet in diameter). The former sat within the pool enclosure; the latter outside of it.[53] The plan of the three pools together made it seem as if the footprint of an Early

C-9. Sunset Pool, summer 1946

CROTONA POOL

Bronx: Crotona Park, East 173rd Street and Fulton
    Avenue
Pool and bathhouse opened July 24, 1936;
    restored 1984
Figs. P-11–17, C-3, 10–11

In the summer of 1934, when the plan to build 23
public swimming pools in New York was announced,
Crotona Park was one of three possible locations in
the Bronx. It was in a predominantly white and
mostly, although not exclusively, Jewish working- and
lower-middle-class neighborhood. The design of the
pool was slated to begin immediately; in the end, it
would be the only public swimming pool in the Bronx
to be constructed during the New Deal.[55] The bathhouse was commensurate with the size of the pool
(330 by 120 feet), accommodating 4,265 people—
2,700 men and 1,600 women. No reason was offered
for the decision to make the pool and bathhouse so
large, but certainly the large park (almost 130 acres)
could easily accommodate a facility of this scale. Like
those at other Moses pools, the bathhouse could be
turned into a gymnasium during the off-season.[56]

The land for Crotona Park was acquired in the
1880s (from the Bathgate family estate). The many
improvements made by WPA relief workers included
the construction of baseball diamonds, tennis courts,
handball courts, playgrounds, public toilets, and a
boathouse as well as the new public swimming pool
and bathhouse.[57] The landscape architects at the
parks department skillfully integrated the enormous
new complex for aquatic recreation into the park and
neighborhood. On a hill at the western edge of the
park, the bathhouse and pool were across the street
from a public school and next to a large wading pool
(110 feet square), which had opened in 1935. The
wading pool, the bathhouse, the swimming pool (330
by 120 feet), and the semicircular diving pool (120
feet in diameter) were arranged in a line, parallel to
Fulton Avenue. Set close to the sidewalk, the pool
enclosure, made of a masonry base and metal fence,
sat on top of a rock outcrop and a stone wall. A monumental flight of stairs, centered on East 173rd
Street, brought swimmers up to the gigantic brick
arch spanning the entry to the bathhouse; the service
entry was farther north on Fulton Avenue.

Herbert Magoon was in charge of the bathhouse.
A successful designer of public architecture that celebrated swimming in the open air, he created a
memorable setting for public spectacle.[58] *Architectural
Forum* touted it as a typical Moses pool: it was sited in
a public park and offered relief from the "semi-slums"

Christian basilica had been imprinted on the park
landscape in Brooklyn. Bleachers completed the
enclosure of the complex on the park side, the bathhouse on the other.

Magoon let his imagination take flight in designing this building, especially the rotunda, where classical motifs and forms were updated to suit the taste
of his 1930s audience. After climbing up a broad
flight of stairs, swimmers faced a curved brick and
glass portico flanked by projecting brick piers and
then walked by fluted concrete columns before entering the building. Inside, the rotunda was lit from windows set into the drum as well as by custom-designed
metal light fixtures suspended from the ceiling. They
surrounded the two-story faceted brick column that
stood in the center of the space, with the ticket kiosk
wrapped around its base. The angled glass panes at
the top served as a fictive capital (in fact, it covered
part of the mechanical system). A thin concrete lintel,
along with a decorative band made up of diamond-
shaped concrete tiles, circled the space; this zigzag
pattern was carried onto the poolside elevation of the
building. The brick piers, between the windows and
mechanical louvers, looked like a colonnade,
especially when set into relief by light flooding in
on a bright sunny day.[54]   — MG

that bordered it on two sides. Illustrating the article, a series of photographs promoted the advantages of the new pool; they showed young New Yorkers, first using fire hydrants on a city street to find relief from the heat and then experiencing the modern world of recreation at the Moses pools, during the summer and off-season.[59]

Although pool technology and construction details were standard, the design of Crotona Pool was exceptional. Magoon bracketed the two-story arched brick entry with brick towers, topped by glass-block skylights and decorated with limestone trim, open-work curved brick details, and modernist clocks. The large rectangular bathhouse block had a small courtyard in the middle, and the locker rooms, spanned by semicircular trusses, were enormous, even by WPA standards. Concrete piers in the form of a pelicanlike bird, designed by the sculptor Frederick G. R. Roth, divided the entries to the men's and women's locker rooms and the corresponding large window on the other side of the building. Giant brick buttresses, edged in limestone and engaged at the base, created the sense of an arcade along the north and south sides of the bathhouse. A retaining wall and concession stands, set into the park embankment, together with a separate filter house (with boiler room inside), established the park side of the pool enclosure.[60] Semicircular concrete bleachers at the end of the elongated enclosure, with a broad terrace between the seats and the diving pool, turned the area into an amphitheatre. Outside the enclosure, concrete stanchions, which Roth designed to look like animals, circled the wading pool. About 3 feet high, they served as fountains, creating showers for small children. — MG

C-10. Crotona Pool, September 8, 1937

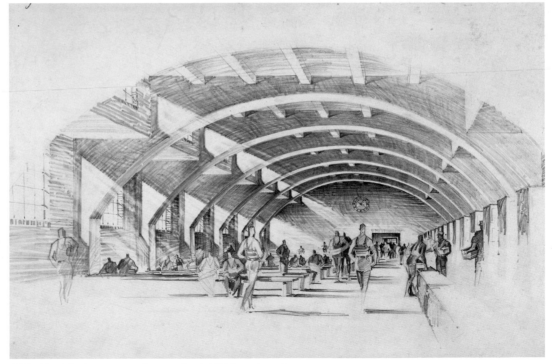

C-11. Men's locker room at Crotona Pool, 1935. Rendering by C. M. F.

McCarren Pool

Brooklyn: McCarren Park, Lorimer Street, between
    Driggs Avenue and Bayard Street
Pool and bathhouse opened July 31, 1936; pool
    closed 1984; bathhouse gutted by fire 1987
Figs. P-24–26, C-12–15

McCarren Pool was the largest of the WPA pools, with
a capacity of 6,800 swimmers. It served the diverse
neighborhoods of northern Brooklyn for forty-seven
years until it was closed for major repairs in 1984.
The renovation, however, was blocked by protesters
from Greenpoint-Williamsburg, who claimed that the
pool had become a magnet for crime and drugs. Many
believe the protests were a racially motivated effort
to keep users from other neighborhoods, minorities
in particular, out of the largely white area. The pool
remains closed today, despite a variety of reuse
proposals made over more than twenty years; lack
of funding and community discord over the size of
the future pool have hindered action. In summer
2005, the structure was stabilized by the New York
City Department of Parks and Recreation and opened
as a temporary performance space.

Its unusual history and picturesque ruins have
given McCarren Pool a unique place in Greenpoint-
Williamsburg: reviled by some as representing a
troubled past, admired by others who see grandeur and
potential in its vast space and monumental architecture.
Oral testimonies collected between 2003 and 2006, by
the author and others, have contributed significantly to
an understanding of the pool and its complex social history, much of which has remained undocumented. This
essay incorporates those testimonies into a general
history of the pool and its communities.

New York City Parks Commissioner Robert Moses
chose Greenpoint-Williamsburg as the location for a
large swimming pool based on the availability of
parkland and the needs of the area's population,
which had more than doubled from 105,000 in 1900
to 248,000 in 1910, forming one of New York City's
most densely populated areas.[61] Composed of distinct
ethnic enclaves of poor immigrants, Greenpoint-
Williamsburg had some of the oldest, most dilapidated housing in Brooklyn. In 1934, 85 percent of
the houses in Greenpoint had been built before 1900,
compared with only 41 percent for all of Brooklyn.
Almost 75 percent of the dwellings were without
central heat or hot water, and 33 percent lacked
private indoor toilets or baths.[62] Such conditions made
the construction of a public pool especially important
as an escape from crowded housing, which was
stiflingly hot during the summer.

C-12. McCarren Bathhouse and Pool, April 15, 1937

Anne F. grew up on Cayler Street during the
1940s and recalled the heat during the summer in
her family's tenement apartment.

ANNE: We were basically . . . poor immigrant
families of factory workers. My family came from
Italy, and I lived amongst Irish, Scotch, German,
and Polish. . . . We walked about five blocks to
the pool. . . . it was so hot in the summer, in those
closed railroad rooms, it was almost impossible
to breathe. There were, at times, something like
seven children living in five rooms.[63]

Regarding recreation, Greenpoint-Williamsburg
was considered one of the most underserved areas of
New York City. Developed largely as an industrial
area, it had little open space and parkland except for
McCarren and McGorlick parks, which were distant
from many residents. According to a survey of recreational needs conducted in 1935, those interviewed
unanimously agreed that Greenpoint was lacking in
such facilities.[64]

Anne F. also recalled the lack of swimming op
portunities and the smell of the local industries.

ANNE: For me, and everybody I knew that went
[to the pool], they were very grateful to have a
place to go to cool down, because, outside of that,
the only other place we had was the Johnny

Pump . . . the fire hydrants. . . . We couldn't go
into the river, it was very polluted. The factory
emptied a lot of the garbage out there and the
smell was pretty bad. It was not recommended to .
. . swim in the river.

Residents of both Greenpoint and Williamsburg
lobbied for the construction of pools in their respective neighborhood. Moses acknowledged that the area
had sparse recreational resources, but he opposed
construction of two separate pools. With limited
funds, he "had to select those areas which needed
such facilities most and where a suitable location
existed."[65] Nevertheless, Moses responded by building the largest WPA pool in McCarren Park, located
in Greenpoint but close to Williamsburg. Comprising
four parcels of land divided by streetcar lines, the
park had been acquired by the city between 1903 and
1905, when it was known as Greenpoint Park; it was
renamed in 1909 for the state senator and former
Williamsburg resident Patrick Henry McCarren.

Hosted by Moses, Mayor Fiorello La Guardia, and
local politicians, the opening of McCarren Pool was
the largest public gathering of the eleven pool
dedications, attended by some 75,000 residents of
Greenpoint-Williamsburg. The festivities featured a
parade led by community groups to the pool entrance,

speeches, a flag-raising, and "elaborate and attractive exhibitions by the parks department aquatic experts." Two hundred ten policemen maintained order as loudspeakers broadcast the ceremony to "the milling thousands in the streets and the crowded rooftops surrounding the park." In his address, Mayor La Guardia said, "I have been opening quite a few of these pools recently, and it is a pleasure to note on this occasion that no pool anywhere has been so much appreciated by the people as this one."[66]

The design of McCarren Pool was chiefly the work of Aymar Embury II, an architect deeply rooted in tradition, whom Moses described as "a living link between two centuries."[67] Embury had little patience for modernism and its emphasis on individual expression, believing an architect's job was to "coordinate units so that they do a required job and at the same time create a pleasant emotion."[68] Despite this, his collaborations with Moses, Gilmore D. Clarke, and Othmar H. Amman produced brilliant modern structures. McCarren Pool mixed classical elements and up-to-date design. Its broad steps and massive Roman arches have been compared to both historic and modern masterpieces, from the Baths of Caracalla in Rome to the Karl Marx Hof in Vienna.[69] The grand entrance courtyard, perhaps the pool's most distinctive feature, included many elements that are missing today, such as bronze doors, flagpoles, lighting, and clocks. A wooden framework is all that remains of the sleekly designed ticket booth, which was made of bronze and black marble and embellished with sculptured figures of swimmers and sea creatures.

To enter the pool, patrons walked up large granite steps, furnished with bronze and oak handrails and flanked by walls of cast-granite blocks. On either side, sculptural groups of bronze art deco eagles supported 60-foot flagpoles topped with gilded copper orbs. Inside, the large courtyard, framed by 30-foot brick arches, was open to the sky; ahead was the vast pool and, to either side, the entrances to the changing rooms.

Former patron Steven K. recalled the impression left by the vast entrance space:

STEVEN: As a kid, it was so big, with these great stairs going up . . . all you would hear [was] the noise of all these people inside and, man, you had to get in there. So you go up these great steps, and I think it was a dime to get in. When you finally got in it was like, eureka! This place is like the Promised Land. 'Cause there were no pools where I lived, trust me, there were no pools. We would hang the hose in the backyard, that was about it.[70]

The simple plan of McCarren Pool is similar to other WPA pools of Olympic size, those at Astoria and Crotona. McCarren Pool features a central entrance courtyard with the men's and women's bathhouses aligned at either side. The bathhouses, which could be used for other sports such as basketball and boxing during the winter, were large rectangular spaces with high ceilings and large windows. The interior layout presented a simple progression from admission booth, through locker rooms, to toilets and shower room. As at other WPA pools, bathers passed through sanitizing footbaths—an antibacterial acid and then pure water—before entering the pool area.

Once patrons exited the bathhouses, they were faced with a vast space full of possible activities, with separate sections for swimming, diving, wading, and sunbathing—all surrounded by wide promenades covered with terra-cotta tile. The main swimming pool, measuring 365 by 165 feet—larger than four Olympic-size pools combined—was four feet deep, with a shallow wading section at the north end that allowed smaller swimmers to stand comfortably in the water. Two small islands in the center of the main pool provided a locus for aeration, lights, and swimmers to rest. At the north and south ends of the main pool were separate hemispherical pools for wading

and diving. Through small arched entrances, patrons could ascend stairs to an area above the pools, to sunbathe or watch events. Or they could sunbathe and observe the passing scene from concrete bleachers located next to the main pool.

Loretta N. preformed water ballet at McCarren Pool, and Leonard S. was a spectator who watched her show.[71]

LORETTA: I started with the pool more or less when it first opened, it was simply nice swimming. You ever see any old pictures of Esther Williams? We'd swim, we'd dive, we'd throw our legs up. It was a lot of practice to get it good; that was show business in itself. People from the surrounding buildings, which I found out later on, would watch from their windows. I just saw it as swimming. . . . I lived for it. . . . That was my summer.

LEONARD: The ballet was something like out of a Busby Berkeley movie. . . . [Loretta] was a standout because she glowed. . . . I'll tell you the ring around the pool to see them perform, everybody would come around, and they'd be lookin' over one another's heads to see, to get a seat.

Former patron Benny D., now a store owner in East Williamsburg, remembers the incredible crowds at the pool, which often exceeded 14,000 swimmers in a single day.

C-13. Axial view of McCarren Pool entry pavilion, March 31, 1947

BENNY: When I came to this country, about forty years ago, everybody used to come from all over, the water was clean, there was everything . . . it was amazing. Our family, we used to go down there, sit down, enjoy a couple hours' sun.[72]

Anne speaks of the special pleasure of swimming at night.

ANNE: It was very beautiful in the evenings, it was completely lighted and the water sparkled a bright aquamarine. . . . this was the age of Esther Williams, she was in the movies, . . . and we swam under a clear, dark blue sky, and looked up at the stars. . . . For people like us, for city people, and for poor people, it all was beautiful.

Those who used the pool from its opening until the 1960s spoke about McCarren Pool, the architecture and the experiences they had there, with great pleasure. Their accounts contrast markedly with the views of those who used the pool primarily in the two decades before its closing. What caused McCarren Pool to decline to the extent that it would close and not reopen? The answers lie both with the economy of New York City during the 1970s and with social and racial issues in Greenpoint-Williamsburg.

Following World War II, New York City experienced the gradual loss of its middle class to the suburbs, which severely eroded its tax base and impacted its ability to provide public services. Furthermore, widespread racial tensions arose from the fragile economic conditions of millions of recent Hispanic immigrants and African-Americans from the south.

As manufacturing decreased nationally, and particularly in New York State, industrial neighborhoods such as Greenpoint-Williamsburg suffered from factory closings and job reductions. Manufacturing jobs in Greenpoint-Williamsburg dropped from 93,000 in 1961 to 12,000 in 1988, causing massive population decline and housing abandonment. In response, the city implemented wide-scale slum clearance projects and built public housing, thus further segregating socioeconomic and racial groups and contributing to the ghettoization of the neighborhood.[73]

The declining economic conditions in Greenpoint-Williamsburg and the rest of the city were amplified in the late 1960s and early 1970s, when the country faced the largest recession since the Great Depression. By 1974, New York City was nearly declared bankrupt. The fiscal crisis led to major cuts in services in New York City public parks. Parks became filled with litter and were vandalized, with buildings covered in graffiti, benches and playground equipment broken, and fields without grass. The city council president Francis X.

Smith claimed that the parks had "never looked so bad, never smelled so bad, never made our people feel so bad."[74]

Without security and staffing, large public facilities such as the pools rapidly declined along with the parks around them. The network of WPA pools, accommodating thousands of swimmers daily, could not function without supervisors, lifeguards, and attendants to operate them, as well as custodians to keep them clean. Lack of security and supervision gradually led to break-ins, fights, and widespread vandalism.

Users of McCarren Pool in the 1970s complained of their feet being cut with broken glass; many reported being intimidated by gangs, muggings, and drug dealing. The problems caused by lack of security and maintenance were compounded by racism. As conditions in public parks deteriorated, the white middle-class majority increasingly sought its recreation outside the city. In 1973, the *New York Times* stated that "very few outsiders will venture into a ghetto pool," citing only four out of twenty-three city pools as being safe.[75] Only one of those was part of the great WPA-era network: Astoria Pool.

Racism is relevant to a discussion of McCarren Pool. The neighborhoods of Greenpoint-Williamsburg consisted of multiple, clearly defined ethnic enclaves. According to the 1930 census, the population of the area was 98.9 percent white.[76] Not surprisingly, during the 1930s and 1940s the users of the pool were predominantly white; nevertheless, during this period it was an integrated facility.

Anne F. and Alan K. recall the diversity of the patrons.

ALAN: I was born in Williamsburg, and [lived there] till I left home when I was 15. McCarren Pool was the center of all the action. . . . it was tremendous, I mean, don't forget that there were so many different ghettos, I mean enclaves, of different ethnic groups. There was the Polish neighborhood, the Puerto Rican neighborhood, the Italian neighborhood, the black neighborhood, the Jewish neighborhood and . . . everybody used to gather there, and there was no fights there, it was very well maintained, well patrolled.[77]

ANNE: There were African-Americans that came, at that time we called them black, and Hispanics. . . . they came by bus, and nobody ever had any fights with anybody. There were no incidents that I can recall. But one of the reasons could have been that it was almost an all-white pool, and it was an all-white neighborhood. Largely white, north Brooklyn in the 1940s was

home to nationalities such as Italians in central Williamsburg; Poles, Ukrainians, and Czechoslovakians in the north and south sides of Williamsburg; and Poles and Irish in Greenpoint. By 1960, the area's population had shifted substantially as immigration from Puerto Rico and Latin America and migration from the American South created areas that were predominantly Hispanic and African-American. Overall, Williamsburg's Hispanic population grew from 5 percent in 1950 to 49 percent by 1980.

Concurrently, white ethnicities dwindled as younger generations moved to the suburbs. The Italian population of Williamsburg dropped from 23,000 in 1960 to 11,000 in 1970, with similar changes in Williamsburg's Polish and Ukrainian communities. The Irish and prewar Orthodox Jews all but disappeared. Despite the decline of the white population, the neighborhoods in the immediate vicinity of McCarren Pool remained predominately Polish and Italian, while the users of the pool were increasingly black and Hispanic.

According to many residents, McCarren Pool in the 1970s became the epicenter of growing neighborhood racial conflicts and crime. Many who had used the pool growing up no longer considered it safe for their own children. Combined with vandalism, criminal activity, and lack of maintenance, the continual ethnic conflicts contributed to decreases in usership and gradual deterioration of the structure. In 1979, addressing the deterioration of the Moses-era pools, the parks department provided nearly $6.5 million in restoration funds for McCarren Pool. Also in this period, the Friends of McCarren Park was organized to "make demands on the parks, police and sanitation department for a cleaner, safer park."[78] The pool was closed for restoration at the end of the 1983 season, but when contractors showed up to work in the summer of 1984, they were barred by a group of protesters. According to the parks department, the protesters "believed that the intended reconstruction did not meet their needs and insisted on a full reconsideration of the project."[79]

The pool remained closed until the conflict could be resolved. Without regular maintenance, the structure rapidly deteriorated. Most of the copper details, including lighting, clocks, ticket booth, and plumbing fixtures, were stripped. The large bronze eagles flanking the stairs were saved by a parks employee as they were being wheeled down Houston Street to an architectural salvage store. Roof failure led to severe structural decay and a fire destroyed much of one bathhouse interior; at one point, a car was driven into the pool.[80]

C-14. Swimmers at McCarren Pool, July 12, 1937

At community board meetings held in 1985 to resolve the conflict, those who had protested the pool's restoration advocated demolishing it or building a smaller pool in its place, while others wanted the pool restored. According to the *Daily News*, the meetings seemed to divide along lines of race; one board member claimed that the "Polish and Irish residents were in favor of a small pool, and the blacks and Hispanics were in favor of a large pool."[81] Those against restoration claimed that the large pool had invited outsiders, who were generally minorities, from other neighborhoods. A small pool, thought to be easily controlled, would serve only the local neighbor-

hood. For others, the push for a small pool implied racial discrimination. Despite resistance from many residents and pool users, Community Board One passed a resolution endorsing the small-pool plan. The parks department had initially rejected the idea of eliminating or reducing the size of the pool but recognized the community board as the official voice of the neighborhood.

The plan called for the demolition of most structures except the entrance courtyard. In 1989, when the city was taking bids to demolish the bathhouses, a preservation effort began, spearheaded by Phyllis Yampolsky. A Greenpoint artist and member of Friends

of McCarren Park, Yampolsky wrote letters to newspapers and gathered support for the pool in the community.[82] Because the parks department had not sought a permit to demolish the bathhouses, she alerted the city's Art Commission, which ordered a halt until the matter could be reviewed. McCarren Pool suddenly became an issue in the press—a battle of words between supporters, detractors, and city officials. Parks Commissioner Henry Stern called McCarren Pool's bathhouses "Moses' eleventh locker room. It's not the Sistine Chapel." He argued that, despite the history of the bathhouses' being used for sports, the ceilings were too low for a modern gymnasium and

C-15. Race at
McCarren Pool,
August 11, 1948

were "not practical for activities involving recreation."[83]

Advocates of the pool, including the architect Robert A. M. Stern, countered that McCarren Pool was "of landmark quality . . . a social vision that was, for once, married to a great architectural statement."[84] Giorgio Cavaglieri, the preservation coordinator for the American Institute of Architects, called the buildings "some of the most remarkable structures designed under Robert Moses."[85] Although McCarren Pool was nominated in 1990 for local and national designation as a landmark, it was not approved. It languished as New York City entered a period of budget deficit, and the funds earmarked for its restoration, nearly $17,500,000, were reallocated. During the 1990s, neighborhood organizations, such as Independent Friends of McCarren Park and McCarren Park Conservancy, created detailed reuse proposals, but these were stymied by continued community disagreement and lack of funding.

In 2001, Community Board One, the parks department, and pool advocates agreed on a $26-million restoration plan for McCarren Pool that preserved the historically significant structures and included a year-round multiuse recreational facility. After the tragic events of September 11, 2001, however, the money for reconstruction once again disappeared. As recently as March 2005, the community board proposed demolishing the pool and replacing it with a soccer field, a decision based in part on the acute need for recreation space created by the recent Greenpoint-Williamsburg rezoning, which will potentially add more than 40,000 new residents to the neighborhood. Additionally, the recent gentrification of Greenpoint-Williamsburg has meant rising numbers of users at McCarren Park, increasing the visibility of the dilapidated pool.

The heightened visibility of McCarren Pool, currently being used as an events space, may ultimately save it. With the success of Noémie LaFrance's "Agora," a dance performance that drew 15,000 in September 2005, large concert producers, such as Clear Channel Communications, have taken note of the pool's potential as a profitable concert venue.

While the Department of Parks sees performance as a temporary use, many area residents have expressed concern that the local community will not benefit. For Williamsburg resident Domenic Fasano, who supports restoration, McCarren Pool represents a broken continuum in the neighborhood. "When I was a baby, my father took me to that pool. To see my sons in the pool is to see myself, but I haven't been able to do that."[86] For Yampolsky, the pool is timeless and "a deep-rooted part of the area's social history. It is as big as a lake, and it is this community's waters."[87]

McCarren Pool, a significant work of architecture and part of New York City history, presents a unique opportunity to restore Robert Moses's grand vision of safe and accessible swimming facilities for all New Yorkers. While a concert venue may generate revenue and serve to stabilize McCarren Pool in the interim, a generation of Greenpoint-Williamsburg's youth has gone without a place to swim. For them, especially on hot summer days, McCarren Pool, designed by master architects and with unprecedented grace, should be a pool once again. — BLM

BETSY HEAD POOL

Originally Betsy Head Bathhouse and Pool, 1915
Brooklyn: Betsy Head Playground, Douglass (Boyland)
   Street, Livonia Avenue, Hopkinson (Strauss) Street,
   Dumont Avenue
Reconstructed and enlarged pool and bathhouse
   opened August 7, 1936; destroyed by fire 1937;
   new bathhouse opened May 27, 1939; pool
   reconstructed 1983
Figs. P-7–10, C-16–18

The ninth pool to open in the summer of 1936 was
located in Betsy Head Memorial Playground, a small
park in Brownsville, Brooklyn.[88] The park was named
in honor of a wealthy British immigrant, who
bequeathed $200,000 to the City of New York in
1907 for the "purchase and improvement of grounds
for the purposes of health and recreation" for
children.[89] The money was spent only when the
Public Recreation Commission took charge of the
project in 1914 and hired Henry B. Herts to design
a playground to be located on land acquired by
Brooklyn property owners for this express purpose.
Ground was broken in May, and the park was turned
over to the Department of Parks after construction
was completed later that year. Just under 11 acres, it
consisted of two blocks, kitty-corner to each other at
the intersection of Douglass (Boyland) Street and
Dumont Avenue, which became the effective center of
the park. Herts designed the smaller plot, across the
street from an elementary school, for younger children
and their mothers: this part of the park held a wading
pool; a playground and playfield; an administration
building incorporating a model farmhouse, milk station, mother's center, and toilets; and a farm school,
with 500 small parcels (8 by 4 feet). The larger plot
was equipped for older children and adults, with an
outdoor swimming pool, a bathhouse, a field house,
and separate gymnasiums for men and women. An
outdoor running track, surrounded by stadium seats,
filled out the rest of the park.[90]

This park was not on Moses's 1934 list of proposed sites for new pools, even though the *Regional
Plan* had suggested improvements were in order. The
study revealed that although the playgrounds were
well attended, more children were found on the
streets and in the movie theaters of Brownsville than
in the park.[91] In 1936, Moses began what became a
series of improvements by modernizing the pool,
which he called decrepit, and the bathhouse. Major
changes were made: the old pool (150 by 50 feet) was
enlarged and turned into a modern pool of Olympic
size, with up-to-date systems for recirculating, purifying, and filtering water. Lockers were removed from

C-16. Entry pavilion at Betsy Head Pool, with stairs to roof bleachers, October 1, 1939

C-17. Locker room at Betsy Head Pool, June 2, 1939

the bathhouse (and replaced with baskets) and the
interior was altered to accommodate 4,660. Other
planned improvements—diving and wading pools
(100 by 50 feet each), a new playground, running
track, and soccer field—were under construction
when the pool opened on August 7, 1936.[92]

No one from the mayor's office or Department of
Parks came to Brownsville on opening day, an exception to the usual fanfare that accompanied these occa-

sions. The explanation offered was that the project
was incomplete, "an interim solution," and that the
mayor and the commissioner would come the following year, when the new bathhouse and the diving and
wading pools were supposed to be finished.[93] Another
reason may have prompted La Guardia and Moses to
avoid the site: Brownsville, largely inhabited by
working-class Jewish immigrants in the 1930s, was a
community well known for radical politics, where the

C-18. Betsy Head Pool, ca. 1940

preceding summer a crowd heckled a public official who spoke at an Independence Day rally; a fistfight developed that had to be quelled by local police.[94] Nevertheless, the absence of elected representatives at the pool opening was startling. The captain of the local precinct, Bernard Rorke, shrugged off the slight. "Commissioners, Aldermen, and such folk aren't expected to use the pool, and they'll not be missed this morning. It's wonderful to have an opening be just that and nothing more." Children were everywhere, drawn by a "grapevine system of communication"; 800 were lined up at the bathhouse entrance an hour before the pool opened. Max Felmer, thirteen years old, was among the first to leave the boys' locker room; Lillian Lutin, eleven, led a group of girls. When queried about the shallow depth, the pool director Peter Bobrowsky explained that this pool, intended for swimming only, had no deep end. A separate diving pool was in the works.[95]

Work continued on the park after the renovated bathhouse, also used by the Department of Parks for administrative purposes, burned down the following summer. The pool remained open, with children advised to arrive wearing their bathing suits. A spectacular new bathhouse, designed by John Matthews Hatton, with E. A. Sears as consulting engineer and S. J. Kessler as structural engineer, opened on May 27, 1939. Other additions to the park were made

through 1941. When finished, the new recreation facilities included—in addition to the bathhouse and in-ground pools—a new baseball diamond, football field, running track, bleachers, softball diamond, and roller-skating rink.[96]

The new bathhouse was built on the site of the burned-down building, which with no land to spare in this small park had been located right on the Hopkinson (Strauss) Street lot line. The sleek modern building, with a cantilevered canopy shading a stepped roof terrace, accommodated 5,500 bathers and occupied most of the park frontage along the street. The new "city play center" quickly won praise in *Architectural Record* for having been designed for "enjoyable use" year-round.[97] While reminiscent of Hatton's bathhouse at the Astoria Pool, the Brooklyn building, stripped of most ornament, was more urbane and even more modernist.[98] Brick piers and panels of glass block, brick, and concrete (incised with curving lines reminiscent of ocean waves) indicated the structural bays of the symmetrical, steel-frame building; large glass-block windows illuminated the locker rooms, and ribbon windows the shower and bathrooms. The walls of the lobby in the middle of the building, open to the air, were clad in dark stone and shiny metal panels; curved glass-block partitions delivered light to offices and storage spaces; and a modernist sculpture stood in the center of the arch-

way on the poolside of the entry. As in all the WPA bathhouses, efficiency in plan was important; the need to protect against vandalism was also cited as a design issue (with the 1937 fire in recent memory). The sturdy materials were supposed to be impervious to graffiti; metal fixtures were designed so they could not be removed; and pool attendants were stationed behind the curved glass-block walls on either side of the entryway, where they could survey the activities.[99]

The coordination of the entry space with the remarkable roof terrace and locker rooms showed the seriousness with which the architects took Moses's directive to design for multiple uses. In this pool, as in others, the mandate prompted inventive, elegant, and even humorous solutions. For example, the circular, tile-clad column in the center of the entryway masked a chimney stack; when it popped out above the roof line, the chimney was clad in glass block and had turned into an oval light fixture, used to illuminate the roof terrace at night. At either end of the roof, on the lower terraces above the shower rooms, the ventilation stacks were also used as lights and enclosed in glass block. Above the locker rooms and entryway, the roof deck had a stepped section, which reduced noise in the spaces below and became a locus for viewing pageants in the pools. As *Architectural Record* pointed out, the roof terrace was an example of design for multiple use in that it recaptured as open space the park area occupied by the bathhouse. Another example was the locker rooms: furnished with up-to-date equipment, during the off-season they could be converted into a gymnasium.

The design of Betsy Head Pool enhanced the potential for spectacle, as the film footage in the parks department archives, probably shot on the opening day of the bathhouse, makes very clear. The public did not have to pay fees to use the rooftop terraces, which were accessible by two flights of stairs located on the city side of the bathhouse (next to the men's and women's shower rooms). On this hot summer day, the residents of Brownsville crowded onto the rooftop stadium, hanging over the pipe rails or seeking shade under the canopy, which hovered above them, supported by eight parabolic arches clad in metal panels, glistening in the sunshine. Swimmers filled the grandstand on the park side of the pool to watch swimming races and diving competitions, judged by lifeguards and the recreation supervisor. As enticing as the film shows the pool to be, however, it also confirms reports that the pool was off-limits to blacks, at least when whites were present: all the bodies, gliding through the air and swimming in the water, were white.[100] — MG

JACKIE ROBINSON POOL AND RECREATION CENTER

Originally Colonial Park Pool
Manhattan: Jackie Robinson Park, Bradhurst Avenue,
    West 145th to West 147th Street
Pools and bathhouse opened August 8, 1936; recent
    renovations include conversion of the diving pool
    to a water play area
Figs. P-18–21, C-19–20

Colonial Pool opened to great acclaim, welcomed by public officials and Harlem residents alike as a long overdue investment in the Harlem community. With the dearth of municipal recreation facilities in central Harlem well known to advocates of public recreation in the 1920s and 1930s, Moses announced in the summer of 1934 that he intended to build one of the WPA-funded pools in this part of Manhattan.[101] Mount Morris Park, now known as Marcus Garvey Park, was selected but abandoned for political reasons: Mount Morris Park sat within Mayor La Guardia's election district, which was also slated to receive a new pool in Thomas Jefferson Park. A new site in Harlem was announced, but not before riots broke out early in the summer of 1935, with the lack of recreation facilities cited as a principal reason for the unrest.[102] The response was fitting if a bit tardy: on the evening of August 9, the mayor and the commissioner attended a bi-weekly dance at Colonial Park (renamed in 1978 to honor Jackie Robinson) sponsored by the parks department and announced that it would be renovated and a new pool and modern recreation center would be built "entirely with local Negro labor," hired with WPA funds.[103] The following year, when the new complex opened, 25,000 cheering Harlem residents attended the festivities. Only half of the bathhouse had been completed; the opening had been expedited for obvious reasons.[104]

The new complex was built on a long narrow strip of land (about 10.5 acres) that the city had acquired for public recreation in the 1890s; the first playground opened in 1911.[105] Embury took charge of the WPA improvements to the park, which when complete extended for ten city blocks, from West 145th Street to West 155th Street, along Bradhurst Avenue. The new pool and bathhouse, a band shell, dance floor, mall, wading pool, playground, athletic fields, and other facilities were arranged in a compact, linear configuration so that they could be constructed on level land, below the rocky escarpment that constituted the western edge of the park. The upper portion of the park was left in "an informal and wooded state," with a new promenade built above the retaining wall along Edgecombe Avenue.[106] In addition to

C-19. Jackie Robinson Park, with pool and recreation areas, September 8, 1937

C-20. Bathhouse at Jackie Robinson Pool, looking south, ca. 1935. Rendering by C. M. F.

Originally Red Hook Recreation Center and Pool
Brooklyn: Red Hook Park, Clinton, Lorraine, Henry,
   and Bay streets
Pool and bathhouse opened August 17, 1936;
   park and bathhouse renovated 1990s
Figs. C-21–22

The 1936 pool-building program culminated on August 17th with the opening of Red Hook Recreation Center and Pool in southwestern Brooklyn. Red Hook, sometimes called the Hell's Kitchen of Brooklyn, was one of the busiest shipping centers in the United States in the first half of the twentieth century; the transport of grain was especially important to the dockyard economy.[112] With tenements and warehouses lining streets near the waterfront, the *Regional Plan* highlighted the lamentable state of public recreation, especially for children in this working-class, largely Italian, immigrant community. Lee Franklin Hanmer observed in the *Regional Plan* that the paucity of public playgrounds, as in Brownsville, encouraged children to go to the movies. "It is a matter of real concern . . . when we find a fifth of the children of a district crowded into the movies for several hours on a pleasant day instead of engaging in active outdoor recreation."[113]

Moses had his eye on this neighborhood in 1934, that is, early in his tenure as parks commissioner; and included it on the list of 23 sites intended for WPA-funded pools.[114] The city had acquired the first parcel of what would become the park in 1913, intending to build a railroad terminal for freight; this piece of land was turned over to the Department of Parks on June 27, 1934, about one month before Moses issued the press release outlining the scope of the pool-building program.[115] Other parcels were obtained, among them 11 acres of swampland; they had been filled in the 1920s by the State Division of Canals but were not needed for an enormous grain elevator built near the waterfront.[116] Another agency in the La Guardia administration had plans in Red Hook: the Tenement House Commission intended to develop 38 acres of land, owned by the city, into public housing. According to Caro, the design of the new housing project had been stalled until Moses expressed an interest in the site and prodded the Tenement House Commission into action. He asked the mayor to instruct the Sinking Fund Commission, which controlled city-owned property, to turn over all vacant and abandoned land to the Department of Parks for development.[117] La Guardia refused in the case of the site for Red Hook Houses, but it took

the precipitous slope, the site presented other challenges: the pool and bathhouse sat on a former streambed, and quicksand and mud complicated construction. Nevertheless, Embury designed an extraordinary two-story brick bathhouse and pool enclosure, whose arched windows, buttresses, towers, and monumental vaulted entry hall recalled medieval and Roman architecture. When finished, the building held about 4,100 people, and like all the other Moses bathhouses could be converted into a gymnasium during the off-season. The swimming pool (236 by 82 feet) and diving pool (82 by 65 feet) were tucked between the bathhouse and the cliff rising up to Edgecombe Avenue.[107] As swimmers jumped into the swimming pool, they could see on the horizon the stone buildings of the City College of New York.

For this site, more than for other pools, the parks department emphasized that the redesigned park included amenities for adults as well as for children. The highlight was the outdoor "granolithic" dance floor and masonry band shell, which allowed the department to bring the dances that it sponsored from streets into the park proper. As the press release announcing the opening of this pool stated, "The addition of these activities [for music and dance] within the heart of the colored section of Manhattan is in keeping with the Park Department's policy to increase adult recreation facilities wherever possible."[108] Does the focus on music and dance, unique to Colonial Pool in the pool-building program, show Moses to be racist in that it conforms to racial stereotypes linking blacks with music and dance? Or is it another example of Moses as savvy publicist, highly skilled in manipulating public opinion? Whatever the answer, the street dances were extraordinarily popular, attracting 1,000 couples who jitterbugged on hot

summer evenings. In some measure, this was due to the quality of the music: Moses used work-relief funds to hire African-American musicians to play in the Colonial Dance Orchestra, a thirteen-piece jazz band; and he invited African-American performers and athletes to participate in the opening day celebration at Colonial Pool.[109]

The improvements to Colonial Park are one example of Moses's using WPA funds to add recreational facilities to black neighborhoods in New York, recreational facilities that African-Americans wanted and pressured the La Guardia administration to provide. The Harlem community benefited from the addition of the grand new pool, even though it and other recreational facilities may have been built to diminish hostility toward the mayor and his administration and to create buffers between black and white neighborhoods.[110] These boundaries could prove to be permeable. As shown in film footage taken in the 1930s and discussed in oral histories, on occasion white children joined African-Americans to swim in Colonial Pool.[111]   — MG

some time for the New York City Housing Authority (NYCHA) to complete the design. At the opening of the Red Hook Recreation Center, La Guardia admitted to a cheering crowd of 40,000 that funding had fallen through for the public housing for the community and called for cooperation among city officials so that his administration could meet its promise to deliver both low-cost housing and recreation amenities to New Yorkers.[118] Eventually, the new recreation center, Red Hook Park, and Red Hook Houses were built, in spite of bitter competition for the control of land during the planning process.

The team at the Department of Parks designed the recreation center according to the usual criteria; Aymar Embury II was probably the lead architect. The bathhouse, which accommodated 4,462 swimmers, and the pools were sited on axis with one another, directly south of the parcel slated for public housing. Two L-shaped buildings, each containing men's and women's locker and shower rooms, bracketed the swimming pool (330 by 130 feet) and the diving pool (150 by 65 feet); the wading pool was outside the enclosure.[119] An open courtyard (since enclosed), shaded by a hipped roof, served as the main entrance to the brick bathhouse, which was decorated with concrete trim and classicizing details, including arches reminiscent of imperial Roman architecture (and Embury's work at Colonial Pool). Portals were cut into the side elevations, offering views into the pool enclosure, and bleachers were constructed over the filter house, at the northern side of the pool enclosure, closest to the public housing site.

Film footage, taken shortly after Red Hook Houses opened in 1939, shows the advantages of this New Deal reform landscape, designed by Gilmore D. Clarke and other architects and landscape architects: gleaming in the summer sun are the pool, the bathhouse, and twenty freestanding brick housing blocks, with 2,545 apartments for dockworkers' families.[120] At long last, working-class New Yorkers, including children, did not have to live, or to swim, in the shadow of tenements. Nevertheless, this housing project, one of the largest in New York and the first in the city to be funded by the United States Housing Authority, was criticized soon after it opened—for its monotony, density, and barracklike appearance. In no small measure, these problems were related to stringent federal guidelines, intended to reduce construction costs, which forced the architects at the NYCHA to amend their initial, more commodious design.[121] Writing in the *New Yorker* in 1940, Lewis Mumford blasted the aspect of the New Deal vision

C-21. Sol Goldman Pool and environs, November 23, 1937

C-22. Main entrance to Sol Goldman Pool, July 18, 1937

for Red Hook that created overcrowding in a part of the city where land costs and densities had been low. Yet, he admitted that building this and three other public housing projects (Harlem River Houses, Queensbridge, and Williamsburg) in record time was "something of a miracle." He praised the planners for creating at each site "an organic unit for living," and at Red Hook he called attention to the recreation facilities nearby, as essential to the community building of the welfare state. "That's a lot," Mumford wrote, "and that is the real reason for demanding a lot more"—meaning even more humane, socially grounded modern architecture for New Yorkers.[122]
— MG

BARGE POOLS

Manhattan: Hudson River, off West 93rd Street and Riverside Drive
Renovated pools opened August 1938; removed 1942
Fig. E-9

In 1938, the Department of Parks addressed another vestige of reforms taken to improve public health: the floating municipal swimming pools from the Progressive Era. The four remaining tanks, in their winter berths in Queens and the Bronx, were in dire need of repair. After Moses wrested control of the pools from the Manhattan borough president, three were reconfigured and towed to the Hudson River for the summer, where they were moored near West 93rd Street and Riverside Park. Piles were driven into the river to create a suitable anchorage; and a gangplank was constructed so swimmers could walk to the pools. Madigan-Hyland, consulting engineers who represented the parks department and the New York Central Railroad in the Westside Improvement, handled the design. Michael John Madigan was also a member of the Moses inner circle.

Made watertight using asbestos tile, two of the floating pools flanked the third barge, which had been reconfigured as a bathhouse. Covered with a great curved roof, it contained dressing rooms, showers, a chlorination room, and a first-aid office. Additional gangplanks brought swimmers to the pools (each 65 by 40 feet), which were surrounded with canopied promenades. The *New York Times* praised the project, finding it to be an "attractive addition" to the new park along the river that allowed "swimmers [to] enjoy the illusion of being immersed in the Hudson," all the while knowing that the water is fresh, pure, and chlorinated according to city regulations.[123]

These pools were used for only a few years, as Moses was unable to convince the city council to fund their upkeep. They fell apart and were abandoned in 1942.[124] — MG

MUNICIPAL BATHHOUSE POOLS

ASSER LEVY RECREATION CENTER
Originally East 23rd Street Municipal Bathhouse, 1908
Manhattan: Asser Levy Place (Avenue A) and East 23rd Street
Outdoor swimming and diving pools opened 1938; rebuilt and refurbished 1990; bathhouse designated a New York City Landmark 1974

CARMINE STREET POOL AND THE TONY DAPOLITO RECREATION CENTER
Originally Carmine Street Municipal Bathhouse, 1908
Manhattan: James J. Walker Park, Seventh Avenue South, and Clarkson Street
Outdoor swimming and diving pools opened 1939; Keith Haring mural August 1987

JOHN JAY POOL AND BATHHOUSE
Originally East 76th Street Municipal Bathhouse, 1906
Manhattan: John Jay Park, East 77th Street and Cherokee Place
Swimming and diving pools opened 1940 and 1942; bathhouse remodeled 1941

RECREATION CENTER 59
Originally West 60th Street Municipal Bathhouse, 1906, and Fieldhouse, 1912
Manhattan: 533 West 59th Street
Outdoor pools opened 1943; closed 1990s

In 1938, when the Department of Parks won control of the city's municipal bathhouses from the Manhattan borough president, Moses started the second phase of the pool-building project. In Manhattan, it resulted in the modernization of four Progressive Era bathhouses and the addition of new outdoor swimming pools to them. As with the 1936 pools, workers, paid with WPA funds, added to, amended, and improved existing infrastructure. The municipal bathhouses, inspired by the public health movement, had been built in response to a change in New York State law that required cities with populations larger than 50,000 to build free bathhouses. In New York City, most of the bathhouses were located in tenement districts and intended to serve a single immigrant or ethnic group.[125]

In the late 1930s and early 1940s, Embury and his colleagues at the Division of Design used the same design standards for the four municipal pools as they had earlier, although due to site constraints the new pools were significantly smaller than those built in 1936. When space permitted, however, separate swimming, diving, and wading pools were provided.

Because entry fees applied, the swimming and diving pools were enclosed; the wading pool was free. They were equipped with similar filtration, purification, and recirculation systems as those used in the earlier pools. Other details included the standard wide pool promenade (over the service tunnel), scum gutters, and sturdy metal plumbing and mechanical fixtures. The connection of these pools to their surroundings is noteworthy, and readily apparent in the films taken of these facilities, with their integration into neighborhood life made possible by their siting and relatively small size.

The municipal bathhouse on East 23rd Street (later named for Asser Levy, one of the earliest Jewish immigrants) was the first to be modernized. Designed by Arnold W. Bruner, with William Martin Aiken, the brick and stone building was intended to look like, or at least recall, an imperial Roman bath. Sitting on a podium, the Beaux-Arts bathhouse was decorated with two monumental round arches framed by giant paired columns and a massive cornice and balustrade. The arches led to separate shower rooms for men and women, which flanked an indoor swimming pool, covered with a great glass roof, retained when the structure was modernized. The parks department added new outdoor swimming and diving pools, along with new playground facilities.[126]

In 1938, plans were also under way to add new pools to three other municipal bathhouses. Renwick, Aspinwall, and Tucker, the architects of the Carmine Street Municipal Bathhouse, conceived it as a multipurpose building; in addition to bathing facilities, it contained a gymnasium and an open-air classroom on the roof.[127] More athletic equipment was added in 1911 and an indoor swimming pool in 1920. The new outdoor diving and swimming pools that opened in 1939, due to the small site, abutted each other, separated by a wall rather than the usual promenade.

The alteration of the East 76th Street Municipal Bathhouse, originally designed by Stoughton & Stoughton, architects, was completed in 1941, after the transfer of the property to the parks department.[128] The park and the bathhouse were part of an impressive node of reform architecture, dating from the Progressive Era, which included the Shively Sanitary Tenements (1911), designed by Henry Atterbury Smith and sponsored by the Vanderbilt family; the York Avenue Estate (1901), designed by Harde and Short and built by the City and Suburban Homes Company; the East End Hotel for Women (1913), another City and Suburban project; a branch of the public library; a settlement house; and a public school. New swimming and diving pools were added behind the bathhouse, close to the East River, and were raised from grade to accommodate the mechanical equipment. The bathhouse was renovated to accommodate almost 1,600 swimmers; the alterations also provided a gymnasium, auditorium, and other amenities.

The last intervention in this sequence was at the West 60th Street Municipal Bathhouse, designed by Werner & Windolph, and at the Fieldhouse, designed by Theodore E. Videto, facing West 59th Street and close to the Hudson River.[129] On land acquired from 1906 onward, and intended to be used in part as a playground, a pair of long narrow buildings had been built back-to-back. The bathhouse, which opened in 1908, was made of limestone and brick and decorated with terra-cotta ornament; it had showers for men and women and an indoor pool, the first to be built in a New York City bathhouse.[130] The fieldhouse was added in 1911, erected on the southern half of the property, which had been set aside for a playground. Located at the edge of Hell's Kitchen and San Juan Hill, these buildings were used by both Irish-Americans and African-Americans and unlike most New York bathhouses were not intended for one ethnic group. Plans to add the swimming pools began in 1938 (when a tenement was cleared); they opened in 1943 and remained in use for about fifty years. — MG

FLUSHING MEADOW POOL

Originally New York State Marine Amphitheatre (1939)
Queens: Flushing Meadows–Corona Park, Long Island Expressway, and Grand Central Parkway
Amphitheater converted to a pool 1940; pool closed 1977, demolished 1996

Robert Moses built a second swimming pool in Queens, in Flushing Meadows Park. The project had been announced in 1934, but its realization took time.[131] The first iteration was the New York State Maritime Amphitheatre, built for the 1939 World's Fair. The enormous brick and cast-stone outdoor theater, designed by Sloan & Robertson, was placed at the head of an artificial lake. A semicircular curved bank of 9,000 seats faced three revolving stages, set into a large pool. Inserted into Fountain Lake, the theater rested on special piles driven precisely for this purpose.[132] Billy Rose, the Broadway impresario, staged the show, which he called the Aquacade; it proved to be one of the most popular, and profitable, events at the fair. "On this stage 'the girl of tomorrow' will perform," the New York Times announced, in a production that would include a water ballet with 200 girls, 100 of them dancing ballet; water shooting 40 feet into the air formed a curtain 260 feet long.[133] Johnnie Weissmuller, the movie star and Olympic champion; Eleanor Holmes, also an Olympic champion; and Gertrude Ederle, the first woman to swim the English Channel, performed, as did stunt divers and the Aquafemmes corps de ballet. To Moses's dismay, Rose insisted on advertising the show with large neon signs—the letters were six feet high. The battle between the commissioner and the impresario went to the governor's office, with Rose prevailing.[134]

After the fair, the amphitheater was converted to a swimming pool (the 9,000 seats were retained) and named for Gertrude Ederle, who came from Flushing Meadows. The pool closed in 1977 and, despite a concerted effort to preserve it, was eventually demolished.[135] — MG

BEACHES

LONG ISLAND STATE PARKS COMMISSION AND JONES BEACH

Created in 1924, the Long Island State Parks Commission (LISPC) built a string of parks linked by landscaped parkways that extended from the city line to Montauk Point, all funded by the state of New York. Planning and construction continued for forty years under the direction of Robert Moses. The original purpose of this innovative and almost universally admired public endeavor was to bring the urban-dwelling middle class to places of recreation. The parks offered active recreation, an idea that looked neither to greensward nor Coney Island but emulated the upper-class leisure landscape of golf, polo, tennis, horseback riding, swimming, and boating. As Lewis Mumford recognized, "Instead of being faced with a small leisured class, we have now to provide recreational facilities for a whole leisured population.[136]

Pressing his agenda in a memorandum to Governor Alfred E. Smith in 1924, Moses wrote, "If the residents of Nassau and Suffolk counties are not to be overrun and the people of New York City and Long Island are to be afforded recreational facilities, the park and parkway plans which have been developed must be put under way immediately."[137] His claim that the parks would contain the urban population ignored the suburban dynamic, but he also knew that such planning was too important to be left to the local towns. The Regional Plan Association's 1928 report on public recreation acknowledged the same point: "If the magnificent beaches of the south shore of Long Island are to be made available for public use, cities, townships, counties, and the State of New York must arrive at some plan of cooperative action for securing and developing these great stretches of waterfront, providing practical means of access to them and safeguarding them against pollution."[138]

Beginning with the Southern State (1925) and ending with Heckscher State (1959), the LISPC built thirteen parkways, including the Wantagh State (1927), the Northern State (1931), and the Meadowbrook State (1932). In its first decade, the LISPC developed a dozen parks, among them Hempstead Lake, Valley Stream, and Belmont Lake. After much legal wrangling, Moses acquired the Taylor Estate, formerly a private hunting preserve abutting the Great South Bay, and transformed it into Heckscher State Park (1929), with facilities for boating, swimming, horseback riding, and picnicking. All the parks were accessible only by private automobile, and each had ample parking.

The LISPC built to the highest standards and utilized the best materials. Attention to detail was legendary. Lampposts and guardrails were of wood with hand-beveled corners; gas stations (most have since been demolished) resembled the outbuildings of a Long Island estate; the design of each stone overpass was unique; and the landscaping was appropriately generous. "Nothing is too good for the people of the Empire State," Moses remarked. These public parks were intended to represent the apex of progressive government, serving the citizenry not because one constituency or another was pushing the state to meet its needs, but because as a first principle the public deserved nothing less.

The parks exemplified both Moses's ideal of recreation and the Regional Plan's concept of regional parks. The RPA suggested that it was "fair that regional parks should be the state's charge. . . . [S]uch a park, when appropriately developed and administered, affords a protection to the local community [and] relieves the locality of the burden of maintaining roads, public utilities, and police within its boundaries."[139] Towns and villages on Long Island established parks for the exclusive use of their residents, supported by local property taxes; nonresidents were either excluded entirely or charged high fees. This effectively channeled visitors from the city to the state parks, a phenomenon that was not particularly significant until the racial and ethnic character of the urban population changed.

Jones Beach was the jewel, and it became the model and justification for transforming beaches within the city when Moses was parks commissioner. The LISPC acquired the barrier beach and bay from the Town of Hempstead in 1926. Tens of thousands of cubic yards of sand were pumped from the bottom of the bay to raise the island (originally only two feet

BEACHES
1934 — 1
1957 — 17.97

= PROPOSED

0   1   MILES   2   3

PLUMB BEACH
BROOKLYN

FERRY POINT BEACH
BRONX

CLEARVIEW BEACH
QUEENS

CANARSIE BEACH
BROOKLYN

MARINE BEACH
BROOKLYN

JAMAICA BAY BEACH
QUEENS

JACOB RIIS
BEACH
QUEENS

ORCHARD BEACH
BRONX

MANHATTAN BEACH
BROOKLYN

GREAT KILLS BEACH
RICHMOND

WOLF'S POND BEACH
RICHMOND

SOUTH BEACH
RICHMOND

CONEY ISLAND-BROOKLYN

ROCKAWAY BEACH
QUEENS

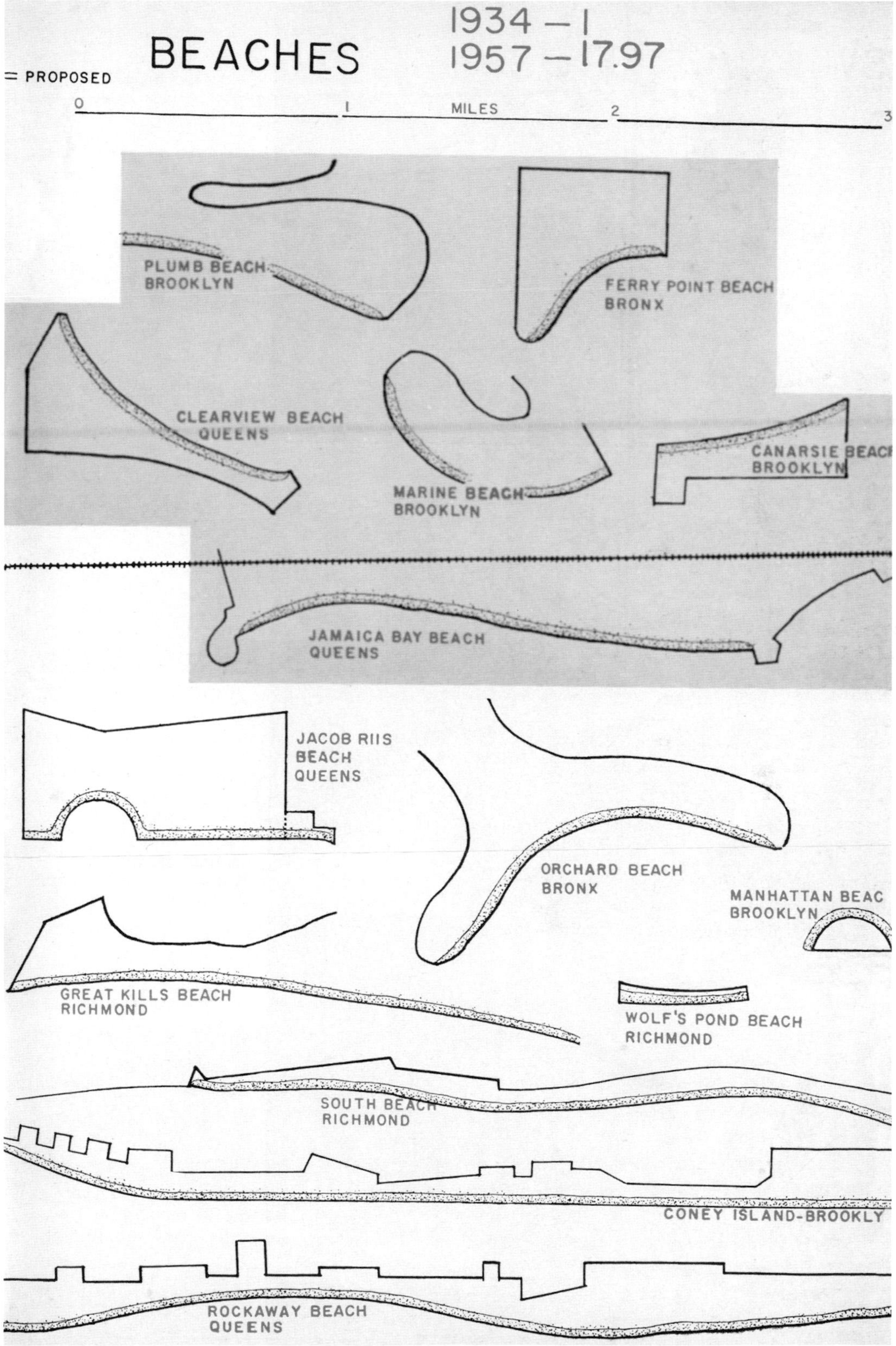

C-23. Schematic plans of beaches built and proposed (shaded) by Moses, January 1958

above sea level), and acres of beach grass were planted to stabilize the new dunes. Handsomely designed and generously proportioned, the bathhouses and concession stands incorporated Barbizon brick and Ohio sandstone; the distinctive water tower was styled in the manner of a Venetian bell tower. Jones Beach opened on August 4, 1929. Even Lewis Mumford, never a Moses fan, admired the achievement, writing in the late 1930s, "The great merit, indeed, of all of Mr. Moses' park developments, from the magnificent seaside park at Jones Beach to his smallest municipal playground, is that every spot that his architects and planners touched bears the mark of highly rational purpose, intelligible design, and esthetic form. No spot is too mean, no function too humble to exist without the benefit of art."[140]

Discussing the history of Jones Beach at the Freeport Historical Society in 1974, Moses recalled in his characteristically brusque style how the LISPC's "concept of a matchless shore front public recreation park open to everyone was still generally regarded by the natives with suspicion and dislike." Even with the benefit of fifty years of hindsight Moses never wavered from his conviction that the only purpose of this "nonpolitical public enterprise" was to build the finest facilities for public recreation.[141] Writing in *The Saturday Evening Post* in 1931, he defended the "Sunday swarms of motorists."[142] Before Jones Beach, "no one had thought to provide

C-24. Jones Beach, with central mall and tower, ca. 1930

a terminus for their excursions. When that terminus is provided, and when it is made as attractive as if it were a private club of rich men, but sufficiently large to prevent overcrowding, something happens. The crowds are well dispersed, quiet, respectable and leisurely. The atmosphere is that of a great public club and the patrons behave like club members." Regarding Prohibition, Moses explained that park officials had no interest in the beverages that visitors consumed; they only wanted to discourage drunkenness. He once proudly proclaimed, "The physical plant at Jones Beach is better than that of any private beach club on Long Island and the beauty certainly would not last unless it were protected. We protect." He also dismissed as "stupid and vicious" the notion that "great public parks in the suburbs shall be only for the poor. If they are properly planned, there

should be facilities for everyone. When you create parks which rich and poor can enjoy, then, we feel you are making democracy function." At the same time, Moses vigorously defended the standards of behavior at Jones Beach, such as enforcing dress codes for the restaurant and prohibiting changing in the parking lots. "There are all kinds of people in this country, and there is no reason why the minority with low standards should prevail."

In 1963, Governor Nelson Rockefeller suggested that Moses yield his chairmanship of State Council of Parks, but in response Moses submitted his resignation as president of the LISPC, a tactic that he had employed against governors and mayors so successfully in the past. On this occasion, Rockefeller finally called Moses's bluff and accepted his resignation. The LISPC passed out of existence in 1972, and all state

parks were transferred to the new Office of Parks and Recreation. Serious cuts to parks funding on Long Island began during the fiscal troubles of the mid-1970s, resulting in reduced maintenance budgets, curtailed hours, and fewer personnel. At the same time, jurisdiction over the parkways was transferred to the Department of Transportation, with the unfortunate result that the distinctive aesthetic features of the system—the lampposts and guardrails, the signage, the stone-faced overpasses—were sacrificed in the name of cost cutting or safety.

During its nearly fifty-year existence, the LISPC set a standard for public architecture and amenities rarely matched, providing an alternative to the pervasive commercial culture. Suburbanites and city dwellers alike have continued to enjoy Long Island's publicly accessible leisure landscape. — JAK

PELHAM BAY PARK

Bronx: Long Island Sound, Hutchinson River,
    Westchester County line
2,766 acres
Established 1888; Orchard Beach reconstructed 1938
Figs. P-28–32, C-25–31

In 1888, the Bronx Parks Department purchased the original 1,700-acre site of Pelham Bay Park, at the northeastern boundary of the Bronx. Before the arrival of Robert Moses as parks commissioner, Pelham Bay Park consisted of a hodgepodge of uncoordinated facilities set amid a largely untamed natural landscape: an 18-hole golf course, a small beach on Long Island Sound, historic mansions, and a World War I memorial erected in 1932. The impressive Bronx Victory Memorial, dedicated to residents of the borough who perished in the war, is a landscaped plaza with a massive Corinthian column topped by a bronze allegorical figure. Moses transformed Pelham Bay Park into a coherent environment, centered around Orchard Beach, comprising discrete but interconnected active recreational resources.

Moses privileged recreation over the preservation of historic structures but accommodated one house in his renovation of the park. The Bartow-Pell Mansion, built in 1836, had been sold to the city at the time of the creation of the park. The city leased the house to the International Garden Club to use as its clubhouse in 1914. During the early years of the twentieth century, many historic homes in the park were demolished, but Bartow-Pell was spared because of the club's residency. The mansion is still run by the International Garden Club and since 1946 has been open to the public as a museum. Moses razed other homes in the park, most notably the Hunter Mansion on Hunter Island, which he demolished to make room for the expansion of Orchard Beach. And, during the summer of 1936, the Bartow-Pell Mansion served a function that categorically prevented Moses from touching it, at least temporarily: Mayor La Guardia and his staff moved into the house for two months and turned it into a "summer city hall."[143]

PELHAM AND SPLIT ROCK GOLF COURSES AND CLUBHOUSE

The recreational system encompassed two adjacent golf courses. The Pell Golf Course opened as early as 1901, with an existing house on the site serving as its clubhouse until 1918, when it was demolished. Claiming that all five existing municipal golf courses

were run-down when he came to power in 1934, Moses restored Pell in 1936 and renamed it the Pelham Golf Course.[144] In 1936, he opened the new Split Rock Golf Course. Under Moses, all the city's golf facilities became self-supporting: golfers were charged for seasonal permits or for each round of golf, and the fees paid for the upkeep of the courses.[145] Moses commissioned John Matthews Hatton, the chief architect for the Astoria Pool and Betsy Head Pool bathhouses, to design a new clubhouse to serve both the new and newly renovated golf courses. The clubhouse, which opened in 1936, was noteworthy enough to be featured in *Architectural Forum*.[146] The more modest of the red brick building's two facades, marked by marble pilasters, faces a circular driveway; the grander facade, fronting on the golf courses, is organized similarly but has a porch defined by six square, white marble columns. The use of marble, even as an accent on an otherwise economical brick structure, is surprising on a Depression-era public building and indicates Moses's commitment to providing luxurious accommodations for those who used

New York City parks. By 1940, he had improved all five of the city's original 18-hole public golf courses, expanded three 9-hole courses to 18-holes, and built two new courses, including Split Rock.

ORCHARD BEACH

Moses's most dramatic change to Pelham Bay Park was the creation of the so-called Bronx Riviera: Orchard Beach. Before 1936, there was a small beach, already known as Orchard Beach, on the Rodman's Neck peninsula. Although the beach was ostensibly public, unrestricted access to the shore was hampered by the residents of a crowded settlement of private bungalows that had grown up during the 1920s. The Bronx Parks Department leased the property to campers, reputedly those with ties to the local Democratic Party. One of Moses's early moves as parks commissioner was to announce, in February 1934, that he was canceling the leases held by all 625 bungalow owners. The campers fought hard to

C-25. Orchard Beach, October 24, 1957

C-26. Club house at golf course, Pelham Bay Park, July 23, 1938

C-27. Interior view, club house at golf course, Pelham Bay Park, ca. 1940

save their summer homes—petitioning the mayor and protesting at City Hall—and received a temporary restraining order. But Moses, adamant that public parks should serve the public at large and not a privileged few, prevailed, and the bungalows were demolished in June 1934.[147]

Moses set about rebuilding the architecture and reconstructing the landscape of Orchard Beach. He immediately ordered the demolition of the low, dark bathhouse complex constructed of granite paving stones, which had only recently been completed, calling it "a monstrosity, atrociously and inadequately planned."[148] He then began to enlarge and reshape the beach itself, sculpting a white sand crescent out of the watery periphery of the Bronx by filling in the shallow area of Long Island Sound dividing Rodman's Neck from Hunter Island. In a typical display of pragmatism, Moses ordered the sanitation department to use ashes as landfill when his budget for importing sand fell short. Despite his request for clean ashes, the incinerated trash was contaminated with garbage, making the beach completely unusable during the summer of 1935. By July 25, 1936, however, a large enough section had been covered with white sand, brought by barge from the Rockaways, to hold the official opening. Yet, the beach would not be completed until 1938, when it extended for a mile and measured 200 feet wide at high tide. Moses's $8-million renovations added 115 acres to Pelham Bay Park: both the

beach and the adjoining parking lot were built on land that had previously been underwater. Orchard Beach was extended once again, in 1947, when Hunter Island was joined with landfill to Twin Islands.

In his transformation of Orchard Beach, Moses followed the model that he had established at Jones Beach in the 1920s. "We will see to it that Orchard Beach is a real beach, where the public will find what it should rightly expect at a beach under the control of the Park Department."[149] This meant a monumental bathhouse complex leading to a wide promenade flanked by opportunities for organized recreation, and a beach tied to a massive parking lot and to efficient

C-28. Site of Orchard Beach, Pelham Bay Park, looking toward City Island, before alterations, April 15, 1935

approach roads. Moses's ideal public beach resort would be defined neither by an Olmstedian natural landscape nor by "an artificial amusement center," like the one he despised at Coney Island. Instead, it would provide "exercise and healthy outdoor recreation": he built tennis courts, baseball diamonds, playgrounds, and picnic groves lining the far side of the promenade from the beach.[150] He revoked all private concessions to prevent the encroachment of unwholesome amusements and made sure that the leisure of the masses would be closely supervised. During the summer of 1937, for instance, in response to "rowdyism and gangsterism," Moses and Mayor

La Guardia assigned extra police to monitor Orchard Beach and set up a seasonal court at a nearby police precinct so that people charged with misconduct at the beach could face a judge immediately.[151]

Moses miscalculated the interests of some Bronx residents, however: my grandmother was a teenager living in the Bronx in the 1930s, and she and her friends preferred the long subway ride to Coney Island over a trip to their local public beach. For poor youth, the games, rides, and vendors at Coney Island guaranteed cheap entertainment, while Orchard Beach was perceived as stodgy and boring. Bronx teenagers might have had a closer amusement park if Moses had not intervened. In 1935, Bronx Borough President James Lyons proposed building games and rides on Hunter Island, asserting that "the people of [this] borough want such recreation." But Moses rejected the plan.[152]

As the designer of many of New York's parkways, Gilmore Clarke, Moses's chief landscape architect, was well qualified to plan a public resort that demanded as much attention be paid to roads and parking lots as to picnic groves and ball fields. A new thoroughfare was built through Pelham Bay Park to connect Orchard Beach to Pelham Parkway. From the inception of the Orchard Beach project, Moses proclaimed his intention to change the course of the road serving the complex, which ran along the shoreline—a convenience to campers. To replace it, Clarke designed a dramatic axial approach consisting of a long road looping around a grassy mall with a bench- and tree-lined perimeter. The mall served as a link between the shore of Long Island Sound and a lagoon that Moses designated as a site for small boating. Drivers approached the beach, dropped off passengers at the bathing pavilion, and then looped back to reach the parking lot—which accommodated 8,000 cars and occupied 45 acres built on top of sanitary landfill. But Orchard Beach was accessible not only by private automobile: a bus terminal was built directly off of the mall, opposite the parking lot. Beach visitors could take the IRT subway to the Pelham Bay Parkway stop and then a bus to the beach, all for a 10-cent fare.

To reach the beach, visitors passed through a 90,000-square-foot pavilion and bathhouse complex. This monumental bathhouse, completed in 1936, stands as a tribute to the public seaside recreation that Moses valued so highly. The structure was designed by Aymar Embury II, the chief consulting architect for the parks department, in a style reminiscent of his other public works, including the Prospect Park Zoo and five swimming pool bathhouses. Embury achieved classical poise using inexpensive

C-29. Orchard Beach crescent, June 2, 1939

C-30. Panoramic view of Orchard Beach, October 27, 1936

modern materials: primarily concrete, with brick and terra-cotta accents. He designed the structure to transform beach-going into an epic experience. The bathhouse complex is composed of a central, raised pavilion, flanked by two wings. From the road, visitors must ascend a flight of stairs to reach the central terrace; only when they walk onto the terrace can they see the landscape of sand, sky, and sea. Two loggias, which reach out like arms embracing the sea, frame the vista. These arcaded hemicycles echo the curve of the manmade, crescent-shaped beach and enhance the drama of the carefully perfected seascape.

Each loggia is two stories tall, the lower level brick and the top level fronted by a colonnade of square concrete columns. The columns mimic the classical orders, their white concrete shafts contrasting with the blue terra-cotta tiles used for the bases, capitals, and entablature. Embury believed that using the orders in modern architecture in a flexible, inventive way brought "dignity and nobility of purpose" to otherwise spare modern buildings. In the exedras of the Orchard Beach bathhouse, his colorful, streamlined orders were meant to produce what he called a "sense of exaltation" in visitors.[153]

Tucked behind the two-story arcade on each side of the bathhouse are brick locker rooms large enough to serve 7,000 people. Bathers approach them along the cross axis of the central terrace through dramatic pavilions. After changing, they exit onto a 50-foot-wide promenade at the end of the hemicycle that parallels the beach. More formal than a boardwalk, the promenade is paved with hexagonal asphalt blocks. The ceremonial quality of the promenade complements the formality of the bathhouse, ennobling the beach-going experience of the masses of New Yorkers who travel to Orchard Beach.

A restaurant is located underneath the terrace, with a landscaped patio containing tables interspersed with trees stretching to the beachfront promenade. The patio has intimate design details like those for which Jones Beach is known: benches, trash cans, and paving stones, for example, are the same shade of blue as the terra-cotta tiles on the columns rising above them. The lower level of the arcade, now filled with shops, in Moses's era was occupied by concession stands run by the parks department, renting chairs and umbrellas. The upper level of the arcade serves as a shaded walk from which visitors can enjoy

views of the beach. A possible model for Embury's bathhouse was Martin Wagner's modern stone beach pavilion built in 1929–30 in Wannsee, on the shore of a lake outside Berlin (fig. E-6).

Orchard Beach, with its harmoniously integrated roads, landscaping, and architecture, still stands as a landmark of generous, well-planned, exquisitely crafted civic design. The quality of the beach and related facilities is a testament to Moses's ability to carry out marvelously cohesive large-scale projects and his commitment to hiring designers capable of producing exceptional public spaces. — KL

C-31. Outdoor restaurant and bathhouse, Orchard Beach, July 18, 1937. Photograph by Max Ulrich

MANHATTAN BEACH

Brooklyn: Atlantic Ocean between Ocean Avenue
and Oriental Boulevard
40.4 acres
Established 1877; opened as city park 1955

After World War II, Robert Moses pressed the city to
acquire the waterfront at Manhattan Beach from the
federal government for a new park. During the war,
Coast Guard and Merchant Marine training stations
occupied the site. It took years of negotiations and
an act of Congress, however, before the state finally
gained possession of the tract in 1950. In the following year, the state transferred 16 acres to the city, and
in 1954 ceded an additional 24 acres. The new city
park at Manhattan Beach opened in 1955. Extending
1,700 feet east of Ocean Avenue between Rockaway
Inlet and Oriental Boulevard, it boasted a clean
beach created with fresh sand, a bathhouse, and
games areas—the same features introduced during
the Moses regime at Rockaway, South Beach, Orchard
Beach, and Coney Island.

In 1954, Moses proposed acquiring the Manhattan
Beach Esplanade, which was accessible only from
local streets (where there was no parking in summer).
Connecting it to the Coney Island boardwalk would
complete a 3-mile promenade running nearly the
length of the island. The local community, however,
vehemently objected to providing public access to
their residential enclave. According to Moses, his
opponents wanted "to make it impossible for persons
on the beach at Coney to walk along the Esplanade,"
regarding such visitors "an intruding and undesirable
element." He argued that transferring the esplanade
to the parks department "would be in the interest of
the people of this city who own these beaches as
opposed to the selfish interest of the Manhattan
Beach Community Group, Inc."[154] But Brooklyn
Borough President John Cashmore supported the
residents, and at his urging the Board of Estimate
blocked the proposal. As a result, the boardwalk
stops at Brighton Beach. — JAK

C-32. Game courts beside the enlarged boardwalk, Coney Island, July 10, 1939

CONEY ISLAND

Brooklyn: Atlantic Ocean between West 37th Street
and Corbin Place
107 acres
Established as seaside resort 1824; expansion of
beach and boardwalk 1938–41
Fig. C-32

In December 1937, just before jurisdiction over the
city's beaches and boardwalks was transferred from the
borough presidents to the parks department, Robert
Moses proposed remaking Coney Island—together with
Rockaway and South Beach—according to the Jones
Beach formula. In a report submitted to Mayor Fiorello
La Guardia, Moses wrote, "There is no use bemoaning
the end of old Coney Island fabled in song and story.
The important thing is not to proceed in the mistaken
belief that it can be revived. There must be a new and
very different resort established in its place."[155] His
plans called for moving the boardwalk 300 feet back
from the water, expanding and replenishing the beach,
and creating an area for games and park facilities 100
feet behind the boardwalk.

By the opening of the summer season in 1940,
nearly a mile of boardwalk had been reconstructed
east of Stillwell Avenue as far as Brighton Beach, and
white sand imported from Suffolk County had been
pumped onto the worn beach. At the same time, parks
department employees began enforcing new regulations for public behavior, including requiring shirts
on the boardwalk and prohibiting changing under the
boardwalk. The carnival atmosphere was not
eliminated, only confined. Even after the Aquarium
opened, in 1957, much of Coney Island remained
immune to the Moses touch. — JAK

NEW YORK AQUARIUM

Brooklyn: Surf Avenue and West 8th Street
Established 1896, Battery Park, Manhattan;
  reopened in Coney Island 1957

Moses succeeded in his effort to relocate the New York Aquarium from Castle Clinton in Battery Park, where it had been operated by the New York Zoological Society since 1902. When it was closed in 1941, during construction of the Brooklyn-Battery Tunnel, many of its 8,000 resident sea creatures were given away to "neighbor aquariums" in nearby cities.[156] Some fish were dumped into the harbor, and others were moved to temporary quarters at the Bronx Zoo. Moses originally proposed building the aquarium a new permanent home there, the headquarters of the New York Zoological Society. Yet when the Coney Island Chamber of Commerce offered the former site of Dreamland Park, on the Boardwalk, Moses jumped at the opportunity to add an educational attraction to Coney Island, which he had been "improving" since 1938. To the dismay of Bronx Borough President James J. Lyons, Mayor La Guardia chose the opening of the African Plains section of the Bronx Zoo in May 1941 to announce that the Bronx would not get the aquarium; it would go wherever Moses wanted.[157] Manhattanites complained that moving the aquarium to Coney Island would make it inaccessible, but Moses retorted that theirs was an elitist perspective and that the facility would actually be accessible to more New Yorkers in Coney Island than Manhattan.[158]

The Zoological Society hired Wallace K. Harrison, the designer of the African Plains exhibition, to design Coney Island's new aquarium. He prepared plans for a one-story building with curves that "hugged the beach" to occupy a 12-acre site between the Boardwalk, Surf Avenue, and West 4th and 8th streets.[159] Construction was stalled when Harrison and his partner, Max Abramovitz, left New York for military service during the war; by the time they returned, the cost of realizing the design had skyrocketed and the size of the building had to be substantially reduced. The 216-foot-long, 120-foot-wide aquarium, comprising "five major halls connected by an overhead passage," opened on June 5, 1957.[160] Served by a new parking lot, the aquarium was accessible through entrances on the street and the Boardwalk. The final design was attributed to the Harrison & Abramovitz firm. The city and the zoological society shared the $1,500,000 construction cost. Whereas the aquarium in Battery Park had been free, this new New York Aquarium charged entry fees of 90 cents for adults and 45 cents for children. At the opening,

the ribbon-cutting responsibility was given to a male penguin named Annie, a former inhabitant of the Battery Park Aquarium who had been biding his time in the Bronx. Annie bit through the ribbon, which was wrapped around a smelt. The *New York Times* report of Moses's speech at the opening reveals his motivation in relocating the aquarium to Coney Island: "Commissioner Moses said he hoped the Aquarium would make Coney Island overcome 'its bad name.' The Aquarium, he predicted, will give to Coney Island 'just the remaining lift it needs, the fine distinction it deserves, the supreme attraction to visitors' that will transform the area into a 'new Coney for healthful outdoor recreation and a year-round community, an ocean resort in the best American tradition.'"[161]

Moving the New York Aquarium to Coney Island was Moses's final touch on his Coney Island Improvement. Turning Coney Island into a wholesome beach resort had been one of his pet projects, and the aquarium provided a family-friendly alternative to the commerce and congestion of the Coney Island of the past that he so despised. In 2006, the Wildlife Conservation Society and the New York Economic Development Corporation announced plans to renovate the facility and held a design competition, which called for a "visually porous, engaging, and inviting" scheme to correct the perceived deficiencies of the 1957 building. — KL

JAMAICA BAY AND MARINE PARK

Jamaica Bay: between Rockaway Peninsula, south-
  western Queens, and southeastern Brooklyn
Marine Park, Brooklyn, at the western inlet of
  Jamaica Bay
798 acres
Park established 1924
Figs. C-33–34

Jamaica Bay had been a productive natural resource since colonial times, but by 1916 the waters had become so polluted that the city banned fishing and swimming. The idea of dredging the bay to create a deep-water port had been advanced by business interests since the early years of the century, and the harbor was included on the official city map. But in the mid-1920s, the Port of New York Authority resolved to redevelop Newark Bay, which essentially killed the plan, though it continued to have its boosters. As parks commissioner, Robert Moses sought to protect the natural attributes of the bay and develop its potential for recreational purposes. During his tenure he advanced park plans and pushed for the construction of new sewage treatment plants to clean the water.

To realize that vision, Moses first organized the Marine Parkway Authority. Established in 1934 with a single member (Moses), the authority opened the Marine Parkway (now Gil Hodges) Bridge in 1937, linking Brooklyn and the Rockaway peninsula. After bondholders and maintenance costs were paid, the surplus from the 15-cent toll collected from every car was to fund the development of Marine Park, an expanse of wetlands and sand at the foot of Flatbush Avenue in Brooklyn. Moses stated that the tolls would be gone in forty years.

In 1916, Alfred T. White and Frederic B. Pratt had donated the first 140 acres to the city for what became Marine Park; by 1934, the site had expanded to more than 1,000 acres through condemnation, purchase, and transfer. The city approved a $40-million plan by the landscape architect Charles Downing Lay in 1931 and construction began two years later using Civil Works Administration labor. After becoming parks commissioner, Moses immediately terminated the project as impractical and too expensive and did not turn his attention to Marine Park until after the war.

In 1938, William F. Carey, the sanitation commissioner, floated a proposal to establish an ash dump and construct a massive incinerator in the middle of Jamaica Bay. Ash from the dump, together with the sand and muck dredged from the bay to carve out shipping channels for possible port development (permitted under existing zoning and still on the

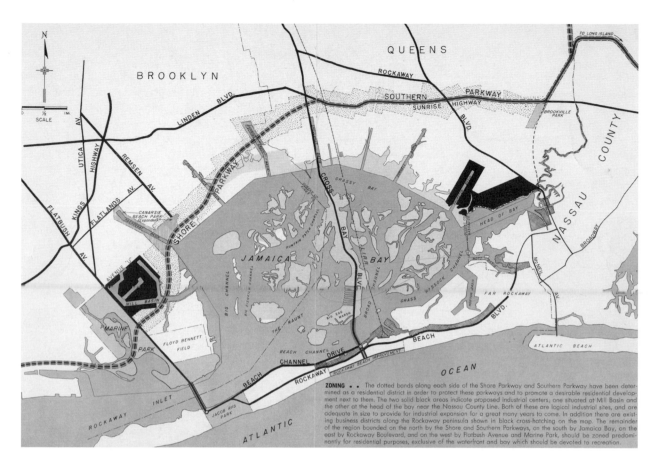

ZONING . . The dotted bands along each side of the Shore Parkway and Southern Parkway have been determined as a residential district in order to protect these parkways and to promote a desirable residential development next to them. The two solid black areas indicate proposed industrial centers, one situated at Mill Basin and the other at the head of the bay near the Nassau County Line. Both of these are logical industrial sites, and are adequate in size to provide for industrial expansion for a great many years to come. In addition there are existing business districts along the Rockaway peninsula shown in black cross-hatching on the map. The remainder of the region bounded on the north by the Shore and Southern Parkways, on the south by Jamaica Bay, on the east by Rockaway Boulevard, and on the west by Flatbush Avenue and Marine Park, should be zoned predominantly for residential purposes, exclusive of the waterfront and bay which should be devoted to recreation.

C-33. Map of Jamaica Bay, with proposed rezoning, ca. 1938

official city map), would provide the fill for two great islands in the center of the bay. With the closing of Rikers Island and the Corona dumps, New York needed a new site for its refuse. But Moses had no intention of allowing the further despoiling of this recreational resource, and he immediately launched an offensive against the plan. In July, the Department of Parks issued *The Future of Jamaica Bay*, a booklet that set forth Moses's own civic values: providing public access to active recreation in a clean environment and eliminating commercial interests in and private control over recreational facilities.

Moses called on the city to decide between the two irreconcilable visions of the bay: a dump and an industrial port or, in his words, "a place within the limits of the city where the strain of our city life can be relieved, where the nerves of tired workers may be soothed, where the old may rest and the young can play." In classic Moses rhetoric, he concluded: "Jamaica Bay faces today the blight of bad planning, polluted water, and garbage dumping. Are we to have here another waterfront slum, depriving millions of

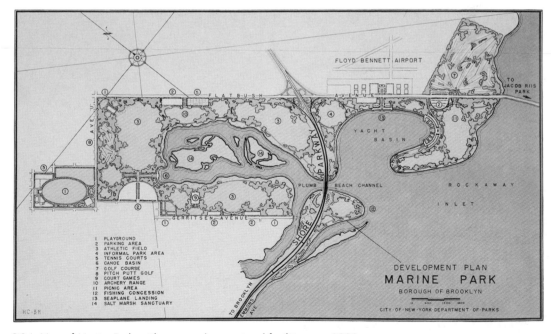

1 PLAYGROUND
2 PARKING AREA
3 ATHLETIC FIELD
4 INFORMAL PARK AREA
5 TENNIS COURTS
6 CANOE BASIN
7 GOLF COURSE
8 PITCH PUTT GOLF
9 COURT GAMES
10 ARCHERY RANGE
11 PICNIC AREA
12 FISHING CONCESSION
13 SEAPLANE LANDING
14 SALT MARSH SANCTUARY

DEVELOPMENT PLAN
MARINE PARK
BOROUGH OF BROOKLYN

CITY·OF·NEW·YORK·DEPARTMENT·OF·PARKS

C-34. Map of Marine Park, with proposed recreational facilities, ca. 1938

future inhabitants of Brooklyn and Queens of the advantages of boating, fishing, and swimming in safe inland waters? . . . Our inheritance at Jamaica Bay is too precious, our investment, present and prospective, in parks, parkways and recreation on its borders is too large to jeopardize them by indifference and bad judgment."[162] The incinerator plan sank.

After 1945, Moses again advanced proposals for recreational facilities in the bay, linking parks development with pollution control. Until the completion of new sewage treatment plants in the early 1950s, rainwater and human waste flowed directly into the bay. From the start, however, the clean-up efforts were compromised. The future park sites were salt marshes and tidal shallows, which would need to be filled. To do so, Moses permitted the dumping of garbage and, at Marine Park, used sludge from the sewage treatment plants for topsoil (much to the distress of local residents). For two decades, beginning in 1949 when the northern rim of the bay from Marine Park to Cross Bay Boulevard was transferred to the parks department, unsightly mountains of malodorous garbage rose between the Belt Parkway and the bay (only in the 1990s was work begun to reclaim the wasteland for a park).

The dumps were integral to his parks plan. As a 1964 parks department publication acknowledged, "Over the years an important factor in [parks] expansion has been the Department of Sanitation's landfill program and the Department of Public Works' sewage disposal program, both vital in reclaiming the waterfront."[163] Nowhere was this more apparent than in Marine Park, where a new golf course opened in 1963, built upon wetlands filled in with garbage and topped with sludge. In 1957, Moses requested funds for a "little Jones Beach" near Broad Channel, an idea that never went forward, largely because additional sewage plants were decades late in coming on line. In 1964, the beaches at Marine Park, described as "proposed" on the parks map still awaited cleaner waters.

In retrospect, Moses deserves credit for saving Jamaica Bay, despite permitting the despoiling of the shoreline. His department indeed recognized the importance of the bay for migratory birds and in the mid-1950s created two freshwater ponds for them on islands in the bay. In 1972, sections of the bay, together with Riis Park, Great Kills on Staten Island, and Sandy Hook in New Jersey, became part of the Gateway National Recreation Area. Today, Jamaica Bay is a thriving wildlife refuge, but the dream of swimming facilities remains just that. — JAK

JACOB RIIS PARK

Queens: Atlantic Ocean between Beach 149th
   and Beach 169th Street
220 acres
Established 1916; Moses's renovations 1936–38
Figs. C-35–38

Land at the western end of the Rockaways was acquired by the city through condemnation in 1912 for use as a public park. Improvements were not made to the shorefront site until 1916, when jetties were constructed to protect the narrow beach from erosion. In 1930, a cinder parking lot was completed, and in 1932 a bathhouse was built using WPA labor. The Moorish-style building, designed by the firm of Stoughton & Plunck, was made of limestone, brick, and cast-stone. Two stories tall, it had a cafeteria on the ground floor and a restaurant opening out to a terrace on the second floor.

Robert Moses examined this elegant structure in 1934 and proclaimed that it extended too far onto the beach: the water came right up to the front of the pavilion at high tide. In August, he announced that he would correct the mistake made by his predecessors by removing 100 feet of the structure. "All we can do is to cut off the front," Moses explained and went on to express his dissatisfaction with the design of the bathhouse. "We also intend to trim off these

gimcracks on it and make it into a decent looking building."[164] With this pronouncement, he set about remodeling an attractive, functional building that had been completed at the cost of $500,000 only two years before. Aymar Embury II supervised the renovation, which was completed in 1936.[165] He eliminated the part of the building that projected onto the beach and replaced it with a conspicuously incongruous concrete facade with squat columns supporting a convex upper floor punctuated by a ribbon window. He added two wings for dressing rooms at either side of the pavilion and spoiled the delicacy of the original towers by topping them with 15 feet of bleak unadorned brick. The heavy brick additions appear to squash the light, intricate stonework of the originals.

A new bathhouse west of the renovated one, called the Central Mall Building (really two discrete structures connected by a patio), was conceived by Embury and opened in 1937.[166] Its organization and style are similar to his bathhouse at Orchard Beach: a pavilion flanked by symmetrical arcades in a streamlined classical style. The hemicycle arcades embrace a view of the beach, echoing the semicircular shoreline. This brick and concrete bathhouse, one story tall, lacks the colorful tiles that enliven the bathhouse at Orchard Beach. One enters the arcades through brick entryways with doors bordered by playful interpretations in concrete of the Doric order: square

C-35. Jacob Riis Park, June 21, 1938

columns, ribbed to mimic fluting, are topped by flat circles representing capitals and by a simplified entablature, complete with triglyphs and metopes. Embury believed that the orders should be imaginatively redefined with modern materials, responding to the qualities of the materials. For him, a building made of concrete was successful when the ornament, although "deriv[ing] from stone forms . . . is obviously cast concrete."[167] Embury simplified and flattened classical forms to suit the building's strong geometrical lines, playfully imitating the classical tradition of stone columns without trying to mask the nature of his economical material. In an attempt to recreate the beckoning water tower at Jones Beach, he placed a clock tower over the western side of the building. The square tower's flat, unadorned brick surfaces make it look drab and looming, not welcoming like the imitation Venetian campanile at Jones Beach. In sum, the clean lines and low horizontal masses of the bathhouse are modern and efficient, but lack the lofty grandeur of Embury's bathhouse at Orchard Beach.

Moses expanded the range of recreational options at Jacob Riis Park with playgrounds; paddle tennis, handball, and shuffleboard courts; and a pitch-and-putt golf course—all beside the mile-long boardwalk. The 40-foot-wide boardwalk was made from Douglas fir imported from the West Coast. To maintain the pristine natural setting, the landscape architect Gilmore Clarke planted shrubs and beach grasses to block the view of the courts and playgrounds from the boardwalk and the beach. Under Moses, Jacob Riis became one of the parks department's revenue-producing properties: small fees were charged for the use of the facilities.[168] Bathers wishing to use the beach for free, however, had only to arrive wearing their swimsuits and avoid sports besides swimming; there was no charge for entering the beach itself. Moses cancelled private concessions at the park as early as 1934, to the dismay of the chamber of commerce of the Rockaways, which objected to the loss to local businesses when the parks department took over services such as parking, food, and entertainment. He defended his position by promising that "uniform low prices for the use of these facilities will be established . . . sufficient to provide for the maintenance cost of the park and no more. . . . The public is entitled to use its own beaches without being forced to rent necessary facilities from private parties."[169] His disapproval of private vendors' profiting from the captive audience at public beaches indicated his commitment to creating noncommercial recreational landscapes, unmarred by loud, unwholesome games and rides like those at Coney Island.

C-36. Game area number 2 and boardwalk, Jacob Riis Park, July 18, 1937

Moses envisioned Jacob Riis in part as a solution to the congestion and chaos of Coney Island. In 1937, he predicted that "the Marine Parkway and Jacob Riis developments will relieve some of the overcrowding at Coney Island, and by force of example will compel an improvement in Coney Island conditions."[170] The *New York Times* affirmed Moses's achievement of a noncommercial public beach resort: "Although Riis Park lies only six miles east of Coney Island it is a million miles away from the so-called Coney Island tradition. Thundering spray, instead of rattling roller coasters, makes the chief music of the beach. Playgrounds for simple games . . . contrast sharply with recreations of the older resort."[171]

Jacob Riis Park was touted simultaneously as the anti–Coney Island and as a second Jones Beach, emulating the paradigm of Moses's highly praised state park built in the 1920s. His faith in the success of importing this Long Island model to the shores of New York City was so strong that he described the creation of a Jones Beach replica at Jacob Riis Park as the "natural" route for the park's development. "The Park Department proposed to develop this park in the way that nature intended it to be developed, along the lines followed with great success and public approval at Jones Beach."[172] Nevertheless, Moses was

not convinced that he had achieved the same triumph in beach planning that he had at Jones Beach, the jewel of his public recreational facilities. He attributed this shortcoming to his having had "to contend with the initial poor planning of Jacob Riis."[173] Still, Jacob Riis succeeded in providing a clean, elegant resort within city limits.

Distinguishing Jacob Riis Park from Jones Beach was its accessibility by public transportation. Robert Caro has claimed that Moses, motivated by racism, built bridges on Long Island that were deliberately low in order to prevent buses—carrying the poor and working class—from reaching the state parks. "In the same way," Caro wrote, Moses "was barring the poor from the best of the city parks, the big parks on the city's outskirts such as Jacob Riis."[174] But Caro misstated the case. Jacob Riis, like Orchard Beach, lay on the "nickel circuit" of public beaches known as subway resorts. By 1937, when the Marine Parkway Bridge opened, New Yorkers dependent upon public transportation could reach Jacob Riis Park via local bus from nearby subway stops in Brooklyn.[175]

In pursuit of his goal of automobility for New Yorkers, Moses planned extensively for automobile traffic to the beach. He created and controlled the Marine Parkway Authority, housed in the Arsenal, to

C-37. Central mall building, Jacob Riis Park, ca. 1936. *Rendering by J. MacGilchrist (detail)*

build both the Marine Parkway Bridge across Rockaway Inlet and a massive parking lot at its terminus at Jacob Riis Park. In a 1935 letter addressed to the Marine Parkway Authority, Moses turned over city-owned land at Jacob Riis to the authority to build the bridge and "incidental facilities," meaning the parking lot. The authority, which was funded by a 25-cent parking fee and, once the bridge opened in 1937, a toll, cooperated with the WPA to finance the construction of the new lot. It replaced an old cinder lot, capable of holding 2,000 cars, with an 80-acre concrete lot for 14,000, promoted as "the largest single paved parking space in the United States."[176] Before the completion of the Marine Parkway Bridge, which connected Jacob Riis directly to Brooklyn, the only way to reach the Rockaways by automobile had been through Queens and over Cross Bay Boulevard. By establishing an integrated system of recreation and transportation, comprising the park and a bridge built specifically to serve it, Moses demonstrated his understanding that convenient access to public parks was as important as the facilities themselves.

Clarke designed a grassy tree-lined mall and pedestrian path leading from the bridge to the beach, a grand axial approach typical of his traditional landscape designs. The road runs parallel to the beach, ending in a turnaround where it meets the mall at a right angle. The mall opens up access to the Central Mall Building and beach at the western end of the park. Moses carried out a scheme of piping in sand, albeit not as dramatically as the earthmoving at Orchard Beach, to make this part of the beach wider and more appealing. The beach at Jacob Riis is naturally long and narrow; Moses doubled its area by adding sand to its west end to create a deep semicircular beach in front of the site of the new bathhouse.

Even though Moses's renovation and expansion of the original Jacob Riis Park bathhouse marred a well-designed building, his provision of recreational resources, a new pavilion, a bathhouse complex, and a new semicircular beach turned the park into a public resort that accommodated masses of water-seeking New Yorkers on hot summer days. His new transportation system—bridge, mall, road, parking lot—brought Jacob Riis within easy reach for these beachgoers.

The beach at Jacob Riis Park is still open to the public, but it is no longer run by the New York City Department of Parks: during the city's fiscal crisis in 1974, it was transferred to the federally run Gateway National Recreation Area. The old bathhouse is currently closed while it undergoes a $22-million renovation. — KL

C-38. Detail of central mall building, Jacob Riis Park, June 15, 1937

ROCKAWAY IMPROVEMENT

Queens: from Beach 1st Street, Far Rockaway,
    to Beach 149th Street, Neponsit
1938–39
Figs. C-39–40

The Rockaway Improvement, part of the unprecedented expansion of public works during the New Deal, provided Robert Moses with the opportunity to repeat the success of Jones Beach, his most widely admired recreational endeavor. With this group of projects, his goal was to remove the private interests that had cluttered the beach with concession stands, hotels, and bungalows and to return to the public a clean and uncluttered recreation landscape. Simultaneously, he improved access to the Rockaways by modernizing existing roads and building new parkways and bridges, while fiercely defending both the beach and Jamaica Bay from new sources of pollution and inappropriate uses. "The Rockaway Improvement may not be a model to be followed in the development of unspoiled beaches," Moses stated. "I believe, however, that it will be a guide to those who seek to reclaim beaches which man has spoiled, and to restore them at least measurably for the purposes to which they were intended by nature."[177]

The first hotel in Far Rockaway had opened in the 1830s, and in 1880 a railroad line was completed across Jamaica Bay. Impressive summer homes and modest bungalow and tent colonies soon dotted the peninsula, and a boardwalk and amusement rides were built in Rockaway Park. In 1924, Cross Bay Boulevard provided access to automobiles, but the two-lane road was inadequate from the day it opened. The Long Island Railroad grade crossings on the peninsula further impeded traffic. According to Moses, Rockaway, like so many other beach resorts, "suffered from the ills brought about by fly-by-night developments and lack of foresight on the part of promoters and public agencies."[178] As parks commissioner, he intended to change that.

In 1937, after a new city charter transferred control of the beaches from the borough presidents to the parks department, Moses proposed a $16-million plan for Coney Island, Rockaway, and South Beach, not to revive what had been but to build a new and very different type of resort. In his report to Mayor Fiorello La Guardia, he wrote, "There must be more land in public ownership, less over-crowding, stricter enforcement of ordinances and rules, better transportation and traffic arrangement, less mechanical noise-making and amusement devices and side-shows, and a more orderly growth of year-round residents, and an increasing respect for permanent, as distinguished from temporary values."[179]

The Board of Estimate approved a $10-million project in April 1938 over the objections of the Rockaway Chamber of Commerce, which asked for a delay until after the summer season. Moses dismissed their arguments as "mostly bunk." "We can't do anything with this project by doing favors for people," he said. "The only way to get it into operation by June 1, 1939, when the World's Fair is here, is to start right away—and I intend to go right ahead."[180] The work was indeed completed by the following May.

Moses financed the Rockaway Improvement by linking it to the $3.75-million Marine Parkway (now Gil Hodges) Bridge (1937) and the reconstruction of Cross Bay Boulevard, widening it to four lanes and constructing a new drawbridge with a 10-cent toll (1939). Instead of being dumped onto the Rockaway streets, cars now flowed over the improved Cross Bay Bridge into a traffic circle and onto Beach Channel Drive and Shore Front Parkway. The drawbridge, however, had the disadvantage of causing serious traffic backups when it was open. In 1970, a new fixed-span bridge opened, now known as Cross Bay Veterans Memorial Bridge.

Along the Rockaway Beach boardwalk from Beach 73rd Street to Beach 108th Street, "a waterfront strip 200 feet wide and 1½ miles long cluttered with unsightly wooden firetrap structures, was cleared of all its encumbrances and developed as an integrated shorefront providing adequate bathing and modern play, landscape and promenade space."[181] A new 100-foot-wide roadway paralleled the improvements. Another key element in the Rockaway Improvement was the elimination of the 39 Long Island Railroad grade crossings. By the end of 1941 a new elevated structure carried the tracks, and an express highway ran underneath and alongside. As part of the Rockaway Improvement, Jacob Riis Park also received a makeover praised for "the decorum which has stamped the administration of all of Mr. Moses' undertakings."[182]

After the war, the city began building sewage treatment plants to clean the recreational waters.

C-39. Brochure published for the opening of Rockaway Improvement, June 3, 1939

In 1952, at the opening of the Rockaway Pollution Control Project, located at Beach Channel Drive and Beach 106th Street, Moses praised the implementation of a modest sewer tax to fund additional water treatment plants. "That's long-range economy," he said. "Good government consists of looking ahead. We've got to spend money to get money back. No apology is needed for the cost of these things."[183]

Moses's attention to the Rockaway beaches remained strong for the rest of his tenure as parks commissioner. He continued to build new parking fields and park facilities and obtained funding for the replenishment of the beach by offshore dredging and hydraulic pumping. In 1958, he prevented the sale of the closed Neponsit Hospital and its 14-acre beachfront for private development, thus assuring that the entire shoreline from Far Rockaway to Fort Tilden would remain public. In 1963, the jetties were rebuilt and new groins added, and in 1964 the section from Beach 9th to Beach 21st Street gained a new comfort station and concession stand. At the same time, Moses proposed extending the public beach all the way to Rockaway Point. In 1972, the beach from Riis Park west became part of the Gateway National Recreation Area.

The Rockaway Improvement, like other Moses initiatives, entailed a number of interconnected projects undertaken simultaneously as pieces of a larger goal. The roads fed into the parks and linked to his other parkways; the tolls on the bridges funded the parks; and sewage treatment plants cleaned up the waters. Together, they represented a strong commitment to the city's future. — JAK

C-40. Rockaway Beach and Crossbay Boulevard and Bridge, ca. 1939. Collection MTA Bridges and Tunnels Special Archive

C-41. South Beach,
June 2, 1939

SOUTH BEACH

Staten Island: Atlantic Ocean at Father Capodanno
   Boulevard
1955
Fig. C-41

Like Coney Island and Rockaway, South Beach on Staten Island was developed as an oceanfront resort in the late nineteenth century, with hotels, bungalows, beer gardens, and amusement parks. The resort area stretched south from Fort Wadsworth through Midland Beach to Great Kills. Many visitors arrived by train from the ferry terminal at St. George. That era ended in 1917, when the city declared the water in the bay too polluted for swimming. Prohibition ruined what businesses survived.

The city did not attempt to revive South Beach until the Great Depression, when Borough President Joseph A. Palma obtained $2 million in Works Progress Administration funds to build a 2.5-mile boardwalk from South Beach to Miller Field. Construction began in August 1935, but a year later not even one section was complete. Although plans

called for replenishing the beach, work on the board-walk began first; as a result, workmen labored in the water when the tide came in. Furthermore, the city owned only the shoreline; private owners retained control over the properties adjacent to the new boardwalk, and the city made no effort to acquire them to create public facilities.

In December 1937, with authority over city beaches scheduled to pass from the borough presidents to the parks department on January 1, Robert Moses announced plans to rebuild South Beach, Coney Island, and Rockaway. Voicing objections to the way work had proceeded at South Beach, he said, "There are already striking evidences of the prophesied deterioration through unfavorable private development back of the Boardwalk. The only answer is to acquire all privately owned property now from the Boardwalk to the present Seaside Boulevard [to] protect the Boardwalk, provide additional beach, afford space for games and substantial parking areas, and also for future bathhouses, and [to] permit the widening and reconstruction of Seaside Boulevard as a genuine 100-foot marginal

roadway."[184] The plan had all the elements that he proposed for Rockaway.

While Moses was able to implement his plans at Rockaway and Coney Island, the regeneration of South Beach, a lower priority, had to wait. In 1953, plans were presented to the city for funding. Moses called the work necessary to "correct very bad sub-standard conditions within the area of the proposed improvement and to reverse the trend of deterioration in the section adjacent." This meant the elimination of the "cheap, dilapidated seasonal bungalows and other seasonal shanties."[185] There were 415 such dwellings and 63 commercial buildings in all. Construction was finally under way in 1955, with a budget of $6.46 million for dredging and beach replenishment and for constructing parking areas, concessions, bathhouses, and a wider marginal road-way (renamed Father Capodanno Boulevard in honor of a priest killed in Vietnam). By then, Moses was already linking the new investment in South Beach to his new Verrazano-Narrows Bridge, just as he had linked Astoria Park and the Triborough Bridge in the 1930s. — JAK

NEIGHBORHOOD PLAYGROUNDS AND PARKS

NEIGHBORHOOD PLAYGROUNDS

Robert Moses did not invent neighborhood playgrounds. He did, however, regularize their design and systematize methods of land acquisition, thus encouraging their rapid development in New York City and making an unprecedented alteration of the built environment. The hundreds of recreation areas built during Moses's tenure as parks commissioner were based on a model created during the Progressive Era by social reformers and playground advocates and identified in New York with the work of Charles Stover.

Charles Stover, who came to New York as a settlement house worker and later became president of the University Settlement House, led a powerful movement for playgrounds in the city and eventually served as parks commissioner from 1910 to 1912. In 1890, Stover founded the Outdoor Recreation League (originally the Lower East Side Recreation Society), an effective advocacy group whose mission was to build experimental playgrounds on unused private and public property in order to prove the social and health benefits of active recreation. It was one of his many contributions. The success of the league's revolutionary playgrounds encouraged the parks department to establish Seward Park. When it opened in 1903, it became the first municipally sponsored playground in America. Designed by Samuel Parsons Jr., the park was New York's earliest effort in providing public spaces for active recreation, which was seen as a means to educate, socialize, and assimilate

immigrants and the poor.[186] A nine-lane running track encircled a children's playground and state-of-the-art gymnastic equipment where children and adults could engage in outdoor exercise supervised by trained play directors. In addition, the park offered a comfort station with showers and lavatories. The playground model that Moses implemented from 1934 to 1961 incorporated elements found in Parsons's design for Seward Park.

Uninterested in design innovations, Moses adopted the Progressive Era prototype for play spaces and rolled them out by the hundreds in every district of New York City. The playgrounds that he built during his tenure as commissioner still retained the basic elements endorsed by Commissioner Stover in 1910: separate spaces for small children, adolescent girls, adolescent boys, and adults; simple iron or steel tubular jungle gyms; restrooms with showers; a stage and space for indoor activities; running track; and courts for handball and basketball that could also be used for roller-skating. Moses's contribution to the development of recreation in America was not in design, but in the vast increase in number of playgrounds in New York City and in his insistence that cities build playgrounds in association with schools, housing projects, and highways.

In addition to adopting the playground model developed by social reformers in the late nineteenth century, Moses also adopted their rhetoric and methods. Much of Stover's success had rested on his ability

to publicize his achievements and the needs of his organization through the press, thus widening his base of support. By circulating photographs of shoeless smiling children swinging energetically on inexpensive jungle gyms, he encouraged the municipal government to build more play spaces for the poor. Similarly, Moses publicized his successes with press releases on the increasing tally of playgrounds. Headlines such as "60 Play Areas to Be Opened Soon," and "310 Playgrounds Opened at Schools" kept his good deeds in the public eye."[187] But by 1940, the Progressive model was outmoded. Moses, however, remained convinced of its efficacy and failed to modernize his playground prototype to satisfy changing ideas about children at play, provoking criticism from recreation experts in the 1960s.

Through the 1930s and 1940s, the *New York Times* published hundreds of articles announcing new playgrounds and praising Moses's ingenuity and administrative prowess. By the mid-1950s, his popularity began to wane as he became involved in political and legal wrangles with the powerful and the influential. In the late 1950s, Moses lost three highly publicized battles in Central Park. Mothers on the West Side defeated his project to build a parking lot for the Tavern on the Green; instead, he erected a new playground. Second, an appellate court of New York State prevented Moses from ousting Joseph Papp's free Shakespeare plays, calling his actions "arbitrary, capricious and unreason-

C-42. Pavilion at Corlear's Hook Playground, summer 1941

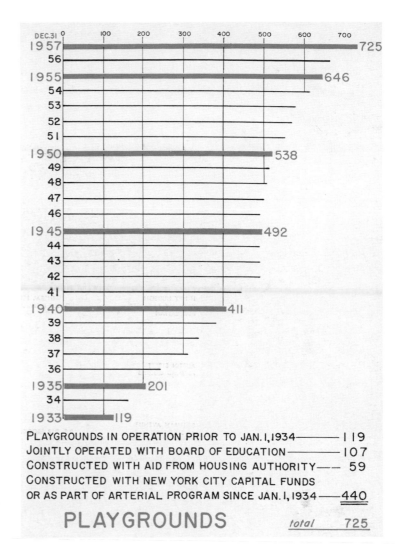

DEC.31	0	100	200	300	400	500	600	700	
1957									725
56									
1955									646
54									
53									
52									
51									
1950									538
49									
48									
47									
46									
1945									492
44									
43									
42									
41									
1940									411
39									
38									
37									
36									
1935									201
34									
1933									119

PLAYGROUNDS IN OPERATION PRIOR TO JAN. 1, 1934———— 119
JOINTLY OPERATED WITH BOARD OF EDUCATION————— 107
CONSTRUCTED WITH AID FROM HOUSING AUTHORITY—— 59
CONSTRUCTED WITH NEW YORK CITY CAPITAL FUNDS
OR AS PART OF ARTERIAL PROGRAM SINCE JAN. 1, 1934——— 440

PLAYGROUNDS   *total*   725

C-43. Graph of playgrounds in operation between 1933 and 1957

able."[188] Yielding to strong public pressure, Moses appealed to the Board of Estimate for funds to build the Delacorte Theater, a permanent home for Papp's summer festival. Lastly, Moses was forced to rehabilitate the Ramble along Calvert Vaux's and Frederick Law Olmsted's original guidelines rather than transform it into a recreation center for the elderly.

Urban planners, academics, and social commentators also criticized Moses. Although park officials praised Sara Delano Roosevelt Park when it opened in 1935 as "one of the finest park developments ever carried out in the city," it had long been a problem.[189] In 1961, Jane Jacobs harshly criticized the "[l]ong strip parks, like the dismally unsuccessful Sara Delano Roosevelt Park in New York and many riverside parks, [which] are frequently designed as if they were rolled out from a die stamper. Sara Delano Roosevelt Park has four identical brick 'recreation' barracks stamped along it at intervals. What can users make of this? The more they move back and forth, the more they are in the same place. It is like a trudge on a treadmill."[190] The banal repetitive design was unappealing; the sunken playgrounds and brick walls attracted drug dealers, gang members, and the homeless.

On the whole, it was Moses's unwillingness to rethink Progressive Era ideas of playground design that led to the failures identified by Jacobs and others. Nevertheless, he accomplished an important goal of many early-twentieth-century play advocates who viewed street-play as a dangerous problem and sought an alternative play space. "Thousands of poor children . . . [are] running wild in the Streets," one reformer wrote, "the establishment of . . . play-grounds . . . will shelter and protect . . . little ones."[191] But Moses, his engineers, and designers did not view street life as a vital element of safe and vibrant neighborhoods. Resistant to criticism, he became belligerent when confronted with problems or failures. In the 1950s, focusing on new building projects, he failed to address growing maintenance problems in existing parks and playgrounds.

In a densely built city like New York, finding playground and park sites was a challenge. Moses's success in fulfilling his recreational vision required ingenuity in meeting this challenge. As outlined in *8 Years of Progress* (1941), he employed several methods to acquire property: reassignment, rehabilitation, landfill, condemnation, and gifts. These methods led to novel sites for playgrounds, which Moses categorized in order to develop an efficient and comprehensive strategy of creating playgrounds: neighborhood, schoolyard, housing, marginal, arterial.[192]

In *The Power Broker*, Robert Caro argued that Moses intentionally located playgrounds in middle-class neighborhoods and ignored poor black neighborhoods, that his highways and housing projects tore neighborhoods apart and created barriers between residents and recreational space. My research of two dozen play spaces, however, does not support Caro's position. Rather, it suggests that Moses's placement of playgrounds was opportunistic, based on the availability of property already owned by the city. The following playgrounds have been selected to highlight these land acquisition and site-selection strategies. — RI

PROTOTYPE: WAR MEMORIAL PLAYGROUNDS

LOUIS ZIMMERMAN PLAYGROUND

Bronx: Barker Avenue, Britton Street, Olinville Avenue
.974 acre

CICCARONE PLAYGROUND

Bronx: East 188 Street, Hughes Avenue, East 187th
Street, Arthur Avenue
.55 acre

WILLIAM E. SHERIDAN PLAYGROUND

Brooklyn: Grand Street, South 1st Street, Wythe
Avenue to Berry Street
.79 acre

WILLIAM McCRAY PLAYGROUND

Manhattan: West 138th Street, between Fifth and
Lenox avenues
.229 acre

JOSEPH C. SAUER PLAYGROUND

Manhattan: East 12th Street, between Avenue A and B
.306 acre

DANIEL M. O'CONNELL PLAYGROUND

Queens: 113 Avenue and 196th Street
2.04 acres

HOWARD A. VON DOHLEN PLAYGROUND

Queens: 138th Street, 18th Place, 91st Avenue,
Archer Avenue
1.38 acres

AUSTIN J. MCDONALD PLAYGROUND

Staten Island: between Forest and Myrtle Avenue,
and Broadway and North Burgher Avenue
1.357 acres

NICHOLAS DE MATTI PLAYGROUND

Staten Island: Tompkins Avenue between Chestnut
Avenue and Shaughnessy Lane
2.343 acres

These playgrounds all opened July 15, 1934.

Upon taking office, Moses surveyed the city's playgrounds and found 119, all of which he considered "not properly laid out, equipped or maintained."[193] He devised a model neighborhood playground composed of indoor and outdoor facilities for all ages and constructed for year-round use. When possible, the playgrounds were equipped with water features such as wading pools, which could be converted into ice-skating rinks. "The playgrounds are not open to all children indiscriminately," the *New York Times* wrote.[194] Instead, small children, boys under sixteen, girls under sixteen, adolescents, and adults were segregated into designated play areas and supervised by playground directors. Play areas for small children were equipped with sandboxes, swings, and slides and surrounded by benches and shade trees for "nurses and guardians."[195] The equipment in boys and girls playgrounds was undifferentiated, but play instruction was carefully geared toward activities considered gender-appropriate: domestic tasks for girls and team sports for boys. A comfort station with bathing facilities was at the center of the playground, "strategically located to be accessible from all sides."[196]

In 1934, his first year as parks commissioner, Moses built nine neighborhood playgrounds (two each in Manhattan, Staten Island, Brooklyn, and Queens, and one in the Bronx) to serve as the prototype for future recreational development in the city. The playgrounds were highlighted in numerous press conferences and were widely covered in the print media, which published drawings and photographs of the planned play spaces. "The design has one major purpose," Moses explained,

C-44. Model playground, between 25th and 30th avenues, Jackson Heights, 1934.
Rendering by Walter W. W. Jones (detail)

to supply recreation to all age groups. Little children and their guardians require wading pools, sandpits, small apparatus and plenty of benches under the trees in an area definitely separated from others, protected and controlled. At the other extreme the old folk, whom we have with us today in increasing numbers, require sitting areas and games tables. Between are those dynamos of energy, the older children, teenagers and young adults. Although an area for larger apparatus is set aside, most of the rest of the playground is laid out for the three good old American games of softball, basketball and handball. Certain playgrounds are large enough, or certain neighborhoods require, other court games such as shuffleboard, paddle tennis, horseshoe pitching and boccie courts. The center of operation of a playground is the building, including comfort stations and maintenance room, strategically located to be accessible from all sides.[197]

The process of acquiring the land for these playgrounds demonstrates Moses's creativity and his aptitude for raising funds. To finance the first model playgrounds, called War Memorial Playgrounds, he harnessed the Arch of Freedom Fund, established in 1921 by police officers who collected donations amounting to $340,000 for the creation of a memorial for fallen World War I soldiers.[198] The donors specified that the fund could not "be used for any other purpose than a war memorial."[199] By March 1934, Moses had convinced the city chamberlain A. A. Berle to use the fund to purchase land in "congested section[s] of each borough" for playgrounds dedicated to the war dead. Moses relied on Civil Works Administration workers and materials to construct the parks.[200] In this way, the playgrounds cost the parks department almost nothing. — RI

C-45. Williamsbridge reservoir, undated. Photograph by 102nd Photo Section, 27th Div. Aviation

REASSIGNMENT

WILLIAMSBRIDGE OVAL

Bronx: Van Cortland Avenue East, Bainbridge Avenue, Reservoir Oval
19.749 acres
Opened September 11, 1937
Figs. C-45–46

SARA DELANO ROOSEVELT PARK

Manhattan: East Houston Street, Chrystie Street, Canal Street, and Forsyth Street
7.85 acres
Opened September 14, 1934
Figs. C-47–48

Using the term *reassignment* for projects built on land already owned by the City of New York, Moses negotiated deals with various departments to transfer derelict property to the parks department. "Abandoned school houses were torn down," he wrote, "reservoirs drained, construction yards cleared, unnecessary streets ripped up, unused State waterfront properties taken over, all to give way to parks and playgrounds."[201] Williamsbridge Oval was one of three reservoirs that Moses converted into play spaces (the others were the Great Lawn in Central Park and Highbridge Pool. Purchased by the city in 1887, the 120-million-gallon reservoir was officially decommis-

C-46. Williamsbridge Oval, converted to park use, June 24, 1938

sioned in 1934; he negotiated a transfer of title from the Department of Water to the Department of Parks.

Originally, Moses had hoped to convert the 41-foot-deep reservoir into an outdoor sports stadium, with a swimming pool at one end and a track and field arena at the other; in the center would be courts that could also be used as a parking lot.[202] Under pressure from local organizations, however, he abandoned this plan in favor of a playground, equipped with a wading pool, basketball court, baseball diamond, slides, seesaws, swings, sand pits, jungle gyms, and recreation areas for the elderly. The 37-foot embankment was cut to 13 feet, creating an 18-acre park below street level to accommodate turf fields, running tracks, 16 tennis courts, a recreation building, and two children's playgrounds (one for boys and one for girls).[203] The final plan also included areas with games for older men: tables for backgammon, checkers, chess, and Ping-Pong, as well as shuffleboard and horseshoe pitching courts.[204]

Sara Delano Roosevelt Park was developed on the Lower East Side on land that had once held nearly two hundred Old-Law tenements. In 1929, the City of New York purchased the tenements. Mayor Jimmy Walker's administration planned to demolish the buildings, widen Chrystie and Forsyth streets, and build model tenements (to be financed by John D. Rockefeller Jr.).[205] In March 1930, the housing was demolished, but the property remained undeveloped for four years, while three plans for model buildings, including designs by Howe and Lescaze, were proposed and rejected.[206] In 1933, the parks commissioner John E. Sheehy, backed by the Municipal Art Society, the Park Association, and the Children's Aid Society, proposed converting the Chrystie-Forsyth thoroughfare into play space for local children.[207] Social reformers such as Lillian Wald, the founder and president of the Henry Street Settlement, argued that the location was undesirable for housing.

Early in 1934, in the second month of his administration, Mayor Fiorello La Guardia scrapped Walker's housing plans and transferred property rites to the Department of Parks for a playground, to be constructed using Civil Works Administration labor.[208] La Guardia and Moses officially opened the facility later that year. Moses insisted on the elimination of four of the six cross streets, leaving only Delancey and Grand streets to facilitate crosstown traffic. Five playgrounds were built: one for general use, two for boys, and two for girls. In addition, there were two wading pools, which could be drained and used for roller-skating, basketball, and ice-skating, and four comfort stations. The parks department and three adjoining public schools jointly operated the playgrounds. As in model playgrounds, park users were segregated by age and gender. Four of the five playgrounds were sunken below street level, and a brick wall enclosed the entire park, "effectively separat[ing] the park itself from the bordering streets and the play areas."[209] — RI

C-47. Site of Sara Delano Roosevelt Park, before conversion, 1931

C-48. Sara Delano Roosevelt Park, upon completion, looking west, September 8, 1937

C 49. Queensbridge Park Playground, beneath Queensboro Bridge, Queens, April 19, 1947

REHABILITATION

QUEENSBORO OVAL

Manhattan: York Avenue, between East 59th
  and East 60th streets
1.24 acres
Opened June 20, 1934

When the Queensboro Bridge (also called the 59th Street Bridge) opened in May 1909, Patrick H. McGowan, the president of the Board of Aldermen, suggested that the city transform the open space beneath the bridge into a playground.[210] The following summer, neighborhood boys began building their own baseball diamond, and the parks commissioner Charles Stover provided them with baseball equipment, backstop, fence, scoreboard, and bases.[211] In 1912, a reinforced-concrete comfort station, with toilet, shower, and locker facilities for boys, was constructed, along with gymnasium apparatus.[212] When Moses took office in 1934, he complained that the playground beneath the bridge was in urgent need of rehabilitation; a few months later, a new playground, opened, following his model playground guidelines.[213]
— RI

LANDFILL

CARL SCHURZ PARK

Manhattan: East End Avenue and the East River,
  between 84th and 90th streets
14.9 acres
Reopened April 27, 1936
Fig. C-50

Landfill, also called reclamation, is a process of making existing land useable or creating new land by adding dirt, trash, and construction debris. In some cases, for example the West Side and East Side highways in Manhattan, landfill together with concrete seawalls was used to extend the boundaries of the island. Moses claimed that his department created an additional 2,500 acres of parkland through landfill from 1934 to 1941, including Williamsbridge Oval and Orchard Beach in the Bronx, Jacob Riis Park in Queens, the Great Lawn in Central Park, and Carl Shurz Park.[214]

In 1891, the parks department acquired an area along the East River from 84th to 86th Street. After the city took possession of Gracie Mansion and its related 11-acre property, East River Park was constructed (1903), based on designs by Calvert Vaux and Samuel Parsons Jr. In 1936, the parks department, in cooperation with the Manhattan borough president, announced plans to rehabilitate the East River shoreline by constructing a highway with adjacent arterial parks and playgrounds. The plans encompassed Gracie Mansion (renovated in 1934), which served as the first home of the Museum of the City of New York, and the former Vaux and Parsons park. The original proposal, which called for a six-lane roadway divided by a shaded mall and lined by parks, underwent revisions when the Brearley School (at 83rd Street and the East River) filed a claim with the city, citing impaired light and air. As a result, engineers designed a two-tiered roadway that swung out over the river; this change added six acres to the park, thus providing students, residents, and museumgoers with unobstructed access to the river. In exchange, the Brearley School transferred property rights to their playground at 81st Street to the city.[215] At the southern end of Carl Schurz Park is a playground, designed by Maud Sargent, with a wading pool, roller-skating rink, swings, sandboxes, and gymnastic equipment for use by both the school and the public.[216] — RI

C-50. Carl Schurz Park, with Gracie Mansion, November 23, 1937

SCHOOL SITES

Moses insisted on building playgrounds in conjunction with virtually all public works, including those outside his purview, such as schools. These playgrounds were open to the community after school hours under parks department supervision. Moses worked with the Department of Education in two additional ways: first, he endeavored to have abandoned school property demolished and redeveloped as playgrounds; second, he demanded that all new schools feature state-of-the-art playgrounds. The parks department opened hundreds of school playgrounds, based on the model established for neighborhood playgrounds.

P.S. 52 (ZEBRA PLAYGROUND)

Brooklyn: East 29th Street, Avenue Z, Nostrand Avenue
2.46 acres
Opened July 15, 1934; reopened July 22, 1951

At the end of each school day and on the last day of school each year, the janitor of P.S. 52 had customarily closed and locked the school's gates, thus preventing neighborhood children from enjoying the safety and fun of the schoolyard. When Moses took office in 1934, he negotiated with the Department of Education to operate this and other school playgrounds in conjunction with the parks department, allowing them to remain open after school and during the summer; they became known as Jointly-Operated Playgrounds (JOPs).[217] He hoped this effort would "guard . . . pupils against the loss of discipline, [and a] tendency toward idleness" during summer vacation.[218] This agreement remained in effect until 1945, when the Kalmon Dolgin Company purchased the school and converted it into a factory.[219]

In September 1950, a new P.S. 52 opened on East 29th Street and Avenue Z. After World War II, the Department of Education and the City of New York initiated a building campaign intended to augment and modernize schools all over the city. According to a plan worked out with the parks department, the new facilities were "designed to meet . . . [a] broader vision for a wider and adult use" including playgrounds and recreation centers available for use year-round and after school.[220] One of nine schools constructed to accommodate the city's largest population boom in a decade, P.S. 52 boasted "nineteen classrooms, a library, nature study room, an auditorium, gymnasium and a combination playroom and lunchroom.[221] A new playground with "a sand pit, swings, slides and seesaws, a wading pool, handball courts, basketball and volley ball courts, ten paddle tennis and two shuffleboard courts, and a large flat area for roller skating and softball" was inaugurated on July 22, 1951.[222] Still jointly operated with the Department of Education, it was renamed Zebra Playground in 2000. — RI

C-51. Evergreen Park Playground at P.S. 68, Queens, March 22, 1943

C-52. Playgrounds at Harlem River Houses, November 23, 1937. Colonial Pool and Park are at top.

HOUSING SITES: HARLEM RIVER HOUSES

HARLEM LANE PLAYGROUND

Manhattan: Harlem River Drive, West 151st to West 153rd Street
1.64 Acres
Opened December 1893; reopened November 27, 1937

COLONEL CHARLES YOUNG TRIANGLE

Manhattan: Seventh Avenue, Macombs Place and West 153rd Street
1.15 acres
Opened November 27, 1937

FREDERICK JOHNSON PARK

Manhattan: Seventh Avenue, West 150th Street to West 151st Street
2.45 acres
Opened March 31, 1939

HOLCOMBE RUCKER PLAYGROUND

Manhattan: West 155th Street, Eighth Avenue to Harlem River
2.5 acres
Opened February 23, 1956

Moses believed that all housing projects should "provide recreation for the surrounding community as well as for residents of the projects."[223] In addition, he viewed the development of low-income housing as an opportunity to provide additional services and amenities, such as clinics, nurseries, and theaters, to needy communities. Like Progressive Era reformers before them, Mayor Fiorello La Guardia and Moses hoped that by packaging housing with public services and recreation they could create "real homes in a community [that people] can take pride in." La Guardia argued that "the chief purpose of public housing is to make better and healthier citizens by giving them a decent place to live, and especially providing proper surrounds for children."[224]

When the Harlem River Houses opened in 1937, there were only two play areas in the vicinity, Harlem Lane Playground and Colonel Charles Young Triangle, to serve more than 500 families. From 1937 to 1956, Moses remedied this lack by increasing play space by 5.5 acres with two new playgrounds, Frederick Johnson Park and Holcombe Rucker Playground. Before that, however, he remodeled Harlem Lane Playground, which was on land acquired by condemnation in 1893 as a spot for viewing the Harlem River. He added a basketball court, gymnasium, recreation center, swings, and a sandpit to the playground, which reopened late in 1937.

Since the housing development had been built on vacant lots used for recreation, the congested neighborhood was left with little play space. For example, residents of the Paul Laurence Dunbar Apartments (Seventh Avenue between West 150th and West 151st Street), a Rockefeller housing development, had used the site.[225] Moses told the Times that he hoped to "find additional land" for playgrounds,[226] and two days after reopening the Harlem Lane Playground, he happily announced that John D. Rockefeller Jr. had agreed to donate two adjacent parcels to the city. The Department of Transportation ceded an additional parcel in December 1937. Less than two years later, Moses opened to the public a 2.45-acre park, equipped with handball, basketball, and tennis courts.[227] The playground was enlarged in 1947. In 1971, the park was named after Frederick Johnson, a well-respected tennis player, best known for coaching Althea Gibson, the first African-American to compete at the national championships.

In 1956, Moses, in collaboration with the Department of Education, opened P.S. 156 Playground, which was subsequently renamed Holcombe Rucker Playground in honor of the Harlem community leader. With a basketball and handball courts, swings, and a gymnasium, the park provided additional recreational space for the residents of Harlem River Houses. — RI

C-53. Playground, Shore Parkway at 17th Avenue, December 13, 1941

ARTERIAL

Moses envisioned arterial parks (also termed arterial by-products) as "shoe-string parks with foot paths, bicycle paths, waterfront promenades, and bordering active recreation areas," where play facilities and playgrounds were built as an integral part of highway development.[228] Unobstructed arterial parks were created in neighborhoods where landowners and community activists fought for more humane park spaces. For example, on the Lower East Side, considered a "super-slum" in 1939, Moses built 55 acres of baseball diamonds, soccer fields, and handball courts.[229]

SHORE ROAD PARK

Brooklyn: Owl's Head Park to Fort Hamilton Parkway, Leif Ericson Drive to Shore Road
58 acres
Opened July 25, 1942
Fig. C-53

Shore Road Park, originally laid out by Frederick Law Olmsted, was expanded and redesigned when the Belt Parkway cut through Brooklyn in 1939.[230] As early as 1860, a number of proposals were made to develop the naturally picturesque shoreline between Bay Ridge and Fort Hamilton into a park. Hired by local equestrians and carriage owners in 1892, Olmsted proposed a 3-mile marine parkway, with routes for drivers, cyclists, and pedestrians, as well as a circular park at Fort Hamilton. His pathways hugged the shore, giving pedestrians and cyclists the best views. In addition to its recreational benefits, the parkway also connected Bay Ridge to Prospect Park via Ocean Parkway.[231]

In 1935, Robert Moses proposed the redevelopment of Shore Drive; Shore Road Park was a by-product. His designers transformed Olmsted's wide curving pathways and undulating hills into a flat parkway surrounded by "landscaped walks and playgrounds."[232] Although Bay Ridge was not a heavily congested neighborhood in dire need of recreational space, Moses understood, as Calvert Vaux and Frederick Law Olmsted had before him, that New York would continue to grow; reserving open space in the less populated regions of the city was imperative. The recreational areas, equipped with benches, comfort stations, promenades, bicycle paths, and athletic facilities, opened in 1942. Access to the park, however, was limited to the pedestrian bridges at 80th and 92nd streets.[233] — RI

HOW MANY PLAYGROUNDS DID ROBERT MOSES BUILD?

Moses's playground-building program was large in scope, but precisely how large was it? The only readily available tally comes from Moses himself. In his last report as parks commissioner, *26 Years of Progress*, published on January 1, 1960, he stated that the number of playgrounds in New York City had grown from 119 at the start of his reign in 1934 to 777 on the eve of his retirement, an increase of 658.[234] When he officially retired as commissioner, on May 23, 1960, the *New York Times* reported a total of 779 playgrounds, a figure that Moses presumably provided.[235] Therefore, by his own calculations, he built 660 playgrounds in the five boroughs of New York.

Because Moses was a brilliant publicist and prone to exaggeration, this number requires independent verification. One source of information is press releases announcing playground openings, but, of course, these were written by Moses and his parks department staff. Moses often staged elaborate opening ceremonies for new playgrounds, but we cannot assume that every opening was publicized. Also, some of the openings listed in press releases were actually reopenings of existing playgrounds that Moses had renovated: he refurbished many derelict playgrounds that were already parks department properties when he became commissioner, and press releases do not always distinguish these from new playgrounds. Further, press releases often announced the openings of playgrounds without providing names or locations, leaving no way of checking the accuracy of the announcement. Similarly, Moses's "years of progress" reports, published irregularly in lieu of annual reports, gave numbers of playgrounds built but not names or locations. *Eight Years of Progress*, for example, quantified playground construction— 42 new playgrounds in 1934, 71 in 1935, 72 in 1936, and 52 in 1937—but did not identify the facilities. *Twelve Years of Progress* cited a total of 492 playgrounds but named only a few: one on Cropsey Avenue in Brooklyn, one at 45th Avenue and 21st Street in Queens, and the Sara Delano Roosevelt Playground in Manhattan.

Determining a number poses another complication: what exactly qualifies as a playground? Properties that Moses categorized as playgrounds varied in size from small pockets of land containing swings, a slide, and a few benches, to Red Hook Park in Brooklyn—called a playground in *12 Years of Progress*—which held a running track, football and baseball fields, and a stadium on a 58.5-acre site. This wide range of facilities stands as a hindrance to surveying all the city's playgrounds built between 1934 and 1960, since Moses may have counted as a playground anything from a single slide on a patch of concrete to a vast complex of playing fields. Counting is particularly problematic where multiple playgrounds were built within a single park property. For example, Moses built the majority of the 34 playgrounds in Central Park, including the 20 placed around its periphery. But similarly detailed information does not exist on most individual playgrounds inside larger parks, playgrounds that Moses may have included in his total. Exact criteria of what constitutes a playground do not exist.

Moses's total, 660, cannot be corroborated by the records available in the parks department.[236] Looking at property numbers, which Moses assigned to all park properties, gives only partial results. He numbered parks sequentially without regard to their uses: playgrounds, parkways, stadiums, swimming pools, and all other types of park property are included in the same list. To disaggregate the playgrounds would require examining every park property file, and there are currently 1,732 properties. Such a search will be simplified when the parks department completes scanning its files and developing a word-searchable database; it should be available within a year. Even then, however, the database will not solve the playground puzzle: not all are inventoried, and opening dates or clear attribution to Moses are not always given. To fill gaps in the parks department records, extensive research in the Municipal Archives would be necessary to track parks department building activities during a twenty-six-year period—a daunting task, indeed.

Just as the number of Moses's playgrounds cannot be confirmed, their geographic distribution cannot be accurately assessed. The question of distribution is important because of the charge Robert Caro made that Moses discriminated against blacks by providing few playgrounds in neighborhoods like Harlem.[237] All the problems described above, including the definition of *playground* and the omission of a playground in a description of a larger park, prevent testing of the accuracy of this claim. The spotty nature of the existing data constrains what can be said about Moses's locational strategies and how playground construction correlates with race, ethnicity, or class.[238]

Although the precise number of playgrounds built between 1934 and 1960 cannot be verified, the claim that Moses built hundreds of playgrounds in a city that badly needed them is indisputable. He did so with his characteristic pragmatism and effectiveness at securing funding: obtaining federal relief funds and a federally financed labor force, convincing philanthropists to donate money, and diverting city funds set aside for a World War I memorial. Moreover, he was ingenious at finding sites. He built playgrounds alongside parkways and underneath bridges and, by coordinating his efforts with those of the New York City Housing Authority and the Board of Education, adjacent to public housing projects and schools. The press and the public rejoiced in his playground accomplishments: in 1938, the *New York Times* raved, "he has taken tens of thousands of children off the streets through the gates of a couple hundred new playgrounds."[239] At a playground opening in 1937, Mayor Fiorello La Guardia declared that Moses had set "a world's record for opening and maintaining playgrounds."[240] The mayor's hyperbole was probably not far from the truth. Whether Moses built 660 playgrounds, as he claimed, or inflated the number, he must be given credit for giving New York City hundreds of public playgrounds where there had been none before. — KL

NEIGHBORHOOD PARKS

BATTERY PARK

Manhattan: State Street, Battery Place, and New York
    Harbor
22.9 acres
Established 19th century; Moses's work 1941–52
Figs. C-54–55

Two of Robert Moses's biggest and most public
failures involved Battery Park: his plans to build
a Brooklyn-Battery bridge and to demolish Castle
Clinton. Despite these defeats, Moses left his mark
on the park and on the institution that he extracted
from it, the New York Aquarium.

Occupying the southernmost tip of the island of
Manhattan, Battery Park was named after the defen-
sive line of guns that were deployed along the shore
during the colonial and revolutionary period. Between
1807 and 1811, the Battery's most recognizable landmark was constructed: a fort called West Battery, built
on an outcropping of rock about 300 feet offshore and
connected to Manhattan by a causeway. The circular
fort, with 8-foot-thick stone walls, was designed by
John McComb Jr. for use in the War of 1812. In 1815,
the fort was renamed Castle Clinton, after Governor
DeWitt Clinton.

The federal government ceded Castle Clinton
to New York City in 1824. Transformed into Castle
Garden, a reception and concert hall, it began its new
life as an open-air venue; a roof was added in 1844.
In 1855, the enclosed structure became the Emigrant
Landing Depot, an immigrant processing facility run
by New York State. Eight million people entered the
country there before it closed in 1890, when the federal government assumed responsibility for screening
immigrants and moved the gateway to the nation to
Ellis Island. In 1896, Castle Clinton acquired yet
another new function, as the home of the New York
Aquarium. The aquarium was initially run by the city,
but in 1902 management responsibilities were transferred to the New York Zoological Society. McKim,
Mead & White expanded the structure to accommodate visitors by adding two stories on top of the massive walls and rearranging its interior; the exterior
was coated in white stucco.

During these changes in Castle Clinton's identity,
Battery Park was gradually expanded through landfill
until the former fort was engulfed and became part of
mainland Manhattan. The final extension of the park
before the Moses era was the addition of a wooden
wharf in 1931. Although many ambitious plans for
the park had been proposed, including one endorsed

C-54. Battery Park and Castle Clinton, before alterations, January 1934

by the Regional Plan Association in the early 1930s
to erect a massive obelisk as a war memorial, none
was carried out. When Moses became parks
commissioner, Battery Park contained a waterfront
promenade and winding paths over which crowds
traveled to reach the aquarium, the park's most
popular attraction.

A plan for a tunnel under the East River running
from the Battery to Brooklyn was already under consideration when Moses came to power. Mayor La
Guardia turned the responsibility of building and
managing the tunnel project over to Moses's
Triborough Bridge Authority. Moses announced in
January 1939, however, that he would build a bridge
instead of a tunnel. The approach ramp to the bridge,
which he envisioned as an elevated road supported by
concrete piers, would have run east-west through the
north end of Battery Park, taking up a substantial
amount of park space and putting a highway between
the park and the city that it was meant to serve.

To quell protests, Moses promoted the reconstruction of Battery Park in tandem with construction of

the bridge. Gilmore Clarke, the parks department's
chief consulting landscape architect, prepared plans
for a $500,000 improvement involving the insertion of
bulkheads into the bay and the expansion of the park
onto them. His design featured a waterfront promenade, a central oval lawn, and a mall creating an
axial corridor between the terminus of Broadway, at
the north end of the park, and the aquarium in Castle
Clinton. After months of promoting the Brooklyn-
Battery Bridge and battling vociferous critics, Moses
was defeated: on July 1, 1939, the day that he had
hoped construction would begin, the United States
Department of War announced that it would not
approve the project, putting a decisive end to his
bridge campaign.

The Triborough Bridge Authority reverted to the
original tunnel plan. The entrance to the tunnel from
the West Side Highway was to be located just west of
Battery Park. In February 1941, Moses announced
the closing of the park for the duration of the tunnel-
building project and the demolition of Castle Clinton
as part of the park renovation. In a letter in the *New*

C-55. Photomontage of proposed redesign of Battery Park and entrance to Brooklyn-Battery Tunnel, October 24, 1941

York Times on February 25, 1941, he defended his plan to raze the fort, calling protesters "woozy with sentiment." He claimed that Castle Clinton had "no history worth writing about"—its guns had never been fired against an enemy, and, as an immigration station, it was "a foul, unsanitary, disgraceful pen through which our prospective citizens were herded like cattle." Moreover, as an aquarium, it was "dark, dingy and badly ventilated." Fish could be better displayed in a new, modern facility to be built at the Bronx Zoo.[241] Moreover, the structure interfered with a key feature of Clarke's revised reconstruction of Battery Park. His plan, although similar to the earlier one, showed the bridge ramp removed and the site of Castle Clinton occupied by a circular plaza. Moses argued that removing the fort opened a site line from Broadway to the Statue of Liberty along Clarke's mall.

The battle to save Castle Clinton dragged on for almost a decade. Moses faced a committed opposition; indeed, the skirmishes at Castle Clinton were a prelude to the widespread preservation movement that developed in the 1960s. He presented himself as

an advocate of historic structures, citing the many buildings that he had saved—including City Hall, the Arsenal, and Jumel and Gracie mansions—as proof of his concern for the city's built history. But those campaigning to save Castle Clinton, whom he painted as weepy sentimentalists, had crossed a line "from history to hysteria."[242] Moses may have preserved some of the city's architectural treasures, but when a historic building stood in the way of his plans he was eager to demolish it.

On October 1, 1941, the park and the aquarium were closed as construction on the tunnel began. The New-York Historical Society published its own history of Castle Clinton to contest Moses's claim that the fort had no historical value and suggested that the former aquarium be turned into a "Museum of the Port of New York."[243] The Fine Arts Federation of New York also entered the fray by hosting a competition to redesign Battery Park with Castle Clinton left intact. Moses's chief architect, Aymar Embury II, protested: "What purpose will the competition serve, other than to . . . harass a public servant?"[244] The competition

went on, and selected entries were put on display at the Architectural League in 1942. The winning design, by Walter W. W. Jones of Brooklyn, was similar to Clarke's scheme but retained Castle Clinton and moved the allée to the east so that it was uninterrupted by the circular structure.

Moses struggled to justify the planned demolition. He claimed that the stability of the fort would be compromised by the digging going on underneath the park, even though the tunnel engineer Ole Singstad reported that no excavation would take place within 170 feet of Castle Clinton. Moses's motivation for fighting so hard and so long to eliminate the old structure is debatable. Robert Caro saw Moses's position as a vengeful reaction to his defeat in the bridge-versus-tunnel battle.[245] Yet Moses tended not to dwell on defeats, of which there were many, but doggedly pursued his goals. Once Clarke had provided him with a vision of the park, he may have simply adhered to it single-mindedly, refusing to admit that the fort could be integrated into Battery Park with only slight modification of the plan. Moses was consistently dismissive of public opinion, and his modernizing zeal to rebuild and relocate the aquarium to a more appropriate site was not without support: the New York Zoological Society expressed delight at the possibility of an up-to-date aquarium facility.

In 1942, Moses reduced the fort to its 8-foot-thick walls of stone. He donated the sheet-iron roof as scrap metal to aid the war effort and removed the additions by McKim, Mead & White. While the war disrupted his momentum and halted tunnel construction, his opposition gained strength. In 1946, the preservationists won a seemingly decisive battle: Congress approved a bill authorizing the federal government to take possession of Castle Clinton and operate it as a national landmark. But because the Department of Interior could not provide funds to begin restoration until the summer of 1948, the New York City Board of Estimate allocated $50,000 for demolition in July 1947. A *New York Times* headline announced: "City Votes Death of Old Aquarium. All Hopes Are Crushed."[246] The paper underestimated Moses's opponents. In 1948, the American Scenic and Historic Preservation Society, led by former Manhattan Borough President George McAneny, filed a lawsuit against Moses arguing that Fort Clinton could not be razed without the approval of the Art Commission, New York's municipal design review board. An injunction was issued against Moses, which he managed to get thrown out by March 1949, but the Preservation Society's delay tactic worked nonetheless. In October 1949, before demolition started,

Congress allocated $165,750 for the restoration of Castle Clinton, and the city ceded the property to the national government. The fort, reopened in 1975, is now called Castle Clinton National Monument and serves as the ticket office for visitors boarding boats to go to Ellis Island and the Statue of Liberty. The National Park Service's exceedingly slow renovation, however, gave Moses plenty of artillery for his continued complaints about the old aquarium's presence in Battery Park.

Moses carried on with the reconstruction of Battery Park, following essentially the plan set forth in 1941 but with Castle Clinton persistently occupying the site of Clarke's proposed circular plaza. Two new acres were added to the park by extending the seawall, and a promenade was constructed along the new shorefront. The park's design integrated formal and picturesque elements. A mall, lined with trees and benches, created an axis between Bowling Green at the end of Broadway and Castle Clinton; the mall widened gradually as it approached the stone building. A raised terrace was added south of Castle Clinton to provide unobstructed views of the harbor. The east side of the park was more informal, with a large teardrop-shaped lawn, winding paths, and a playground. A few vestiges of the former park remained, including a 1909 statue of Giovanni da Verrazano facing the harbor. The reconstruction cost a total of $2,377,000.

Two tunnels hummed with vehicular activity beneath the revamped Battery Park: the Brooklyn-Battery Tunnel, opened May 25, 1950, and the Battery Park Underpass, which linked the West Side and East Side highways. Eight thousand people attended the reopening of the park on July 15, 1952; they were treated to speeches by Moses and Mayor Vincent Impellitteri, music, and a show put on by a fleet of fireboats shooting water into the air. Moses's new Battery Park and the Brooklyn-Battery Tunnel under it can be seen as his triumphant coordination, after two forced compromises, of agencies under his control—the parks department and the Triborough Bridge and Tunnel Authority—to combine recreation and transportation, two components that he saw as essential to the modern city, at this prominent site at the southern tip of Manhattan. — KL

BRYANT PARK

Manhattan: between Fifth and Sixth avenues,
    40th and 42nd streets
9.6 acres[247]
Established 1847; reconstructed 1934; restored
    1988–92
Fig. C-56

Bryant Park, the only substantial open space in Manhattan's bustling midtown, was in shambles: on January 22, 1934, the *New York Times* described it as "an unsightly vacant lot" comprised of "four acres of mud and dirt."[248] The restoration of the park was one of the first projects that Moses tackled as parks commissioner. By the end of the month, his workers were cleaning it up; plans for the park's complete reconstruction were released a month later. Moses may have been responding to its visibility as well as to its deplorable condition. An editorial in the *Times* singled it out as the park most in need of repair:

"No doubt all the parks are crying out to the new commissioner for prompt and intelligent attention, yet no other can be in so serious a plight as Bryant Park. It is a sad spectacle seen by of tens of thousands every day."[249] For Moses, its reconstruction marked a regime change: "It had become a kind of symbol of municipal inefficiency. We are trying to cure that."[250] The plans were based on the winning entry from a competition sponsored by the Architects Emergency Employment Committee. The first-prize design, submitted by Lusby Simpson, an architect from Queens, was adapted and executed by the parks department landscape architect Gilmore Clarke and its architect Aymar Embury II.

The fast-tracked reconstruction was executed by two shifts of federally funded relief workers, 340 during the day and 160 at night. The park reopened on September 14, 1934, and Moses was credited for the feat of completing reconstruction in just nine months. Two thousand people attended the reopening

C-56. Bryant Park, looking east from Sixth Avenue, 1935. Photograph by Nathan Schwartz

ceremony, which included the first appearance of the newly formed parks department band. Two guests of honor—the great-granddaughter of William Cullen Bryant, the noted poet and editor after whom the park was named, and the sister of Josephine Shaw Lowell, to whom the park's Lowell Memorial Fountain was dedicated—threw rose petals into the fountain, which, along with the new sprinkler system in the lawn, was turned on for the occasion. The whole affair was broadcast on the radio. Moses and Mayor La Guardia, busy opening parks all over the city in the 1930s, left the celebration to preside over another opening: the playgrounds at Chrystie-Forsyth Park.

Moses called the overhaul of Bryant Park a "housekeeping job." This was not merely an expression of modesty; compared with his other park projects, which had extensive recreational facilities, architecturally ambitious buildings, and transportation, Bryant Park was a simple endeavor, involving a rearrangement of existing elements and a new landscape design. The final product was a formal garden marked by classical symmetry and order; its layout, Moses commented, was intended to complement "the dignity of the western facade of the New York Public Library."[251]

Although the design was uncomplicated, Bryant Park was nonetheless dramatically transformed. The ground level was raised four feet above the street, and the park was surrounded by a granite wall, topped by the same wrought-iron fence that had enclosed the site since it was a potter's field. The principal feature of the park was a central rectangular lawn, 250 feet long and 140 feet wide. The central axis was punctuated at its east end by a statue of William Cullen Bryant, in its original place on the library's rear terrace, and by the Lowell Memorial Fountain, which was moved from the terrace to the west end of the park. The black granite fountain, designed by the architect Charles A. Platt, had been dedicated in 1913 in honor of Josephine Shaw Lowell, the first woman member of the New York State Board of Charities. In its new location, the fountain became part of a circular plaza at the park's main entrance, reached by a stairway from Sixth Avenue. The central lawn was flanked by a scroll planting, a straight hedge culminating in volutes near the fountain. An automatic, subsurface sprinkler system watered the expanse of grass. The lawn was surrounded by a promenade, but the grass itself was fenced in, for observation only. Recessed a few feet below the grade of the surrounding park, the lawn was bordered by a stone balustrade and framed by four rows of plane trees, 270 trees in total. The trees were planted in beds of English ivy that were regularly interspersed with flagstone walks lined with benches.

The new Bryant Park received mixed reviews. Lewis Mumford was its harshest critic. He liked the lawn, proclaiming, "Nothing could be more restful than that lush expanse of grass."[252] But he complained that the axis of the garden directed attention toward the elevated train tracks on Sixth Avenue, "as dingy a piece of urban architecture as was ever used to close a vista." Moreover, Mumford faulted the inaccessibility of the lawn: "The grand effect of the design is to invite one to slump on a backless bench and look through a toothless balustrade at a piece of green one mustn't walk on and cannot see. If I stayed on one of those benches long enough, I'd be prepared to lead an uprising on the part of the unemployed for the purpose of tearing down the balustrade and providing the benches with backs."[253] Other responses were more positive. In November 1934, the American Institute of Architects commended Lusby Simpson for his design, and in 1936 *Architecture* magazine suggested that Bryant Park "might well serve as a pattern and inspiration for other city open spaces."[254] Local civic groups were also thrilled with the renovation and hoped the cleaned-up park would boost property values and retail revenues.

Bryant Park was designated a Scenic Landmark by the Landmarks Preservation Commission in 1974. Nevertheless, it deteriorated during the 1970s and 1980s, becoming dangerous and uninviting. Between 1988 and 1992, the Bryant Park Restoration Corporation, formed in 1980, carried out an extensive redesign that altered Clarke's formal scheme. The park has been crowded with visitors ever since. Moses's fenced-off lawn is now full of chairs, which along with food kiosks attract lunchtime crowds. The park is home to New York Fashion Week twice a year and to a free outdoor film festival in the summers. Although a public, parks department property, it is managed and maintained by the nonprofit Bryant Park Corporation. — KL

EAST RIVER PARK

Manhattan: FDR Drive, between Montgomery and East 12th streets
57.457 acres
Opened 1939
Figs. C-57–59

Moses sculpted East River Park from landfill and a highway project. Largely overlooked, it is nevertheless important: a typical example of his opportunistic park-siting strategy, a demonstration of the role of a park in neighborhood transformation, and a model of his effective coordination with public works that he did not control. In 1935, Mayor La Guardia secured federal funding from the WPA to build the section of the East Rive Drive between Grand and 14th Street, the area where the Lower East Side elbows out into the East River. Groundbreaking and clearance followed swiftly in August 1935, and the road, which was funded by the Manhattan borough president, opened in June 1937. Housing reformers saw the East River Drive as an opportunity to clear slums, and their efforts led to the development of Vladeck Houses, located along Corlears Hook Park, south of Grand Street. Announced in 1938 and opened in 1940, Vladeck Houses was the first New York City Housing Authority project on the Lower East Side.

East River Park is a tribute to Moses's aggressive championing of a parks agenda and a pendant to his contemporary recreational facilities along the Hudson River. Moses fought to set the East River Drive (later renamed the FDR Drive) slightly inland in order to claim the shoreline for park purposes. As with the West Side Improvement, he expanded the site by a landfill operation, which the 1938 aerial photograph shows under way. East River Park is a ribbon park running between road and river for a 1.5-mile stretch. In the first phase of construction, the park reached from Grand Street, a block south of the Williamsburg Bridge, to 12th Street, an area of 35 acres. In 1937, the Board of Estimate approved the project estimated to cost $750,000; the photograph from 1939 documents the park upon completion. Its chain of game courts, tennis courts, wading pool (in winter, a skating rink), baseball diamonds, and running track illustrate Moses's characteristic emphasis on active recreation.

In the second phase of building, completed in 1941, the park was expanded south to Jackson Street, bringing the total area to more than 57 acres and linking with Corlears Hook Park (1903), which was remodeled at this time. The highlight of the southern extension was a concrete amphitheater for public concerts, with seating for 2,500 people. A wide

C-57. Landfill operation for East River Park, looking north, September 8, 1937

pedestrian bridge over East River Drive provided access to the theater from Corlears Hook Park, where people from multiple directions could gather at a roundabout, punctuated by a flagpole. The roundabout launched an axial approach to the theater and offered sweeping views of the East River, highlighting the transformation of the park from a sawtooth fringe of commercial docks to a recreational green ribbon. The landscape design is unsigned but bears the hallmarks of Gilmore Clarke's flexible but formal planning; even in its current, less than pristine condition, a gracious, processional quality is evident.

East River Drive separates the waterfront park from the city, and access is limited to pedestrian overpasses, but the distancing effects of the road are less severe than may be expected. The roadway is relatively narrow, and the grade is flat, unlike the more difficult conditions of the West Side Improvement, where the grade drops substantially between Riverside Drive and the recreational facilities along the Hudson River.

Moreover, the inconvenience of crossing East River Drive is outweighed by the waterfront location, which magnifies the sense of openness otherwise unobtainable in a strip park. East River Park is an underappreciated jewel and a model for the ongoing transformation of Manhattan's shoreline into a recreational landscape.

East River Park initially served a tenement district, but, as envisioned in the late 1930s, public housing colonized the area in the postwar years, and the park was a major neighborhood asset. The wall of

C-58. East River Park, with Williamsburg Bridge, looking north, June 2, 1939

public housing flanked the park, beginning with Jacob Riis Houses (1946) at the north end and continuing south, and in chronological order, with Lillian Wald Houses (1947) and Baruch Houses (1953), north of the Williamsburg Bridge. Under Moses's leadership the area immediately south of the bridge, the last available segment of quasi-park frontage, was chosen for a middle-income housing development, the Corlears Hook Title I. Its success, too, owes something to the waterfront park. — HB

C-59. View from Corlear's Hook Park of East River Drive overpass and amphitheater in East River Park, August 22, 1941

CITY PARKS

CENTRAL PARK

Manhattan: 59th to 110th Street, Fifth Avenue
    to Central Park West
843 acres
Opened 1859; Moses's additions 1934–62
Figs. C-60–63

By 1934, many areas of Central Park had fallen into disrepair. Moses, taking advantage of the labor and supplies available to him from the Civil Works Administration, implemented extensive park improvements, including the construction of athletic facilities, renovations, replanting, and tree pruning. Upon taking office as parks commissioner, he articulated a vision for Central Park that sought to accommodate various users and to balance passive and active recreational activities. Wishing to preserve the park's picturesque beauty and special qualities as a tranquil oasis, he nevertheless recognized that recreational needs had changed since the mid-nineteenth century when Frederick Law Olmsted and Calvert Vaux designed the park. Moses built active play spaces for children, adolescents, adults, and the elderly, along with washrooms, making an effort not to distract from the overall experience of the landscape. If his interest in athletics conflicted with Olmsted's idea of the landscape, they shared a bias against commercial activities. Moses sought to replace the numerous ugly food stands that had infiltrated the park with simply designed and

strategically placed concessions that provided food at any budget. He also tried to balance amenities for the upper class, such horseback riding and expensive meals, with the needs of the poor and working classes who traveled greater distances to enjoy the park.

Moses's plan for the park underwent drastic change after World War II. Where his ideas for the park in the 1930s were balanced, by the 1950s his approach was unilateral, shortsighted, and even irresponsible. He endorsed vast changes to Olmsted and Vaux's original design and the destruction of some of the most treasured enclaves of the park. In 1956, he proposed to build a recreation center for the elderly in the Ramble. The plans, calling for the destruction of much of the Ramble and the insertion of locked gates, parking lots, and clubhouses with television and game rooms, were blocked by a huge public outcry. Many of his decisions seemed arbitrary and designed solely to demonstrate his authority. In 1959, Moses unexpectedly refused to allow Joseph Papp to produce Shakespeare's plays in the park. His effort backfired; news media decried Moses's unsympathetic act, and New York State Appellate Court ruled in favor of the permit.

MARGINAL PLAYGROUNDS
Billy Johnson Playground (67th Street and Fifth Avenue)
East 72nd Street Playground (72nd Street and Fifth Avenue)

Levin Playground (77th Street and Fifth Avenue)
East 96th Street Playground (96th Street and Fifth Avenue)
Benheim Playground (100th Street and Fifth Avenue)
Bernard Playground (108th Street and Fifth Avenue)
Lenox Avenue Playground (110th Street and Lenox Avenue)
West 110th Street Playground (110th Street between Seventh and Eighth avenues)
West 100th Street Playground (100th Street and Central Park West)
Rudin Playground (96th Street and Central Park West)
Safari Playground (91st Street and Central Park West)
Spector Playground (86th Street and Central Park West)
Mariner's Playground (84th Street and Central Park West)
Diana Ross Playground (81st Street and Central Park West)
Adventure Playground (68th Street and Central Park West)
Opened April to August 1936

In April 1934, the New York City police jailed Mrs. Fella Biro and her two-year-old son when she refused to pay a two-dollar fine for allowing him to dig a small hole in the Sheepfold. In her defense, she claimed that the city's greatest park ignored the needs of children. At the time, the only playground in Central Park was Hecksher Playground, north of Central Park South at Seventh Avenue. In order to provide play space for children and to "protect the natural beauty of the greater areas within," Moses built fifteen "marginal" play-

C-60. Central Park, looking north, June 24, 1938

grounds at park entrances to "intercept the little potential destroyers on the perimeter of the park."[255] In September 1935, the parks department broke ground on the first marginal playground in Central Park. By the spring, Mrs. Biro's son could happily—and legally—dig a hole in any of the playground sandpits.[256] Oval in shape and roughly 30,000 square feet in area, the marginal playgrounds followed the standard design that Moses developed in 1934. The shaded playgrounds were equipped with benches, sandboxes, slides, seesaws, and swings, as well as a concave circle of concrete where a shower could be set up on hot days.[257]

NORTH MEADOW
West 97th to West 101st Street
25 acres
Opened May 18, 1934

New Yorkers had been using the North Meadow for baseball, soccer, and football since the late nineteenth century. In 1934, Moses formalized its use as a recreational space when he laid out fifteen baseball diamonds, transformed a stable at the north side of

the 97th Street Transverse into a field house, and installed handball courts and two roller skating arenas.[258] Some have viewed Moses's campaign to build baseball and soccer fields in Central Park as an attack on Olmsted and Vaux's landscape. Others see the park as landscape architecture that must respond to changing societal values and needs. Since the completion of the park, real estate developers, reformers, and landscape architects have made hundreds of proposals to add recreation areas, entertainment venues, museums, schools, and eateries. Moses's transformation of the North Meadow was a modest alteration that responded to requests of reformers, neighbors, and sports enthusiasts for more active recreation areas throughout the city.

GREAT LAWN
Midpark between 79th and 85th streets
13 acres
Opened November 21, 1936

When the Department of Water hinted in 1898 that the lower reservoir would soon be obsolete, architects,

landscape architects, and play enthusiasts saw an opportunity to transform the 32 acres into play space. Proposals included playgrounds, wading pools, a museum, war memorials, a stadium, and a sunken garden.[259] In 1917, Thomas Hastings, whose partnership with John M. Carrère is best known for the design of the New York Public Library, proposed a sunken Beaux-Arts garden prominently situated at the midpoint of an "intermuseum promenade" between the American Museum of Natural History and the Metropolitan Museum of Art. Frederick MacMonnies's acclaimed sculpture *Barge of State*, exhibited at the World's Columbian Exposition in Chicago in 1893, served as the focal point of the design, composed of a garden amphitheater and formal mall.[260]

In 1931, the American Society of Landscape Architects (ASLA) presented a modified version of Hastings's design. A. F. Brinkerhoff proposed to transform the lower reservoir into a great green meadow called the Great Lawn. The new design retained some of Hastings's Beaux-Arts elements, including a formal mall over the 86th Street Transverse that extended to the upper reservoir and an east-west walkway connecting the two museums. It also accommodated active recreation in the form of two children's playgrounds, with shallow wading pools, on either side of the mall. To the south, Brinkerhoff proposed a small lake (today called Turtle Pond) northeast of Belvedere Castle.[261] Two years later, the Tammany mayor John L. O'Brien and his new parks commissioner John Sheehy devised a plan to transform the lower reservoir into playground and athletic facilities with five baseball diamonds and several wading pools. Within weeks of taking office, Sheehy ordered workers to steamroll the ground and begin laying a one-mile cinder running track.

In 1934, Moses discarded Sheehy's plan and proposed to modify Brinkerhoff's plan by doubling the two playgrounds (to 4 acres each) and providing recreation space for adults.[262] The main feature of the new design was a large oval lawn with a small lake at the south end and a mall at the north end extending to the upper reservoir; children's playgrounds were on either side of the mall, with the rest of the area devoted to walks, clusters of trees, shrubs, and spaces for adult games such as shuffleboard, croquet, and boccie. Equipped with a jungle gym, the playground to the east of the mall was designated for older children; the westerly playground was reserved for younger children. When it opened in November 1937, the oval lawn was closed to the public to protect the grass.

The plan exemplified Moses's balanced vision for Central Park in the first decade of his tenure as commissioner. It respected Olmsted and Vaux's undu-

lating picturesque landscape and provided ample
space for passive leisure activities such as walking
and reading. At the same time, Moses responded to
contemporary ideas about the importance of active
recreation in combating disease and improving physical fitness in children as well as adults. Finally, he
rejected the two elements that were most beloved by
New York's wealthy and powerful residents, the intermuseum promenade and Thomas Hastings's Beaux-
Arts sunken garden. In doing so, he respected
Olmsted's wish to shield the park from shifts in architectural fashion and prevented the American Museum
of Natural History and the Metropolitan Museum of
Art from laying claim to land within the park.

MARY HARRIMAN RUMSEY PLAYGROUND
East Drive and 72nd Street
1.25 acres
Opened May 7, 1937

Many city residents considered the Casino
Restaurant, opened in 1929 during Mayor Jimmy
Walker's administration, "a gross misuse of the city's
property and an affront to the millions of common
people and their children who were kept away from
it." During its five years of operation, the Casino
grossed $3,096,155 but remitted only $42,000 to the
parks department.[263] When Moses took office in 1934,
he demanded that the operators of the restaurant, the
Dieppe Corporation, lower the exorbitant cover
charges and food prices or risk eviction. After a year
of legal wrangling, the New York State Supreme Court
upheld Moses's right to end the corporation's lease.[264]

Moses demolished the Casino in 1936 and created
Rumsey Playground, furnishing it with swings, slides,
and other equipment; a large oval wading pool; a roller-
skating track; benches for mothers and nurses; and
shade trees.[265] Calvert Vaux had designed the original
building as a Ladies' Refreshment Saloon in 1862;
Mayor Walker commissioned Joseph Urban to remodel
it in 1928, and it became one of the most exclusive
nightclubs in the city.[266] Moses destroyed a beautiful
landmark in favor of a grand gesture publicizing his
triumph over Walker's corruption and extravagance.

TAVERN ON THE GREEN
Central Park West and 67th Street
Opened June 9, 1934

As Moses was fighting with the Diepe Corporation
over concession rights for the Casino, he demolished

C-61. Central Park Zoo, January 30, 1936

a shepherd's house designed by Jacob Wray Mould in
1870 to house 200 sheep and their keeper. In its
place, Moses built the Tavern on the Green, which
was designed by Civil Works Administration architects to provide "table d'hote luncheon . . . service
within reach of the average purse."[267] Community
organizations, including the Central Park West and
Columbus Avenue associations, opposed the new
restaurant, expecting it to cause traffic congestion and
"draw an undesirable class of patrons from 'Tenth
Avenue and the Lower East Side.'"[268] The Tavern on
the Green opened in 1934, and the sheep were moved
to the Sheep Meadow in Prospect Park, Brooklyn.[269]

In January 1956, Moses announced plans to
increase the size of Tavern on the Green's parking
lot.[270] A large group of mothers, who used the half acre
as a playground, protested; with toddlers and infants
in their arms, they surrounded the bulldozers and prevented work for two days. On April 24, Moses ordered

work to begin before dawn; the area was flattened
before the women arrived. Two days later, a court
halted the work as an attorney for the mothers argued
that, like the Casino Restaurant, "the Tavern-on-the-
Green was too expensive to be an acceptable feature
of Central Park."[271] In July, the Board of Estimate and
Corporation Counsel asked Moses to back down. The
publicity finally encouraged the city council minority
leader Stanley M. Isaacs to collaborate with the
Citizens Union to draft legislation to limit the parks
commissioner's powers to negotiate concessions.[272]

BETHESDA TERRACE RESTAURANT
Midpark at 72nd Street
Opened July 1935

In addition to his battles with the Casino and his creation of Tavern on the Green, Moses introduced

another official concession into the park during the first years of his administration. In May 1935, the parks department began to restore Terrace Bridge, which had been designed by Calvert Vaux and Jacob Wrey Mould in 1865. The new plans, intended to accommodate visitors to musical programs on the mall, included building a restaurant under the bridge and placing chairs and tables on the terrace. The "scheme . . . create[d] a beer garden . . . spreading its tables over the brick-paved esplanade about the Bethesda Fountain."[273] The restaurant, serving sandwiches, soft drinks, and beer, was managed by Central Park Catering Corporation, the same firm that ran the Tavern on the Green.[274] Civil Works Administration artists painted a mural on the walls of the restaurant and the arcade under Terrace Bridge.[275]

ZOO
Fifth Avenue between 63rd and 65th streets
5.5 Acres
Opened December 2, 1934; extensively remodeled 1988

Calvert Vaux and Frederick Law Olmsted purposely omitted a menagerie from Central Park, although New York State in 1861 had allocated funds to build a small zoo. Numerous proposals were made, including a design by Calvert Vaux, but none was realized. Nevertheless, an unofficial zoo took up residence in the area surrounding the Arsenal. In the last decades of the nineteenth century, William Conklin, the menagerie's director, oversaw the construction of several Victorian-style buildings. By the time Moses took office, the zoo, never first-rate, had become dilapidated and was an inhumane setting for animals.

In 1934, Aymar Embury II and his team redesigned the Central Park Zoo in sixteen days, transforming the site into a small wonderland that functioned like a children's picture book. As children and their families stepped into the zoo, each successive page revealed a new and wondrous animal from across the world. The zoo's orientation was simple and geometric. The main feature was a rectangular pool for seals (267 by 290 feet), surrounded by a wide shaded path. The houses with the most active and exciting animals—monkeys, bears, elephants, and birds—were placed at the corners where the animals could be viewed from both inside and outside the zoo. The zoo was bound by the Arsenal on the east; a restaurant, known as Kelly's Café, on the west; and the Lion House on the north. To the south of the seal pool, Embury placed the large Antelope House,

positioned to block parkgoers' views of the garage and maintenance buildings. The buildings to the north and south were connected with arcades.[276]

The zoo was decorated throughout with an elaborate program of animal-themed art designed by Frederick G. R. Roth and Hunt Diederich, including a bronze dancing goat and bear, limestone reliefs, a painted mural, and wrought-iron weathervanes.

CONSERVATORY GARDEN
Fifth Avenue from 103rd to 106th Street
6 acres
Opened August 1937

In 1934, Moses began construction of the Conservatory Gardens. Twenty-two greenhouses, which had been costing the city $8,000 a year to maintain, were demolished to make way for formally planted gardens. Designed by Gilmore Clarke to evoke French, Italian, and English models, the new garden and was divided into three plots: a sunken garden, a pool, and a semicircular arbor for wisteria.

In 1938, Gertrude Vanderbilt Whitney donated gates that had been designed by George B. Post for Cornelius Vanderbilt's mansion on Fifth Avenue at 58th Street (demolished); they were installed at 105th Street, the entrance of the Conservatory Garden.[277]

RAMBLE
South of the 79th Street Transverse
38 acres

When Calvert Vaux and Frederick Law Olmsted created the Greensward Plan, they were determined Central Park have the physical and visual variety found in nature. Reformers and physicians blamed the congestion and noise of the cities and their repetitive grid layouts for numerous physical and psychological disorders; they viewed nature as the only remedy. The human body, doctors argued, required fresh air, sunlight, and contrasting visual experiences. Influenced by these views, Vaux and Olmsted designed Central Park's Ramble—wild rocky terrain, twisting paths, densely planted trees, secluded

C-62. Conservatory Garden, Central Park, September 8, 1937

glades, and a tumbling stream—to closely echoed the most sublime areas of the Adirondack Mountains. Olmsted called it a "wild garden." Owing to its diversity of tree and plant material, the Ramble quickly became a sanctuary for birds and a popular destination for bird watchers.

Although it continued to attract migratory birds, by the 1950s the Ramble had become one of the most dilapidated and dangerous areas of the park. In 1955, Moses announced a $250,000 grant from the Florina Lasker Foundation to transform 14 acres into a recreation center for the elderly. Described by one writer as "suburbanization" of the park, the plans called for an indoor center equipped with a food bar, television, radio, records, and game rooms; a social hall; a terrace; outdoor recreational areas for horseshoe pitching, croquet, shuffleboard, and game tables; and parking lots and locked gates. Bird-watchers, park enthusiasts, scientists, and conservationists denounced the plans and criticized Moses as uncaring and arrogant. The *New York Times* published letters from across the country; writers complained that the Lasker Recreation Center would disrupt the migratory pattern of birds and limit the Ramble's use by parkgoers.[278] Only one organization, the Park Association of New York City, supported Moses, stating: "it must be kept in mind that there has been a vast change in the conception of the function of public parks since the days of Mr. Olmsted."[279] Most New Yorkers disagreed and in letter after letter asked Moses to preserve and renovate the Ramble. After six months of scathing articles and reports, the Lasker Foundation withdrew its grant.[280] Acknowledging public sentiment, Moses petitioned the Board of Estimate for $220,000. Once the money was approved, the parks department immediately began a two-year campaign to prune trees, clear paths, and reconstruct bridges and shelters, following Vaux's original designs.

DELACORTE THEATER
South of the Great Lawn, near Central Park West and 79th Street
Opened 1962

Moses was soon engaged in a second, failed battle in Central Park. Despite the immense popularity of Joseph Papp's free Shakespeare productions, in 1959 Moses threatened to revoke Papp's permit unless he began to charge $2 per ticket and remit 10 percent of the proceeds to the parks department to defray "erosion" costs.[281] Enraged, Papp complained that he risked breaching his contracts with the actors' union

and supply companies if he charged admission fees. Over the next two months, Papp and Moses exchanged barbs in the press. At the end of May, Moses revoked Papp's permit.[282] After an appellate court ruled against Moses, calling his action "arbitrary, capricious and unreasonable," he petitioned the Board of Estimate to allot $20,000 to build fences and benches to pave the way for permanent facilities. In August, the City Planning Commission approved $250,000 for a permanent facility.[283] Built as a temporary structure in 1962, the Delacorte Theatre still stands today. Although it functions well, its utilitarian design is at odds with the gothic-style architecture of Vaux's Belvedere Castle nearby, which complements the park's picturesque setting.

LOEB BOATHOUSE
On the Lake, midpark at 74th Street
Opened 1952

In 1867, Calvert Vaux designed a small Victorian-style building to house small boats for public use. By 1924, the boathouse had fallen into disrepair; the parks department demolished it and built another. Over the next few decades, demand for boats grew. In 1952, Mr. and Mrs. Carl M. Loeb donated $250,000 to build a new boathouse to accommodate the nearly 500,000 people who used the facility each year.[284] Stuart Constable designed the building to resemble Vaux's original design. Parkgoers can rent boats; purchase hotdogs, drinks, and sandwiches;

and dine in a restaurant alongside the lake at this one-story brick building with a metal roof.

KERBS BOATHOUSE
Conservatory Water, Fifth Avenue near East 74th Street
Opened 1953

In 1953, Mrs. J. E. Kerbs donated $85,000 to construct a small boathouse on Conservatory Water. The Kerbs Boathouse, which includes a concession stand and restroom facilities, has storage for model sailboats that can be rented by park visitors. Designed by Stuart Constable in the Victorian style, it has a terrace for watching boats on the pond.[285]

WOLLMAN MEMORIAL SKATING RINK
Southeast corner of the park, near the Pond
Opened 1950

Wollman Rink was constructed with funds donated by the philanthropist Kate Wollman in memory of her father and brothers. Built for use in the winter for ice-skating, the rink can be converted for roller-skating, dancing and, concerts in warm weather. Stuart Constable's design included a semicircular building to hold refrigeration equipment, dressing rooms, concessions, and a skate shop. On top of the building was a playground with swings, seesaws, a sandpit, and a shower basin.[286] — RI

C-63. Model of a proposed restaurant in Central Park at 59th Street.
Design by Edward Durell Stone. Courtesy MTA Bridges and Tunnels Special Archive

PROSPECT PARK

Brooklyn: Prospect Park West and Flatbush Avenue
    (Grand Army Plaza), Parkside and Ocean avenues
526.25 acres
Opened 1868; Moses's additions 1934–61
Figs. C-64–65

Following their collaboration in the creation of
Central Park, Frederick Law Olmsted and Calvert
Vaux designed the 526-acre Prospect Park in
Brooklyn. It opened in 1868, with work continuing
into the 1870s. When Moses was appointed parks
commissioner in 1934, he immediately dispatched
relief workers to clean and renovate Prospect Park,
as he had done at Central Park. This federally
funded labor force also constructed seven new playgrounds distributed around the park's periphery.
Other additions that Moses made included a zoo, a
band shell, baseball diamonds, and an ice-skating
rink. While many critics were furious at his intrusion
into the park's bucolic landscape, Moses's insertion
of popular attractions and active recreational facilities updated the masterfully designed park for modern users.

PROSPECT PARK ZOO

Flatbush Avenue
8 acres
Established 1890; new zoo opened July 3, 1935;
    renovated 1989–93

A small menagerie had been in the park since the
late nineteenth century, but Moses and his planners
moved it to the site of a duck pond near Flatbush
Avenue. The pond was drained and construction
began in 1934. The concern soon arose that there
would not be enough animals to fill the zoo once it
was completed: 30 percent of the animals from the
old zoo had been disposed of because they were sick
and elderly, and the parks department emphasized
that city zoos would "serve no longer as an 'old animals home,' to which decrepit and senile pets may
be sent when their owners tire of them."[287] Moses
tried to secure city money to purchase animals but
failed, observing that "public officials are sensitive
about voting money for animals in a time of unemployment."[288] His inspired solution was to appoint
Alfred E. Smith to serve as "rental agent" for the
Prospect Park Zoo, entrusting the former governor
with obtaining new animals. In addition to his other
municipal position as night superintendent of the
Central Park Zoo, Smith generously agreed to take on

C-64. Prospect Park Zoo, September 8, 1937

the responsibility of renting homes to suitable animal
tenants. He was presented with a floor plan of the
Prospect Park Zoo on which various accommodations
were described: "Bearville Arms, nine suites with
bath" and "large duplex apartment available for Mr.
and Mrs. Giraffe" were among the properties he
would be renting. On May 28, 1935, Smith initiated
a campaign to obtain the 160 animals needed to fill
the zoo to capacity. He asked New Yorkers to donate
50 cents or a dollar toward animal purchases. One
Manhattan businessman, S. Klein, upped the ante
with a $5,000 donation under the condition that his
twelve-year-old daughter, Phyllis, choose the animals
to be bought with his money. The *New York Times*
reported that "Phyllis's list ranges from sea lions
to monkeys, enough exhibits for twenty cages."[289]
Smith asked governors to send animals native
to their states. Vermont sent fawns and foxes,
Connecticut raccoons and quails, Maryland muskrats
and terrapins. A man in Philadelphia, who heard
word of the zoo drive, contributed a 60-pound
chimpanzee named Gustave. By the time the zoo
opened its cages were two-thirds full.

Three thousand people attended the opening of
the $500,000 zoo, but Moses and Mayor La Guardia
were not among them. In the midst of a feud, they
each avoided the celebration to spite the other:
Moses had demanded to be sworn in for his second
term as parks commissioner before the opening ceremony, and La Guardia had scheduled the swearing
in for the following Wednesday. Moses had threatened to resign from the position altogether if he
were not reappointed before the zoo opened;
instead, he boycotted the opening in protest. In
Moses and La Guardia's absence, Smith officiated
at the ceremony. He used the opportunity to express
his support of Moses, saying that "it would be a
regretful thing for the people of the City of New
York if any back-alley politics was to interfere with
the progress of the work under the direction of
Commissioner Moses."[290] The next day, the *New
York Times* emphatically praised his triumphant
accomplishment: "Mr. Moses' rod has worked its
modern miracles. Graceful structures of concrete
and pale red brick have taken the place of dilapidated and unsanitary buildings."[291]

These "graceful" new buildings were designed by Aymar Embury II, the chief consulting architect for the parks department and the architect behind the Central Park Zoo reconstruction. Moses deemed Embury's second attempt at zoo planning more successful than his first, in part because there was more available space in Prospect than in Central Park.[292] Lewis Mumford agreed with his assessment: "Brooklyn has all the luck. . . . After a first stab at planning the Central Park menagerie, more to occupy the unemployed hastily than to exhibit animals, Mr. Aymar Embury II has gone to Brooklyn and has done one of the handsomest small zoos that the country can boast—the best, as far as buildings go, that I have seen anywhere."[293]

With more time (he had designed the Central Park Zoo in sixteen days) and more space at Prospect Park, Embury produced an architectural masterpiece for animals with an immediately comprehensible, formal layout. Visitors entered the zoo from Flatbush Avenue through a pair of brick gates topped by limestone panels depicting in relief scenes from Rudyard Kipling's *The Jungle Book*; similar plaques decorated other zoo buildings. A pair of curving staircases led down an embankment to a semicircular group of buildings looping around a seal pool. At the top of the hemicycle was the elephant house, crowned with two square brick towers flanking a flat, blue-tiled dome constructed by the Guastavino company. Two curving wings, comprising brick and concrete animal houses connected by covered passageways, extended from either side of the elephant house. Outdoor runs radiated from the animal houses. Wherever possible, moats separated the animals from viewers, providing a more naturalistic experience. Otherwise, wrought-iron cages enclosed the animals. Bear pits, located along Flatbush Avenue, were surrounded by moats instead of bars, to dramatic effect. A ventilation system and interior illumination insured that each display was clean and clearly visible. The semicircle culminated in a cafeteria on one side and a comfort station on the other, each opening onto a terrace with tables and benches from which visitors could watch the seals.

Embury's formal organization of the zoo around a circle is typical of his classical designs for other parks department projects: the arms of the animal houses embracing the seal pool at the Prospect Park Zoo are reminiscent of the Orchard Beach bathhouse arcades framing the view of the beach. The design of the zoo illustrates the observation that in Embury's architecture "the theme of the circle in all its parts and pieces reverberates."[294] He used inexpensive, WPA-approved materials—brick, concrete, and blue terra-cotta tile—and the logic of simple geometrical form to create an elegant public menagerie that is both noble and accessible. Although the zoo underwent a $37-million renovation beginning in 1989, when management was transferred from the parks department to the Wildlife Conservation Society, much of the original design remains.

BAND SHELL
Near Prospect Park West and 9th Street
Opened 1939

Embury also designed a band shell, consisting of a concrete acoustic shell and brick lower walls. The structure opens onto a paved semicircular plaza that seats 2,000 spectators; performances can also be viewed from a surrounding lawn. Defenders of Olmsted and Vaux's original rural park design balked at the insertion of the band shell into Prospect Park. One critic claimed that the concert venue "looks as out of place in this simulated rural setting as a colossal overturned piano box"; another called it "the crowning affront to the park's pastoral atmosphere."[295] Still, the band shell has many fans: it is the home of the immensely popular Celebrate Brooklyn! a summer festival of free music, dance, and film events, now in its twenty-eighth season.

BASEBALL DIAMONDS
South end of Long Meadow
Opened 1959

Moses built baseball diamonds in the Prospect Park Parade Ground, a formal rectangular field at the southeast corner of the park. He also dramatically transformed the Long Meadow, one of the park's central features. In his overhaul of the park in 1934, he removed the meadow's flock of sheep, Olmsted and Vaux's method of trimming the lawn. Many years later, in 1959, Moses inserted seven baseball diamonds into the southern end of the Long Meadow in order to expand the park's active recreational facilities. The ball fields were originally surrounded by chain-link fences and flanked by concrete and brick bleachers, but these were removed in the 1980s so that the fields would not so blatantly disrupt the Long Meadow's nearly mile-long flowing pasture.

C-65. Parade ground with baseball diamonds, Prospect Park, September 8, 1937

Moses's final addition to Prospect Park was Wollman Rink; he secured funding for the outdoor skating rink in 1959, and it opened on December 22, 1961. A portion of the money for the rink was donated by Kate Wollman, the chairwoman of the William J. Wollman Foundation, who also financed the construction of a rink in Central Park in 1949. The donor gave $300,000, and the city paid $600,000. Moses explained that "the City or state often has to 'piece out' or supplement gifts which are inadequate to accomplish the entire purpose. Sometimes in the end the City contribution exceeds the gift."[296] The 28,000-square foot concrete rink and adjoining concession building, designed by the architectural firm of Hopf & Adler, is located on the shore of Prospect Lake, near the park's East Drive. This facility, popular with the public, provoked the fury of critics opposed to any change of the original park design. One complained that the "structure is what one would expect to find serving as a snack bar on a busy freeway, and its self-conscious geometry and artificial materials could not look more out of place than in this sylvan setting."[297]

Despite criticism from purists, Moses's incursions into Prospect Park created attractions that are still popular today. The expansive park can easily accommodate these facilities without disrupting its overall pastoral effect. "There is no excuse for having . . . a place of detention for animals, a roofless concert hall, a ball park, or an artificial skating rink within a landscape garden," one detractor complained. On the contrary, there is a good excuse: the enjoyment of their many users.[298] There was, however, one negative effect of the changes made to the park during Moses's reign: maintenance was neglected even as money poured in for new construction, and by the 1960s Prospect Park was in a derelict state. Moses added new facilities without insuring that they, and the park into which they were inserted, would be taken care of. An organization called Friends of Prospect Park has restored Olmsted and Vaux's park so that its original design and Moses's attractions are now integrated into a uniformly beautiful whole. — KL

C-66. Flushing Meadows, before alteration, ca. 1934

FLUSHING MEADOWS–CORONA PARK

Originally Flushing Meadow Park
Queens: Grand Central Parkway and Van Wyck
   Expressway
1255.42 acres
Established 1939 as site of World's Fair; opened
   as a park June 3, 1967
Figs. C-66–69

Like Central Park, Flushing Meadows–Corona Park is an artificial creation built from a degraded landscape. The Flushing River cut into Queens from the East River to the terminal moraine, and the expansive wetlands on either side of the channel yielded marsh grasses much prized by early settlers as fodder and bedding for livestock. Flushing Meadows retained its pastoral aspect until the first decade of the last century, when the contractor and developer Michael Degnon began transforming it into an industrial park and dredging Flushing Bay to create a deep-water port. Subsidiaries of his Degnon Realty and Terminal Improvement Company received a five-year contract with the city for the removal of ashes and street sweepings (i.e., manure) from Brooklyn, with the refuse used to build up the meadows for development. The Brooklyn Rapid Transit Company inserted itself into the deal, setting up the Brooklyn Ash Removal Company, a subsidiary controlled by the Tammany-connected Fishhooks McCarthy, to funnel refuse along their trolley lines overnight. Dumping began in the winter of 1910, with as many as five garbage scows a day depositing their noxious cargo. It did not take long for neighbors to complain about the "nauseating stench of rotting garbage decomposing in the summer heat," for all manner of refuse was dumped along with the clean ashes and manure.[299]

In 1913, the state legislature allocated funds for straightening and dredging the Flushing River and for preparing an engineering survey for canals that would cut through the borough, linking the river with Newtown Creek and Jamaica Bay.[300] The dredging pumped silt and mud from the bottom of the bay directly onto Degnon's property, and within a year the surface rose as high as 14 feet above the original wetlands. By 1917, as much as 10,000,000 cubic yards of fill had been deposited on the site, and nearly two miles of new bulkheads were under construction. The port and barge terminal, if not the canals, seemed well on the way to realization when the First World War brought activity to a halt. Degnon defaulted on his obligations, and the property was sold at auction in October 1924; he died within months.[301]

In 1929, the Board of Estimate approved a plan for the city to acquire 325 acres from the Brooklyn Ash Removal Company by condemnation and create Flushing River Park, with a golf course, tennis courts, ball fields, and other facilities.[302] This was precisely the kind of small, and by implication corrupt, thinking that Robert Moses abhorred. At the time, his Grand Central Parkway was under construction through the dump, and Moses envisioned in that valley of ashes a great public park, built on a scale to rival Central Park. At first, however, he could find no way to fund his vision. The answer was the World's Fair.

The original purpose of the 1939 World's Fair was to commemorate the 150th anniversary of George Washington's inauguration as president. Moses seized on the fair as a vehicle to fund the infrastructure for his new park, including the permanent New York City Building, and to advance other projects, including the Whitestone Bridge.[303] Regrading was completed in 190 working days, a remarkable feat, which eliminated Mount Corona and spread the fill evenly over the site. At the same time, workers dug out 146 acres for two lakes, using the muck as topsoil (which worked well, once it dried and the odor dissipated). The lakes, together with a dam across the remnants of the Flushing River, meant that an entirely new drainage system had to be devised to redirect the natural flow. New storm sewers would empty waste water from the grounds directly into Flushing Bay, already polluted from years of industrial and residential waste. Sewage treatment plants went on line at Tallmans

Island in College Point and Bowery Bay to prevent further degradation of the water quality.

When the fair closed, Moses was ready, for he had designed the site with the successor park in mind. In "From Dump to Glory," written for the *Saturday Evening Post* (January 15, 1938), he declared that the park would be "more romantic and interesting than anything of a temporary nature, no matter how astonishing or uplifting. For like the mirage in the desert, the Fair will be gone in 1940, and at that time Flushing Meadow park will come into its own." Francis Cormier and Gilmore Clarke, with Aymar Embury II as consulting architect, designed the new 1,260-acre park, incorporating "informal landscaped areas, formal gardens evocative of those of Versailles, a Japanese garden, a bird sanctuary, lakes, and a wide range of facilities for public events and active recreation, including a pitch-and-put golf course, a boat basin fronting Flushing Bay, bridle paths, bicycle paths." The Aquacade remained, as did Embury's New York City Building, with a popular rink for ice- and roller-skating. Construction was to have been funded by anticipated profits from the fair, but unfortunately, for all its glory, it repaid investors only 33 cents on the dollar. The federal government, the funding stream that Moses had tapped so successfully in the past, was

then being redirected to the war. There would be no more federal dollars for municipal parks.[304]

In 1946, the park might have been permanently derailed. The United Nations had selected New York for its headquarters, and the city offered 350 acres in the former fairgrounds for a world capital. The General Assembly convened in the New York City Building, meeting for the first time on October 24, 1946. The city willingly provided funds to convert the building for the UN, and Moses reallocated part of that stream for parking, access roads, and landscaping. The committee charged with finding a permanent home for the UN included Nelson A. Rockefeller, Thomas J. Watson of IBM, Democratic Party insider James A. Farley, Grover Whalen, Winthrop W. Aldrich, and Arthur H. Sulzberger of the *New York Times*, together with Queens Borough President James A. Burke and Bronx Borough President James Lyons. Moses, not surprisingly, was the chairman. "We are not simply turning over to you so many barren acres," Burke said. "We are giving to you the best portion of a park which was becoming of more and more value in use to our people."[305]

In the *New York Times Magazine* (October 20, 1946), Moses made his case for locating the UN's world capital in Flushing Meadow Park, declaring that site preferable to either Manhattan or Westchester because it "is central, but not crowded, equally accessible to city and suburbs, protected by parks, parkways, bay and lakes and other buffers and barriers and by zoning against future undesirable developments; because it is already furnished with most of the basic utilities and because it involves no disturbances of homes or business, no condemnation, no local tax problems and no unhappy suburban controversies." To bolster his case, Moses commissioned the renowned architectural delineator Hugh Ferriss to create evocative charcoal renderings. He also convinced New York banks to fund construction of Parkway Village, a quiet garden apartment complex in Kew Gardens Hills for delegates' families. The United Nations, however, wanted to be
in Manhattan, and it was ultimately the wealth of the Rockefellers that secured property along the East River from William Zeckendorf. Moses may not have had the chance to build the world capital, but at least he could complete his park.

Flushing Meadows scarcely had time to mature as a park when ground was broken for the second World's Fair. In 1960, Moses was named president of the World's Fair Corporation, and from that post approved inclusion of a 50,000-seat baseball stadium in the plans. This was the first time that part of the park was

C-67. View of World's Fair, 1939. Photograph by Skyviews

C-68. Flushing Meadow Park, August 2, 1951. Photograph by McLaughlin Air Service

C-69. Shea Stadium, 1973

handed over to private interests (Moses had tried to lure the Brooklyn Dodgers to a stadium there in 1957, but Walter O'Malley was intent on Los Angeles). Originally approved for a team in the new Continental League, Shea Stadium was ultimately occupied by the New York Mets. Although a year behind schedule, it opened in time for the 1964 season—and the World's Fair. In conjunction with the second world's fair, Moses pushed forward a new arterial highway program, including the extension of the Van Wyck Expressway and the widening of Grand Central Parkway. He expected the profits from the fair to fund not only reconstruction of the Flushing Meadows–Corona Park, as it was renamed in 1964, but also a string of parks from Kissena Corridor to Alley Pond. "What is left of

the fairgrounds and its environs is at least as important to us as the successes and imprint of the fair itself," he said.[306] Like the earlier fair, however, the second also failed to yield a surplus.

Still, the 1964 fair did leave behind several structures intended to be permanent features of the park. Joining the two veterans of the World of Tomorrow in 1939—the New York City Building, now with the Panorama, a scale model of the five boroughs; and the Aquacade—were the Federal Building, the New York State Pavilion, the Singer Bowl, the Port Authority Building (with a heliport), and the Hall of Science (which reopened as a museum in 1966), as well as the Unisphere. The site plan, essentially unchanged since 1939, remained, with fountains, sculptures, and utili-

ties. While the onset of the war prevented the realization of Moses's park in the 1940s, the new Flushing Meadows–Corona Park (as it was officially renamed in 1964) opened to the public on June 3, 1967, less than two years after the fair closed. The Queens Zoo opened on the grounds, incorporating Buckminster Fuller's geodesic dome, originally built to house a tribute to Winston Churchill. Just east of the park was the Queens Botanical Garden, which grew out of Gardens on Parade, an exhibit at the '39 fair. Flushing Meadows–Corona Park was poised to become a cultural and recreational mecca. The timing, however, was hardly auspicious.

During the years when John Lindsay was mayor, the new park almost immediately began to suffer from benign neglect. The fountains stopped working and became stagnant, filled with garbage and weeds. The city found no use for the New York State Pavilion, designed by Philip Johnson; the revolving restaurant atop its towers never reopened after the fair and was finally removed. Queens Theatre in the Park was established in part of the pavilion, but the enormous open space under the Tent of Tomorrow, with its detailed terrazzo map of New York State, was left exposed and the map literally disintegrated, a process that accelerated when the space was used as a roller-skating rink. The fate of the Singer Bowl, the site of the opening ceremonies, athletic contests, and musical performances during the fair's two-year run, was equally depressing, as the city abandoned it after a few one-time events. The Federal Building remained empty and was eventually demolished, and funds for the Hall of Science dried up. The Queens Museum of Art, however, opened in the New York City Building in 1971. The fate of the Aquacade is another scandalous chapter in this park's story. The parks department closed the pool in the early 1980s and, in a familiar pattern, abandoned the structure to vandals and the elements; despite the protests of preservationists, it was demolished in 1996.

Although he ardently opposed commercial ventures within his parks (with the notable exception of Shea Stadium and the Jones Beach Amphitheater), Moses enthusiastically used the commercialism of the two world's fairs to achieve a public purpose: the construction of a great public park. In recent decades, however, the city has accelerated the privatization of the park, with the construction of the Arthur Ashe Tennis Stadium and a new pool and skating complex, and it was willing to hand over virtually the entire park when the city bid for the 2012 Olympics. Nevertheless, the park remains one of the most heavily used in the city. But the question arises: why is Olmsted and Vaux's Central Park venerated as one of the great achievements of American urbanism, while Robert Moses's Flushing Meadows–Corona Park is viewed as a blank slate rather than as a historic landscape? — JAK

RANDALL'S AND WARDS ISLANDS

East River between Manhattan, Queens, and the Bronx
528.4 acres
1934–68
Figs. C-70–72

Robert Moses reshaped Randall's and Wards islands by coordinating recreation and transportation in his simultaneous roles as parks commissioner and head of the Triborough Bridge Authority. He envisioned the islands, in the shadow of the future Triborough Bridge, as the site for an extensive recreational development, a "water-bound pleasure ground," far larger than park sites available in the crowded boroughs surrounding the islands.[307] Moses was not the first to imagine parks on these islands but, as with other large-scale public works projects, was the first to attempt to build them. He was not entirely successful: the islands had tenants before Moses came along and expelling them proved difficult. His battle for parks on this site dragged on for the duration of his career, and the various nonrecreational institutions that reside there today attest to his defeats by other factions of city government. Moses built his headquarters on Randall's Island, below the toll booths of the Triborough Bridge. The island landscape stands for both his immense power and the powerful constraints on it.

Randall's and Wards islands became New York City property in 1835. Their names derive from their previous private owners, Jonathan Randel and the brothers Jaspar and Bartholomew Ward. Once under municipal control, the islands' separation from the surrounding city made them a convenient home for undesirable inhabitants and institutions. Wards Island was used as a potter's field, and in 1863 the New York City Asylum for the Insane opened there. Transferred to the state in 1899, it became the Manhattan State Hospital for the Insane, which was still crowded with patients when Moses set his sights on redeveloping the islands in 1934. The Wards Island Sewage Treatment Works, begun in 1931, was under construction in 1934. Randall's Island was also a dumping ground for the unwanted: it held the House of Refuge, a home for juvenile delinquents, and the Idiot Asylum, later called the New York City Children's Hospital, for mentally ill children.

Randall's Island, the smaller of the two, lay to the north of Wards Island. Separating them was a body of water called Little Hell Gate. To the east of Randall's Island, there was a small, marshy, uninhabited island called Sunken Meadow, which Moses called "a geological slopover of Randall's and Ward's Islands."[308] He connected and enlarged these islands over the course of more than three decades. In 1946, the shoreline of Randall's Island was extended northward by filling in the Bronx Kill, which separated it from the Bronx. In 1955, it was announced that the landfill operation to join Randall's Island to Sunken Meadow,

C-70. Triborough Bridge Authority Administration Building, Randall's Island, ca. 1937. Photograph by Richard Averill Smith. Collection MTA Bridges and Tunnels Special Archive

first proposed by Moses in 1934, would commence. The project, coordinated by the Triborough Bridge and Tunnel Authority, was virtually free of cost; the TBTA provided a place for private contractors to dump their waste, and they provided the fill. The landfill ultimately united Randall's and Wards islands into a single landmass by connecting the northeastern tip of Wards to Sunken Meadow and filling in some of Little Hell Gate.

As early as 1926, the Regional Plan for New York studied the possibility of park development on the islands and touted their value to the densely populated neighboring residential areas. In 1930, the Regional Plan Association presented a more detailed plan, calling for a public amusement park on Randall's Island. The same year, the Metropolitan Conference on Parks, chaired by Moses, endorsed this proposal and suggested removing the islands' institutions to make room for city parks. The state government approved of this approach: Governor Franklin D. Roosevelt criticized the outdated, over-crowded Manhattan State Hospital and advocated its closure, and in 1933 the state legislature passed a bill calling for removal of the facilities from Randall's Island within two years and of the hospital on Wards Island within ten years. Moses accepted the impossibility of exiling the sewage plant from Wards Island, given that Mayor La Guardia planned to complete it using federal relief grants.

This legislation paved the way for Moses's announcement in March 1934 that the islands would soon become parks. Work on Randall's Island did not begin for another year because the city hospital commissioner Sigismund S. Goldwater fought the eviction of the House of Refuge and the Children's Hospital. Delays persisted until the young offenders and patients could be moved into new institutions. By May 1935, construction started on the site of the House of Refuge. By August, the Children's Hospital was vacated: some patients were transferred to the mental hospital on Wards Island and the rest were moved temporarily to a vacant school in Flushing.

The centerpiece of the Randall's Island park was a municipal stadium, which Moses initially hoped would have 70,000 seats; he later settled on 22,000. He attempted to pay for the construction of the stadium with federal Triborough Bridge funds, arguing that it would attract traffic to the bridge and thereby increase tolls, but Secretary of the Interior Harold Ickes, the administrator of the PWA loans and grants allocated to finance the bridge's completion, rejected this arrangement. Moses ultimately secured a combination of city and federal relief funds to construct the

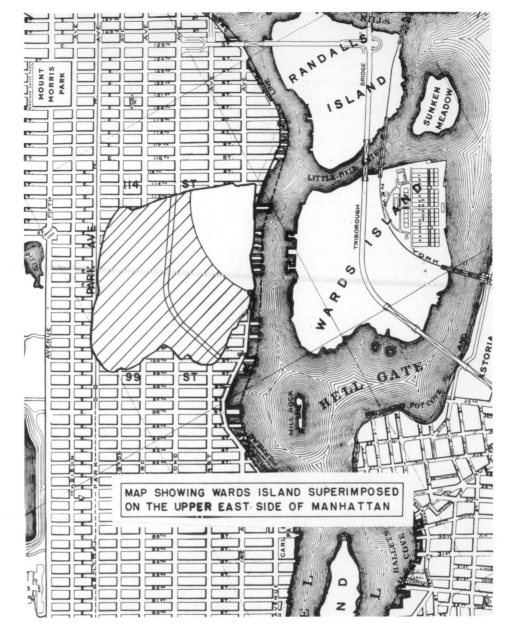

C-71. Map with Wards Island superimposed on the Upper East Side of Manhattan, ca. 1937

$1,000,000 stadium under the auspices of the parks department, without skimming off the bridge budget. The opening of Randall's Island Stadium was staged to coincide with the opening of the Triborough Bridge, on July 11, 1936. Following the bridge dedication, Moses and La Guardia descended to the stadium and addressed a below-capacity audience of 15,000 people; after the ceremony, tryouts for the Olympic track and field team commenced. The day was oppressively hot and the public address system failed, but the

patient if frustrated spectators were rewarded by witnessing Jesse Owens's qualification to travel to Berlin for the Olympics. The open-air stadium, made of brick with concrete stands, enclosed a football field and quarter-mile running track and was served by 4,300 parking spaces underneath the Randall's Island span of the bridge. Moses made the stadium a revenue-producing facility: fees paid by visitors to sports events and concerts covered maintenance and operation. In 1955, it was renamed Downing Stadium in memory of John J. Downing, a longtime parks department employee.

After the stadium opening, other park features were developed on Randall's Island, including football fields, baseball diamonds, tennis courts, open play areas, landscaped paths, a waterfront promenade, comfort stations, and food concessions. Plans for the 150-acre park were prepared jointly by the Department of Parks and the Triborough Bridge Authority. The *New York Times* praised Moses's coordination of the two agencies under his control: "He can relate the park work on Randall's Island with the bridge work across it so that there will be no conflict of effort, no duplication, no waste."[309] The construction of the headquarters of the Triborough Bridge Authority is an example of the close relation between the two Moses-run organizations. He had Aymar Embury II, the chief architect of the parks department, create a command center for the TBA on parks department-owned land below the massive toll plaza and traffic junction on Randall's Island. Resembling an Italian Renaissance villa, the three-story limestone building had arched windows on the ground floor; an exedra and a circular driveway marked its entrance. The headquarters was actually an extension of the bridge itself, jutting from the north side of the road leading from the toll plaza to the Manhattan-bound section of the bridge. A tower hovering above the headquarters appeared to be part of the office structure, emphasizing its grandeur, although the tower really belonged to the bridge.

Construction of the park on Wards Island progressed more slowly. Before the parks department released a plan, a 77-acre sewage plant opened in October 1937. The Department of Sanitation completed construction of the plant with the help of an $11,360,250 PWA grant. At the dedication of the Wards Island Sewage Treatment Works, Secretary Ickes and Mayor La Guardia predicted that the plant would "do much toward reclaiming the polluted waters surrounding the city," and even voiced the hope that East River swimming beaches could be reopened eventually.[310] Sewage that was previously dumped into the river from Manhattan and the Bronx traveled through tunnels to reach Wards Island, where it was purified through the activated sludge process. Sludge was then shipped far out to sea. The technology, the most advanced available, could not, however, contain odors; the island smelled of sewage—and still does. Now called the Wards Island Pollution Control Plant, stench from the facility continues to permeate the island.

Nevertheless, Moses forged ahead with plans for a park on Wards Island. He expected the Manhattan

C-72. Wards Island Pedestrian Bridge, undated. Collection MTA Bridges and Tunnels Special Archive

State Hospital for the Insane to evacuate the island by 1943, leaving all but the site of the sewage plant open for redevelopment. The plans submitted by the parks department to the Board of Estimate in November 1937 called for three playing fields, an open meadow, a field house, comfort stations, and a medical museum, to be called the American Museum of Health, which would take over buildings vacated by the mental hospital. All these facilities would add up to "a carefully balanced combination of passive and active recreation."[311] Moses anticipated that the park would serve residents of Manhattan's East Side from 86th to 114th Street; he produced maps illustrating the density of this area's population and superimposing Wards Island on the Upper East Side to demonstrate the exceptional recreational opportunity that the park would provide for Manhattan. Property of equivalent size in Manhattan, he estimated, would cost $65,000,000 to reclaim for parks. Wards Island would be like a new Central Park, created without displacing residents other than the occupants of the hospital.

Moses built two bridges besides the Triborough to facilitate access to the island parks. He was determined to shut down the ferry service that had transported people to the islands before the completion of

the Triborough. Once it opened, automobile off-ramps and pedestrian stairways allowed visitors coming from Manhattan, Queens, and the Bronx to reach Randall's Island. Wards Island was accessible from Randall's by the Little Hell Gate Bridge, which opened in May 1937. Ferry service was terminated permanently after the bridge was completed. Built by Moses's Triborough Bridge Authority for $530,000, the concrete and steel bridge was designed by Triborough engineer Othmar Ammann. The low span, hovering just 40 feet above the water on three arches, was in between the Triborough and the Hell Gate railroad bridges but was invisible from these structures because it lay so far below their decks. The Little Hell Gate Bridge was 24 feet wide, with walkways cantilevered from either side of the central automobile passage. It was demolished in 1996, long after landfill had closed off Little Hell Gate, uniting Randall's and Wards islands and making the bridge obsolete.

Moses also proposed a pedestrian bridge between 103rd Street and Wards Island. He insisted that it was "desirable and essential if the city is to take advantage of this extremely valuable piece of city property. . . . The same people who would have to walk 3 miles to reach the island, by the present method, would have their walking distance cut to approximately 1,000 feet by the construction of this bridge."[312] Contrary to his usual commitment to automobile transportation, Moses never suggested that this East River crossing accommodate cars. The bridge would be particularly convenient for occupants of the East River Houses, a public housing project adjacent to East River Drive between 102nd and 105th Streets. A *New York Times* editorial praised the bridge scheme: compared to recently built bridges that "all have the same lack of intimacy . . . there is something rather jolly and homelike in Commissioner Moses' proposal for a footbridge (no automobiles, no buses, no trucks)."[313]

Progress on Wards Island Park and Pedestrian Bridge was gradual. In 1938, the southeastern corner of the island was transferred to the parks department and landscaping and park construction began. In 1942, Parks opened a playground on East River Drive to serve the East River Houses, and a 40-foot-wide concrete walk was built at its center to make room for a ramp to the future footbridge. Work on the bridge, designed by Ammann in 1939, was delayed by World War II and finally began in 1949. Robert Caro depicted Moses's completion of the bridge at this time as a strategy to help Mayor William O'Dwyer defeat Newbold Morris in the 1949 mayoral election. Morris had criticized Moses for neglecting Harlem in his provision of recreational facilities, leading Caro to claim that the bridge connecting East Harlem to Wards Island was meant to counter this criticism.[314] But Caro's argument does not stand up in light of Moses's decade-long fight for the bridge.

The Wards Island Pedestrian Bridge and the park, still incomplete and awaiting a land transfer from the Manhattan State Hospital, opened on May 18, 1951. Its simple design was based on an earlier plan by Ammann, who supervised construction although he was no longer employed by the Triborough Authority. The authority, now called the Triborough Bridge and Tunnel Authority because of its operation of the Brooklyn-Battery Tunnel, paid for the $2,100,000 bridge and then turned it over to the Department of Public Works. The steel bridge is 956 feet long, with a 12-foot-wide walkway and a central vertical-lift span that can be raised to allow tall ships to pass. Access is from the promenade on East River Drive and from a ramp that runs over the highway from the East River Houses playground. Ammann called it "the Little Green Bridge"; it was one of his favorite creations despite its diminutive size relative to his other works.[315]

In a brochure for opening day ceremonies in 1951, Moses presented the park and bridge as "a step in the redevelopment and rehabilitation of an entire sector,

the Hell Gate waterfront." In response to planners who criticized him for building "scattered, uncoordinated" projects, Moses decided that the bridge and park were part of the improvement of a neighborhood that included the east side of Manhattan from 86th to 125th Street, Astoria in Queens, and the southern Bronx.[316] Hell Gate waterfront, which he pointed out was home to a great deal of public housing, was served by an array of Moses's facilities: the Triborough Bridge, East River Drive, Astoria Pool, Thomas Jefferson Pool, ten playgrounds in East Harlem, the park on Randall's Island, and now the Wards Island park and pedestrian bridge. While Moses was justified in demanding recognition from his critics, the "long-haired planners," for his numerous contributions to the so-called Hell Gate waterfront, it was inaccurate to suggest that the Triborough had united areas in three boroughs into a single neighborhood. East Harlem and the Upper East Side maintained separate identities, not to mention Astoria and Mott Haven.

The park that opened on Wards Island in 1951 was meant to be only the beginning of a larger development, but the persistent presence of the Manhattan State Hospital for the Insane hindered plans for expansion. The hospital was initially ordered to vacate the island by 1943, but in 1941 Governor Herbert H. Lehman passed a bill postponing this deadline because no new facilities had been built to house the patients. In 1952, the state decided to retain its part of the island, demolish the outdated hospital buildings, and replace them with a modern institution. After years of trying to banish the mental hospital, Moses, in his role as the city construction coordinator, ultimately supported the plan for the new hospital "on the ground that the advantages to New York of a centrally located mental hospital outweighed the value that the land would have for park development."[317] Moses fought hard for projects he believed in, but once he lost a battle he tended to "drop the whole idea and get on to the next order of business," sometimes supporting projects that he had long opposed.[318] The hospital on Wards Island, now called Manhattan Psychiatric Center, remains open.

Only one-third of Wards Island, the southeastern 68 acres unused by the psychiatric and sanitary facilities, was developed as a park. Containing two playgrounds, baseball and softball diamonds, playing fields, meadows, benches, a shorefront promenade, and a concession building, this small park has always been underused. In 1954, the *Times* reported that Wards Island Park was "languishing from the lack of use."[319] The concession stand was shut down because

visitors were so scarce. Although the park was accessible by the pedestrian bridge, people considered the trip long and inconvenient. Moses understood that "bridge approaches are the despair of experienced park officials. No matter how close they are to congested housing and how attractive their recreation facilities, the short walk over water seems to prevent a psychological obstacle."[320] A recent trip to Wards Island indicated that little has changed: besides a few picnicking families and softball teams, the park was eerily empty on a sunny summer weekend afternoon.

Moses's final addition to the islands was a 50-acre park on Sunken Meadow; it opened on June 15, 1968. He spoke at the dedication although he had recently lost control of the TBTA when it was folded into the MTA. The park contained five baseball diamonds, one with floodlights to allow for evening play, four horseshoe courts, four boccie courts, a picnic area, and a field house. Moses cited the park, paid for by the TBTA, as an example of the history of cooperation between the TBTA and the parks department and of the TBTA's provision of incidental recreational facilities to complement its transportation projects. At the opening, he insisted that he had proven that "a road or bridge need not be a mere gasoline gully for fast-moving cars" by lining roads with playgrounds and building parks in the shadow of bridges.[321]

After this last attempt by Moses to devote Randall's and Wards Islands to recreation, nonrecreational facilities have continued to penetrate the islands. The Fire Department Training Academy opened on Randall's Island in 1975. Its burn building, made entirely of steel, is routinely set on fire as practice for novice firefighters. The Charles Gay Homeless Shelter opened on Wards Island in 1979. These facilities, along with the Psychiatric Center and the Pollution Control Plant, dominate the islands, which are difficult to traverse because of the gouges cut across them by bridge piers.

Moses's parks are still open and reachable by the Wards Island Pedestrian Bridge, which is open from April through October; in the winter it is left in the raised position. Moses's sports fields are frequented by local high school teams that lack their own grounds, but otherwise the parks are still underused. An organization founded in 1992, the Randall's Island Sports Foundation, is looking to change that. Using a combination of public and private funding, the foundation plans to introduce popular attractions. The first big project advanced by RISF was the replacement of Downing Stadium with Icahn Stadium in 2005; plans for the future include the creation of a water park. — KL

ROADS AND CROSSINGS

MANHATTAN LOOP

The highway loop around Manhattan, a crucial link in the city's infrastructure, was built in bits and pieces over many decades. The oldest portion, along the Harlem River, was constructed in 1898 as a racetrack for horse-drawn carriages, whereas sections on the East Side were not completed until the 1960s. In all, the loop includes five separate and distinct highways: the elevated West Side Highway (also known as the Miller Highway), the Henry Hudson Parkway, the Harlem River Drive, the Triborough Bridge approach (actually a stretch of highway more than 1.5 miles long), and the East River Drive (later renamed the Franklin Delano Roosevelt Drive). Robert Moses participated in the construction of each of these separate projects, some more than others. He was primarily responsible for the Henry Hudson Parkway and the Triborough Bridge approach, while he played less important roles on the West Side Highway and the Harlem River Drive projects, and was only peripherally involved in the completion of the East River Drive.

The entire loop, based upon preliminary planning work by the municipal engineer Nelson P. Lewis, was first formally proposed in the Manhattan borough president's annual report for 1922. As early as 1915, Lewis had called for new north-south express routes to rectify the east-west orientation of the city's original grid, which had established numerous river-to-river cross streets and few avenues running the length of the island. Two great waterfront highways seemed to

be the solution, one along the Hudson River and the other along the East and Harlem rivers. The Regional Plan Association embraced his idea and eventually pushed it forward by prominently including it in their published plans, including the landmark 1929 *Regional Plan of New York and Its Environs*.[323]

By 1928, Mayor James J. Walker and Manhattan Borough President Julius Miller obtained state and city approval for the elevated West Side Highway, from Canal Street up to 72nd Street. Although the onset of the Depression slowed progress, the first section, from Canal Street to 23rd Street, was completed in 1930. The remaining portions were opened in 1932 (59th Street to 72nd Street), 1935 (23rd to 45th), and 1937 (45th to 59th). Primary responsibility remained with Miller (for whom the highway was eventually named) and his successor, Samuel Levy; Moses was involved only in the completion of the last two sections, since by the mid-1930s he controlled all federal work-relief projects conducted in New York. He was significantly more instrumental, however, in the 1937 completion of the ambitious West Side Improvement, which included the Henry Hudson Parkway, as well as the Henry Hudson Memorial Bridge and the expansion and relandscaping of Riverside Park. At this same time, he also facilitated the construction of the first East River portion of the loop, the approach to the Triborough Bridge. This section, from 92nd Street up to the

bridge itself at 125th, opened in 1936. The vast majority of the work on the rest of the East River Drive, southward from 92nd Street, took place between 1937 and 1942, under the guidance of Manhattan Borough President Stanley Isaacs and his staff engineer Walter Binger. Moses's only responsibility for this section involved the various parks created by Isaacs and Binger along the route. While many of these were tiny vest-pocket parks or small stand-alone playgrounds, there were two significant park projects that Moses oversaw along the East River Drive: East River Park, and the expansion and redesign of Carl Schurz Park.

Later, as the city construction coordinator, Moses presided over numerous expansions and improvements to eastern portions of the loop, most of which had been designed earlier by Binger but had been deferred because of limited funds. These included an elevated section near 23rd Street to eliminate traffic lights at 18th, 20th, and 23rd streets (1949); the Battery Park underpass, which connected the East Side half of the loop to the West Side piece (1951); modifications to accommodate the United Nations headquarters (1952); an exit/overpass at Houston Street to eliminate a traffic light (1953); and finally, both the South Street viaduct and the 96th Street overpass, which included new playgrounds and pedestrian access to John Finley Walk, the 3-mile path along the East River from 63rd to 125th Street

(1954). Moses had also arranged for the construction of pedestrian overpasses at 103rd, 111th, and 118th streets in 1950, thereby eliminating the traffic lights along the Triborough Bridge approach. The final traffic light was removed in 1967 with the completion of an elevated viaduct at the 34th Street intersection.

Occasionally, however, Moses's efforts were obstructive rather than helpful. In the 1940s, he refused to provide funds for the completion of the last link in the loop, the section of the Harlem River Drive from 125th Street up to 162nd Street, where it could meet up with the turn-of-the-century Harlem River Speedway, which ran alongside the river to 208th Street. His refusal was intended as revenge on Stanley Isaacs after Isaacs had successfully opposed him in the debate over whether the Brooklyn-Battery crossing should be a tunnel or a bridge. Despite his public proclamations supporting the Harlem River Drive, Moses in a letter to Isaacs bluntly explained why he would prevent its funding: "If you had been a little

more statesmanlike in your approach to this problem and a little less dogmatic about your conception of bridge esthetics, the Harlem River Drive would now be under construction." As a result of Moses's opposition, work on the Harlem River Drive was postponed until long after Isaacs was no longer Manhattan borough president. It was not completed until 1964, although by that time it had Moses's blessing and had been expanded to include a repaving and modernization of the Speedway section above 162nd, as well as the addition of the Harlem River Drive Extension, an elevated viaduct that climbed from 172nd Street through Highbridge Park to connect with the 178th–179th Street tunnel and the George Washington Bridge. Moses also did his best to delay or prevent the construction of ramps connecting the loop to toll-free bridges that competed with his Triborough Bridge and Tunnel Authority. Many of the toll-free Harlem River crossings are not directly connected to the Harlem River Drive, and the ramps between the FDR Drive

and the Brooklyn Bridge were not built until 1970, after Moses lost power.

In the 1970s, after decades of neglect and deferred maintenance, several sections of the loop highway—not those, however, built by Moses—began to fall apart. Parts of the West Side Highway and the FDR Drive collapsed, literally swallowing cars and trucks. Most of the West Side Highway, from lower Manhattan all the way up to 57th Street, was entirely dismantled. Westway, an ambitious replacement highway that would have included extensive landfill and the creation of new parkland as well as a massive Interstate-designated superhighway, was defeated in 1985 after lengthy debate and considerable controversy. In its place, West Street was restored as a local thoroughfare, with at-grade intersections controlled by numerous traffic lights. For the other portions of the loop, along both rivers, a process of repair or replacement that began in the 1980s is still ongoing. — OG

WEST SIDE IMPROVEMENT PROJECT

Manhattan: Henry Hudson Parkway from 72nd Street
to the Henry Hudson Memorial Bridge, and
Riverside Park Expansion
Bronx: Henry Hudson Parkway to the Westchester
County line
Completed 1937
Figs. C-74–79

Like many of Robert Moses's projects, most of the
West Side Improvement had been originally proposed
years before he became involved. These plans had
languished, however, until Moses adopted the undertaking and guided it to a rapid and efficient completion. The outcome, which included the Henry Hudson
Parkway, the Henry Hudson Memorial Bridge, and
the expanded and relandscaped Riverside Park,
would later be collectively regarded as one of his
most notable legacies.[322]

Plans to cover the railroad tracks along the
Hudson River waterfront were first advanced in
1891, when the neighboring Riverside Park was
more an eyesore than an amenity. It was filled with
rubble and scarred by the exposed train tracks,
decaying garbage dumps, unmaintained paths, and
crumbling walls. By the early 1930s, the landfill
under the train tracks was starting to leak out into
the river through an inadequate seawall; homeless
people caught by the Great Depression had established squatter settlements. As conditions deteriorated, more and more plans emerged to rehabilitate
the waterfront. In the decade of the 1920s, at least
four different proposals were published, suggesting
various combinations of the elements that Moses
would eventually integrate into the West Side
Improvement: additional landfill to provide new park
acreage; an elegantly landscaped express roadway;
and a wide array of sports facilities, including playing fields, tennis courts, and playgrounds.

When Moses took charge of the project in 1934,
work on covering the train tracks above 72nd Street,
based upon plans by McKim, Mead & White, had
been under way for five years. In addition, Manhattan
Borough President Samuel Levy had initiated construction of a new roadway atop the covered tracks.
But Moses, who had followed the debates for years
and had his own thoughts about how to reshape the
neglected waterfront, suspended work and brought in
his own team of designers, architects, and engineers
to sort through the dozens of proposals from the preceding decades. Remarkably, by 1937, less than three
years later, Moses had presided over the completion
of the entire project, including enclosing the tracks

C-74. Riverside Park at 79th Street, with railway, before the West Side Improvement, 1934.
Photograph by Percy Loomis Sperr

C-75. Railroad tunnel under construction in Riverside Park at 100th Street, looking north, May 11, 1937

south of 125th Street, transforming Riverside Park, and building the brand-new Henry Hudson Parkway and the Henry Hudson Memorial Bridge.

The bridge, too, along with its approaches, had been on the drawing boards for many years, with work advancing haltingly. Legislative appropriations for a bridge over the Harlem Ship Canal had begun in 1904. In 1909, the city bought land for the Bronx side of the span, in the village of Spuyten Duyvil. In 1913, Frederick Law Olmsted Jr. had completed plans to extend Riverside Drive from its terminus at 158th Street up to the Spuyten Duyvil bridge site near the end of Dyckman Street. The design included a 60-foot-wide landscaped roadway, gently curved for pleasure driving, alongside a stone-walled sidewalk overlooking the river, with a carefully arranged view across to the New Jersey Palisades. A neoclassical colonnaded temple was planned for the most scenic spot, to be named Inspiration Point. Work proceeded slowly. The new driveway and scenic walkway were not finished until 1925, and there had been no progress at all on the bridge when Moses and his team stepped in, in 1934.

Moses hired Gilmore Clarke as the lead landscape architect for the parkway and for the renovations and expansions in Riverside Park. After his groundbreaking designs on the Bronx River Parkway and his work for Moses on the Long Island parkways, Clarke was already a leader in the field. To provide the necessary technical support, Moses retained his favorite engineering firm, Madigan-Hyland, which assigned Emil H. Praeger as chief engineer. To design the bridge, Moses hired David P. Steinman of Robinson & Steinman, and, to round out the team, Moses appointed Aymar Embury II as architect.

The resultant design for the West Side Improvement was a blend of the preceding plans. To the south, especially where work on covering the train tracks had already started, from 72nd Street to 83rd, many elements of McKim, Mead & White's plans were retained. To the north, from 181st to Dyckman Street, elements of Olmsted's driveway were integrated into the new parkway. In particular, the section of Riverside Drive completed in the 1920s became the northbound roadway of the parkway. And, for the bridge, the Moses team followed the original route closely and drew extensively from the design in Steinman's 1909 thesis. The team, however, did not solely rely on these existing off-the-shelf schemes. They also incorporated new and state-of-the-art features into the final design for the West Side Improvement, particularly along the parkway and at the rotunda for the 79th Street Boat Basin.

C-76. Play areas in Riverside Park, north of 100th Street, November 1938

C-77. Athletic field, Riverside Park, October 27, 1940

For the Henry Hudson Parkway, Clarke applied lessons from the advancing science of parkway design while continuing to improve on his own pathbreaking innovations from the Bronx River Parkway and the early Long Island parkways and continuing to improve on these precedents. The Henry Hudson Parkway would be grade separated and limited access throughout its length. No commercial traffic was permitted. Following the example of the Mount Vernon Memorial Highway in Virginia, completed in 1932, curves were arranged according to the new "spiral" technique that incorporated gradually eased arcs. The outcome, with three lanes in each direction for much of its length, carried more traffic more efficiently than its predecessors and yet was still clearly a parkway, with scenic landscaping and artfully designed vistas. Travelers along the route are treated to an orchestrated parade of breathtaking scenery: ever-changing views of the river, forested parkland, and cliffs (both the Palisades in New Jersey and Fort Tryon Park in Manhattan), interspersed with impressive glimpses of the George Washington Bridge and the famous New York City skyline.

Yet, some of the parkway features proved problematic for a road that would quickly evolve from a pleasure route into a high-volume commuter corridor. Its ten-foot lanes were narrow compared with later expressway designs. There were no full-size shoulders or break-down lanes. Many of the exits and entrances had very tight curves and short acceleration/deceleration lanes. Initially, there was no median divider in the segments where traffic in opposite directions shared the same alignment. Nor were there any guardrails except along the river side of parts of the southbound roadway. Some of the design flaws were later rectified: emergency turnouts were added in 1947, many paved with Belgian blocks; guardrails were installed during the 1960s. Although many of these improvements made the parkway safer and more efficient, they undermined the original design aesthetic. For example, the original old-fashioned, wrought-iron incandescent streetlights were eventually replaced with new, modern, high-intensity discharge units mounted on characterless aluminum poles.

The Henry Hudson Parkway connects five major parks, four in Manhattan and one in the Bronx. From south to north, these are Riverside Park, Fort Washington Park, Fort Tryon Park, Inwood Hill Park, and Van Cortland Park. Of these, only Riverside Park was thoroughly renovated as part of the West Side Improvement project. Moses arranged for a series of playgrounds, easily accessible from Riverside Drive, including larger facilities at 76th, 86th, 91st, 97th, and 123rd streets, with smaller ones interspersed. Extensive sports facilities were also constructed, mostly between 95th Street and 112th, where there were two multicourt tennis complexes, four baseball fields, a soccer field, and a half dozen basketball courts. Crude paths were realigned and paved with decorative blocks, crumbling rustic-style stone walls were replaced with granite-faced concrete, and benches and walkways were positioned to offer visitors myriad options for enjoying the vistas. Moses's well-oiled publicity machine made sure that the public knew of the 132 acres of new parkland that were created in Riverside Park as a result of seawall reconstruction and covering the unattractive train tracks. But these claims were misleading, since they did not take into account the many acres of parkland that were ultimately lost to the parkway's roads and ramps in all five parks. Furthermore, despite the carefully laid-out pedestrian crossing and tunnels, the design clearly privileged drivers' enjoyment of the waterfront over pedestrians'. For example, the temple-like overlook and walkway at Inspiration Point, completed only a decade earlier, was cut off by the layout of the new parkway and rendered virtually inaccessible; it was reachable only through a single obscure entrance many blocks away, followed by a long path alongside the northbound roadway. In effect, the pavilion became an elaborate decoration, glimpsed fleetingly by motorists.

North of the bridge, the Henry Hudson Parkway resumed, initially passing along the path of the old Spuyten Duyvil Parkway, which had been a two-lane, tree-lined main thoroughfare in a small Bronx neighborhood. Then, it proceeded through Riverdale, passing under more than a dozen bridges that allowed local traffic to cross without interruption. These distinctive bridges, most of which were designed by Clarke, were modern steel and concrete structures, disguised by rustic-style masonry. Some of the bridges along this section of the Henry Hudson Parkway, like those on other Moses parkways, had low clearances—less than ten feet—because commercial traffic was not permitted. Thus, the route could not be adapted for bus use without extensive

C-78. Henry Hudson Parkway at 79th Street, ca. 1938

grade crossings, $5 million from a similar federal fund administered by the Public Works Administration, and $12 million from a different program intended for transportation improvements. To complete the budget, Moses borrowed money through a specially created public-benefit corporation that would pay back the loan using the tolls collected on the bridge.

One of the most remarkable components of the West Side Improvement Project was the 79th Street Boat Basin, which Moses had creatively yet misleadingly described as a grade crossing in order to obtain funding from the federal government. This multilevel structure, tucked between the parkway and the riverfront, is sometimes referred to as the rotunda. It includes a traffic roundabout on its top level, which connects the southbound off- and on-ramps to an underpass at the foot of 79th Street. On the middle level, unseen by the motorists hurrying above, is a café and colonnaded terrace. Below that is the access to the actual marina, which provides municipally operated berths and facilities for sailboats, day cruisers, and small yachts. On the lowest level, Moses's team included a garage.

Most of the new recreational facilities in Riverside Park were easily accessible from the adjacent neighborhoods. Farther north, however, getting to the riverfront and to the recreational facilities that Moses had built between 145th and 152nd streets and at the foot of Dyckman Street was more difficult. Changes in topography and the location of the train tracks made direct access a problem. In fact, many swaths of the northerly parkland were virtually impossible to reach, requiring long detours, and as a result served only as scenic surroundings for the parkway. This north-south imbalance in the original scheme was somewhat rectified when the 28-acre Riverbank State Park was built from 1972 to 1986, atop the North River Pollution Control Plant on new landfill between 138th and 145th streets. Two new walkways spanned the parkway and the tracks, providing straight and easy connections to the park from West Harlem and allowing upper Manhattan residents easier access to a wide range of new facilities including athletic fields, baseball diamonds, basketball courts, and running tracks. — OG

C-79. Henry Hudson Parkway at Fort Tryon Park, with George Washington Bridge, 1938

reconstruction. As Moses imagined a future in which everyone would own or have access to an automobile, the design of his parkways reflected this expectation.

The financing of the West Side Improvement was typical of Moses's public works projects. Drawing upon his remarkable political and administrative skills, he assembled funds from a range of available sources: $30 million from the Civil Works Administration for a "park access road," $13.5 million from a state fund created to eliminate railroad

C-80. Henry Hudson Bridge with single deck, 1937.
Photograph by Richard Averill Smith. Collection MTA Bridges and Tunnels Special Archive

C-81. Henry Hudson Bridge seen from New Jersey, with the necklace lighting of the Throgs Neck (left) and the Bronx-Whitestone (right) bridges on the horizon, 1936. Photograph by O. Winston Link.
Collection MTA Bridges and Tunnels Special Archive

HENRY HUDSON BRIDGE

Originally Henry Hudson Memorial Bridge
From Manhattan (Inwood Hill Park) to the Bronx
(Spuyten Duyvil section of Riverdale) across
the Harlem River
Opened 1936
Figs. C-80–82

The Henry Hudson Bridge connects the northern tip of Manhattan Island to the Spuyten Duyvil section of Riverdale in the Bronx. The bridge had been proposed by civic groups as early as 1901 to memorialize the explorer and was to be completed in time for the 1909 Hudson-Fulton celebration, a major event being planned in the city to honor the two historic figures. The 1901 proposal included a scheme by Alfred P. Boller, the designer of the Macombs Dam, Madison Avenue, and 145th Street bridges, for an elaborate stone structure with a 500-foot steel arch over the water and ornate triumphal arches over its abutments. In 1906, after seeing no progress on his original plan, Boller and the architectural firm of Walker & Morris proposed a less ornate design with an 800-foot steel arch, resembling the Washington Bridge between Manhattan and the Bronx at 181st Street. The Art Commission, which considered the new design too utilitarian for a memorial, rejected it, and the celebration passed without a new bridge. In 1909, William Hubert Burr, a professor of civil engineering at Columbia University, proposed a concrete arch that could carry future subway tracks on its lower deck. Leon Moisseiff of the Department of Bridges was appointed engineer in charge of the project; Whitney Warren of the firm Warren & Wetmore, designers of Grand Central Terminal, was the architect. The Art Commission approved this design, but, like the others, it never got beyond the drawing board because funding could not be found.

During the time that these proposals were being made, a plan to extend Riverside Drive north from its terminus at 155th Street was gaining support. The roadway, which would go along the Hudson to the northern tip of Manhattan, required a new bridge to the Bronx in order to continue to the city line at Westchester County. It was this plan that made the construction of the Henry Hudson Bridge possible. In 1930, the Metropolitan Conference of City and State Park Authorities, chaired by Robert Moses, proposed the route as a parkway. Public demand for the project increased after the George Washington Bridge opened in 1931.

Following his appointment as city parks commissioner in 1934, Moses and his engineers

began planning the design and financing of the roadway, which became the Henry Hudson Parkway, and secured money from several sources for its construction. The Henry Hudson Parkway Authority, created by the legislature in 1934 with Moses as the sole member, financed and constructed the Henry Hudson Bridge to carry the parkway between northern Manhattan and the Bronx.

Although prominently visible from the Hudson River, an arch bridge placed at this location was more than aesthetic. The body of water it crosses is the United States Ship Canal, which runs between the Hudson and Harlem rivers. Built in stages between 1888 and 1938, the canal allows boats coming down the Hudson to reach the Harlem and East rivers without going around the southern tip of Manhattan. To accommodate these vessels, all bridges had to be high enough for ships to pass underneath or have a movable lift or swing span. Port activity in the city was still bustling in the 1930s, and an arch between the steep hills on each side of the canal would avoid the disruptions that a movable bridge would create.

By the 1930s, Inwood Hill Park was the last area of native forest in Manhattan, and several civic groups pressed to have the parkway approach to the bridge skirt the east edge of the park instead of running along its forested ridge. Moses refused to change his plan: the route through the park would avoid right-of-way expenses and qualify the parkway as a park access road, making it eligible for federal relief funding from the Civil Works Administration. The route around the park would also have been at a lower level, requiring a moveable bridge instead of an arch.

Madigan-Hyland were the engineers for the entire parkway and bridge project, with Emil H. Praeger, the firm's chief engineer. Robinson & Steinman were the consulting engineers for the bridge itself. It closely resembled a bridge that David B. Steinman designed for the site as his thesis, "Design of the Henry Hudson Memorial Bridge as a Steel Arch," written in 1909 while he was a graduate student at Columbia University. Clinton F. Loyd was chief of architectural design and Aymar Embury II was consulting architect.

In 1936, the 800-foot arch was the longest plate girder steel arch and the longest fixed arch in the world, though the record has since been surpassed. The wide span cleared the tracks of the New York Central's Hudson Line on the Bronx side; its midspan clearance of 142.5 feet above mean high water allowed large ships to pass.

The bridge opened on December 12, 1936, with a single deck. The underwriters, believing that only a limited number of motorists would pay the dime toll, because the nearby Broadway Bridge was free, agreed to back only a $3.1-million bond issue for a four-lane crossing instead of the six lanes that Moses claimed would be necessary. Convinced of the need for the additional lanes, however, he had the bridge designed to allow for a second deck. Traffic demands soon proved him right, and the second deck was completed in 1938, eighteen months after the bridge first opened. The total cost of the bridge was just over $5.1 million. In 1937, 6,419,000 vehicles crossed the bridge; by 2005, the number had increased almost four-fold to 24,136,000. — LR

CROSSTOWN
EXPRESSWAYS

To understand the expressway projects, consider New York from the viewpoint of a trucker. To most truckers, Manhattan Island is an obstacle 13 miles long. It is directly accessible from New Jersey by only three Hudson River crossings, and it blocks west-east and southwest-northeast connections. Manhattan is a great separator—separating mainland America from Brooklyn, Queens, and Long Island, and separating New Jersey and everywhere south and west from Connecticut and everywhere north and east. In a dynamic nation characterized by high levels of consumption and a long history of emphasizing road and neglecting rail, the trucker is vital and every trucking delay has its costs.

By the 1920s, many motorists, business owners, and financiers were complaining that Manhattan Island was congested and difficult to access. Complaints were also rife about the inefficiencies of the port of New York and the high costs of moving people, vehicles, and cargo across the Hudson. Initially, the problem was seen mainly as one of building tunnels and bridges across the Hudson and East rivers in order to replace ferries. Numerous bridges spanned the narrow Harlem River, but only four bridges—Brooklyn (opened 1883), Williamsburg (opened 1903), Manhattan (opened 1905), and Queensboro (opened 1909)—were available to carry vehicles across the East River. As new bridges and tunnels were built, however, traffic congestion and parking problems in Manhattan increased and p ressure grew for ways to speed the flow of through-traffic, particularly trucks, across the island.

The policy response to the trucking problem came in four main stages, each complicated by the necessity to blend city, state, and federal standards, authorizations, and funding. First was the establishment of the Port of New York Authority in 1921, which led to the planning and construction of vehicular connections across the wide Hudson River: the Holland Tunnel (opened 1927), the George Washington Bridge (opened 1931), and the Lincoln Tunnel (opened 1937). The Port Authority also connected New Jersey to Staten Island with the Goethals and Outerbridge crossings (both opened in 1928) and engaged in lengthy discussions about two additional Hudson River bridges, which in the end were not built: one around 57th Street and the other around 125th Street.

Second was the preparation between 1921 and 1929 of the *Regional Plan of New York and Its Environs*, a major eight-year nongovernmental planning effort sponsored by the Russell Sage Foundation and many local businesses and dignitaries. The first volume, called *The Graphic Regional Plan* (1929), proposed an ambitious tri-state system of bridges, tunnels, expressways, parkways, railways, and mass-transit lines (see fig. E-17). It included four expressways crossing Manhattan, and circumferential highways to bypass Manhattan running across Westchester County to the north and across Staten Island and Brooklyn to the south. A new bridge across the Hudson, which became the George Washington, and a tunnel across the Narrows between Staten Island and Brooklyn were envisaged as carrying both road and rail traffic. The Regional Plan vision for New York City was largely ratified by the New York City Planning Commission in 1940 and 1941, in the preparation of its draft comprehensive plan. Substantial portions of the Regional Plan referring to highway and park systems were implemented between the 1930s and the 1960s, with Robert Moses playing a lead role as advocate and executor of public works. In sharp contrast, the Regional Plan's recommendations on railways and mass transit were largely forgotten. The neglect of investment in railroads and mass transit during the period from 1930 to 1970 reflected the priority that federal, state, and city governments gave to highways, the growing influence of the automobile and petroleum corporations, and the vital significance of cars and homeownership in the growth in prosperity and mass consumption following World War II.

Third was the formation of the Triborough Bridge Authority early in 1933 at the initiative of Moses as a means to fund the ongoing Triborough Bridge construction. Triborough became the prime base for Moses's power, and it was a New York State authority rather than a city authority. Thus, it focused not just on linking the five boroughs of New York City but also on linking Long Island and the lower Hudson Valley more effectively into the metropolitan region. Trucking and commuting flows were visualized and addressed on a regional scale, and outward metropolitan sprawl was facilitated by Triborough's investments in transportation infrastructure. More trucks and more automobile commuters signified more revenue and, in the long term, more infrastructural investments to facilitate additional travel.

Fourth was the historic alliance of the Port and Triborough authorities to prepare the *Joint Study of Arterial Facilities* (1955), a two-state plan anticipating the interstate coordination that would be required

under the anticipated National Interstate and Defense Highways Act, signed by President Dwight D. Eisenhower in 1956. This legislation ensured that federal funding would be available to cover 90 percent of the costs of any expressway that was approved as part of the national system.

During these various planning processes, five major west-east expressway crossings of Manhattan were considered, but only one—the northernmost, around 178th Street, connecting the George Washington Bridge to the Cross-Bronx Expressway—was actually built. This Trans-Manhattan Expressway traverses a narrow strip of upper Manhattan, far from the prestigious business districts and residential neighborhoods of midtown and downtown.

Two other crosstown expressways, around 57th Street and 125th Street, were discussed for decades but never got close to construction because Hudson River bridges were not built in the areas. The 57th Street project, which would have channeled heavy traffic directly into the heart of midtown Manhattan, was based on Gustav Lindenthal's 1920 Hudson suspension bridge design. It was effectively dropped in the late 1920s when the Port Authority opted for Othmar Ammann's 178th Street bridge. In turn, the heavy use of Ammann's George Washington Bridge led to his being commissioned by the Port Authority in 1954 to design a bridge at 125th Street. Based on the recommendations of the *Joint Study*, Triborough then outlined a plan for an elevated cross-Harlem expressway along the axis of 125th Street, linking directly to the Triborough Bridge. In the late 1950s, however, this project lost momentum as attention focused on expanding the capacity of the George Washington Bridge and building the Verrazano-Narrows Bridge, thus strengthening the Metropolitan Loop and shifting the pressure of heavy traffic to the outer boroughs.

The other two crosstown links, the proposed Lower Manhattan Expressway (LME) to connect the Holland Tunnel with the Manhattan and Williamsburg bridges and the Mid-Manhattan Expressway (MME) to connect the Lincoln Tunnel with the Queens Midtown Tunnel, had been frequently discussed for more than half a century. From the early 1940s until the late 1960s, Moses vigorously supported them, and the Port and Triborough authorities' *Joint Study* gave them high priority, in part because both already had their tunnel and bridge links across the Hudson and East rivers. That the LME and MME were never built is an important sign that Moses and their major institutional advocates—the Regional Plan Association, the Port Authority, the Triborough Authority, and the

Tri-State Transportation Commission—were far from omnipotent, especially when faced with conflicting political forces; lukewarm responses from the mayor, the Board of Estimate, and the governor of New York State; and growing community opposition.

Although Moses remained a steadfast advocate of building both the LME and the MME as elevated highways, mayors Robert Wagner and John Lindsay flip-flopped and called for more studies, considered surface and tunneling options, and often argued that one or other should be built, but not both. In 1966, Lindsay terminated Moses's role as City Arterial Highway Coordinator, the last vestige of his broader role as City Construction Coordinator, a position that Moses had held from 1946 until 1960. Then, in 1968, sensing an opportunity to build his own power base by advocating mass transit, Governor Nelson Rockefeller forced Moses's resignation from the Triborough Bridge and Tunnel Authority and merged it into the new Metropolitan Transportation Authority (MTA). Left with no institutional power base, Moses continued to argue for the LME and the MME, but both projects were soon shelved. In March 1971, Rockefeller officially recommended that they be "de-mapped," and they were removed from all official lists of future projects. — RB

LOWER MANHATTAN EXPRESSWAY

Unexecuted
From the Holland Tunnel to the Williamsburg Bridge, with a branch to the Manhattan Bridge
Initially proposed 1940
Figs. C-83–84

The Lower Manhattan Expressway (LME), nicknamed "Lomex," came considerably closer to construction than the MME. Together with the Brooklyn-Queens Expressway (BQE), the Harlem River Drive, and part of the New England Thruway, it was included in a $65-million Defense Highways proposal presented by Moses to Mayor La Guardia in November 1940. Although city funding was not forthcoming, Moses continued to press for the project during World War II, maintaining that it was essential both to open bottlenecks and to facilitate evacuation of the city. In 1946, the Triborough Authority prepared a preliminary design study for a $22.3-million, 1.5-mile elevated highway to be built 30 to 40 feet above the ground. The study ruled out any consideration of tunneling, citing its prohibitive expense because the tunnel would have to pass below all the north-south subway lines. The route chosen followed Broome Street for most of the distance between the twin-tube Holland Tunnel and the Williamsburg Bridge, with a branch southward at Mott Street that would cross Canal Street and connect to the Manhattan Bridge. It would pass through portions of Soho, Little Italy, the Bowery, Chinatown, and the Lower East Side. Triborough claimed that the route selected was the one that would have least impact on the built fabric of the area.

After 1956, with the impetus of promised Interstate Highway funding, more detailed design studies were prepared for an elevated LME. A plan was completed by Relocation and Management Associates Inc. in October 1960 in preparation for the eviction of 1,972 households and 804 businesses along the route. Nevertheless, there was little progress beyond the construction of an "approach" at Christie and Broome streets costing slightly under $1 million. Property owners, tenants, and civic and religious leaders organized into a Joint Committee to Stop the Lower Manhattan Expressway and launched a lobbying, letter-writing, and petitioning campaign. Mayor Wagner and the Board of Estimate postponed key decisions.

The deadlock continued until 1965, when Moses committed the TBTA to building a $10-million housing project beside the LME to house 460 families that would be displaced by the project. Mayor

Wagner then announced that the LME would be constructed at an estimated cost of $110 million, promising that most of the displaced households who could not be rehoused in the new TBTA project would be given top priority in the allocation of lower Manhattan public housing. Representative John Lindsay, who was a candidate to succeed Wagner, expressed his strong opposition to the project. Nevertheless, after his election, Mayor Lindsay changed his mind and began reviewing alternative designs, including a tunnel and a skyway 80 feet above the ground. Eventually, and after eliminating Moses's role as city coordinator of arterial highways, Lindsay opted for a combined tunnel-and-ditch design, which reduced the number of evictions and demolitions to 650 housing units and 400 commercial and industrial structures. The new proposal also included air-rights housing and a school built above the expressway.

Despite Wagner's late endorsement, Lindsay's conversion, and the wide range of alternative designs and housing projects that had been discussed, by 1967 public opposition to the LME project was gaining momentum. Protest movements against urban renewal projects and expressway construction were gathering force in many American cities, and New York was in the vanguard. By 1967, two hundred religious, civic, and social welfare groups had declared their opposition to the Lower Manhattan Expressway. Many of the leading protesters came from Greenwich Village, including Jane Jacobs, already a major public figure because of her best-selling book *The Death and Life of Great American Cities* (1961). Jacobs advocated "attrition of automobiles"—not building highways, narrowing streets, and improving transit services, so as to reduce vehicle use—a doctrine dramatically opposed to Moses's vision. In the 1950s, Jacobs and other Greenwich Village activists had battled Moses over local housing and road projects and had defeated the southward extension of Fifth Avenue through Washington Square Park.

In April 1968, with the costs of the LME estimated at $150 million, and with the Lindsay administration pressing hard for its construction and also for a "linear city" cross-Brooklyn expressway that would channel traffic to the Verrazano-Narrows Bridge, Jane Jacobs was arrested, accused of trying to disrupt a public hearing on the LME. Because of her international celebrity, Jacobs's arrest helped mobilize public sympathy. Petitions and marches vigorously asserted her mantra that "people are more important than highways," and public concern about

highway-related noise and air pollution rose rapidly. In July 1969, with Moses removed from all official public positions, Mayor Lindsay finally dropped his advocacy of both the LME and cross-Brooklyn projects. — RB

C-83. Lower Manhattan Expressway (proposed), with roadway enclosed in buildings, looking east on Broome Street, late 1950s. Rendering by Gero. Collection MTA Bridges and Tunnels Special Archive

C-84. Model of the Lower Manhattan Expressway (proposed), including Delancey, Christie, and Forsythe streets, late 1950s. Collection MTA Bridges and Tunnels Special Archive

C-85. Mid-Manhattan Expressway (proposed), looking east from the Hudson River, before March 1959. *Rendering by Julian Michele. Collection MTA Bridges and Tunnels Special Archive*

C-86. Mid-Manhattan Expressway (proposed), with roadway enclosed in buildings, 1950s. *Rendering by Julian Michele. Collection MTA Bridges and Tunnels Special Archive*

MID-MANHATTAN EXPRESSWAY

Unexecuted
From the Lincoln Tunnel to the Queens Midtown Tunnel
Design study 1950
Figs. C-85–87

The Triborough Authority prepared a design study for a mid-Manhattan expressway in 1950. A direct link between the Lincoln Tunnel and the Queens Midtown Tunnel would logically pass along 40th, 41st, or 42nd Street in Manhattan. Because of the great number of major buildings, institutions, and transportation terminals in the area, however, it was decided that a connecting expressway would have to pass farther south, along the axis of 30th Street. This route went through more workaday areas of apartments and small-to-medium-size businesses, including many fur and garment manufacturers, avoiding Times Square, Grand Central Terminal, Penn Station, Herald Square, the Empire State Building, and other major landmarks. The Triborough Authority's recommendation was to build an elevated two-way, six-lane highway, widening the 30th Street axis by demolishing the buildings on the south side. Triborough rejected a mid-Manhattan tunnel on grounds of cost and ruled out a surface highway because of the problems it would create for local traffic. When the elevated highway project was announced by Mayor William O'Dwyer, a dispute erupted over the rejection of the tunnel option, an idea that had been floated in the 1930s and early 1940s by the Regional Plan Association and the City Planning Commission. Moses took a firm and very personal stance, arguing that a tunnel would be absurdly expensive.

In 1956, the project gained new momentum when it became eligible for federal Interstate Highway

215

C-87. Model of the Mid-Manhattan Expressway (proposed), 1950s. Collection MTA Bridges and Tunnels Special Archive

funding; in 1958, it was officially designated I-495, with the intention of uniting the I-495 segment in New Jersey with the I-495 Long Island Expressway. Moses announced that the crosstown route, estimated at that time to cost $88 million, would solve "the worst problem of traffic strangulation in history." Triborough commissioned and circulated spectacular artists' impressions showing skyscrapers, which would be developed using air rights, above the elevated expressway and normal street traffic passing below. Nevertheless, the Thirtieth Street Association, the fur industry, the Murray Hill Home Owners Association, and the Midtown Realty Owners Association were steadfast in their opposition.

The original Lincoln Tunnel, opened in 1937, had just one tube with two lanes. In 1945, however, the

Port Authority opened a second tube, and in 1957 it opened a third. The increasing traffic pressure on Manhattan strengthened the arguments for the expressway. Moses responded by proposing a third tube for the Queens Midtown Tunnel, which had originally been built with twin tubes, two lanes in each direction. He argued vehemently that the MME and expanded Queens Midtown Tunnel would create jobs, relieve traffic congestion, and support industrial and warehousing activity in Manhattan, Queens, and Brooklyn. In December 1965, Triborough took a first tentative step toward building the MME by purchasing a parcel of land at Second Avenue and 29th Street for $1 million. The day after that land acquisition was announced, Mayor Lindsay publicly declared his opposition to the MME and Queens Midtown Tunnel

expansion. The public alarm that the two projects generated strengthened the resolve of both Mayor Lindsay and Governor Rockefeller and led to the definitive cancellation of both projects. Triborough's parcel at Second and 29th eventually became the Vincent F. Albano Jr. Playground, an ironic memorial to the MME that was never built. — RB

CROSS-BRONX EXPRESSWAY

Bronx: from the Alexander Hamilton Bridge and the
  Major Deegan Expressway to the Throgs Neck
  Expressway
1948–63
Figs. P-35–37, C-88

In the New York metropolitan region a vital distinction was established in the 1930s and 1940s between *parkways*, designed to be beautiful and engineered for automobiles, and *expressways*, utilitarian routes engineered for large trucks and open to all forms of traffic. To be sure, a few highways have been mislabeled, like the Gowanus viaduct in Brooklyn, which was named a parkway when it was initiated in 1939 and renamed an expressway in 1957 when it was expanded. For the most part, however, this separation of standards and traffic has been maintained through to the present—wonderful for the motorists who can use the parkways but miserable for those who have to use the expressways.

Many millions of Americans and foreign visitors see little more of the Bronx than what is visible from their vehicle along the seven miles of the Cross-Bronx Expressway (CBE). On good days, the CBE does exactly what its name implies: it carries traffic across the Bronx as swiftly as possible. On bad days, it is heavily congested for most of its length. Either way, it is a utilitarian crossing built to carry trucks and cars. It connects the George Washington Bridge and Trans-Manhattan Expressway with the Major Deegan, Sheridan and Bruckner expressways, the New England Thruway, and the Bronx-Whitestone and Throgs Neck bridges. It is sunken when it crosses ridges and elevated as a viaduct when it crosses valleys, and for most of its length it passes through working-class neighborhoods. While the Grand Concourse and the Bronx parkways (Moshulu, Pelham, Saw Mill, Bronx River, and Hutchinson) were designed to be beautiful, the CBE has no such ambitions. The parkways have extensive tree-planting and often curve to follow contours; the CBE simply cuts through the cityscape.

A SEGMENT IN A SYSTEM

Since the 1920s, most transportation planners have viewed individual highway segments as parts of existing or future regional and national systems. West of the Bruckner Expressway, the CBE is I-95, the East Coast Interstate highway linking Florida to Maine. A vital connection between northern New Jersey, northern Manhattan, and Queens and Long Island, the

CBE is also a designated route for heavy trucks. Not surprisingly, therefore, it is often congested, and bottlenecks are particularly common at the west end. When compared with highways of similar significance in other cities—for example, the Dan Ryan Expressway in Chicago, the Central Expressway in Dallas, Beltway 8 in Houston, and King's Highway 401 in Toronto—the CBE is meager: it has only three lanes in each direction, with no real hard shoulders in many areas and no parallel service roads for most of its length. North America's widest urban expressways have hard shoulders and up to eight lanes in each direction, including express, local, and parallel service roads. Admittedly, most were built after the Cross-Bronx, in advance of urban development and to supposedly higher standards. Although the Cross-Bronx is not beautiful, in the areas west of the Bronx River the design engineers made a genuine effort to keep the axis of demolition relatively narrow and to allow for numerous bridges and decking across part of the cutting that separates East Tremont from Crotona Park North. The result is a highway that seems small, congested, and substandard to most of the motorists who use it, and generates more air pollution than a wider and less crowded highway would.

The origins of the CBE date back to the 1920s, and to decisions in which Robert Moses played no part. In 1921, the Port of New York Authority was established to improve transportation across the Hudson River. In the same year, the Russell Sage Foundation made its first grant in support of a regional plan for New York and its environs. During the planning process, which lasted until the publication of the *Graphic Regional Plan* in 1929, many studies and policy debates focused on the future metropolitan regional transportation system and the location of new bridges and tunnels. The most important decision was for the Port Authority to build the George Washington Bridge across the Hudson at 178th Street in Manhattan. Construction began in 1927, and when the six-lane bridge was opened in 1931 it was by far the longest suspension bridge in the world. It was built to accommodate a second deck, which was added later, opening in 1962 and expanding capacity to 14 lanes.

The *Graphic Regional Plan* proposed a grand regional system of express highways and parkways whose most prominent element was the Metropolitan Loop, a circumferential expressway to carry heavy trucks. Going eastward from the George Washington Bridge, the loop was projected to cross northern Manhattan, the Harlem River, and the Bronx and to connect with a new bridge over the East River (com-

pleted as the Bronx-Whitestone in 1939). Continuing south toward Jamaica Bay, then west to a projected Verrazano-Narrows tunnel, the loop crossed Staten Island to Elizabeth, New Jersey, before going north to meet the George Washington Bridge. The Port Authority and the Regional Plan rejected the 57th Street Hudson River Bridge project promoted by Gustav Lindenthal and the North River Bridge Company, arguing that it would interfere with port activity. Instead, they prioritized the Loop, marginalized the 57th Street idea, and argued that additional crosstown expressways were needed at 125th Street, around 30th Street, and around Canal Street. The Port Authority's George Washington Bridge was like a giant cannon pointed directly at northern Manhattan and the South Bronx, the dense urban area that had to be crossed to reach New England, Queens, and Long Island.

The Regional Plan's vision of the Metropolitan Loop became a template guiding Robert Moses in his roles as the chairman of the Triborough Bridge and Tunnel Authority and as New York City Construction Coordinator. He was not so much planner as executor, an efficient and determined administrator seeking to push highway projects through. Traffic densities increased rapidly as the metropolitan region grew in population and economic activity and as the suburbs sprawled outward. Soon the old bridges across the Harlem River and the existing street systems of northern Manhattan and the Bronx were clogged with cars and trucks.

ROUTING, CONSTRUCTION,
AND THE "ONE MILE" PROTEST

The Regional Plan's Metropolitan Loop axis went directly from the George Washington to the projected Whitestone Bridge, passing just south of Claremont and Crotona parks. By the early 1940s, however, the Triborough Authority was envisaging another link farther east, which became the Throgs Neck Bridge, opened in 1961. Therefore, the route for the newly named Cross-Bronx Expressway was revised to pass north of Claremont and Crotona parks and head directly toward the Throgs Neck, with connections along the way to the Hutchinson River Parkway and the Whitestone Bridge. The route was made final in 1945, and early in 1946 the first eviction notices were served to 540 households in the Unionport neighborhood, northwest of the Whitestone Bridge. Mayor O'Dwyer and Commissioner Moses promised relocation assistance, but many residents and political leaders were skeptical.

Moses started work on the CBE east of the Bronx River, because population density was lower and the topography was much easier, thus greatly reducing the costs of eviction, demolition, excavation, and bridging. Nevertheless, construction of the eastern portions of the CBE proceeded rather slowly in the late 1940s and early 1950s because federal, state, and city funds did not come through as rapidly as anticipated. Each year there were eviction notices, protests, and relocations as the highway advanced westward, but the project received little media attention until evictions and demolitions were imminent in the hillier and more densely populated areas west of the Bronx River.

The greatest controversy, documented by Robert Caro in a three-chapter, 58-page case study in *The Power Broker*, began in December 1952 with the serving of eviction notices to 1,530 households along a "one mile" section of the designated expressway route in the Bathgate, East Tremont, and West Farms areas. Community protest was vigorous, not just because of the number of families involved but because a viable alternative route was apparently available two to three blocks farther south, along the northern edge of Crotona Park. The alternative route, advocated by the Crotona Park Tenants Committee for an Alternative Highway and endorsed by professional engineers, would have required much less demolition and would have displaced only nineteen households. For Moses, however, the protests raised issues of "principle"—first, that every time a project was delayed by hearings and reroutings, funding was also delayed and costs increased; and second, that damaging a park may be worse than reducing the density of a residential neighborhood lacking adequate green space. Eventually, Moses got his way when, in November 1954, the Board of Estimate unanimously ruled in favor of the original routing. The decision emphasized Triborough's power, Moses's inflexibility, and the preeminence of three planning objectives: facilitating regional traffic flows, protecting parks, and reducing residential densities in low-income neighborhoods. Moses overcame strong community pressure and pushed his Bronx highway project through. Within a few years, however, he would be defeated by community opposition to highway projects that he advocated for Greenwich Village, mid-Manhattan, and lower Manhattan.

In their *Joint Study of Arterial Facilities* (1955), the Port and Triborough authorities emphasized the importance of the CBE and recommended the expansion of the George Washington Bridge, which would greatly increase traffic flows between New York and New Jersey and in turn require the construction of the Alexander Hamilton Bridge over the Harlem River to supplement the capacity of the old Washington Bridge. The flow of funds for CBE construction increased dramatically after the Interstate and Defense Highways Act was passed in 1956, providing federal funding to cover 90 percent of approved project costs. Ironically, though, increased federal funding sharply reduced Moses's role in the CBE project, as the New York State Department of Public Works was the principal liaison with the federal government.

Between 1957 and 1963, the most technically complex portions of the CBE were constructed: the eight-lane Alexander Hamilton Bridge, the complicated interchange with the Major Deegan Expressway, the deep east-west cut and tunnel through the ridge that carries the Grand Concourse, and construction or reinforcement of 13 bridges over the CBE to reconnect the old north-south avenues, subways, and els west of Webster Avenue. The CBE axis was also extended eastward from the Hutchinson Parkway to the Throgs Neck Bridge as I-295. Complementing these works, the Port Authority added new approach roads and the second deck to the George Washington Bridge. The CBE was officially opened in 1963, but the interchange with the Major Deegan was not completed until 1964; the interchange with the Bruckner Expressway and Hutchinson River Parkway was finished only in 1974. According to Triborough, the total number of households displaced and relocated for the CBE was 3,866. This figure covered the housing units in the direct path of the expressway, but it failed to account for many households in the adjacent blocks who moved away because their lives were disrupted by the traffic, noise, dust, dirt, and the interruption of vital services caused by the construction.

SISTER PROJECTS: THE TRANS-MANHATTAN, MAJOR DEEGAN, BRUCKNER, AND SHERIDAN EXPRESSWAYS

As part of the George Washington Bridge project, the Port Authority built several approach roads across northern Manhattan. The first was the two-lane 178th Street Tunnel, completed in 1940. A second two-lane tunnel, along the axis of 179th Street, opened in 1951. Both linked the George Washington Bridge to the Harlem River Drive and to the Washington Bridge, which spanned the Harlem River. The current half-mile Trans-Manhattan Expressway was planned in 1955 as a 12-lane connection from the expanded George Washington Bridge to the projected Alexander

Hamilton Bridge and the Major Deegan and the Cross-Bronx expressways; it was completed in 1962. Triborough reported that 1,824 families had to be displaced and relocated for this short segment of highway. Because of high land values in Manhattan, architects and planners in the 1960s were eager to utilize air rights; here they constructed a bus terminal and four high-rise apartment buildings directly above the highway.

The Triborough Authority initiated the Major Deegan in 1935 as a one-mile approach road from the Grand Concourse to the Triborough Bridge, and the six-lane highway opened in 1939. In 1945, Moses proposed to extend the Deegan 7.5 miles north to the New York City line, so that it would serve as a continuation of the New York State Thruway, a grandiose project approved by the state legislature and Governor Herbert Lehman in 1942 to connect New York City, Albany, and Buffalo. Delayed by the war, construction began near Syracuse in 1946. Progress was slow until 1950, when Governor Thomas E. Dewey created the New York State Thruway Authority, modeled on Moses's Triborough Authority, and charged it with implementing the nation's most ambitious toll road. With funding from bonds and the assurance of future toll revenues, the 427-mile highway between the New York City line and Buffalo was built swiftly and relatively cheaply. Bertram Tallamy, a New York State engineer who went on to oversee the construction of the Interstate system, directed the work.

Construction of the Major Deegan extension began in 1950 and was completed in 1956, coinciding with the completion of the Thruway. The route selected required little demolition of housing. From south to north, it runs along the Harlem River and the Hudson Line railroad for most of its length, and then it cuts through an old industrial area in the valley between Kingsbridge Heights and Riverdale, crossing Van Cortlandt Park to meet the Thruway. The main opposition to the project focused on the ecological impact of the park crossing, a problem that Moses claimed to have resolved with a complex three-way land swop, adding land to one side of the park in exchange for cutting across it. A few years later, however, his experience with defenders of Van Cortlandt Park may have strengthened his resolve not to give in to the "one mile" alternative route put forth by proponents of the CBE, who advocated infringing on Crotona Park so as to save neighborhoods and housing stock.

The 7.6-mile Bruckner Expressway connects the Triborough Bridge to the Cross-Bronx Expressway and the Hutchinson Parkway before going northward as I-95, crossing Pelham Parkway, and becoming the

C-88. Cross-Bronx Expressway under construction, looking east, with Jessup Avenue Bridge in the foreground, 1963. Collection MTA Bridges and Tunnels Special Archive.

After the CBE was completed in 1963, the Bronx, and especially the southwestern portions of the borough, entered a period of crisis that continued into the early 1980s. It is easy to make a simple chain of causality: Moses built the CBE, the Bronx "fell," and so Moses caused the fall of the Bronx. The problems with this logic are fairly obvious. Even if Moses had never lived, the CBE would probably have been built, and approximately in its current location. The basic concept and routing of a CBE were developed before Moses became involved, and subsequent state and federal plans and funding endorsed the early visions. Large volumes of heavy traffic were directed across the Bronx because of the location, construction, and expansion of the George Washington Bridge. Resistance to crosstown expressway projects farther south, to building freeways through the Palisades Park, and to directing heavy trucks across the Palisades and Westchester were other factors. The Bronx was "dumped on" to save areas in Manhattan and the suburbs that were more highly valued.

Expressways were built in all of America's major cities. Hundreds of cities across the Northeast and Midwest were in "crisis" in the 1970s. Although New York overall was much less affected than Detroit, Saint Louis, Cleveland, or Buffalo, the South Bronx was ravaged by abandonment, arson, and out-migration. But many of the hardest hit areas, like Melrose, Morrisania, and the notorious Charlotte Street, were quite distant from expressways. Some areas of Brooklyn that never got an expressway, like Brownsville and Flatbush, were just as severely hit. Clearly, something much broader than the negative impact of expressways on neighborhoods was at work: the results of decades of disinvestment and suburbanization, compounded by urban renewal, deindustrialization, racism, fraud, and city, state, and federal policies favoring Manhattan and the suburbs.

To be sure, the construction of the CBE caused disruption along its axis and hardship for many of the households that were displaced, but it was just one of thousands of post–World War II demolition and construction projects that traumatized America's cities. More than any other project in New York City, however, it became the vantage point for motorists to survey the 1970s urban crisis: abandoned and burned-out buildings, mainly in the Bathgate, East Tremont, and West Farms areas. For many Manhattanites and suburbanites who had never ventured out of their cars in the Bronx, this became its enduring image. Even though the level of destruction

New England Thruway. From the Triborough Bridge to the Sheridan Expressway and Bronx River, it is an elevated viaduct, but farther north it runs at grade or slightly below. Its southern portion, constructed between 1957 and 1962, follows the route of the old Bruckner Boulevard, a wide surface street over which the expressway viaduct was constructed. The depressed northern section of the highway from the CBE and Hutchinson Parkway intersection to Pelham Parkway was constructed quickly, between 1959 and 1961. In contrast, construction of the middle section of the Bruckner, including a comprehensive remodeling of the intersection with the CBE and Hutchinson Parkway, was initiated only in 1964 and not completed until 1974.

The Sheridan Expressway, first proposed in *The Graphic Regional Plan* of 1929 as an upgraded Boston Post Road express highway, was included in the *Joint Study of Arterial Facilities* (1955) as a 5.1-mile, south-north link from the Bruckner Viaduct to the New England Thruway. Construction of the 1.2-mile southern portion along the west bank of the Bronx River began in 1958 and was completed in

1962. The projected 4-mile northern portion of the expressway would have required considerable demolition of housing and retail businesses; construction was never initiated. In 1971, Governor Rockefeller formally declared his support for demapping; the project was terminated. The short, southern segment remains, an underused highway connecting the Bruckner to the CBE about one mile west of the primary intersection of the two expressways.

The rapidity of construction of the Trans-Manhattan and Major Deegan expressways indicates their crucial regional significance as well as the coordinated efforts of Triborough, the Port Authority, the Thruway Authority, and the New York State Department of Public Works. In contrast, the delays of the Bruckner and noncompletion of the Sheridan resulted from the fact that Moses and the Triborough Authority often worked alone on these projects, delaying them when funds were scarce in order to push through those with higher priorities. By the 1960s, funds were more abundant, but further delays ensued as Moses's power was gradually cut by Governor Rockefeller and mayors Wagner and Lindsay.

was less than in areas farther south and away from the expressways, the CBE axis became the public face of urban tragedy. And then, to compound the injury, tragedy became farce in the early 1980s when New York City used federal highway funds to decorate the windows of abandoned buildings overlooking the expressway with faux blinds and flowers.

Since the late 1980s, however, the CBE has become a window on the revitalization of the Bronx. Vacant buildings have been rehabilitated and re-occupied, new housing has been built on vacant lots, and new industrial and commercial facilities have been constructed. The CBE still awaits upgrading and beautification, but the surrounding areas have undergone considerable improvement. — RB

PARKWAYS AND EXPRESSWAYS IN BROOKLYN AND QUEENS

Parkways: Grand Central (1933–36); Interborough (1936); Belt (1941); Laurelton (1940); Cross Island (1940); Whitestone (1939); Gowanus (1941)
Expressways: Brooklyn-Queens (1964); Van Wyck (1950–63); Long Island (1955–72); Prospect (1962); Gowanus (1964); Whitestone (1963); Clearview (1963)
Figs. E-21–23, C-89–96

The first generation of parkways built by the Long Island State Parks Commission in the 1920s provided a model for the construction of new highways in New York City in the 1930s, when New Deal agencies made federal funds available for local highway projects for the first time. Indeed, with Robert Moses in charge, it was inevitable that the city would adopt the model of ribbon parks that he had established on Long Island. As president of both the State Council of Parks and the Metropolitan Conference of Parks,

C-89. Robert Moses speaking at opening ceremony of the Interborough Parkway, November 12, 1935

Moses unveiled a comprehensive plan for new parks and parkways at the annual dinner of the Park Association of New York City on February 25, 1930. The proposed highways generally followed the network suggested in the 1929 *Regional Plan of New York and Its Environs*. Moses saw his new roads as part of a regional network, linking the parks and parkways of Long Island with Westchester and New Jersey.

Construction of the Grand Central Parkway began in 1931, and the first section, from Kew Gardens in Queens to the Nassau County line, opened in 1933. Funding came from the state's Temporary Emergency Relief Administration, the first outlay of state money for road construction in the city. As chairman of the Triborough Bridge Authority, Moses ordered modifications to the design of the Triborough—most famously eliminating the granite facing—and reallocated the funds to build an approach through Astoria and along the water to connect with the Grand Central. He considered it inefficient to construct a bridge without adequate approach roads connecting to existing or planned parkways.

Work on the four-lane, undivided—hence extremely dangerous—Interborough Parkway (renamed for Jackie Robinson in 1997) began in 1933. Opened in 1936, the serpentine Interborough ran west from the Grand Central Parkway in Kew Gardens through Forest Park and Cypress Hills Cemetery to East New York in Brooklyn. Modified with the addition of concrete barriers in the late 1980s, it has proven impervious to further safety modifications. Moses wanted to extend the parkway south along Pennsylvania Avenue to link up with the Belt Parkway, but the idea never went further. The marvelous confluence of the Grand Central, the Interborough, Union Turnpike, and Queens Boulevard in Kew Gardens was immediately dubbed the "pretzel." Construction of the Van Wyck Expressway in 1952 added another layer of complexity, and thousands of more cares, to the interchange.

Begun in 1934, the Belt Parkway (originally called Marginal Boulevard, then the Circumferential Parkway) runs along the south shore of Brooklyn from Owl's Head Park in Bay Ridge and meets the Marine Parkway Bridge to the Rockaways, before continuing east to link with the Cross Island Parkway and Southern State via the Laurelton Parkway (until the 1970s each section of the Belt retained its own name). The Cross Island hugs the Nassau County line and meets the Whitestone Bridge. The Whitestone Parkway continues until it meets the Grand Central. These highways had parks, bike paths, and greenery

C-90. Map of arterial roads in the New York Metropolitan area, 1955. Courtesy MTA Bridges and Tunnels Special Archive

along much of the route, following the pattern of the Long Island parkways. With the opening of the elevated Gowanus Parkway in 1941, the Belt was complete, a continuous limited access parkway from the Triborough Bridge to Red Hook. A gap remained, however, from the Triborough to the Gowanus; it was filled by the Brooklyn-Queens Expressway after the war. (For a fuller discussion of the Belt Parkway, see pp. 225–27.)

Originally only four lanes, the Cross Island and Belt were constructed to allow for expansion to six, which was accomplished in the late 1940s. That expansion maintained the original design aesthetic, but in recent decades the demands of safety engineers and lower standards of maintenance have eroded many original elements, including railings, lights, and signage. After the proposed Bushwick and Cross-Brooklyn expressways were cancelled in 1971,

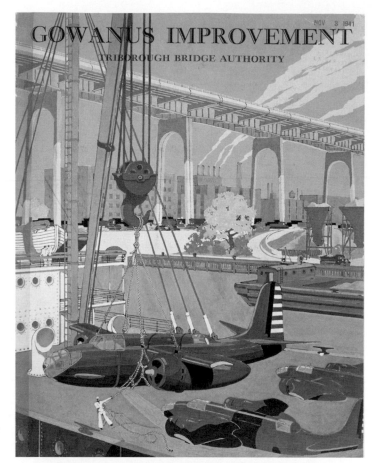

C-91. Brochure cover, Gowanus Improvement, November 1, 1941

C-92. View of arches supporting the Gowanus Parkway, at drawbridge gate, February 9, 1942

Governor Nelson Rockefeller proposed expanding the Belt into an Interstate, but that was neither financially nor politically feasible.

Although roadway construction was impossible during the war years, planning continued, and in 1946 construction on the city-wide arterial highway program was again under way. There would be no parkways, however, only expressways, serving both commercial vehicles and passenger cars. The era of the ribbon parks was over; the new highways were to have neither amenities nor charm. The expanded network included the construction of the Brooklyn-Queens, Van Wyck, Long Island, and Clearview expressways, and the transformation of the Gowanus and Whitestone parkways into expressways. Funding came from a combination of federal, state, and municipal sources.

Bridging the era of parkway construction in the 1930s and the expressways in the postwar years was the Brooklyn-Queens Expressway (BQE), begun in 1937 and completed (if that is the word) in 1964. The Kosciuszko Bridge, rising high above Newtown Creek, had opened before the war, and completing the BQE was clearly key to Moses's postwar plans. The design incorporated innovative triple-decking of the roadways and the public esplanade in Brooklyn Heights, but the BQE also cut through Red Hook and Cobble Hill, demolishing blocks of historic residences, including half of the Riverside, a model tenement complex built in Brooklyn Heights by the philanthropist Alfred Treadway White in 1890. The neighborhoods could have been preserved had the BQE been built closer to the water, an option that was certainly possible.

The first section of the Van Wyck (named for Robert Van Wyck, the first mayor of Greater New York), between New York International Airport/Idlewild (now JFK) and the Belt Parkway, opened in 1950, and it was extended to the Pretzel in 1952. Because of the postwar housing shortage, dozens of homes were relocated from the path of the highway to adjacent blocks rather than being simply bulldozed. Although the Van Wyck crossed both the Long Island Railroad and the IND subway line, extending rail service to the airport along the highway was never a consideration, despite its being both feasible and affordable when the expressway was built. As a result, the Van Wyck is plagued with perpetual traffic. In 2003, the Port Authority's Airtrain began running to JFK, but most travelers must negotiate an inconvenient transfer in Jamaica to the subway or the LIRR.

The New York State Department of Public Works had first recommended construction of an expressway to run the length of Long Island in 1949. Four years later, Moses announced plans for a 70-mile, six-lane road from the Queens Midtown Tunnel to Riverhead. Writing to Governor Thomas E. Dewey, Moses contended that completion of this mixed-use arterial "is the only logical solution to the intolerable congestion resulting from the rapid increase of building subdivisions, extraordinary population growth and large increase in motor vehicle registration." As always, he stressed that it was imperative to begin immediately, for the costs of acquiring land would only rise. In 1954 construction began on the Long Island Expressway (originally called the Horace Harding Expressway, after the banker who had advocated the construction of the road in the 1920s), and the last section to Riverhead opened in 1972. Officially, the western section, from the Queens Midtown Tunnel to Queens Boulevard, was called the Queens Midtown Expressway, and had been planned since 1942. Almost from the day it opened in 1955, the LIE was known as the world's longest parking lot. To relieve congestion, a second deck was added in 1966, running 1.5 miles east from the BQE interchange; in the 1990s, a fourth lane was inserted from the Cross Island Parkway east into Nassau County.

In 1955, Moses chaired the Joint Study of Arterial Facilities, bringing together his Triborough Bridge and Tunnel Authority and the Port of New York Authority, an unlikely and long-overdue collaboration. The result was the last set of plans for arterial expansion prepared under Moses, and the last master plan for highway construction in the city to be even partially implemented. The final report, authored by Moses, recommended the long-sought Narrows crossing and a Throgs Neck bridge together with additional expressways, construction projects that would benefit the Port Authority as much as the TBTA. A Narrows crossing and Staten Island expressway would feed traffic to the Port Authority's underutilized bridges: the Outerbridge, Goethals, and Bayonne. Blessedly, neither the Bushwick Expressway, proposed to cut through Brooklyn from the Williamsburgh Bridge to the Southern State, nor the Cross-Brooklyn Expressway, which would have cut through south Brooklyn from the Gowanus Expressway to the Queens County line, progressed further than dotted lines on a map, for they would have devastated far more neighborhoods than the legendary Cross-Bronx Expressway.

During the late 1930s, Moses justified the rush to complete his projects by linking them with the 1939 World's Fair. He approached the 1964 fair the same way. As the Whitestone Bridge and Parkway were

C-93. Gowanus Parkway superimposed on an aerial view of the neighborhood, ca. 1941

C-94. Construction of below-grade segment of the Brooklyn-Queens Expressway, August 18, 1948

C-95. Brooklyn-Queens Expressway in Brooklyn Heights showing three-level roadway, undated

C-96. Aerial view of the Brooklyn-Queens Expressway, looking north from Metropolitan Avenue toward the Kosciuszko Bridge, September 17, 1950

crucial in 1939, so in the early 1960s were the Verrazano-Narrows and Throgs Neck bridges, the Clearview Expressway, the Van Wyck Extension north from Kew Gardens, and the conversion of the Whitestone Parkway into an expressway.

The Clearview Expressway was intended as a north-south route across Long Island, from the Throgs Neck Bridge (1961) to Idlewild Airport. By 1963, it was open to Hillside Avenue, but there it stopped. Community opposition stalled the project, and in

1971 Governor Rockefeller officially eliminated the lower section. Similarly, the Prospect Expressway was to funnel traffic across Brooklyn from Coney Island to the Brooklyn-Battery Tunnel. When completed in 1962 after nearly nine years of construction, the Prospect ran only from the Gowanus to Ocean Parkway, one of the original parkways designed by Olmsted and Vaux. Eliminating historic Ocean Parkway in favor of a high-speed, limited-access expressway would have been a tragic loss for the city.

The parkways built in the 1930s facilitated suburban development in outer Brooklyn and Queens after the war. The postwar expressways were intended to speed commercial traffic through the boroughs, but they were jammed to capacity almost from the day that they opened. Most of Moses's plans were realized, but the goal—free-flowing traffic—remains elusive. — JAK

BELT PARKWAY

Segments: Shore Parkway, Southern Parkway,
    Laurelton Parkway, and Cross Island Parkway
From Brooklyn (Owls Head Park) to Queens
    (Whitestone Bridge)
Opened 1934–41
Figs. C-97–99

The culmination of Robert Moses's parkways before World War II, the Belt Parkway is a multimodal transportation system of arterial roadways and parkways around the periphery of Brooklyn and Queens.[326] The roadways of the Belt Parkway system, most of which were constructed between 1939 and 1941, extend for 33 miles from southwest Brooklyn, across Queens to the Nassau County line, and north to the Whitestone Bridge. The comprehensive design is of lasting significance because of its regional connectivity and its design qualities. Moses's attentiveness to many scales and levels of detail, shown in this and his other civic amenities, enabled such projects to achieve a highly articulate spatial character, shaped by buildings, structures, landscaping, and site furnishings.

CONCEPTION AND DESIGN

Moses wrote enthusiastically about the design characteristics of the Belt Parkway and how it accommodated "our restless modern life": banked curves; sight distances exceeding 1,000 feet; a landscaped center dividing strip; concrete pavement; 400-candlepower streetlamps; and neon sign lighting.[327] He also described how parkway grade eliminations that "were marveled at twenty years ago are now commonplace" and how his public works benefited from engineering innovations and aesthetic enhancements.[328] "Landscaped parkways, restricted to pleasure vehicles, have proven not only to be the most efficient way of providing for a smooth flow of traffic, but also to be great neighborhood assets . . . especially if provision is made for neighborhood playgrounds and walks along these parkways so that they can be enjoyed by local residents and pedestrians as well as motorists."[329] Moses and his team conceived and built the parkway for 35-mph traffic. He frequently stressed the leisurely, park-oriented aspects of the project, at the same time recognizing that many motorists ignored the speed limit and used the road as a high-speed traffic artery rather than for a scenic pleasure drive.

The Belt Parkway system demonstrated Moses's commitment to richly landscaped hybrid corridors that interwove the movement of cars, bicycles, pedestrians, horses, and boats. Professional teams of collaborators executed his vision. The architect Aymar Embury II supervised the design of the buildings, included roadside gas stations, that shaped the character of the Belt Parkway. Yet it is arguably the relative absence of buildings, in particular along the Shore Parkway segment—made possible in some areas through zoning restrictions and the demolition of ramshackle constructions near the road—that

C-97. Shore Parkway
at Owl's Head Park,
Brooklyn, September 8,
1937

reveals Moses's desire to present drivers with views of the landscape and the adjacent bodies of water, such as Jamaica Bay and the Verrazano Narrows.

Massive vehicular bridges, many executed under the direction of chief engineer Emil Praeger of Madigan-Hyland Engineers, carried the parkway over land and water and allowed for innovative grade-separated interchanges. Forming a recurring design element along the length of the "shoestring park," the

bridges had sleekly angled stone and concrete wing walls and abutments, and expressive radiatorlike curving steelwork. The vehicular bridges were complemented by gracefully shaped steel pedestrian bridges, spanning the parkways and linking the shorefront promenade to parklands on the inland side of the road. The most remarkable bridge was the 27th Avenue Pedestrian Bridge in Brooklyn, a three-hinged arch designed under L. W. Wendell and

financed through the Triborough Bridge Authority, which was featured along other icons of modern architecture and design from the 1930s and 1940s in the Museum of Modern Art's 1944 exhibition and catalog *Built in U.S.A.*

Among the essential components of the landscape design were a tree-lined waterfront promenade, informal plantings along the roadway corridor, and specific pine plantings framing the bridge abutments and views beyond. The segment beginning near Owl's Head Park took advantage of the Olmsted design for Shore Road Park, completed in 1892. New plantings were used to articulate areas around the pedestrian and bicycle paths, which paralleled the vehicular lanes and connected to nearby parks and recreational areas. Picturesque and rustic elements, such as rough timber rails, fences, and light poles similar to those on Moses's earlier parkways were integrated with urbane, streamlined metal fixtures characteristic of modern bridge detailing to create a naturalistic setting along the urban periphery that could be enjoyed by both drivers and pedestrians. These pedestrian areas included carefully integrated plantings, surface treatments, seating, and lighting.

The consulting landscape architect who oversaw these and other aspects of the Belt Parkway was Gilmore Clarke, who built his career through strong political connections to Harold Ickes, Franklin Delano Roosevelt, and Robert Moses. Among the primary parks department staff members who contributed to the Belt Parkway were the longtime assistant to the commissioner George E. Spargo, the landscape architects Francis Cormier and Allyn Jennings, the architect and book designer Clinton Loyd, and the engineer William H. Latham, who later presided over the construction of the Niagara Project hydroelectric works.

FUNDING AND IMPLEMENTATION

The Belt Parkway was largely funded by the Public Works Administration (PWA), started in 1933, and the Works Progress Administration (WPA), established in 1935. The parkway's final stretch, completed in 1941 along Sheepshead Bay, was financed by the Triborough Bridge Authority under Moses's direction. His effective strategies to finance infrastructure projects like the Belt Parkway allowed New York City to obtain a disproportionately large portion of the total national funding through WPA and PWA sources from 1933 through 1940.[330] He used $12 million from the PWA in order to build the initial phases from 1938 to 1940. These funds were dispersed in

C-98. Cloverleaf on the Shore Parkway, ca. 1941. Photograph by Fairchild Aerial Surveys, Inc.

C-99. Pedestrian bridge over the Shore Parkway, December 14, 1940

. . . Study the maps of the Belt System and the neglected and reclaimed territory, which it will open up. Anticipate, if you can, its effect on travel, recreation, residence, transportation and industry. But first see it yourself because the average New Yorker knows little of the community outside of the orbit of his daily travels. Then show it to visitors. . . . Just let the road unfurl and the town speak for itself.[335]

At the opening ceremony, Mayor Fiorello La Guardia applauded Moses's effectiveness: the parkway "is another one of those obviously needed public improvements indicated on the city plans for more than a generation and now translated into reality." Among its benefits was creation of a spectacular urban landscape: "There is no finer or more scenic waterfront in the city than the view across the Narrows and over the Lower Bay. It is unsurpassed on the Atlantic Seaboard."[336]

Aerial photographs taken within the first few years of completion indicate that the Belt Parkway was already overloaded with commuters. By 1944, plans were in place for the addition of a third lane in each direction, as anticipated in the original design, but World War II interrupted construction. Even as the parkway evolved, Moses continued to insist on design quality. Correspondence between the designers and Moses following the construction demonstrates how this landscape and urban design project was actively managed—and changed—by a team that included many of the original designers.[337]

Moses regarded the Belt Parkway as the most innovative design of his career to that point and the linchpin of the well-connected transportation system that he had built over the previous two decades. In total, the entire Belt Parkway system in Brooklyn and Queens included 65 bridges and overpasses, connecting 26 park areas totaling 3,550 acres, many of which were upgraded as part of the parkway construction. Furthermore, the technical aspects of traffic engineering and lighting made this project one that Moses viewed as the "last word in parkway construction, planning and design," a standard that would be imitated widely by turnpike and highway designs after World War II.[338] At the dedication of the Belt Parkway on June 29, 1940, the *New York Times* hailed it as the greatest municipal venture of its type ever attempted in an urban setting. The multimodal parkway exemplifies Moses's multiple pursuits of transportation and recreation, of modern engineering and picturesque rusticism, and of careful aesthetic detailing and systematic efficiency at a regional scale. — DMF

dozens of contracts for various trades, thus achieving the WPA's stated aim of encouraging economic viability through the channels of private enterprise. The project was among those frequently cited by the federal government as a positive result of its interventions: "PWA funds are now building the great East River Drive and Belt Parkways, almost 40 miles of new-type highway destined to speed traffic around congested centers. . . . It is a scene in which PWA could be allegorically depicted as striking the traffic chains, which bound the city."[331]

Moses's understanding of federal funding strategies hastened the completion of the Belt Parkway. Its origins, however, dated from several years earlier. On February 25, 1930, at the annual dinner of the Park Association, with hundreds of civic leaders in attendance, Moses unveiled a giant map of new roadways, including a diagrammatic route of a "marginal boulevard" around the coast of Brooklyn and along the eastern border of Queens—the route that became the Belt Parkway. His master plan synthesizing roadway design with park proposals was significant not only for its audacious expense and scope but also for its regional approach to planning. The parkway, Moses argued, had the benefit of "opening territories which have been dead, relieving the pressure on other parts of the city, connecting the city with the suburbs and the rest of the country, raising tax values, encouraging building and spreading our population."[332]

As construction continued, Moses's penchant for "simple Anglo-Saxon words used and interpreted in the same way by everyone" led him to abandon "circumferential" and "marginal" in favor of "Belt Parkway."[333] He opposed naming it after a person, choosing to emphasize its geographic and diagrammatic role as a connection between and to other parkways. The Shore Parkway, Southern Parkway, and Cross Island Parkway, segments of the Belt system, were named in the same spirit.[334] The whole project was completed in nineteen months, a very short time to build a $28-million project.

Moses's savvy encompassed publicity as well as design, financing, and logistics. The brochure published for the opening on July 1, 1940, championed the heroic effort and perfect sense of timing required to build the parkway and bring about its transformative effects.

It takes more than a good idea to make a great public improvement. The fact is that such things happen when there are leaders available ready and eager to take advantage of the logic of events. . . . Efforts a few months too early are wasted. Six months of delay may be fatal. It sounds foolish, but so it is.

Many people—officials of national and state as well as municipal governments, engineers, contractors, workers, citizens in groups and individually, and of course the representation of the press have contributed to this particular end.

RICHMOND PARKWAY AND WILLOWBROOK PARKWAY

Staten Island
1962–64
Fig. C-100

In the decades after World War II, Robert Moses sought to build interconnected highways throughout Staten Island, but local opposition in the 1960s prevented him from completing his program. From the start, his plans resembled the proposals offered in the 1929 *Regional Plan of New York and Its Environs*, an ambitious and farsighted scheme intended both to open up the borough for residential and recreational development and to integrate the island into the regional highway network.

The key was a bridge across the Narrows and an expressway across the island to the Goethals Bridge. The Regional Plan Association also called for one parkway to run north-south through what is now the Greenbelt, connecting the Outerbridge Crossing and the Narrows crossing, and another from the Goethals Bridge to a proposed park at Great Kills. According to the plan, "a considerable part of this route passes through park lands acquired in 1928 as well as through additional proposed parks. . . . Although there will be some difficulties of a topographic nature . . . they are not insurmountable and a parkway thus located would constitute one of the largest assets possible in the development of Staten Island."[339]

From the planners' perspective in the 1920s, the Greenbelt was merely empty space, suitable for development and parkland. The route was chosen "because it required few relocations of residents and because the costs of acquiring the site would be low. The fact that the ravine and forest . . . are a remarkable natural area within the larger Staten Island Greenbelt was not—in Moses' time—much of a concern."[340]

The Staten Island parkways had been part of Moses's master plan since 1930, although no work was done until the 1960s when construction of the Verrazano-Narrows Bridge and the Staten Island Expressway was under way. Richmond Parkway was to run from the Outerbridge Crossing through the Greenbelt to meet the expressway at an interchange at Sunnyside; only the 4.5-mile lower section (renamed the Korean War Veterans Parkway in 1997) below Arthur Kill Road was completed, as was the unused interchange with the expressway. Willowbrook Parkway was to have run from the Bayonne Bridge to Great Kills, traversing Latourette Park, with interchanges at the expressway and Richmond Parkway; between 1962 and 1964, the 2.6-mile section

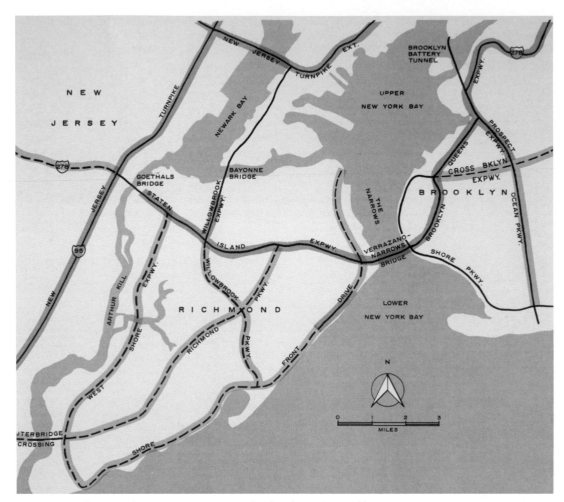

C-100. Map of proposed expressways in Staten Island and western Brooklyn, ca. 1965

between the bridge and the expressway was completed (renamed the Dr. Martin Luther King Jr. Expressway in 1988), but there construction stopped.

Mayor John Lindsay had initially endorsed the parkways, but opposition by supporters of the Greenbelt, the Staten Island Citizens Planning Committee, and his own planning advisers convinced him to put the parkways on hold in 1966. In 1967, with construction stopped, Moses replied to his critics, "We are not despoilers of beauty, as alleged by the so-called Staten Island Citizens Planning Committee. The Richmond Parkway follows closely the natural terrain. Great care has been taken to preserve existing trees and shrubbery. . . . We are firm in our position that the original Richmond Parkway route is the only suitable and practical one between the Verrazano Narrows Bridge and the Outerbridge Crossing. All alternative routes have been examined by our consulting engineers and have been found to be excessively costly. They do not meet traffic patterns, and do not serve the anticipated development of Staten Island. . . . As to the charge that the Richmond Parkway will destroy the green areas of Staten Island, we have shown that nature paths, bicycle paths and bridle paths can be better provided and more practically constructed as part of the parkway within the present right-of-way."[341]

Opponents proposed and Mayor Lindsay accepted an alternative route for Richmond Parkway that would have run to the west of the Greenbelt, but Governor Nelson Rockefeller adamantly rejected that option, insisting on a route that would link up with the completed Sunnyside interchange. The state's intransigence, together with the environmentalists' persistence in advocating for the Greenbelt, ultimately doomed the roads to remain unconnected fragments. — JAK

TRIBOROUGH BRIDGE

From Astoria, Queens, to Wards Island over the East
River (suspension span); from East 125th Street,
Manhattan, to Randall's Island over the Harlem
River (vertical-lift span); from the Bronx to Randall's
Island over the Bronx Kills (truss span)
Opened July 11, 1936
Figs. C-101–103

The Triborough Bridge, connecting the boroughs of
Manhattan, the Bronx, and Queens, opened on July
11, 1936, as the first bridge completed by Robert
Moses and the Triborough Bridge Authority. More than
just a bridge, the 3.5-mile structure was built to link
the boroughs with three major spans and nearly two
miles of viaduct over Randall's and Wards islands.

Unlike the four older East River bridges, all carrying
rail at the time, the Triborough was designed to carry
only vehicular traffic. Instead of feeding traffic into
local streets, it was built with 14 miles of approach
roads connecting it directly to the new system of traffic arteries then being built in New York City and on
Long Island. It was a bridge for the automobile age.

C-101. Triborough Bridge, looking north, ca. 1936. Manhattan (left), the Bronx (top),
Queens (right), Wards Island and Randall's Island (center), and Astoria Pool (right).
Photograph by McLaughllin Aerial Surveys. Collection MTA Bridges and Tunnels Special Archive

The Triborough was originally a municipal project to be financed by city bonds or corporate stock. Designed by the New York City Department of Plant and Structures under the direction of its chief engineer Edward A. Byrne, its layout would have been essentially the same as the current structure, and it was to carry only vehicular traffic. Stylistically, it would have resembled the Brooklyn and Manhattan bridges, even though they had been designed to carry rail and horse-drawn vehicles. The arches supporting its viaducts, and its anchorages and piers would have been clad in ornate granite. The steel suspension span towers, each with a pair of gothic arches soaring over the roadway, would have supported four cables instead of the two as built; the additional cables were for a future second deck that would have doubled the capacity of the eight-lane span. There was, however, no provision for adequate approach roads.

Mayor James J. Walker used a silver-plated pick and spade to break ground for the bridge at a ceremony in Astoria Park on October 25, 1929, the day after the Black Thursday stock market crash that ushered the Great Depression. Three years later, the city was broke and all that had been built were a few piers and the suspension span's unclad anchorages on Wards Island and in Astoria Park.

The project was revived in 1932 after the federal government created the Reconstruction Finance Corporation to fund the construction of self-liquidating public works. The bridge topped the list of projects in New York, chosen by the State Emergency Public Works Commission, chaired by Robert Moses. Governor Herbert Lehman signed an act on April 7, 1933, that established the Triborough Bridge Authority, charged with completing the bridge. The act also provided for the construction of adequate approaches and connections, absent from the original plan. A separate bill was passed declaring the intent of the state and city to vacate and demolish the institutions for the sick and poor on Wards and Randall's islands, in order to make way for parkland.

The RFC's role in the project was subsequently transferred to the Public Works Administration, which financed the bridge with a $35-million loan and a $9.2-million grant. The TBA was authorized to issue bonds, secured by tolls, to repay the loan. The city paid the rest of the $60.3-million cost, including $5.4 million appropriated before the creation of the TBA and $10.7 million for land to build the expanded highway approaches. The new authority began work, with Byrne continuing as chief engineer.

The three TBA commissioners were appointees of the mayor. When Fiorello La Guardia took office on

C-102. Triborough Bridge, vertical-lift span, Manhattan approach, July 1, 1965

January 1, 1934, he restructured the authority and, on February 3, appointed Moses secretary and chief executive officer. Finding Byrne unwilling to modify his design, Moses arranged with the Port of New York Authority (now the Port Authority of New York and New Jersey) to "borrow" Othmar Hermann Ammann on a half-time schedule to replace him. Ammann, already famous as the chief engineer for the George Washington Bridge, determined that 16 lanes would never be required on the Triborough's suspension span and that the granite cladding would be too ornate and costly. The suspension span towers, redesigned to support only two cables, were streamlined with minimal art deco detailing. Instead of the previously specified granite-covered arches, eight-sided concrete columns would support the viaducts. The anchorage enclosures would also be concrete, ornamented only with bold diagonal and vertical lines reflecting the bridge's structural elements. Eliminating the ornate stonework and two of the four cables reduced the cost, freeing funds for the bridge approaches. Ammann's design team included Allston Dana as engineer of design and Aymar Embury II as architect.

The crossing between Wards Island and Astoria, Queens, is a suspension span. This type of structure

allows for a deck high enough for ships to pass under and long enough between its towers to span a body of water as wide as the East River. The bridge's Manhattan arm, over the narrower Harlem River between Randall's Island and 125th Street, is a six-lane, vertical-lift span, which goes up and down like an elevator to allow ships to pass underneath. The world's largest lift span in 1936, its low roadway did not require the lengthy approach ramps needed to reach the deck of a suspension span. The six-lane Bronx arm has a 360-foot-long truss span that could have been converted to a lift span if the Bronx Kills were to become navigable; instead, the Kills has been narrowed with landfill and the span has remained fixed. The consulting engineers for the Manhattan and Bronx spans were Waddell & Hardesty, who specialized in movable bridge design.

Viaducts connect the three spans to an enormous junction on Randall's Island, where traffic moving between the three boroughs and to Randall's Island Park is sorted out. Two toll plazas, originally with a total of only 11 toll booths, are located on the junction. When the junction was expanded in 1969 to handle increased traffic, the number of toll booths more than tripled. A separate low-level bridge,

C-103. Triborough Bridge, suspension span, with Manhattan in distance, undated

demolished in the 1990s, carried traffic between Wards and Randall's Island before they were joined with landfill. In 1951, TBTA built a vertical-lift bridge for pedestrians between East 103rd Street and Wards Island. Consulting engineers for that bridge, which was turned over to the city upon completion, were O. H. Ammann, and Waddell & Hardesty.

The TBA Administration Building, now called the Robert Moses Building, was built on Randall's Island adjacent to the toll plaza closest to Manhattan. The formal symmetry and minimal ornamentation recalling classical motifs on the small building's limestone exterior are typical of Aymar Embury's style. The center of operations for the bridge, it became a major base of operations for the authority as the number of its facilities increased. For more than four decades, Moses spent more time in this building than at any of his other offices. Later additions extended the north end of the building, including a large room added in 1966 for the display of models.

The Triborough Bridge and its approaches became major components of the city's arterial road system. For the original Bronx approach, Whitlock Avenue was rebuilt as a boulevard and Eastern Boulevard was repaved all the way to Pelham Bay Park and the Westchester parkway system. Today, the Bruckner Expressway, built in stages in the 1960s, follows this route and is part of Interstates 278 and 95 leading to the New England Thruway.

The Queens approach was built by widening Astoria Boulevard and extending the Grand Central Parkway. The parkway connected directly to the Long Island parkway system, but had terminated near Flushing Bay. When extended, it curved along the west side of Flushing Bay, near the edge of what is now LaGuardia Airport, and then converged with the widened Astoria Boulevard at 75th Street to become an eight-lane depressed highway leading directly to the bridge a mile away. As the first direct connection to the Queens parkway system from Manhattan and the Bronx, the bridge became an important factor in the suburbanization of Long Island.

For the Manhattan approach, the TBA built the section of the East River Drive from 92nd Street to the 122nd Street ramps, which connect to the bridge at 125th Street. The city had made the decision to locate the Manhattan arm of the bridge at that location nearly two decades earlier. As Manhattan's only thoroughfare running river to river north of Central Park, 125th Street was the commercial heart of Harlem. As traffic increased, its property owners and business leaders had been among the first to press for a vehicular bridge to connect it to Queens and the Bronx. In response, Byrne had prepared a preliminary proposal for the bridge in 1916, which located its Manhattan arm at that location. The TBA inherited this location, although 103rd Street would have been much closer to Manhattan's main business districts and the Queens arm of the bridge. In *Public Works: A Dangerous Trade*, Moses wrote, "Hearst real estate interests, that had procured the 125th Street arm in the first place would probably have stymied the entire project if we had insisted on 103rd Street. We reluctantly accepted 125th Street, on the theory that a misplaced arm is better than no bridge at all." To save travel time, however, the TBA built the East River Drive approach, which became a segment of what is now the Franklin D. Roosevelt Drive, completed by the city in 1942.

Throughout his career, Moses combined parks with roads and bridges, beginning with the parkways he built on Long Island in the 1920s and 1930s that led to Jones Beach and other state parks. In New York City, he was appointed parks commissioner less than two weeks before his appointment to the TBA. As part of the Triborough Bridge project, TBA, the parks department, and relief agencies transformed Randall's Island and parts of Wards Island into parkland. These new recreation areas, reachable by the bridge's walkways or by car, included expansive lawns, athletic fields, and a stadium (replaced by the new Icahn Stadium in 2005). The same agencies added a play center with an enormous swimming pool in Astoria Park. Playgrounds and small sitting parks were added along the Queens and Manhattan approaches, and the East River Drive was constructed with a waterfront promenade.

By the time the bridge opened, Robert Moses had been appointed TBA chairman. The bridge's immediate success provided the framework for the TBA to evolve into the Triborough Bridge and Tunnel Authority, which built every major vehicular bridge and tunnel in the city after 1936. Since 1994, the TBTA has been known as MTA Bridges and Tunnels. After seven decades of operation, the Triborough is now undergoing a multiyear renewal to redeck the entire roadway, add a ramp to Wards Island to accommodate renewed recreational development there, reconfigure its toll plazas, and make other improvements. In 1937, the first full year of operation, 11,043,000 vehicles crossed the bridge. By 2005, the number had climbed to 62,841,000. — LR

BRONX-WHITESTONE BRIDGE

From Queens (Whitestone) to the Bronx (Old Ferry
    Point), across the East River
Opened April 29, 1939
Figs. C-104, 106

The Bronx-Whitestone Bridge opened one day before
the opening of the 1939 New York World's Fair in
Flushing Meadow Park. Billed as the fair's Gateway
from the North, the new East River suspension
bridge linked the new parkway systems in the Bronx
and Queens and allowed traffic between Long Island
and the mainland to bypass more congested parts
of the city.

The bridge was the second built by the Triborough
Bridge Authority. In 1937, the state legislature
amended the Triborough Act to authorize the
authority to refinance the Triborough Bridge, purchase the outstanding bonds from the Reconstruction
Finance Corporation at a profit to that corporation,
and sell a larger bond issue to the general public
through ordinary private banking channels. Of the
proceeds, $18 million was designated for construction
of the new bridge. Less than a year after the
Triborough opened, construction on the Bronx-
Whitestone was proceeding at a rapid pace. The sinking of the tower pier caissons and the preparation of
the pedestals for the towers took just five months,
and the 377-foot-high towers were each erected in 18
days. The entire bridge was built in only 23 months.

The bridge's 2,300-foot main suspension span was
then the world's fourth longest. Although not a record-
breaker, its sleek, unadorned design captured the
nation's attention. The suspended roadway was stiffened by 11-foot-high ribbons of solid plate girders at
its edges instead of the much taller system of zigzagging trusses used on most bridges. From a distance,
the stiffening girders gave the roadway the appearance of a clean, gently arched line over the East
River; from the roadway, this type of construction
allowed for an unobstructed view of the river and
surrounding landscape. The slender steel towers
supporting the deck had no trusses or diagonal cross
bracing to detract from the sleek profile. In the
brochure issued on its opening day, Moses called the
Bronx-Whitestone "architecturally the finest suspension bridge of them all, without comparison in
cleanliness and simplicity of design, in lightness
and the absence of pretentious ornamentation."

Having the bridge completed in time for the
World's Fair dovetailed with Moses's broad plans. Two
years later he wrote: "From the beginning it has been
our conception that the function of the Authority is

C-104. Bronx-Whitestone Bridge
after the installation of diagonal
stay wires and before the installation of stiffening trusses,
ca. 1940

not merely to build and maintain certain water crossings within the city, but to help solve metropolitan
arterial and recreational problems." Bringing the fair
to Queens enabled the Department of Parks to transform the infamous Corona Ash Dump into what is now
the 1,255-acre Flushing Meadows–Corona Park. In
The Great Gatsby (1925), F. Scott Fitzgerald described
the dump as the "valley of ashes" that Jay Gatsby
drove through to reach his estate on the north shore of
Long Island. A decade later, Moses was building the
Grand Central Parkway along the dump's western
edge. Covering the swampy dump with landfill and
constructing the fairgrounds provided the infrastructure for the park after the fair was over, with the
additional benefit of improving the scenery around
the Grand Central Parkway. At the same time, the
Whitestone Parkway was built as a direct link
between the bridge, the fairgrounds, and the Grand
Central Parkway. Since that time, the Whitestone
Parkway has become part of the Interstate system.

Moses also built a park at each end of the bridge,
in sites that first functioned as construction and stag-

ing areas for the bridge and were then developed for
recreation. The parks department acquired the land
for Francis Lewis Park on the Queens side in 1937.
Dedicated a year after the bridge opened, the 17-acre
waterfront park has winding paths that lead to over-
looks and a beach with views of the bridge and East
River. That same year, the city purchased 171 acres
of land at Old Ferry Point for the Bronx end of the
bridge. Since that time, land acquisitions and landfill
have increased the size of Ferry Point Park to 413
acres. Through the 1940s, Moses intended to build a
beach there, but his plan was never carried out.
Currently, the parks department is working with a
developer on a planned golf course in the park to the
east of the bridge. The section of the park to the west
of the bridge has ball fields, lawns, picnic areas, and
a parking lot.

When the Bronx-Whitestone was under construction, wind engineering was new and the limits of
streamlining were still being explored. Although the
bridge proved safe, the public became concerned
when the four-month-old Tacoma-Narrows Bridge over

Puget Sound in Washington State collapsed on November 7, 1940. The wild undulations of that bridge's roadway earned it the nickname Galloping Gertie, and the film footage of its collapse is still familiar to millions. The Tacoma-Narrows was streamlined beyond the safe limit: its towers were 18 percent higher than those of the Bronx-Whitestone, its 2,800-foot main span was 22 percent longer, and its two-lane roadway little more than half as wide, stiffened with plate girders only 8-feet high. After its collapse, Othmar Ammann participated in the investigation that led to the creation of new guidelines for the aerodynamics of suspension bridge design.

Although all suspension bridges sway and undulate to some degree, the movements on the Bronx-Whitestone sometimes reached the point of discomfort for people walking or driving across it. Ammann determined that it was safe, but, in response to public fears after the Tacoma collapse, four diagonal stay cables were installed between each of the towers and the roadway in 1940. In 1945, 14-foot-high stiffening trusses were attached to the tops of the plate girders at the deck's edges for added stability, though at the cost of impairing both the bridge's streamlined appearance and the views of the East River and Long Island Sound from the roadway. At the same time, the roadway was widened from four to six lanes, requiring the removal of the walkways on each side of the roadway.

The modifications made in 1945 added a great deal of weight to the suspended roadway. A major rehabilitation to lighten the load of the roadway and improve its aerodynamic stability has recently been completed. In 2003, the steel trusses were replaced with more effective and much lighter fiber-reinforced polymer aerodynamic fairings. Attached to the sides of the plate girders, the fairings have a triangular shape that slices the wind and prevents it from hitting the deck head-on. Unlike the trusses, the fairings are barely noticeable on the bridge; thus its streamlined appearance and the unobstructed views from the roadway are restored. In 2006, the roadway load was further lightened by the replacement of the concrete deck with a much lighter steel deck, overlaid with a bonded-aggregate driving surface.

Othmar Ammann was the chief engineer, Allston Dana was the engineer of design, and Aymar Embury II was the architect. The consulting engineers were Waddell & Hardesty; Moran, Proctor & Freeman; Madigan-Hyland; Leon Moisseiff; and Charles P. Berkey. In 1940, its first full year of operation, 6,318,000 vehicles crossed the Bronx-Whitestone, in 2005, the number reached 41,198,000. — LR

THROGS NECK BRIDGE

From the Bronx (Locust Point) to Queens (Little Bay near Cryders Point), across the East River
Opened January 11, 1961
Figs. C-105–106

The Throgs Neck Bridge crosses the East River where it meets Long Island Sound. The name Throgs Neck comes from the name of John Throckmorton, who settled in the Bronx in 1643.

The *Joint Study of Arterial Facilities New York-New Jersey Metropolitan Area*, published by the Port of New York Authority and Triborough Bridge and Tunnel Authority in January 1955, had recommended a bridge to relieve traffic on the Triborough and Bronx-Whitestone bridges and to be part of a northerly bypass route around Manhattan. The bypass also required the addition of the second deck of the George Washington Bridge and the construction of the Trans-Manhattan and Cross-Bronx expressways between the Throgs Neck and the George Washington bridges. Construction of the Clearview Expressway, which was to connect to the Long Island Expressway, the Grand Central Parkway, and, farther south, the

planned Nassau Expressway, was recommended as the Queens approach to the bridge.

As TBTA chairman, Robert Moses was charged with the funding and building of the bridge; as New York City Construction Coordinator, he oversaw the construction of all federally funded projects in the city, including the Interstate highways that would be the bridge's approaches. Upon passage of the Federal-Aid Highway Act of 1956, federal and state funds were made available for the expressway approaches, but controversies over the route of the Clearview Expressway, not resolved until September 1957, delayed groundbreaking for the bridge until October 22 of that year. Its entire $92,503,000 construction cost was paid by the TBTA.

The Throgs Neck opened on January 11, 1961, as the first major bridge in the city built as a link in the National System of Interstate and Defense Highways. Two years later, most of the bypass route was in place: the Cross-Bronx and Trans-Manhattan expressways and the second deck of the George Washington Bridge had opened and the Clearview Expressway, with connections to the Long Island Expressway and Grand Central Parkway, was completed to Hillside

C-105. Throgs Neck Bridge from the Bronx showing the suspension span under construction, June 28, 1960.
Photograph by Mal Gurian Associates. Collection MTA Bridges and Tunnels Special Archive

C-106. Bronx-Whitestone (foreground) and Throgs Neck bridges, 1964.
Photograph by Skyviews. Collection MTA Bridges andTunnels Special Archive

Avenue, just south of the Grand Central Parkway. The expressway still dead-ends at that location, the result of state and city priorities shifting away from building new roads through populated areas in the late 1960s. For the same reason, only about 4 miles of the Nassau Expressway were built, terminating about 9.5 miles away from the Clearview.

At first, the bridge greatly reduced traffic on the Bronx-Whitestone. In 1962, its first full year of operation, 23,065,000 toll vehicles crossed the Throgs Neck and 17,159,000 crossed the Bronx-Whitestone, about half its 1960 count of 33,196,000. By 1983,

however, annual traffic on each bridge exceeded 34,000,000 vehicles. In 2005, 41,199,000 vehicles crossed the Throgs Neck and 41,198,000 crossed the Bronx-Whitestone.

The Throgs Neck consists of a steel suspension bridge with a center span of 1,800 feet and two side spans of 555 feet each; a 4,100-foot viaduct connects with the Clearview Expressway in Queens, and a 6,400-foot viaduct over the Throgs Neck peninsula links to the Cross-Bronx and Throgs Neck expressways. The suspension span of the Throgs Neck, which is often referred to as the sister bridge of the Bronx-

Whitestone, appears to be a shorter and wider version of the older bridge.

Ammann & Whitney, the engineering firm that O. H. Ammann established in partnership with the engineer Charles S. Whitney in 1946, were the consulting engineers for the suspension span. E. Lionel Pavlo was the consulting engineer for the viaduct approaches, and Emil H. Praeger was consulting engineer for the foundations. Consulting architects were Aymar Embury II, A. Gordon Lorimer, John Peterkin, and Theodore J. Young. — LR

MARINE PARKWAY GIL HODGES MEMORIAL BRIDGE

Originally Marine Parkway Bridge
From Brooklyn (Flatbush Avenue) to Queens
   (Rockaway Peninsula), over Rockaway Inlet
Opened July 3, 1937
Fig. P-27

The four-lane Marine Parkway Bridge has a 540-foot-long vertical lift span, which in 1937 was the world's longest for vehicular traffic; it still ranks among the longest of its type. The construction of the bridge was coordinated with the park department's expansion of Jacob Riis Park near the bridge's south end on Rockaway Peninsula. The tapering, curled tops of the bridge's towers add a playful note to its design. Madigan-Hyland were the engineers of the entire parkway project and Emil H. Praeger was chief engineer. Robinson & Steinman were the consulting engineers for the approach spans, and Waddell & Hardesty were consulting engineers for the lift span. The chief of architectural design was Clinton F. Loyd and the architect was Aymar Embury II. The bridge was renamed in 1978 to honor the Brooklyn Dodgers' first baseman and later the manager of the New York Mets.

Robert Moses held the title Sole Member of the Marine Parkway Authority, which was established in 1934 to build the bridge. The authority also built the Marine Parkway between the bridge and Riis Park's 70-acre parking field, then the largest in the world. More than just a route to the beach, the bridge and parkway would be a spur of the planned Belt System, providing a new express route for people from the rest of the city to reach Marine Park, Jacob Riis Park, and the Rockaway Peninsula.

Unlike many parkway facilities, the bridge has always accommodated trucks and busses. Before it opened, most people reached Riis Park and the western part of Rockaway Peninsula by municipal ferry service from the end of Flatbush Avenue or by using Cross Bay Boulevard, 5.5 miles to the east. Ferry service ended when the bridge opened, but public transportation service became available. The city made an agreement with Green Bus Lines to extend an existing route from the Flatbush-Nostrand Avenue subway station, allowing people to get to the beach for a dime. There was also a bus connection from the Long Island Railroad Rockaway Beach Line until 1950, when the rail trestle across Jamaica Bay burned. The city purchased the railroad's right-of-way in 1953 and three years later reconstructed the tracks as an extension of the A subway line, with bus connections to the beach.

The Marine Parkway Authority financed the bridge, parkway, and parking field with a $6-million bond issue. After a series of consolidations, the authority became part of the Triborough Bridge Authority in 1940. The bridge remains a facility of MTA Bridges and Tunnels. The parking field was an authority facility until 1985, when it was turned over to the National Park Service and incorporated into the Gateway National Recreation Area.

The annual number of vehicle crossings in 1938 was 1,889,000; in 2005, the number had more than quadrupled to 7,673,000. In 2002, after more than 60 years of operation, the entire deck of the bridge was replaced. At the same time, a new sidewalk was cantilevered out from the roadway, which allowed for an additional foot in each traffic lane and space for a centerline median. — LR

BROOKLYN-BATTERY TUNNEL AND PROPOSED BRIDGE

From Brooklyn (Red Hook) to lower Manhattan
Opened May 15, 1950
Figs. C-107–110

The Brooklyn-Battery Tunnel, connecting lower Manhattan to Brooklyn, was the second project of the New York City Tunnel Authority, created by the state in 1936. Public Works Administration funding was quickly obtained for the authority's first project, the Queens Midtown Tunnel, and construction began that year. Financing the Brooklyn-Battery Tunnel was more difficult because the cost and length of time required to build exceeded PWA limits at that time. At 9,117 feet, 40 percent longer than the Queens Midtown, it would be the longest continuous underwater vehicular tunnel in the nation. Four years later, ground was broken after the Reconstruction Finance Corporation made a $57-million loan available for plaza-to-plaza construction. The city purchased the real estate for the approaches, and the Triborough Bridge Authority agreed to construct connections to the new Belt System in Brooklyn and to the highway system then being built around the edges of Manhattan.

During the tunnel authority's struggle to obtain financing, Robert Moses proposed that a bridge be built instead. He argued that it could be achieved at half the cost and construction time, be less expensive to maintain, and carry six lanes of traffic instead of four. O. H. Ammann designed the proposed bridge, which would have had two suspension spans in tandem, meeting in the harbor near Governors Island. On April 4, 1939, the state passed legislation authorizing construction, but the cost-saving plan was controversial. For the roadway to be high enough for ships to pass under, Battery Park and adjacent streets would have been overrun with elevated approach ramps, and historic Castle Clinton would likely have been demolished. The bridge would also have required an enormous anchorage near the end of State Street and a soaring tower near where the Battery Maritime Building now stands. In all, the bridge would have created a barrier around Manhattan's southern tip and blocked the celebrated view of its skyline from the harbor.

The most famous opponent was First Lady Eleanor Roosevelt, who expressed her concerns in her column "My Day" in the *New York World-Telegram* the day after the legislation was passed. Secretary of War Harry H. Woodring ended the controversy on July 17 by declaring that the construction of a bridge seaward of the Brooklyn Navy Yard would be a war hazard. Noting that the Brooklyn and Manhattan bridges were

C-107. Photocollage of New York Harbor with proposed Brooklyn-Battery Bridge, 1939. Photograph by Fairchild Aerial Surveys, Inc., with alterations. Courtesy MTA Bridges and Tunnels Special Archive

C-108. Elevation and plan of proposed Brooklyn-Battery Bridge, 1939. Courtesy MTA Bridges and Tunnels Special Archive

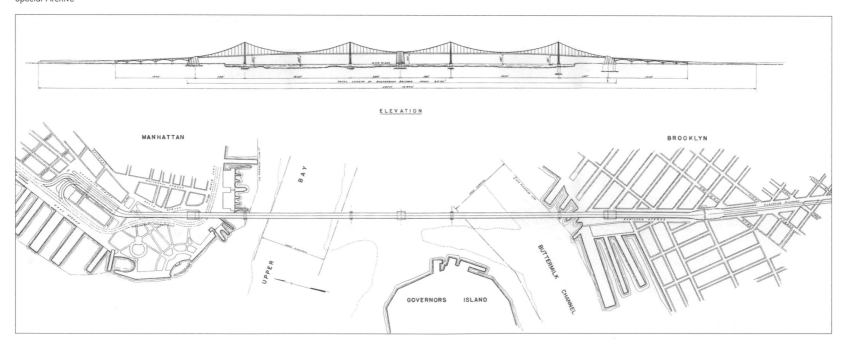

both seaward of the navy yard, he added that they should be replaced by tunnels when they reached the end of their safe life. President Franklin D. Roosevelt, who attended the groundbreaking ceremony for the tunnel on October 28, 1940, was widely believed to have been behind the decision to stop the bridge. Roosevelt responded that he was just standing by the advice of his war secretary.

Construction of the tunnel progressed until late 1942, when wartime iron and steel shortages caused the project to shut down until the end of 1945. The tunnel authority, in serious financial trouble from escalating construction costs and the impact of the war on toll revenues at the Queens Midtown Tunnel, was consolidated with the Triborough Bridge Authority by the State on April 22, 1946. The new agency, Triborough Bridge and Tunnel Authority, with Robert Moses at the helm, assumed responsibility for the tunnel's completion.

Ole Singstad, the acclaimed chief engineer for the Queens Midtown and Brooklyn-Battery tunnels, had been a vocal opponent of the bridge plan. After the consolidation, Moses immediately replaced him with Ralph Smillie, who had been a senior member of the Port Authority's engineering team for the Lincoln Tunnel, headed by Ammann. The tunnel authority's architect, Erling Owre, remained through the entire project. Consulting architects for the tunnel's ventilation building, just off Governors Island, were McKim, Mead & White, who won a design competition held by the tunnel authority in 1941.

The tunnel consists of two parallel cast-iron tubes, 31 feet in diameter, 15 feet apart, and 9,117 feet long between portals, with a maximum roadway depth of 115 feet below mean high water. The tubes were excavated through the earth and dynamited rock under the riverbed by 400-ton circular cutting devices called shields. A cranelike arm on the back of each shield was used to assemble the cast-iron rings that line the tunnel. Unlike some of today's tunneling equipment that grinds through the earth, the shields were hydraulically shoved from opposite shorelines until they met deep in the earth under the harbor.

A decade after construction began, the four-lane tunnel opened to traffic on May 15, 1950; the cost had been $90,568,000. A total of 53 enormous supply and exhaust fans, in ventilation buildings at each end of the tunnel and near Governors Island, provide a complete air change every 90 seconds. It remains the nation's longest continuous subaqueous tunnel. In 1951, the first full year of operation, 15,057,000 vehicles passed through the tunnel; in 2005, the number was 17,426,000. — LR

C-109. Robert Moses with model of revised proposal for Brooklyn-Battery Bridge, March 1939. Model by J. J. Wenner.

C-110. Brooklyn-Battery Tunnel portals and ventilation building, with clock by the sculptor R. M. Fischer, Manhattan side, 1992. Photograph by Paul Warchol. Collection MTA Bridges and Tunnels Special Archive

VERRAZANO-NARROWS BRIDGE

From Brooklyn (Bay Ridge) to Staten Island
(Fort Wadsworth area), across the Narrows
Opened November 21, 1964
Figs. C-111–112

The Verrazano-Narrows Bridge, spanning the strait between Upper and Lower New York Bay, was the last major bridge built by Robert Moses and the Triborough Bridge and Tunnel Authority. It remains, in fact, the last major bridge built in the city. The groundbreaking ceremony on August 13, 1959, followed seven decades of failed attempts by railroad companies, politicians, and engineers to build a Narrows crossing to connect Staten Island to Brooklyn.

In 1888, the Baltimore and Ohio Railroad put forth the first serious plan for a freight tunnel under the Narrows. The railroad had just built a bridge over Arthur Kill to extend its tracks from New Jersey to Staten Island but still had to ferry trains across the Narrows to Brooklyn. The tunnel would have allowed freight to be carried from the mainland to Brooklyn, Queens, and the rest of Long Island via Staten Island, but the cost proved prohibitive.

In 1923, Mayor John Hylan broke ground for a combined freight and passenger rail tunnel, and by the following year the city had spent $1.3 million to sink shafts on either side of the Narrows. The tunnel would do more than connect the rail systems of the mainland and Long Island. At that time, the city was proposing to transform Jamaica Bay into a large industrial port; this rail freight connection would have been an important factor in that development. The passenger rail service through the Narrows tunnel, with a connection to the BMT Fourth Avenue line in Bay Ridge, would enable a faster commute from Staten Island to the four other boroughs. Although the B & O was the only major freight carrier that terminated on Staten Island, the mayor argued that other

C-111. Verrazano-Narrows Bridge nearing completion, September 9, 1964.
Photograph by Skyviews. Collection MTA Bridges and Tunnels Special Archive

freight carriers would be able to hook up to the line. The state opposed the city's plan, however, because it did not fit with the Port Authority's comprehensive plan to build a rail connection, incorporating many of the mainland trunk lines that terminated in New Jersey, to a cross-harbor tunnel between Greenville Yards south of Jersey City and Bay Ridge. Governor Alfred E. Smith, a member of the Port Authority, signed legislation on April 1925 that removed the freight component of the Narrows tunnel. The city, counting on freight revenue to pay for the passenger rail service, abandoned the project.

By then, automobile ownership was rapidly increasing, and the city was planning a new system of traffic arteries. A vehicular crossing at the Narrows was seen not only as a local connection between Brooklyn and Staten Island but as a link in a proposed highway that would allow traffic to move between Long Island and the mainland without passing through traffic-clogged Manhattan. Walker, who succeeded Hylan as mayor in 1926, supported plans for a bridge and then a tunnel, neither of which got beyond the planning stages.

David B. Steinman, a well-known bridge engineer backed by a group of investors, proposed the Liberty Bridge in 1926, a suspension span supported by 800-foot gothic-detailed steel towers, each featuring observation balconies, beacons, and a carillon. The project met with resistance from Congressman Fiorello La Guardia, who felt that the private sector should not profit from a major transportation facility. Nevertheless, Steinman continued fighting for this bridge until the early 1950s.

In 1937, New York State authorized the New York City Tunnel Authority to construct a vehicular tunnel at the Narrows, but World War II delayed the project. A year after the financially troubled authority was consolidated with the Triborough Bridge Authority in 1946, Robert Moses made his first formal proposal for a bridge at the Narrows. After extensive hearings before the Joint Army-Navy-Air Force Board in 1949, the TBTA was granted a federal permit to construct a bridge. This action reversed the War Department's decision in 1939 that no bridge could be built seaward of the Brooklyn Navy Yard, a ruling that had prevented the construction of the Brooklyn-Battery Bridge.

The final plans for the bridge followed the release of a report by the TBTA and the Port Authority, the *Joint Study of Arterial Facilities: New York-New Jersey Metropolitan Area* in 1955. This report recommended three major projects that together would form the links required for the long-planned highway system to

C-112. Verrazano-Narrows Bridge, from Staten Island, ca. 1964. Collection MTA Bridges and Tunnels Special Archive

connect Long Island, including Queens and Brooklyn, to the mainland without passing through the more congested parts of Manhattan: the construction of the Throgs Neck and Verrazano-Narrows bridges and the addition of a lower deck on the George Washington Bridge. The study had been conducted while President Dwight D. Eisenhower and Congress were hammering out the National Defense Highways Act of 1956, whereby the federal government would contribute 90 percent of construction and right-of-way costs. This program would build and finance the Interstate expressway approaches to the three crossings proposed in the *Joint Study*. The TBTA and the Port Authority would be responsible for the bridges to link them. Originally, the Port Authority was to fund and construct the Verrazano, because the TBTA was not in a financial position to do so; the TBTA was later to buy it back with the proceeds of a bond issue. By subsequent agreement between the two authorities, four months after construction began the TBTA assumed the entire financing and construction of the $320,126,000 project and repaid the $30 million already spent by the Port Authority. Ammann & Whitney were the consulting engineers, and John B. Peterkin, Aymar Embury II, and Edward Durell Stone served as consulting architects.

The bridge opened on November 21, 1964. At that time, its 4,260-foot main suspension span was the world's longest, surpassing the Golden Gate by 60 feet. It still remains the longest in the U.S. Not only was the Verrazano-Narrows the last major bridge built by Moses and the TBTA, it was also the last bridge designed by Othmar H. Ammann, who died on September 22, 1965, at the age of 86. The clean lines of its towers are reminiscent of those of the Bronx-Whitestone, but they have sturdier proportions and are nearly twice the height. The monumental 693-foot-high towers are 1 5/8 inches farther apart at their tops than at their bases because the great distance between them made it necessary to compensate for the earth's curvature. Between anchorages, the double-deck roadway measures 6,690 feet. The two six-lane roadway decks and the trusses between them were designed as a unit to be resistant against dynamic wind action. For this reason, both decks were in place when the bridge opened, although the volume of traffic did not require the opening of the lower one until June 28, 1969. The four cables from which the roadway is suspended are made up of 143,000 miles of pencil-thin steel wire, whose seasonal contractions and expansions cause the roadway to be 12 feet lower in the summer than in the winter.

At 60 degrees Fahrenheit, the center span clearance above mean high water is 228 feet.

The bridge and its expressway connections had a tremendous impact in both Brooklyn and Staten Island. Nearly 3,000 families in the two boroughs had to be relocated, even though the immediate approaches were built on army property: Fort Hamilton in Brooklyn and Fort Wadsworth in Staten Island. As the only vehicular crossing between Staten Island and the city's four other boroughs, the bridge spurred tremendous growth in Staten Island, which had a population of only 221,991 in 1960 but by 2000 had doubled to 443,728.

In 1965, its first full year of operation, 17,626,000 vehicles crossed the bridge; the 2005 count at 69,980,000 was nearly four times greater. It was originally to be called the Narrows Bridge, but near the time of its completion, the state legislature added the name of Giovanni da Verrazano, who, in 1524, became the first recorded European explorer to sail into New York Harbor. — LR

RYE-OYSTER BAY BRIDGE

Unexecuted
From Westchester County (Rye) to Nassau County
   (Oyster Bay), across Long Island Sound
Feasibility study released July 1, 1965
Fig. C-113

The Long Island Sound Crossing between Rye and Oyster Bay was the last bridge proposed by Robert Moses and the Triborough Bridge and Tunnel Authority. It would have provided direct travel between Long Island and the mainland, completing an expressway loop around the New York metropolitan area that linked the Seaford-Oyster Bay Expressway in Nassau County to the Cross Westchester Expressway and the New England Thruway on the mainland.

Proposals for the crossing date back to the 1950s, but it was not until 1964 that the TBTA and the State Department of Public Works commissioned Madigan-Hyland to prepare a feasibility study. Released on July 1, 1965, the report touted the benefits of easier travel, greater accessibility between outlying areas, and savings in time and distance. The Westchester end of the bridge would have been in Rye; the Long Island bridgehead would have been in the village of Bayville in the town of Oyster Bay. The estimated cost was $130 million, including property acquisition; construction of the immediate approaches, toll plaza, and service structures; and engineering and administration expenses. At 6.5 miles from shore to shore, it would have been the longest water crossing built by TBTA but not the longest in the nation. The Chesapeake Bay Bridge-Tunnel had opened in 1964 with a shore-to-shore length of just over 17.5 miles.

The report concluded that the bridge would be economically feasible as a self-supporting toll project and proposed that the state create a new authority to build and finance it with revenue bonds. The TBTA was a logical agency for the job, but legal limitations prevented it from building outside the city. Instead, the proposed new authority would have a three-member board headed by the chairman of the TBTA. The two other members would be the county executives of Nassau and Westchester. At that time, Governor Nelson Rockefeller was not ready to support the project, causing the plan to languish for two years. Studies commissioned by the State Department of Public Works for three alternate routes between Suffolk County and Connecticut dropped out of sight.

The project was revived in 1967, this time with Rockefeller at the helm. The governor was preparing legislation to expand the Metropolitan Commuter

Transportation Authority (MCTA), created in 1965 to buy and run the financially troubled Long Island Rail Road. The MCTA would become the Metropolitan Transportation Authority (MTA), an umbrella agency whose mission was to provide unified policy direction and control over several existing transportation agencies. In addition to the Long Island Rail Road, it would initially oversee the New York City Transit Authority and later add other regional rail and bus agencies. The only non-mass-transit agency that would immediately come under the umbrella would be the TBTA, whose surplus revenues, formerly used to finance projects for the automobile, would be redirected to mass transit. Rockefeller announced his support for the Rye-Oyster Bay Bridge and signed legislation in March 1967, authorizing the MTA to build the bridge and, at a future date, a second crossing farther east.

At first, Moses vehemently opposed Rockefeller's MTA plan, but announced his support less than two weeks before legislation was passed to build the bridge. Rumors were reported in the press that he had changed his mind because Rockefeller had promised to give him a key position in the new agency and let him be in charge of building the bridge. When the legislature created the MTA on March 1, 1968, Moses discovered that he was not on its board and no longer head of the TBTA; he was allowed to maintain an office at the TBTA, but only as a consultant.

Although the project was supported by businesses and organized labor, controversy had loomed over it from the start. Rye and Oyster Bay were determined to stop it from coming through their communities. In 1968, Rye filed a lawsuit. That same year, Oyster Bay donated 3,100 acres in the bridge's path to the federal government as a wildlife refuge, which meant the state could not use the land without Washington's permission. The terms of the donation also provided that if the Department of the Interior allowed encroachments on the property, it would revert to the town.

In spite of mounting opposition, in 1972 the MTA and the New York State Department of Transportation released a draft environmental impact statement (DEIS), examining four alternate approaches within the town of Rye and three in Oyster Bay. Madigan-Hyland's design was never finalized, but the proposed crossing in the DEIS had a series of spans with four lanes divided by a median barrier carrying traffic over 6.5 miles of water. Commercial vessels would have passed under the main span, a cable-stiffened box girder with a 135-foot clearance above mean high water, located 1.5 to 2 miles off the Long Island

C-113. Rye-Oyster Bay Bridge (proposed), ca. 1965. Rendering by Rudolph Associates NYC.
Collection MTA Bridges and Tunnels Special Archive

shore. Near the Westchester shore, there was to be a span with a 55-foot clearance for recreational boating and shallow-draft commercial vessels. The remaining spans were to have a minimum 25-foot clearance. The Federal Highway Administration approved the DEIS. By this time, the cost was estimated to be between $258 and $274 million.

Resistance continued to grow. Lawsuits prompted the postponement of hearings on the bridge approach roads originally scheduled for mid-January 1973. On March 16, 1973, the Department of the Interior blocked all three proposed routes on the Nassau County side because they went through the Oyster Bay National Wildlife Refuge, deeded to the federal government five years earlier. The following month, U.S. Senator Abraham A. Ribicoff of Connecticut added another impediment: legislation that would bar

federal highway aid for the project unless it were approved by both New York and Connecticut.

After years of fighting for the project, including twice vetoing bills against it, Rockefeller announced his decision to discontinue plans for its construction on June 20, 1973. Referring to the crossing, he said, "It is part of a long standing plan to link Long Island to the mainland and to enhance the role of the Island in the commerce and industry of the State. However, in recent years the people of our State and country have gradually come to adopt new values in relation to our environment and evidenced a willingness to forego certain economic advantages to achieve these values. The Rye-Oyster Bay Bridge has become a lighting rod in this period of evolution. . . . It is clear that the people want to take a more careful look at decisions which affect the face of their land."[342] — LR

HOUSING AND URBAN RENEWAL

REDEVELOPMENT COMPANIES LAW

Moses's first efforts to involve private capital in slum clearance were accomplished through the framework of the Redevelopment Companies Law, which was passed by the New York State Legislature in 1942. Subscribing to the mainstream view of housing as a domain of the private sector, he hoped that the law would entice private developers to invest in large-scale housing projects combined with slum clearance. The law authorized the city to exercise eminent domain in site assemblage on behalf of a private developer and to grant a tax exemption for a period of twenty years on the increased value of the property after improvements. In exchange for these public benefits, the developer had three obligations: certify that site tenants found adequate replacement housing, a flimsy requirement that fell short of actually finding the new housing; build interior streets and parks, a requirement that Moses inserted in the law; and accept a limited return on investment in the form of rent controls for the duration of the tax-exempt period. The law also removed state restrictions that prevented saving banks and life insurance companies from investing in housing construction. New York was in the vanguard, but not alone. Illinois and Michigan passed comparable laws to stimulate slum clearance by private entities.

After passage of the Redevelopment Companies Law, Moses expectantly proposed housing sites on the Lower East Side to the New York Life Insurance Company. Although New York Life had lobbied for the law and was consulted by lawmakers when it was drafted, the company turned down the land offers. Moses approached several other financial institutions, which reacted in the same way, hence his eagerness to accommodate the Metropolitan Life Insurance Company when it responded positively. Met Life had recently completed Parkchester (1938–42), a complex of 51 buildings with 12,200 apartments, on 125 largely vacant acres in the Bronx. Moses's goal was to redirect the firm's appetite for big building to slum-covered, central city land. At his instigation, the state legislature amended the Redevelopment Companies Law in 1943 to address concerns of Met Life and to loosen regulatory controls. As amended, the law extended the partial tax exemption (based on preimprovement, 1943 valuations) to 25 years, ended the certification requirement on replacement housing, and lifted income limits on residents. Rental controls, however, remained in place.

In April 1943, Met Life unveiled its plan for Stuyvesant Town in Manhattan, the first project under the Redevelopment Companies Law. The company combined 18 square blocks into one 60-acre superblock running from 14th to 20th Street between First Avenue and Avenue C. The size of Stuyvesant Town, a feat made possible by eminent domain, was considered a vital step toward urban health. "The greatest danger to successful urban redevelopment is that it will be attempted in a timid, piecemeal fashion and will fail for that one reason," Tracy Augur, planner of the Tennessee Valley Authority, wrote in an appreciative article about Stuyvesant Town. "Little islands of redevelopment in a big sea of blight have little chance of survival."[343]

The human consequences of large-scale clearance had not, however, been thought through. Met Life hired the relocation firm of James Felt, a reputable real estate man who would become chairman of the City Planning Commission in the 1950s and an opponent of the renewal work of Moses. Felt's job was to find replacement housing for the 10,000 displaced site residents, but his success rate was shockingly low. Apartments were not available at the low rental levels, below $10 per room, affordable by the site population.

Stuyvesant Town (1947) was designed by Irwin Clavin, H.F. Richardson, George Gore, and Andrew Eken, under the direction of Gilmore Clarke, Moses's man in charge of large-scale landscape design for the Department of Parks. Displeased by the preliminary scheme, Moses requested building setbacks and height variations, with low buildings at the periphery and taller buildings in midblock, "to get away from a box-like institutional appearance of most big developments of this kind. I know this is unorthodox, but I think it is the right thing to do."[344] The complex housed 24,000 people in 35 buildings, comprising a total of 8,775 apartments. At the center was an oval park and playgrounds in a cruciform arrangement. The buildings, cross-bar in plan, were arranged like spokes around the oval and in open quadrangles around the periphery of the block.

Although Stuyvesant Town had a porous plan, it was dubbed the walled city because it barred non-white residents. Martha Biondi discusses the battle over racial exclusion earlier in this volume. Suffice it to say here that Moses backed Met Life's right to segregate and accepted the racist norms of the housing market in a desperate attempt to appease his one and only private slum clearer. The state court upheld Met Life's exclusionary housing policy on the grounds that Stuyvesant Town was a private development. Yet Moses himself called it quasi-public housing, a term that captured the middle ground of public and private cooperation encouraged by the Redevelopment Companies Law.

Met Life built another limited-dividend project, Riverton Houses in Harlem, between 135th and 138th streets along the East River Drive, a de facto black-only project intended to balance Stuyvesant Town. With 1,232 units, it was tiny by comparison, which had the benefit of shrinking the relocation problem. Met Life built a third project, Peter Cooper Village (1946–47), adjacent to Stuyvesant Town, but it was outside the framework of the Redevelopment Companies Law and had unrestricted rents.

After Met Life's two tax-exempt, limited-dividend projects, the Redevelopment Companies Law had no sequel. Mayor Fiorello La Guardia signed an agreement with seven New York savings banks in July 1945 to build a rent-controlled housing project called Colonial Village north of the Polo Grounds in Manhattan. The site, however, was a rail yard, not a slum, and within two years the savings banks backed out. The New York City Housing Authority took over the site and built a limited-subsidy project, Colonial Park Houses (now called the Ralph J. Rangel Houses), which opened in 1951. Moses regarded the Redevelopment Companies Law as a failure and concluded that the powers it afforded were insufficient to motivate private developers to participate in slum clearance. Deeper subsidies were needed.

In the immediate aftermath of World War II, the urgent need for housing sidelined the destructive and cumbersome methods of slum clearance in favor of faster, easier solutions. The solution embraced by the New York City Housing Authority, developers, and housing reformers alike was to build on vacant land at the edges of the city. Moses fiercely opposed this approach, which left the central city to fester, removed housing from transportation and employment, and abandoned the investment in urban infrastructure. His primary commitment was to slum clearance. "In July, 1948 . . . I had to admit that 'savings banks failed to contribute to the construction of new housing.'" Accordingly Moses redirected his attention. "We pushed for enactment of the Taft-Ellender-Wagner bill, which incorporated a novel Federal aid system for middle-income housing."[345] This was Title I, which gave Moses a second chance to attack the slums and, as he saw it, rescue the city. — HB

TITLE I DEVELOPMENTS

WASHINGTON SQUARE SOUTH TITLE I

Unexecuted
Manhattan: Washington Square South, Mercer Street, West Houston, and Sixth Avenue
40 acres
Plan published January 1951

WASHINGTON SQUARE SOUTHEAST TITLE I

New York University: Weaver Hall, Tisch Hall, Bobst Library, 1966–72
Washington Square Village, 1956–59
Silver Towers and 110 Bleecker Street (originally University Village), 1961–66
Manhattan: West 4th Street and Washington Square South, Mercer Street, West Houston Street, West Broadway
17.68 acres
Plan published August 1953
Figs. P-46–48, C-114–119

Washington Square South and its sister project, South Village, were a joint assault on Greenwich Village. Together they encompassed close to 53 acres and reformatted 27 Village blocks into 10 superblocks. They illustrated not only the overbearing, destructive side of Moses's large-scale thinking, but also the limitations on what he could do.

Washington Square South divided 40 acres into three sections (see fig. E-27). The first section, bordering the square, was assigned to New York University for educational purposes. The second section (Washington Square Village), between West 3rd and Bleecker streets, was programmed for market-rate housing. The third section, between Bleecker and Houston streets, combined low-income housing (Houston Houses), a new public school, and playgrounds. It also incorporated the MacDougall-Sullivan Gardens, a group of historic townhouses and communal garden, which was to be preserved. The scheme was bisected by West Broadway, enlarged into a boulevard with a central median and renamed Fifth Avenue South. Although it was not aligned with Fifth Avenue, Moses proposed to link the streets with a curving road cut through Washington Square.

Confronted by protests from business and community groups, which deprived him of political backing, Moses promptly withdrew the project.[346] Washington Square South and South Village were the first of several slum clearance projects Moses abandoned or scaled back in 1951 and 1952, the first years of the Title I program. Skillfully responding to these set-backs, he revised his approach in future urban renewal projects and, with the exception of the Lincoln Square Title I, never again proposed a project as large as Washington Square South.

In August 1953, Moses introduced a scaled-back plan, Washington Square Southeast, encompassing nine blocks, less than half the area of the original project. The revised plan called for three superblocks. As before, the northern block was assigned to NYU, and the rest of the site was devoted to housing with supporting commercial uses. But public housing was removed from the mix and shifted to the adjacent site previously designated for South Village.

Moses's renewal plan had a local precedent. In 1946, the Washington Square Association, which represented Village property owners, hired Holden, McLaughlin Architects to develop a master plan to

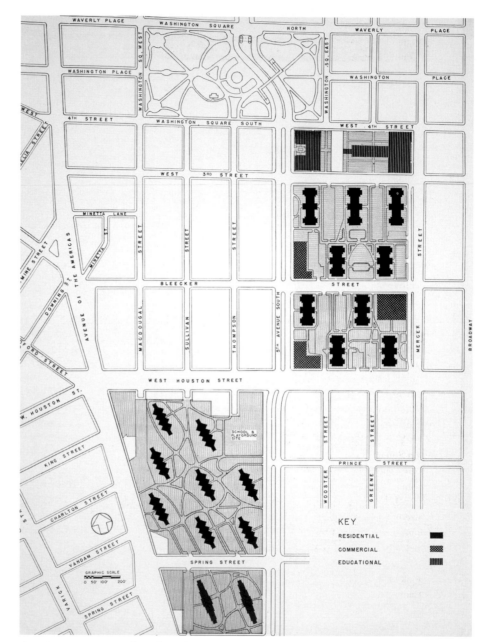

C-114. Composite site plan of Washington Square Southeast and South Village, August 1953

address neighborhood deterioration and traffic congestion. The similarities between their plan and Moses's approach to renewal underscores the conventional cast of his ideas. Foreshadowing Moses's crosstown expressways, Holden, McLauglin proposed an expressway on Houston Street with a 200-foot setback on either side to keep residential buildings a safe distance from traffic. Their plans emphasized the need for quality middle-income housing and found building sites by clearing lofts and tenements. Even preservation advocates, such as the Washington Square Neighbors, believed there should be some "revamping" of the area. The architect Robert Weinberg, writing for the group, "endorsed the . . . large-scale clearance and reconstruction . . . of the blighted area lying between Washington Square and Houston Street."[347]

In addition to its compatibility with local prorenewal sentiment, the project had another advantage: the targeted area had few residents. Of 191 buildings, 175 had commercial or industrial uses, 16 were residential. The Slum Committee's tenant survey counted only 132 residential tenants in the project area. But if residential relocation was a minor issue, the impact on small businesses was significant; commercial tenants received no compensation under the 1949 Title I legislation. The displaced businesses protested the project, but the Greenwich Village Chamber of Commerce and the Washington Square Association joined NYU in backing the plan. The City Planning Commission and Board of Estimate approved Washington Square Southeast in January 1954. "If we waited for unanimous or even majority approval of people threatened with eviction from blighted areas," the *New York Times* editorialized, "we would never make any headway at rebuilding New York's slums. Responsible officials have to take the long view of the greatest good for the greatest number, and a few brickbats along with it."[348]

What provoked sustained community protests was the road plan, which was eventually defeated. In 1956, the plan to enlarge West Broadway from 75 to 120 feet was dropped, and traffic was permanently banned from the park in 1959, a story that Robert Fishman recounts earlier in this volume.[349]

Moses chose the architectural firm of Eggers and Higgins to prepare the site plan because he admired their historicist design of Vanderbilt Hall (1950), home of the NYU Law School, on Washington Square South. Eggers and Higgins, the descendant firm of John Russell Pope, were masters of historical styles. Moses appreciated their aesthetic conservatism, which he thought was aligned with public taste, and

believed that NYU's new buildings should defer to the historical character of the Village. Odd though it may seem, the Slum Clearance Committee sounded a note of respect for the historic fabric. The proposal "will not prejudice the character of Greenwich Village and Washington Square nor will the historical concepts of these areas be infringed upon. The lands assigned to educational use will be redeveloped with attractive low buildings in Washington Square consistent with present architecture."[350]

Indeed, the rendering by Eggers and Higgins shows traditional academic buildings at Washington Square, but the design otherwise looks like a generic housing project. Nine apartment buildings are set on grassy islands amid parking lots. Two boxy shopping centers with glass walls face Fifth Avenue South, and a multistory garage rises on the northeast corner of the superblock. The scale of the project and underlying template of superblock urbanism voided whatever historical gestures the architects might have contemplated.

In any event, the Eggers and Higgins scheme was only a diagram. "Actual building locations and other site details will be agreed upon between the redeveloper and the Committee on Slum Clearance," the committee noted.[351] Although the public hearings considered the Eggers and Higgins plan, it was schematic and nonbinding. The sponsors's actual plans were established at a later date, after public review.

A WASHINGTON SQUARE CAMPUS FOR NYU

Washington Square became an extension of NYU, thanks in large part to Title I. Although established at the square in 1832, the university had only a modest presence there until urban renewal facilitated large land acquisitions.

The area was already considered deteriorating in 1894 when NYU moved its college to a bucolic campus in the Bronx designed by McKim, Mead & White. "At this time," wrote a university historian, "it didn't seem probable that the old residential section surrounding Washington Square, which was being transformed into a manufacturing center, would become a residential or university center."[352] The professional schools remained in the Village and were joined in 1914 by a new undergraduate program. As enrollments increased, NYU's lack of facilities at Washington Square and its poor environs became a growing problem. "The limitation of our physical facilities has made it almost impossible for us to care properly for the development of our students' bodies and for their social life," the historian observed in 1932, as American institutions of higher education were expanding their mission and assuming responsibility for the social as well as the academic part of student life.[353]

After World War II, with enrollments booming, NYU sought to expand at Washington Square South.

C-115. Proposal for Washington Square Southeast, looking north from Houston Street, 1953.
Design by Eggers and Higgins; rendering by R. T. Eggers

It acquired the block between MacDougal and Sullivan streets, where it built a new law school (Vanderbilt Hall). But the real estate drama that played out on the adjacent block indicated NYU's stiff competition from better-funded private developers, who envisioned the Village as an apartment district. In 1945, Anthony Campagna, a prominent developer of Upper East Side luxury apartments, bought the block between Thompson Street and West Broadway, cleared the site, and prepared to build a 14-story apartment building; but in July 1948, Moses intervened and prevailed upon him to sell the block to NYU.[354] The site was used as a playground for a decade before NYU built the Loeb Student Center (1957–60), designed by Harrison & Abramovitz.

The Title I legislation in 1949 gave Moses and NYU a tool more powerful than personal persuasion with which to challenge the real estate market. The 1951 renewal scheme would have given NYU the seven blocks from Sixth Avenue to Mercer Street, including the entire southern frontage of Washington Square, and have swept away McKim, Mead & White's Judson Memorial Church (1892). In the executed 1953 scheme, NYU acquired the three blocks between West Broadway and Mercer Street, an area of 3 acres, including the extant School of Commerce (later renamed Shimkin Hall), a 1926 building already owned by NYU.

Moses expected the university to robustly defend slum clearance. The silence of Chancellor James Madden in the face of public protests annoyed him, but he found a stalwart partner in Henry T. Heald, who became chancellor in 1952. Heald had been a slum-clearance pioneer in Chicago and introduced the planning strategy Moses pursued to facilitate university expansion in New York. As president of the Armour Institute and Illinois Institute of Technology from 1937 to 1951, Heald had used slum clearance to expand the grounds from 9 to 85 acres and made possible Mies van der Rohe's iconic campus. Heald understood that urban renewal could solve NYU's space problem and enable the institution to transform itself in the postwar era. In June 1952, Moses contacted the new chancellor to determine his interest in a scaled-back renewal project. Heald enthusiastically replied, "I feel that the University has an important stake in whatever solution may be arrived at. . . . I shall be glad to help in any way that I can in developing such a program."[355]

NYU and the Slum Clearance Committee negotiated the terms of a new project in February 1953. NYU agreed to contribute $15,000 to $20,000 to defray the committee's cost of developing a new renewal plan. The university also agreed to clear its sites within three to four years, but it could delay construction fifteen to twenty years, or as long as it took to raise building funds. The committee denied Heald's request to include land west of West Broadway and stipulated that "Commissioner Moses will expect the University to stand by any commitments in public and private. This is important because of possible organized popular voices which may be raised against any change in the neighborhood."[356]

NYU was painfully slow to build. In 1964, the university hired Philip Johnson and Richard Foster as master planners and de facto university architects. Their plan guided the development of the Title I land. Construction proceeded from east to west, beginning with Warren Weaver Hall (1966), designed by Warner, Burns, Toan & Lunde, on Mercer Street; Tisch Hall (1972), designed by Johnson and Foster, in the middle of the block; and the forbidding Elmer Holmes Bobst Library (1972), also by Johnson and Foster, at the corner of La Guardia Place.

Heald left NYU in 1956 to become president of the Ford Foundation, where, among other things, he funded the first generation of academic studies of Title I renewal. Although his tenure was brief, his effective partnership with Moses in the Washington Square renewal enabled NYU to modernize and to become a major physical presence in New York, merging its identity with Greenwich Village, just as Columbia University had done a half century before with Morningside Heights. Of course, Heald could not have anticipated that over time NYU would gain possession of the entire renewal area.

WASHINGTON SQUARE VILLAGE

The sponsor of the residential component was Morton S. Wolf, a hotel operator whose company Spencer-Taylor managed some of New York's finest hotels. Wolf had been involved in the redevelopment of the Golden Triangle in Pittsburgh, a model of private urban renewal, and he recruited as his partner the prominent builder Paul Tishman.[357]

Wolf and Tishman had architectural ambitions. They disregarded the Eggers and Higgins plan and

C-116. Proposal for Washington Square Village, looking north from Houston Street, undated.
Design by Paul Lester Wiener and S. J. Kessler & Sons; rendering by unknown artist

hired Paul Lester Wiener as consulting site planner and designer to work with S. J. Kessler and Sons, the Title I specialists.[358] Wiener was a Viennese émigré rooted in the tradition of European modernist housing. In 1945, he and José Luis Sert cofounded Town Planning Associates and in the following years developed master plans for several South American cities featuring long apartment slabs akin to Washington Square Village. After Sert became dean of the Harvard Graduate School of Design, the partnership dissolved, and Wiener opened a solo practice in Manhattan. Although an independent design, Washington Square Village grew out of Wiener's work with Sert; it is an important if flawed attempt to introduce a modernist idiom, one heavily indebted to Le Corbusier and associated with CIAM (Congrès international d'architecture moderne) in New York City.

Wiener designed three apartment buildings, distinguished by their extreme length: each three blocks long (580 feet) and 17 stories tall. Two buildings were set on the perimeter of the middle superblock, along West 3rd and Bleecker streets, with a park and underground garage in between. The third apartment building was located on the Houston Street superblock and buffered from heavy crosstown traffic by commercial buildings positioned along the street. The rental brochure promised "a new kind of urban living" with "no city-mass-of-stone look but instead a feeling of country-like space, air and light."[359] Phase one, consisting of the two buildings on the middle superblock, was completed in 1959. Wiener attempted to enliven and give dimension to the extra-long slabs by various means: boldly colored walls of glazed brick, rhythmic setbacks, balconies in alternating bays, driveways and sightlines that extend across the two city streets (Wooster and Greene) subsumed in the superblock. But the problem of scale remains and is aggravated by the open-ended superblock—a playground on the east and a row of single-story shops on the west provide no closure and invite views across the superblock—and by the failure of the interior park to function as a compelling space. The park sits above the underground garage and is raised several feet above grade; it is difficult to enter and not designed for use.

In 1959, the developers were rethinking their plan for the remaining superblock. The two completed buildings contained 1,292 apartments. Tenants were striking over poor building conditions, and the second building was not fully rented. Rents were high: forecast in 1953 at $48 a room per month, actual rents were $75 to $100 a room per month. The Houston Street building had a less desirable location and

C-117. Washington Square Village, looking south from West Broadway, September 14, 1961

therefore less command on high rents; and there were concerns about the negative impact of a public housing project slated south of Houston Street or a requirement to incorporate public units on site. "The problem of Negro and Puerto Rican applicants would become an increasingly difficult one to handle particularly if it becomes necessary to build apartments for open public housing at lower rentals. Any influx of such occupancies would make the two units already occupied less attractive," explained an NYU vice president.[360] To generate more revenue, the sponsors proposed increasing the height of the third building from 17 to 20 stories and the amount of commercial space. Federal renewal officials at the Housing and Home Finance Agency indicated that the changes might result in a surcharge of $400,000 due to the increased value of the development. The developers withdrew the revised plan in late 1959 and sold the unbuilt superblock to NYU in 1960.[361]

NYU projected a population of 50,000 students in the next decade, most coming from outside the region and in need of housing. In 1963, anticipating an

enormous demand for student housing, NYU purchased Washington Square Village and converted it to a graduate student residence. The purchases in 1960 and 1963, which gave NYU ownership of the entire Title I site, and other acquisitions that further enlarged the university holdings in the area set the stage for NYU's sale of its Bronx campus in 1973 and the consolidation of its undergraduate facilities in Greenwich Village.

UNIVERSITY VILLAGE: THE I. M. PEI TOWERS

In September 1960, after nine months of public hearings, the Board of Estimate approved the sale of the 5.5-acre, undeveloped superblock to NYU. It was clear of all buildings except a supermarket at the northwest corner, which had been built in conjunction with Washington Square Village. NYU paid $10.50 per square foot for the land, the same price the sponsors had originally paid. The land was significantly underpriced, brokers observed; nearby property had recently sold for $31 per square foot. But Title I regulations prevented sponsors from profiteering on the land; the parties were locked into the original price. NYU's plan was to build housing for faculty and graduate students and, on the east end of the site, an experimental elementary school. As a condition of approval, the Board of Estimate required NYU to dedicate a third of the housing to middle-income cooperatives under the Mitchell-Lama program.

In 1960, NYU hired I. M. Pei to design the project. His first scheme, in January 1961, combined four buildings: a 16-story cooperative tower on West Broadway; a 29-story tower for NYU faculty; a 6-story serpentine building for graduate students and faculty families, modeled on typical New York City brownstones; and a low-rise school in the southeast corner. The varied scale of these buildings was an important feature, a development of the combination of townhouses and towers at Pei's Society Hill (1957–64) in Philadelphia. But the scheme was too expensive and the land coverage was too high.[362] The second scheme, in 1962, reduced the land coverage while retaining low and high-rise buildings; it featured two 30-story towers and an L-shaped 7-story building. The varied scales were lost in Pei's final design in 1964, which consisted of three 30-story towers, reflecting the logic of midcentury renewal and its fixation on reduced ground coverage.

The NYU towers culminated a series of designs by Pei that began with two Title I–Zeckendorf projects, Town Center Plaza (1953–61) in Washington, D.C., and Kips Bay Plaza in New York City. Pei had been striving to bring concrete construction to a new level of refinement and economy; he met at least the first goal. The gridded wall of University Village is the building structure, revealing the module of the interior rooms and integrating mechanical systems; the air-conditioning vents are set in the spandrels, unlike Kips Bay where the air-conditioning units were not integrated in the design. And the contrast between the sheer walls and grid establishes a rich dialogue between light and shadow, surface and recess, solid and transparent.[363] Pei also created a sense of place by setting the towers around a plaza where Picasso's 36-foot-tall sculpture *Sylvette* introduces an intermediate scale. Each tower is oriented differently and preserves sightlines along the city streets, which become pedestrian paths when they traverse the superblock. The complex breaks the scale and texture of the traditional fabric; along Houston Street in particular there is a void. Nevertheless, in the context of midcentury renewal in New York City, University Village was a considerable achievement.

Construction of University Village began in 1964 and was completed in 1966. The cooperative occupies the west tower, 110 Bleecker Street. The two NYU towers were renamed Silver Towers in 1974 in honor of the university benefactor Julius Silver. On the east end of the site, where an elementary school had been planned, NYU built a gym, the Coles Sports and Recreation Center, which opened in 1982. A movement to landmark the three towers is under way; NYU opposes the designation and is reportedly developing plans for a new academic building on the supermarket site. — HB

C-118. Model of first project for University Village, looking north from Houston Street, 1961.
Design by I. M. Pei & Associates

C-119. University Village (now Silver Towers and 110 Bleecker Street), looking northwest, ca. 1966.
Design by I. M. Pei & Associates

SOUTH VILLAGE TITLE I

Unexecuted
Manhattan: Sixth Avenue, West Houston Street,
    West Broadway, and Spring Street
14 acres
Plan published January 1951
Fig. C-120

South Village was part of a plan to transform more than 50 acres in the heart of Greenwich Village. Although it was far smaller and more intelligently planned than the companion project, Washington Square South, it was nevertheless alarming. The Slum Clearance Committee gave two reasons for selecting the site south of West Houston: to provide improved housing near lower Manhattan and to stabilize Greenwich Village and protect it from creeping slums. The committee's brochure painted a picture of inhumane living conditions in old- and new-law tenements without elevators, 75 percent without private bathrooms and 68 percent without central heat. Yet the committee's real estate consultant, Charles F. Noyes Co., noted elsewhere in the report that 16 percent of the apartments lacked individual toilets.[364] With discrepancies like this, it is no wonder that community groups challenged the validity of the Slum Clearance Committee's data.

The redevelopment plan by Voorhees Walker Foley & Smith conveys a pervasive faith in sunlight and open space to improve urban conditions. Six apartment buildings, of 15 and 20 stories, surround a green quadrangle in the center of the site, with nonresidential uses providing buffering along the streets. As shading on the site plan indicates, the architects considered the solar orientation of the apartment buildings, and "cross vistas were arranged to allow a depth of view from all exposures."[365] Existing land coverage was 85 percent; in the residential areas of the redevelopment, it dropped to 13 percent. The only recreational space in the neighborhood was the Thompson Street Playground, which was 100 by 75 feet, equivalent to three standard row-house lots. It was to be replaced by a 1.3-acre playground.

In response to the artistic character of the area, South Village was to include artist studios (they are not, however, shown in the building plans) and a gallery, which was incorporated in a row of commercial buildings on West Broadway, widened and renamed Fifth Avenue South. The commercial row backs onto Thompson Street, which was retained to provide access to a parking lot. In addition to their urban benefits, the shops were attractive to developers. The Voorhees plan shows seven apartment build-

C-120. Proposal for South Village, 1951. Design by Voorhees Walker Foley & Smith

ings, but financial reasons led the committee to designate the building at the corner of West Houston and Sixth Avenue for commercial use.

Although the scheme called for substantial clearance, the site plan accommodated several existing buildings: a parochial school and church on West Houston Street and a modern apartment building and library facility on Sixth Avenue were preserved. In order to create a civic hub, a new police station was located beside the library building, at the corner of Sixth Avenue and Spring Street, where there was a subway station. With such convenient access to mass transit, the three parking lots (for 213 cars) look superfluous, but they were required by the zoning law: the formula was on-site parking for 30 percent of the apartments in new construction.

The Slum Clearance Committee developed the plan on speculation, in effect, hoping subsequently to attract a developer. It reported an offer from the Foundation for the Improvement of Urban Living, a nonprofit charitable corporation that proposed a tax-exempt project with rents of $20 per room (the committee's business plan projected rents at $33 per room) and offered to pay $4 per square foot. The committee accepted this price for the residential land only and required $6 for the commercial area.

South Village never reached the next step in the process, a public hearing before the Board of Estimate. In the face of strong community protests, Mayor Vincent R. Impellitteri delayed the hearings, and in short order Moses abandoned the project. By 1953, the South Village site was passed on to the NYC Housing Authority for a low-income housing project, provisionally named the Mary K. Simkhovitch Houses, but it was never built. — HB

DELANCEY STREET TITLE I

Unexecuted
Manhattan: East Houston, Allen, Delancey,
 and Forsyth streets
10.6 acres
Plan published January 1951
Fig. C-121

Delancey Street, the third slum clearance plan to be released, was a high priority, yet it never advanced, probably because Moses could not find a sponsor. The project targeted six blocks in the heart of the Lower East Side, in a neighborhood where the city had already invested in public improvements. Sara Delano Roosevelt Park, which Moses had created in the 1930s, bordered the site on the west, and the bounding streets—East Houston to the north, Allen to the east, and Delancey to the south—had been enlarged and furnished with malls and sitting areas.

The redevelopment scheme had two distinguishing features: it mixed uses and incorporated some extant buildings. Eight apartment buildings were proposed for the center of a superblock: five at 20 stories, three at 18 stories. Low-rise shopping centers were placed along the heavily trafficked north and south streets, with parking lots for 250 cars behind the stores. A 1903 bath house on Allen Street and two public schools (P.S. 20 and P.S. 91) on Forsyth Street were retained, although many other public-use buildings were slated for demolition: three synagogues, two theaters, and the University Settlement on Eldridge Street, the oldest settlement house in the city. As a result of a significant reduction in land coverage—the residential building coverage would drop from 75 percent of the lot area to 11.4 percent—playgrounds and landscaped areas were introduced in the center of the block.

The site plan was designed by William Wilson, a politically connected engineer-architect. Mayor La Guardia's commissioner of housing and buildings from 1939 to 1945 and a longtime member of the NYC Housing Authority, Wilson was a Moses ally and represented his interests on the Housing Authority and State Power Commission. William I. Hohauser was the associate architect.

The primary goals of the project were to replace inferior tenements with modern, affordable housing and to involve private capital in the renewal of the Lower East Side. Of the 98 residential buildings on the site, close to 60 percent lacked bathrooms and central heating. The plan acknowledged that the area was not attractive to private investment and required "the intervention of the municipality charged with the

C-121. Revised proposal for Delancey Street Title I, with retail shops on Delancey Street (foreground) and Houston Street (background), 1957. Sara Delano Roosevelt Park is at left. Design by S. J. Kessler & Sons. Collection MTA Bridges and Tunnels Special Archive

well being of its citizens."[366] The financial plan aimed at rentals of $25 to $27 per room per month. In New York, such low rents could usually be achieved only with the aid of tax exemptions or subsidies; otherwise, new construction such as that projected at Delancey Street resulted in high-cost rentals. Moses hoped to avoid this outcome and to make the development more attractive financially by including commercial space. The Delancey Street plan anticipated that high rentals for the stores would make the low-rent apartments affordable for the developer. But the project was problematic from a social as well as business perspective. It promised a net loss in dwelling units, from 1569 to 1189, and the dislocation of as many poor families, most of whom would not be able to afford the new housing.

While Moses completed two projects nearby— Corlears Hook and Seward Park—Delancey Street stalled. In 1957, he attempted to relaunch it with a revised plan by S. J. Kessler & Sons that changed the configuration of apartment buildings, resulting in four I-shaped slabs. The new scheme retained only one of

the extant schools but proposed a new $1-million building for the University Settlement House.

Although Moses kept Delancey Street on his list of future projects, it never reached the stage of public hearings. The lesson that he learned was the necessity of securing a sponsor at the earliest stage of planning; otherwise, a project had no future. — HB

TITLE I AND THE LIMITED-EQUITY CO-OP

The cooperative, or co-op, is a form of homeownership in which buyers purchase shares of stock in a corporation that owns the entire building; in return they receive a long-term lease granting rights to a particular space. This system, which was first developed in New York City in the 1880s, is distinct from the condominium mechanism, introduced to the U.S. after World War II, in which each owner receives a deed to an individual unit. For many years, few lenders were willing to make money available for co-ops; prospective homeowners therefore had to contribute most of the cost in cash. This practice all but prohibited working-class families from participating, and as a result most co-ops were built for very well-to-do families, originally on Manhattan's East Side.[367]

During the severe housing crisis that followed World War I, however, philanthropists, leaders of trade unions, and others concerned with improving housing for working-class families in the city became interested in cooperatives. Their primary objective was to lower the cost of housing and to protect working families from the vicissitudes of the city's housing market, which during periods of economic instability, such as wartime, made tenants vulnerable to steep and frequent rent increases. Monthly maintenance charges in any co-op or condominium—charges that cover the owners' share of utilities, taxes, upkeep—always run below rents for comparable units in buildings owned by a single party. For the most part, this savings is achieved because individual ownership of units obviates the problem of vacancies, which even at the best of times cost a landlord 10 to 15 percent of her income.

A second goal was ideological. Housing reformers had long believed that conventional housing markets caused slum conditions and had sought alternatives to the capitalist system for the production and ownership of housing. The prevailing solution had been "philanthropy and 5 percent," which encouraged developers to run "model" tenements at a reduced profit. By replacing the landlord with a corporation controlled by residents, the co-op promised to achieve a similar end at yet lower operating costs.

Philanthropists, unions, and leftist fraternal organizations each financed several co-op projects in New York in the 1920s. To ensure affordability in perpetuity, these projects introduced the novel limited-equity component whereby any rise in value was to benefit the corporation rather than the individual. In prac-

tice, this meant that resales were permitted only to the corporation and only for the original price paid. Any profit from resale of the shares was to benefit all owners in the form of reduced maintenance charges. Given the successful completion and operation of these prewar projects, the limited-equity co-op came to be widely admired by housing reformers, both locally and nationally. By World War II, many came to see it as a necessary complement to the public housing program, uniquely capable of producing privately developed and owned housing at significantly lower costs than might be possible otherwise. Indeed, throughout the postwar period, it operated in New York State as a de facto public housing program—albeit one privately administered—for families too well off to meet the federal government's low income limits for publicly owned housing.

To aid the limited-equity co-op, and privately built low-rent housing generally, New York State introduced a series of laws. The first was the Housing Law of 1926, which offered discounted property taxes and low-interest construction loans to projects for which the developer agreed to take a reduced profit. The second was the Redevelopment Companies Law of 1942, which, like the national Title I of 1949, enabled private, low-rent housing projects to acquire sites using eminent domain. The third was the Limited Profit Housing Companies Law of 1955, popularly known as Mitchell-Lama, named for its sponsors, which replaced the 1926 law. Nationally, Congress supported the limited-equity co-op through the Federal Housing Administration's numerous programs for multifamily "rental" housing and, after 1950, though Section 213 of the National Housing Act, which was introduced specifically to finance privately built co-ops.

Although limited-equity co-ops had been built by a variety of individuals and organizations in the 1920s, trade unions came to dominate the field after World War II. In an era of strong labor, the city's prosperous and well-organized unions were uniquely able—and willing—to finance projects with their multimillion-dollar pension funds. Furthermore, the city's labor community possessed effective leadership deeply committed to the alternative to capitalism embodied by the limited-equity co-op. First and foremost among these men was Abraham Kazan of the Amalgamated Clothing Workers of America.

A Jewish immigrant from the Ukrainian countryside, Kazan spent his first years in the U.S. at Carmel, one of several agricultural communes in southern New Jersey operated by Eastern European Jews in the late nineteenth and early twentieth cen-

turies. There he became acquainted with the Western European consumers' cooperative movement, a network of clubs organized by working men and women for the exchange of groceries and other goods and services at wholesale prices. Kazan believed that this movement offered the working classes a more politically expedient alternative to capitalism than socialism, the political ideology that predominated in his social milieu. During the housing crisis of the 1920s, he came to see the limited-equity co-op as a integral part of the "cooperative" political economy that he envisioned for America—a vision that continued to guide his efforts for the rest of his life. While in the employ of the Amalgamated, he orchestrated the union's efforts to build two large limited-equity complexes, the Amalgamated Housing Cooperative in the Bronx (1926–27, 1929–37) and the Amalgamated Dwellings on Manhattan's Lower East Side (1930).

Before the close of WWII, Kazan began work on additional projects for the Amalgamated, including Hillman Houses on the Lower East Side. Conceived as an addition to the Amalgamated Dwellings of the 1930s, Hillman included 807 units in three 12-story buildings designed by Springsteen and Jessor, architects of all of Kazan's co-ops. Ground was broken in 1947 and construction was completed in 1950. Perhaps more significantly, Kazan began assisting other groups plan and build projects after the war.

First among these was Queensview in Long Island City, developed by Louis H. Pink and Gerard Swope, for which Kazan served as consultant on "cooperative practice." Pink was a longtime public servant in New York City and State, and Swope was an ex-president of General Electric, who had served briefly as head of the city's housing authority. Like Kazan, they were committed to the production of sustainable low-rent housing in the city. Begun in 1949 and completed in 1951, Queensview comprised 728 apartments in four 14-story buildings designed by Brown & Guenther, who also went on to design several additional limited-equity co-ops, including an addition, Queensview West; Kingsview, a sister project realized as part of the Fort Green Title I project; and four Mitchell-Lama co-ops in the Inwood section of northern Manhattan, for which the firm also served as developer.

Following the completion of Queensview, and to further encourage use of the limited-equity format, Kazan and Pink established an advocacy group called the United Housing Foundation in 1951, complete with a subsidiary, Cooperative Services, Inc., which operated as a general contractor and project manager. Kazan served as chairman and Pink as president;

after Pink died in 1955, his post was assumed by James Felt, a longtime real estate operator who also chaired the city's planning commission between 1956 and 1963. During the course of the 1950s and 1960s, the UHF developed some 31,000 cooperative apartments in eight complexes and assisted countless other groups—mainly trade unions—with the development and operation of tens of thousands of units in scores of other projects.

The majority of these projects, both UHF and otherwise, were built on the outskirts of the city, particularly in suburban Queens and the northern Bronx, where the lower cost of land, in combination with Mitchell-Lama and FHA financing, permitted share prices under $650 a room and maintenance charges under $21 a room per month. For many years, and despite rising incomes of the residents, these rates were considered by public officials and housing reformers an inviolable threshold, no matter how arbitrary. Hillman Houses and Queensview had been able to sustain such prices because they had been begun in the 1940s. But maintaining such prices at new projects in Manhattan and Brooklyn in the 1950s came to require additional subsidies. Title I offered this support and in practice enabled developers to build at outdated prices, at least until inflation began to accelerate in the 1960s. Kazan was quick to grasp this opportunity and immediately following enactment of Title I began planning the first of three Title I projects for Manhattan: Corlears Hook, followed by Seward Park and Penn Station South. Louis Pink, meanwhile, began planning Kingsview.

By most measures, these and other Title I limited-equity projects—including Morningside Gardens, Chatham Green, and Chatham Towers—were a resounding success. Projects were planned, executed, and occupied without delay, satisfying the demands of Robert Moses and the Committee on Slum Clearance. Furthermore, relocation of existing residents was achieved smoothly and without undue hardship. Perhaps most importantly, public funds allowed prices that met political demands.

Under typical financing plans, these projects sold shares at a rate of $625 to $650 per room, with a two-bedroom apartment requiring a cash investment of less than $3,000 (roughly $25,000 in today's dollars). And thanks to discounted taxes, most buildings were able to operate with maintenance, or carrying, charges of around $17 to $21 a room per month, or roughly $1,100 a year for the same two-bedroom unit. By comparison, co-ops built in Manhattan in the 1950s without Title I charged at least twice these rates for shares and maintenance, and typically far

more, while new rental buildings of comparable quality charged at least $40 a room per month.

During the 1960s, however, both Title I and the limited-equity co-op generally lost viability. As the national economy soured, construction and operating costs skyrocketed, as did interest rates and property taxes. By the early 1970s, average maintenance charges in newer limited-equity projects, Title I or otherwise, ran upward of $75 a room per month. This situation was exacerbated by efforts to lower bars to tenant ownership by reducing share prices and increasing the size of construction loans—and residents' debt burden. Shareholders in the newer, larger projects tended to feel less like homeowners than tenants and began to rebel, organizing "rent" strikes and forcing dozens of projects into debt. Meanwhile, the city's own fiscal woes, which essentially bankrupted the Mitchell-Lama program, and antipathy toward slum clearance all but shut down the UHF and the limited-equity program by 1973, although the organization has continued ever since to operate as a shell of its former self.

Any effort to revive the limited-equity program in the absence of Title I and Mitchell-Lama would likely have required federal assistance. Yet, while the co-op briefly commanded national interest after WWII and a handful of limited-equity projects were realized in other cities, without local leaders as committed to the system as Kazan and, perhaps more importantly, in the absence of significant demand on the part of working- and lower-middle-class families outside of Greater New York for owner-occupied apartments, efforts to introduce the limited-equity co-op elsewhere proved isolated and experimental.

Today, the limited-equity model has fallen from favor even in New York, in part because significant subsidies for new low-rent housing are no longer politically expedient, but in larger part because New Yorkers, like most Americans, have demonstrated a strong preference for more traditional forms of homeownership. Indeed, as city tax breaks that bind projects to the limited-equity format expire, many residents are abandoning it, voting to permit themselves to sell their units at market prices. That said, others, including those at Penn Station South and the Amalgamated Cooperative in the Bronx, have resisted such changes. These buildings remain living examples of Kazan's critique of the conventional housing market. — MGL

CORLEARS HOOK TITLE I

East River Houses, 1954–56
Shopping center, 1954–56
Manhattan: FDR Drive, Delancey, Lewis,
    Grand, Jackson, and Cherry streets
14.66 acres
Plan published January 1951
Figs. C-122–124

Corlears Hook was the fourth Title I plan published by the Committee on Slum Clearance and the first to be completed. Conceived as an expansion of the Amalgamated Dwellings of 1930, it was the second of three large housing projects sponsored by Abraham Kazan on the Lower East Side of Manhattan after World War II. Together with the Hillman Houses and Seward Park, the four housing complexes are known collectively as Cooperative Village.

Even before the end of the war, Kazan had decided to extend the Amalgamated Dwellings, announcing the Hillman Houses, which opened in 1950. The number of qualified applicants far exceeded capacity, however, and Kazan immediately began plans for the East River Houses on a nearby parcel proposed by Moses. The site was adjacent to East River Park, which Moses had built in the 1930s, and comprised nearly 15 acres distributed among all or part of eleven blocks sandwiched between the FDR Drive to the east, Corlears Hook Park to the south, and Hillman Houses and the public Vladeck Houses to the west.

To persuade the city to allow him to use the site, Kazan established a development company, the East River Houses Corporation, in late 1950 and undertook a preliminary plan using a grant from the Edward A. Filene Good Will Fund. Filene, a New England department store magnate, had supported consumers' cooperatives since the 1930s and had established the foundation to encourage co-ops of all types, including limited-equity housing. Kazan's plan called for 1,672 units in four high-rise slabs with variegated facades arranged as a series of Maltese crosses. The buildings, two of 21 stories and two of 22, were to be distributed equally between two new superblocks, one north of Grand Street and one south of Grand and Madison streets. No existing buildings were retained.

Simultaneously, the Committee on Slum Clearance commissioned a different plan. Prepared by the architects and engineers Lorimer and Rose, it called for an identical superblock configuration; but rather than four buildings it suggested seven rectangular slabs of 20 stories with roughly 200 units each, for a total of 1,400 apartments. Four of these buildings were to be

C-122. East River Houses, below the Williamsburg Bridge, looking north, March 14, 1956

north of Grand and three south. The firm's design principal, A. Gordon Lorimer, was a Scottish architect who had first worked for Moses during the New Deal on several public works projects and served during the 1940s as the chief architect of the city's Department of Public Works.

Kazan's plan, which was the work of the architects George W. Springsteen and Herman J. Jessor, improved on the city's and was approved. Springsteen and Jessor had designed several other low-rent housing projects in the city, including Hillman Houses, whose buildings were similar, and the original Amalgamated co-ops of the 1920s. Both men were from Kazan's social and political milieu and were committed to the UHF's ideological program. Springsteen died in the early 1950s, but Jessor lived to design some 40,000 limited-equity apartments, mostly for Kazan and the UHF.

Apart from accommodating 272 additional units in fewer buildings, which permitted additional economies

of scale, by substituting a cruciform plan for Lorimer's slabs the Springsteen and Jessor plan allowed every apartment but one per floor to have two outside exposures and cross-ventilation. As in Lorimer's scheme, the buildings were oriented roughly parallel to one another on north-south axes so that most apartments did not directly face another building and all units, at least on higher floors, enjoyed views of the lower Manhattan skyline or the East River. Given that production of housing was Kazan's chief priority, the plan as built resulted in higher land coverage and population density than the city's proposal would have: The Lorimer plan called for coverage of just under 20 percent and densities of 334 people per acre, while the Springsteen and Jessor plan called for 25 percent and 350 people, respectively. By contrast, the existing coverage was more than 90 percent, with about 217 residents per acre.

Suites were of 617 to 1,294 square feet and came in four basic layouts, ranging from two and a half

rooms—bedroom, living room, and foyer with kitchenette—to five and half rooms—three bedrooms, kitchen, living room, and foyer. Most units had only one bathroom, but nearly 60 percent were given a balcony or, if at a setback, a terrace. Each building comprised three cruciform sections, each with its own service core and elevator bank, an arrangement that meant only seven apartments shared a public corridor.

In addition to the residential buildings, the project included shops and an auditorium on the small triangular block bounded by Jackson, Grand, and Madison streets; a central heating plant at the corner of Delancey and Lewis streets; and a parking lot along the remaining Delancey Street frontage. In the retail and meeting complex were a cooperative grocery store at street level and a 1,000-seat auditorium on the second floor. Rents from the shops were to benefit residents by helping to defray maintenance costs. As was the fashion at the time, the buildings occupied very little of the site, with the high-rises consuming fewer

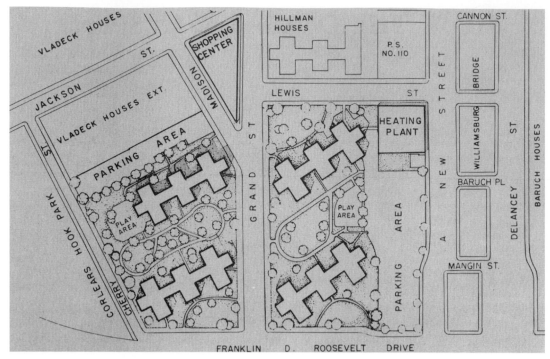

C-123. Site plan for East River Houses, ca. 1957

C-124. East River Houses and East River Park, ca. 1957

than 2.25 acres and the community and service structures consuming an additional acre, leaving 11 acres for gardens, two playgrounds, and the parking lot.

As with the majority of projects that Kazan initiated in the postwar period, he found an outside sponsor, in this case the International Ladies' Garment Workers' Union, which offered $15 million in mortgage loans. The ILGWU, led by David Dubinsky, chose to fund the project less to house its membership—it was expected that only a third of the residents would ever be union members—than to make a good investment for members' pension funds and to bolster the union's public image.

With preliminary approvals in place, East River Houses went on sale in August 1952. More than 5,000 families applied, patiently waiting in lines that stretched for blocks. All had learned about the project by word of mouth or through news coverage; demand was such that advertisements were unnecessary. Units were priced at $625 a room, with the smallest one-bedrooms selling for about $1,560 and the largest three-bedrooms for about $3,440. These amounts represented only the buyer's share; with the ILGWU's loans covering roughly 80 percent of the total, true costs ranged from roughly $7,800 to $17,200 (about $80,000 to $180,000 today). Projected maintenance, which covered each owner's share of the complex's mortgage payments, ranged from $13 to $21 a room per month.

Families that had been living on the site were given priority, and a solid majority of those admitted were residents of the Lower East Side. Although like all publicly aided housing in New York State at the time the project was open to people of all races, creeds, and colors, most of the first families were Jewish or Italian, reflecting the area's traditional ethnic composition.

A groundbreaking ceremony took place in November 1953, with Kazan, Moses, and Dubinsky wielding the shovel; construction did not begin until early 1954. Residents of the first building took occupancy in late 1955, and the project was completed in mid-1956—according to plan, within cost estimates, and on schedule. East River Houses has now operated successfully for half a century. That said, as the project became free of its financial obligations to the city in the late 1980s, residents began plans to convert the project into a market-rate co-op, and the new system was phased in during the 1990s. Today, the original units sell for $400,000 to $850,000, with $320 to $800 in monthly maintenance; larger units, where two or more have been combined, command as much as $1.4 million. — MGL

HARLEM TITLE I

Lenox Terrace, 1957–60
Manhattan: West 132nd to West 135th Street,
    Fifth to Lenox Avenue
12 acres
Plan published January 1951
Figs. P-40–41, E-30, 37

The Harlem Title I, along with the North Harlem Title I a few blocks away, demonstrated Moses's determination to bring quality housing to Harlem. He attached a high priority to the two Harlem projects: announced in January 1951, they were among the first plans introduced by the Slum Clearance Committee and among the first submitted to the Board of Estimate, which approved them in May 1952. Moses's advocacy of Title I projects for black Harlem was consistent with his long-standing opposition to integrated housing. Rather than promote the entry of middle-class blacks into racially mixed developments, he reinforced the color line. Nevertheless, these projects show an unexpected determination to bring private investment to Harlem. As Moses saw it, Harlem should have adequate housing for the black middle class. "The fiction that the only people who will stay in Harlem are those who can't move and those who are provided for in the lowest rental public housing dies a hard death," he commented in 1958, as the Harlem Title I project approached completion. "The fact is that there is a demand for all sorts of good, new housing right in Harlem coming from people who manifestly want to stay there. This, of course, does not square with some ideologies—but there it is."[368]

The location of this project took advantage of, and was meant to reinforce, public facilities already in the area. Harlem Hospital was one block to the north (on Lenox between 136th and 137th streets) and was formulating plans to expand toward 135th Street. The corner of Lenox Avenue and 135th Street was the cultural center of Harlem: the public library, later expanded as the Schomburg Center for Research in Black Culture, attracted the leaders of the Harlem Renaissance. A subway entrance and public school occupied the same corner, and to the east, running from Fifth Avenue to the Harlem River, were two new housing developments: the Abraham Lincoln Houses (132nd to 135th Street), a low-income project of the NYCHA opened in 1948; and the Riverton Houses (135th to 138th Street), a moderate-rent development of the Metropolitan Life Insurance Company opened in 1949.

The Title I project was originally named the Godfrey Nurse Houses, after the Harlem-based sur-

C-125. Delano Village, before and during construction, 1955–60

geon who had led the effort in the 1930s to integrate Harlem Hospital and worked to remove professional obstacles facing black doctors. Nurse (1888–1968), who was also active in the Democratic Party, presumably had a role in the formative stages of the project, but he was not involved in its execution. Symptomatic of the difficulty in finding viable Title I developers, sponsorship changed twice before Moses designated Robert S. Olnick as the developer in July 1952.

Olnick would become a real estate titan—CEO and chairman of Starrett Brothers & Eken (later Starrett Housing Corporation), which he acquired in 1961—but in 1952, he was a thirty-seven-year-old lawyer turned investor-builder near the start of his career. Returning from World War II, he built a number of large apartment buildings in Riverdale and housing for defense workers near Poughkeepsie. Recognizing the development opportunities that flowed from federal funding, Olnick took on the Harlem Title I project, which he renamed Lenox Terrace.

Lenox Terrace illustrates what went wrong with Title I in the early years. Although the city approved the project in 1952, construction did not begin until 1957. Newspaper articles chronicled the dark side of slum clearance: tenants living in deteriorating conditions while awaiting relocation; partially cleared sites used for parking; and a sponsor given no guidance in the delicate process of tenant relocation. Like other early sponsors, Olnick was encumbered by federal obstacles and the experimental nature of the program. Initially, the FHA withheld approval of Lenox Terrace because of a statute requiring that a project be consistent with the character of the surrounding area or be large enough in scale to change the area. Lenox Terrace did not meet these criteria: it was purposefully different in character from the surrounding area and too small in size to cause area-wide change. Not until 1955 were FHA regulations adjusted to eliminate these conditions. In November 1956, the FHA at last approved mortgage insurance for the Harlem Title I, but Olnick could not obtain financing. Lenders were deterred by a FHA ruling setting a maximum construction cost per room; the FHA would not make an exception for high-cost areas like New York City.

Unable to change federal policy, Moses pressed local lending institutions to invest in Harlem real estate. The stalemate was broken in 1957, when, with Moses's help, Olnick secured the necessary loans. Borough President Hulan Jack told the dignitaries at the opening ceremony, "the project sponsors 'had broken the barrier' that banks had long maintained against substantial investment in new housing for Harlem."[369] Construction began in April 1957. The first three buildings were dedicated in October 1958; the remaining buildings were completed in 1960. Among the structures swept away was 67 West 134th Street, the office of Philip A. Payton Jr., Harlem's first major black realtor, whose rise in the early 1900s was linked with the creation of black Harlem.

The redevelopment scheme by Skidmore, Owings & Merrill, published in January 1951, disrupted the vernacular of tenements on small lots. The plan merged three city blocks into a superblock with eight free-standing apartment buildings, each 20 stories; parking lots and sitting areas blanketed the extensive open spaces. In 1956, Olnick replaced the SOM scheme with a slightly improved site plan by S. J. Kessler & Sons; the architecture, however, lacked distinction. The number of apartment buildings dropped from eight to six, and height was reduced from 20 to 16 stories. The bulk of the buildings, however, increased as did the number of dwelling units, which went from 1,105 projected in the 1951 plan to 1,716 units as built. The greatest missed opportunity was relinquishing the ample open space to on-site parking for about 400 cars.

Nevertheless, the site plan responded to local conditions in two commendable respects. Stores were located on 135th Street and Lenox Avenue, where they maintained the commercial character of those streets, and the site plan incorporated several extant community buildings: a play center and playground run by the Children's Aid Society and a public bath were absorbed in the center of the superblock; a church (formerly Lincoln Theater, where Fats Waller debuted in 1925) was accommodated in the commercial strip on 135th Street; and a public service building and power substation on 132nd Street were left intact. Indeed, the Kessler site plan appears restrained compared to the Harlem redevelopment scheme by William Lescaze, published in *Architectural Forum* in April 1944; Lescaze proposed clearing ten blocks and forming two superblocks with "superbuilding units" turned 30 degrees to the avenues.

The most important aspect of Lenox Terrace was captured in a *New York Times* headline on opening day (October 17, 1958): "Luxury Housing Opens in Harlem." Lenox Terrace gave Harlem its first buildings with 24-hour doorman service. The apartments offered picture windows, air-conditioning, ceramic tile bathrooms, modern kitchen appliances, and Venetian blinds; most had generous balconies. At the time of the opening, monthly rentals averaged $40 per room. The original building names—Americana, Fontainebleau, Eden Roc, Devonshire, the Continental, and the Buckingham—were more Miami Beach than Harlem and did not catch on, but Lenox Terrace was a success and quickly became "Harlem's most desirable address," as the *New York Times* reported in 1968. A survey in 1965 indicated that 30 percent of the tenants had moved to Lenox Terrace from Westchester, Long Island, or other suburbs. The roster of residents included judges, politicians, government employees, civic l eaders, teachers, doctors, and nurses. "To me, Lenox Terrace is an oasis in Harlem, with all the East Side luxuries," a resident commented in 1968. "When I give my address to a client, he says, 'Oh, Lenox Terrace!' It's more than just another building in the area."[370]

Like the high-quality residences, the new stores were also a community benefit. The Slum Clearance plan had noted the inadequate number of stores for the population density. The Lenox Terrace stores included national retailers: Liggett Drugs, S. H. Kress, Thomas McAn Shoes, A & P, and Safeway, whose 11,000-square-foot space made it one of the first—possibly the first—large supermarkets in Harlem. Olnick also had a policy of recruiting and assisting local businessmen. One such establishment was the coffee shop at 22 West 135th Street, which was famously frequented by Malcolm X. — HB

NORTH HARLEM TITLE I

Delano Village, 1956–62
Manhattan: West 139th to West 141st Street, Fifth to Lenox Avenue, half block from 141st to 142nd Street on Lenox Avenue, and Lenox Avenue frontage from 142nd to 143rd Street
12 acres
Plan published January 1951
Figs. C-126–127

This development was conceived in conjunction with Lenox Terrace, its sister project four blocks away, to provide modern, upscale housing for Harlem's professional class. Moses rejected the argument of the Urban League and others that the site should be used for public housing; he firmly believed that Harlem needed middle-class housing, which Title I was intended to stimulate.

Located at the north end of Lenox Avenue, the 2.5-block site was a ragged industrial borderland with a mixture of tenements and warehouses, supply shops, storage yards, and parking lots. Moses recognized that its potential for residential use depended on government intervention to direct market forces; without such leadership, the area would not attract investment and would continue to deteriorate. The North Harlem Title I was both a reclamation project, remaking an underutilized manufacturing zone into a residential area, and a consolidation effort, reinforcing the already significant public and private investment in East Harlem housing.

Unlike the prime location of Lenox Terrace, the North Harlem Title I site was in a fringe area. It had several neighborhood assets—a playground one block to the north, public schools and Harlem Hospital to the south—but other structures diminished the area's residential appeal: a Department of Sanitation facility and the Harlem River Drive to the east; the 369th Regiment Armory, home of the Harlem Hell Fighters, and manufacturing plants to the north. A Borden Ice Cream Company plant on the half block from 141st to 142nd Street on Fifth Avenue was omitted from the project. It represented the manufacturing activities that had located in the area beginning in the late nineteenth century to take advantage of river access a block away.

This mixed pattern of land usage led to low density. The Slum Clearance Committee counted only 920 families living on the 12 acres (the sponsor later put the number at 1,200 families). Although landmarks such as older churches were often incorporated in Title I sites, Moses made no allowance for those of popular and commercial culture. And this clearance project swept away a Harlem landmark: the Savoy Ballroom, the legendary jazz hall on Lenox between 140th and 141st streets, which had been operating under the same management since 1926. (The original Cotton Club had been located on Lenox Avenue between 142nd and 143rd streets, but it moved from this location in 1936.)

By the time the plan was published, in January 1951, the committee had worked out a development plan with a sponsor who guaranteed to bid at the public auction for the prenegotiated terms. The sponsor, Charles Axelrod and his sons, Bernard and Carlin, had recently built their first apartment building, a 440-unit complex in Riverdale. Although the Axelrods owned numerous buildings, they were far from being major builders; Moses's receptivity to their overture revealed his eagerness to work with the relatively few developers who came forward in 1950. Bernard Axelrod remembers contacting Moses's office after reading in the newspaper that the commissioner was seeking Title I sponsors.[371] "Pretty soon they called me out to Randall's Island to the headquarters of the Slum Clearance Committee," Charles Axelrod recalled in 1959, "handed me a map of Manhattan with the slums marked on it, and asked me what I would like to have."[372] The Axelrods chose the North Harlem site and named the project Delano Village after an early Harlem landowner and Franklin Delano Roosevelt.

The site plan published in the Slum Clearance Committee brochure followed the standard renewal recipe: high-rise apartment buildings floating on a superblock, stores on an avenue (Lenox), parking lots and playgrounds in the residual open space. (The Lenox Avenue frontage between 142nd and 143rd streets was also incorporated in the plan and designated for parking.) It was atypical, however, for the brochure to reproduce two rival building plans and apartment layouts: one by SOM, proposed by Moses; the other by Maxon-Sells Architects, later Maxon, Sells and Ficke, proposed by the Axelrods. "The unit plan of the apartments proposed by the developer is not as good as ours," the Slum Clearance Committee wrote, "but it is adequate and is the type of apartment this group wants to build and which they know has been acceptable in other areas."[373] The Moses/SOM proposal called for seven 20-story buildings with a total of 1,120 dwelling units; the sponsor's proposal was for ten 8-story buildings, cruciform in shape and much bulkier than SOM's sleek slabs. The Axelrods ultimately built seven 16-story buildings with 1,800 dwelling units, a 60 percent increase over the number of apartments projected in the Moses plan. Maxon,

C-126. Proposal for North Harlem Title I, 1951. Design by Skidmore, Owings & Merrill

C-127. Delano Village, 1952. Design by Maxon, Sells and Ficke; rendering by G. C. Rudolph

Sells and Ficke specialized in nondescript apartment buildings and in the 1950s designed several large-scale developments on the outskirts of the expanding metropolitan area: Far Rockaway, New Rochelle, Pelham Bay. Delano Village was more spartan than those projects; cost-cutting evidently eliminated the "luxury" amenities that distinguished Lenox Terrace.

The Axelrods also substantially reduced the number of stores. SOM specified three commercial blocks on Lenox Avenue; as built, Delano Village included only one block of stores. As Bernard Axelrod explained, the family was experienced in residential construction; commercial development and leasing was out of their ken. They proposed building a new Savoy Ballroom on the block between 142nd and 143rd streets, but its owners rejected the offer. Stretched by Delano Village, the Axelrods sold that property. Bethune Tower, a Mitchell-Lama apartment building, was built on the quarter-block and opened in 1970.

After a fast start, the North Harlem project demonstrated the obstacles facing slum redevelopments. The Slum Clearance Committee plan was published in January 1951 and was immediately sent to the Board of Estimate (along with Corlears Hook, which also had a committed sponsor); it was approved in April. Then the project stalled because the Axelrods could not get financing. Taking a cue from Corlears Hook, which was moving ahead, Charles Axelrod restructured the development as a cooperative and in May 1952 won approval from the Board of Estimate for the revised project. He then reverted to the original rental development, having concluded that a cooperative was not viable in the neighborhood, but he still could not obtain financing. Moses pressed him to clear the site: clearance was a sign of progress and prevented Title I sponsors from behaving like slum lords, collecting rent from their condemned properties. The Axelrods, like the developers of Manhattantown and other stalled Title I projects, made the case that the rents were needed to defray the carrying charges on the property during the prolonged waiting period. Moses again played the middle man, hammering the federal government to change FHA mortgage insurance policy, urging private lenders to provide financing, pressing the sponsors to maintain their properties, and defending their right to make a profit to the press.

The stalemate ended with the passage of the U.S. Housing Act of 1954, which authorized the FHA to issue mortgage insurance on urban renewal projects. Delano Village was the first Title I project in the nation to receive FHA mortgage insurance, a decision announced in September 1955. Construction proceeded quickly from that point on: the first three buildings (on the east side of the site) opened in September 1957, two others followed in 1960, and the final pair in 1962.

Delano Village had mixed results in the 1960s. From the city's fiscal perspective, it was a success. The property on which the first three towers were built had previously produced $35,000 in taxes; the tax yield on the new apartments was approximately $225,000 in the early years. But the tenants were unhappy; they complained about inadequate maintenance and poor security, and repeatedly asked for better locks and doormen, as provided at Lenox Terance. In the mid-1960s, Delano Village was hard hit by crime.

The Axelrod brothers sold Delano Village in 2006 for $175 million. — HB

WILLIAMSBURG TITLE I

Unexecuted
Brooklyn: Wilson Avenue, Division Avenue, Marcy Avenue, Hewes Street, and Wythe Avenue
45 acres
Plan published January 1951
Fig. C-128

The Williamsburg Title I project was conceived in relation to the Brooklyn-Queens Expressway (BQE), which bisected the site. In 1940, Moses initiated what was originally called the Brooklyn-Queens Connecting Highway to link the Brooklyn-Battery Tunnel with the Triborough Bridge (or more precisely the Queens access road, Grand Central Parkway). When the Williamsburg Title I plan was published in January 1951, the seventh issued by the Slum Clearance Committee, Moses evidently expected imminent construction of the adjacent road segment between the Williamsburg Bridge and the Brooklyn Navy Yard. The project was intended to take advantage of the clearance involved in the road construction while replacing a tenement area with middle-income housing.

Like the Delancey Street project, the Williamsburg Title I was another rare instance when Moses published a plan before securing a sponsor. Because he had a free hand in shaping the redevelopment scheme, Williamsburg Title I, although unexecuted, provides a clear picture of the Moses planning paradigm.

Skidmore, Owings & Merrill, the consulting architects of the Slum Clearance Committee, devised the site plan, which responds to the axis of the BQE. The highway segments the site into two large triangular areas, each divided into three blocks. Fifteen apartment towers are evenly distributed on the three largest blocks. Placed parallel to the diagonal cut of the highway, the apartments turn against the local grid and face east-west to capture sunlight. The three other blocks, all irregularly shaped, have community facilities. A shopping center is at the busiest intersection, close to the Marcy Avenue subway station. A commercial garage rises beside a highway exit, where the BQE changes from a sunken to an elevated road. A new junior high school and playground occupy another block, and a park fills an adjacent leftover parcel. Although the site plan called for closing the east-west streets, the north-south streets, Lee and Bedford avenues, were retained and bridge the sunken highway.

In an area of two- and three-story row houses, SOM's proposal for 20-story apartment buildings

C-128. Proposal for Williamsburg Title I, ca. 1951. Shopping center is at lower left, junior high school center top.
Design by Skidmore, Owings & Merrill; rendering by G. C. Rudolph & Associates.

entailed a radical change of scale. In establishing a foundation for its planning work, the Slum Clearance Committee initiated a comparative cost study of buildings at varying heights and found that the cost of three 14-story buildings was comparable to two 20-story buildings. "The advantage to the site plan of achieving the same density of population in fewer buildings was obvious. It meant taller buildings with more space between them for light and air."[374] The residential land coverage dropped from 58 percent to 7.8 percent in the SOM scheme. This strategy of reducing land coverage, increasing building height, and holding population density steady was adopted in every Moses Title I project.

The Williamsburg Title I would have caused serious social dislocation. There were 12,539 residents on the site. The redevelopment would house 9,300, but only 37.5 percent of the site residents were projected to move into the new Title I housing, and such estimates were generally inflated. Nevertheless, Moses saw the housing as a compensatory response to the highway displacement and intended to make the Title I developer responsible for relocating tenants on

the expressway right-of-way, thereby transferring the city's responsibility to the private builder. The Williamsburg Title I in combination with the BQE set a precedent for Moses's later proposal for Lower Manhattan Expressway housing.

Delays in constructing the BQE, in particular the segment between the Williamsburg Bridge and the Brooklyn Navy Yard, put the Title I project on the back burner. The city did not acquire the land for that portion of the road until 1952, and redevelopment plans resurfaced only when the road was completed at the end of the decade. In 1959, the Seafarers International Union offered to build a Title I cooperative housing development modeled on the ILGWU–United Housing Foundation Title I projects. In place of 20-story buildings, the union proposed 8-story buildings on a smaller site west of the original area, a 6-acre strip closer to the water bounded by Wythe and Kent streets, Division Street and the highway. Nothing came of this proposal, but in the 1960s the area remained a priority of the Housing and Redevelopment Board, the successor agency to Moses's Slum Clearance Committee. Ada Louise

Huxtable reported in the *New York Times* (June 19, 1969) that Constantinos Doxiadis, whom the board hired as a consultant, designed a scheme "closing off Williamsburg from the sea with a Chinese wall of construction."

By the late 1950s, the New York City Housing Authority had also targeted the area south of the Williamsburg Bridge for slum clearance; at the same time, the anticipated closing of the naval yard in 1966 inflicted further economic damage. In this blighted territory, the NYCHA built three public housing projects: Jonathan Williams Plaza (completed in 1964), Independence Houses (completed 1965), and Taylor Wythe Houses (completed 1974). The latter two projects were built on the original Title I site, and, in a reprise of the 1951 SOM scheme, Independence Houses consisted of six 20-story buildings. The Orthodox Jewish community acquired a large portion of the original site and in the early 1970s developed a middle-income cooperative of low-rise buildings. These housing colonies encircled by the BQE encapsulate the postwar history of urban renewal in New York City. — HB

MORNINGSIDE-MANHATTANVILLE TITLE I

Morningside Gardens, 1955–57
Manhattan: Amsterdam Avenue to Broadway,
    123rd to La Salle Street
9.97 acres (net)
Plan published September 1951
Figs. P-38–39, E-30

Morningside Gardens was Moses's gold standard of how to do a Title I project. It had responsible leadership, proceeded without delays, handled relocation responsibly, and embraced integration. It met the goal of providing middle-class housing while coordinating with low-income public housing and other community improvements. What distinguishes the project above all is the role of the sponsor, Morningside Heights, Inc., and its young president, David Rockefeller. His impressive debut in urban renewal work on Morningside Heights was the prelude to a still more ambitious initiative launched in the mid-1950s to redevelop lower Manhattan, as discussed in the entry on Battery Park Title I.

The origins of the project went back to 1946 when Riverside Church, International House, and Columbia University mobilized to confront slum conditions in their environs. After undertaking a study of neighborhood conditions, the institutions established in July 1947 a nonprofit corporation to pursue concrete actions. The mission of Morningside Heights, Inc., was "to foster, plan, develop and promote the improvement, redevelopment and advancement of the Morningside Heights district . . . as an attractive residential, and educational and cultural area; to collect, study and disseminate information, research and data affecting the improvement, redevelopment and advancement of this district; . . . and to acquire property, provided it is necessary for these purposes." It was supported by fourteen local universities, seminaries, churches, and hospitals.[375] Morningside Heights, Inc., responded to the institutional anxiety about the impact of creeping slums by forging a progressive social and planning agenda.

The president of Morningside Heights, Inc. was David Rockefeller, then thirty-one years old and continuing his family's deep involvement with Morningside Heights. His father John D. Rockefeller Jr. had financed the construction of International House (1924)—David was chairman of its board—and of Riverside Church (1930).[376] The group's vice president was Grayson L. Kirk, the president of Columbia University, and the executive director was planner Lawrence M. Orton, a member

of the City Planning Commission since its creation in 1938 (he continued to serve until 1969). The approach to planning of Morningside Heights, Inc., was shaped in these early years by Orton, Rockefeller, the Rockefeller family architect Wallace Harrison, and General Otto Nelson, the vice president of New York Life Insurance in charge of its substantial housing program.[377]

Providing housing for the middle-class employees of the Morningside institutions was a priority. A neighborhood study by Columbia faculty revealed that three-quarters of the staff of the local institutions lived outside the area; most would have preferred to live nearer their jobs but were dissatisfied with housing options on the hill. New York's so-called Acropolis was belted by overcrowded tenements and single-room-occupancy hotels that served a rising tide of blacks and Puerto Ricans spreading south from Harlem. The worry was this tide would flood Morningside Heights and absorb it into Harlem. Morningside Heights, Inc., pursued a two-pronged approach to the housing problem: it proposed to sponsor a middle-income Title I project, and it persuaded the New York City Housing Authority to build two low-income public housing projects nearby.

With funding from the Rockefeller Brothers Fund, Morningside Heights, Inc., developed a proposal for the Morningside-Manhattanville Title I project, which Moses approved in February 1951. The group's plans and research were then worked up into a Slum Clearance Committee brochure and published in September 1951. Title I made it possible to reduce the land costs from $14.50 per square foot (according to the acquisition appraisal) to $3 per square foot, the resale price. But even with discounted land costs, the challenge of financing the project was considerable and restricted it to a relatively small area: two blocks directly north of the Jewish Theological Seminary, from West 123rd to La Salle Street, a total of 10 acres, compared to 15 acres for the neighboring public housing.

The Slum Clearance Committee brochure presented two financial scenarios: a cooperative with down payments of $1,000 per room and monthly carrying charges of $25 per room, and a rental project with monthly rents of $31 per room. Moses had resisted the initial request of Morningside Heights, Inc., for partial tax exemption. It was not that he opposed tax-exempt cooperatives; on the contrary, they were a defining component of his approach to Title I. His resistance was tactical: he correctly anticipated that the Board of Estimate would readily grant tax exemptions when confronted by community protests at the public

hearings.[378] The partial tax exemptions made it possible for Morningside Gardens to revise its financial plan and offer monthly carrying charges of $16 to $22 with down payments of about $700 per room. Orton enlisted Shirley Boden to set up the cooperative. Boden had been schooled in cooperative housing with the master of the field Abraham Kazan; and after Morningside Gardens he went on to establish the Middle Income Housing Corporation, which was responsible for two Title I projects, Park Row and Park Row Extension, among other housing cooperatives.

The initial scheme for Morningside Gardens was designed by Wallace Harrison and Harmon Goldstone, who a decade later became the first chairman of the Landmarks Commission. The two-block project area had been covered by walk-up tenements; a quarter of the dwelling units lacked a private bathroom, and buildings covered 91 percent of the site, leaving only the streets and sidewalks for recreation. Harrison and Goldstone's scheme published in September 1951 proposed six brick apartment buildings arranged diagonally in two rows, with generous playgrounds in the middle of the block. Stores were located on Broadway, and a surface parking lot was laid out along La Salle Street, across the street from the public housing and where the site was flat.

The design of Morningside Gardens was subsequently revised by Harrison & Abramovitz, with Harrison continuing as the designer. His executed scheme offered the typical benefits of modernist urbanism—reduced land coverage, automobile amenities, and improved housing—plus better than average landscaping and responsiveness to site conditions. At the recommendation of the Federal Housing Administration, an indoor garage was added on the Broadway frontage, where the blank garage wall faces the subway as it emerges from underground. The sloping site allowed the garage entrance to be located on La Salle Street while providing access to rooftop parking from the higher ground on 123rd Street. The stores were shifted to Amsterdam Avenue, where they maintain the street wall; the apartment buildings were realigned with the city grid, in contrast to the diagonal orientation of the adjacent General Grant Houses. By reorienting the apartment buildings and pulling them out toward the perimeter of the site, the architects opened up the center of the double block where a hilly park makes the unusual topography of the site visible.

Although displaced tenants from the site had priority in the cooperative, few could afford to buy into Morningside Gardens. In an effort to alleviate the relocation problem, Morningside Heights, Inc., lobbied the New York City Housing Authority to invest in the area. In November 1951, the Housing Authority selected a site bordering Morningside Gardens, on La Salle Street and Amsterdam Avenue. The General Grant Houses were built between 1953 and 1957, the same time as Morningside Gardens, with federal aid, which made it possible to offer very low rents ($9 per month per room) but also imposed stringent eligibility requirements: an income ceiling of $4,000 and no single-person families.[379] These eligibility standards excluded a high percentage of those displaced by the slum clearance projects. For those who fell between the financial requirements of the Grant Houses and Morningside Gardens, the Housing Authority agreed to build a second project, using state rather than federal funds, which allowed for a higher income ceiling of about $6,000. Manhattanville Houses was approved in 1954 and completed in 1961, on a five-block site between 129th and 133rd streets, Amsterdam Avenue and Broadway; the rents were about $14 per room.[380]

Morningside Gardens and the Grant Houses are often described as a barricade separating Morningside Heights from Harlem, but this description does not adequately capture the innovative and progressive character of the housing program. First, the housing did not stop at 125th Street but reached into Harlem. And three projects were involved, each targeted at a different income. This three-part program was brought about by the cooperation of the Housing Authority, the Slum Clearance Committee, and a nonprofit community organization. Although not much of a team player, Moses subsequently emulated the strategy of coordinating Title I and public housing, but as the experience of Morningside Gardens illustrates, this approach could not solve the relocation problem. The three Morningside housing projects cleared a total of 35 acres and displaced more people than they could rehouse. Morningside Gardens alone displaced 1,626 families of which only 248 found haven in public housing. The remainder landed in other slums, some just a few blocks away. Far from a barricade, the new housing set in motion a local migration. "Slums Engulfing Columbia Section" was the headline of a 1958 New York Times story about the failure of the Morningside institutions to halt the "vicious cancer of slum housing" that was further eroding the area.[381]

The experience of Morningside Gardens and the Grant Houses also demonstrated the built-in conflicts of race and class. The sponsors of the Title I cooperative were committed to open housing and, for the period, achieved a relatively integrated community; in Morningside Gardens, where about one-third of the residents were affiliated with the sponsoring institutions, 75 percent of the residents were white, and 21 percent were black and Puerto Rican. In the General Grant Houses, with its low income ceiling, the numbers were more skewed the other way: 11 percent of residents were white, 89 percent were black and Puerto Rican.[382]

The large ambitions of Morningside Heights, Inc., were not satisfied by one small Title I project, and it tried to interest Moses in another redevelopment, from 108th to 110th Street between Central Park West and Columbus Avenue. "It has long seemed to us," Orton wrote to Moses in 1955, "that there are opportunities for, in effect, linking the upper end of Central Park with the lower end of Morningside Park by means of a low-coverage residential development which would provide open spaces bordered by modern apartments in the gap between the two parks." In a polite reply, Moses explained the steps that the group would have to go through to propose another Title I project, but he gave David Rockefeller a franker assessment: "It does not seem to me that my group could possibly extend its activities in this area. We have helped in every possible way even going a considerable distance beyond our official responsibilities. There is such a thing as getting spread too thin."[383]

The Title I project was only one part of a comprehensive effort by Morningside Heights, Inc., to improve social conditions in the area. The corporation assisted in housing rehabilitation, funded music classes in the public school, organized crime prevention and street patrols to combat gang violence, and developed an athletic program with a popular baseball league that played at Columbia's Baker Field. Athletics was the context of another town-gown partnership: in 1957, Columbia built athletic fields and a field house on 6 acres at the south end of Morningside Park. "I don't think that a university such as ours ought to exist as an enclave of a city," President Kirk had stated in 1955. "Its cultural resources ought in so far as possible to be made available to the people of the community."[384] The Columbia-Community Athletic Field was jointly used without disturbance for a decade, and the proposal in 1960 to build a gym on the site was a natural extension of ongoing activities. By 1968, however, the gym was regarded as a sign of institutional racism. The bitter debacle of the gym underscores the different circumstances that prevailed in the 1950s, when Morningside Heights, Inc., acted in the name of community improvement and built Morningside Gardens as the crown jewel in its program.

An event in 2006 testified to the success of Morningside Gardens as a diverse middle-class community. In order to preserve Morningside Gardens as a moderate-income community, the sale price of units was regulated from the start, as at the other Title I cooperatives. The gentrification of Morningside Heights widened the gap between the regulated sale price at Morningside Gardens and the value of the apartments if they could be sold on the open market, creating an apparently irresistible temptation of "going to market." In March 2006, the resident-owners voted to raise the maximum sale price to 80 percent of market value but imposed a 15-percent tax on profits to benefit the co-op. The immediate impact of the vote was to triple sale prices. Over time, the policy will squeeze out the middle class for whom this Title I project was built. — HB

MANHATTANTOWN TITLE I

Park West Village, 1957–61
Manhattan: West 97th to West 100th Street,
    Central Park West to Amsterdam Avenue
23 acres
Plan published September 1951
Fig. C-129

Manhattantown was the most notorious Title I project, emblematic of sponsor abuses. According to Moses, the project was suggested by Representative Franklin Delano Roosevelt Jr. and the West Side Housing Committee, a coalition of social action and neighborhood groups.[385] Roosevelt and Representative Adam Clayton Powell blessed the project in 1952 when it came before the City Planning Commission, which granted approval despite community objections to the vague relocation plan. Five years later, the site had not been cleared and living conditions had declined, but the nonperforming sponsors were making money.

The abuses at Manhattantown were publicly exposed in September 1954, when the Senate Committee on Banking and Commerce held public hearings on the inactive Title I project. The committee was conducting a national investigation of abuses of the FHA mortgage insurance program, tracking down cases where developers inflated construction estimates to get a cut of the federal money. Manhattantown was one of the first Title I projects to be scrutinized by the Senate. The investigation revealed inflated expenses on the Manhattantown application for FHA mortgage insurance: fees of 5 percent of construction costs for the architect Melvin Kessler and the builder Jack Ferman, who was also a sponsor and the president of Manhattantown, Inc.; their actual fees were 1.25 percent.

The testimony of Samuel Caspert, a spokesman for and the secretary of Manhattantown, Inc., revealed a variety of other seedy money-making practices. For example, Caspert's son-in-law bought the refrigerators and gas appliances in the tenements, leased them to Manhattantown, Inc., and at the end of the year sold the appliances back, making about $150,000 from the fake transactions.[386] One demolition expert who had been denied site work informed Moses that Caspert was "milking" the city "with under the table deals for apartments, kickbacks on moving expenses, sale of fixtures, ordering of excess fuel and resale of same, padding of pay rolls and kickbacks from contractors."[387] The Senate report found that the Manhattantown principals took $649,215 out of the project in the first 18 months.

After the Senate exposé, there were some changes

C-129. Site of Manhattantown Title I, looking east, with Trinity Evangelical Lutheran Church and P.S. 105 on cleared block, ca. 1958. The Frederick Douglass Houses (left), a NYCHA project, are under construction.

at Manhattantown, Inc., but without visible effect. Caspert withdrew from the project, and, in 1956, the FHA issued mortgage insurance on the first three buildings, known as West Park. Among the shareholders identified on the FHA application was Melvin Kessler, the Title I architect. Kessler later disclosed that he had invested $18,000 in the project (a 1.75 percent share of the corporation), as had his father and brother, and made $3,600 when he cashed out.[388] Kessler's investment on top of his extensive Title I work became a scandal in 1959 and resulted in Mayor Wagner's banning him from future involvement with the program.[389] By 1957, Manhattantown was owned by two shareholders: Jack Ferman and Seymour Milstein, then 37 years old and president of Mastic Tile Company, a family-owned building materials company. Ferman was about to slide from public view. Milstein within a decade emerged as a real estate titan.

No one wanted results more than Moses. In June 1957, he threatened Ferman and Milstein with foreclosure and prevailed upon them to sell a majority interest in Manhattantown to Webb & Knapp. William Zeckendorf, the principal of Webb & Knapp, was Moses's white knight; one week earlier he had taken

over the stalled NYU–Bellevue project. The change in ownership, the *New York Times* reported, "is viewed in building circles as the squeezing out from the slum clearance program of some of the early promoters who had little or no construction know-how."[390] Webb & Knapp paid the back taxes owed by the original sponsors and set the project in forward motion.

Manhattantown was an ideal Title I site: underutilized land, run-down housing, prime Central Park location. A profitable slum like Manhattantown, Moses argued, required government intervention and aggressive clearance; private owners had no economic incentive to improve conditions.[391] The six targeted blocks were packed with 4- to 5-story walk-up tenements, many used as rooming houses. Overcrowding pushed the population density to 910 persons per net housing acre in 1950, as compared to 650 persons in 1940. Redevelopment would lower density to 422 persons, which translated to a drop in the site population from 11,200 to 8,840.

The reduced density and increased rent levels in the replacement market-rate housing meant not only massive relocation and social upheaval but also racial resorting. One of the distinguishing features of Manhattantown was its racially mixed population.

According to data that Moses collected, the site population was almost evenly split between white families (1,953) and nonwhite families (2,132). No other Title I site was as integrated.[392] The effect of redevelopment was to segregate this 6-block site, as the expensive new rentals generally priced out nonwhite tenants. Existing monthly rentals averaged about $30 per room; the apartments at Park West Village started around $50 per room.

Moses privatized the relocation problem by shifting responsibility to the Title I sponsors and counted on public housing to house evictees. The planning of Manhattantown was coordinated with the development of a New York City Housing Authority project on an adjacent site, seen in the lower left corner of the aerial photograph. The Frederick Douglass Houses were located from 100th to 104th Street, between Manhattan and Amsterdam avenues, a 22-acre site comparable to the area of Manhattantown. Both projects developed at about the same pace: they were approved by the City Planning Commission in 1952, and the Douglass Houses opened in 1958, slightly before Manhattantown. The Douglass Houses did not solve the relocation problem at the Title I site, but the coordinated construction of public and Title I housing was an attempt to create a racially integrated, mixed-income neighborhood.

The original site plan by S. J. Kessler & Sons for the Slum Clearance Committee was a grim, monotonous scheme. Seventeen uniform apartment buildings were arranged in three staggered rows on two superblocks, with alternating parking lots and play areas in the open spaces. Commercial buildings fronted Amsterdam and Columbus avenues, and public facilities, including a playground and new police station, were grouped on 97th Street In a revised scheme from around 1956, Kessler reduced the number of buildings to nine and enlarged their volume but retained the same arrangement in rows.

In 1957, Zeckendorf rechristened the project Park West Village and, more importantly, had I. M. Pei improve the site plan, although Kessler remained as architect.[393] The buildings were rearranged around a mall running through the center of the Central Park West superblock and continuing across Columbus Avenue to the middle of the second superblock. Four 20-story buildings frame the central open space on the east block; their east-west alignment gives every apartment a view of the park. The three 16-story buildings west of Columbus Avenue stand at the head of the mall, their long sides facing east and west to close the composition.[394] They are disposed around a midblock driveway/promenade that extends the central axis of the overall scheme, but Amsterdam Avenue and the tennis courts and stores that border the street break the development into two distinct parts. Webb & Knapp marketed Park West Village as a way "to enjoy the charm of country living in the very heart of the city." Resident families to this day commend the openness, park access, and play facilities of Park West. Unfortunately, the mall achieved no higher purpose than a parking lot.

Webb & Knapp developed the project in two phases: the three towers and shops west of Columbus opened in September 1959; the four towers on the Central Park West block followed in February 1961. As originally planned, a row of storefronts was built on Amsterdam at the corner of 100th Street in 1960; the stores were vacated in 2006 as a prelude to redevelopment. A 16-story, subsidized apartment building was erected in 1965 on the 97th Street corner.

In addition to housing, commercial, and recreational facilities, the Title I site reserved a strip near Amsterdam Avenue for public facilities. A new public school, P.S. 105, was built on 97th Street. A health center operated by the Department of Health (Riverside Health Center) and a new Bloomingdale branch of the New York Public Library were built on 100th Street, beside Trinity Evangelical Lutheran Church (1909), the only building on the site that was preserved. If the standard practice applied, Webb & Knapp was expected to provide the cleared building site and the city paid for the improvements. Across 100th Street, on the grounds of the Douglass Houses, the NYCHA project, a new police station, fire station, and armory were built.

Sponsor malfeasance, tenant evictions, and resegregation shaped the sad beginning of Manhattantown, but the project had other significant features that belong in the urban renewal story. They include the coordination of Title I and public housing, the provision of public facilities, the creation of an appealing middle-class community with playgrounds, and the privileged use of open space for parking. — HB

COLUMBUS CIRCLE TITLE I

New York Coliseum, 1953–56; demolished 2000
Coliseum Park Apartments, 1956–57
Manhattan: Columbus Circle to Columbus Avenue, West 58th to West 60th Street
6.32 acres
Plan published December 1952
Figs. C-130–132

Moses devised the Columbus Circle Title I to provide the city with a modern convention center. The project epitomized the high-handed and combative Moses style and relentless pursuit of his city-building agenda. He manipulated numbers, twisted the Title I law, and bullied federal officials to get what he wanted: a federal subsidy for a high-priority city project. The Coliseum sparked congressional hearings and became a national symbol of the misuse of the Title I program for commercial development, yet the Coliseum was atypical of Moses's approach to Title I: of his 17 executed urban renewal projects, it was the only one that focused on commercial use, although the Coliseum was a public building.

Before the Coliseum opened in 1956, the city had two convention venues, both small and out-of-date. The main facility was Grand Central Palace, on Lexington Avenue between 46th and 47th streets, built in 1911 by the New York Central Railroad in conjunction with its reconstruction of Grand Central Terminal. The building contained 180,000 square feet, but it was split on 6 floors, chopped up by columns, and unsuitable for the increasingly large floor areas required for trade shows.[395] The other option was Madison Square Garden, on Eighth Avenue between 49th and 50th streets, built in 1927. With a seating capacity of 18,000, it was useful for large meetings but largely unavailable because the Garden was heavily booked with sporting events.

Conventions were an economic stimulus, and their numbers were trending upward: bigger shows, higher attendance, more revenues. In 1946, conventions brought $150 million into New York, according to the New York Convention and Visitors Bureau, but the city was losing ground; in 1949, 65 conventions were too big for New York's outdated facilities. The city's main rival, Chicago, had two much larger venues, the Chicago Navy Pier with 350,000 square feet and the Chicago International Amphitheatre with 250,000 square feet. And other cities were investing in exhibition halls and auditoriums: Atlantic City opened a convention hall in 1929 with a capacity to seat 41,000 people; and, in 1946, Los Angeles was plan-

C-130. Site of the future New York Coliseum, May 14, 1954. Photograph by Richie Productions, Inc.
Collection MTA Bridges and Tunnels Special Archive

ning a 30,000-seat hall. To secure New York's stake in the booming, multimillion-dollar convention business, the city needed to build a state-of-the art facility in Manhattan, where hotels, tourism, and business were centered.

Moses was the city's designated point person to tackle the problem. His Triborough Bridge and Tunnel Authority had the proven ability to build big projects and the means to finance them, with high bond ratings backed by a "silver stream" of tolls, as Caro put it, and without encumbering the city's debt limit. In order for the TBTA to assume this role, the state had to pass enabling legislation and raise the authority's bond limit. There was some opposition to expanding the already expansive role of the TBTA. The state legislature considered establishing another authority to build the convention center, but the mayor and dozens of business groups backed the

TBTA option, and in April 1948 Governor Thomas E. Dewey signed a bill empowering it to do the job.[396]

But the TBTA could not do the job alone; committed as it was to self-supporting enterprises, the authority needed a partner to lease the hall when absent conventions. In 1946, Moses teamed up with Madison Square Garden to plan a joint sports arena and convention facility. (The president of Madison Square Garden, General John Reed Kilpatrick, described Moses as the father of the project.) Mayor O'Dwyer was on hand to unveil the scheme in November 1946. The site was one of the most prominent and potentially imposing in the city, on Columbus Circle, at the southwest corner of Central Park, from 58th to 60th Street. The project consisted of a 25,000-seat sports arena in a circular structure, an abutting rectangular wing with 200,000 square feet of exhibition and meeting space dubbed the

Coliseum, and a garage for 2,000 cars. Chicago had larger facilities, but this inconvenient fact did not stop boosters from celebrating the new Madison Square Garden as the largest convention center in the world. The structure bridged 59th Street, which remained intact, and accommodated two existing buildings on the northern block: the Cosmopolitan Theatre and the towering Manufacturers Trust Company Building.[397] The 1946 scheme was designed by Leon Levy and Lionel Levy, architects probably chosen by Madison Square Garden. The Levys, who were unrelated and met as students at the Georgia Institute of Technology in the 1920s, specialized in sports arenas and race tracks.

Negotiations between the TBTA and the Garden broke down in 1949. The Garden board was split over the desirability of opening a second sports venue, uncertain about the impact of television on attendance, and reluctant to assume financial responsibility for leasing the entire Columbus Circle facility—the sports arena, convention center, and garage—as Moses insisted. The project stalled for two years, until he figured out another way to move forward.[398]

In 1951, Moses reimagined the Coliseum in two ways. First, he restructured the convention center as a Title I project in order to tap a government subsidy and reduce site acquisition costs. Smack in the middle of the site was the Manufacturers Trust Company Building, a valuable 22-story skyscraper assessed at $1.5 million; the write-down made it affordable to buy this property and clear the site completely. Second, in May 1951, Moses invited the Metropolitan Opera to replace the Garden and offered it the Columbus Circle frontage between 58th and 59th streets. He envisioned a city musical center involving the New York Philharmonic-Symphony Society and perhaps the ballet, but those programmatic questions were to be addressed at later date. The first step for the Opera was to raise $1.2 million for site acquisition.

When Moses vetted the project with federal urban renewal officials, he was told that the land uses did not satisfy Title I requirements. The proposed mixture of convention center, opera house, and a small amount of housing required a ruling that the Columbus Circle site was a "primarily residential" slum. The Title I law imposed no restrictions on redevelopment of such areas; if a slum were "primarily nonresidential," however, the redevelopment had to be weighted toward housing. According to the numbers Moses published in the Slum Clearance brochure in 1952, existing land uses were as follows: tenements, 10 percent; parking lots, 33.7 percent; and commercial buildings, 39 percent (the remaining

17 percent was not mentioned in the brochure but elsewhere classified as residential).[399] The parking lots and commercial buildings add up (in whole numbers) to 73 percent nonresidential, which led to a federal ruling that the Columbus Circle site was primarily nonresidential. In order to obtain Title I financing, Moses had to raise the residential component of the redevelopment to at least 51 percent. As a result, in March 1952, he eliminated the Metropolitan Opera from the project. "The important thing is that we have an agreement with the people in Washington to erect a Coliseum," Moses explained. "The Metropolitan would have taken up too much space."[400] More room was needed for housing.

The plan published by the Slum Clearance Committee in December 1952 was the result of its reprogramming to meet the 51 percent residential rule. The site plan proposed complete clearance, closed 59th Street, and divided the double block roughly in half, with the Coliseum facing Columbus Circle and two apartment buildings on the Ninth Avenue side. The plan hinged on one calculation, which was clearly explained: "the area devoted to housing is 147,874 square feet, or 53.4 percent of the

area. This includes 18,000 square feet of parking space reserved in the public garage for cars of tenants in the housing project."[401] Remove the 18,000 square feet of parking beneath the Coliseum from the calculation and only 47 percent of the area was allocated to housing, below the Title I requirement. (It is curious that Moses did not extend this principle to include the apartment garage in the residential calculation.) The Title I officials accepted Moses's creative math.

The 1952 brochure describes the Coliseum as a multipurpose civic facility, serving exhibitions, large meetings, and other public functions. The building has five stories, with four floors of exhibition space, 6,000 fixed seats, meeting rooms on the top floor, and a two-story underground garage for 800 cars. The Levys' revised design shows a windowless block with concave facade, a holdover from the sports arena, overscaled fluting, and a projecting glass pavilion. Like a beached whale, the building was oblivious to its magnificent site.

The Columbus Circle Title I was approved by the city in December 1952 and by the Housing and Home Finance Agency (HHFA) in January 1953. The city acquired the two-block area for $11.7 million and

resold it for $2.2 million; the federal government paid for two-thirds of the $9.5 million write-down.[402] In short, Moses wrested a $6 million subsidy from the federal government for a municipal convention center. Relocation and clearance were delayed for the better part of 1953 by a legal challenge to the city's claim of eminent domain, which a state court eventually affirmed. Then, with construction one month away, Moses dramatically changed the project.

In March 1954, Moses filed a revised scheme without obtaining prior approval from the HHFA as required. The height of the twin apartment buildings was raised from 12 to 14 stories. The Coliseum lost its concave facade and became a blunt rectangular block; inside the fixed seating was removed. But the last-minute change that astonished Washington, snubbed urban renewal protocol, and wholly disregarded the law was the addition of a $10-million, 26-story office building, with 550,000 (gross) square feet. Moses held that the office building was needed to subsidize the Coliseum. Members of Congress and the HHFA held that Moses had abused Title I. The House passed an appropriation bill with a rider putting strict limits on the nonresidential components of

C-131. First scheme for New York Coliseum and Coliseum Park Apartments, ca. 1952. Design by Leon and Lionel Levy. Collection MTA Bridges and Tunnels Special Archives

to remove the land beneath the office building from the Title I project.

Moses would not let go of the lucrative, tax-exempt office tower. While Mayor Wagner attempted to negotiate an amicable truce, Moses mounted a public counterattack. In an indignant letter to the HHFA director that was published in the *New York Times*, Moses claimed the high ground of fiscal responsibility.

> The use of these air rights to produce additional revenue for Triborough was necessitated by the higher cost of construction and to keep faith with our bond holders. We told you . . . that Triborough is not a money making authority . . . that we undertook the Coliseum in answer to widespread public demand; that to realize it our act was amended by the State Legislature . . . that the amendments clearly indicated the need and approval of additional revenue producing facilities; that we have no revenues to apply to the Coliseum except those which it earns by itself, and that only enough revenue will be obtained in any event to amortize principal, pay interest and upkeep and some city taxes.

If the federal government reduced the write-down, Moses threatened to "make an announcement to the public of your repudiation, at the same time releasing five years of correspondence with the Federal agency on this subject, and throwing the whole matter into the courts."[404] Then he brazenly proceeded with the groundbreaking ceremony on April 13, 1954, which the Voice of America broadcast around the world, presenting the Coliseum as proof of American urban progress.

Of course, Moses prevailed. In December 1954, federal officials recategorized the original site as a primarily residential slum. This was done by counting the existing surface parking lots as residential land use on the grounds that they occupied land previously used for tenements. As *Architectural Forum* noted, the HHFA ruling lifted all restrictions on the redevelopment; Moses could have built the Coliseum without any housing.[405]

The Coliseum opened in April 1956 with three simultaneous trade shows (stamp, photo, and international auto). A half-million visitors were expected during the nine-day run. The Coliseum may have been "a $35,000,000 investment in the gregariousness of man," as the *New York Times* kindly put it; above all, it was a smart investment in the future of New York as a magnet for trade and tourism.[406] Four free-span floors contained 323,000 square feet of

C-132. New York Coliseum and office building at Columbus Circle, looking south, May 1, 1956.
Courtesy MTA Bridges and Tunnels Special Archives

"primarily residential" Title I projects. When the bill came before the Senate, Mayor Wagner and Moses led a large New York delegation to protest the rider; they were joined by redevelopment officers from across the country and even the HHFA director, Albert Cole, who asserted that the bill's broad language would unduly restrict redevelopment. The Senate dropped the bill in May 1954.[403]

Meanwhile, Moses battled the Housing and Home Finance Agency. James Follin, the head of the New York office, informed Moses that the office tower endangered the eligibility of the Columbus Circle project for Title I financing and at the least necessitated a recalculation of the federal write-down. "As you well know, the determination that the re-use under the original redevelopment plan was predominantly residential was a very close decision and has been severely criticized. From a preliminary examination of the [new scheme] . . . it seems highly unlikely that such a determination could have been reached had the present plans been submitted in connection with your original application." Follin's solution was

flexible exhibition space. The building was designed to facilitate efficient loading and unloading: one loading dock allowed 18-wheel tractor trailers to drive onto the first exhibition floor; another, ramped loading dock let trucks drive onto the second floors; and giant freight elevators lifted trucks to the upper floors. A hidden structural wonder were the 120-foot-long steel trusses supporting the roof.

The merits of the Coliseum as a building were all internal; as a work of public architecture, it was a failure. Windowless, the six-story block was clad in white brick and decorated with four large cast-aluminum panels, designed by Paul Manship, with the seals of the Coliseum's sponsors—the federal, state, and city governments and the TBTA. Rising from the south end of the block was the office tower, known as 10 Columbus Circle, faced with a grid of small windows in an intentional rebuke of glass-walled modernist towers. The editor of *Art News* denounced the project at a banquet with Moses in attendance, a confrontation that drew from the *New York Times* a rare article on the subject of urban design. The *Art News* editor criticized "the completely dictatorial way in which Mr. Moses is imposing this design upon the public without anyone getting in a word of dissent" and the Coliseum's "total lack of relation to its site. . . . The Coliseum plan looks as if it really disdained, as well as ignored, the arc of the circus on which it is to stand (O shades of Nash's Quadrant!)—as if it merely faced another shoddy loft building instead of, diagonally across the axis of Columbus Circle, the matching concave double-entry into Central Park's acres of greenery." Pouncing on the criticism of his "antiquarian" taste in architecture, Moses declared that "public officials had no right to experiment" with public architecture.[407] Moses had appointed an advisory group of architects—Aymar Embury, Eggers and Higgins, and John B. Peterkin—whom he trusted to enforce the conservative bias of public taste; what effect if any they had on the Levys' design is unknown.

The Coliseum Park Apartments were developed by Charles Punia and Robert Marx, a Brooklyn-based real estate investment firm, in association with Israel Orlian, with whom they frequently partnered on developments. In 1954, at Senate hearings on windfall profits from FHA mortgage insurance, Charles Punia testified that he made $2.8 million on 25 rental projects from FHA mortgage insurance before the buildings were even completed. As a result, Punia and Marx were disqualified from obtaining FHA mortgage insurance on the Coliseum housing, but without consequence as they obtained private financing. The Coliseum Park Apartments consisted of two

14-story buildings, designed by Sylvan Bien, a prolific architect known for luxury apartment buildings in Manhattan, and his son Robert L. Bien. The Coliseum apartments fronted on the side streets, offered ground-floor professional suites, and framed a central garden; beneath the garden was a garage. Construction began in April 1956 (when the Coliseum opened), and the 590 apartments and ground-floor professional suites were ready for occupancy in September 1957. Rents started at $50 a room, well above the $43 room rate outlined in the Slum Clearance brochure.

By 1968, the Coliseum was too small. Robert Moses acknowledged that the city would need a new building in about twelve years, but proposed an interim expansion by bridging 60th Street and building on the southeast corner of 60th and Broadway.[408] His proposal was no more than a provocation; the TBTA was about to be absorbed in the MTA. The administration of Mayor John Lindsay resisted the idea, favoring a new hall at a different location. Plans for the Javits Convention Center were announced in 1979. In 1986, a year before it opened, the Coliseum closed; the city sold it in 1987. In a swan song, it reopened from 1992 to 1998 for occasional exhibitions. In 2000, the Coliseum was demolished to make way for the Time Warner Center.

Moses's hardball tactics with the Coliseum served the city's interests. In addition to convention-related revenue, the building stimulated new construction and raised property values in the area. Moses conceived the Columbus Circle Title I as "the nucleus of the general rehabilitation" of the West Side, and it was associated with the more extensive transformation accomplished by the Lincoln Square Title I. But if good for New York, the Coliseum raised legitimate policy questions about Title I. Was it appropriate for federal funds to subsidize the construction of a convention center in New York? "We suppose an argument may be made for Federal funds for slum clearance," the *Wall Street Journal* opined, "though it seems to us that even that is the responsibility of the cities where the slums are, and not of the federal government. But certainly to leap from helping people get better housing to helping cities build pretty places and 20 story office buildings is a big jump indeed."[409] The Coliseum was decidedly not a pretty place, which leads to another policy issue. Given the civic stature of the Coliseum and its location on Columbus Circle, "a natural setting for a civic building" in the words of the Slum Clearance Committee, why did the city fail to set high design standards? — HB

FORT GREENE TITLE I

Kingsview, 1955–57
University Terrace, 1957–58
Shopping center, 1957–58
LIU dormitory, 1958–59
Brooklyn: St. Edward Street, Willoughby Street, Ashland Place, De Kalb Avenue, De Bevoise and Fleet places, Fair and Prince streets, and Myrtle Avenue
20.45 acres
Plan published December 1952
Fig. C-133

The Fort Greene slum clearance plan, published in December 1952, was the eleventh Title I program proposed for the city and among the first group of renewal projects proposed for Brooklyn. In the summer of 1951, the Committee on Slum Clearance received a grant from the federal government to study the site, which comprised about 20 acres of mostly commercial land on all or part of 17 blocks extending west from Fort Greene Park, Brooklyn Hospital, and the old Kings County Jail to Flatbush Avenue Extension, and north to the recently completed public Fort Greene Houses.

The project was undertaken to benefit two institutions, Brooklyn Hospital and Long Island University, and to provide land for a shopping center and two middle-class housing developments, one rental and the other a limited-equity co-op. According to the slum clearance plan, the hospital, which had long occupied a site adjacent to the clearance area, needed two acres to extend its facilities on the western side of Ashland Place. The college, which for twenty-five years had occupied various rented quarters in the borough, sought 7.5 acres to build a permanent campus. The shopping center, to occupy nearly 3 acres on Myrtle as part of the rental housing complex, was understood as necessary to serve both the new housing and the recently completed Fort Greene public housing projects. The housing complexes were intended to improve the character of the area with economically stable families.

Another party with an interest in the site was the owner of the Brooklyn Dodgers, Walter O'Malley. For several years, O'Malley had been searching for land for a new stadium to replace the aging Ebbets Field, four miles down Flatbush Avenue. Though the sale of Ebbets Field promised to generate sufficient cash to undertake his project privately, with the introduction of Title I O'Malley became determined that the city should help him realize his plan. When he learned of the city's plans for the Fort Greene slum clearance project, he wrote to Moses requesting the site. Moses,

C-133. Fort Greene Title I, with Long Island University (right), University Towers (left),
and Kingview Homes (the towers beyond), 1963. Rendering by R. Corbelletti

who seems to have had a personal dislike for both
O'Malley and professional sports, rejected the idea on
the grounds that a stadium did not represent an
appropriate use of Title I funds.

According to preliminary plans by the architects
Kahn & Jacobs, all or part of six interior streets were
to be eliminated to create three superblocks: one of 3
acres bounded by the park, Willoughby, Ashland, and
Myrtle; one of roughly 9 acres bounded by the hospital and jail, De Kalb, De Bevoise, and Willoughby;
and one of about 8 acres bounded by Ashland,
Willoughby, Fleet, Fair, Prince, and Myrtle. The old
Kings County Jail, also known as the Raymond Street
Jail, was to be replaced by a playground and ball
field, but excluded were six parcels within the general boundaries of the project, including the former
Brooklyn Paramount Theatre, used by LIU as an aca-

demic building; an electric substation; a parking
garage; and several commercial buildings. The hospital and university were to share the southern
superblock; the rental housing, which was eventually
realized as University Towers, and the shopping center were planned for the one to the northwest, and the
co-op for the one to the northeast, facing the park—a
privileged site designed to enhance the appeal of the
apartments.

At the initial hearings, several local business owners spoke in opposition, and later filed a suit against
the city, which was dismissed by the state supreme
court. Several officials questioned the use of public
funds for expansion of the Long Island University
campus. Despite these concerns, the project and the
necessary agreements with Washington were approved
by the city in early 1953. That spring, the co-op

apartments, called Kingsview, went on sale. Both
Kingsview and the project as a whole enjoyed the
support of Frank D. Schroth Jr., the vice president of
the *Brooklyn Eagle*, whose father had first proposed
the nearby Pratt Institute renewal area to Robert
Moses; initially the sales offices were housed in the
Eagle building on Johnson Street. Unlike Title I
co-ops in Manhattan, which had a ready market,
those in other boroughs had to advertise to generate
interest. Kingsview advertised heavily in local and
regional papers, running a series of display ads
between the spring of 1953 and the summer of 1955
that featured site plans for the renewal area and floor
plans of the units.

Kingsview was conceived by Louis H. Pink and
Gerard Swope, who had developed Queensview in
Long Island City and were working there on an

extension, Queensview West. Like these projects, Kingsview was designed by George D. Brown Jr. and Bernard W. Guenther. The buildings, atypically small for a Title I project, were modeled on those at Queensview, where they had been proven to work well. Each tower was to have around 55 units, arranged four to a floor in suites of three and a half, four and a half, and five and a half rooms, for a total of 275 units. Also atypical of comparable Title I co-op projects was that 75 percent of the suites had two or three bedrooms, rather than the usual 40 to 50 percent. As a result of public demand, plans were revised a year into sales in order to accommodate 42 studio apartments of two and a half rooms, raising the total number of units to 290.

Shares were priced at $625 a room with maintenance averaging around $19 per month, which was about $2 less than initial estimates suggested. In practice, units ranged from $1,550 with a monthly maintenance of $49 for a studio up to $3,200 with a monthly charge as much as $104 for three bedrooms. As at Corlears Hook, shareholders' contributions comprised 20 percent of the equity in the project, with the remainder provided through a mortgage, in this case courtesy the Bowery Savings Bank. With all but a handful of the larger units sold, construction started in late 1955 and the project was completed in the spring of 1957. By the early 1980s, the shareholders abandoned the limited-equity format, and today one-bedroom units sell for about $300,000, with $600 in monthly maintenance. As built, the buildings occupy about 16 percent of the site, with a population density of about 364 persons per acre. The plan also called for 55 parking spaces, which sold on the cooperative plan for $300 and had a monthly maintenance of about $8. The ground floor of each building was devoted to community rooms and storage for baby carriages.

Of Fort Greene's multiple components, only Kingsview proceeded as planned. The institutional projects languished. Brooklyn Hospital built nothing on its parcel, and the site is used today as surface parking for employees of LIU. The college, meanwhile, proved unable to afford anything resembling that in the Kahn & Jacobs plan. Faced with insufficient room for its growing number of students, LIU had been looking for space for a permanent campus for several years. The college's president, Tristram Walker Metcalfe, proposed moving to Nassau County. But William Zeckendorf, who had joined the university's board in 1943 and played a lead role in its affairs, learned of Moses's intention to apply for federal funds to clear the Fort Greene site and insisted

on pursuing the Brooklyn location. The university decided to move ahead with both ideas, constructing a Long Island campus, which opened in Brookville in 1954, while negotiating sponsorship for a portion of the Title I area from the city.

The plan that secured this sponsorship called for a dormitory, a student union building, a library, a gymnasium, and a field house. It also called for the college to purchase, and occupy, the old but solid Paramount Theatre at the northeast corner of De Bevoise and De Kalb, which it did in 1952. To cover the cost of acquiring the remainder of its portion of the site from the city, Zeckendorf made a gift to the university of $500,000; in recognition, it named the campus for him. Once the site had been cleared, however, the college lacked sufficient funds to proceed and broke ground for its first new building only in late 1958. That project, a 16-story residential building with dormitory rooms for students and apartments for faculty, was designed by Melvin E. Kessler of S. J. Kessler & Sons and completed in 1959. The remainder of the site was used for parking and athletic fields and filled in with buildings only gradually.

The rental project and shopping center, meanwhile, were also delayed for several years. The original developer selected by Moses was Fred C. Trump, one of the city's most prolific builders of middle-class rental housing, but he was unwilling or unable to realize the project after purchasing the site from the city in 1954. Eventually, the parcel was transferred to Benjamin Neisloss, Arnold Praver, and the architect Benjamin Braunstein, and ground was broken in 1957. Both the apartment complex and shopping center were completed in late 1958.

The apartments were built more or less according to initial plans, though situated differently within the superblock, with one facing Ashland, another facing Willoughby, and the third perpendicular to Willoughby at the center of the site. Each rises 15 stories and contains 182 units of two to five and a half rooms, which initially rented from $98 to $205 a month. These buildings occupy about 10 percent of the superblock, with a population density of about 182 people per acre. Most of the open space is devoted to surface parking. Unfortunately, the project never proved profitable at prevailing rents, and in 1964 the developers sold the complex to LIU for faculty and student housing. The college in turn resold the buildings for conversion to market-rate co-ops in the late 1980s. The shopping center, whose anchor tenant was a Safeway supermarket, was designed by Braunstein. — MGL

NYU–BELLEVUE TITLE I

Kips Bay Plaza, 1957–63
Medical office building
Shopping center
Manhattan: East 31st to East 33rd Street,
    First to Second Avenue
10.63 acres
Plan published [1953]
Figs. P-42–45, C-134–138

Moses proposed the NYU–Bellevue Title I project to reinforce a concerted effort by the city beginning in the 1940s to develop the Kips Bay area as a medical center. The purpose of the project was to provide middle-income housing for the doctors and medical personnel working in the area.

The project took its name from the NYU–Bellevue Medical Center, which was located across the street from the redevelopment site, on the east side of First Avenue. The medical center was established in 1944, when NYU's College of Medicine merged with Bellevue Hospital, the oldest city hospital. Driving the merger was an ambitious social vision of comprehensive medical care for low- and middle-income patients and of an integrated system of teaching, research, and treatment. The university and city leaders who teamed up to create the NYU–Bellevue Medical Center envisioned it as a regional center of specialized postgraduate medical training and as a world-class facility serving the international community attached to the United Nations, a few blocks away.[410]

By 1946, NYU had acquired the medical center site, 11 acres from 30th to 34th Street between First Avenue and East River Drive, which was largely covered with industrial and commercial structures.[411] The city closed four streets (30th through 33rd) and ceded the roadbeds to form a superblock. Skidmore, Owings & Merrill designed a modern medical campus, consisting of a hospital, medical school, the Rusk Institute of Physical Medicine and Rehabilitation, a clinic, and residential hall.[412] Construction of the NYU buildings continued through the 1950s, with the first four completed in 1956. In keeping with the alignment of public and private goals, the university recruited former city officials to realize the medical center. In 1947, Edwin Salmon resigned as chairman of the City Planning Commission to direct the NYU building project.[413] He had helped to devise the city's master plan for public hospitals and chaired the City Planning Commission when the NYU–Bellevue Medical Center was approved. The City Commissioner of Hospitals, Dr. Edward M.

Bernecker, also resigned his post and became administrator of hospital services at the new medical center. Throughout the 1940s, Moses, in his role as City Construction Coordinator, facilitated the project.[414]

The new NYU facilities accelerated the development of a medical zone on First Avenue from 24th to 34th Street comprising federal, municipal, and private institutions. In 1947, the federal government announced a new Veteran's Administration Hospital to be built between 24th and 25th streets, which opened in 1954.[415] The city agreed to fund a multi-million-dollar expansion of Bellevue Hospital and to build the chief medical examiner's office and city morgue at the corner of 30th Street and First Avenue, on land donated by NYU.[416] The NYU School of Dentistry and the Bellevue School of Nursing were also located in this corridor.

With upgrading of the East Side waterfront under way, Moses turned his attention inland where, he noted, "a great deal remains to be done."[417] The greatest need, as he saw it, was modern housing to complement the substantial institutional investments in the area and to allow medical staff to live near their jobs. In 1949, Moses was contemplating a state housing project opposite Bellevue Hospital when passage of the Title I legislation paved the way for a private sector development. In 1952, he secured funding from the trustees of the NYU–Bellevue Medical Center, chaired by Winthrop Rockefeller, for a study of the costs of condemnation and rebuilding, the first step in the Title I planning process.[418] The NYU–Bellevue Title I plan followed in 1953, the twelfth issued by the Mayor's Committee on Slum Clearance. The City Planning Commission and Board of Estimate quickly approved it, and, in September 1954, the Housing and Home Finance Administration allocated $4 million for the federal portion of the write-down, whereupon the Board of Estimate approved the sponsor chosen by Moses, University Center, Inc., and authorized condemnation proceedings. Thirteen hundred tenants on the site were uprooted.[419] Among the demolished buildings was the first model housing built by Phipps Houses, on East 31st Street.

It is a mystery why Moses chose as sponsor University Center, Inc., a syndicate of 93 investors headed by David Moss, an executive of a local construction firm with neither development experience nor financial muscle.[420] Whatever Moses's reason, it must have been compelling because he selected it over a higher bid from James H. Scheuer. In 1953, Scheuer was a bright young thirty-three-year-old without a track record, but his family owned a successful real estate firm with a portfolio of significant

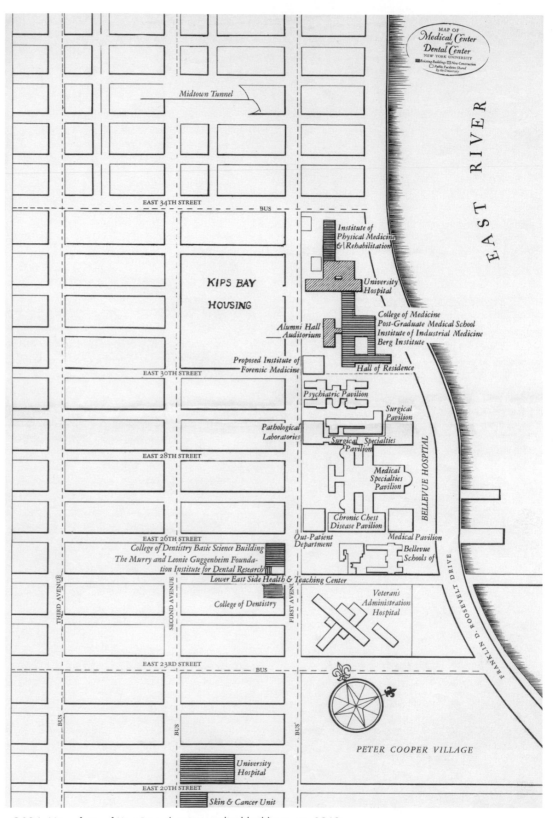

C-134. Map of site of Kips Bay, showing medical buildings, ca. 1960

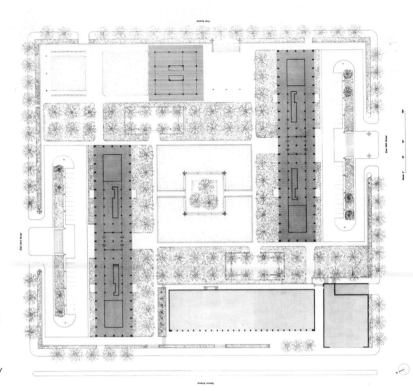

C-135. Site plan of Kips Bay Plaza, 1957. Second Avenue is at bottom. Design by I. M. Pei.

C-136. Sketch of Kips Bay Plaza, looking east, ca. 1958. Design by I. M. Pei

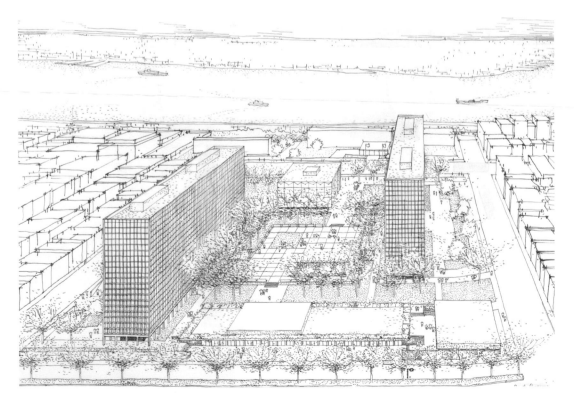

properties. Scheuer complained that Moses gave him the runaround and arranged for Moss to outbid him. (The Slum Clearance Committee later acknowledged that Scheuer had the high bid but said it was late and disqualified it—a wholly unconvincing explanation.) Shut out of Moses's Title I program, Scheuer went on to sponsor Title I projects across the country, including the Southeast Washington development. Unlike Moses, Scheuer actively promoted integration in his projects and became a vocal critic of Moses's approach to renewal. He headed the Citizens Housing and Planning Council, and his housing activism launched a long political career, beginning in 1964 when, as a reform Democrat, he was first elected to the U.S. House of Representatives. Whether Scheuer's political posture was already defined in 1953 and the cause of Moses's hostility is an intriguing and open question.[421]

University Center, Inc., acquired the redevelopment site in December 1954, whereupon the project stalled as Moss tried and failed over and over again to obtain private financing. Thirty lending institutions reportedly turned him down. After two years, Moss saw no other option but to apply for federal mortgage insurance, but the application process was slow and likely to take a half year or more.[422] Moses was not prepared to wait any longer.

In June 1957, with the city poised to reclaim the land for unpaid taxes, Moses recruited William Zeckendorf, one of the most active and imaginative Title I developers in the country. Zeckendorf did more than rescue the project; he improved it.[423] Renaming it Kips Bay Plaza, he rejected the original scheme by S. J. Kessler & Sons and, beginning in 1957, had his talented in-house architect I. M. Pei redesign the project, making this one of the rare instances of a Title I sponsor committed to architectural quality with an architect up to the task. The Committee on Slum Clearance approved the revised design in April 1958, and construction at long last began in April 1959.

The site comprised three city blocks merged into one. Two streets (31st and 32nd) were eliminated, and the bordering streets (30th and 33rd) were enlarged to accommodate the displaced crosstown traffic.[424] Kessler's dismal site plan, published in the Slum Clearance Committee brochure, proposed five apartment buildings (with 840 units), set parallel to the avenues and spread across the site amid a patchwork of playgrounds and surface parking. The site plan was open and barren.

Pei revised the norms of superblock urbanism in two important ways: he began to restitch the superblock back into the urban fabric and

C-137. Kips Bay Plaza from East 31st Street, looking north, ca. 1962. The shopping center is at left.

inally open to the public, and neighborhood children gathered at Kips Bay Plaza. This openness, underscored in Pei's renderings, is now lost, with the once-permeable features of Pei's site plan sealed shut. The point of entry through the shopping center was filled in during a remodeling, and elsewhere gates and security guards keep outsiders off the grounds.

A medical office building was sited on First Avenue to serve physicians at the medical center across the street. Pei's office did not design the office building. NYU acquired the parcel in 1966 and erected a dormitory in 1986.

As with the site plan, Pei fundamentally rethought the structure and design of the apartment buildings. "At that time, we had only one thing in mind," Pei recalled, "how to break out of the straightjacket of Peter Cooper Village and Stuyvesant Town."[425] He did more than break the dull standard of brick housing projects; substituting a load-bearing wall for a skeletal frame, he also rejected the high-modernist language of curtain wall and steel. Taking cues from Le Corbusier's recent housing project in Marseilles, the Unité d'Habitation (1945–52), Pei designed a long slab with an exposed concrete structure. At the Denver Hilton Hotel (1954–60), he had experimented with a concrete frame, but the structure was masked by precast exterior wall units cantilevered from the floor slabs. At Kips Bay, Pei turned the wall itself into structure.[426]

With Zeckendorf footing the bills, Pei's office undertook research into concrete technology to determine how to achieve the desired structural and aesthetic effects. He originally intended to use precast concrete, but as Edward Friedman, who headed the research effort, explained, it quickly became clear that "because of cost and local code restrictions governing structural continuity, only cast-in-place concrete could be considered."[427] Pei's desire for a smooth surface and uniform color, in contrast to the textured concrete of the Unité and its Brutalist offspring, presented multiple challenges. In order to achieve the desired finish, the architects tested different pouring methods, concrete recipes, and colors; they developed a new type of formwork and designed expansion joints and "pour lines" to cope with concrete drip, absorb thermal movement, and reduce surface spalling. Finally, they erected a full-scale model of a structural bay on site to test their new methods of concrete construction.

The structure was based on a window module 5 feet 8 inches in width, repeated without variation; thus, the gridded facade did not reflect the interior layout of rooms. The window heads curve gracefully at

concentrated the open space in a publicly accessible garden. He placed two superlong slabs, each 410 feet, parallel to the cross streets and offset them in relation to each other, with the north building pulled toward Second Avenue and the south building pulled toward First Avenue. A shopping center was located on Second Avenue and an office building on First Avenue.

These buildings framed a garden square at the heart of the block. Two of the paths bounding the garden were aligned with the city streets; the other two were aligned with the entry axes of the apartment buildings. The resulting garden was both tranquil and urban, protected and permeable. Pei had wanted to install a large Picasso sculpture in the center of the plaza, but the idea was abandoned in favor of landscaping, a budgetary choice imposed by Zeckendorf. (Pei succeeded in placing the sculpture at his Title I project for NYU).

Although Pei could not entirely escape the car-oriented standards of Title I planning, he managed to contain the automobile. The apartment buildings are

set back from the sidewalk by driveways and parking lots that provide drive-up convenience for residents, but most of the parking is underground, in a garage entered from First Avenue and extending beneath the garden. An unsatisfactory feature of the site plan is the forbidding blind wall on 33rd Street that encloses the garage.

The shopping center on Second Avenue translated the traditional commercial character of the street into new forms. A big box at the corner 31st Street was planned for a supermarket; the long, low block beside it combined small neighborhood shops with a movie theater. To improve traffic flow, a service road was inserted in front of the stores. Drawings of the shopping center, many of which are signed by James Freed, reveal the effort to coordinate the shopping center with the residential complex and to impose the same governing geometry. A carefully designed plaza between the two commercial buildings led to a playground tucked behind the shopping center. Although privately owned, the playground and garden were orig-

the corners, and the columns are tapered, with setbacks at the fifth and tenth floors, to represent the diminishing structural load.[428] In contrast to the varied pattern of Le Corbusier's housing block, its muscular pilotis, and massive effect, Pei's wall grid was uniform, weightless, elegant, and smooth. The density of the grid opened up at ground level where the building was encircled by an open-air arcade with bays 17 feet in width (three modules wide). The fascia above the arcade read as a cornice, and, in another gesture to the classical tradition, the column faces were shaped as pilasters that die into the cornice. The achievement of this refined concrete construction is to merge structure, form, and decoration into an organic unity.

Zeckendorf financed the project with FHA mortgage insurance, which entailed regulatory controls. He retained Kessler as consulting architect because of the firm's experience with such matters, but Pei, who served on the FHA Advisory Board, needed no help. The FHA calculated mortgage insurance on the basis of the number of rooms in the dwelling units. The FHA formula counted a balcony—but not a bathroom—as a room. Pei would not add balconies "to fatten the room count."[429] At Kips Bay, however, the glass wall was set 14.5 inches behind the concrete frame, and Pei convinced the FHA to give partial credit for balconies because of the deep wall

recesses. The recesses, of course, were not usable as balconies, but they served to a limited extent as sun screens, and the chiaroscuro effects produced by the deep reveals enlivened the long, repetitive walls.

As an experimental project, Kips Bay Plaza inevitably had some less successful features. The concrete refinements are overwhelmed by the length of the slabs, which look particularly daunting from the street, whereas from the garden the facades tend to visually recede. The structural system had the benefit of largely removing interior supports from the apartments, but the modular system produced some inflexibility in apartment layout. The air-conditioning units, which were not adequately integrated into the structural wall, make the facades look pockmarked. Pei revised these features—building scale, modular dimensions, apartment layout, and mechanical systems—in his other closely related Title I projects: Hyde Park in Chicago, Society Hill in Philadelphia, Town Centre Plaza in Washington, D.C., and University Village in New York City.

Numerous factors drove up the cost of housing at Kips Bay Plaza. After reviewing Pei's revised scheme, the federal government reevaluated the write-down and required Zeckendorf to make an additional payment to accommodate several changes in the program.[430] Although Pei's intention had been to

reduce construction costs, he estimated that the project cost 7 percent more than conventional housing.[431] Meanwhile, Zeckendorf's firm, Webb & Knapp, was overextended, and the financial pressures led to cost cutting on a variety of elements, from hardware to mechanical equipment, in particular the air-conditioning.[432] The south building opened in 1961, and the north building followed in 1963. They contained 1,120 apartments in all: 560 units per building, 28 units per floor, 21 floors per building.

Moses did not get the moderate-rent project he had planned in 1953, with rentals of $31 to $35 per room per month. Efficiency apartments in Kips Bay Plaza rented for $130 and three-bedroom apartments for $309.[433] The displaced site residents had paid $25 to $50 a month; they could not afford the new housing, nor could the nurses, technicians, and young hospital staff for whom the project had been intended. What began as a middle-income project ended up as luxury housing. The percentage of medical center employees among the original residents of Kips Bay Plaza is unknown; one of the original residents recalls many doctors among the first settlers. Although a successful renewal project in many respects, it failed to meet Moses's social vision, as he fully recognized. That is why he tried again and introduced the Bellevue South Title I in a continuing effort to provide affordable housing.

Moses realized he needed a nonprofit sponsor in order to produce affordable housing for medical center staff. Rejecting a bid from Zeckendorf, in August 1959 he designated Phipps Houses, a charitable organization founded in 1901 to build nonprofit workers' housing, as developer of Bellevue South. The project was located across the street from Bellevue Hospital, between First and Second avenues, from 24th to 29th Street. According to a hospital study, Bellevue faced a serious nursing shortage because of inadequate housing and unsafe conditions in the area. Moses's original plan called for 2,500 apartments, with a building reserved for nurses. The urban renewal project thus drew strong support from the Bellevue Hospital School of Nursing and its influential board chairman, Ellen Zinsser McCloy, the wife of John J. McCloy, who at the time was chairman of Chase Manhattan Bank, the Ford Foundation, and the Council of Foreign Relations. With the benefit of Mitchell-Lama subsidies, Phipps Houses guaranteed rents of no more than $30 per room per month. The city approved Bellevue South in 1964, and the four apartment buildings known as Phipps Plaza, designed by Frederick G. Frost Jr. and Associates, were completed between 1970 and 1976. Priority renting went to hospital personnel. — HB

C-138. Full-scale model of one module of wall structure, Kips Bay Plaza, 1958

273

PRATT INSTITUTE TITLE I

Pratt dormitories, 1954–55
Willoughby Walk, 1957–61
University Terrace, 1962–64
Brooklyn: Myrtle Avenue, Emerson Place, Classon
    Avenue, Lafayette Avenue, St. James Place,
    Hall Street
41.59 acres
Plan published July 1953
Fig. C-139

The Pratt Institute urban renewal plan for the Clinton Hill section of Brooklyn was the thirteenth Title I project proposed by the Committee on Slum Clearance. The scheme was first proposed to the city by Frank D. Schroth Sr., a trustee of Pratt and owner of the *Brooklyn Eagle*. Schroth's objective was twofold: to create a single quadrangle from the five city blocks surrounding the college's existing buildings and to convert the once-genteel adjacent blocks to upper-middle-class housing. The plan proposed a site of about 42 acres on 14 blocks. In addition to the college's Main Building, library, and Memorial Hall, all facing Ryerson Street between De Kalb and Willoughby, two factory buildings, an apartment house, and a police station, all on De Kalb, were preserved.

The plan called for three superblocks, with Pratt forging a new campus on the central one of about 19 acres and a private developer building luxury rental housing on those that bordered it to the north and south. The northern block was to comprise 9.25 acres and the southern one 13.5. Preliminary drawings were done by the architectural firm of McKim, Mead & White for the Pratt block and by Melvin E. Kessler of S. J. Kessler & Sons, who had worked on several other Title I projects, for the others. Plans for the campus called for additions to the library, three new dormitories, several new classroom buildings, a large athletic complex, and three surface parking lots. The housing complex was to include nine high-rise slabs of 14 stories, each with 168 or 224 units, as well as a public school, three playgrounds, nine surface parking lots, a parking garage, and three blocks of shops.

Following approval of the plan by the city in early 1954, Pratt began its portion of the project, yet work never progressed much beyond clearance of the site and closing of the through streets. Two dormitories designed by McKim, Mead & White, one for men and one for women, were begun in late 1954 and opened in the fall of 1955. The men's building, near the northeast corner Hall and De Kalb, today operates as De Kalb Hall. The women's, near the southeast corner of Hall and Willoughby, is now known as the ISC

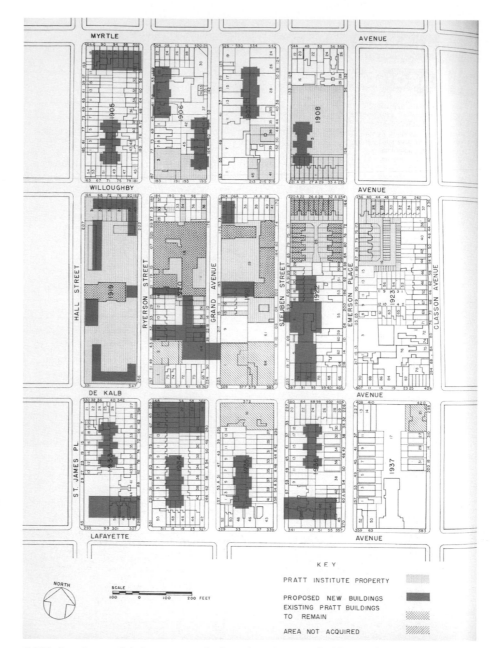

C-139. Pratt Institute Title I project, overlaid on plan of existing buildings, July 1953.

Building. No other portion of the original plan was completed; however, a classroom building called North Hall facing Willoughby was completed in 1958 on a site originally slated for parking.

Plans for the other superblocks also suffered; although eventually completed, they too departed from the original expectations. The developer initially selected to undertake the housing component was a consortium of thirty-one investors, about twenty of

whom were also investors in a similar organization set up to undertake the Manhattantown Title I project. As at Manhattantown, these men proved unable to see the project through, and they backed out of the project in 1956. In 1957, Moses found a new developer, Herbert S. Greenwald's Metropolitan Corporation of America. Chicago's rival to William Zeckendorf's Webb & Knapp, Metropolitan had completed several Title I projects in the Midwest. At the time, Moses was busy recruiting men like Greenwald and Zeckendorf to replace developers at several Title I projects that had foundered without the sponsorship of an institution with construction money at the ready, like the UHF, a university, or the New York City Housing Authority (see Battery Park Title I entry).

Proceeding with existing plans, which had since been modified to accommodate three buildings on the northern block and four on the southern, Greenwald began work on the northern portion. He called the project Willoughby Walk. Each of the buildings consisted of one 16-story slab with 267 units, resulting in a population density of about 234 persons per acre. Meanwhile, Greenwald commissioned Mies van der Rohe to redesign the southern block. And while Mies's office drafted several preliminary plans under the working title "Quadrangle Apartment Buildings," no sooner had the first two buildings at the northern superblock rented than Greenwald died and all work stopped for eighteen months.

During the hiatus, Mies's association with the project was terminated and Greenwald's involvement in the project came up for public scrutiny as questions mounted about irregularities and favoritism in the selection of developers for the Title I project generally—questions that contributed to the dismantling of the Committee on Slum Clearance. When his former business partners resumed work in the fall of 1960, they finished the third building as planned but hired Kelly & Gruzen, the architects of Park Row and Park Row Extension, and the contractor Tishman Realty and Construction to redesign and build the southern block, where in lieu of a school the city had in the interim built Classon Playground.

The new plans resulted in construction of three limited-equity co-ops, each of 24 stories with 326 units of three and a half to six and a half rooms, with a population density of roughly 280 people per acre. Named Pratt Towers, Ryerson Towers, and St. James Towers and collectively known as University Terrace, the buildings were financed through the Mitchell-Lama program and, thanks to unusually long fifty-year construction loans, sold for only $485 a room with $22 a room in monthly maintenance. Kelly & Gruzen's design placed recessed balconies on three sides of each building, permitting all but a few of the smallest apartments private outdoor space. Because the double-loaded corridor plan precluded cross ventilation, all were equipped with outlets for air-conditioners.

Unlike other Title I co-ops, the project was not affiliated directly with Abraham Kazan or Louis Pink, whose UHF always handled sales directly. The developers therefore made use of a private agent to promote the project and screen applicants; the firm of Herbert Charles, one of the city's leading real estate brokers with much experience in the sales and management of middle-income co-ops. Nevertheless, with the support of Tishman and the UHF, a group of area residents operating as the University-Clinton Area Renewal Effort (U-CARE) stationed volunteers from the nearby Kingsview co-op at the sales office to educate prospective buyers about the limited-equity format. They also served to assure middle-class buyers that they would feel comfortable living in what remained a rough neighborhood.

Despite these efforts, the project sold slowly and in the summer of 1962, after a year on the market, Tishman took the unusual step of introducing a second mortgage program, which enabled down payments on shares as low as $200 per unit, with the balance to be repaid over ten years. After eighteen months of advertisements, the buildings finally sold out in early 1964. Because work could not begin without the shareholders' equity, construction was delayed, with the last building, Pratt Towers, not getting under way until mid-1963.

The project's troubles did not end once it was completed. Within two years, residents found themselves unable to meet expenses. Rather than increase maintenance, an emergency appeal was made to the city for additional tax breaks. Many residents stopped paying maintenance above what had been promised during the initial sales period. Tax breaks were extended in 1968. Nevertheless, the "rent" strike continued and the city began foreclosure, which, in effect, empowered it to evict nonpaying residents and seize their equity.

The rental buildings at Willoughby Walk fared little better. Despite highly competitive rents, the developer had been forced to offer turkey dinners and savings bonds to fill them in the early 1960s. Then, unable to make the buildings pay at rents mandated by the city, Metropolitan defaulted on the complex in 1965. It tried to sell the complex to Pratt for student and faculty housing, but protests on the part of tenants led to nearly a decade of struggle. Eventually, Pratt took one building and the other two ended up in the hand of the federal government. These, at the insistence of tenants, were converted to co-ops in 1977. Today, these two buildings operate on the market-rate plan, and two-bedroom units sell for around $400,000 with $750 in monthly maintenance. The buildings of University Terrace, meanwhile, remain limited-equity co-ops, at least until their loans are retired in the early 2010s. — MGL

SEASIDE ROCKAWAY TITLE I

Surfside Park, 1962–66
Dayton Towers West, 1964–66
Queens: Beach 108th Street, elevated
    subway, Beach 102nd Street, and
    Shore Front Parkway
35 acres
Plan published October 1954
Figs. C-140–142

HAMMELS ROCKAWAY TITLE I

Dayton Beach Park, 1962–66
Dayton Towers East, 1964–66
Queens: Beach 90th Street, Rockaway Beach
    Boulevard, Beach 74th Street, and
    Shore Front Parkway
45.17 acres
Plan published November 12, 1956
Figs. C-140, 143

Robert Moses envisioned the Seaside Rockaway and Hammels Rockaway Title I projects as a unified effort to transform Rockaway from a seasonal "resort slum" into a year-round residential community. The Title I projects, located 12 blocks apart on Shore Front Parkway facing the Atlantic Ocean, extended his prior incursions into the Rockaways in the areas of recreation, transportation, and public housing to complete his makeover of the peninsula.

Moses proposed building housing in the center of Rockaway as early as 1938. In his view, housing and recreation had to be integrated in order for either to be successful: "There is no such thing as a sound recreation policy for this city which is not based upon close coordination with slum clearance, low-rent housing, and indeed, housing or rehousing of every kind."[434] The Rockaways provided an ideal testing ground for this theory: Moses's redevelopment of Rockaway Beach, known as the Rockaway Improvement, was completed in 1939. The renovation of Rockaway Beach was typical of his public beach projects. He exiled private concessions and amusements; built promenades, playgrounds, and handball courts; and made the beach more automobile accessible by constructing the Shore Front Parkway, running parallel to the beach, and elevating the Long Island Railroad train tracks to eliminate grade crossings on local streets. Moses proposed a limited-dividend housing development on Shore Front Parkway between Beach 73rd and 95th streets to be funded by an insurance company with support from the city in the form of tax exemption and the use of eminent domain to clear the site. Although World War II put an end to the project, some features of the early site plan anticipated the

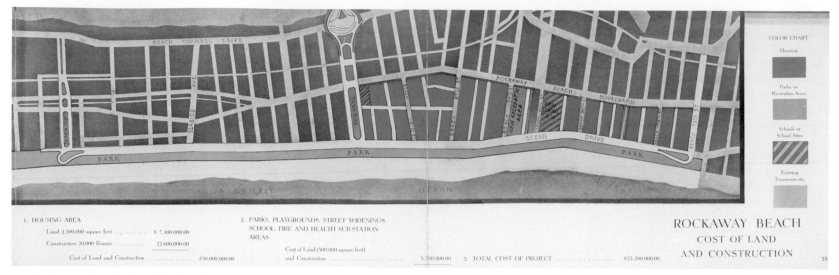

C-140. Moses's plan for limited-dividend housing to complement Rockaway Improvement, ca. 1938

Title I plans to come: several of the small north-south streets were to be closed to create a series of superblocks that contained buildings "so constructed as to take advantage of the ocean air and view."[435] The project would have entailed razing the wood frame houses that Moses viewed as blighted and replacing them with modern apartment towers, thus fulfilling his hope that the "great Rockaway improvement should be flanked by the right kind of residence."[436]

After the passage of the Housing Act of 1949, Moses resumed planning for housing in the Rockaways. In 1953, he suggested to the Rockaway Chamber of Commerce that the Seaside neighborhood would make an apt site for a Title I project. The organization was enthusiastic about Title I but lobbied to move the projects into Hammels, an adjacent neighborhood to the east. The choice between the two sites raised issues of expediency and race. Moses selected Seaside, where he had already eliminated the amusement parks in his improvement of Rockaway Beach; a white neighborhood, it had relatively few year-round residents and would be easy to clear. Hammels, the preference of the Chamber of Commerce, was a crowded slum with primarily black occupants. According to Lawrence and Carol Kaplan, the Chamber of Commerce saw slum clearance in Hammels as "the removal of black people from the Rockaways, not the destruction of a white area, to be the main purpose of a Title I project."[437] Moses refused to consider relocating the Seaside project, but at a Chamber of Commerce dinner in June 1954 he offered a compromise: a Title I project would be planned for Hammels as well. In announcing the joint

projects at Seaside and Hammels, the *New York Times* endorsed Moses's vision of a united attack on the "resort slums" that plagued the Rockaways: "This will mean that a sweeping slum clearance program can be advanced over a 100-acre tract occupied mostly by ramshackle frame summer bungalows. . . . The twin projects are part of an over-all plan to eliminate substandard areas in the Rockaways and substitute sound year-round housing accommodations."[438]

The Slum Clearance Committee proposed the coordinated projects in separate brochures, but Moses wanted to see them developed simultaneously by the same sponsor. Both brochures advanced the same argument: new housing in the Rockaways would be part of the solution to the citywide housing shortage and "an outlet for the densely populated areas of Manhattan and Brooklyn."[439] Both sites were touted for their proximity to the beach and to public transportation: the Rockaway line of the Long Island Railroad, shut down in 1950 after a trestle fire, was in the process of being converted into an elevated subway line. This conversion was under way in 1954, when Seaside Title I was proposed, and almost complete by November 1956, when the Hammels brochure was published.

Seaside and Hammels had the same wood frame architecture but entirely different social dynamics. Seaside swelled with summer renters and then emptied in the winter, taking "on the bleak nature of a ghost town during the unseasonal months of the year."[440] Hammels had a steady year-round population, although the Slum Clearance brochure disguised this fact. While Seaside was nearly empty during the

winter, with only 142 full-time families in need of relocation, Hammels had 1,763 year-round families, and 75 percent were minorities, predominantly black and some Puerto Rican. Almost 30 percent of Hammels residents were dependent upon welfare. Moses hoped to coordinate Title I with the many public housing projects in the Rockaways, including Hammel, Arverne, Redfern Houses, and especially Edgemere Houses, the largest public housing complex in Rockaway, which was in an early planning stage in 1956. He anticipated that the new NYCHA project would open in time to accommodate many of the displaced residents of Hammels, 40 percent of whom were expected to qualify for public housing, and hoped that the NYCHA would give them preference over other applicants.

The two SCC plans—prepared by Chapman, Evans & Delehanty, architects and engineers; and Skidmore, Owings & Merrill, coordinating architects—were standard. The Seaside site contained 17 blocks and the Hammels site 15 blocks; both site plans called for closing streets to create superblocks and widening the remaining streets. Both included parking, in garages and in outdoor lots, and a shopping center. The Seaside plan called for twenty 8-story buildings, all oriented so that their long sides faced east and west to maximize the number of apartments with at least partial views of the Atlantic Ocean. The plan for Hammels was more dynamic than the parallel rows of buildings at Seaside: some of the twenty-eight 8-story buildings were perpendicular to the ocean, but others were T-shaped and situated diagonally. In both site plans, the buildings were distributed around the superblocks amid landscaped walks, plazas, and play areas. Residential land coverage would be minimal: at Seaside 14.6 percent and at Hammels 14.9 percent.

Clearance of the Rockaway sites did not begin until December 1959. Moses described the setbacks that stalled the launch of the projects in *Public Works: A Dangerous Trade*, using Seaside and Hammels as examples of the typical difficulties and delays that plagued Title I planning. In 1957, the Federal Housing Administration insured mortgages for Seaside but refused to do so for Hammels, concerned that the development would not attract tenants at the proposed high rental rates. Perhaps the FHA hesitated, as the Kaplans suggest, out of fear that middle- and upper-middle-class families would not choose to live next to public housing. In order to lower the rents in Hammels Title I, Moses asked the city for tax exemption; he faced outspoken opposition, most notably from Queens Borough President James J. Crisona, who depicted the proposal as a $21,000,000 giveaway.[441] Tax exemption was finally granted at the end of 1958, the City Planning Commission approved the plans for both Rockaway Title I projects in January 1959, and federal grants were received in April of the same year.

Delays were also caused by controversies surrounding the prospective developer. In 1958, the SCC named Zukerman Brothers, Brooklyn-based builders and developers, as the tentative sponsor of Seaside and Hammels Title I. Before the firm was able to purchase the sites from the city, however, the SCC decided, for the first time in the history of Title I in New York City, to hold an open bidding process. Frouge Construction Company of Bridgeport, Connecticut, was approved to bid on the properties, but ultimately failed to come up with the required pre-auction deposit, leaving Zukerman Brothers as the only eligible developer. So much discussion of multiple bidders, so inconsequential. After purchasing the Seaside and Hammels sites for $4,388,851.60 on November 2, 1959, Zukerman Brothers announced that they had contracted the architectural firm S. J. Kessler & Sons to design the buildings. Criticism was immediate. Mayor Robert F. Wagner had banned the Kessler firm from working on Title I projects after the involvement of Melvin E. Kessler in the corruption that surrounded Manhattantown Title I. William Zukerman, one of four Zukerman Brothers, defended their choice: "They have more Title I experience than all the other architects put together."[442]

S. J. Kessler & Sons were kept on as architects, and their plans for the Rockaway sites were revealed at a ceremony marking the beginning of clearance in December 1959. Instead of twenty 8-story buildings at Seaside, there would be six 16-story buildings; instead of twenty-eight 8-story buildings at Hammels, there would be nine 16-story buildings. Charles Zukerman, another brother, promoted the design as a way to create a "more park-like area." But civic groups erupted in protest, fearing that the height of the buildings would force planes leaving Idlewild Airport to take off more steeply, thus inflicting more noise on the residents.[443] The City Planning Commission stepped in to resolve the dispute and set a height limit of 12 stories. In the completed design, all the buildings adhered to the limit, and the number of buildings at each site (six at Seaside, nine at Hammels) remained as in the 1959 Kessler proposal.

Clearance of the sites provoked charges of racism. A church with a black congregation was slated to be demolished to make room for the Hammels project, and the church had only recently completed a new building after its original home was razed when the Hammel Houses were constructed. Black civic groups protested, and their charge of racism was far from unfounded. Moreover, two other religious institutions on the Hammels site, St. Rose of Lima Roman Catholic Church and Temple Israel Synagogue, had been singled out in the original 1956 Title I plan to be preserved—and were saved. Such an exception was not made for the black church, however, which ultimately agreed to move, amid rumors that its leaders had been paid off. Racial conflict also surrounded the relocation of Hammels residents. The New York City welfare department sent some of its more intractable cases to Hammels, which became a predominantly black neighborhood.[444] These were single mothers and people with criminal records or histories of mental health problems, and they were refused admittance into the peninsula's many public housing projects precisely because of these disadvantages. In Hammels, they lived crowded into the wood frame homes that Moses was so eager to eliminate. He hoped that these families would be placed in Edgemere Houses, but by the time clearance began in early 1960 he had fallen from power and could not persuade the NYCHA to give displaced Hammels residents preference. Because of the dissolution of the Slum Clearance Committee and Moses's loss of control over New York City housing, the Kaplans conclude that "after 1960, there would be no further link between Title I and low-income projects."[445] In the end, the Zukermans hired the Urban Relocation Company to find new homes for Hammels families. The company moved many families from substandard, inadequately winterized homes in Hammels to similar

C-141. Surfside Park at Beach 107th Street and Rockaway Beach, 1968.

C-142. Proposal for Seaside Rockaway, ca. 1954. Design by Chapman, Evans & Delehanty; rendering by J. Floyd Yewell

C-143. Proposal for Hammels Rockaway, 1956. Design by Chapman, Evans & Delehanty; rendering by Jimenez. Courtesy MTA Bridges and Tunnels Special Archive

housing in neighboring Arverne, where a new slum was created that would become the target of clearance plans just a few years later.

Construction began on two apartment complexes in 1962: Surfside Park in Seaside, and Dayton Beach Park in Hammels. The first two of six planned buildings in Surfside Park opened in 1963; a third opened in 1966. By March 1964, Surfside Park, consisting of two finished buildings and one yet-to-be-built structure between Beach 108th and 105th streets, was all that remained under the control of the Zukermans. Leon D. DeMatteis & Sons, a builder based in Elmont, Long Island, completed the remainder of Seaside and constructed the entire Hammels project. DeMatteis built three apartment complexes: one in Seaside, Dayton Towers West, comprising three new buildings between Beach 105th and 102nd streets and two in Hammels, Dayton Beach Park, five buildings between Beach 90th and 81st, and Dayton Towers East, four buildings between Beach 81st and 74th. Originally, Seaside and Hammels had been envisioned as rentals, at rates ranging from $35 to $38 per room per month. The Zukermans built Surfside Park as a rental development, with studios starting at $97 a month and three-bedrooms at $221. But all three DeMatteis complexes, completed in 1966, were middle-income cooperatives subsidized by Mitchell-Lama aid from the city. At the time of their opening, Dayton Beach Park co-ops cost between $1,500 and $3,250, with monthly carrying charges of $78 for studios and $178 for three-bedroom units.

The four complexes, two on each Title I site, are set within superblocks containing on-site parking, swimming pools, and play areas. Each Title I site got its own shopping center on Rockaway Beach Boulevard: Dayton Shopping Plaza was designed by the architect Lawrence H. Furman in 1966, and the Zukerman Brothers completed Surfside Park Shopping Center in 1968. All the apartments were advertised as year-round vacation homes, desirable because of their proximity to the beach. An advertisement for Dayton Beach Park proclaimed that "at unbelievably low cost, you can enjoy 12 months of resort living. . . .All only a swift subway ride from New York City."[446] Another advertisement promised that "People who like long vacations . . . 12 months a year . . . will find Dayton Towers the answer to their dreams."[447] It seems that the ad agencies hired by the Zukerman and DeMatteis groups overlooked the bitter cold of New York City winters, which would undoubtedly put a damper on a year-long vacation in the Rockaways.

Kessler's Rockaway buildings are marked by a shared mediocrity. The fifteen buildings of the four developments are all 12-story, blonde-brick slabs punctuated by terraces.[448] All the complexes except Dayton Towers West are arranged so that the buildings are parallel to one another and perpendicular to the beach to maximize the number of apartments with ocean views. At Dayton Towers West, three buildings form an open square embracing a central driveway that curves around a fenced-in swimming pool.

Moses realized his vision of providing year-round housing in the Rockaways to complement its recreational assets. The prediction in the *New York Times* in 1958 that Rockaway's "Transformation from Slum Resort to a Residential Suburb Is Expected" came true: between 1960 and 1966 the year-round population of the peninsula rose from 68,000 to 90,000.[449] The Rockaways may no longer be a slum resort, but the landscape of repetitive, drab apartment buildings lining the shore is oppressive and uninviting and has probably made the Rockaways less desirable as a destination for the summer visitors that Moses had hoped to attract to the public beaches. — KL

LINCOLN SQUARE TITLE I

Fordham University, 1962–69
Lincoln Center for the Performing Arts, 1958–69
    Philharmonic Hall (now Avery Fischer Hall), 1962
    New York State Theater, 1964
    Vivian Beaumont Theater, 1965
    Library & Museum of the Performing Arts (now Library for the Performing Arts), New York Public Library, 1965
    Metropolitan Opera House, 1966
    The Juilliard School, 1969
    Damrosch Park and Guggenheim Band Shell, 1969
American Red Cross New York Headquarters, 1963
P.S. 199, 1963
Lincoln Towers, 1961–64
Princess Gardens, 1960

Manhattan: West 60th to West 66th Street, Columbus to Amsterdam Avenue; and West 66th to West 70th Street, Amsterdam Avenue to New York Central Railroad
45.19 acres (as built)
Plan published May 28, 1956
Figs. P-49–50, C-144–152

"The scythe of progress must move north." Thus Moses ordained after completing the Coliseum.[450] Lincoln Square, the sixteenth plan issued by the Slum Clearance Committee, was the next step in his program to transform the West Side. It was New York City's biggest Title I project, covering 53 acres as originally planned; the earlier projects were 14.6 acres on average, and the Manhattan projects were even smaller at 12.5 acres on average.[451] Apart from its size, Lincoln Square was the most ambitious Title I project in conception, the most complicated to execute, and the most influential in urban renewal. These superlatives are solely attributable to Lincoln Center for the Performing Arts, the centerpiece of the Lincoln Square development. Lincoln Center demonstrated the potential of the arts as an engine of economic development and opened a new era of cultural expansion, transforming the performing arts from an elite privilege to a middle-class entertainment.[452] The leadership challenge that Lincoln Square presented to Moses was balancing his instinct to think big with his competing drive to contain costs and get results.

Looking at the south-facing aerial view on the cover of the Slum Clearance brochure, the logic behind the site selection becomes evident. Between the Coliseum, Broadway, and the riverfront rail yards lies an L-shaped field of low-rise tenements, typical specimens of the nineteenth-century grid. They wrap around two standout structures that were not part of the clearance area: circular gas tanks, which were replaced by a more decorous substation as the redevelopment proceeded, and Amsterdam Houses (1948), a low-rise public housing project between 61st and 64th streets on Amsterdam Avenue. Moses's techniques of slum clearance were no different from those the New York City Housing Authority had used to build Amsterdam Houses: wholesale demolition, superblocking, and social displacement. Leveraging the public investment already made in the area (the Coliseum, public housing, and a new school, P.S. 191), Moses recruited private, including nonprofit, developers to clear the remaining tenements and to rebuild.

The area met the prevailing definition of a slum. According to a house-to-house survey, most buildings (77 percent) were built before 1901; 30 percent lacked central heating, and 40 percent lacked private bathrooms. The *New York Times* saw a "dreary, dismal neighborhood with no future . . . except . . . certain decline."[453] According to the Slum Clearance Committee's real estate consultant, it would be cost effective to renovate only 10 of the 585 structures on the site. The area was primarily residential; 5,268 families (including single-person households) called it home, and population density was rising, which meant overcrowding, deteriorating living conditions, and rooming-house conversions. The residents were poor: 77 percent had annual incomes of less than $4,000 or lived on pensions and relief. The neighborhood was racially mixed: 76 percent were white, 18 percent Puerto Rican, and 4 percent Negro. Redevelopment would result in economic and racial resorting.

Opposition to Lincoln Square attracted extensive publicity because of its high-profile sponsors, Lincoln Center and Fordham University, whereas the relocation of 2,100 households in the housing section, almost half the site families, escaped public notice. Yet, the joint relocation effort of the two nonprofit institutions exemplified the best practices at that time. Instead of allowing condemned properties to deteriorate during the planning stages, as was the norm, the sponsors corrected code violations and spent money on building maintenance. Their relocation firm staffed an on-site office where public housing officials were also on call. Families that self-relocated were offered cash payments on a sliding scale pegged to apartment size, and although there was no such legal obligation, commercial tenants obtained up to $3,000 in relocation assistance. An analysis of the first 500 families to relocate revealed a troubling jump in rents: the average rent on site was $51.82; the average new rent was $65.26, a 26 per-

cent increase that was only partially due to improvements in living standards.[454] The report did not overlay rent and income to measure the increased housing costs in relation to household income, nor did it comment on the segregating effects of relocation. These problems were caused by large-scale forces in the housing market and beyond the ability of any sponsor to resolve.

Moses began entertaining ideas for Lincoln Square in 1953. A fashion center, engineering headquarters, and television studios were considered, and Moses suggested to Harry Guggenheim that he build his Frank Lloyd Wright–designed museum on a Lincoln Square site.[455] By mid-1955, Lincoln Square was blocked out, Moses was in negotiation with designated sponsors, and their architects were at work on preliminary site plans.

The first published plan, in the Slum Clearance Committee brochure of May 1956, reorganized 18 blocks into 5 superblocks, with one nineteenth-century block left in tact. The constituents included Fordham University, a "music and arts center," a commercial development, and market-rate housing with supporting public uses: a park, elementary school, church, police station, and parking garage. The land auction and title transfer were deferred until February 1958, an unusually long wait during which Moses wrangled with federal officials over their funding level and resale appraisals, and waited out lawsuits challenging the constitutionality of the project.

ROGER STEVENS'S COMMERCIAL COMPLEX

The 1956 plan included a commercial section in the triangular area from 65th to 70th Street between Broadway and Columbus Avenue, comprising stores, an office building, hotel, and garage as well as a commercial theater complex on the east half of the block from 65th to 66th Street. The designated sponsor of the commercial section was Roger L. Stevens, a successful theatrical producer and major real estate developer. Stevens's first brush with Title I seems to have come in 1952, when he represented ANTA (American National Theatre and Academy) in discussions about participating with the Metropolitan Opera in the Columbus Circle Title I project. In 1955–56, he set his sights on Lincoln Square and hired the architectural firm of Pereira and Luckman to design a multitheater structure. (No rendering has been found in their archives.) Moses considered the scheme dramatic but objected to a garage located on Broadway, insisting on maximum underground parking.[456]

The federal government balked at the large write-down that Moses requested for Lincoln Square. He asked for $42 million; the government granted $25 million. Moses responded by raising the land costs of the cultural sponsors, but the primary savings came from eliminating the five- block commercial section. Cut from the project, Stevens redirected his appetite for Title I redevelopment to New Haven and Washington, D.C., where he sponsored major projects. Yet, Lincoln Square changed his life in an unforeseen way: at the request of President John F. Kennedy in 1961, Stevens established what became the Kennedy Center for the Performing Arts in the nation's capital, based on the model of Lincoln Center.[457]

FORDHAM UNIVERSITY

Fordham needed in-town facilities to complement its pastoral campus in the Bronx, where the traditional undergraduate program was located. Since the turn of the century, the Roman Catholic university had rented scattered spaces in Manhattan to accommodate its part-time students, numbering about 5,000 in 1950. For a time, the Law School was installed on the 28th floor of the Woolworth Building, the School of Education was on Duane Street, and the School of Social Work on 39th Street. In 1949, in need of more and better space to meet the postwar student boom, the university formed a real estate advisory committee to conduct a search. At a meeting in the fall of 1954, committee member George A. Hammer suggested asking Moses if Fordham could rent five floors in the Coliseum tower. Hammer was one of the city's star real estate brokers (he had famously brokered the sale of the Empire State Building in 1951) and vice president of the Charles F. Noyes Co., a real estate firm that the Slum Clearance Committee retained to provide resale appraisals for its Title I plans. Moses will turn down the request, Hammer predicted. "I think he will say, why don't you let me bring you in on the urban development program at 9th Avenue and 59th Street." "What's an urban renewal development?" the president of Fordham, the Reverend Laurence McGinley, innocently replied.[458]

McGinley requested the Coliseum space in November 1954, and Moses responded as predicted. In a letter of December 8, 1954, he described the inadequacies of the Coliseum for university uses and offered Fordham a piece of Lincoln Square.[459] In February 1955, after a quick study of the area, Fordham chose the two southern blocks (60th to 62nd Street) and gave as reasons the proximity of the subway at Columbus

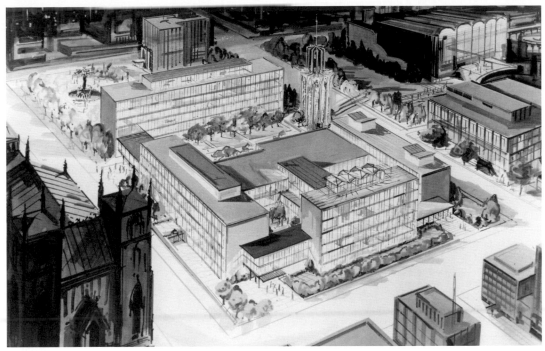

C-144. Second scheme for Fordham University campus, 1959.
Design by Voorhees Walker Smith and Smith; rendering by Marinsky

Circle and of St. Paul's Church on Amsterdam Avenue, which met the need for a university church.

Why Fordham? Robert Caro has teased out the web of mutual interests linking Moses to the Archdiocese of New York, which might explain why he bestowed Title I land on the Roman Catholic institution.[460] Personal and political connections were significant factors, but the selection of Fordham also fit with Moses's well-established renewal strategy of advancing higher education. Before Fordham, he had initiated Title I projects benefiting New York University, NYU Medical Center, Long Island University, Pratt, and the academic institutions on Morningside Heights, either directly by providing land for campus expansion or indirectly by stimulating housing construction. In the context of a legal proceeding to block the Fordham project, Appellate Justice Charles D. Breitel asked Fordham's attorney if other educational institutions were likely to bid for the site. The attorney, Porter R. Chandler, a member of the Board of Higher Education, acknowledged that the site would be fine for Hunter or City College, but "'the city fathers' had not made money available for such a project."[461] Although that was no doubt true, Moses consistently reserved the tools of Title I for private-sector institutions, and probably made no overture to public universities.

A lawsuit challenging Fordham's involvement in Title I charged that the university's land purchase constituted a state subsidy of religion and violated the constitutional separation of church and state. The New York Court of Appeals unanimously sided with Fordham in May 1958, and the Supreme Court refused to review the decision.[462] In an ecumenical gesture perhaps intended to quell the Fordham controversy, Moses offered Yeshiva University a part of the Riverside-Amsterdam Title I.

Fordham's Lincoln Square campus was devoted to the schools of law, business, education, social work and general studies. Construction moved slowly because resources were limited as was the architectural imagination of Fordham and its architects. The university turned to Voorhees, Walker, Smith & Smith, the architects of its Bronx student center (1958).[463] The first campus plan (May 1956) confined the Fordham buildings to the south half of the superblock. The north half was occupied by the Iona Powers Memorial Academy, a parochial high school where basketball star Lew Alcindor (Kareem Abdul-Jabbar) played in the 1960s. A short segment of 61st Street was also retained to provide access to the school. The park on the northeast corner of the site, at Columbus and 62nd Street, was a placeholder. The city's first armory, built in 1887, stood on the site,

and late in 1955 the university learned that it would be included in the clearance project. The Voorhees plan oriented the campus to 60th Street and arranged three buildings around a circular driveway.

In the second scheme, of January 1959, the campus expanded to 62nd Street in a more conventional quadrangular plan. The dominant element was a plaza oriented to 62nd Street, with a monumental bell tower and campus entrance aligned with the cross-axis of Lincoln Center. Only two fragments of this plan were completed: a three-story wing on 62nd Street and a perpendicular wing housing the Law School. Ground was broken in 1959, and the Law School was dedicated in November 1961. Although the design was banal, the Voorhees plan had the virtue of making the campus accessible at street level.

Fordham then abandoned the Voorhees plan and reorganized the campus as a series of freestanding buildings set on a podium high above street level. Buildings on Columbus Avenue and 62nd Street disregarded their street frontage and turned toward the landscaped podium. This scheme envisioned a stepped plaza on 62nd Street dominated by a theater building, designed both programmatically and stylistically to echo Lincoln Center. Renderings of the view from 62nd Street evoke a still-permeable environment with easy movement up to the main plaza level, but the staircases as built failed to mitigate the distancing effects of the elevated plaza. The second phase of construction included the plaza and the Leon Lowenstein Center (1965–69), a 12-story multipurpose academic building on 60th Street designed by Slingerland & Booss. In 1975, Perkins and Will devised a new master plan for extensions on Columbus Avenue and 60th Street, where Fordham eventually built a 20-story dormitory. As the campus expanded, it increasingly turned inward, with gates and guards barring entry to the public.

The Lincoln Square campus now serves about 8,000 students, more than the sprawling campus in the Bronx. Yet McGinley's founding vision of a metropolitan campus, participating in city life, is undermined by its physical design. Unlike the leaders of Lincoln Center, Fordham did not take advantage of the opportunity to shape a coherent campus. Construction was slow, and to this day the Amsterdam Avenue frontage remains undeveloped. In 1984, the Congregation of Christian Brothers demolished the Powers Memorial Academy, which was excluded from the Lincoln Square project area, and sold the property for redevelopment as a condominium tower. Fordham has sought to move in a similar direction. Although obliged by the Lincoln Square renewal plan to develop the land for educational uses, Fordham was granted a waiver from the city to sell the parcel for redevelopment as a residential tower.[464] In 2005, the university unveiled plans to replace many of the original buildings with a high-rise campus and to finance construction by selling the vacant corner properties on Amsterdam Avenue for condominium development.[465]

LINCOLN CENTER FOR THE PERFORMING ARTS

In 1938, Mayor La Guardia floated the idea of a municipal music and arts center and asked Moses, his building maestro, to conduct a feasibility study. "As a matter of personal opinion," he informed La Guardia, "I am not at all sure that we must have a center of this kind, because it seems to me that Grand Opera, as we have known it, is on its way out, that symphonic music can find homes elsewhere and, along with operatic and other serious music, will more and more reach millions of people in their homes over the air, and finally, because I believe that centralization of such efforts as distinguished from neighborhood provision may be a step in the wrong direction."[466] This report marks Moses's first, unfriendly encounter with an idea that he would resurrect twenty years later. Over the next dozen years, he discovered two things that changed his mind: the value of the arts in city building, and the hardship caused by New York's expensive real estate market on nonprofit institutions.

The Metropolitan Opera, on Broadway at 39th Street, was handicapped by an aging building built in 1883, with good acoustics but obstructed sightlines and no backstage. Successive rebuilding prospects, most famously at Rockefeller Center in 1928, failed for lack of funds.[467] Both Moses and the Met saw discounted Title I land as a solution to an entrenched real estate problem. In May 1951, Moses offered the opera a superb location on Columbus Circle but withdrew it in March 1952 after the federal government required housing in the Columbus Circle Title I plan. The Met pressed for another site, and in November 1952 Moses offered 5 acres south of Washington Square, part of the Washington Square Southeast Title I, anticipating that the suggestion would not please the Met directors "who live in the past, [and] cling to

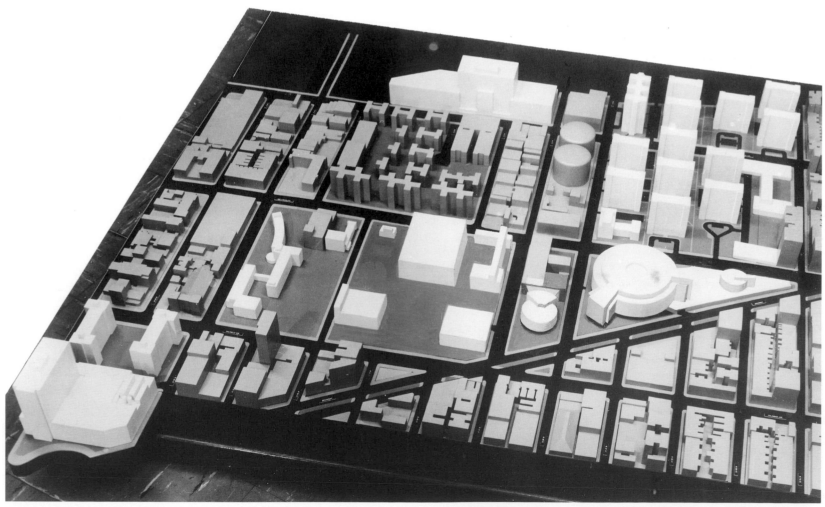

C-145. Model (now lost) of proposed Lincoln Square Title I, 1956. Courtesy MTA Bridges and Tunnels Special Archive

C-146. Representatives of Lincoln Center member institutions with architectural model, January 19, 1960. Photograph by Arnold Newman. From left to right: ballerina Alicia Markova; dancer Martha Graham; Juilliard president William Schuman and student Dorothy Pixley; soprano Lucine Amara; Metropolitan Opera director Rudolf Bing; Lincoln Center executive director Reginald Allen; Philaharmonic managing director George E. Judd Jr.; conductor Leonard Bernstein; theatrical producer Robert Whitehead; actress Julie Harris.

what they regard as 'fashionable' neighborhoods."[468] As predicted, the opera rejected the site.

After striking out with two sites, Moses offered the Lincoln Square property to the Metropolitan Opera in 1954. The opera's conservative leadership hesitated until 1955, when Charles M. Spofford took charge of the Opera Association and seized the opportunity. A partnership with the Philharmonic-Symphony Society had been under consideration for the Columbus Circle site, and that idea was also reinstated. Spofford had supported La Guardia's aborted music and arts center. Thus, when news that the Philharmonic-Symphony Society would soon be homeless (its Carnegie Hall lease ended in 1959, when the building was slated for demolition), both Spofford and Moses were receptive to joint action.[469]

The large size of the Lincoln Square project area made possible still more expansive thinking. The idea of aggregating several cultural institutions came from the Exploratory Committee for a Municipal Arts Center, which was formed in December 1955, with John D. Rockefeller 3rd as chairman, in order "to consider whether the removal of these two great institutions [the Metropolitan Opera and Philharmonic-Symphony] to the Lincoln Square location presented an opportunity to develop a music or cultural center of vastly greater significance to the people of the City than would be possible by the two institutions acting alone or jointly."[470] By May 1956, when the Slum Clearance Committee unveiled the renewal plan, the arts center encompassed a museum for the display of musical instru-

ments, a New York Public Library branch for the performing arts, a repertory theater, restaurant, and plaza in addition to a concert hall, opera house, and public park, on which Moses insisted. A month later, in June 1956, Lincoln Center for the Performing Arts was incorporated, its name clarifying the principle of inclusion, and Rockefeller was elected president.

In order to accommodate this ambitious program, the boundaries of Lincoln Center expanded four times. At the outset, in 1955, Moses thought the two anchor institutions would occupy the two blocks from 62nd to 64th Street and that the office building owned by Joseph P. Kennedy on the Columbus Avenue frontage of the south block would remain standing. A model by Wallace Harrison reflects this straitened condition, with the concert hall tucked behind the 12-story Kennedy building.[471] The Exploratory Committee requested first an additional block, from 64th to 65th Street, then the site of the Kennedy building, in January and April 1956 respectively, and for both expansions cited the same reason: to "make possible architectural treatment which would enhance the dignity and impressiveness of the whole Music Center."[472] In October 1958, Lincoln Center grew again to accommodate the Juilliard School, which had joined the organization in 1957. Lincoln Center acquired the Broadway half of the block from 65th to 66th Street, where Stevens had hoped to build his theater center. Finally, in 1962, Juilliard took over the remainder of the block fronting on 65th Street.[473]

Lincoln Center underscores the nature of Moses's planning intelligence and particular capacity as a creative thinker. He was not the mastermind behind the arts center but established the necessary preconditions to create it by providing the land and affirming the strategic value of aggregating similar institutions. After those foundational decisions, he played the role of budget watchdog and taskmaster. He never lost track of the city's budget and debt limit as he tried to stretch federal grants, contain city outlays, shift costs to the private sector, and prevent the inflation of program and budget beyond achievable goals. Thus, his responses swung from encouraging Rockefeller to seek more Title I aid so as to expand Lincoln Center to pressing him to consolidate the building program so as to reduce city costs. As budget master, he made Lincoln Center partially subsidize three public improvements that reverted to the city upon completion: Damrosch Park, the underground garage, and the main plaza.[474] Moses was particularly fortunate in having John D. Rockefeller 3rd as partner in this enterprise. Rockefeller showed an exceptional commitment to architectural quality and bravely accepted sky-rocketing budgets and fundraising targets to support campus expansion and the design goals of high-minded architects oblivious to the bottom line. As a result, Lincoln Center achieved a far higher quality of urban design than any other New York Title I project.

In the summer of 1957, federal officials challenged the resale appraisals submitted by Moses and required a new set of appraisals. Moses and the sponsors had negotiated resale land prices of $6.75 per square foot for Lincoln Center and Fordham and $7 per square foot for Webb & Knapp, the housing sponsor. The Housing and Home Finance Agency position was that fair reuse values should be for the highest use and thus should not vary for commercial and nonprofit sponsors. But Moses and the nonprofit sponsors objected that their nonprofit reuse justified lower land costs. "The crux of the appraisal controversy appears to be a fear on the part of some federal officials that the city wants to sell sites to the university and the arts center for less than a true resale value," the *New York Times* reported.[475] The compromise solution preserved variable rates but on a higher scale: the tax-exempt cooperative paid $4.24 per square foot; Fordham and the Red Cross, $7; Webb & Knapp, $7.70; and Lincoln Center, $10.60 for the main area, $13.28 for the half block to the north. The Lincoln Center costs were ratcheted up by the $1.5-million price tag on the Kennedy building.[476]

The creation of Lincoln Center was transformative in several respects. The gargantuan sums required to build the campus led to cranking up an unprecedented fund-raising machine; and, with thousands of seats to fill, the center pursued a broad outreach effort to attract audiences, opening the preserves of high society to the middle class. It was visionary of the center to make arts education a part of its mission. Leonard Bernstein's concert series for young people was only the most visible part of a multifaceted effort to bring the performing arts into classrooms and school children to Lincoln Center. An achievement of Lincoln Center was the democratization of high culture. It has become commonplace to fault the aloofness of the center, but this reading looks strictly at the physical form of the campus and disregards its social mission.

LINCOLN CENTER: SITE PLANNING

A persistent issue revived by the 2005 redesign of Lincoln Center is its detachment from the urban context. The theaters sit on a plinth above street level, and staircases bring visitors to a travertine, temple-like precinct. The following discussion focuses on the site planning process that brought about this urban posture; the design of individual buildings is beyond the scope of this entry. In his first scheme of May 1956, Harrison organized the buildings around a circular plaza inspired by Bernini's colonnaded piazza in front of St. Peter's in Rome and serving similar functions. Harrison's colonnade dramatized the approach to the opera house, the dominating axial building; shaped a central gathering place; and screened the structures in the outlying areas. In addition to the opera house, the other element whose location would remain fixed was the public park.

Moses positioned it at the corner of Amsterdam Avenue and 62nd Street, the closest spot to the housing project and parochial school across the street.

In October 1956, Harrison convened five architects—Alvar Aalto, Sven Markelius, Pietro Belluschi, Marcel Breuer, and Henry Bulfinch—to consult on design issues. Whereas Harrison saw Lincoln Center as a city square, the visitors imagined an enclosed cloister. "With the realization that for the arts and for music one needs to get out of the maelstrom and into a quiet place, the consultants were unanimous in agreeing that the Lincoln Center for the Performing Arts be an area isolated from the hubbub of New York City. The Center will be a special place, concentrated upon an inner space and inward-looking."[477] Aalto envisioned the center as "a casbah with high walls to the outside world. . . . When one entered the piazza and the number of decibels dropped there would be a psychological feeling of quiet, preparatory to the complete silence of the interior of each hall." The architects commended the Piazza San Marco in Venice as a model; later schemes invoked this idea by surrounding Lincoln Center with arcades or colonnades.

At the root of the desire to wall out the city was a view of it as an alien place, a mindset conveyed by this stunning remark: "Although the people of New York do not walk generally because the city is not generally a pleasant place in which to stroll, [the architects] . . . agreed the Center should not be planned with the idea that people will arrive only here by bus, subway or by car." In 1956, it evidently took a leap of faith to imagine approaching Lincoln Center on foot. Harrison, the only one thinking about city connections, suggested an approach from Central Park. Yet he bowed to the majority view in his revised site plan dated October 23, 1956, with a north-south plaza enclosed in the middle of the superblock and detached from the surrounding streets. Rather than an important opening on Columbus Avenue, there was a closed wall consisting of two side-by-side theaters and a thick grove of trees.

Moses objected to this new approach on procedural rather than planning grounds. The revised plan "would necessitate going back to Washington, then to the Board of Estimate, resubmission, renewal of the entire debate, loss of momentum, etc. Probably 6-7 months would be lost and we would then be in a municipal campaign." He called for a return to the "previously approved framework."[478] Accordingly, in November 1956, the Lincoln Center leadership reinstated the Columbus Avenue plaza. New designs were drawn up with a more open and permeable plaza. The opera returned to the head of the plaza; the dance

and produced a coordinated design. The Department of Parks hired Eggers and Higgins to design the band shell. Dan Kiley landscaped the park and north plaza. Harrison nominally chaired the group of so-called collaborating architects, but the term was a misnomer as these strong-willed talents found it difficult to agree, let alone collaborate.

Their robust disagreements led the architects to articulate guiding principles in an effort to arrive at a more integrated approach. The center would have a "spirit of unification rather than of diversification," a central plaza and secondary spaces, buildings of common height, and "a definite space relationship between the Center and the surrounding city."[479] Yet the architects remained divided on the site plan and character of the main plaza, as the study models produced in January and February 1959 illustrate. Philip Johnson proposed an enclosed plaza with a colonnaded screen on Columbus Avenue. Harrison and Abramovitz proposed two connecting plazas opening onto the avenue and punctuated by an obelisk. Bunshaft moved the plaza to the symphony's corner site, where it opened onto two streets. Saarinen considered the "campus effect" undesirable and insisted on enclosing the center with a "fence" and setting it apart from the city. The most significant feature of the resulting site plan, miraculously approved in February 1959, was the affirmation of an open plaza facing Columbus Avenue, with a cross axis reaching the side streets.[480]

The plaza's classical aspect was shaped by decisions in late 1959 and 1960. The chosen materials were glass, to provide transparency between lobby and plaza, and travertine, the stone of ancient Rome.[481] Philip Johnson designed a circular fountain with a radial paving pattern that refers to the Campidoglio, Michelangelo's great civic square in Rome. Bunshaft dissented; he wanted concrete and considered the fountain "too archaeological." His aversion to the historicizing elements was echoed in contemporary criticism of the plaza's classical guise. Our temporal distance, however, has kindled a new affection for the midcentury modernism of Lincoln Center, and its status has changed from glittering intruder to iconic New York landmark. Indeed, Lincoln Center ranks as one of the city's great public spaces. Although individual buildings disappoint, the quality and impact of the whole composition surpass that of any component part, and the experience of the illuminated plaza on a performance night dispels the notion of its urban detachment. In fact, the plaza occupies an in-between status as both a constitutive part of the city and an out-of-the-ordinary, ennobling

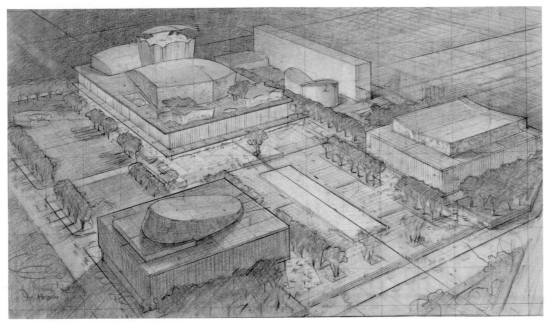

C-147. Perspective of Lincoln Center campus, September 1957.
Design by Harrison & Abramovitz; rendering by Hugh Ferriss

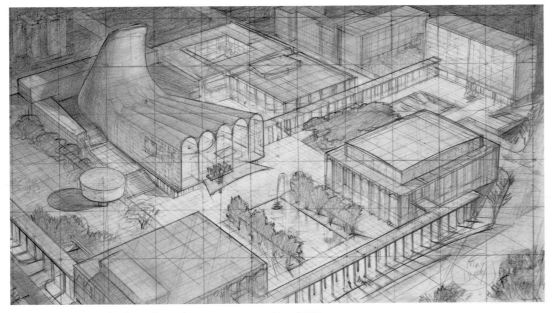

C-148. Perspective of enlarged Lincoln Center campus, May 1959.
Design by Harrison & Abramovitz; rendering by Hugh Ferriss

theater and concert hall were on either side. The buildings stood free, stripped of connecting screens.

The addition of the Juilliard School in 1957 crowded the site and led to the campus expansion to 66th Street a year later. By then the team of architects was established. In addition to Harrison for the opera house and Max Abramovitz for Philharmonic Hall,

Philip Johnson was chosen for the dance theater, Eero Saarinen for the Vivian Beaumont (repertory) Theater, Gordon Bunshaft of Skidmore, Owings & Merrill for the Library and Museum of the Performing Arts, and Pietro Belluschi for the Juilliard School. Because their site in the northwest corner of the campus was so tight, Saarinen and Bunshaft joined their buildings

place. Its civic valence and public character are unmistakable.

That said, the streetscapes are lifeless because the design channels social activity to the elevated plinth. Amsterdam Avenue was always treated as the invisible back of the campus; the result is an impermeable cliff of large-scale forms. Damrosch Park was the biggest missed opportunity. The campus plinth lifted the park above street level, and the unwelcoming view from Amsterdam Houses was of a blind wall and the outside curve of the band shell. The base of the opera tower became the truck entrance; if the architects had had their way, cars also would have entered and exited the garage here. The only street-oriented facility on Amsterdam Avenue was in the base of the museum-library, and pedestrian access to the campus was limited to a staircase at 65th Street, where the grade was lowest and the ascent to plaza level consequently steepest. The cross streets were regarded as traffic conduits to Lincoln Center's underground garage.

The north plaza raised issues of access because a bridge to Juilliard, staircase to 65th Street, and garage entrances converged at this point. In November 1959, a lively debate erupted over models of the north plaza by Saarinen and Bunshaft, who were responsible for the Beaumont Theater and library–museum on the west side. Saarinen proposed a broad flight of stairs, as wide as the plaza, leading down to 65th Street, with a narrow, bronze-covered bridge at each side. Belluschi objected that the monumental stair led nowhere and that the bridges created "a visual slum."[482] Bunshaft favored a wide bridge to better integrate Juilliard with the main campus and to hide street traffic. The effects of a wide bridge on the street below were not mentioned; evidently they were considered irrelevant. Saarinen's proposal for a pool and sculpture was combined with landscaping by Kiley in the executed scheme, and the bridge grew into a 200-foot-wide deck as its role in joining the two parts of the campus took over. That vacant, wind-swept platform was demolished in 2006 and will be replaced by a transparent structure in an attempt to animate 65th Street.

Automobile access was a major concern of Moses and the Lincoln Center directors, especially the opera officials, because their house was farthest from the street. Moses suggested a loop road to allow passenger drop off at the opera. "You can't dump people on the Avenue and make them walk all the way across the plaza to the opera," he announced.[483] Johnson also favored automobile access but for aesthetic reasons— to avoid ugly canopies in inclement weather. But the

C-149. Model by Harrison & Abramovitz, February 11, 1959

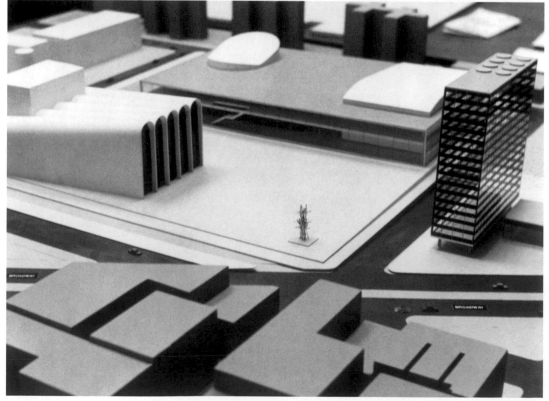

C-150. Model by Gordon Bunshaft of Skidmore, Owings & Merrill, January 19, 1959

C-151. Model by Eero Saarinen, January 19, 1959

C-152. Model by Philip Johnson, January 19, 1959

prevailing view was that vehicular access belonged underground (a pedestrian passage was also built from the subway). The service road at the edge of the plaza parallel to Columbus Avenue was added for ceremonial reasons: "to insure adequate access for the public and state dignitaries and visitors. This treatment will provide the facilities for major public events to be conducted in keeping with the stature of the Center without interference with normal operations and activities in the neighborhood."[484] Above all else, automobile convenience was pitched to the suburbs, a primary part of Lincoln Center's catchment area. Edgar Young, Lincoln Center's executive vice president, who commuted from Summit, New Jersey, correctly saw Lincoln Center as a regional magnet. "It can mean that we will all think of ourselves as residents of the metropolitan community of . . . which New York is only the core."[485]

Moses played a limited role as the project went into construction. He cut through the city bureaucracy to speed up approvals, pushed for coordination among the disparate parts, and prodded the players to move forward. Lincoln Center appointed Otto L. Nelson executive director of construction. A retired major general, he had had extensive experience in slum clearance, largely in Chicago, where as vice president in charge of housing at the New York Life Insurance Company he led the Lake Meadows urban renewal project. The first building to open at Lincoln Center was Philharmonic Hall, in September 1962. It was followed by the New York State Theater in April 1964, the Vivian Beaumont Theater in October 1965, the Library and Museum of the Performing Arts the next month, the Metropolitan Opera House in September 1966, and finally the Juilliard School in October 1969.

Lincoln Center was still a chrysalis, the buildings not yet out of the ground, when it began to change the area. The architects worried about undignified commercialism on the adjacent blocks, and Moses dissuaded Columbia University, the owner of a property opposite Lincoln Center, from renting to a funeral parlor, but market forces were a more effective deterrent to such unwelcome uses.[486] Lincoln Center immediately drove up land values and sparked a high-rise building boom. Lincoln Square Motor Inn, Dorchester Towers, American Broadcasting, Banker's Trust, and American Bible Society were the first ripple of a sea change. Jane Jacobs categorically condemned the centralizing strategy on the grounds that dispersed institutions produced a greater benefit by stimulating several different neighborhoods.[487] A single building might have the power to vitalize one street but was less likely to transform a large urban area and attract an international spotlight, as Lincoln Center did. Its actual and symbolic effects required a collection of buildings, a concentration of people, and steady flow of activity and dollars, with a dash of glamour and spectacle.

At Lincoln Center, Moses did more than bid for neighborhood change. His larger-scale objective was to establish a world-class institution and showcase the city's preeminence. President Dwight Eisenhower and Moses evoked the symbolic power of Lincoln Center at the groundbreaking in May 1959. Lincoln Center, they said, symbolized America's cultural coming-of-age and successful assault on urban blight, and Moses summed up his global ambition: "Here we stake our claim that New York will become the world center of the performing arts."[488]

THE HOUSING SUPERBLOCKS

In 1955, Moses named Joseph Weiser, an inexperienced developer, as sponsor of the housing section of the Lincoln Square Title I, and Weiser paid a $200,000 deposit. But in 1957, Moses rescinded the agreement and designated William Zeckendorf as the housing sponsor; Weiser's lawyer protested that his client had been eliminated without cause.[489] Moses rewarded Zeckendorf with the Lincoln Square housing at the time that he was rescuing two stalled Title I projects, Manhattantown and NYU–Bellevue, where nonperforming sponsors were giving Title I a black eye.

The plan in the Slum Clearance Committee brochure projected twelve buildings on two superblocks bordering West End Avenue, from 66th to 70th Street. The scheme by S. J. Kessler and Sons was typical of the firm's Title I work, with rows of freestanding apartment buildings separated by surface parking lots and play areas that squandered an opportunity to shape a magnetic communal space. Each building was 20 stories, with 17 apartments per floor, amounting to a total of 4,080 residential units. The site plan also included four low-rise commercial rows facing the avenues, a parking garage, church, and public school on 70th Street. Two fine apartment buildings from the 1920s at the corner of 70th Street and Columbus Avenue were excluded from the project area.

As at Kips Bay Plaza, Zeckendorf relied on his architect I. M. Pei to redesign the housing. The only surviving record of Pei's design (none have been found in his archives) is a sketch published in the *New York Times* on December 8, 1957. It indicates Pei's desire to vary the scale of housing with a combination of high-rise apartment buildings and 400 single-family residences in low-rise blocks, an approach that he employed at the Title I projects for Zeckendorf in Philadelphia (Society Hill) and Chicago (Hyde Park). Zeckendorf resented that his bankers forced him to sacrifice Pei. Lazard Frères "brought in an 'expert' at putting up the pseudo-luxury, builders' housing that blankets so much of Manhattan. . . . I'm not proud of the final product; I am ashamed of it. For a relatively very minor increase in costs, Lincoln Towers could have been one of the wonders of Manhattan, but this was not to be. When these towers are torn down, no one will mourn their passing, but the builder or politician who moves to tear down Kips Bay will have some angry citizens' groups on his hands. Kips Bay was no surrender, but a genuine advance in quality of city living." Zeckendorf's judgment was correct.

Lincoln Towers was built according to a revised design by S. J. Kessler and Sons. The dozen buildings originally envisioned were consolidated into six much larger units, each 28 or 29 stories, with about 3,800 apartments, allowing for more open space on the 20-acre site. (Of the six structures, two have different street numbers, thus reports sometimes erroneously mention eight buildings.) Construction began in 1961, and the buildings opened in 1964. The layout is designed for automobile convenience, with long circular driveways, surface parking lots, and underground garages. The structures are overscaled, and their relentless sameness and cheap mix of brick and concrete ledges stink of "projectitis." The complex included two blocks of small-scale retail along Amsterdam and West End avenues. The commercial block on West End Avenue at 70th Street was sold in 2006 for $97.5 million; the single-story row was demolished and an apartment tower will be built on the site. The stores originally projected for West End Avenue at 66th Street were not built.

Lincoln Towers fell into the luxury class. Monthly rents began at $130 for studios and $272 for two-bedroom apartments. (The room rate projected in the Slum Clearance plan of 1956 was $47.50 per room.) Lincoln Towers was the largest luxury project built through Moses's Title I program. He justified the development of market-rate housing on financial grounds; having removed Lincoln Center and Fordham from the tax rolls, his balance sheet required a fully taxpaying development in the housing section. "You cannot provide in this program exclusively for tax-exempt, low or partially tax-exempt middle-income families and wholly tax-exempt educational, charitable and cultural purposes. Someone has to pay the real estate taxes. And that's where the speculative builder who charges higher rentals and pays full taxes comes in." Distressed by the high social cost of displacement, housing advocates called for racially and economically mixed housing. Moses was unreceptive to this sort of social experimentation, but, to appease his critics, he added a middle-income cooperative to the housing program.

The cooperative was located on the west end of 60th Street, a shabby industrial fringe land. Consolidated Edison gas tanks and substation, a Chrysler garage, New York Times printing plant, and rail yards were the neighbors. It took a leap of imagination to see the area as Zeckendorf and Moses did, as fit for housing. After the New York Teachers Guild rejected the site, a private developer named Stanley J. Harte came forward and in 1958 became the sponsor with a bid of $225,000. The 20-story building, named Princess Gardens, was a banal U-shaped structure designed by Kelly & Gruzen, without the architectural distinction of the firm's Title I projects downtown, Chatham Green and Chatham Towers. The co-op had 420 units and opened with a waiting list of 1,500. Down payments were $890 a room, and monthly carrying charges were about $30, low rates made possible by a 25-year real estate tax exemption.

Moses reserved a portion of the housing superblock for a public school and playground. In 1960, in an unusual effort to recruit high-profile design architects in the school expansion program, the Board of Education commissioned Edward Durell Stone to build the K-6 elementary school. P.S. 199, which opened in 1963, had ribbed facades, recessed windows, decorative glazed brick, and a wafer-thin cantilevered roof. The unexpected delicacy of Stone's building stood in sharp contrast to the standard, stolid brick school box.

AMERICAN RED CROSS

The property at the corner of Amsterdam Avenue and 66th Street was originally reserved for St. Matthew's Roman Catholic Church and parochial school, which had been uprooted from elsewhere in the project area. Redevelopment, however, had banished the congregation. Unable to resurrect itself on the new terrain, the church withdrew from the project and in 1957 was replaced by the International Red Cross, in part because of a Rockefeller family connection. The chairman of the Red Cross's building development committee was James Stillman Rockefeller, the president of National City Bank and cousin of the Lincoln Center chairman. Designed by Skidmore, Owings & Merrill, the 5-story gridded structure is set back from the street by a stepped granite plaza which lies at the highest point of the sloping site. At the corner of 67th Street, the low point of the site, a chilling blind wall faces pedestrians. The design conveys civic polish and institutional hauteur, an odd tone for a social service organization and certainly unwelcoming to donors bound for the blood center. The building also contained laboratories, first-aid classrooms, administrative offices, and parking garage. The Red Cross bought the site in 1958 for $350,000 and sold it in 2004 for $72.3 million. The purchaser, A. & R. Kalimian Realty, plans to build an apartment building. — HB

SEWARD PARK TITLE I

Seward Park Housing, 1958–60
Office building, 1958–60
Shopping centers, 1958–60
Manhattan: East Broadway, Grand Street, Essex
    Street, Seward Park
15.21 acres
Plan published August 29, 1956
Figs. C-153–154

The Seward Park co-op, built on a narrow triangular site on the Lower East Side, was the seventeenth Title I one project endorsed by the Committee on Slum Clearance, the second Title I project undertaken by Abraham Kazan and the United Housing Foundation, and the fourth and final section of Kazan's Lower East Side limited-equity housing complex.

Planning began in the mid-1950s while work on Corlears Hook was under way, and the city approved the project in 1957, despite the protests of a handful of residents and small-business owners who objected to their being relocated. Removal of the area's 1,481 families began in early 1958 and was completed in the summer of 1959. Around half of these families were Jewish, a third Puerto Rican, and most of the remainder Chinese. Construction began in the summer of 1958 and was completed in 1960. The UHF received about 3,500 applications for the units, including 300 from families living on the site, of which two-thirds were approved. These households were permitted to remain in a few of the existing buildings whose demolition was postponed until the new apartments were ready.

The site comprised all or part of twelve blocks. Ten interior streets were eliminated to form three superblocks: one to the east of Pitt Street, one between Pitt and Clinton streets, and one to the west of Clinton. As part of the redevelopment, Grand, Pitt, and Clinton streets were widened. As was the case at several other urban renewal areas, older institutional buildings were preserved: a Jewish home for the aged on East Broadway near Clinton Street and a branch of the New York Public Library on East Broadway just east of the adjacent Seward Park. The park, and later the co-op, were named for the nineteenth-century politician William Henry Seward.

Plans by the architect Herman J. Jessor called for 1,728 units in four buildings, two small shopping centers, a theater, freestanding offices for the UHF, two playgrounds, a small city park, and a subterranean garage for 275 cars. The larger western and central superblocks contained the housing, shops, and garage, with the apartments oriented to provide

views of either midtown Manhattan or downtown Brooklyn. The UHF offices and park occupied the much smaller eastern superblock. The residential buildings were virtually identical to those designed by Springsteen and Jessor for Corlears Hook: triple cruciform towers of 20 stories with seven or eight units off each corridor. As at Corlears, the top three stories of the buildings were set back, offering terraces to many units on these floors. Land coverage declined from between 75 and 100 percent to about 26 percent, while population density rose from around 325 persons per acre to 380.

The most significant innovation over Corlears was the inclusion of two-room studio apartments of 500 square feet in addition to the one-, two-, and three-bedroom units similar to those in the earlier project. The studio units had a foyer and a small separate kitchen; all the three-bedroom suites included two bathrooms. Curiously, the plan allowed fewer units with balconies or terraces and fewer units with cross-ventilation than at Corlears. The first floor of each tower featured laundry, carriage, and storage rooms; public meeting rooms; and lobbies. Each lobby was decorated with a mural by Hugo Gellert, a leftist artist best known for his political works of the 1930s. The murals depicted Thomas Jefferson, Abraham Lincoln, Albert Einstein, and Franklin D. Roosevelt. As at Corlears Hook, a cooperative supermarket was among the shopping facilities.

Shares sold at a rate of $650 a room, or $1,950 to $3,575 per unit (roughly $15,500 to $28,500 today). Owing to increased costs and higher interest rates than prevailed at the time Corlears was financed, Seward's monthly charges were about 25 percent greater, averaging $21 a room in contrast to the earlier project's $17. In practice, these charges ranged from as little as $33.50 for two rooms on a low floor to $139.50 for four and a half rooms with a terrace ($3,000 to $12,500, annually, in 2004 dollars). As in most UHF co-ops, cash generated by the sale of shares covered a fifth of the construction costs. For the balance—some $18 million—Kazan relied upon several sources rather than a single lender as he had done at Corlears, taking six separate mortgages ranging in value from $1 million to $7 million.

Lenders included two local savings banks; Workmen's Circle, a well-established Jewish consumers' cooperative and mutual-aid society; and three trade unions: the Brotherhood of Painters, Decorators and Paperhangers of America; the International Brotherhood of Electrical Workers; and the United Hatters, Cap and Millinery Workers International Union. The hatters had been one of several unions to

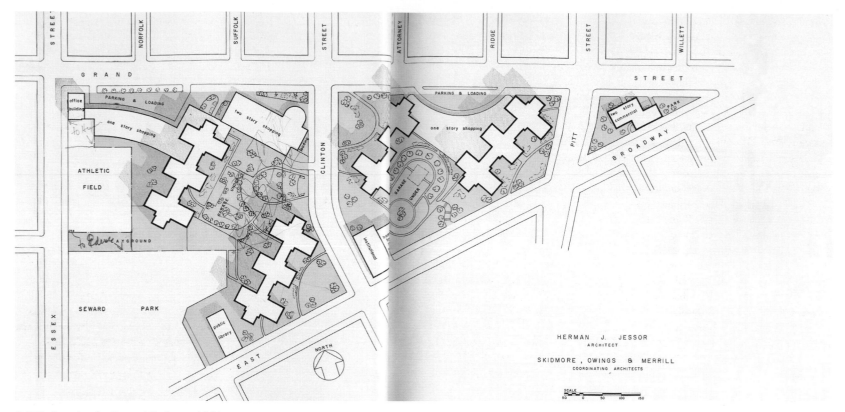

C-153. Site plan for Seward Park, ca. 1956. Design by Herman J. Jessor

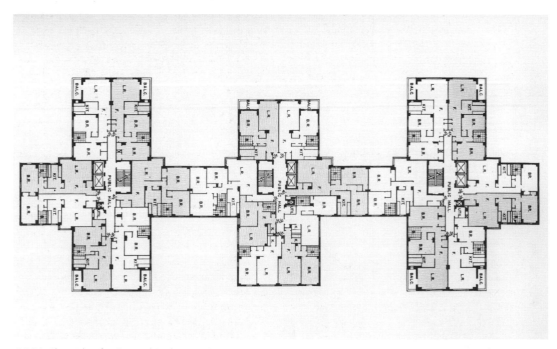

C-154. Floor plan for Seward Park, ca. 1956

make an unsuccessful bid for a limited-equity co-op in the Bronx in the 1920s, and the electrical workers had financed the 2,225-unit Electchester limited-equity co-op on the site of an old country club in Flushing, Queens, in the early 1950s. Like the ILGWU at Corlears, however, these groups made the loans to Seward Park primarily because they understood the project as a secure investment. Indeed, among the original residents, only 174 were members of the Workmen's Circle or one of the unions. Three-quarters of the residents moved to the complex from elsewhere on the Lower East Side, including 185 displaced households.

The project was executed quickly, thanks to rapid sales, and almost entirely in accord with initial plans. The only significant departure from the published plan was the orientation of the shopping centers. Instead of being set back from the road at odd angles, the shops fronted directly on Grand and Clinton streets. Demand for the housing was such that during construction Kazan conceived of an addition, called Seward Park Extension, for a site to the immediate north, bounded by Willett, Grand, Essex, Broome, and Delancey streets. Although Moses and the Committee on Slum Clearance—and after Moses's removal, the new Housing and Redevelopment Board—were eager to proceed, leaders of two houses of worship on the site who wielded significant power in City Hall effectively blocked it from even reaching initial hearings, and the idea was abandoned.

Like residents of the Amalgamated Dwellings, Hillman Houses, and the East River Houses, those of Seward Park began plans to convert the building to the market-rate format in the late 1980s. Today, shares fetch from $350,000 for studios to $825,000 for three bedrooms. Larger, combined units with 1,600 or 1,800 square feet sell for $1.1 to $1.5 million. To help defray maintenance, owners pay a "flip tax" fee to the cooperative corporation when they sell. While many newer residents seem to dislike the towers-in-the-park plan, which they feel isolates the project from the city, the buildings remain well cared for and offer the types of well-planned, naturally lighted spaces difficult to find in Manhattan at any price. — MGL

PARK ROW TITLE I

Chatham Green, 1959–62
Shops, 1959–62
Manhattan: Pearl Street, Park Row, and St. James Place
5.24 acres
Plan published October 15, 1956
Figs. P-51, C-155, 161

The Park Row slum clearance plan was the eighteenth Title I scheme proposed by the Committee on Slum Clearance. It noted that the site was selected because of general "blight," "nuisance conditions," and over-crowding. Indeed, the area was at the core of the Lower East Side's oldest slum district, just a short block from Five Points, the present-day corner of Baxter and Worth streets. Yet, after decades of out-migration from the Lower East Side, the Park Row renewal area was by 1956 home only to 410 families, with 1,042 persons in 36 residential buildings, for a population density of about 230 people per acre. Apart from three boarding houses, the majority of the land was occupied by a mix of small business buildings and vacant lots.

Clearance of this section of town had been a priority of housing reformers and civic leaders for more than a century. Among the city's very first slum clearance projects was the construction in 1897 of Jacob Riis Park (today Columbus Park), between Baxter and Mulberry streets south of Bayard Street, on the site of Mulberry Bend, one of Five Points' most unhealthful and densely populated sections. In the late 1940s, the entire area extending north from City Hall, the Municipal Building, and the law courts at Foley Square up to Canal Street had been projected in a nonbinding plan for redevelopment as a new civic center. Although not specifically mentioned in this post–World War II plan, the Park Row site and adjacent blocks appeared in bird's-eye renderings as rebuilt with clusters of towers-in-the-park.

The Committee on Slum Clearance affiliated the Park Row project with the lower Manhattan financial district. Implicit was the hope that the site would prove popular as middle-class, walk-to-work housing for civil servants and financial services employees. Despite the assertion, however, the Park Row site was not part of the financial district; it was part of Chinatown. And the committee's proposal was in direct competition with a separate set of plans formulated by private citizens to redevelop the area in a way that would preserve its roles as tourist attraction, residential center, and regional marketplace for greater New York's Chinese-American community. These plans, sponsored by a local American Legion post and the University Neighborhood Project settle-

ment house and developed by MIT architecture students in 1947 and 1948, called for the creation of a "China Village," complete with new housing and extensive retail space for local merchants in culturally sensitive structures that combined modernist planning principles with traditional Chinese design elements.

Largely ignored by city leaders, the China Village plan had the support of Herman T. Stichman, New York State's commissioner of housing. Stichman unveiled it to the public in 1950 at a series of community meetings in Chinatown. As a state official, however, he had no authority to initiate redevelopment projects in the city; he could only make recommendations. And while the Committee on Slum Clearance had not yet formulated specific plans of its own for the area, Moses attacked China Village with vitriol, arguing that its idiosyncratic designs would be impossible to pay for with the public purse, despite Stichman's offer of substantial state aid. Moses further chastised Stichman for taking the plan public without his endorsement. In a letter to Stichman, Moses asked if he planned to fund the project with "Chinese money" and suggested that his "exuberant celestial promises represent what might be called a Slip of the Tong."[493] Stichman let go of the plan.

By comparison with China Village, Park Row Title I was conventional. It called for the clearance of all existing structures, the closing of all but one interior street, and the creation of two superblocks. At the southern end of the site, bounded on the north by Madison Street, a small superblock of one-third of an acre was to be created by eliminating New Chambers and Chestnut streets. It was designated for a park, today called James Madison Plaza. North of Madison, Roosevelt and James streets were to be eliminated to create a larger superblock of more than four acres. Because the original parcels were so small, combining them yielded an area similar in size to a standard Manhattan block. This site was designated for redevelopment as a limited-equity co-op called Chatham Green, two surface parking lots with space for 106 cars, an underground parking lot with space for 69 cars, and two blocks of shops.

The developer of the complex was Chatham Green, Inc., which Shirley F. Boden and William Reid organized to undertake the project in 1955. Boden had assisted Abraham Kazan with the Corlears Hook Title I project and had helped to develop the cooperative plan for Morningside Gardens, then under way. At the time, he was also at work on a limited-equity co-op in Yonkers called Sunset Green. Reid was a lifelong civil servant who had begun his career in 1913 in the city controller's office. By the mid-1950s, he had assumed, among other roles, the presidency of the city's Municipal Credit Union, the New York State Credit Union, and the Credit Union National Association. The first two of these, under Reid's guidance, promised to serve as the project's primary sponsor. Like the trade unions that had financed other limited-equity co-ops, the credit unions, with tens of thousands of members and tens of millions of dollars in deposits, had plenty of cash to invest. Somewhat later, Boden and Reid brought on board the New York State Teachers Retirement Fund, which made the bulk of mortgage loans for the project.

Boden and Reid gave their architects, Kelly & Gruzen, considerable freedom in design. Since its establishment by Colonel Hugh A. Kelly and Barnett Sumner Gruzen in Jersey City in 1936, the firm had specialized in commercial buildings and multifamily housing, designing scores of schools, shops, and apartment complexes in New York and northern New Jersey. Their work was not avant-garde, yet the firm brought a fresh eye and keen imagination to its city commissions, which to date had included the Hamilton Fish Park branch library and Junior High School 22 at East Houston and Columbia streets (1956).

In stark contrast to the rigid geometry of other Title I projects, Kelly & Gruzen's proposal was for a long, undulating slab of 21 stories that curved through the site like a serpent. It was flanked by a one-story row of shops attached to the main structure at the northeast corner of Madison and Pearl; a free-standing two-story block of shops and professional suites at the acute intersection of Park Row and St. James Place faced Chatham Square. This latter building, in which Boden himself took an office, was also unconventional in design; along the St. James side it had a saw-tooth plan, which served to increase visibility from the Chinatown shopping district running north along the Bowery from Chatham Square. In contrast to the shopping centers at other Title I projects, which were almost entirely of brick, this building was distinguished by a wall of plate glass at the main entrance rising the full two stories.

Long buildings were typically avoided in redevelopment projects so as to maximize the number of angles and exposures, which in turn promised to fill apartments with the most fresh air and sunlight. Kelly & Gruzen, however, achieved the same result by arranging suites only one room deep and by eliminating the double-loaded interior corridor. Apartments were accessed by covered outdoor catwalks running the length of the building along the northwest facade. While common in luxury apartment buildings in Latin America and Florida for decades, catwalks appeared in northern cities like New York only after World War II—and largely at public housing projects as an experimental, cost-saving measure. At Chatham Green, however, this arrangement had less to do with economy than with achieving a playful form without sacrificing light and air: the plan permitted each of the 20 units per floor to have windows at both the front and back, and those at the ends of each floor to have three exposures. For additional privacy and convenience, each floor was divided into three sections of six to eight suites, with each portion served by a separate entrance at the ground floor and a bank of two elevators.

The project was also atypical in its unexpected juxtaposition of otherwise everyday materials. At a distance, the apartments appear to be faced entirely in red brick, though in a shade paler than in most other Title I projects. Yet, on the northwest side of the building, only the catwalks and service cores are brick; the walls, set back from the corridors, are unpainted cinderblock. On the southeast side of the building, meanwhile, the structure is composed primarily of unbroken ribbons of windows, separated at each story by a narrow band of brick. In addition, above the sixth floor all but one suite per floor have balconies, which besides providing most units with private outdoor space serve to break the monotony of the facade and work as a brise-soleil.

The building's 420 units, which yielded a nearly identical population density before and after redevelopment despite a reduction in land coverage from about 75 to 20 percent, were configured in four basic plans: studios with two and a half rooms, one-bedrooms with four rooms, two-bedrooms with five rooms, and three-bedrooms with six and a half rooms. As in most other Title I co-ops, owners' equity covered 20 percent of the project's cost. Units sold at a rate of around $850 a room, with projected maintenance of $25.50 a room per month. Due to rising costs, these rates were somewhat higher than the $625 in equity and $22.50 in maintenance initially anticipated.

Despite opposition by a group of prominent Italian-Americans who wished to preserve their community's historic St. Joachim's Church at the northeast corner of Roosevelt Street and St. James Place, the City Planning Commission and the Board of Estimate approved Kelly & Gruzen's plan. Relocation began in the spring of 1957, and the land was officially condemned and sold to Chatham Green, Inc. a year later. Ground was broken in September 1959 and the building was completed, almost precisely as originally designed, in March 1962. In the early 1980s, owners overwhelmingly approved plans to convert it to a market-rate co-op. Today, one-bedroom apartments of 880 square feet sell for approximately $550,000, with $575 in monthly maintenance. — MGL

C-155. Chatham Green, detail of open-air corridors, 2005. Photograph by Matthew Gordon Lasner

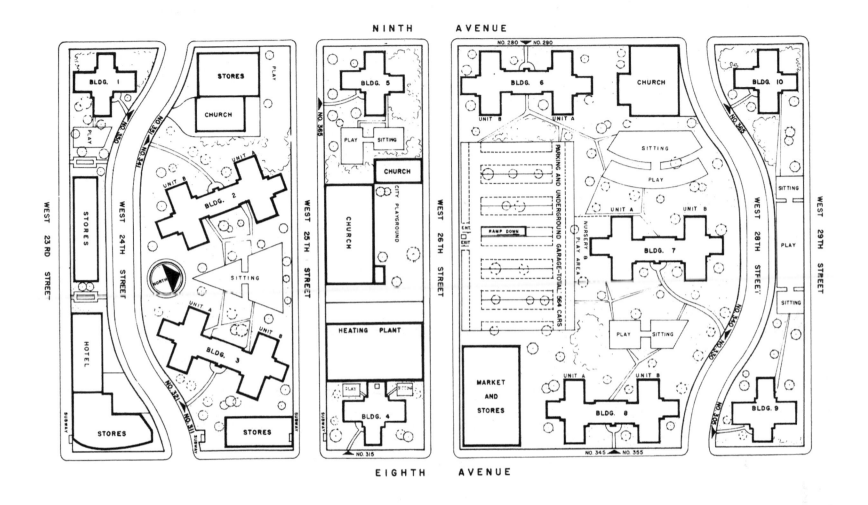

C-156. Site plan of Penn Station South, 1962

PENN STATION SOUTH TITLE I

Penn Station South, 1962
Shopping centers
Churches
Manhattan: West 23rd to West 29th Street, Eighth
   to Ninth Avenue
23.45 acres
Plan published August 1957
Figs. C-156–157

As work neared completion at the Corlears Hook
urban renewal project, Abraham Kazan persuaded
David Dubinsky of the International Ladies' Garment

Workers' Union to finance a second development of
limited-equity co-ops. Robert Moses first proposed
to Kazan a midtown site on the East Side. The UHF,
however, preferred the idea of a community within
walking distance of the garment district, which was
centered around Seventh Avenue in the lower 30s,
and proposed a site between West 23rd and 29th
streets, from Eight to Ninth Avenue. For generations,
this section of Chelsea had been considered a slum.
Indeed, in the late nineteenth century, Chelsea
boasted the second highest residential densities in
the city after the Lower East Side. It was home to a
mix of aging warehouses, smaller walk-up apartment

buildings, and rooming houses carved from old three-
story row houses. Moses happily developed a plan to
use Title I to purchase the site.

As at other large UHF projects, Kazan hired the
architect Herman J. Jessor, who undertook a plan for
the Committee on Slum Clearance, its twentieth Title
I proposal. The scheme realigned West 24th and West
28th streets in curvilinear fashion and created one
superblock by eliminating West 27th Street. Initially,
UHF had hoped to eliminate most of the interior
streets, but elected officials objected on grounds that
doing so would inhibit the flow of commercial traffic
to and from the West Side piers and further congest

C-157. Aerial view of Penn Station South, 1962

23rd Street. As a compromise, Jessor devised the curvilinear plan, which created larger blocks without disturbing traffic.

Three existing buildings were preserved: the Protestant Episcopal Church of the Holy Apostles at West 28th Street and Ninth Avenue, St. Columba's Roman Catholic Church and school midblock on West 25th Street, and the 12-story Cornish Arms Hotel (today a market-rate co-op called the Broadmoor) on West 23rd Street just west of Eighth Avenue. Built in 1925, the hotel had a public hall that had been used for decades as a meeting room for unions and leftist groups based in the neighborhood. It was one of the few modern structures on site. Two churches were razed and given new lots elsewhere in the project.

The initial plan called for 2,520 apartments in nine 20- and 21-story buildings. Later a tenth building was added, and the number of stories raised to a uniform 22, allowing a total of 2,820 units. The plan also called for a series of one- and two-story shopping centers along the two avenues and West 23rd Street, a theater, a cinema, an indoor tennis center, a 3-story office building, a central heating plant (today a cogeneration plant that produces electricity for the entire complex), and a central parking area along the

north side of West 26th Street. Together, these facilities and the apartments occupied about 5 acres, or about 21 percent of the site. Previous buildings had covered 70 to 99 percent. Population density, of 360 persons per acre, was to remain comparable before and after redevelopment.

There was a significant amount of opposition to Penn Station South among the 2,646 existing site families. The activist Jane Wood, a long-time tenants' rights advocate and radical leftist, established a group called Chelsea Coalition on Housing, which staged protests at City Hall and filed a lawsuit against the city in the summer of 1959. The project was also singled out for criticism by the city's controller, Lawrence Gerosa, who believed that the extension of real estate tax breaks to projects built through Title I was fiscally irresponsible. Nevertheless, the application for Title I funding went through and sales were under way by early 1958. As clearance proceeded, the press closely monitored the process. But as at other UHF Title I sites, relocation went smoothly.

The residential buildings recall those at Corlears Hook and Seward Park, although they are significantly smaller. Five single-core buildings of 188 units form one cruciform tower and five double-core buildings

of 376 units form two. Each tower contains nine suites per floor arranged along a T-plan corridor. The double buildings are served by a single lobby on the ground floor. As at Corlears Hook and Seward Park, the buildings step back at the upper three stories. In accordance with Manhattan's gridiron street plan, most of the residential buildings and all the secondary facilities are aligned with the streets and avenues. The units themselves are arranged in ten different plans and sizes, ranging from two rooms in 520 square feet to six and a half rooms in 1,696 square feet. Sales of shares, which were priced at a rate of $650 per room, contributed 20 percent of construction costs. Two-thirds of the rest came from a mortgage made by the ILGWU and the remainder from a mortgage, arranged once construction had begun, from the New York State Teachers' Retirement System.

The first families moved in in May 1962, after a dedication ceremony attended by President John F. Kennedy and Eleanor Roosevelt, as well as Mayor Robert Wagner and Governor Nelson Rockefeller. Among the residents were 300 families displaced from the site—a proportion consistent with other UHF projects—and 715 members of the ILGWU. More than half of the first residents moved from elsewhere in Manhattan; most of the rest came from the other boroughs. The atypically high number of residents who were union members or who had previously lived outside the neighborhood was a result of the project's highly desirable, central location.

Before moving in, all residents received mandatory pre-occupancy training designed to imbue them with a sense of the UHF's ideological mission—a practice that began at Queensview West and was eventually extended to all new UHF co-ops. Thanks to this training and to strong leadership by the co-op's board of directors, Penn Station South has remained a vibrant oasis of affordable housing in otherwise costly Chelsea. In the mid-1980s, while the residents of many other limited-equity co-ops formulated plans to convert their homes to market rate, Penn Station South voted to extend the limited-equity format in return for an additional twenty-five years of tax relief from the city. Faced with mounting taxes in spite of this break, shareholders reached a second agreement with the city in 2001 for a yet-steeper discount in return for retaining remaining limited equity until 2022.

At Kazan's four Lower East Side complexes, where more than 80 percent of the shareholders voted to abandon the limited-equity program (as compared to only 5 percent at Penn Station South), many of the older residents had left the community, typically to retire in Florida, choosing to sublet their units to renters rather then sell them back to the co-op under the limited-equity system. They seem to have understood their vote for change as an opportunity to profit from their many years of commitment to the community. At Chelsea, by contrast, subleasing was rare, thanks to active vigilance by the residents. As a result, the shareholders, by an overwhelming margin, remained committed to continuing Kazan's program. Shares, now jointly administered by the co-op and city as part of the tax arrangement, sell today for just under $10,000 a room. Maintenance remains under $150 a room. The project has a waiting list of about 10,000 families; they can expect to wait for ten to twenty years. — MGL

RIVERSIDE-AMSTERDAM TITLE I

Unexecuted
Manhattan: Riverside Drive to Amsterdam Avenue,
    West 83rd to West 86th Street
24.58 acres
Plan published November 10, 1958
Fig. C-158

The Riverside-Amsterdam urban renewal project, a controversial and ill-fated plan to revitalize nine residential blocks on Manhattan's West Side, was the brainchild of the attorney and real estate investor Sidney J. Ungar. In March 1955, Ungar had purchased a 16-story apartment building in a rough neighborhood, at the corner of West 85th Street and Amsterdam Avenue. When he discovered the difficulty of retaining tenants, he began to look for ways to fight the social and physical deterioration on his block and turned to redevelopment as a potential solution for the neighborhood's problems.[494]

Although this part of the West Side had a number of modern apartment buildings like Ungar's, it was still largely a neighborhood of aging brownstones and tenements. Many of them had been subdivided into small apartments or converted into rooming houses, whose overcrowding and physical deterioration contributed to the neighborhood's decline. In a series of meetings with members of the Slum Clearance Committee, city officials, architects, and engineers, Ungar began to formulate an approach to physical planning intended to halt this decline. A nine-block area, from West 83rd to West 86th Street and from Riverside Drive to Amsterdam Avenue, was targeted for redevelopment, but only certain buildings, primarily the substandard brownstones and tenements, would be demolished. Other buildings, generally the modern apartment buildings and a limited number of institutional structures, would be exempted from the plan. New luxury housing would be constructed on scattered sites, improving the overall quality of the neighborhood's housing stock without total clearance of the area.

Robert Moses had misgivings about this approach. As he wrote to the Manhattan borough president Hulan Jack in June 1956, Ungar's project made no provisions for "features of good planning," such as street widening and the creation of superblocks. Moreover, Moses anticipated objections to the project, notably on the grounds that it required too much relocation and could be seen—especially in light of Ungar's financial interest in one of the exempted buildings—as an attempt to improve the property values of specific building owners. But Ungar, a

Tammany Hall insider and a one-time congressional candidate, had political ties, including a close personal relationship with Jack, that would help to promote this redevelopment project. Moses needed the borough president's vote on the Board of Estimate to ensure the approval of other Manhattan projects, and he seemed to have been willing to recommend this one as a favor to Jack.[495]

Riverside-Amsterdam thus became the Slum Clearance Committee's first spot-clearance project. Ungar was designated its tentative sponsor in October 1956, and the first round of federal funds for the $36-million project was approved in December 1957. After several months of further study, the SCC published its own plan for the area in November 1958. In this plan, 116 structures out of approximately 170 in the nine-block area would be cleared, requiring the relocation of 593 families, 188 single people, and 1,048 roomers.[496] New high-rise apartment buildings would be constructed on cleared land on eight of the nine blocks in the project area. The veteran Title I architects S. J. Kessler & Sons designed double-loaded corridor buildings—12, 16, and 20 stories in height—oriented according to the existing street grid. In total, 1,843 new market-rate units were planned in eight buildings, with monthly rentals projected at $49 per room. The proposed development also included extensive outdoor sitting and play areas adjoining the residential buildings, a medical building, outdoor parking, a parking garage, and commercial space. Although the individual residential structures proposed in the plan are very similar to those in other SCC projects, the site planning marks a departure from the towers-in-the-park paradigm. The street grid has been retained; the new construction is situated within the block and oriented toward the street; and land coverage, while lower than existing conditions, is still high.[497]

Spot clearance also differed from the SCC's usual physical planning strategies. Typically, redevelopment projects in New York City involved total demolition of existing structures and the elimination of through streets to form superblocks, although existing public buildings and religious structures were occasionally exempted from redevelopment plans. Increasingly throughout the 1950s, however, planners and policy makers were reconsidering the merits of total clearance. Reviewing the nation's first Title I projects in 1953, an advisory committee appointed by President Dwight Eisenhower made a series of recommendations that were incorporated into the landmark 1954 Housing Act: redevelopment of slum areas alone would not solve the nation's housing problems and

C-158. Proposal for Riverside-Amsterdam, November 1958. Design by S. J. Kessler and Sons

overcrowded and deteriorated but not yet a slum. It is not surprising, then, that the plan found widespread support. Shortly after its publication, Mayor Wagner heralded the plan as a new approach to the city's housing problems; the *New York Times* commented that it was "in line with the trend toward renewing old neighborhoods through preserving what is good"; and the *World Telegram and Sun* praised it for "avoiding needless upheaval and dislocation."[498]

Yet, in important ways, this plan was deeply conservative. Other experiments in the late 1950s calling for limited clearance—notably the West Side Urban Renewal Area, a pilot project of New York's Urban Renewal Board, located in the blocks between West 86th and West 96th Street, Amsterdam Avenue and Central Park West; or the highly regarded Wooster Square project in New Haven—combined targeted demolition and new construction with rehabilitation, aggressive code enforcement, and community outreach to help landlords and homeowners understand and comply with the city's program. Moses, however, believed that rehabilitation was not financially feasible in New York and was openly skeptical about the outlook for the Urban Renewal Board's West Side project. Riverside-Amsterdam may have broken with the top-down planning techniques of the 1950s, but it did not embrace the neighborhood-oriented programs that would become widely used in the 1960s.

Like the city's Title I program itself, the Riverside-Amsterdam project spent most of 1959 in the public eye, awash in scandal. The first erupted in February, when the *New York Post* revealed that Ungar had a financial interest in five properties in Harlem whose condition was so poor that he had been charged with 157 violations of the housing code. Not only did the *Post* point out the glaring conflict between Ungar's behavior as a landlord in Harlem and his aspirations to neighborhood revitalization on the West Side, but it also noted his political connections and his donations to the Jack and Wagner campaigns. Although Ungar threatened a libel suit, the *Post* had turned the spotlight on the legitimacy of his sponsorship and his problematic prospects as a landlord at Riverside-Amsterdam. Moses recommended dropping the project, and the Board of Estimate, which had scheduled a hearing on it on February 26, a crucial stage in the approval process, postponed the hearing until April 9.[499]

Charges of corruption in the selection of sponsors and reports of criminal behavior by sponsors acting as landlords plagued the SCC in the late 1950s. By spring 1959, Riverside-Amsterdam was one of a number of projects—including Washington Square Southeast and Gramercy Park in Manhattan and Pratt

should be accompanied by a program of targeted clearance, housing code enforcement, zoning code revision, and city-wide planning to arrest decline in marginal neighborhoods.

Moreover, by the late 1950s, the so-called bulldozer approach was also coming under attack from both community groups and the press, which were beginning to question the social effects of total clearance and relocation. Both community protest and editorial commentary placed pressure on those public officials whose support was essential to the planning process. Nowhere was this more evident than in New

York, whose Title I program was the largest in the country and also one of the most closely scrutinized. As a physical planning strategy, spot clearance, which was less destructive of marginal housing and seemed to require less displacement, was fast becoming more politically palatable than projects requiring total clearance.

The SCC itself described the Riverside-Amsterdam plan as "a positive means of arresting blight and deterioration before it infests a whole neighborhood," an especially appropriate strategy for the Upper West Side, an area of the city that city officials considered

Institute in Brooklyn—that were under investigation by citizens' groups and the press. At the Board of Estimate meeting on April 9, critics of the project protested Ungar's sponsorship, and the group deferred its decision in order to investigate charges against Ungar. A week later, the Housing and Home Finance Agency announced that it would withhold funding.[500]

With Ungar's participation in question, the SCC revisited its plans for Riverside-Amsterdam and began discussions with another potential sponsor, Yeshiva University. In the fall of 1958, Yeshiva's trustees, interested in a new downtown campus, had approached the SCC with an interest in purchasing land adjacent to the Lincoln Square redevelopment project. The following spring, when that plan proved unsuccessful, they began considering the Riverside-Amsterdam area and in June announced their intention of becoming partial sponsors for this project. Facilities for Yeshiva's Stern College for Women and its graduate schools of education, social work, and mathematical science and physics, as well as residential dormitories, would occupy those parcels on the three easternmost blocks of the project area, between West 83rd and West 86th and Broadway and Amsterdam, that had been slated for residential reconstruction in the original plan. Plans for clearance and residential development for the six western blocks were left essentially intact.[501]

Although not much had changed in the physical planning of the nine blocks in the project area, the new sponsorship represented new life for the project. Yeshiva University was the kind of reliable institutional sponsor that the SCC preferred.[502] In October 1959, the SCC announced a coalition of sponsors that would carry the project forward: Yeshiva University, responsible for the institutional development, and two firms that would redevelop the residential areas, Dworman Associates, a national construction company, and Seymore and Jerome Berger, local realty management experts.

Ungar continued to fight aggressively for sponsorship of the project that he had initiated, although his approval seemed less and less likely as the year progressed. In June, another major scandal developed involving a "good faith" deposit that Ungar made in SCC member Thomas Shanahan's Federation Bank and Trust Company.[503] In December, the ultimate storm broke: a contractor told the *Post* that he was unable to collect full payment from Ungar for the expenses he had incurred at Ungar's behest while remodeling Hulan Jack's apartment in the spring of 1958.

Unlike the previous Riverside-Amsterdam scandals, which had cast doubt on Ungar's character and on the ethics of SCC's sponsor selection process, this one offered concrete evidence of graft between a sponsor and an elected official whose approval was essential to the project's realization. It also threatened a major figure in city politics: Jack, a former state assemblyman who was elected borough president of Manhattan in 1953 and 1957, was an important player in Tammany politics; when he was indicted in January 1960, he held the highest elected administrative post of any African-American in the country.

During Jack's trial in June 1960, Ungar testified that he had paid for the remodeling because he believed Jack "probably could do favors for me." Moses testified that Jack had told the SCC that they "couldn't do better than go ahead with [Ungar's] sponsorship" of the Riverside-Amsterdam project and that, when Ungar's sponsorship came under scrutiny in 1959, Jack had asked him not to take a public stand against Ungar. Jack was convicted in December 1960 on one charge of conspiracy to obstruct justice and three violations of the city charter and was removed from office.[504]

One of the central social and economic arguments in favor of spot clearance as a physical planning strategy was that a focused attack on only the very worst housing would have a revitalizing effect at the local level. The large-scale bulldozer projects of the 1950s were metropolitan or even regional; entire neighborhoods were sacrificed to bolster the municipal tax base and the status of the central city. Spot clearance, however, opened up the possibility of turning around a single marginal or struggling neighborhood through targeted physical intervention. In the late 1950s and early 1960s, a new politics of redevelopment emerged. Stakeholders likely to benefit from a renewal plan—often homeowners and middle-class renters—threw their support behind spot clearance, and those who were most likely to be displaced by it—working-class and poor renters and residents of SROs—opposed renewal.

This dynamic developed in the Riverside-Amsterdam project area. As early as the fall of 1959, two project-area residents—Louis Beck, a salesman, and Laurence Housman, an accountant, both residents of 310 West 85th Street, an apartment building not scheduled for demolition—began to organize their neighbors. They established the Neighborhood Improvement Association, one of the first community organizations to be formed in support of renewal and the Riverside-Amsterdam plan. In December 1959, a group of local residents presented to President Samuel Belkin of Yeshiva University, the project's main sponsor, a petition in favor of the project with the signatures of 1,500 residents of the urban renewal area.[505]

The new politics of redevelopment was complex. A wide array of groups, not just middle-class residents of the project area, were campaigning for the improvement of housing conditions in declining neighborhoods like the West Side, supporting the Riverside-Amsterdam plan, even arguing for its enlargement.[506] As in the conflicts that would characterize urban renewal projects in the 1960s, politicians and community leaders recognized the racial overtones of selective demolition. In Riverside-Amsterdam, where substandard SROs housed a growing Puerto Rican community, spot clearance would clearly have displaced a significant part of the neighborhood's minority population. In January 1960, just after the presentation of the petition, one local politician speculated that fears of racial succession in the neighborhood motivated its proponents and accused the project's supporters of a thinly veiled racism.[507]

National attitudes toward the construction of luxury housing in renewal and redevelopment areas were also changing. In 1962, Milton Mollen, the chairman of the Housing and Redevelopment Board (HRB), declared that the agency would no longer pursue renewal projects intended solely to provide luxury housing; the agency's priority was now the provision of middle-income housing. Riverside-Amsterdam, one of 28 SCC projects inherited by the HRB in 1960, was among those slated for further study. It was scaled back and revised once again in 1963, when the three easternmost blocks were eliminated and annexed to the adjacent Museum General Neighborhood Renewal Plan, which emphasized rehabilitation and conservation rather than redevelopment.[508] Until Riverside-Amsterdam was canceled in 1966, it retained a certain amount of support among area residents who believed that spot clearance and new housing would revitalize the neighborhood. Approximately 200 people gathered to protest its end.[509]

Conceived by a slumlord, sealed with a backroom deal, and never executed, Riverside-Amsterdam would be easy to dismiss. As a social effort, its goals were dubious; as an experiment in physical revitalization, it was limited and conservative in comparison with other contemporary projects. But in the context of the numerous physical and social planning experiments that took place on Manhattan's West Side in the 1950s and 1960s, it stands as a transitional project whose history reflects changing attitudes toward the social and economic possibilities of limited clearance and redevelopment. —JH

C-159. Battery Park Title I apartments (proposed), ca. 1959. Design by Mies van der Rohe; photomontage by Hedrich Blessing. Chicago History Museum, neg. HB22411B

BATTERY PARK TITLE I

Unexecuted
Manhattan: South, Whitehall, Water, Broad, and Pearl streets, and Coenties Slip
4.91 acres
Plan published January 19, 1959
Fig. C-159

This project was linked to the campaign to modernize lower Manhattan launched by David Rockefeller with strong support from civic and business groups. The decision of Chase Manhattan Bank in February 1955 to resist the migration of banking institutions to midtown and to build its new headquarters downtown sparked the redevelopment effort. (The Chase Manhattan Bank building on William and Pine streets, designed by SOM, was built from 1957 to 1960.) Rockefeller, the executive vice president of the bank in charge of the headquarters project, went to see Moses about closing a city block (Cedar Street between Nassau and William streets) in order to create an enlarged site for the new bank building and plaza. As Rockefeller recalled in his *Memoirs* (2002), Moses raised the issue of the surrounding neighborhood and cautioned: "'You'll be wasting your money unless others follow suit.' He pointed out that many Wall Street businesses had already moved uptown or were about to leave the City altogether. If any more left, Chase's decision to remain would be viewed as a colossal blunder. Moses suggested that I put together an organization that could speak on behalf of the downtown financial community and offer a cohesive plan for the physical redevelopment of Wall Street to persuade the politicians to allocate the necessary resources."[510]

In 1956, persuaded by Moses's broad urban perspective, Rockefeller formed the Committee on Lower Manhattan to pursue collective action. Renamed the Downtown-Lower Manhattan Association in 1958, the group issued a far-reaching master plan to remake the historic heart of Manhattan as a modern residential and financial district. The plan envisioned extensive clearance, huge public investments in infrastructure (including the Lower Manhattan Expressway), and private redevelopment. A key recommendation was to transform the East River waterfront into a residential corridor. Moses assisted by developing plans for three Title I projects: Battery Park, Battery Park North, and Brooklyn Bridge, named for the adjacent landmarks.

The Battery Park Title I project was the only one to reach the stage of a published plan. Studies began in 1956, and the plan, the 22nd to be issued by the Slum Clearance Committee, was published in January 1959. The project aimed to turn the derelict commercial waterfront into an upscale residential district within walking distance of Wall Street offices. The site plan by S. J. Kessler & Sons, with SOM as consulting architects, merged six small blocks into two superblocks. Three 24-story apartment buildings were situated perpendicular to the river to provide scenic harbor views for residents in the proposed 1,224 dwelling units and to keep view corridors open for inland towers. A shopping center, parking lots, and playgrounds filled out the superblocks. The open space was expanded by incorporating Jeannette Park, at the north end of the site, into the site plan. Relocation was a minor issue with this project: of the 97 extant structures recorded in the site survey, only 5 were residential. On the other hand, the project raised the issue of historic preservation at a time when aggressive slum clearance was beginning to galvanize activists in New York City. In fact, Moses decided to preserve Fraunces Tavern and the neigh-

boring eighteenth-century buildings on Whitehall Street, which were excluded from the project, although the renewal plan did not mention their historic value. Evidently, the logic of the decision to save these buildings was too threatening to expose.

Moses chose Herbert Greenwald to develop the Battery Park Title I as well as Battery Park North Title I, which was in early planning for an adjacent site. A Chicago-based developer, Greenwald (1915–1959) had significant Title I projects under way in Detroit (Lafayette Park) and Newark, N.J. (Colonnade Park), as well as Brooklyn, where he was building the housing in the Fort Greene Title I. In the annals of architectural history, Greenwald is celebrated as the client of Mies van der Rohe's twin towers in Chicago at 860 and 880 Lake Shore Drive. While nurturing Mies's experiments in design, materials, and building technology in a series of important commissions in the 1950s, Greenwald also pursued his own social vision and commitment to the city in Title I work (see the essay by Hilary Ballon). "The city may be damned, but it is by no means doomed. . . . Let's rebuild it," he cheered himself on. "We can prevent families from fleeing to the suburbs if we give them good city accommodations.'"[511]

Dissatisfied with Kessler's work at Fort Greene, Greenwald involved Mies, as he had with his Title I ventures in Detroit and Newark. Mies treated Battery Park and Battery Park North as one site, from Whitehall Street to Old Slip, and proposed three sleek towers, each on its own superblock. The repetitive forms and wide open spaces dramatically contrasted with the dense bouquet of spiky skyscrapers in the center of island. But the photomontage is no more than a preliminary proposal. Mies ceased working on the design when Greenwald died, killed in an airplane crash in the East River, on February 3, 1959. Five months later, on July 20, the *New York Times* reported on a revised scheme with two towers of 42 stories, a 10-story garage, and a restaurant that bridged Broad Street. It is unclear who was behind this scheme, but it died when Moses resigned from the Slum Clearance Committee in 1960.

Renewal ambitions for the area, however, remained alive. In 1962, the city announced plans to relocate the New York Stock Exchange on the site. The tortured history of that project ended in 1966, when the stock exchange abandoned the project. The Battery Park and Battery Park North sites were then privately developed; the city approved the formation of superblocks, much as Moses had originally proposed, but instead of apartment buildings, four giant office buildings (1, 2, and 4 New York Plaza and 55

Water Street), built in the late 1960s and early 1970s, commanded the waterfront like a bastioned wall.

Moses did not get far with the third downtown renewal project, the Brooklyn Bridge Title I. In August 1959, he selected Tishman Realty and Construction Company as tentative sponsor; a 19-acre area from the Brooklyn Bridge to Fulton Street, and from the East River to Gold Street, was under study. It was left to Moses's successors to shape the project in the 1960s. Because the Fulton Fish Market could not be relocated, redevelopment was restricted to 10 acres west of Water Street, where Moses's recipe of public and residential land uses was faithfully followed. The Brooklyn Bridge renewal included Southbridge Towers, a middle-income cooperative subsidized by New York State Mitchell-Lama funding and designed by Kelly & Gruzen; a campus for Pace College; and NYU Downtown Hospital.

The renewal of the East River waterfront, which happened after Moses, underscores the sustained support for his approach to urban renewal. — HB

GRAMERCY TITLE I

Unexecuted
Manhattan: East 24th to East 27th Street, Second to
    Third Avenue
8.3 acres
Plan published February 16, 1959

This late project illustrates the deterioration of
Moses's Title I program from a cause to a racket (to
borrow Scott Greer's description of the national program).[512] There was no debate that the area was
blighted. Although some apartment buildings and
shops were in good condition, "most of the area is a
grotesquerie of deteriorated tenements, industrial
lofts, rooming houses and shabby stores, including
many that are vacant," the New York Times reported.
A significant number of buildings could be saved
with extensive renovation, but even the Citizen's
Housing and Planning Council, an advocacy group
hostile to Moses, concluded that this approach was
not "economically feasible."[513] The Slum Clearance
Committee plan, developed by S. J. Kessler & Sons,
did not bother to save even the economically viable
apartment buildings; it called for complete clearance.
In those renewal plans where Moses exercised spot
preservation, he typically did so for public facilities,
but he had no qualms about taking private property
when it came to slum clearance.

The Gramercy project was small, only three
blocks, and barely altered the city grid; only one
street (25th) was to be closed. The plan consisted of
five 16-story apartment buildings with commercial
use on the corners and a new fire house. Its worst
aspect was the predominance of parking, with the
recouped open space—80 percent in the residential
areas—dedicated to parking lots. The dream of reinserting nature in the city through reduced land coverage had dissolved into paved patches for cars.

The neighborhood organized effectively to protest
the renewal project; the Gramercy Neighbors called
for spot clearance and challenged the relocation plan.
But the issue that got most traction in the press was
the closed process of sponsor selection. Moses chose
a syndicate represented by the local assemblyman
Joseph J. Weiser, an attorney in the real estate business, whom Tammany supported for election in 1954.
Weiser had a financial interest in the Gramercy project: his wife and other family members were investors
in the syndicate.[514] Critics charged that Moses
selected Weiser as "the result of a pay-off for his
involuntary withdrawal" from the Lincoln Square
project. According to Weiser's complaints two years
earlier, in 1957, Moses accepted his bid for the hous-

ing portion of Lincoln Square along with a $200,000
escrow payment, then without cause ousted Weiser
and designated William Zeckendorf as the new
sponsor.[515]

Although uncorroborated, the story is eminently
plausible. In 1957, involving Zeckendorf in the New
York Title I program was a top Moses priority. It was
strategic to sacrifice Weiser and to compensate him
with a project in his own assembly district, where he
would have to manage the political fight. Weiser initially told his Gramercy constituents that he would
contest the Title I project, but after obtaining the
sponsorship he reversed his position. The Gramercy
Neighbors understandably felt betrayed. In June
1959, facing defeat at the Board of Estimate, Moses
withdrew the Gramercy Title I project and redirected
the allocated federal funds to Bellevue South, a better
project to which Moses was more committed. In 1964,
Weiser was defeated in his bid for reelection by a
reform Democrat. — HB

SOUNDVIEW TITLE I

Unexecuted
Bronx: O'Brien Avenue, White Plains Road, Bronx
    River
92.3 acres
Plan published March 1959

The effort to develop an area in the Soundview section of the Bronx was among the last Title I projects
proposed by the Slum Clearance Committee. In
March 1959, Moses and the committee presented a
plan to transform an area of modest single-family
homes adjacent to the Bronx River into a higher-
density apartment complex. The plan, by the architectural firm of Kelly & Gruzen, called for fourteen
8-story buildings, with a total of 1,818 apartments.
The height of the buildings was limited by the site's
location within the flight paths of LaGuardia Airport.
The project also called for building new access roads
and an expansion and improvement of the existing
Soundview Park.

By June 1959, the Slum Clearance Committee was
calling the project Bronxview Village. It was structured as a middle-income cooperative, sponsored by
the Building Construction and Trades Council of
Greater New York and a consortium of building trades
unions. The apartments were to have down payments
of $650 per room and carrying charges of $24 per
room. The total cost of the development was to be
$30.6 million.[516] There were 276 residential struc-
tures, most of them small bungalows and private
homes built early in the twentieth century as summer
homes, that would have to be torn down to make way
for the new cooperative. The report of the Slum
Clearance Committee concluded that all the units
were substandard.[517]

The summer of 1959 would prove to be one of dis-
content for Moses, with allegations of financial impro-
priety raised in connection with several housing
projects and an unprecedented scrutiny and criticism
of his actions and managerial style by the city's press.
News of the Soundview Title I project generated
unwanted headlines for Moses. In June 1959, the
owner of record for most of the land to be acquired,
Helen G. Nugent, the private secretary to Monroe
Goldwater, was a revealed to be a "dummy owner."
Goldwater was a longtime power in Bronx politics,
the law partner of the late Bronx County Democratic
leader Edward J. Flynn and one of Robert Moses's
favorite lawyers.[518] The actual owners were eight
men, all clients of Goldwater's, including three labor
lawyers and two architects, who had acquired the
land in 1953 for $500,000 with the intention of

reselling it for development as cooperative housing. An appraisal prepared for the Slum Clearance Committee estimated the land acquisition costs at $1.3 million.[519]

As was his wont, Moses vigorously counterattacked and challenged the allegations. Writing to the *New York Times*, he denied that the owners of the property would stand to make the sort of profit that the *Times* alleged, and asserted that the $1.3 million figure covered a larger area than the land owned by Goldwater's clients and also included additional costs, such as the acquisition of housing structures. In stating claims of financial malfeasance, Moses wrote that the *Times* reporter had been "either very befuddled or deliberately malicious." He further defended the development at Soundview as a benefit to the local region and a source of new middle-income housing. Increasingly sensitive to criticism of his tenant removal policies, he claimed that the "prime reason" for Soundview was the rare opportunity it presented to build middle-income cooperative housing on sparsely settled land requiring only a modest number of residential relocations.[520] (He would make a similar claim that year in regard to the proposed development of Jamaica Race Track, which became Rochdale Village.)

This time, Moses's defense failed. The Board of Estimate did not approve the Soundview project. Although Mayor Robert Wagner talked of reviving it in the fall of 1959, this trial balloon stalled, and the project was stillborn.[521] In the next few years, considerable building of both low-income public housing and middle-income Mitchell-Lama private-rental housing took place in the Soundview neighborhood, but the area designated in the 1959 Title I proposal remains undeveloped.[522] The perception that Moses had abetted wrongdoing and insider dealing in his plans for the project contributed to his growing political problems. Within a year after the Soundview proposal, he announced his plans to resign from the Slum Clearance Committee and as City Construction Coordinator, which marked the beginning of the end of his long dominance of New York City's housing policy. — PE

CADMAN PLAZA TITLE I

Cadman Plaza North, completed 1967
Whitman Close, completed 1968
Cadman Towers, 1973
Brooklyn: Clark Street, Henry Street, and
    Cadman Plaza West
6.67 acres
Plan published April 20, 1959
Fig. C-160

Moses conceived this Title I project as a contribution to the development of the Brooklyn Civic Center. The Civic Center, proposed in 1941 and begun in 1944, had involved the clearance of 65 acres in downtown Brooklyn around Borough Hall, built in the 1840s to serve as the city hall for the then-independent city of Brooklyn. Moses and the Brooklyn borough president John Cashmore believed that a monumental civic center with government buildings would be an incentive for private business to invest in downtown Brooklyn. The master plan for the Civic Center was prepared by the landscape architect Gilmore Clarke, the engineer W. Earle Andrews, and the architect Lorimer Rich; Clarke and Andrews were both long-time associates of Moses. A new section of the Brooklyn-Queens Expressway was built to serve the neighborhood, elevated train lines were torn down, new approaches to the Brooklyn and Manhattan bridges were constructed, and Cadman Plaza itself was created. Laid out between 1950 and 1960, Cadman Plaza is an 8-acre grassy mall stretching from Borough Hall to the approach to the Brooklyn Bridge; it contains the Brooklyn War Memorial, erected in 1951, also a component of the Civic Center scheme. New municipal buildings constructed to complement Borough Hall included the headquarters of the New York City Board of Transportation (1951), the Welfare Center Building (1955), the Brooklyn Men's House of Detention (1956), a courthouse for the New York State Supreme Court (1958), a federal courthouse (1962), and a branch of the Brooklyn Public Library (1962).

Moses insisted that this program of government offices and public buildings required a contiguous housing component "to complete the Brooklyn Civic Center redevelopment." He planned the Cadman Plaza Title I housing project to serve as this missing residential element and to realize his vision of "comprehensive urban renewal" for downtown Brooklyn.[523]

The Slum Clearance Committee had considered a Title I project at Cadman Plaza as early as 1956, but a lack of federal funds kept it in the preliminary planning stage until 1959, when the slum clearance

brochure for the site was published. The plan called for the creation of a superblock by closing three streets between Fulton (now Cadman Plaza West) and Henry streets. This would produce a unified wedge-shaped site with a small appendage at its southeast end comprising half the block below Clark Street between Cadman Plaza West and Monroe Place. The brochure predicted that the site would cost $4,500,000 to acquire and that the total cost of the project would be $15,444,615. Redevelopment required clearance of 77 existing buildings, all but two of which were classified by the committee as substandard.

Sponsors of the project included Seon Pierre Bonan, his partner T. Roland Berner, and Bonan's Bonwit Construction Company. Bonan, an attorney, formed the Bonwit Construction Company in 1947 and began his career building suburban homes on Long Island and in Westchester and Stamford, Connecticut. In the late 1950s, he became involved in large-scale urban redevelopment and went on to sponsor Title I renewal projects in cities all over the country. His redevelopment of Stamford's downtown was based on a plan, devised by the architect and planner Victor Gruen, to close the city's Main Street and turn it into a pedestrian mall. Gruen also designed Charles River Park, Bonan's project in Boston's West End. Both the Stamford and Boston renewal projects, which covered 66 and 40 acres respectively, were massive compared to the 6.67-acre site of Cadman Plaza.

The published plan for Cadman Plaza was prepared by the architectural firm of Harrison & Abramovitz. At the northern end of the site was a single 20-story apartment building, raised on a plinth over underground parking for 536 cars; five small retail buildings were distributed around its southern end. The long slab of the building was oriented so that apartments faced either west, with views of the East River and lower Manhattan, or east, with views overlooking Cadman Plaza; Moses promised that the "elevation of the building provides light and air and unusual vistas for most apartments."[524] Land coverage would be greatly reduced—from 90 percent to 53 percent—leaving open space for landscaped plazas. The new building would provide 722 apartments, most of them two bedrooms, with rents of $53 per room per month.

The Cadman Plaza Title I project provoked controversy even before Moses and Bonan's plans were published: on April 10, 1959, the Brooklyn Heights Community Conservation and Improvement Council protested that small luxury rental apartments were not appropriate for a middle-class, family-oriented

C-160. Proposal for Cadman Plaza Title I apartments and retail stores, April 1959. Designed by Harrison & Abramovitz

neighborhood. Instead of rentals, they demanded affordable cooperative apartments large enough for families. They informed Moses that they had lined up a developer who would build fully tax-paying co-ops, assuring that the city would not lose money by having to provide tax exemptions for the cooperative development, which was the usual arrangement for Title I co-ops. On April 30, the *New York Times* reported that the Slum Clearance Committee would consider building co-ops instead of the planned rentals, but no decision was made before the committee was dissolved in March 1960. Mayor Robert Wagner replaced the SCC with the Housing and Redevelopment Board, which inherited the debate over luxury rentals versus middle-income cooperatives. After much uproar from community groups, now led by the Brooklyn Heights Association, the board finally announced in November 1961 that the entire Cadman Plaza site would be devoted to cooperative housing. Although this plan was approved by the City Planning Commission in 1962, the site was not cleared until 1964.

The delay was caused by a new round of protests inspired by the historic preservation movement: a pamphlet written by Martin S. James, a professor of art at Brooklyn College, argued that wholesale clearance of the site would destroy many historically or architecturally significant buildings and would intro-

duce "intrusive 'downtown' conceptions" into a peaceful residential neighborhood.[525] He proposed that the site be revitalized through spot clearance, demolishing only those buildings that were unsalvageable and constructing new buildings to match the low-rise scale of the neighborhood.

Ultimately, three high-rise buildings, all taller than the single 20-story building proposed by Moses, were built on the site, sacrificing the low density and minimal land coverage that Moses valued. Bonan remained as sponsor of two of the three high-rises: Cadman Plaza North, completed in 1967, and Whitman Close, completed in 1968, both cooperatives for middle-class families. Designed by Bonan's new architect Morris Lapidus & Associates, they are identical brick and concrete towers, raised up from the street on concrete pillars and set on plinths above parking garages. Whitman Close, named for the poet Walt Whitman, whose house was bulldozed to make room for it, is separated from Cadman Plaza North by the Whitman Close townhouses. The townhouses represent an attempt to mediate between the low-rise houses of the neighborhood and the high-rises, but the tall brick walls surrounding them block them from the street and ruin this desired outcome.

The third component of the site is Cadman Towers, built by the Long Island-based developer

Max Mishkin, with Mitchell-Lama aid from the city, and completed in 1973. Comprising one 32-story tower, one 13-story tower, and 36 townhouses, Cadman Towers is architecturally more successful than its neighbors. Designed by Glass & Glass and Conklin & Rossant, it won an award from the New York State Association of Architects for what Paul Goldberger called its "skillful interplay of towers and low-rise units."[526] Constructed of concrete and ribbed concrete blocks, the zigzagging facades of the towers are more dynamic than those of Whitman Close and Cadman Plaza North, which are both repetitively gridded with balconies.

The projects that were eventually built on the Title I site maintained some elements of Moses's 1959 proposal: a superblock was created by closing off the same streets that Moses had suggested, some retail shops were integrated into the plan along a pedestrian thoroughfare called Pineapple Walk, and a small landscaped plaza was retained in the middle of the site facing Cadman Plaza. The neighborhood benefited from the availability of cooperative apartments that were affordable for middle-class families. But if Harrison & Abramovitz's original plan for a single residential building had been carried out, the site would have offered more open park space to neighborhood residents. — KL

PARK ROW EXTENSION TITLE I

Chatham Towers, 1963–65
Manhattan: Park Row, Worth Street, Centre Street,
   and Columbus Park south of Mosco Street
3.30 acres
Plan published June 8, 1959
Figs. P-52, C-161–162

Park Row Extension was the twenty-sixth and final Title I plan prepared by the Committee on Slum Clearance. Although published in 1959, it had been conceived several years earlier as part of the Park Row Title I plan, where it appeared as a "possible future extension." At that time, however, the site had been reserved for another city project. As noted in the entry on Park Row, the redevelopment of Chinatown had long been contested. Earlier in the 1950s, New York State Housing Commissioner Herman T. Stichman had, at the insistence of Robert Moses, given up plans to redevelop the area as China Village. In 1954, however, Stichman submitted to the city a much more modest plan, still called China Village (later renamed Cathay Houses), for the site in question.

Stichman's plan called for two modernistic residential towers capped by pagoda roofs, to be built by the New York City Housing Authority, and two commercial buildings, also incorporating Chinese design elements. In accord with local housing needs, several floors were to be reserved for bachelors (as a result of the Chinese Exclusion Act, about four out of five residents of Chinatown were single men). Despite Moses's previous opposition, Stichman garnered the support of the NYCHA director Philip J. Cruise. In early 1955, the plans were approved by the City Planning Commission and the Board of Estimate. Just before relocation for Park Row got under way in early 1957, however, NYCHA announced, without a word of explanation, that the project was to move to a site well outside Chinatown, bounded by Pike, Madison, Rutgers, and Cherry streets.

Because Park Row Extension eliminated so many streets, the location is difficult to describe. North of Worth Street it included a small triangular block of about two-thirds of an acre between Baxter and Mulberry streets, which was retained by the city for an expansion to Columbus Park. South of Worth Street, the project was to comprise two small blocks bounded by Park Row, Worth, and Baxter streets, together with a portion of the block west of Baxter that contained the New York County Courthouse. These parcels, which were to form a small superblock of about two acres, were designated for housing, parking, and a small block of shops.

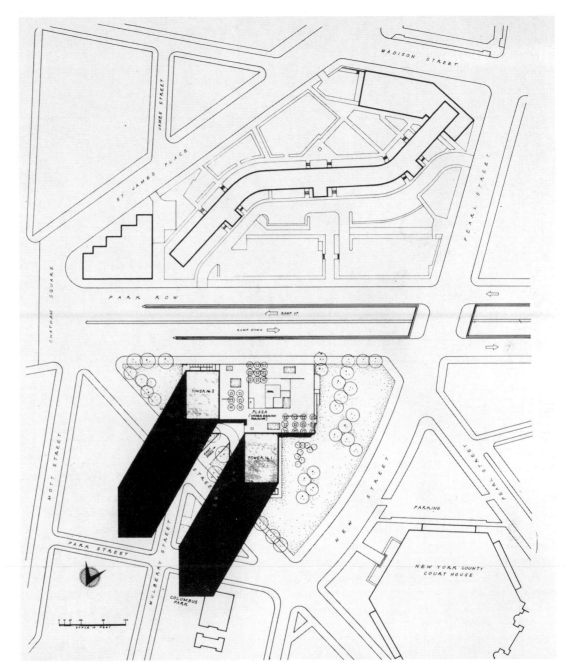

C-161. Site plan of Chatham Green and Chatham Towers, ca. 1965

Chatham Towers was conceived as a companion to Chatham Green. Again, the sponsor was the Municipal Credit Union and the New York State Credit Union League under the leadership of Shirley F. Boden and William Reid. Since the publication of the Park Row plan, Boden had established his own counterpart to Abraham Kazan's United Housing Foundation, called the Fund for Urban Improvement.

Like Kazan's body, the fund had a subsidiary designed to implement projects, named the Middle Income Housing Corporation. Around 1959, Boden and the Committee on Slum Clearance also formulated plans for a third Title I co-op for the Chatham Square area, on a site between the Bowery, East Broadway, and Market, Bayard, and Catherine streets. After the dissolution of the Committee on Slum Clearance in 1960,

C-162. View of Chatham Towers, ca. 1967

however, the new Housing and Redevelopment Board thought that the neighborhood had seen too much redevelopment too quickly and shelved the project until the late 1960s, when the site was slated for redevelopment as Confucius Plaza (1976).

Plans for Chatham Towers and the extension of Columbus Park called for razing all buildings on the two sites. Of these, about half were commercial and half residential—249 families and 564 people, for a population density of about 220 persons per acre. Among them were a group of model tenements erected in the 1860s, two of Chinatown's five Chinese-language theaters (most operating as cinemas by the early 1960s), and a well-known saloon called Diamond Dan O'Rourke's, which was said to have been so popular in the late nineteenth century that the Women's Christian Temperance Union allowed it to operate in peace.

As at Park Row, Boden and Reid commissioned Kelly & Gruzen to design the apartments and shops. Although the firm conceived the plans while working on Chatham Green, the design for Chatham Towers was entirely different. The architects believed the confluence of streets at the site (notwithstanding that most were to be eliminated) demanded strong vertical lines, and from the earliest discussions it was decided the suites should be arranged in slender towers rather

than as a slab. Unveiled in 1959, the plan, which was executed by Kelly & Gruzen designer George Shimamoto, called for two 25-story glass and steel buildings, each with 112 units of two and a half to six and a half rooms. These were laid out four and five to a floor, ensuring that all but studios, which were sandwiched between one-bedrooms opposite the elevator cores on certain floors, were at corners.

The site was also to accommodate three surface parking lots for residents with a total of 50 spaces, a commercial building at the corner of Park Row and Worth, and a small parking lot for the courthouse. The landscape architect M. Paul Friedberg was hired to design a plaza with formal gardens and a children's playground between the towers. The suites, which went on sale in the spring of 1960, were initially priced at $900 a room, with expected maintenance of $33 a room per month; due to construction delays, however, these prices rose to $1,100 and $40. The project was approved by the City Planning Commission and the Board of Estimate in spring 1961, and relocation and clearance were completed by fall of 1962. Construction, though, did not begin for nearly a year.

In response to ever-evolving ideas for the area around City Hall, the sponsors were forced to release the western portion of the site for a projected off-ramp

from the Brooklyn Bridge, reducing the parcel from roughly 2.1 to 1.6 acres. As a result, the commercial building was eliminated; Friedberg's plaza was repositioned behind the buildings; and parking was moved underground, directly beneath the plaza, but the number of parking spaces was more than doubled to 125. An unintended consequence of this change was that the land coverage at the project dropped to an unusually low 14 percent. The off-ramp was never built, and the site was used for parking until construction of a new federal courthouse in the early 1990s. Kelly & Gruzen, using the delay to rethink the design of the towers, substituted reinforced concrete, in the emergent Brutalist style, for the more traditional modernist glass and steel originally projected. Furthermore, several smaller suites were added, raising the total number of apartments to 240.

Although the tower plan was fundamentally more generic than Chatham Green's serpentine slab, several design innovations, including the use of exposed concrete, drew considerable attention from architects and critics. Half the corner units, for example, had private balconies—two adjacent floors with, two without. From the street, this pattern appeared, in the words of one critic, like a "serrated silhouette" that contrasted well with the structures' otherwise strong vertical lines.[527] Among other elements that fascinated the design community were double-glazed windows that had Venetian blinds built in between two panes of glass, and dry wall rather than wet plaster for interior partitions, which saved a large amount of labor.

Owners disliked the vinyl flooring in every room, found the closet space inadequate, and thought that the exposed concrete required paint. Perhaps to their surprise, the press described the project as "luxurious."[528] Juries agreed: after the project was completed in November 1965, it received awards from the New York chapter of the American Institute of Architects for use of materials and from the City Club of New York for making an "astounding exception" to the red-brick design of most low- and moderate-income housing in the city.[529] Friedberg's plaza too was commended. Isolated from city life by the towers and a tall wall along Park Row, it had lush plantings, abstract follies, and a reflecting pool that transformed what might otherwise have been dreary space atop the garage into a private oasis. Like Chatham Green, Chatham Towers abandoned the limited-equity format after its 25-year tax abatements expired in 1990. Today, 800-square-foot apartments with one bedroom and no terrace sell for upward of $600,000, with $800 in monthly maintenance. — MGL

FUTURE TITLE I PROJECTS

In 1959, Mayor Wagner appointed J. Anthony Panuch, a reorganization expert, to evaluate New York's urban renewal program. Moses took preemptive action and decided to dissolve his Slum Clearance Committee. It "has done what it was originally established to do," he informed Panuch on January 28, 1960, "namely enable New York City in the face of enormous difficulties and obstacles to take full advantage of Title One. It has finished the job for which it was formed. . . . The time has apparently come when the functions of the Committee should be turned over to some other agency in the regular City organization."[530] With one word, "apparently," Moses acknowledged that external forces had controlled his fate.

The issuance of Panuch's report on March 1, 1960, was coordinated with a surprisingly low-key public announcement of Moses's resignation. Per Panuch's recommendation, the Slum Clearance Committee and Urban Renewal Board, chaired by James Felt, were merged into the newly formed Housing and Redevelopment Board. The three-member group was chaired by J. Clarence Davies Jr., the commissioner of the Department of Real Estate, and included Walter S. Fried, former regional administrator of the Housing and Home Finance Agency with whom Moses had so often battled, and Robert C. Weaver, whom President Johnson would name in 1966 as the first secretary of the Department of Housing and Urban Development. The board's first job was to review Moses's pending renewal projects.

Despite mounting protests in the late 1950s, Moses did not temper or modify his planning efforts. The portfolio bequeathed to the successor board included seven projects already funded by federal survey and planning grants: Riverside-Amsterdam, Battery Park, Soundview, Cadman Plaza, and Park Row Extension, which had been unveiled in published brochures, as well as two not yet publicly announced, Cooper Square and Lindsay Park in Brooklyn. Moses also had a large store of projects in waiting. At the head of the list were Bellevue South, Mid-Harlem, Seward Park Extension, Delancey Street, Division Street, Brooklyn Bridge Southwest, Bronx Park South, Battery Park North, Atlantic Avenue, and Flatbush Avenue. Still others were described as future projects: Arverne-Rockaway, South Brooklyn, Houston Street, Chelsea, Jamaica, Bronx Park, Heyward-Bedford, Fulton Market, Atlantic Avenue, and Willowtown. Most were no more than pipe dreams; even so, the audacious quantity is staggering.

The Housing and Redevelopment Board brought about a bigger change in personnel and rhetoric than actual policy, at least in the early years. While calling for a breathing spell, it immediately endorsed nine Moses projects: Battery Park, Park Row Extension, Riverside-Amsterdam, Seward Park Extension, and Bellevue South, all in Manhattan; Cadman Plaza, Lindsay Park, and Brooklyn Bridge Southwest in Brooklyn; and Bronx Park South. Moses's plans were revised over the course of their development, nevertheless his site selection remained in force. In 1961, the board officially dropped four controversial projects: Chelsea, Cooper Square, Delancey, and Division Streets. An examination of the projects continued by the Housing and Redevelopment Board is beyond the scope of this catalog, but the continuity of policy and renewal problems underscores the intractable nature of the issues Moses battled.

One of the major criticisms of Moses, certainly among the planning community, was that he failed to coordinate his projects with a master zoning plan for the whole city. Comprehensive planning was the code word for this more integrated approach. Though no friend of Moses, Panuch soberly questioned the assumption that "a meaningful 'coordinated plan' for New York City, which does not even have a modern zoning ordinance, is feasible," and he formulated the fundamental challenge that bedeviled Moses as well as his renewal successors. "How does one evolve a 'consistent pattern' of urban redevelopment in a non-totalitarian society, in a city such as New York, where private builders and investors respond only to market opportunities?"[531] — HB

MITCHELL-LAMA HOUSING

The Limited-Profit Housing Companies Law of 1955, commonly known as the Mitchell-Lama Act after its two sponsors, Republican State Senator MacNeil Mitchell and Democratic Assemblyman Alfred Lama, was one of the most important of many efforts by city and state officials to encourage the building of middle-income housing in New York City in the 1950s. Its provisions called for the state or municipal government to lend up to 90 percent of construction costs to builders who agreed to restrict their profits to no more than 6 percent on their investment. Mitchell-Lama projects were entitled to a tax abatement up to 40 percent on their assessment for 30 years. In return, Mitchell-Lama projects had to impose income limits for residents (those exceeding the limits were required to pay a surcharge) and were subject to close regulation and supervision by state or municipal agencies.

In 1953, Robert Wagner's successful campaign for the mayoralty included a proposal for additional state aid for private middle-income housing, which resembled the eventual Mitchell-Lama Act.[532] According to Warren Moscow, a veteran political reporter who served as a special assistant on housing in the first Wagner administration, Robert Moses at first supported Wagner's initiative, then opposed it when Wagner let Moscow—instead of Moses—present it to Board of Estimate. Moses reacted to this apparent challenge to his authority over housing in the city by denouncing Moscow and introducing a similar proposal of his own. The Board of Estimate approved Wagner's proposal and sent it on to Albany.[533] Whatever the backroom negotiations between Wagner and Moses, the initiative remained identified with Wagner, with Moses relegated to a secondary and supportive role.[534] The legislature rejected Wagner's proposal in 1954 because of opposition from the administration of the outgoing Republican governor, Thomas E. Dewey. But with the support of a newly elected Democratic governor, Averell Harriman, the Mitchell-Lama legislation was approved the following year.

The Mitchell-Lama Act was a great success, and by 1958, 25 cooperatives developed under its auspices were either in planning or under construction.[535] Nonetheless, Moses did not make extensive use of the program in its early years. In 1956, he rejected Mitchell's suggestion to seek Mitchell-Lama status for Title I projects and insisted that the two funding alternatives be kept separate. He considered

Mitchell-Lama useful for "small projects or projects on vacant land."[536] Perhaps his reluctance was a result of his lack of control over the Mitchell-Lama program, or his concern that projects carrying both Mitchell-Lama tax abatements and Title I aid in land acquisition costs made too tempting a target for his critics.[537]

By late 1959, Moses seems to have had a change of heart. The possibility of using Mitchell-Lama funding for projects on vacant or nearly vacant sites became an attractive alternative to cumbersome Title I procedures, related controversies over tenant relocation, and difficulties in obtaining tax abatements for middle- income cooperative Title I projects from City Comptroller Lawrence Gerosa. "Where federal funds are concerned," Moses wrote in November 1959, "there has been tremendous red tape and delay in approvals and little courageous, effective, prompt and sympathetic cooperation in the Housing and Home Finance Agency in Washington and its regional office. . . . The obstruction tactics . . . are appalling, and the lack of reliable local administrative support results in some of it being matched in the Board of Estimate and the City Comptroller's Office."[538]

Mitchell-Lama funding was used for three limited-equity cooperatives that Moses developed in conjunction with the United Housing Foundation in the 1960s: Amalgamated Warbasse Houses in Brooklyn (completed in 1965), Rochdale Village in Queens (1965), and Co-op City in the Bronx (1972). These three enormous cooperatives, with more than 23,000 apartments among them, accounted for almost a quarter of all housing built under the state Mitchell-Lama program (269 developments with 105,000 units).[539] Because they were built on vacant or nearly vacant land, they did not involve Title I assistance in land acquisition. The Mitchell-Lama program was of great help in keeping the cooperatives' monthly carrying charges at the lower end of the middle-income spectrum.

The heyday of the Mitchell-Lama program did not long survive Moses's exit from the housing scene in 1960. By the early 1970s, it was seriously troubled as increased costs of construction and maintenance placed many of the projects under financial strain; the fiscal crisis of 1975 ended further Mitchell-Lama construction.[540] Since the 1980s, it has been possible for cooperatives organized under the Mitchell-Lama Act to leave the program and privatize their housing stock at market rates, and a number of cooperatives have opted for such a buy-out. Although this option has been widely discussed in Amalgamated Warbasse Houses, Rochdale Village, and Co-op City, as of 2006 they remain limited-equity cooperatives. — PE

CO-OP CITY

Bronx: Co-op City Boulevard, Peartree Mall, Bartow Avenue, Cross-Bronx Expressway, and Hutchinson River Parkway; Section 5 bounded by Goose Island, Hunter Avenue, Metro-North Railroad, and Hutchinson River Parkway
300 acres
1965–72

Co-op City is a limited-equity cooperative in the Baychester area of the Bronx. One of the largest housing developments ever built, Co-op City contains 15,373 apartments in 35 cruciform apartment buildings—24, 27, and 33 stories—along with seven clusters of townhouses containing 236 units. There are also three shopping malls, three elementary schools, two intermediate schools, and a high school. The buildings are connected by a gently undulating greensward with paths and playgrounds. The first families moved in in December 1968. The period of initial occupancy lasted until March 1972.[541]

Co-op City rose on the site of Freedomland, a short-lived attempt (1960–64) by William Zeckendorf to build a version of Disneyland in the marshland of the East Bronx. After the demise of Freedomland, Robert Moses and Governor Nelson Rockefeller played a critical role in developing the area for middle-income cooperative housing, with Moses steering the project to his frequent partner in large-scale cooperative housing, the United Housing Foundation (UHF). In 1965, the state provided a $261-million mortgage to the UHF. Since the land was without previous housing structures, Moses and the UHF avoided the contentious battles over tenant relocation that had bedeviled their development efforts in Manhattan, such as Lincoln Center and Cooper Square.

The immense scope of Co-Op City attracted much attention and attendant controversy. Almost from the time that the project was announced, there were complaints that Co-op City was becoming a giant magnet, drawing the remaining Jewish families out of the West Bronx and Grand Concourse area and hastening the decline of the Bronx. But Co-op City was only one of many factors involved in the exodus of white middle-class families from large sections of the West and South Bronx, which had been under way for at least a decade before plans for Co-op City were announced.

Another controversy concerned architectural style. The chief architect was Herman Jessor, who had been the main architect for most of the large UHF cooperatives. Co-op City, except for its size and scale, was very similar in interior and exterior details to his designs for other UHF cooperatives, including Penn

South, Warbasse Houses, and Rochdale Village. Nevertheless, of all Jessor's designs, Co-op City attracted by far the most critical brickbats. *Time* magazine said that "it is relentlessly ugly: its buildings are overbearing bullies of concrete and brick," its layout "dreary" and lacking any sense of community.[542] The doyenne of New York City architectural critics, Ada Louise Huxtable, wrote in the *New York Times* in 1968 that its monumental scale was balanced by its minimal attention to environmental and social planning.[543]

Co-op City had its defenders as well. Denise Scott Brown and Robert Venturi argued that the criticisms were hyperbolic, and Co-op City was simply a conventional housing project on a mammoth scale, well suited to its purpose.[544] Not surprisingly, this was also the point of view of Jessor and the UHF, who were proud of the plainness of the exteriors of their cooperatives, arguing that their focus was on interior apartment space and that architectural embellishment would simply have added to the cost without enhancing livability. Whatever the merits of the contending sides, most residents at Co-op City seemed at first to be very pleased with their attractive and inexpensive housing. Huxtable, returning to Co-op City for a second look in 1971, conceded that it contained more than 15,000 "well-planned apartments . . . no mean achievement" and provided affordable housing for many New Yorkers.[545]

Nonetheless, by the mid-1970s, there was considerable tension at Co-op City. When the project was originally announced, the average per-room carrying charge was to be $23 per month.[546] This proved impossible to sustain, because of higher costs from unanticipated difficulties in building on marshy ground only a few feet above sea level, the general rate of inflation, and the skyrocketing price of heating oil. The carrying charges underwent steep increases, from $27 per room in 1968 to $42 per room in 1974. The announcement of another sharp rise in 1975 precipitated a contentious rent strike that lasted thirteen months.[547] The rent strikers were largely victorious, but the UHF, stung by the strike and faced with unfavorable conditions for building affordable middle-income housing, withdrew from the development of new cop-ops. Co-op City was UHF's final housing cooperative, and one of Robert Moses's last efforts to build housing in New York City. In the early twenty-first century, it remains a successful middle-income development. Its residents, originally 80 percent white, are now approximately 65 percent minority. Nothing of remotely comparable size, scale, or ambition has been attempted in New York City in the 35 years since Co-op City opened. — PE

ROCHDALE VILLAGE

Queens: New York (now Guy Brewer) Boulevard,
   Baisley Boulevard, Bedell Street, and 137th
   Avenue
170 acres
1963

Rochdale Village, a limited-equity, middle-income housing cooperative, is located in South Jamaica on the site of the former Jamaica Race Track. When it opened in December 1963, it was the largest housing cooperative in the world, with 5,800 apartments. The complex was developed by the United Housing Foundation (UHF) and was designed by its chief architect, Herman Jessor. The cooperative, occupying a single superblock with no through streets, consists of twenty cruciform 14-story buildings, each divided into three sections with separate elevator systems. The buildings are clustered into five sections, distributed along a cul-de-sac permitting external vehicular access and connected by pedestrian paths on a greensward. The cooperative also contains two shopping malls, one designed by the well-known architect Victor Gruen; two elementary schools and an intermediate school; and a community center with an auditorium seating more than 1,500. Having its own power plant, Rochdale was one of the first middle-income cooperatives to offer central air-conditioning. Jessor's design, typical of his many UHF projects including Co-op City, offered plain red-brick exteriors balanced by spacious and well-designed apartments that proved attractive to families on the lower end of the middle-income spectrum.

Plans to close Jamaica Race Track had been rumored as early as 1953. In his capacity as the city construction coordinator and slum clearance commissioner, in 1955 Robert Moses suggested that the area could be used for a new stadium for the Brooklyn Dodgers or for a mix of lower- and middle-income housing.[548] By 1956, he announced his preference for a middle-income cooperative, to be built by the UHF.[549] After several years of difficult negotiations, the UHF—always shepherded by Moses—signed an agreement in January 1960 with New York State, in which the state promised to lend the UHF the $86 million in outside funds needed for the development of the cooperative.[550] As Abraham Kazan, the president of the UHF stated, "Rochdale Village owes its existence to Robert Moses."[551]

Rochdale Village is located in the third largest African-American neighborhood in New York City. It was conceived as a racially mixed project and was at its opening the largest experiment in integrated housing in New York City—and very likely the largest such experiment in the United States. At that time, its racial breakdown was approximately 80 percent white, and 20 percent African-American. The white families were overwhelmingly Jewish. Its schools, shared with the surrounding community, were fully integrated.

Moses's support of a huge experiment in integrated housing might seem at first paradoxical. In the 1930s and 1940s, he had been a prominent opponent of civil rights and open-housing legislation, arguing that requiring racially nondiscriminatory access would frighten away scarce private funding for large-scale urban development. In the late 1950s, he continued to be very skeptical of open-housing legislation, doubting its wisdom and efficacy.[552] While adamant in his opposition to an aggressive enforcement of laws against private homeowners and developers, Moses recognized that nondiscrimination was a requirement for projects involving state funding and powers of eminent domain.[553] He had often worked with private developers committed to an open-housing policy, including the UHF.[554] In early 1959, Moses wrote to Elmer Carter, the chairman of the State Commission against Discrimination, that while "handsome gestures are no good" in the field of integrated housing, the development of the Jamaica Race Track was the sort of civil rights effort the state should be backing.[555]

There was considerable opposition to the development of the Jamaica site as integrated middle-income housing. The large labor unions, the usual backers of UHF cooperatives, were leery of the project. Abraham Kazan related in his memoirs that prominent labor leaders were "very cool" about it because of its location in a black neighborhood and worried about the possibilities of large numbers of unsold apartments.[556] Moses tried, unsuccessfully, to interest other private sources in financing the cooperative. Finally concluding that only the state government had the resources and the ability to take the necessary risk in developing the racetrack for housing, he convinced Governor Nelson Rockefeller to assume the burden.

For Moses, the main attractions of the Jamaica project were the size of the site, the absence of tenants to relocate, and the opportunity to build integrated housing—probably in that order.[557] He planned bus excursions to Rochdale from the 1964 World's Fair in Flushing Meadows to show it off to national and international visitors. Moses ranked it as one of his greatest achievements, comparable to Jones Beach and Lincoln Center, and until the end of his career praised it as a model for integrated housing and for the revitalization of older neighborhoods.[558]

In its early years, Rochdale Village was indeed a model of integrated housing. As was widely noted at the time, whites and blacks moved to Rochdale, not because of a commitment to civil rights or cooperative living but because "the apartments represented such an unusual bargain that the pressing need for economical housing overcame fear and uneasiness."[559] Rochdale's social life was vibrant and integrated, with 150 organizations and community groups formed in its early years. Although vigorous, its internal politics were not divided along racial lines; in fact, the first president of the House Congress was African-American. Children from Rochdale integrated the previously all-black schools in the surrounding South Jamaica community. And in 1966, the local newspaper proclaimed a widely shared sentiment of the time that "the advocates of Open Housing may look to Rochdale and say to the nation that integrated housing exists and works!"[560]

Alas, amid the pressures of the late 1960s, Rochdale did not stay integrated. The divisive school strike of 1968, which pitted Jews against blacks in bitter acrimony, was the turning point. Local schools deteriorated, crime became an increasing problem, and white families started moving out in large numbers. Rochdale Village today remains a successful middle-class cooperative, with a proud 40-year history; but with a population 98 percent black, it is no longer integrated.

In the four decades since Rochdale opened, large-scale integrated housing in New York City remains for a number of reasons a path largely not taken. Even though its fame has been eclipsed by better-known projects, Moses was right to see Rochdale Village as one of his greatest achievements. — PE

MISCELLANEOUS PROJECTS

BATTERY PARKING GARAGE

Manhattan: at the Brooklyn-Battery Tunnel, between
    Washington and Greenwich streets
Opened 1950

The rise of automobility in the 1920s and 1930s
presented American cities with problems of traffic
flow and automobile storage. In Moses's analysis,
storage was a private-sector matter. From the start of
his building career in New York City, he tackled the
traffic problem by building new roads and argued
that the city should stay away from building garages,
which was better left to the private sector. Yet rising
public and commercial concern over the parking
problem drew political leaders into the issue, and
in 1937 Mayor La Guardia raised the possibility of
building municipal lots, an approach Moses opposed.
He believed the city's role should be limited to the
installation of parking meters on the street (the city
installed the first meters on an experimental basis in
1951) and insisted that the city should not get into
the garage business. In 1944, Mayor La Guardia
appointed Moses the chair of a committee to study the
parking problem. While affirming Moses's view of
garages as a private-sector business, the report nevertheless proposed municipal construction of three
"auto and bus terminals," each at the Manhattan
outlet of a tunnel crossing. As outlined in this plan,

the Port of New York Authority built a bus terminal
near the Lincoln Tunnel with rooftop parking for
private vehicles, and the Triborough Bridge and
Tunnel Authority built an airline bus terminal, also
with some parking capacity, near the Queens Midtown
Tunnel. The bus component of the third terminal was
dropped by January 1945 when preliminary plans for
a six-story parking garage north of the Brooklyn-
Battery Tunnel were filed.

This structure was inaccurately touted as the city's
first public-owned garage. The city provided the land,
and the Triborough Bridge and Tunnel Authority did
the rest: secured the financing, incurred the debt,
constructed the structure while completing the
adjacent tunnel, and collected the parking revenues.
The Brooklyn-Battery garage was a TBTA facility.
Construction started in August 1948, and the
1,050-car garage, with seven floors of self-parking,
opened in June 1950; an addition made in 1968
increased capacity to 2,117 cars. The revenue
stream impressed Moses, who became more enth
usiastic about garage construction, but other public
officials blocked the TBTA from playing any further
role in sponsoring municipal garages. — HB

EAST SIDE AIRLINES TERMINAL

Manhattan, First Avenue between 37th and 38th
    streets
1953; demolished 1986
Fig. C-163

Until 1953, shuttle buses traveling between midtown
Manhattan and the airports in Newark and Queens
departed from a terminal at 80 East 42nd Street,
opposite Grand Central Terminal. But with a boom in
air travel, the old facility could no longer accommodate the growing crowds.[561] Furthermore, the 550
airport buses that passed through midtown each day
produced massive congestion in the Grand Central
neighborhood. In 1951, Robert Moses proposed a new
bus terminal to be located on First Avenue between
37th and 38th streets and built under the auspices of
his Triborough Bridge and Tunnel Authority. While
he saw reduced street traffic as a benefit of a new bus
terminal, he also considered the benefit to TBTA
coffers of rerouting buses through the authority's
Queens Midtown Tunnel, which charged a toll,
instead of the toll-free Queensborough Bridge.

The three-story, $7.5-million building, designed
by the architect John B. Peterkin, included a rooftop
parking lot for 275 cars and a basement garage for
100 buses, which were operated by the Carey
Transportation Company.[562] The TBTA leased the

C-163. East Side Airlines Terminal, 1967. Photograph by O. Winston Link. Collection MTA Bridges and Tunnels Archive

land and building to the East Side Airlines Terminal Corporation, established by ten domestic carriers. Under the conditions of a 20-year lease, the corporation was required to repay the $5.5 million invested by the authority, plus interest.[563]

Passengers first stepped through the doors of the East Side Airlines Terminal on December 1, 1953, following the settlement of a strike by the International Brotherhood of Teamsters, which had delayed the opening for three months. Ten international carriers shared space in the new building with ten domestic airlines. The new depot served all New York metropolitan airports until 1955, when a smaller bus terminal for Newark passengers was completed on the West Side.[564] Designed to handle 6,500 travelers per day, the East Side Airlines Terminal often accommodated up to 10,000 on busy Fridays.[565]

Its lobby, three times the size of that in the previous building, included a gift shop, restaurant, bar, and cocktail lounge. The terminal was an immediate success, pleasing passengers and benefiting the TBTA, which boasted record earnings in 1954.[566]

But the building had one major flaw: its location. Although being near the Queens Midtown Tunnel entrance shaved off five minutes from each bus trip, the terminal lacked convenient access to the subway system. With taxi fares from LaGuardia to midtown not significantly higher than the bus fares, many passengers chose cabs. Still, the Carey Bus Company estimated that it served 30 percent of the passengers from LaGuardia and 50 percent of the passengers from Idlewild (now John F. Kennedy International Airport).

By the time its lease expired in October 1973, the East Side Airlines Corporation was routinely seeing deficits of $1 million per year. With a 20 percent decrease in traffic from 1967 to 1972, the corporation wanted to close the facility.[567] Fifteen city council members assailed the plan, urging the city to pay the deficits and keep the building open.[568] The Triborough Bridge and Tunnel Authority soon agreed to assume responsibility for the terminal's finances, but inadequate revenues led to the building's closure in 1984. A real estate partnership headed by Bernard Spitzer and Peter Malkin purchased the East Side Airlines Terminal at an MTA auction in 1985 for $90.6 million and constructed a 54-story office and condominium tower on the site.[569] — JK

C-164. Panorama of the City of New York, detail showing Brooklyn, Manhattan, and Williamsburg bridges, 1964.
Photograph by Eileen Costa, 2004

PANORAMA OF THE CITY OF NEW YORK

Wood, plastic, brass, and paper, mounted on ure-
   thane foam, Formica, and wood, 154.5 ft. x 137 ft.
Collection the Queens Museum of Art
Completed 1964; periodically updated through 1992
Fig. C-164

One of the most prominent exhibits at the 1964–65
New York World's Fair was the *Panorama of the City
of New York*, a comprehensive scale model of the
metropolis. On permanent display in the Queens

Museum of Art since 1972, it offers visitors an aerial
view over the vast expanse of the city. The *Panorama*
is a gigantic "miniature": with more than 895,000
individual structures in the scale of 1:1,200 (1 inch
equals 100 feet), it occupies 9,335 square feet. On it,
the Empire State Building is only 15 inches tall. To
this day, the *Panorama* remains the largest architectural model of an urban environment in the world.

Commissioned for the fair by Robert Moses, the
Panorama was once experienced as an eight-minute
sky-ride, during which visitors slowly circled its
periphery in railcars and listened to Lowell Thomas's

recorded narration. In the early 1990s, Rafael Viñoly,
a New York City–based architect, replaced the ride
with a sky-walk around the periphery. The original
dawn-to-dusk lighting cycle is still in place,
enhancing the experience of the miniature.

The *Panorama* took three years to build. Moses
entrusted its construction to his chief model maker,
Raymond Lester (1911–1983). At his architectural
firm, Lester Associates, in West Nyack, New York,
two hundred workers diligently transformed geological and survey maps and aerial photographs into the
273 large rectangular blocks that comprised the epic

Panorama. Yet, the model was more than an accurate representation of the metropolis; it was a monument to Moses's achievements as a city builder for over three decades. The bridges were made of brass, unlike the wood and plaster of the rest of the structures, and were slightly larger in scale, to emphasize his role in connecting the boroughs.

Moses's public works often disrupted the urban fabric and in the process of development displaced communities. The *Panorama*, which was created at the end of his career, did not show the painful process of urban transformation. Rather, New York appears as an idealized cityscape: clean, clear-cut, connected—perhaps his belated master plan for the city. Moses insisted that the model be a "living" representation of the city, by which he meant not unchanging replicas of people and their movements (in fact, its only moving object is a frequently malfunctioning small metal plane landing at and taking off from LaGuardia Airport), but an architecturally up-to-date model. The *Panorama*, last revised in 1992, has not kept up with the rapidly changing city.

The model may be a static, old-fashioned medium of envisioning space, but it is unsurpassed for showing an urban environment as a three-dimensional totality. In calling the model a panorama, Moses suggested a curious reversal in viewing experience. Visitors to panoramas, those 360-degree paintings of cityscapes, battles, and religious scenes popular in Europe and North America in the eighteenth and nineteenth centuries, were surrounded by the picture as they stood on an elevated platform in its center and turned around to see the entire image. In contrast, visitors to the New York City *Panorama* surround the model and must circle around it to see its entirety.

Walking, an activity extending over time, transforms the static *Panorama* into a dynamic experience: as visitors stride like giants above and around the model, they can spot their own houses, famous landmarks, and little-known sites among the miniature structures; direct laser pointers at them; and share personal stories about them. Soon, the still city is animated by memories as visitors connect two cities: the visible one of the museum model and the invisible one inhabited by recollections. Thus, despite its many paradoxes—panoramic yet not a panorama, living yet unpopulated, accurate yet ideological, aerial yet pedestrian, miniature yet gigantic—the *Panorama of the City of New York* serves as a unique memory palace and an ideal site for exploring how cities are represented, experienced, and remembered. —BM

UNITED NATIONS HEADQUARTERS

Manhattan: East 42nd to East 48th Street, Second Avenue to the East River (headquarters and surrounding improvements)
1946–53
Fig. C-165

Soon after its founding in 1945, the United Nations established a Headquarters Committee to select a location for its permanent home. Many American cities campaigned to become the base for the new international organization: Philadelphia, San Francisco, and Boston would prove to be New York City's toughest competition. From the helm of the various city agencies under his control, Robert Moses spearheaded New York's successful bid to be the world capital and, after a headquarters site was chosen, coordinated the city's effort to make room for the UN in Manhattan's crowded grid.

New York got a leg up in the competition in early 1946, when the organization agreed to move temporarily to the city while awaiting a permanent home. After initial meetings at Hunter College, the Secretariat met at the Sperry Plant, a former war factory in Lake Success on Long Island, and the General Assembly convened in the New York City Building in Flushing Meadow Park. In his capacity as parks commissioner, Moses was charged by the Board of Estimate with converting the City Building, built for the 1939 World's Fair, into a functional meeting and office space. He hired Aymar Embury II, the building's original architect, and Skidmore, Owings & Merrill to plan the transformation. The roller-skating rink was hidden beneath carpeting and turned into an auditorium (because Moses insisted on later reopening the rink, its floor had to be disguised, not removed); a new cafeteria building was constructed, and offices were carved out of former recreation space. Flags of many nations lined the circular driveway, heralding the new function of the building. The General Assembly first gathered in Queens in October 1946 and continued to meet there until 1950. While occupying this temporary headquarters, the UN took some of its most important actions, including creating the state of Israel.

Moses, always on the lookout for opportunities to improve parks, used the provisional home of the UN in Flushing Meadow as a chance to restore the park that he had reclaimed from marshland for the 1939 World's Fair. Although he had expected the park to extend beyond the life of the fair, the war had halted construction. In the $2.2-million budget for the conversion of the City Building was $900,000 for sur-

rounding park improvements. Under the pretext of creating an appealing backdrop for the UN, Moses restored 250 acres of Flushing Meadow Park: repaving roads and walkways, replacing overgrown lawns, and building new parking lots and playgrounds. He hoped that the refurbished park would serve as the permanent site for the UN headquarters.

Mayor William O'Dwyer named Moses chairman of the Committee on Plan and Scope, charged with convincing the UN to remain in New York. Moses invited powerful New Yorkers like Nelson Rockefeller and Arthur Hayes Sulzberger to serve on the committee, and he appointed a board of design that included his preferred architect, landscape architect, and engineer—Aymar Embury II, Gilmore Clarke, and Earl Andrews—as well as Wallace Harrison and Louis Skidmore. In October 1946, the city formally invited the UN to make Flushing Meadow its permanent home, offering to donate 350 acres of the park, estimated to be worth $7 million, to the world organization. In an article published in the *New York Times* on October 20, Moses made "the case for New York, and Flushing Meadows, as the capital of the world." He explained that Manhattan was not a viable option because of "congestion, atmosphere and cost," and he dismissed the possibility of an "international compound" in a suburban area like Westchester because delegates would be isolated and unhappy, "fenced off from the surrounding world" in a Brasilia-like city devoted solely to governing.[570] Flushing Meadow Park was touted as an ideal site, both in Moses's editorial and in the promotional brochure presented to Secretary General Trygve Lie: it would not require clearance of any residents or businesses; it was easily accessible by car and by public transportation and was convenient to New York's two airports, LaGuardia and Idlewild; and the park was large enough to allow for future expansion of the headquarters.

The park was also close to housing. As City Construction Coordinator, Moses arranged for the development of Parkway Village, a complex of two-story garden apartments on Grand Central Parkway in Jamaica. The project, funded by the Savings Banks Trust Company, was set aside exclusively to house UN employees. Moses also convinced the Metropolitan Life Insurance Company to reserve 600 apartments in Peter Cooper Village in Manhattan and New York Life to make a similar commitment with half the apartments in its new Fresh Meadows complex in Queens. This same housing would ultimately serve UN personnel when the headquarters moved to Manhattan in 1952.

The design proposed in 1946 for the Flushing Meadow Park headquarters was for a fanciful, monumental complex consisting of four main buildings. Visitors would enter by crossing a bridge over a moat and passing through a colonnade of massive piers. The central feature of the headquarters was a domed General Assembly building fronting on a landscaped formal terrace. All other UN offices were to be housed in three long, horizontal two-story buildings, situated so that they could easily be extended as more nations joined the nascent world organization.

Shortly before the December 31 deadline for selecting a site, Tyrgve Lie informed Moses and O'Dwyer that the Headquarters Committee would not approve the Flushing proposal. The delegates preferred either a suburban location or, if they were going to be in New York City, a site in Manhattan. Moses blamed the "long-range European planners, notably M. LeCorbusier" for this development. Corbusier disapproved of any New York City location because he saw the city as "terrifying" and "menacing," expressing particular disdain for Queens: "Flushing Meadow is not the site for the headquarters of the United Nations because Flushing Meadow is inescapably a suburb of New York, a dependency of New York."[571] It looked like New York would lose the UN to Philadelphia, which had become the frontrunner.

In a telephone conversation on December 6, 1946, Lie, Moses, and O'Dwyer discussed the possibility of the Turtle Bay neighborhood in Manhattan for the headquarters. In his autobiography, Lie credited Moses with the idea: "I believe Robert Moses, Park Commissioner and Coordinator of Planning, was the first to mention it as a prospect; the solution appealed to him as a practical idealist and city planner."[572] The developer William Zeckendorf owned the Turtle Bay site. He had been buying up land along the East River occupied by slaughterhouses and commissioned Wallace Harrison to design a mixed-use complex of apartments, offices, and a hotel, called X City. In his own autobiography, Zeckendorf remembered having come up with the idea to sell his X City land to the UN himself. Moses referred to Lie's recollection in *Public Works: A Dangerous Trade* but failed to address Zeckendorf's contention. Whoever initiated the process, Zeckendorf offered the land to the UN, and John D. Rockefeller Jr. donated $8.5 million to purchase the site. The deal was concluded on December 14, 1946, when the General Assembly voted to approve the construction of the permanent headquarters of the UN in Manhattan between 42nd and 48th streets, First Avenue and the East River. In a desper-

C-165. Site of the United Nations, view east from the 12th floor of Tudor City, April 1948. Rendering by Hugh Ferriss

ate rush to keep the UN in New York, 17 acres of prime Manhattan real estate had been secured in less than two weeks.

Moses put his weight behind the Manhattan location in spite of his persistent belief that Flushing was preferable to the small East River site. He compromised so that New York would not lose the opportunity to serve as the world capital. Exercising his ability to turn defeat into victory, he led the city's negotiations with the UN on improvements to accommodate increased traffic and to create an attractive approach for visitors from all over the world.

In January 1947, Mayor O'Dwyer assigned Moses to be the liaison between the city and the UN and to coordinate the city's contributions to the construction of the new headquarters. These included the improvement of surrounding streets, closing the numbered streets on the site between First Avenue and the FDR Drive, giving the organization an aerial easement so that a platform could be built over the drive, granting tax exemption, and passing zoning legislation to restrict building type and height and the erection of new billboards in the area surrounding the headquarters. Billboards were forbidden even in the section of

Queens across the river from the UN, and no new breweries, crematories, or dance halls were permitted to open in Turtle Bay. The city also condemned the block east of First Avenue between 47th and 48th streets and closed a playground between 42nd and 43rd streets, turning over the land to the UN. The city spent a total of $25,806,300 on improving the neighborhood; Moses maintained that the clearance of the slaughterhouse district and the increased value of property surrounding the headquarters justified this investment.

Moses altered three streets to provide access to the UN: First Avenue between 41st and 48th streets, 42nd Street and 47th Street, both between First and Second avenues. Forty-seventh Street was redesigned with the intention that it would serve as the main approach to the UN. When this decision was made, the team of architects planning the headquarters under Wallace Harrison's supervision was envisioning the Secretariat at the north end of the site. Although the Secretariat was moved to the south end, 47th Street was nevertheless developed as an approach, but it now culminated in blank space. Widened to 160 feet, the street was divided into two lanes separated by a landscaped mall.

The southern strip was turned into a park, named Dag Hammarskjöld Plaza in 1961. Moses could not have predicted that the plaza, which he expected would offer "passive recreation to local residents and employees," would become a popular gathering place for protesters.[573]

Moses faced heavy criticism for what many saw as his failure to provide an appropriately grand approach to the United Nations. The New York chapter of the American Institute of Architects encouraged the city to produce a master plan for the UN neighborhood. Lewis Mumford expressed his disapproval: "To think that a strip of formal park will create the necessary atmosphere is not to think at all."[574] The most aggressive critic was Zeckendorf, who in the summer of 1947 submitted to the Board of Estimate an alternative plan for the development of the area. He wanted the city to condemn a huge swath of city property between First and Third avenues from 46th to 49th Street and sell it to him. He would create a superblock and build the United Nations Concourse, comprising a mall surrounded by eight 16-story buildings. The mall would culminate in a plaza adjacent to the UN containing a fountain and "a vastly tall openwork steel pylon, guyed in place by cables."[575] In a letter to the New York Times, Zeckendorf advocated monumentality: "Surely the City of New York could not think in less grandiose terms than those for the permanent approach to the United Nations."[576] At a rowdy hearing, Zeckendorf attacked Moses, who was absent; Mayor O'Dwyer defended his prized commissioner. The Board of Estimate rejected Zeckendorf's plan and approved Moses's proposal. Moses maintained that his widened, landscaped streets and parks would serve as "a dignified setting" and provide for the "quiet, orderly enjoyment of the premises of delegates and visitors alike."[577] His solution did not allow for an impressive approach to the UN buildings, but neither did it require the displacement of hundreds of businesses and residences that Zeckendorf's would have. Moses and Zeckendorf later reconciled and, appreciating each other's vast talents, collaborated on many urban renewal projects.

The other streets altered to accommodate the UN followed the precedent of 47th Street: changes were practical and modest, eschewing monumentality by adhering to the street grid. Avoiding traffic congestion and providing incidental parks were the primary goals of Moses's street improvements. The First Avenue tunnel, designed by the engineering firm of Andrews & Clark, diverted through traffic so that the surface level of First Avenue served only local and UN traffic.

The six-lane tunnel, completed in 1953, also diminished noise and thus made the UN site more peaceful. The widened section of First Avenue under which the tunnel travels was renamed, with Moses's encouragement, United Nations Plaza. A small park, also designed by Andrews & Clark, was inserted on the west side of First Avenue; it is now called Ralph Bunche Park. A new ramp was built linking 42nd Street to the FDR Drive. The bridge connecting Tudor City across 42nd Street was replaced by a masonry span with a wider underpass at street level. Forty-second Street was also widened by removing ramps that had carried traffic up to Tudor City and replacing them with steep, ornamental staircases. Two new playgrounds were built in Tudor City, on either side of 42nd Street.

A dispute arose over Moses's insistence that a playground be built as part of the plaza at the north end of the UN site. He first proposed the playground in December 1949 and was immediately turned down by Lie, who said that if Moses "sees a little bit of land . . . he wants it at once for playgrounds and swimming pools. . . . I do not think there will be any swimming pool or playground on the site of the United Nations."[578] In April 1951, Lie, after persistent badgering from Moses, agreed to a playground in the northeast corner of the plaza. Three prominent women who lived in the neighborhood commissioned the sculptor Isamu Noguchi and the architect Julian Whittlesey to design a sculptural playground; they offered to contribute $75,000 to the construction of this model playground, meant to promote freedom and creativity in the play of its young users. Moses, uninterested in inventive design, favored a conventional playground based on parks department prototypes designed by Gilmore Clarke, with swings, slides, and seesaws enclosed by a fence.[579] Siding with Moses, the UN built the traditional playground. This incident serves as an example of Moses's influence beyond the bounds of his official jurisdiction: although the playground was built by the UN on UN land, the powerful parks commissioner dictated the design of playgrounds even when they were not parks department property. The Noguchi and Whittlesey model was later put on display at the Museum of Modern Art, where it was described as "the most creative and imaginative play area yet devised."[580]

Moses's final UN-related quarrel was over parking. He insisted that, in exchange for the city's improvements to surrounding streets, the UN build an underground parking garage to hold 1,500 cars, in order to prevent the widened streets from becoming clogged. In 1953, Dag Hammarskjöld, Lie's successor as

Secretary General, claimed 250 parking spots for use as storage. Furious, Moses accused the UN of being a poor neighbor by taking up street parking. He sent six photographs of congested streets in the area to both Hammarskjöld and the New York Times. This trick brought the UN enough bad publicity to convince Hammarskjöld to return half the appropriated parking spaces to their intended use.

In spite of these various conflicts and his own misgivings about the East River site, Moses played an essential role in bringing the United Nations to New York. He believed that the city "must be rebuilt, not abandoned," and that attractions like the UN headquarters would contribute to its lasting vitality.[581] His accomplishment did not go unrecognized: "Almost everywhere, as rubble makes way for a startling renaissance, Moses can be found riding the bulldozer. Without him we might have lost the United Nations headquarters, which caps the new East River skyline and adds to our pre-eminence as a world capital." — KL

NOTES

See Selected Bibliography for full citations of abbreviated references.

1. "$1,000,000 City Pool Opens Wednesday," *New York Times*, June 21, 1936; "Parks Kept Open at Night by Mayor," *New York Times*, July 10, 1936.
2. "Pattern for Parks," 505.
3. New York City Landmarks Preservation Commission, "Astoria Park Pool and Play Center," Designation Report, 2006, 6–7, 9; "Pattern for Parks," 499–501; Rodgers, *Robert Moses*, 84.
4. My discussion of procedure and pool design and technology is based on drawings and other materials in the archives of the Department of Parks and Recreation. Also see Latham, "Swimming Pool Construction," 33–34; "Pattern for Parks," 505–6.
5. "Pattern for Parks," 507.
6. For the term *scum gutter*, see Latham, "Swimming Pool Construction," 34; "Pattern for Parks," 506.
7. For a detailed discussion of the locker rooms at McCarren Pool, see Marcus, "Last One In," 52–57.
8. Latham, "Swimming Pool Construction," 33.
9. "23 Bathing Pools Planned by Moses," *New York Times*, July 23, 1934.
10. Filter house operators, who were uniformed civil service parks department employees, received special training for handling dangerous chemicals, such as chlorine gas and ammonia. See oral interview of Phyllis Robinson by John Mattera, April 11, 2006, New York City Department of Parks and Recreation Archives.
11. I am grateful to Kate Nichols for information about pool water temperature.
12. "Pattern for Parks," 505.
13. For the typical design, see Kocher and Davison, "Swimming Pools," 71–73. For the Moses scum gutters, see Latham, "Swimming Pool Construction," 33–34; "Pattern for Parks," 506.
14. The colored tile on the basin walls helped to mask the "scum" that collected in the pool water. See Kocher and Davison, "Swimming Pools," 71–73.
15. "Views of New York," 1938–49, New York City Department of Parks and Recreation, 16mm film, VHS tape 1, 4.
16. Marcus, "Last One In," 60. For the term *concrete beach*, see "Pattern for Parks," 506.
17. As stated in the press release announcing the opening of the Hamilton Fish Pool (June 24, 1936), "Boys and girls, men and women, may use the pools at the same time, permitting entire families to swim together." See also "Views of New York," VHS tape 1, 4.
18. "East Side Cheers as City Opens Pool," *New York Times*, June 25, 1936.
19. Ibid.
20. Moses, "Public Swimming Facilities"; "Park Work Is Begun on 2 Bathing Pools," *New York Times*, October 4, 1934. Also see Hanmer, *Public Recreation*, 167.
21. For this and other pool entries, I have drawn on sources cited in my essay (see pp. 83–85) as well as the guide to the history of New York City's parks on the Web site of the Department of Parks and Recreation. For this park, see www.nycgovparks.org/sub_your_park/historical_signs/hs_historical_sign.php?id=6457. Also see Iannacone, "Open Space for the Underclass," 114–19.
22. "Hamilton Fish Swimming Pool," press release, June 24, 1936, New York City Department of Parks.
23. Ibid.
24. "$1,000,000 City Pool Opens Wednesday."
25. "Mayor Dedicates Big Harlem Pool," *New York Times*, June 28, 1936. See Moses, "Public Swimming Facilities"; "23 Bathing Pools Planned by Moses."
26. Iannacone, "Open Space for the Underclass," 155–57. Also www.nycgovparks.org/sub_your_park/historical_signs/hs_historical_sign.php?id=6499.
27. Hanmer, *Public Recreation*, 169.
28. "Oases in New York's Heat Wave: The New Public Swimming Pools," *New York Times*, July 19, 1936.
29. "Mayor Dedicates Big Harlem Pool."
30. Mumford, "The Sky Line: Parks and Playgrounds—New Buildings for Old" (October 24, 1936), in *Sidewalk Critic*, 170.
31. Caro, *Power Broker*, 514. See also p. 82 above.
32. Moses, "Public Swimming Facilities"; "Park Work Is Begun on 2 Bathing Pools." Also see on Astoria Pool, www.nycgovparks.org/sub_your_park/historical_signs/hs_historical_sign.php?id=8892; New York City Landmarks Preservation Commission, "Astoria Park Pool and Play Center."
33. "Astoria Pool Pavilion, John Matthews Hatton, Architect," *Architectural Forum* 67 (August 1937), 127–28.
34. "Astoria Swimming Pool," press release, July 1, 1936, New York City Department of Parks.
35. "Mayor Occupies Summer City Hall," *New York Times*, July 3, 1936.
36. In these races, men and women competed for a place on the team that would represent the United States in Berlin; the team sailed for Germany on July 14. "Largest United States Olympic Team Will Leave for Berlin on Wednesday," *New York Times*, July 12, 1936.
37. "Views of New York," VHS tape 1, 4.

38. "Staten Island Pool Is Opened by Mayor," *New York Times*, July 8, 1936.

39. Moses, "Public Swimming"; also see "Joseph H. Lyons Pool," www.nycgovparks.org/sub_your_park/historical_signs/hs_historical_sign.php?id=112.

40. "Mayor to Dedicate Swim Pool Tuesday," *New York Times*, July 5, 1936; "Tompkinsville Swimming Pool," press release, July 5, 1936, New York City Department of Parks.

41. Moses, "Municipal Recreation," 21–32.

42. "Joseph H. Lyons Pool" (as in n. 39).

43. "2 Reservoir Sites to Serve as Parks," *New York Times*, April 4, 1934; "Moses to Get Two Unneeded Reservoirs as Sites for Stadium and Swimming Pool," *New York Times*, April 5, 1934.

44. For Highbridge Park, see www.nycgovparks.org/sub_your_park/historical_signs/hs_historical_sign.php?id=12805; for Highbridge Pool and Recreation Center, see www.nycgovparks.org/sub_your_park/historical_signs/hs_historical_sign.php?id=7732.

45. See n. 43.

46. "Park Work Is Begun on 2 Bathing Pools."

47. "Highbridge Swimming Pool," press release, July 13, 1936, New York City Department of Parks; "Pool Opens Tomorrow," *New York Times*, July 13, 1936.

48. "Views of New York," VHS tape 4.

49. Marcus, "Last One In," 75.

50. "Mayor Opens Pool in Brooklyn Park," *New York Times*, July 21, 1936. This pool was on the list of sites that Moses circulated in the summer of 1934, identifying places where design of a new pool was expected to begin immediately. See Moses, "Public Swimming Facilities"; "23 Bathing Pools Planned by Moses."

51. Snyder-Grenier, "Sunset Park," 1143–44.

52. For Sunset Park and Pool, see www.nycgovparks.org/sub_your_park/historical_signs/hs-historical-sign.php?id=166.

53. "Sunset Swimming Pool," press release, July 19, 1936, New York City Department of Parks. Also see "5,000 in the Bronx at Pool Opening," *New York Times*, July 25, 1936.

54. "Views of New York," VHS tape 4.

55. Moses, "Public Swimming Facilities." For an insightful account of Moses's effect on the Jewish South Bronx, see Berman, *All That Is Solid*, 298–308.

56. "Park Work Is Begun on 2 Bathing Pools." Also see "Pattern for Parks," 490–510.

57. For Crotona Park, see www.nycgovparks.org/sub_your_park/historical_signs/hs-historical-sign.php?id=11153.

58. On the importance of spectacle, see Berman, *All That Is Solid*, 300. Also see "Views of New York," VHS tape 4.

59. "Pattern for Parks." Also see "Pool: Crotona Park, New York City, Park Department," *Architectural Forum* 65, no. 4 (October 1936), 369.

60. "Crotona Swimming Pool," press release, July 23, 1936, New York City Department of Parks. Also see "Crowds at Brooklyn Pool," *New York Times*, July 22, 1936.

61. Toby Sanchez, *The Williamsburg Neighborhood Profile* (New York: Brooklyn in Touch Information Center, 1990), 5.

62. M. Elizabeth Smith, *Greenpoint: A Neighborhood Study* (New York: Council for Social Planning, 1940), 8.

63. Anne F., telephone interview by Benjamin Marcus, February 24, 2006.

64. Smith, *Greenpoint*, 48.

65. "Moses to Ignore Protests on Pools" *New York Times*, August 9, 1934.

66. "75,000 Hail Opening of Pool in Greenpoint" *Brooklyn Daily Eagle*, August 1, 1936.

67. "Aymar Embury, Architect, Dead" *New York Times*, November 15, 1966.

68. Ibid.

69. Phyllis Yampolsky, letter to the editor, *New York Times*, August 1, 1991.

70. Steven K., interview by Elliot Malby and Sarah Eichner of Thread Collective Architecture, 2003, www.poolproject.org/future_stories2.html (accessed December 10, 2005; site now discontinued.)

71. Loretta N. and Leonard S., interviews by Amanda Aronczyk, "The Next Best Thing: Everything about a Pool" (show #251), WNYC, August 25, 2002.

72. Benny D., interview by Benjamin Marcus, April 10, 2006.

73. Sanchez, *Williamsburg Neighborhood Profile*, 3.

74. "The Mayoralty: Parks," editorial, *New York Times*, October 13, 1969.

75. "Six Splendid Ways to Make a Splash and Avoid the Mob at the Beaches" *New York Times*, July 8, 1973.

76. There were only 2,902 blacks living in Greenpoint-Williamsburg, and 254 Hispanics, with the remaining population of 279,920 deemed "white." *Population in Health Areas, New York City, 1930: Color, Nativity, Parentage, Sex and Age* (New York: Research Bureau, Welfare Council of New York City, 1931), 17.

77. Alan K., interview by Dean Olsher, "The Next Best Thing: Everything about a Pool" (show #251), WNYC, August 25, 2002.

78. Bob Kappstatter, "Neighbors Band Together to Save McCarren Park" *New York Daily News*, August 10, 1979.

79. Richard Schwartz [Director of Capital Projects, New York City Department of Parks], letter to Meyar Braiterman," August 23, 1989, New York City Parks Department, Arsenal Library, McCarren Pool File.

80. Merle English, "McCarren Pool: A Controversy of Olympic Proportions" *Newsday*, March 17, 1989.

81. Larry Celona, "Greenpoint Park Plans Offered" *New York Daily News*, March 23, 1986.

82. Sarah Baar, "Sink or Swim?" *Block Magazine* 2, no. 22 (June 2005), 9.

83. David W. Dunlap. "Old Bathhouse Defended as Brooklyn Landmark" *New York Times*, March 6, 1989.

84. Ibid.

85. Giorgio Cavaglieri, letter to the editor, *New York Times*, August 18, 1990.

86. Nadine Brozan, "A Crumbling Pool Divides a Neighborhood," *New York Times*, July 30, 1990.

87. Phyllis Yampolsky, "In Brooklyn, People Say, 'I Grew Up at McCarren Pool,'" *New York Times*, August 18, 1990.

88. Pritchett, *Brownsville, Brooklyn*; Rawson, "Brownsville," 163.

89. As cited in "Betsy Head Playground," www.nycgovparks.org/sub_your_park/historical_signs/hs-historical-sign.php?id=164. Betsy Head, a British immigrant, was the housekeeper of George C. Taylor, a reclusive banker and merchant; she died on June 15, 1907; Taylor the following September. Mrs. Head disowned her daughter, who married a coachman, and left her money to charities for children, as well as for the purchase and improvement of land for health and recreation. See "May Share Taylor Millions," *New York Times*, September 19, 1907; "Mrs. Betsy Head Is Dead," *New York Times*, June 15, 1907; "New Brownsville Playground Planned as Most Elaborate in City," *New York Times Sunday Magazine* (May 17, 1914), 8.

90. "New Brownsville Playground." The design attracted attention; and the parks department included a model of the playground in its exhibit at the Panama-Pacific International Exposition in San Francisco (1915), where the department won first prize. See www.nycgovparks.org/sub_your_park/historical_signs/hs-historical-sign.php?id=164.

91. Hanmer, *Public Recreation*, 172; Moses, "Public Swimming Facilities."

92. "Betsy Head Swimming Pool," press release, August 5, 1936, New York City Department of Parks.

93. "City Pool Is Opened without Ceremonies," *New York Times*, August 8, 1936; "New Swimming Pool Will Open Tomorrow," *New York Times*, August 7, 1936.

94. "Alderman Hart Fells Red Heckler in Fight with 150 Radicals at Fourth Celebration," *New York Times*, July 5, 1935.

95. "City Pool Is Opened without Ceremonies."

96. "Fire in Park Building," *New York Times*, August 18, 1937; "Park Is Nearing Completion," *New York Times*, June 24, 1941.

97. "City Play Center for All-Year Use," *Architectural Record* 90 (September 1941), 84.

98. Stern, Gilmartin, and Mellins, *New York 1930*, 717.

99. "City Play Center for All-Year Use," 86.

100. "Views of New York," VHS tape 4.

101. See, for example, Hanmer, *Public Recreation*, 170; also Moses, "Public Swimming Facilities."

102. See sources cited p. 85, n. 85. I am indebted to Kate Louis and other Columbia students—Katherine Gressel, Peter Lederman, Diane Simonson, and Julia Werb—for information about site selection offered in a classroom presentation, "Robert Moses and Racism: A Study of Public Pools," at Columbia University, May 3, 2006.

103. "Harlem Gets News of Big Play Centre," *New York Times*, August 9, 1935. Plans to build the public housing project that would be called Harlem River Houses were also announced at this meeting.

104. "25,000 at Opening of Harlem Pool," *New York Times*, August 9, 1936; "New Swimming Pool Will Open Tomorrow," *New York Times*, August 7, 1936.

105. "Jackie Robinson Park," www.nycgovparks.org/sub_your_park/historical_signs/hs_historical_sign.php?id=11614.

106. "Harlem Gets News of Big Play Centre." Also see the aerial photo of the park in Cormier, "Some New York City Parks and Parkways," 133.

107. "Colonial Swimming Pool," press release, August 7, 1936, New York City Department of Parks.

108. Ibid.

109. "25,000 at Opening of Harlem Pool"; "Harlem Gets News of Big Play Centre."

110. Davidson, "Federal Government and the Democratization of Public Recreational Sport," 181, 200.

111. "Views of New York," VHS tape 4.

112. Fletcher and Gallagher, "Red Hook," 991–92.

113. Hanmer, *Public Recreation*, 173.

114. "23 Bathing Pools Planned by Moses"; Moses, "Public Swimming Facilities."

115. For Red Hook Park, see www.nycgovparks.org/sub_your_park/historical_signs/hs-historical-sign.php?id=12487.

116. Caro, *Power Broker*, 376.

117. Ibid., 375.

118. "40,000 at Opening of Red Hook Pool," *New York Times*, August 18, 1936.

119. Ibid.; and Web site in n. 115.

120. "Views of New York," VHS tape 4.

121. Plunz, *History of Housing in New York City*, 236–38.

122. Mumford, "The Sky Line: Versailles for the Millions" (February 17, 1940), in *Sidewalk Critic*, 260–61.

123. "Antiquated Barges Become Floating Pools and Bathhouse, Madigan & Hyland, Engineers," *Architectural Record* 84 (December 1938), 57; "New Type of Pool to Open in Hudson," *New York Times*, August 3, 1938.

124. Buttenwieser, "Awash in New York City," 11; idem, "Awash in New York," 19.

125. Renner, "Nation that Bathes Together," 5–12; Williams, *Washing the Great Unwashed*, 61, 63.

126. "Asser Levy Recreation Center, Pool, and Playground," www.nycgovparks.org/sub_your_park/historical_signs/hs_historical_sign.php?id= 9722; Renner, "Nation that Bathes Together," 27, 63; Williams, *Washing the Great Unwashed*, 61, 63.

127. "Carmine Street Mural," www.nycgovparks.org/sub_your_park/historical_signs/hs_historical_sign.php?id=11966; "Tony Dapolito Recreation Center," www.nycgovparks.org/sub_your_park/historical_sign.php?id=6422.

128. "John Jay Park," www.nycgovparks.org/sub_your_park/historical_signs/hs_historical_sign.php?id=6466.

129. "Recreation Center 59," www.nycgovparks.org/sub_your_park/historical_signs/hs_historical_sign.php?id=7723.

130. "Branch Public Bath, West 60th Street, New York, N.Y., Werner & Windolph, Architects," *American Architect and Building News* 90, pt. 1, no. 1600 (August 1906), 71–72.

131. Moses, "Public Swimming Facilities."

132. "First Pile Driven on State Fair Site," *New York Times*, April 2, 1938.

133. Christopher Gray, "Streetscapes/New York State Marine Amphitheatre: 'At Old Aquacade, Things Aren't Going Swimmingly,'" *New York Times*, May 28, 1995; August Loeb, "Varied Amusements for the Fair," *New York Times*, March 12, 1939. Also see "Ederle Amphitheatre," www.nycgovparks.org/sub_your_park/historical_signs.hs_historical-sign.php?id=12065.

134. "Billy Rose Signs Opposed by Moses," *New York Times*, April 8, 1939; "Moses Ready to Carry His Fight on Aquacade Signs to Governor," *New York Times*, April 17, 1939; "Rose Defends Sign, Cites Moses 'Flops,'" *New York Times*, April 18, 1939.

135. For the conversion, see "Park Tourists See Conversion of Fair," *New York Times*, May 28, 1941. For the decay of the pool, see Gray, "New York State Marine Amphitheatre"; Lori Nickel, "End Near for Once-Grand Pool," *New York Times*, July 24, 1994.

136. Lewis Mumford, *The Urban Prospect* (New York: Harcourt, Brace & World, 1968), 81.

137. Moses, letter to Smith, January 9, 1924, New York Public Library, Manuscripts and Archives Division, Moses Papers (hereafter NYPL Moses Papers).

138. Hanmer, *Public Recreation*, 27.

139. Ibid., 193–94.

140. Lewis Mumford, "Report on Honolulu" (1938), in *City Development: Studies in Disintegration and Renewal* (New York: Harcourt, Brace, 1945), 133–34.

141. Transcript of talk given at a meeting of the Freeport Historical Society, February 26, 1974, in Krieg, *Robert Moses*, 135–39.

142. Robert Moses, "Hordes from the City," *Saturday Evening Post*, October 31, 1931, 14ff.

143. "'Summer City Hall' Is Chosen in Bronx," *New York Times*, June 26, 1936.

144. New York City Department of Parks, *Six Years of Progress*.

145. In 1940, seasonal permits cost $5. With a permit, weekday play was free and weekend play cost 50 cents. Without a permit, one round of golf cost 75 cents on weekdays and $1 on weekends.

146. "Club House for Golf Course, Pelham Bay Park, Bronx, NYC," *Architectural Forum* 67 (December 1937), 482–83.

147. Mayor La Guardia initially supported the soon-to-be-displaced campers, and his decision to back the clearing of the site is a telling example of his deference to Moses. La Guardia announced that "The bungalow colony will go. I took a different view of the matter, but after I talked it over with Mr. Moses I agreed with his viewpoint. Next year there will be a fine public beach there. . . . I have a fine Park Commissioner who knows his business." "Mayor Backs Moses on Orchard Beach," *New York Times*, April 10, 1934.

148. "New 'Jones Beach' Planned in Bronx," *New York Times*, February 28, 1934.

149. Ibid.

150. Department of Parks, City of New York, *The Improvement of Coney Island, Rockaway and South Beaches*, November 30, 1937. Small fees were charged for the games areas and for other services—parking, locker rental, use of the bathhouse, chair and umbrella rental.

151. "Rowdyism Fought at Orchard Beach," *New York Times*, July 17, 1937.

152. "Moses Bars City Amusement Park in Bronx as Improper Enterprise for Municipal Board," *New York Times*, June 1, 1935.

153. Aymar Embury II, "Using the Orders with Freedom," *Architecture* 54, no. 5 (November 1926), 324.

154. "Moses Asks Support of Plan for Beaches," *New York Times*, August 17, 1955.

155. "Moses Seeks $16,150,000 to Remake 3 City Beaches," *New York Times*, December 2, 1937.

156. "10,000 Visit Aquarium in Day as Moving of Specimens Begins," *New York Times*, September 24, 1941.

157. "Mayor Opens Zoo's New 'Veldt'; Doubts Aquarium Will Be Moved," *New York Times*, May 2, 1941.

158. The *New York Times* (October 12, 1941) published a poem, "Farewell to the Aquarium," by Arthur Guiterman lamenting Manhattan's loss of the aquarium:

> Displaced by a tunnel,
> A submarine funnel
> From Brooklyn to Battery Park . . .
> No habeas corpus
> Could save us a porpoise,
> A seahorse, a fluke or a ray.
> Commissioner Moses
> Who opens and closes
> Has moved our fish circus away!

159. Newhouse, *Wallace K. Harrison*, 73.

160. "Plan of Aquarium at Coney Approved," *New York Times*, October 23, 1953.

161. "City Welcomes Coney Aquarium," *New York Times*, June 6, 1957.

162. *The Future of Jamaica Bay* (New York: New York City Department of Parks, 1938).

163. New York City Department of Parks, *30 Years of Progress*, 79.

164. "Moses to Develop Riis Park as Model," *New York Times*, August 7, 1934.

165. Some sources say that Embury worked together with Clifton Lloyd on the renovation, while others mention only Embury. Despite the collaborative nature of parks department designs, produced by a team of architects based in the Arsenal, it is nevertheless accurate to attribute buildings to Embury, who was Moses's chief consulting architect and whose style is unmistakable in both the refurbished and the new Jacob Riis bathhouses.

166. This design has also been attributed to the team of Embury and designer Frank Willis.

167. Embury, "Aesthetics of Concrete," 279.

168. Handball, paddle tennis, and shuffleboard were 10 cents per half hour of play; golf cost 50 cents per player per round; locker rentals cost 15 cents for children and 25 cents for adults; use of the bathhouse cost 50 cents; and 10, 50, and 25 cents respectively were charged for renting towels, bathing suits, and chairs and umbrellas.

169. "Beach Park Plan Upheld by Moses," *New York Times*, November 22, 1934.

170. *Marine Parkway*, brochure signed by Moses, published by the Marine Parkway Authority (July 3, 1937).

171. "Beach Treks Begin Soon: More and Better Bathing Facilities Have Been Made Available for New Yorkers," *New York Times*, June 13, 1937.

172. "Beach Park Plan Upheld by Moses," *New York Times*, November 22, 1934.

173. *Marine Parkway*.

174. Caro, *Power Broker*, 492.

175. "Boom for the Beaches," *New York Times*, June 13, 1943; "Beaches to Open Memorial Day," *New York Times*, May 25, 1941.

176. *Marine Parkway*.

177. Robert Moses, "Restoring Rockaway's Beach Front," *Rockaway Review*, June 1941, 5–6.

178. Ibid.

179. "Moses Seeks $16,150,000 to Remake 3 City Beaches," *New York Times*, December 2, 1937.

180. "City Refuses to Postpone Rockaway Job," *Long Island Daily Press*, April 29, 1938.

181. Moses, "Restoring Rockaway's Beach Front."

182. *Queens Evening News*, June 16, 1937.

183. *New York Times*, August 8, 1952.

184. "Moses Seeks $16,150,000 to Remake 3 City Beaches."

185. "South Beach Plan Presented to City," *New York Times*, May 18, 1953.

186. For a history of the Play Movement in America, see Richard F. Knapp and Charles E. Hartsoe *Play for America, The National Recreation Association 1906–1965* (Arlington, Va.: National Recreation and Park Association, 1979). Dominick Cavallo explores the social aspects of play in *Muscles and Morals, Organized Playgrounds and Urban Reform, 1889–1920* (Philadelphia: University of Pennsylvania Press, 1981). I am grateful to the New York City Department of Parks and Recreation for allowing me to use the library and resources from the Parklands office. I extend special thanks to John Mattera, the parks librarian, for his assistance in gathering research materials.

187. *New York Times*, April 8, 1934, and March 21, 1934.

188. "Court Bids Moses Retreat on Bard," *New York Times*, June 18, 1959.

189. "7-Block Play Area Nearly Finished," *New York Times*, July 28, 1935.

190. Jacobs, *Death and Life of the Great American City*, 105.

191. George A. Kells, letter to Mayor Strong, 16 October 1895, William L. Strong Papers (1895–1897), Parks Department File, New York City Department of Records and Information Services.

192. The terminology and photography used during Moses's tenure speaks to the low status of playgrounds in his hierarchy of urban development. The terms *arterial by-product* and *marginal playground* indicate that park and playground spaces were secondary areas created to supplement slum clearance projects and congestion relief or to prevent damage to more important parks. In the Progressive Era, reformers circulated photographs of children swinging and running in playgrounds in order to advertise their importance and success. Moses published photographs devoid of parkgoers and happy children.

193. City of New York Department of Parks, *8 Years of Park Progress*, 14–15.

194. "7-Block Play Area Nearly Finished," *New York Times*, July 28, 1935.

195. *8 Years of Park Progress*, 14–15

196. City of New York Department of Parks, *20 Years of Park Progress*, 26.

197. Ibid.

198. "Police War Fund to Buy Play Sties," *New York Times*, March 2, 1934.

199. "Large Police Fund May Go to Charity," *New York Times*, February 9, 1934.

200. "Police War Fun to Buy Play Sties."

201. *8 Years of Park Progress*, 11

202. "Moses to Get Two Unneeded Reservoirs As Sites for Stadium and Swimming Pool," *New York Times*, April 5, 1934.

203. "Promenade to Cap Huge Play Centre," *New York Times*, May 9, 1935.

204. News release, 12 February 1938, City of New York Department of Parks.

205. In 1933, the Seabury Investigation uncovered corruption related to the purchase of the Chrystie-Forsyth thoroughfare. The infamous State Supreme Court Justice Joseph Force Crater, whose disappearance was called one of the most notorious missing person cases in America, sold a hotel to the city for $2.85 million that he purchased months earlier for $75,000. This corruption and the overwhelming cost of the property (totaling $15,000,000) explain the delay in developing the property.

206. "City Clears Site for Model Housing," *New York Times*, October 12, 1930; "Model Housing Site Is Urged for a Park," *New York Times*, March 14, 1931. The Howe and Lescaze plans were unveiled on September 27, 1932, at an exhibition on modern architecture. "Third Housing Plan Offers Low Rent," *New York Times*, September 27, 1932.

207. "City Lots for Play Sought by Sheehy," *New York Times*, May 27, 1933.

208. "La Guardia Scraps Chrystie St. Plans," *New York Times*, February 1, 1934.

209. "Roosevelt Park Will Open Friday," *New York Times*, September 9, 1934.

210. "Morgenthau Fights Evils of Congestion," *New York Times*, May 4, 1909.

211. "Boys Clear Playground," *New York Times*, July 31, 1910.

212. City of New York Department of Parks, Annual report, 1912, 13.

213. "New Playground Opened on East Side," *New York Times*, June 20, 1934.

214. *8 Years of Park Progress*, 13

215. "Two Agreements Aid East River Drive," *New York Times*, April 14, 1939; "East River Drive is 15% Completed," *New York Times*, July 22, 1939.

216. "Old Gracie Home Nearly Restored," *New York Times*, March 15, 1936; "Historic Mansions Restored by City," New York Times, April 17, 1936; "Design of Tunnel for the East River Drive," *New York Times*, January 8, 1940.

217. *8 Years of Park Progress*, 46

218. "392 Playgrounds Will Open July 2," *New York Times*, June 17, 1934.

219. "Brooklyn School Sold," *New York Times*, October 8, 1945.

220. Clara F. Blitzer, "Schools Suited to Functions Seen as Post-War Need," *New York Times*, November 14, 1943.

221. "Public School 98 Begun," *New York Times*, January 27, 1949; "894,500 to Enroll in City's Schools" *New York Times*, August 28, 1950.

222. "2 Playgrounds Opened," *New York Times*, July 22, 1951.

223. City of New York Department of Parks, *18 Years of Park Progress* (1952), 12

224. "New Standard in Harlem Housing Is Set by Clinic and Amphitheatre," *New York Times*, June 14, 1936.

225. "3 Playgrounds Opened," *New York Times*, November 27, 1937; "Rockefeller Gives Harlem Plot to the City for a Playground," *New York Times*, November 29, 1937.

226. Ibid.

227. "Two Harlem Playgrounds to Open Tomorrow," *New York Times*, March 31, 1939.

228. *18 Years of Park Progress*, 10.

229. Lynn Preston, "New Beauty for Old East Side," *New York Times*, November 5, 1939.

230. The "Circumferential Parkway" was originally proposed during Mayor Walker's administration to relieve traffic congestion in Brooklyn and Queens. "A Constructive Traffic Plan," *New York Times*, January 4, 1929.

231. "Brooklyn City's Beautiful Suburbs," *New York Times*, March 31, 1895.

232. "Charm of Brooklyn's Shore Road Being Revived as Park Project," *New York Times*, August 4, 1935.

233. "New Playgrounds Overlook the Bay," *New York Times*, July 25, 1942.

234. This is the total given by Caro, *Power Broker*, 7.

235. "Moses Steams on Minus His Park Job," *New York Times*, May 24, 1960.

236. My understanding of the limitations of using parks department documents to determine the exact number of playgrounds that Moses claimed to have built comes from conversations and correspondence with John Mattera, the librarian of the Department of Parks and Recreation, who was generous with his time and expertise.

237. Caro, *Power Broker*, 510.

238. My research on the locations of Moses's swimming pools suggests that, regardless of his own prejudices and the racist and classist climate of the 1930s, his choice of sites for playgrounds was opportunistic, not prejudicial. Moses built recreational facilities where space was available, and he built the greatest number of them in the most densely populated boroughs—Manhattan and Brooklyn—where they were more direly needed.

239. "Our Park Creator Extraordinary—Robert Moses: Over the City and State He Flings a Network of Fine Roads, Bridges and Busy Playgrounds," *New York Times*, March 20, 1938.

240. "Mayor Says City Set Playsite Mark," *New York Times*, July 31, 1937.

241. Letters to the *Times*, "Mr. Moses and the Aquarium; Tracing Somewhat Tarnished Past, He Insists It Be Banished From Battery," *New York Times*, February 25, 1941.

242. "Preserving Historic Sites," *New York Times*, December 31, 1948.

243. "Aquarium Barrage Turned on Moses," *New York Times*, March 24, 1941.

244. Aymar Embury II, "Letters from Readers," *New Pencil Points* 23 (September 1942), 8.

245. Caro, *Power Broker*, 678–88.

246. *New York Times*, July 25, 1947.

247. The acreage varies depending on whether the New York Public Library is considered part of the site. Without the library, Bryant Park is approximately 4 acres; the parks department counts the entire 9.6-acre site as park property.

248. "Plan Suggested for the Beautification of Bryant Park," *New York Times*, January 21, 1934.

249. "Bryant Park," *New York Times*, January 22, 1934.

250. "New Bryant Park Formally Opened," *New York Times*, September 15, 1934.

251. Ibid.

252. Mumford, "The Sky Line: Modern Design and the New Bryant Park" (December 1, 1934), in *Sidewalk Critic*, 122.

253. Ibid, 123.

254. "Bryant Park, New York City," *Architecture* 72, no. 3 (March 1936), 145.

255. "Perimeter Playgrounds," *New York Times*, September 14, 1935.

256. "Playgrounds Open Today," *New York Times*, April 4, 1936; "13 New Play Sites to be Open Today," *New York Times*, 4 May 1936; "11 New Play Areas Will Open Today," *New York Times*, June 26, 1936.

257. "Leisure de Luxe Provided by Park," *New York Times*, April 12, 1936.

258. "Central Park Gets More Play Areas," *New York Times*, May 18, 1934.

259. "What Might Be Done in Central Park," *New York Times*, June 13, 1909; "The Central Park Plan," *New York Times*, 3 June 1910; "The Park Invaders," *New York Times*, March 12, 1912.

260. "To Alter Reservoir into Sunken Garden," *New York Times*, July 20, 1917; "Plans Memorial for Central Park," *New York Times*, 1 February 1920; "Plans for the Reservoir Site," *New York Times*, April 23, 1930; "Plan for Reservoir Adopted by Herrick," *New York Times*, June 3, 1930; "Lawn Plan Chosen for Park Reservoir," *New York Times*, March 4, 1931.

261. "Lawn Plan Chosen for Park Reservoir."

262. "Sheehy Park Plan Dropped by Moses," *New York Times*, April 6, 1934; "Play Area to Open in Central Park," *New York Times*, November 20, 1936.

263. "No Park de Luxe," *New York Times*, May 25, 1934; "Casino in 5 Years Grossed $3,096,155," *New York Times*, March 12, 1935.

264. "High Casino Prices Fought by Moses," *New York Times*, February 20, 1934; "Park Casino Loses Fight on Eviction," *New York Times*, April 10, 1935.

265. "Wants Casino Razed," *New York Times*, January 9, 1936; "Rumsey Playground Will Be Opened Today," *New York Times*, May 7, 1937.

266. "Razing of Casino Will Begin Today," *New York Times*, May 5, 1936.

267. "Sheepfold in Park to Become Tavern," *New York Times*, February 28, 1934.

268. "Park Tavern Plan Brings Protests," *New York Times*, March 10, 1934.

269. "Ban on Inn Dancing Laid to High Price," *New York Times*, June 9, 1934.

270. "Only a Half Acre—But," *New York Times*, April 20, 1956.

271. "Court Stops Job in Central Park," *New York Times*, April 27, 1956; "Court Adjourned to Lot in the Park," *New York Times*, April 28, 1956.

272. "Moses Yields to Mothers; Drops Tavern Parking Lot," *New York Times*, July 18, 1956; Charles G. Bennett, "Controls Sought on Park Outlays, Tavern Dispute Inspires Bill by the Citizens Union and Isaacs on Concessions," *New York Times*, August 29, 1956.

273. "Central Park Dons a New Dress," *New York Times*, December 30, 1934; "Third Restaurant for Central Park," *New York Times*, April 14, 1935.

274. "Ban on Inn Dancing Laid to High Price," *New York Times*, June 9, 1934.

275. "Artists Start Murals in Park to Relieve Mall's Somber Aspect," *New York Times*, August 3, 1935.

276. Central Park Wildlife Conservation Center, www.nycgovparks.org/sub_your_park/historical_signs/hs_historical_sign.php?id=11048.

277. "City to Demolish Park Greenhouses," *New York Times*, November 8, 1934. "New Garden Rises in Central Park," *New York Times*, August 17, 1937; "Vanderbilt Contract Let," *New York Times*, December 18, 1938.

278. "For the Older People," *New York Times*, June 1, 1955.

279. Daniel Chased [executive director, Park Association], letter to the editor, *New York Times*, 14 June 1955.

280. "Paul Crowell, Naturalists Win Battle of Ramble," *New York Times*, December 1, 1955.

281. "Park Troupe Told to End Free Plays," *New York Times*, 16 April 1959.

282. "Shakespeare in the Park," *New York Times*, April 18, 1959; "State Judge Offers to Mediate Dispute Over Plays in Park," *New York Times*, May 21, 1959.

283. "Court Bids Moses Retreat on Bard," *New York Times*, June 18, 1959; "Moses Asks Funds by City for Plays," *New York Times*, June 20, 1959; "Shakespeare in the Park," *New York Times*, August 22, 1959.

284. "Park Boat House is Gift of Couple," *New York Times*, September 2, 1952.

285. "New Model Yacht Boathouse Is Gift of Mrs. J. E. Kerbs to Central Park," *New York Times*, February 2, 1953; "New $305,000 Boathouse at Central Park Lake Will Be Opened Today," *New York Times*, March 12, 1954.

286. "Constructing a New Skating Rink in Central Park," *New York Times*, November 22, 1950; "New Skating Rink in Central Park to be Opened to Public Thursday," *New York Times*, December 18, 1950; "City Has Yule Gift of a Skating Rink," *New York Times*, December 22, 1950; "Roof-top Playground Opened in Central Park," *New York Times*, June 20, 1951.

287. "City Zoos Will Eliminate 30 Per Cent of Their Animals as Too Old or Unfit," *New York Times*, September 18, 1934.

288. "Smith Now 'Agent' For Prospect Park Zoo," *New York Times*, May 10, 1935.

289. "'Pep' Talk By Smith Opens Zoo Drive," *New York Times*, May 28, 1935.

290. "Smith Decries 'Back-Alley Politics' of La Guardia in Row with Moses," *New York Times*, July 4, 1935.

291. "Zoologically Speaking," *New York Times*, July 5, 1935.

292. Robert Moses, "Zoos in Particular," in *Public Works*, 28.

293. Mumford, "The Sky Line: Menageries and Piers" (October 12, 1935), in *Sidewalk Critic*, 134.

294. Kaufman, *Designing the Moses Era*.

295. Clay Lancaster, *Prospect Park Handbook* (New York: Walton H. Rawls, 1967), 97; Graff, *Central Park Prospect Park*, 150.

296. Moses, "Central Park," *Public Works*, 17.

297. Lancaster, *Prospect Park Handbook*, 98–99.

298. Ibid., 101.

299. Vincent F. Seyfried, *Corona: From Farmland to City Suburb, 1650–1935* (Garden City, N.Y.: 1986), 67–68.

300. *New York Times*, April 20, 1913; March 12, 1913; and May 19, 1913. See also Seyfried, *Corona*, 68.

301. *Queensborough* [monthly magazine of the Queens Chamber of Commerce], May 1916; Seyfried, *Corona*, 68–70.

302. Seyfried, *Corona*, 90.

303. Caro, *Power Broker*, 1082?–85; David Oats, "The World in a Park," *Queens Tribune*, July 3–9, 1980, and July 10–16, 1980.

304. Stern, Gilmartin, and Mellins, *New York 1930*, 723.

305. *Long Island Star Journal*, October 18, 1946, and October 19, 1946; *New York Times*, October 19, 1946.

306. *New York Times*, May 17, 1964.

307. "Huge Park Program," *New York Times*, March 8, 1936.

308. Ibid.

309. "Moses's Many Projects Are All Tied Together," *New York Times*, Feb. 10, 1935.

310. "New Sewage Plant To Be Ready Today," *New York Times*, October 23, 1937.

311. "Park To Be Begun On Wards Island," *New York Times*, January 10, 1938.

312. "Foot Bridge Urged For Wards Island," *New York Times*, November 8, 1937.

313. "Plans For Wards Island," *New York Times*, Nov. 9, 1937.

314. Caro, *Power Broker*, 779.

315. Rastorfer, *Six Bridges*, 171.

316. Robert Moses, *Ward's Island Park, Ward's Island Pedestrian Bridge, Hell Gate Waterfront* (New York: Department of Parks and Triborough Bridge and Tunnel Authority, May 18, 1951), 1.

317. "State Will Retain Wards Island Site," *New York Times*, February 12, 1952.

318. "The Achievements of Robert Moses," *New York Times*, December 13, 1953.

319. "Wards Island Park," *New York Times*, July 13, 1954.

320. Moses, *Public Works*, 238.

321. "City Gets a Park on Randall's Island and a Speech from Robert Moses," *New York Times*, June 16, 1968.

322. Elizabeth Michell and Katherine Reed, "Henry Hudson Parkway," HAER No. NY–334, Historic American Engineering Record (HAER), National Park Service, U.S. Department of the Interior, 2005.

323. Nelson P. Lewis [chief engineer for the New York City Board of Estimate], untitled city planning pamphlet (New York: 1915); Manhattan Borough President, *1922 Annual Report*, 35; and *Regional Plan of New York and Its Environs*, vols. 1 and 2.

324. Moses, letter to Stanley Isaacs, April 23, 1941, NYPL, Stanley Isaacs Papers. For additional information on Moses's relation with Isaacs and other matters pertaining to the loop highway, see Owen D. Gutfreund, "The Path of Prosperity: The Story of Manhattan's East River Drive" (master's thesis, Columbia University, 1991).

325. For Long Island Expressway, see www.nycroads.com/roads/long-island.

326. I have drawn extensively on primary sources as well as on the Historic Inventory Report for the Shore (Belt) Parkway, written by Pressley Associates Landscape Architects and McGinley Kalsow Associates as consultants to URS Corporation for the New York City Department of Transportation and the New York City Department of Parks and Recreation. The principal in charge of that work was Marion Pressley FASLA; the project manager was Lauren Meier ASLA. During the project, from 2004 to 2006, I was an intern under their supervision.

327. Robert Moses, "The Comprehensive Parkway System of the New York Metropolitan Region," *Civil Engineering* 9, no. 3 (March 1939), 161.

328. Ibid., 162.

329. Ethan Carr, "The Parkway in New York City," in *Parkways: Past, Present, and Future, Proceedings of the Second Biennial Linear Parks Conference, 1987* (Boone, N.C.: Appalachian Consortium Press, 1989), 4, citing the New York City Parks Department's brochure "New Parkways in New York City" (1937).

330. John D. Millett, *The Works Progress Administration in New York City* (Chicago: Public Administration Service), 1938, vii.

331. United States Public Works Administration, *America Builds: The Record of PWA Prepared in the Division of Information* (Washington, D.C.: US Government Printing Office, 1939), 186.

332. Moses, letter to Reagan McCrary [of the *New York Daily Mirror*], December 3, 1938, NYPL, Moses Papers, Box 97.

333. Robert Moses, "How to Plan and Pay for Better Highways, First National Better Highways Awards Contest" (Detroit: General Motors, 1952), 10.

334. Clinton Loyd, *The Belt Parkway: Published on the Occasion of the Opening* (New York: Robley, 1940), 34.

335. Ibid., 3.

336. Triborough Bridge Authority, *Sheepshead Bay Section of the Belt Parkway, May 30, 1941* (New York: Robley, 1941), 8.

337. Moses, letter to Charles K. Panish [Army Corps of Engineers], November 30, 1944, New York City Municipal Archives.

338. Moses, "Comprehensive Parkway System," 161.

339. Regional Plan Association, *Graphic Regional Plan*, vol. 1 (repr. New York: Arno, 1974), 285.

340. Elliot Willensky and Norval White, *AIA Guide to New York City* (New York: Harcourt, Brace, Jovanovich, 1988), 845.

341. See www.nycroads.com/roads/korean-war-vets/.

342. "Statement by Governor Nelson A. Rockefeller," press release, June 3, 1973, State of New York, Executive Chamber.

343. Tracy B. Augur, "An Analysis of the Plan of Stuyvesant Town," *Journal of the American Institute of Planners* (autumn 1944), 9.

344. Cited by Schwartz, *New York Approach*, 94.

345. Moses, *Public Works*, 435.

346. Mayor Vincent Impellitteri twice delayed Board of Estimate hearings, after which Moses abandoned the project. "Hearings Proposed on Village Projects," *New York Times*, March 31, 1951; "Two Areas Approved for Housing," *New York Times*, April 3, 1951.

347. Schwartz, *New York Approach*, 146–50.

348. "A Slum Clearance Victory," *New York Times*, January 30, 1954.

349. Washington Square Village, however, was built with the expectation of an enlarged street; the extra wide setback of the sidewalk on La Guardia Place resulted from the decision not to widen the street.

350. Mayor's Committee on Slum Clearance. *Washington Square Southeast*, 3.

351. Ibid., 18.

352. James B. Munn, "The Washington Square College," in *New York University 1832–1932*, ed. Theodore Francis Jones (New York: New York University Press, 1933), 380.

353. Ibid., 387.

354. The block included a row of historic townhouses facing the square known as Genius Row, after its famous resident writers. On the transaction between NYU and Campagna, see Schwartz, *New York Approach*, 138; "City to Scan Sale in Washington Sq.," *New York Times*, July 17, 1948; "Moses Faces Sale Query," *New York Times*, July 20, 1948. In December 1943, Mayor La Guardia appointed Campagna to the Board of Education, and two years later he took charge of the school construction program, tapping his professional expertise to run the city's postwar school expansion. Although Moses was consistently supportive of NYU, his attitude toward Washington Square fluctuated. In 1945, he intervened on the neighborhood's behalf to limit the negative impact of a bulky apartment building on Washington Square; the result of this conflict was a height limit of 7 to 8 stories around the square; see "Against the Rootless," *Architectural Forum* 82 (April 1945), 12, 16. At the same time, he supported plans to build a road through the park.

355. The IIT expansion was a small part of Chicago's South Side Renewal Project which Heald helped to organize. On Heald's role at IIT, see Sarah Whiting, "Bas-Relief Urbanism: Chicago's Figured Field," in *Mies in America*, ed. Phyllis Lambert (New York: Whitney Museum of American Art, and Montreal: Canadian Center for Architecture, 2001), 656, 668, 676; Cammie McAtee, "Aline #5044325: Mies's First Trip to America," in *Mies in America*, 150–52; and Daniel Bluestone, "Chicago's Mecca Flat Blues," *Journal of the Society of Architectural Historians* 57 (December 1998), 393–98. The quotation is from a letter from Heald to Moses, July 3, 1952, NYU Archives, Office of the President, Box 12, Folder 5: Plant and Properties, Washington Square Southeast Project, November 1952–October 1953.

356. Memo, February 6, 1953, NYU Archives (as in n. 355).

357. In 1959, Tishman disclosed that he bought out S. Pierre Bonan, president of the Bonwit Construction Company, who had originated the project. For further information on Bonan, see the entry on Cadman Plaza Title I (p. 299).

358. The Eggers and Higgins plan called for nine 14-story buildings with a total of 2,184 apartments, a garage at the corner of Bleecker and Mercer streets, surface parking lots throughout, and stores along West Broadway. On Paul Lester Wiener (1895–1967), see "Paul Lester Wiener, Architect and City Planner is Dead at 72," *New York Times*, November 18, 1967; Paul Lester Wiener and José Luis Sert, "Work of Town Planning Associates in Latin America, 1945–1956," *Architectural Design* 27 (1957), 190–213; Sigfried Giedion, "Washington Square Village, New York," *L'Architecture d'aujourd'hui* 31 (1960), 68–75. On Wiener's partnership with Sert, see *Sert arquitecto en Nueva York* (Barcelona: Museu d'Art Contemporani de Barcelona, 1997).

359. Washington Square Village rental brochure, New York Public Library, Milstein Division, Real Estate Brochure Collection.

360. George F. Baughman, letter to Dudley L. Miller, December 21, 1959, NYU Archives, Buckley Collection, Box 43. Baughman was the treasurer and CFO of NYU. Miller, an attorney at the firm Gerdes, Montgomery & Miller, represented NYU.

361. George F. Baughman, letter to Morton S. Wolf, November 24, 1959, NYU Archives, Eileen Buckley Collection, Box 43.

362. Minutes of planning meeting, January 9, 1961, NYU Archives, Roberto Collection, Box 18, Folder: Silver Towers, 1962.

363. At the time of completion, the towers were known as University Plaza. They were well reviewed in the architectural press but, like Pei's other Title I work, have yet to receive the rigorous study they merit. "Bright Landmarks on Changing Urban Scene," *Architectural Forum* 125 (December 1966), 21–29; Douglas Haskell, "10 Buildings that Climax an Era," *Fortune* 74 (December 1966), 156–62; "The 1967 Honor Awards," *AIA Journal* 47 (June 1967), 44.

364. Mayor's Committee on Slum Clearance, *South Village*, 49.

365. Ibid., 7.

366. Mayor's Committee on Slum Clearance, *Delancey Street*, 49.

367. Research for this essay, involving hundreds of primary sources, was done in conjunction with my doctoral dissertation, Matthew Gordon Lasner, "No Lawn to Mow: Cooperatives, Condominiums and the American Dream, 1881–1973" (Harvard University, 2007); a more complete history of cooperative and condominium housing and ownership in the U.S. can be found there.

368. Moses, letter to Lester Markel, March 7, 1958, NYPL, Moses Papers, Box 117, Folder 1, Committee on Slum Clearance 1958.

369. Charles Grutzner, "Luxury Housing Opens in Harlem," *New York Times*, October 17, 1958.

370. Ernest Dunbar, "The View from Lenox Terrace," *New York Times*, March 3, 1968.

371. Conversation with author, May 15, 2006.

372. *New York Times*, July 1, 1959.

373. Mayor's Committee on Slum Clearance, *North Harlem*, 3.

374. Mayor's Committee on Slum Clearance, *Williamsburg*, 14.

375. Elizabeth R. Hepner, *Morningside-Manhattanville Rebuilds . . . A Chronological Account of Redevelopment in the Morningside-Manhattanville Area with Special Reference to the Development of Morningside Gardens* (New York: Morningside Heights Housing Corporation and Morningside Heights, Inc., 1955), n.p. The member institutions were Barnard College, St. John the Divine, Columbia University, Corpus Christi Church, Home for Old Men and Aged Couples, International House, Jewish Theological Seminary, the Juilliard School, St.

Luke's Home for Aged Women, St. Luke's Hospital, Teachers College, Riverside Church, Union Theological Seminary, and the Woman's Hospital Division of St. Luke's Hospital.

376. As Morningside Gardens was under way, the Rockefeller family funded construction of the two new buildings: the Interchurch Center (1954–58), which served as the headquarters of the National Council of Churches of Christ, on Riverside Drive and 119th Street; and the parish house of Riverside Church (1955–57) on Riverside Drive and 120th Street.

377. The housing program of the New York Life Insurance Company has not yet been properly studied. In addition to Lake Meadows in Chicago, it included Fresh Meadows (1946–49) in Queens, and Manhattan House (1949–50) on Second Avenue between 65th and 66th streets. Nelson was later hired to oversee the construction of Lincoln Center for the Performing Arts.

378. Moses, letter to Margaret Bartlett [associate executive director of Morningside Heights], October 16, 1957, NYPL, Moses Papers, Box 116, Folder 2.

379. The General Grant Houses contained 1,943 apartments in nine buildings: eight buildings with 21 stories and one with 14 stories. It had about twice as many units as Morningside Gardens on a site 50 percent bigger.

380. Manhattanville Houses contained 1,272 apartments in six 20-story towers. The site covered about 10 acres.

381. Wayne Phillips, "Slums Engulfing Columbia Section," New York Times, June 9, 1958.

382. Charles Grutzner, "City's 'Acropolis' Combatting Slums," New York Times, May 21, 1957.

383. Morningside Heights, Inc., letter to Moses, December 15, 1955, NYPL, Moses Papers, Box 116, Folder "Housing Corres. for Mr. Moses' Library Project Jan. 1, 1955 to Dec. 31, 1955." Moses, letter to David Rockefeller, February 26, 1957, Box 116, Folder 2.

384. Gertrude Samuels, "Rebirth of a Community," New York Times Magazine (September 25, 1955), 26.

385. "Roosevelt Jr. Bid Is Cited by Moses," New York Times, May 21, 1959.

386. On the Senate hearings chaired by Senator Homer E. Capehart, see Charles Grutzner, "Senate Inquiry Opens Here Today on $14 Million Housing Windfalls," New York Times, September 27, 1954; idem, "Huge Yield on 'Slum Clearance' Cited at Senate F.H.A. Hearing," New York Times, October 2, 1954; "New York's Title I Controversy Spotlights Architect Kessler: A Combination of Know-How and Know-Who," Architectural Forum 3, no. 2 (August 1959), 13–14.

387. A. Hoffman [demolition consultant], letter to Moses, undated (early October 1954), NYPL, Robert Moses Papers, Box 116, Folder: Housing 1954.

388. "New York's Title I Controversy," 13–14.

389. At Wagner's request, Moses produced a report on Kessler's Title I work. The firm was working for the Slum Clearance Committee and under the supervision of Skidmore, Owings & Merrill on the housing in six projects: Manhattantown, NYU–Bellevue, Lincoln Square, Battery Park, Gramercy Park, and Riverside-Amsterdam. In addition, the private sponsors hired Kessler to work on five Title I developments: Harlem (Lenox Terrace), Manhattantown, NYU–Bellevue (Kips Bay), Pratt, and Washington Square Southeast (Washington Square Village). The list omitted Lincoln Towers at Lincoln Square. Mayor Wagner banned Kessler from any future Title I work, but it did not hold: he was hired for the two projects on Rockaway Beach. Moses, letter to Robert F. Wagner, July 1, 1959, NYPL, Moses Papers, Box 118. Charles Grutzner, "Wagner and Moses Will Confer on Title I Disclosures Today," New York Times, June 26, 1959; Wayne Phillips, "Barred Designer Has 2 Slum Jobs," New York Times, November 2, 1959; idem, "Project Site Sold Despite City ban," New York Times, November 3, 1959.

390. Charles Grutzner, "City Acts to Spur Housing Project," New York Times, June 20, 1957.

391. The Slum Clearance Committee brochure (Manhattantown, 49) stated: "Although showing a rather satisfactory yield based upon the depressed value of these old buildings, it would nevertheless be insufficient to return a reasonable profit upon the reconstruction value of the various structures. . . . This unique condition is one of the many factors preventing the elimination of slums by the investment of private capital without the intervention of the municipality charged with the well being of its citizens."

392. NYPL, Moses Papers, Box 116, Folder: Housing 1954.

393. No records concerning Manhattantown have been found in the Pei archives.

394. Despite substantial changes in the site plan, the number of apartments remained steady at around 2,600.

395. Grand Central Palace was an air-rights development over the train tracks. During World War II, it served as a recruitment and enlistment center for the U.S. Army, and in 1953 it was leased by the IRS. During these extended periods, the building was unavailable for exhibitions. It was demolished in 1964.

396. "Way Seen Cleared for New 'Garden,'" New York Times, February 17, 1948; "Dewey Signs Bill for Huge Garden," New York Times, April 13, 1948. After the TBTA repaid its debt, ownership of the Coliseum was to pass to the city.

397. Leo Egan, "New Sports Arena Will Seat 25,000," New York Times, November 15, 1946. The published rendering was not accompanied by a plan, thus it is impossible to determine if the intention at the outset was to extend the convention center to Ninth Avenue.

398. The TBTA quietly dropped the project in 1950. "Triborough Authority Drops Plan to Build New York Coliseum," New York Times, January 29, 1951.

399. Mayor's Committee on Slum Clearance, Columbus Circle, 38; "Nation's Costliest Redevelopment Project, New York Coliseum Gets Legal Green Light," Architectural Forum 99, no. 5 (November 1953), 123.

400. "Plan is Abandoned for 'Uptown' Opera," New York Times, March 29, 1952.

401. Mayor's Committee on Slum Clearance, Columbus Circle, 6.

402. Charles Grutzner, "Coliseum Hailed as Tax Producer," New York Times, April 18, 1956.

403. The rider read: "no funds in this act shall be available for . . . grants . . . involving the development or redevelopment of a project for predominantly residential uses where incidental uses are not restricted to those normally essential for residential uses." "Threat to Urban Redevelopment," Architectural Forum 100, no. 5 (May 1954), 37. Also see, "New Coliseum Jeopardized by Rider to U.S. Funds Bill," Architectural Forum, April 10, 1954; "Coliseum Funds in Sight," New York Times, May 20, 1954.

404. "Texts of Moses and Follin Letters on the City's Coliseum Project," New York Times, April 19, 1954.

405. "HHFA bows to New York in Coliseum Site Dispute," Architectural Forum 102, no. 5 (May 1955), 17.

406. Charles Grutzner, "Coliseum to Open in Fanfare Today," New York Times, April 28, 1956. The TBTA paid most of the $35-million cost of the Coliseum in cash, borrowing only $9.5 million on short-term notes. Because of its strong financial position, it was able to obtain a substantial cut in interest payments, presumably better terms than the city could have negotiated. Clayton Knowles, "Bridge Revenues Built New Center," New York Times, April 28, 1956.

407. "Art News Assails Coliseum Plans but Moses Declines to 'Get Mad,'" New York Times, March 31, 1954; "Where'll Moses Be When the Lights Go On?" editorial, Art News 53, no. 2 (April 1954), 15.

408. "Larger Coliseum Urged by Moses," New York Times, February 12, 1968.

409. "Clearing the Slums," Wall Street Journal, April 27, 1956.

410. "Medical Center Planned by N.Y.U.," New York Times, October 27, 1944.

411. Lee E. Cooper, "N.Y.U. Acquires Site of Medical Center," New York Times, November 3, 1946.

412. Stern, Mellins, and Fishman, New York 1960, 287. On the formation of the NYU–Bellevue Medical Center, see Schwartz, New York Approach, 214–17.

413. "Salmon to be Head of Medical Center," New York Times, May 7, 1947.

414. Moses, for example, helped to demap the streets to create the medical center superblock. "Parking Is Settled in Medical Center," New York Times, July 29, 1949.

415. "East Side Chosen for U.S. Hospital," New York Times, March 25, 1947. The V.A. Hospital was designed by Eggers and Higgins, and Charles B. Meyers. See Stern, Mellins, and Fishman, New York 1960, 287.

416. "New Medical Units To Shut 4 Streets," New York Times, July 24, 1947. The Chief Medical Examiner's Office, located at 520 First Avenue, was opened in 1960; the building was designed by DeYoung, Moskowitz and Rosenburg.

417. Richard H. Parke, "N.Y.U.-Bellevue Plan Grows with Cost at $32,744,000," New York Times, January 17, 1949.

418. "NYU-Bellevue Center Aids in Moses Slum-Area Study," New York Times, November 8, 1952.

419. "$4 Million U.S. Aid Granted Slum Job," New York Times, September 18, 1954.

420. Maurice Foley, "Builders Acquire East Side Blocks," New York Times, December 19, 1954.

421. Scheuer's Title I work has not received the attention it deserves. For his views on urban renewal and argument against the federal government's auction process, see James H. Scheuer, Eli Goldston, and Wilton S. Sogg, "Disposition of Urban Renewal Land: A Fundamental Problem in the Rebuilding of Our Cities," Columbia Law Review 62 (1962), 959–91.

422. Charles Grutzner, "Three Slum Projects Explain Delays," New York Times, January 30, 1957.

423. The city had sold the site to University Center, Inc., for $2,898,078, of which $1,983,751 was a city mortgage. Webb & Knapp paid about $1 million and also acquired Industrial

Engineering, the company headed by David Moss, the displaced sponsor. Charles Grutzner, "Title I Developer to Try Again Here," *New York Times*, September 6, 1959; idem, "Housing Projects Getting New Life," *New York Times*, June 14, 1957; "Land Cost Raised for Slum Project," *New York Times*, January 20, 1960.

424. The *Slum Clearance Plan* put the total at 9.44 acres, but the area was enlarged to 10.63 acres by the time it was approved by the Board of Estimate. Paul Crowell, "City to Take Land for New Housing," *New York Times*, September 24, 1954.

425. Address at YMHA, New York City, November 29, 1983, cited by Cannell, *I. M. Pei*, 145.

426. The structure of Kips Bay Plaza realized an idea that Frank Lloyd Wright introduced in his San Francisco Call Building project (1912), which combined load-bearing walls and clear-span floors. Aldo Cossutta, a partner in Pei's firm, evokes the Wrightian ethos of organic structure in his account of Pei's concrete structures, "From Precast Concrete to Integral Architecture," *Progressive Architecture* 47, no. 10 (October 1966), 196–207.

427. Edward L. Friedman, "Cast-in-Place Technique Restudied," *Progressive Architecture* 41, no. 10 (October 1960), 158–75.

428. Among the contemporary writings on Kips Bay Plaza, the most informative are James Marston Fitch, "Housing in New York, Washington, Chicago and Philadelphia: Architect: I. M. Pei," *Architectural Review* 134, no. 799 (September 1963), 192–200; and Friedman, "Cast-in-Place Technique Restudied."

429. Pei's expressive description is cited in Walter McQuade, "Pei's Apartments Round the Corner, *Architectural Forum* 115 (August 1961), 11.

430. Compared to the scheme by Kessler for University Center, Inc., Zeckendorf added 9,000 square feet of commercial space and 320 apartments and doubled the capacity of the garage to 320 cars.

431. "What Price City Living?" *Architectural Forum* 119 (March 1964), 89.

432. No sooner were the buildings completed than Zeckendorf sold them in a failed effort to keep Webb & Knapp afloat. In 1964, the Alcoa Corporation bought Kips Bay Plaza, among several Title I projects that it acquired from Zeckendorf.

433. Murray Schumach, "Folk on Bellevue Housing Site Sad over Severing Neighborhood Ties," *New York Times*, March 1, 1954.

434. Moses, *Housing and Recreation*, 2.

435. Ibid., 29.

436. Ibid.

437. Kaplan and Kaplan, *Between Ocean and City*, 92.

438. "Rockaway Slums Are Slated to Go," *New York Times*, July 28, 1955.

439. Mayor's Committee on Slum Clearance, *Seaside Rockaway*, 3; and Mayor's Committee on Slum Clearance, *Hammels Rockaway*, 3.

440. *Seaside Rockaway*, 48.

441. "'Give-away' Seen in Slum Projects," *New York Times*, November 22, 1958.

442. "Barred Designer Has 2 Slum Jobs," *New York Times*, November 2, 1959.

443. "Clearance Begins on Rockaway Site," *New York Times*, December 18, 1959.

444. Kaplan and Kaplan, *Between Ocean and City*, 6.

445. Ibid., 103.

446. *New York Times*, August 26, 1962.

447. *New York Times*, July 17, 1966.

448. Dayton Beach Park is currently undergoing renovation, and brick accents are being added to the upper level exteriors of the five buildings.

449. "Rockaway Boom Slated to Begin," *New York Times*, October 26, 1958.

450. Charles Grutzner, "Stevens Expands Lincoln Sq. Plans," *New York Times*, October 27, 1956.

451. These calculations are based on figures in Mayor's Committee on Slum Clearance, *New York City Title I Progress. Quarterly Report on Slum Clearance* (April 1959), 24–25.

452. On the proliferation of arts centers in the 1960s, see Martin Mayer, *Bricks, Mortar and the Performing Arts: Report on the Twentieth Century Fund Task Force on Performing Arts Centers* (New York: Twentieth Century Fund, 1970). Between 1962 and 1969, 173 arts centers and theaters were completed in the U.S. and 179 were in planning. For a cost-benefit analysis, also see William J. Baumol and William G. Bowen, *Performing Arts: The Economic Dilemma* (New York: Twentieth Century Fund, 1966).

453. "The West Side's Turn," *New York Times*, April 25, 1955. The data about site conditions in this paragraph are drawn from the Slum Clearance Committee brochure.

454. Braislin, Porter and Wheelock, Inc. *The First 500 Families: A Relocation Analysis* (New York: [1958]).

455. Moses, letter to Harry Guggenheim [Solomon R. Guggenheim Foundation], August 24, 1953, NYPL, Moses Papers 9, Box 90.

456. Moses, telegram to Judge Samuel Rosenman, October 17, 1956, NYPL, Moses Papers, Box 116.

457. After his removal from Lincoln Square, Stevens proposed a new slum clearance project, combining theaters and housing near the Broadway theater district, from 45th to 48th Street west of Eighth Avenue, but it was opposed by theater interests and went nowhere. Stevens was a sponsor of the Southwest Washington Title I project in Washington, D.C., and the Church Street project in New Haven. See Lowe, *Cities in a Race with Time*, 178–79, 192–93, 427–63; and Allan R. Talbot, *The Mayor's Game: Richard Lee of New Haven and the Politics of Change* (New York: Harper & Row, 1967), chap. 9.

458. The Reverend Laurence J. McGinley [president of Fordham, 1949–63], interview by the Reverend Edward C. Zogby, July 9, 1982, and June 17, 1986, Fordham University Archives, Oral History Project. McGinley's recollection of the timing of the events he describes is not consistent with other documentary evidence. See Moses, letter to Laurence McGinley, December 8, 1954, and George A. Hammer, letter to William Lebwohl, January 18, 1955, and related documents in Fordham University Archives, Box Lin-Lu, Folder Lincoln Center Library for the Performing Arts. On Hammer see, "G. A. Hammer Sr. of Noyes Co. Dies," *New York Times*, August 11, 1957.

459. Moses, letter to Laurence J. McGinley, November 8, 1954, Fordham University Archives, Box Lin-Lu, Folder Lincoln Center C.L.C.

460. Caro, *Power Broker*, 1155–57.

461. Charles Grutzner, "Judge Questions Lincoln Sq. Plan," *New York Times*, February 14, 1958.

462. The *New York Times* extensively covered the lawsuit in 1958; see, in particular, "Text of Court [of Appeals] Ruling, *New York Times*, May 2, 1958; and Anthony Lewis, "Lincoln Sq. Plan Wins Clearance in Supreme Court," *New York Times*, June 10, 1958.

463. Dubbed a "business architect" by his detractors, Stephen Voorhees was the kind of architect Moses liked. Voorhees was chief architect of the 1939 New York World's Fair, designed Army bases during World War II, specialized in university design (he was supervising architect of Princeton from 1930 to 1949), and involved the firm in large housing projects, notably Fresh Meadows (1949), the 3,000-unit development built by the New York Life Insurance Company in Queens. "Stephen Francis Voorhees, 86, Designer of Skyscrapers, Dies," *New York Times*, January 25, 1965.

464. "Fordham Would Sell Parcel to a Developer," *New York Times*, February 23, 1986.

465. David W. Dunlap, "Cramped Fordham Plans to Expand at Lincoln Center, Mostly Skyward," *New York Times*, February 23, 2005.

466. Report to the Mayor from the Park Commissioner on the Proposed Municipal Music Art Center, September 20, 1938, typescript, NYPL Performing Arts; manuscript copy in NYPL, Moses Papers, Box 97.

467. On the history of the Metropolitan Opera House and Wallace Harrison's design of the new opera at Lincoln Center, see Victoria Newhouse's judicious account in *Wallace K. Harrison, Architect*, chaps. 17 and 18. Subsequent to the book, the Harrison archives were donated to Columbia University, Avery Architectural and Fine Arts, Library, Drawings and Archives Collection.

468. The site was bounded by West Broadway, Bleecker, Greene, and West 3rd streets. The price Moses proposed was $1.3 million, or $6 per square foot. Moses, letter to Col. Joseph M. Hartfield, November 10, 1952. NYPL, Moses Papers, Box 90.

469. The *New York Times* reported on April 9, 1955, that the Slum Clearance Committee "hoped to create a music and drama center in a group of new buildings into which the Metropolitan Opera, Philharmonic-Symphony and City Center might move," but the opera and symphony "had not shown interest." Russell Porter, "U.S. Aid Awaited on Slum Razing," *New York Times*, April 9, 1955. On Spofford's role, see *Performing Arts* 1, no. 9 (September 17, 1959).

470. An informal planning group began meeting in October 1955 but did not formally constitute itself as the Exploratory Committee until December. John D. Rockefeller 3rd, draft letter to Moses, April 5, 1957. Rockefeller Archive Center, Pocantico Hills, N.Y., Record Group III 17B, Box 51, Folder 541.

471. Columbia University, Avery Library, Drawings and Archives Collection, Max Abramovitz Architectural Drawings and Papers Collection, Project Records, Photographs from AKS Office Files, 81g.

472. Anthony A. Bliss [president, Metropolitan Opera Association], letters to Moses, January 30, 1956, and April 3, 1956. Rockefeller Archive Center, Record Group III 17B, Box 51, Folder 641.

473. The Board of Education originally planned to enlarge the School of Commerce on West 65th Street to include the High School of Performing Arts. In 1961, the board decided to combine the performing arts school with the larger High School of Music and Art, and commissioned Pietro Belluschi to design the high school in order to integrate it with his design of the neighboring Juilliard School. In 1963, the high school was relocated to a new Title I site on Amsterdam Avenue between 64th and 65th streets, and the West 65th Street site was made available for a Juilliard expansion.

474. After Rockefeller successfully lobbied federal officials for aid, Moses asked him to press for an expansion of the Title I area. He wanted to incorporate an educational television studio in Lincoln Square. Moses, letter to John D. Rockefeller 3rd, September 25, 1959, NYPL, Moses Papers, Box 118.

475. Charles Grutzner, "Moses Scores U.S. over Lincoln Sq." *New York Times*, July 24, 1957.

476. Kennedy rented the building to the U.S. Immigration Service and the U.S. Atomic Energy Commission. In a deal negotiated by Kennedy and Rockefeller and approved by Moses, the building was sold for $2.5 million, of which Lincoln Center was to pay $1.5 million and the city the balance. After the building was included in the project area, the leaders of Lincoln Center wanted the Title I discount extended to the Kennedy property, but Moses refused to revisit the terms of the deal, probably because he wanted to preserve any available Title I funds for another project and felt Lincoln Center could absorb the cost.

477. Minutes, Lincoln Center meeting, October 2–12, 1956, Columbia University, Avery Library, Abramovitz Collection, Box 18, Folder 5.

478. Moses, letter to Samuel Rosenman, October 20, 1956; Moses, memo to William S Lebwohl, October 22, 1956, NYPL Moses Papers, Box 116, Folder 4.

479. Minutes, meeting of the collaborating architects, December 20, 1958, Columbia University, Avery Library, Abramovitz Collection, Box 18, Folder 7.

480. Photographs of the models are located in Columbia University, Avery Library, Abramovitz Collection, Box 18, Folder 8.

481. Minutes, meeting of the collaborating architects, October 28, 1959, Columbia University, Avery Library, Abramovitz Collection, Box 18, Folder 8.

482. Minutes, Lincoln Center meeting, November 20, 1959, Columbia University, Avery Library, Abramovitz Collection, Box 18, Folder 9.

483. Moses, letter to Wallace K. Harrison, December 24, 1957, NYPL, Moses Papers, Box 116.

484. Otto L. Nelson [executive director of construction, Lincoln Center], letter to Walter S. Fried [administrator, Housing and Home Finance Agency], September 28, 1959. Rockefeller Archive Group, Rockefeller Family, Record Group 17B, Associates—Edgar B. Young, Series 1.9 Planning Construction, Box 43, Folder 532.

485. *Performing Arts* 3, no. 13 (January 26, 1962).

486. Moses, letter to Grayson Kirk [president of Columbia University], September 1, 1959, and Kirk's reply, September 3, NYPL, Moses Papers, Box 118.

487. Jacobs, *Death and Life of Great American Cities*, 168.

488. "Addresses by Eisenhower and Moses," *New York Times*, May 15, 1959.

489. Nathaniel Goldstein [attorney for Joseph Weiser], letter to Moses, September 3, 1957, NYPL, Moses Papers, Box 116, Folder 4.

490. Zeckendorf, with McCreary, *Autobiography*, 238.

491. Ownership of Lincoln Towers passed from Zeckendorf to Alcoa to William Zeckendorf Jr. and through several other hands before the buildings were converted to cooperative ownership in 1986.

492. Moses made these remarks at the groundbreaking ceremony for Lincoln Center, an inappropriate occasion for self-justification. "Addresses by Eisenhower and Moses," *New York Times*, May 15, 1969.

493. Quoted in "Moses Ridicules Chinatown Plan," *New York Times*, June 4, 1950.

494. Sidney J. Ungar, memo on the Riverside-Amsterdam project, undated [1959]. NYPL, Moses Papers, Box 118, Folder "Committee on Slum Clearance 1959."

495. Despite his reservations about the Riverside-Amsterdam plan, Moses said he would "recommend approval [of the project] to the Committee because I respect your judgment and want your support." Moses, letter to Hulan Jack, June 22, 1956, NYPL, Moses Papers, Box 116, Folder "1956 Robert Moses' Library Correspondence from Housing File Folder 1 of 3."

496. As Ungar had originally proposed, the structures the SCC recommended demolishing were primarily the smaller brownstones and tenements, while those to be left intact were primarily the larger, more modern apartment buildings. Thus, even though the percentage of structures to be demolished appears high at almost 70 percent, the plan proposes demolition on approximately half the land in the nine-block area.

497. Mayor's Committee on Slum Clearance, *Riverside-Amsterdam*. See also "New Slum Plans Drawn by Moses," *New York Times*, November 10, 1958.

498. Mayor's Committee on Slum Clearance, *Riverside-Amsterdam*, 3; "New Slum Plans Drawn by Moses"; "Title I Improvements," *World Telegram and Sun*, November 11, 1958; "Mayor Sees Need to Study Housing," *New York Times*, November 23, 1958.

499. For the exposé and Ungar's response, see "The Slum Properties of an Anti-Slum Leader," *New York Post*, February 14, 1959; "Landlord Loses Subpoena Pleas," *New York Times*, February 27, 1959. For Moses's recommendation, see memo from Moses to William Lebwohl, March 20, 1959, NYPL, Moses Papers, Box 118, Folder "Committee on Slum Clearance 1959." Charges for all but one of the buildings were dismissed on a technicality in early March; Ungar was acquitted on the remaining charges in June.

500. "City Vote Backs a Ban on Traffic in Washington Square," *New York Times*, April 10, 1959.

501. On Yeshiva's plans, see "Yeshiva May Seek Riverside Campus," *New York Times*, June 12, 1959; "Yeshiva is Seeking Co-Sponsor in Bid for Riverside Plan," *New York Times*, June 18, 1959; "Plan Body Scored At Slum Hearing," *New York Times*, February 4, 1960.

502. Yeshiva's interest must also have come as something of a relief to Moses, who had faced public criticism for including religious institutions as Title I sponsors in 1958, a debate sparked by Fordham University's participation in the Lincoln Square plan.

503. "Bank Deal Linked to Slum Project," *New York Times*, June 10, 1959.

504. For statements delivered at a news conference on December 17, 1959, see "Texts of the Statements by Ungar and Jack," *New York Times*, December 18, 1959. See also "Ungar Says He Aided Jack in Hope of Winning Favors," *New York Times*, June 21, 1960; "Moses Says Jack Cited Obligation to Aid Ungar Plan," *New York Times*, June 29, 1960.

505. "Tenants Support West Side Title I," *New York Times*, October 25, 1959; "1500 on West Side Back Title I Plan," *New York Times*, December 25, 1959.

506. At hearings held by the City Planning Commission in December 1958, the Reverend James Gusweller, the rector of the Episcopal Church of St. Matthew and St. Timothy, located a few blocks away from the project area, testified that it should be expanded to include the blocks between Amsterdam and Central Park West, pointing out that conditions there were even worse than in the project area. "City Weighs Drive on Slum 'Jungle,'" *New York Times*, January 3, 1959.

507. Gilbert Jonas, the president of the Reform Independent Democrats of the Fifth Assembly District South, accused backers of "exploiting the fears and ignorance of many West Side residents . . . [and] assert[ing] that the new project would rid the neighborhood of 'those undesirable nonwhites,' namely the Puerto Rican and Negro citizens." At Riverside-Amsterdam, almost all those slated for relocation were renters, and a high proportion of them—47 percent of the families, 55 percent of the single people, and 54 percent of the roomers—were African-American or Puerto Rican. "Project Backers Accused on Race," *New York Times*, January 12, 1960.

508. "City Reactivates Riverside-Amsterdam Project," *New York Times*, June 28, 1963.

509. "Decision Nearing on Renewal Projects Planned under Mayor Wagner," *New York Times*, May 5, 1966.

510. David Rockefeller, *Memoirs* (New York: Random House, 2002), 387–88.

511. Austin C. Wehrwein, "Project Builder Tries to Bring Suburban Amenities to Cities," *New York Times*, February 16, 1958. In 1958, Greenwald's commissions accounted for two-thirds of the work in Mies's office (Phyllis Lambert, "Mies Immersion," in *Mies in America* [New York, 2002], 361).

512. Greer, *Urban Renewal and American Cities*, chap. 3.

513. Charles Grutzner, "Gramercy Group Protests Razing," *New York Times*, March 5, 1959.

514. The syndicate included the Moritz Oestreicher Trust and William Oestreicher. Weiser's wife was Ruth Oestreicher.

515. "Gramercy Award Decried to Mayor," *New York Times*, March 7, 1959.

516. Thomas W. Ennis, "Large Co-ops Due in the East Bronx," *New York Times*, June 14, 1959.

517. "City Urged to Push Bronx Housing Unit," *New York Times*, March 16, 1959.

518. For Goldwater's connection to Moses, see Caro, *Power Broker*, 720–21.

519. Wayne Phillips, "Slum 'Deal' Data Sent to City Hall," *New York Times*, June 18, 1959; idem, "Politician's Aide Owns Housing Site," *New York Times*, June 19, 1959.

520. "Text of Statements by Moses on Project in Bronx," *New York Times*, June 22, 1959.

521. "Mayor Revives Bronx Project," *New York Times*, October 8, 1959.

522. Theodore Jones, "City Wasteland Gets a New Face," *New York Times*, June 24, 1962.

523. Mayor's Committee on Slum Clearance, *Cadman Plaza*, 22.

524. Ibid., 14.

525. Martin S. James, *Cadman Plaza in Brooklyn Heights: A Study of the Misuse of Public Power and Funds in Urban Renewal* (New York: Brooklyn College, 1961), 18.

526. Paul Goldberger, "Design Awards: Skill, But No Innovation," *New York Times*, October 27, 1974.

527. "Chatham Towers," *Empire State Architect* (March–April 1965), 28

528. Ellen Perry, "Middle Income Project in Lower Manhattan," *Progressive Architecture* (February 1966), 132–39.

529. Quoted in "1967 Bard Awards Announced," *Empire State Architect* (May–June 1967), 7.

530. J. Anthony Panuch, *Building a Better New York. Final Report to Mayor Robert F. Wagner* (New York: Office of the Mayor, 1960), 22.

531. Ibid., 94.

532. Peter Kihss, "City Candidates Offer Plans for New Housing and Schools," *New York Times*, October 19, 1953.

533. Warren Moscow, *What Have You Done For Me Lately? The Ins and Outs of New York City Politics* (Englewood Cliffs, N.J.: Prentice-Hall, 1967), 203–4.

534. See "Mayor Rebuffed on Housing Plan," *New York Times*, March 19, 1954; Charles Grutzner, "Billion Spent in Housing Since '36 Yet One in Five Here Is Slum Dweller," *New York Times*, March 15, 1954.

535. Thomas W. Ennis, "State or City Aid Given to 25 Co-ops," *New York Times*, June 29, 1959.

536. MacNeil Mitchell, letter to Moses, June 22, 1956; Moses, letter to MacNeil Mitchell, July 5, 1956; Folder M, 1956; Moses, "For Mr. J. Anthony Panunch, Rough Miscellaneous Notes," November 30, 1959, NYPL, Moses Papers, Folder P, 1959.

537. The first possibility is suggested by Caro, *Power Broker*, 891. One exception to the mixing of Title I and Mitchell-Lama funds occurred after Moses's exit as City Construction Coordinator, when the Board of Estimate required NYU to build middle-income Mitchell-Lama cooperatives on part of Title I land they had acquired; see the entry on Washington Square South Title I.

538. Moses, "For Mr. J. Anthony Panunch,"

539. New York State Division of Housing and Community Renewal, "Mitchell-Lama Housing Program," www.dhrc.state.ny.us/ohm/progs/mitchlam/ohmprgmi.htm.

540. State Study Commission for New York City, "New York City's Mitchell-Lama Housing Program: The Management of the Middle-Income Housing Project by the Housing and Development Administration of New York City," 1973.

541. See also Stern, Gilmartin, and Mellins, *New York 1930*, 969–71; and Paul D. Naish, "Fantasia Bronxiana: Freedomland and Co-op City," *New York History* 82 (2001), 259–85.

542. "The Lessons of Co-op City," *Time* 93 (January 24, 1969), 30.

543. Ada Louise Huxtable, "A Singularly New York Product," *New York Times*, November 25, 1968.

544. Denise Scott Brown and Robert Venturi, "Co-op City: Learning to Like It," *Progressive Architecture* 51 (February 1970), 64–73.

545. Ada Louise Huxtable, "Co-op City's Grounds: After Three Years, A Success," *New York Times*, October 26, 1971.

546. Moses, *Public Works*, 470.

547. For an account of the rent strike from the perspective of the strike leaders, see Ian Frazier, "Utopia, the Bronx: Co-op City and Its People," *New Yorker* (June 26, 2006), 54–65.

548. Moses, letter to John Cashmore, August 22, 1955, NYPL, Moses Papers, Box 44, folder B; Moses, letter to F.M. Flynn [publisher of the Daily News], August 22, 1955, Box 44, folder C.

549. For the text of his speech on the use of the Jamaica Race Track, see Robert Moses, "The Role of Housing Cooperatives in Urban Development," *Co-op Contact*, November 1956.

550. Moses, letter to Nelson Rockefeller, January 14, 1960, New York City Municipal Archives, Robert F Wagner Papers, Subject Files, Housing–Rochdale.

551. "The Reminiscences of Abraham Kazan" (1970), 493, in the Oral History Collection of Columbia University.

552. For Moses's opposition to antidiscrimination legislation in the mid-1940s, see Biondi, *To Stand and Fight*, 19, 121–36. His views on civil rights in the late 1950s defy a neat summary. He is quoted in 1956 as saying his fight against open-housing legislation was necessary to keep private capital available for urban housing, though he also felt that the efforts of Metropolitan Life to keep blacks out of its Stuyvesant Town development had been "grievously ill-advised" (*New York Post*, July 1, 1956). Also in the same year, writing to his friend Herbert Bayard Swope, a member of the city's Commission on Intergroup Relations, Moses argued that the agenda of the committee if "fanatically attempted [will] set the clock back a quarter of a century." His fundamental belief seems to have been that all progress in the area of civil rights needed "to be evolutionary and not forced." Moses, letter to Herbert Bayard Swope, NYPL, Moses Papers, January 6, 1956, Box 45, folder Swope.

553. As early as 1946, he wrote to a private developer that a nondiscriminatory clause would be a requirement for any use of city's eminent domain power, saying that "certainly some respectable colored families won't hurt the project." Cited in Schwartz, *New York Approach*, 126.

554. Ibid., 136–43. See also Kaplan and Kaplan, *Between Ocean and City*, 88–89. On the UHF's commitment to open housing, see Bea and Jack Moss, "One of Queensview's Most Distinguished Families," *Co-op Contact* (March 1956), on Henry Lee Moon, the NAACP's director of publicity, who became a member of the board of Queensview and later served on the board of directors of the UHF and Rochdale Village. See also Eleanor Roosevelt, "Housing for Everyone," *Co-op Contact* (May 1956).

555. Moses, letter to Elmer Carter, March 13, 1959, NYPL, Moses Papers, folder C, 1959.

556. "Reminiscences of Abraham Kazan," 504. This is confirmed by Nicholas Gyory, telephone interview with author, October 2005.

557. "Jamaica Project Please Moses," *New York Times*, May 18, 1959. Moses closed his plea to Rockefeller by stating, "I need not emphasize the fact that this is the largest and most sufficient middle income coop project in the country and that it does not involve moving people." Robert Moses, letter to Nelson Rockefeller, January 14, 1960, New York City, Municipal Archives, Robert F Wagner Papers, Subject Files, Housing—Rochdale.

558. Robert Moses, "Rochdale: Master Planner Moses Views a Master Housing Plan," *Long Island Press*, December 1, 1963. See also Moses, "Rochdale Village: A Model for the Future," *Newsday*, February 3, 1968.

559. Harvey Swados, "Where Black and White Live Together," *New York Times Magazine* (November 13, 1966), 47, 102ff.

560. Bernard Seeman, "Rochdale Village Must Set an Example," *Inside Rochdale*, November 26, 1966.

561. Bliss K. Thorne, "Aviation: New Terminal," *New York Times*, July 12, 1953.

562. Armand Schwab Jr., "New York's New Air Terminal," *New York Times*, November 8, 1953.

563. "Contracts Signed for Airline Depot," *New York Times*, July 4, 1951.

564. "New Terminal to Get All Airport Buses," *New York Times*, September 25, 1953.

565. Schwab, "Progress Report," *New York Times*, July 15, 1954.

566. "Triborough Sets Traffic Record," *New York Times*, March 7, 1955.

567. Frank J. Prial, "East Side Airline Terminal to Remain Open, for Now," *New York Times*, October 17, 1973.

568. "Metropolitan Briefs: Airline Terminal Closing Fought," *New York Times*, September 26, 1973.

569. Alan S. Oser, "Zone Shift Spurs Housing on the East Side," *New York Times*, September 12, 1986.

570. Robert Moses, "'Natural and Proper Home of the UN'—Moses States the Case for New York, and Flushing Meadows, as the Capital of the World," *New York Times*, October 20 1946.

571. Moses, *Public Works*, 485.

572. Trygve Lie, *In the Cause of Peace: Seven Years with the United Nations* (New York: Macmillan, 1954), 112.

573. Robert P. Wagner, Jr., Borough President of Manhattan, and Robert Moses, City Construction Coordinator, *The United Nations and the City of New York*, November 1951 (brochure).

574. Quoted in Stern, Mellins, and Fishman, *New York 1960*, 617.

575. Stern, Mellins, and Fishman, *New York 1960*, 614.

576. "William Zeckendorf, "Proposed UN Concourse," *New York Times*, August 12, 1947.

577. *United Nations and the City of New York*.

578. "Moses Faces Rebuff on U.N. Playground," *New York Times*, December 17, 1949.

579. Gilmore Clarke was also commissioned to design the landscaping of the UN site.

580. "Approve Final Plan for Disputed U.N. Playground," *Architectural Record* 112 (October 1952), 366.

581. Moses, quoted in "Striking a Balance on Robert Moses," *New York Times*, July 15, 1956.

SELECTED BIBLIOGRAPHY

Abrams, Charles. *The City Is the Frontier*. New York: Harper and Row, 1965.

———. *Forbidden Neighbors: A Study of Prejudice in Housing*. New York: Harper, 1955.

Altshuler, Alan A., and David Luberoff. *Mega-Projects: The Changing Politics of Urban Investment*. Washington: Brookings Institution, 2003.

Anderson, Martin. *The Federal Bulldozer: A Critical Analysis of Urban Renewal, 1949–1962*. Cambridge, Mass.: M.I.T. Press, 1964.

"Astoria Pool Pavilion, John Matthews Hatton, Architect." *Architectural Forum* 67 (August 1937), 127–28.

Augur, Tracy B. "An Analysis of the Plan of Stuyvesant Town." *Journal of the American Institute of Planners* (autumn 1944), 9.

Bachin, Robin. *Building the South Side: Urban Space and Civic Culture in Chicago, 1890–1919*. Chicago: University of Chicago Press, 2004.

Barlow Rogers, Elizabeth. *Rebuilding Central Park*. Cambridge, Mass.: M.I.T. Press, 1987.

Bellush, Jewel, and Murray Hausknecht, eds. *Urban Renewal: People, Politics and Planning*. Garden City, N.Y.: Anchor Books, 1967.

Berman, Marshall. *All That Is Solid Melts into Air: The Experience of Modernity*. New York: Simon and Schuster, 1982.

Biondi, Martha. *To Stand and Fight: The Struggle for Civil Rights in Postwar New York*. Cambridge, Mass.: Harvard University Press, 2003.

Black, Elinor G. *Manhattantown Two Years Later: A Second Look at Tenant Relocation*. New York: Women's Club of New York, 1956.

Blumberg, Barbara. *The New Deal and the Unemployed: The View from New York City*. Lewisburg, Pa.: Bucknell University Press, 1979.

Bracher, Howard, et al. Recreation, special issue, "The World at Play" 25, no. 8 (November 1931).

Bressi, Todd W. "Parkway, Beach, and Promenade: Robert Moses' Regional Vision." Places 6, no. 2 (1990), 90–91.

Bullard, Robert D., Glenn S. Johnson, and Angel O. Torres, eds. *Highway Robbery: Transportation Racism and New Routes to Equity*. Cambridge, Mass.: South End Press, 2004.

Buttenwieser, Ann L. "Awash in New York: A Chronicle of the City's Floating Baths." *Seaport* 18, no. 1 (1984), 12–19.

———. "Awash in New York City: A Chronicle of the City's Floating Baths." *New York Archives* 2, no. 1 (2002), 8–11.

———. *Manhattan Water-Bound: Planning and Developing Manhattan's Waterfront from the Seventeenth Century to the Present*. New York: New York University Press, 1987.

———. "Shelter for What and For Whom? On the Route Toward Vladeck Houses, 1930 to 1940." *Journal of Urban History* 12, no. 4 (August 1986), 391–413.

Campanella, Thomas J. "American Curves: Gilmore D. Clarke and the Modern Civil Landscape." *Harvard Design Magazine* 1, no. 2 (1997), 40–43.

Cannell, Michael. *I. M. Pei: Mandarin of Modernism*. New York: Carol Southern, 1995.

Caro, Robert A. *The Power Broker: Robert Moses and the Fall of New York*. New York: Knopf, 1974.

Cavaglieri, Giorgio. "Ten W.P.A. Play Centers." New York: Building Structure Inventory Form, New York State Office of Parks, Recreation and Historic Preservation, 1990.

City of New York Department of Parks. *Six Years of Progress*, report to the mayor. January 1940.

———. *Eight Years of Progress*, report to the mayor. October 1941.

———. *12 Years of Progress*, report to the mayor. October 1945.

———. *18 Years of Progress: Report to the Mayor and the Board of Estimate*. March 1952.

———. *20 Years of Progress: Report to the Mayor and the Board of Estimate*. March 1954.

———. *24 Years of Progress: Report to the Mayor and the Board of Estimate*. January 1958.

———. *26 Years of Progress: Report to the Mayor and the Board of Estimate*. January 1960.

———. *28 Years of Progress: Report to the Mayor and the Board of Estimate*. June 1962.

———. *30 Years of Progress: Report to the Mayor and the Board of Estimate*. June 1964.

Clurman, David, et al. *Condominiums and Cooperatives*. Second ed. New York: Wiley, 1984.

Condit, Carl W. *The Port of New York: A History of the Rail and Terminal System from the Grand Central Electrification to the Present*. Chicago: University of Chicago Press, 1981.

Coplan, Joseph. "Urban Waters." *Metropolis* (July–August 1987), 66–70.

Cormier, Francis. "Some New York City Parks and Parkways: Recreational Developments Made since 1934." *Landscape Architecture* 29 (April 1939), 124–36.

Cranz, Galen. *The Politics of Park Design: A History of Urban Parks in America*. Cambridge, Mass.: M.I.T. Press, 1982.

Curran, Cynthia Ann. *Administration of Subsidized Housing in New York State Co-op City: A Case Study of the Largest Subsidized Cooperative Housing Development in the Nation*. Ann Arbor: UMI, 1978.

Cutler, Phoebe. *The Public Landscape of the New Deal*. New Haven: Yale University Press, 1985.

Davidson, Judith Anne. "The Federal Government and the Democratization of Public Recreational Sport: New York City, 1933–43." Ph.D. diss., University of Massachusetts, 1983.

Davies, J. Clarence, III. *Neighborhood Groups and Urban Renewal*. New York: Columbia University Press, 1966.

Davis, Timothy. "Mount Vernon Memorial Highway and the Evolution of the American Parkway." Ph.D. diss., University of Texas, 1997.

Doig, Jameson W. *Empire on the Hudson: Entrepreneurial Vision and Political Power at the Port of New York Authority*. New York: Columbia University Press, 2001.

Duffy, John. *A History of Public Health in New York City*. New York: Russell Sage Foundation, 1974.

Dulles, Foster Rhea. America Learns to Play. New York: D. Appleton-Century, 1940.

Elias, Norbert. *The Civilizing Process: The History of Manners*. Trans. Edmund Jephcott. Vol. 1. New York: Urizen Books, 1978.

Embury II, Aymar. "Using the Orders with Freedom." *Architecture* 54, no. 5 (November 1926), 323–28.

———. "Aesthetics of Concrete." *Pencil Points* 19 (May 1938), 266–79.

Felt, James, New York City Department of City Planning. *A Report on the West Side Urban Renewal Study to Mayor Robert F. Wagner and the Board of Estimate of the City of New York, and to the Urban Renewal Administration* [1958].

Field, Corinne T., and Marilyn Thornton Williams. "Bathhouses." In Jackson, ed., *Encyclopedia of New York City*, 87–88.

Fletcher, Ellen, and John J. Gallagher. "Red Hook." In Jackson, ed., *Encyclopedia of New York City*, 991–92.

Frykman, Jonas. "On the Move: The Struggle for the Body in Sweden." In C. Nadia Seremetakis, ed., *The Senses Still: Perception and Memory as Material Culture in Modernity*, 63–86. Chicago: University of Chicago Press, 1994.

Foster, Mark S. *From Streetcar to Superhighway: American City Planners and Urban Transportation, 1900–1940*. Temple University Press, 1981.

Gans, Herbert J. "The Human Implications of Current Redevelopment and Relocation Planning." *Journal of the American Institute of Planners* (February 1959), 16–25.

———. "The Failure of Urban Renewal: A Critique and Some Proposals." *Commentary* (April 1965.), 29–37.

Garvin, Alexander. *The American City: What Works, What Doesn't*. New York: McGraw-Hill, 1996.

Gelfand, Mark I. *A Nation of Cities. The Federal Government and Urban America, 1933–1965*. New York: Oxford University Press, 1975.

Genevro, Rosalie. "Site Selection and the New York City Housing Authority, 1934–39." *Journal of Urban History* 12, no. 4 (August 1986), 334–52.

Goldberger, Paul. "Robert Moses, Master Builder, Is Dead at 92," *New York Times*, July 30, 1981.

Goodman, Percival. "Lincoln Center, Emporium of the Arts." *Dissent* (summer 1961), 333–38.

Graff, M. M. *Central Park, Prospect Park: A New Perspective*. New York: Greensward Foundation, 1985.

Greer, Scott A. *Urban Renewal and American Cities: The Dilemma of Democratic Intervention*. Indianapolis: Bobbs-Merrill, 1965.

Gutfreund, Owen D. "The Path of Prosperity: New York City's East River Drive, 1922–1990." *Journal of Urban History* 21, no. 2 (January 1995), 147–83.

———. "Robert Moses" in *American National Biography*. New York: Oxford University Press, 2006.

———. *Twentieth-Century Sprawl: Highways and the Reshaping of the American Landscape*. New York: Oxford University Press, 2004.

Gutman, Marta. "What Kind of City: The Charitable Landscape That Women Built in Oakland, California." Chicago: University of Chicago Press, forthcoming.

Hamlin, Talbot F. "The Battery Park Competition." *New Pencil Points* (November 1942), 71–74.

Hanmer, Lee Franklin. *Public Recreation: A Study of Parks, Playgrounds, and Other Outdoor Recreation Facilities*. Edited by Thomas Adams, Frederick W. Loede Jr., Charles J. Storey and Frank B. Williams. Vol. 5, *Regional Survey of New York and Its Environs*. New York: Regional Plan of New York and Environs, 1928.

Henderson, A. Scott. *Housing and the Democratic Ideal: The Life and Thought of Charles Abrams*. New York: Columbia University Press, 2000.

Herring, Hugo. "Robert Moses and His Parks." *Harper's Magazine* 176 (December 1937), 26–37.

Iannacone, Rachel E. "Open Space for the Underclass: New York's Small Parks (1880–1915)." Ph.D. diss., University of Pennsylvania, 2005.

Irving, Carter. "Parks for Seven Million: A Vision Realized." *New York Times Sunday Magazine*, (August 16, 1936), 10–11, 19.

Jackson, Kenneth T., ed. *The Encyclopedia of New York City*. New Haven and New York: Yale University Press and the New-York Historical Society, 1995.

Jackson, Kenneth T. "Robert Moses and the Planned Environment: A Re-Evaluation." In Krieg, ed., *Robert Moses*, 21–30.

Jacobs, Jane. *The Death and Life of Great American Cities*. New York: Random House, 1961.

Joint Study of Arterial Facilities, New York-New Jersey Metropolitan Area. New York: Port of New York Authority and Triborough Bridge and Tunnel Authority, 1955.

Kaplan, Harold. *Urban Renewal Politics. Slum Clearance in Newark*. New York: Columbia University Press, 1963.

———, and Carol P. Kaplan. *Between Ocean and City: The Transformation of Rockaway, New York*. New York: Columbia University Press, 2003.

Kaufman, Peter S. *Designing the Moses Era: The Architecture and Engineering of Aymar Embury II*. Hempstead, N.Y.: Hofstra University, 1988.

Kessner, Thomas. *Fiorello H. La Guardia and the Making of Modern New York*. New York: McGraw-Hill, 1989.

Kocher, A. Lawrence, and Robert L. Davison, "Swimming Pools (Standards for Design and Construction)." *Architectural Record* 65, no. 1 (January 1929), 71–73.

Kohn, Margaret. *Radical Space: Building the House of the People*. Ithaca, N.Y.: Cornell University Press, 2003.

Krieg, Joann P., ed. *Robert Moses: Single-Minded Genius*. Long Island Studies Conference, Hofstra University, 1988. Interlocken, N.Y.: Heart of Lakes Press, 1989.

Kroessler, Jeffrey A. "Robert Moses and the New Deal in Queens." In Krieg, ed., *Robert Moses: Single-Minded Genius*, 101–8.

———, and Nina S. Rappaport. *Historic Preservation in Queens*. Sunnyside, N.Y.: Queensboro Preservation League, 1990.

Latham, William H. "Swimming Pool Construction." *American Architect and Architecture* 149 (November 1936), 33–34.

Lawson, Ronald, ed. *The Tenant Movement in New York City, 1904–1984*. New Brunswick, N.J.: Rutgers University Press, 1986.

Leighninger Jr., Robert D. "Cultural Infrastructure: The Legacy of New Deal Public Space." *Journal of Architectural Education* 49, no. 4 (May 1996), 226–36.

Lopate, Phillip. "Rethinking Robert Moses." *Metropolis* (August–September 2002), 42–48.

Lowe, Jeanne R. *Cities in a Race with Time: Progress and Poverty in America's Renewing Cities*. New York: Random House, 1967.

Lubar, Harvey. *Building Orchard Beach*. New York: Department of Parks and Recreation, July 25, 1986.

Marcus, Benjamin Luke. "Last One In: Community, Conflict, and the Preservation of McCarren Park Pool." Master's thesis, Columbia University, 2006.

Marcuse, Peter. "The Beginnings of Public Housing in New York." *Journal of Urban History* 12, no. 4 (August 1986), 353–90.

Mayor's Committee on Slum Clearance. *Battery Park: Slum Clearance Plan Under Title I of the Housing Act of 1949* (Plan 22). New York: January 19, 1959.

———. *Cadman Plaza. Slum Clearance Plan Under Title I of the Housing Act of 1949* (Plan 25). New York: April 20, 1959.

———. *Columbus Circle: Slum Clearance Plan Under Title I of the Housing Act of 1949* (Plan 10). New York: December 1952.

———. *Corlears Hook: Slum Clearance Plan Under Title I of the Housing Act of 1949* (Plan 4). New York: January 1951.

———. *Delancey Street: Slum Clearance Plan Under Title I of the Housing Act of 1949* (Plan 3). New York: January 1951.

———. *Fort Greene: Slum Clearance Plan Under Title I of the Housing Act of 1949* (Plan 11). New York: December 1952.

———. *Gramercy Park: Slum Clearance Plan Under Title I of the Housing Act of 1949* (Plan 23). New York: January 16, 1959.

———. *Hammels Rockaway: Slum Clearance Plan Under Title I of the Housing Act of 1949* (Plan 19). New York: November 12, 1956.

———. *Harlem: Slum Clearance Plan Under Title I of the Housing Act of 1949* (Plan 5). New York: January 1951.

———. *Lincoln Square: Slum Clearance Plan Under Title I of the Housing Act of 1949* (Plan 16). New York: May 28, 1956.

———. *Manhattantown: Slum Clearance Plan Under Title I of the Housing Act of 1949* (Plan 9). New York: September 1951.

———. *Morningside-Manhattanville: Slum Clearance Plan Under Title I of the Housing Act of 1949* (Plan 8). New York: September 1951.

———. *North Harlem: Slum Clearance Plan Under Title I of the Housing Act of 1949* (Plan 6). New York: January 1951.

———. *NYU-Bellevue: Slum Clearance Plan Under Title I of the Housing Act of 1949* (Plan 12). New York: [1953].

———. *Park Row: Slum Clearance Plan Under Title I of the Housing Act of 1949* (Plan 18). October 15, 1956.

———. *Park Row Extension: Slum Clearance Plan Under Title I of the Housing Act of 1949* (Plan 26). New York: June 8, 1959.

———. *Penn Station South: Slum Clearance Plan Under Title I of the Housing Act of 1949* (Plan 20). New York: August 19, 1957.

———. *Pratt Institute Area: Slum Clearance Plan Under Title I of the Housing Act of 1949* (Plan 13). New York: July 1953.

———. *Preliminary Report on Initial New York City Projects under Title I of the Housing Act of 1949*. New York: July 14, 1949.

———. *Riverside-Amsterdam: Slum Clearance Plan Under Title I of the Housing Act of 1949* (Plan 21). New York: November 10, 1958.

———. *Seaside Rockaway: Slum Clearance Plan Under Title I of the Housing Act of 1949* (Plan 15). New York: October 1954.

———. *Second Report to Mayor William O'Dwyer from the Mayor's Committee on Slum Clearance by Private Capital*. New York: January 23, 1950.

———. *Seward Park: Slum Clearance Plan Under Title I of the Housing Act of 1949* (Plan 17). New York: August 29, 1956.

———. *Soundview: Slum Clearance Plan Under Title I of the Housing Act of 1949* (Plan 24). New York: March 16, 1959.

———. *South Village: Slum Clearance Plan Under Title I of the Housing Act of 1949* (Plan 2). New York: January 1951.

———. *Washington Square South: Slum Clearance Plan Under Title I of the Housing Act of 1949* (Plan 1). New York: January 1951.

———. *Washington Square Southeast: Slum Clearance Plan Under Title I of the Housing Act of 1949* (Plan 14). New York: August 1953.

———. *Williamsburg: Slum Clearance Plan Under Title I of the Housing Act of 1949* (Plan 7). New York: January 1951.

Metropolitan Conference on Parks. *Program for Extension of Parks and Parkways in the Metropolitan Region*. New York: 1930.

Meyerson, Martin, and Edward C. Banfield. *Politics, Planning and the Public Interest: The Case of Public Housing in Chicago*. New York: Free Press, 1955.

M'Gonigle, G. C. M., and J. Kirby. *Poverty and Public Health*. London: V. Gollancz, 1936.

Miller, Richard A. "Lincoln Center: 'A New Kind of Institution.'" *Architectural Forum* 109 (August 1958), 74–78.

Miller, Sara Cedar. *Central Park: An American Masterpiece*. New York: Harry N. Abrams, 2003.

Millett, John D. *The Works Progress Administration in New York City*. Chicago: Committee on Public Administration, Social Science Research Council, 1938.

Moses, Robert. *The Civil Service of Great Britain*. New York: Columbia University Press, 1914.

———. Housing and Recreation. New York: DeVinne Brown, 1938.

———. *La Guardia: A Salute and a Memoir*. New York: Simon and Schuster, 1957.

———. "Mr. Moses Dissects the 'Long-Haired Planners.'" *New York Times Magazine* (June 25, 1944), 16–17, 38, 39.

———. "Municipal Recreation." *American Architect and Architecture* 149 (November 1936), 21–32.

———. "Parks, Parkways, Express Arteries, and Related Plans for New York City after the War." *American City* 58 (December 1943), 53–58.

———. "Plan and Performance," in *A Century of Social Thought: A Series of Lectures Delivered at Duke University* . . . Durham, N.C.: Duke University Press, 1939, 126–42.

———. "Public Swimming Facilities in New York City." Press release, New York City Department of Parks, July 23, 1934.

———. *Public Works: A Dangerous Trade*. New York: McGraw-Hill, 1970.

———. "What Happened to Haussmann?" *Architectural Forum* 77 (July 1942), 57–66.

———. "What's the Matter with New York?" *New York Times Magazine* (August 1, 1943), 8.

———. *Working for the People: Promise and Performance in Public Service*. New York: Harper, 1956.

Mulholland, James V. "The Multiple Uses of Recreation Facilities." *Recreation* 33, no. 1 (April 1939), 28–30.

Lewis Mumford. *The City in History: Its Origins, Its Transformations, and Its Prospects*. New York: Harcourt, Brace, and World, 1961.

———. *The Highway and the City*. New York: New American Library, 1964.

———. *Sidewalk Critic: Lewis Mumford's Writings on New York*. Edited by Robert Wojtowicz. New York: Princeton Architectural Press, 2000.

Nasaw, David. *Children of the City: At Work and at Play*. Garden City, N.Y.: Anchor /Doubleday, 1985.

Newhouse, Victoria. *Wallace K. Harrison, Architect*. New York: Rizzoli, 1989.

Panuch, J. Anthony. *Building a Better New York: Final Report to Mayor Robert F. Wagner*. New York: Office of the Mayor, March 1, 1960.

"Pattern for Parks." *Architectural Forum* 65 (December 1936), 490–510.

Petroski, Henry. *Engineers of Dreams: Great Bridge Builders and the Spanning of America*. New York: Alfred A. Knopf, 1975.

Plunz, Richard. *A History of Housing in New York City: Dwelling Type and Social Change in the Metropolis*. New York: Columbia University Press, 1990.

Pritchett, Wendell. *Brownsville, Brooklyn: Blacks, Jews, and the Changing Face of the Ghetto*. Chicago: University of Chicago Press, 2002.

Rapkin, Chester. *The Real Estate Market in an Urban Renewal Area. Tenure Ownership and Price of Residential Real Property in a Twenty-Block Area of Manhattan's West Side*. New York: Planning Commission, 1959.

Rastorfer, Darl. *Six Bridges: The Legacy of Othmar H. Ammann*. New Haven: Yale University Press, 2000.

Rawson, Elizabeth Reich. "Brownsville." In Jackson, ed., *Encyclopedia of New York City*, 163.

"Redevelopment Today." *Architectural Forum* 108 (April 1958), 108–13.

Regional Plan Association. *Regional Plan of New York and Its Environs*, 2 vols. New York: 1929, 1931.

———. *Regional Survey of New York and Its Environs*, vol. 3. New York: 1927.

Reier, Sharon. *The Bridges of New York*. New York: Quadrant, 1977.

The Reminiscences of Abraham Kazan, 1968. Oral History Collection of Columbia University.

Renner, Andrea. "A Nation that Bathes Together: The Structuring of Morality and Class in New York City's Progressive Era Public Baths." Master's thesis, University of Delaware, 2005.

"Robert (or-I'll-Resign) Moses." *Fortune* 17, no. 6 (June 1938), 71–79ff.

"Robert Moses—Park Creator Extraordinary." *Recreation* 32, no. 5 (August 1938), 289–91.

Robbins, L. H. "Gay Days for the City Parks." *New York Times Sunday Magazine* (August 30, 1936), 10, 17.

Rodgers, Cleveland. *Robert Moses: Builder for Democracy*. New York: Henry Holt, 1952.

Rose, Mark H. *Interstate: Express Highway Politics 1939–1989*. Revised ed. Knoxville: University of Tennessee, (1979) 1990.

Rosenzweig, Roy, and Elizabeth Blackmar. *The Park and the People: A History of Central Park*. Ithaca, N.Y.: Cornell University Press, 1992.

Schwartz, Joel. "Moses, Robert." In Jackson, ed. *Encyclopedia of New York City*, 774–75.

———. *The New York Approach: Robert Moses, Urban Liberals, and Redevelopment of the Inner City*. Columbus: Ohio State University Press, 1993.

Seely, Bruce A. *Building the American Highway System*. Philadelphia: Temple University Press, 1987.

Sert, José Luis. *Can Our Cities Survive?* Cambridge, Mass.: Harvard University Press, 1942.

Short, C. W., and R. Stanley-Brown. *Public Buildings: A Survey of Architecture of Projects Constructed by Federal and Other Governmental Bodies between the Years 1933 and 1939 with the Assistance of the Public Works Administration*. Washington, D.C.: Government Printing Office, 1939.

Snyder-Grenier, Ellen Marie. "Sunset Park." In Jackson, ed., *Encyclopedia of New York City*, 1143–44.

Spears, Betty, and Richard A. Swanson. *History of Sport and Physical Activity in the United States*. Edited by Elaine T. Smith. 2nd ed. Dubuque, Iowa:William C. Brown, 1983.

Stern, Robert A. M., Gregory Gilmartin, and Thomas Mellins. *New York 1930: Architecture and Urbanism between the Two World Wars*. New York: Rizzoli, 1987.

———, Thomas Mellins, and David Fishman. *New York 1960: Architecture and Urbanism between the Second World War and the Bicentennial*. New York: Monacelli, 1995.

Triborough Bridge Authority. *Brooklyn Battery Bridge*. New York: January 23, 1939.

———. *The Triborough Bridge Authority Fifth Anniversary*. New York: 1941.

Triborough Bridge and Tunnel Authority. *Spanning the Narrows*. New York: November 21, 1964.

Van Leeuwen, Thomas A. P. *The Springboard in the Pond: An Intimate History of the Swimming Pool*. Cambridge, Mass.: M.I.T. Press, 1998.

Vernon, Raymond. *Metropolis 1985: An Interpretation of the Findings of the New York Metropolitan Region Study*. Cambridge, Mass.: Harvard University Press, 1960.

Vural, Leyla F. *Unionism as a Way of Life: The Community Orientation of the International Ladies' Garment Workers' Union and the Amalgamated Clothing Workers of America*. Ann Arbor: UMI, 1994

Waldheim, Charles, ed., *CASE: Hilberseimer/Mies van der Rohe*. Lafayette Park Detroit. Munich, 2004.

Weaver, Robert C. *The Urban Complex: Human Values in Urban Life*. Garden City, N.Y.: Doubleday, 1964.

Williams, Marilyn Thornton. *Washing the Great Unwashed: Public Baths in Urban America, 1840–1920*. Columbus: Ohio State University Press, 1991.

Wilson, James Q., ed. *Urban Renewal: The Record and the Controversy*. Cambridge, Mass.: M.I.T. Press, 1966.

Worpole, Ken. *Here Comes the Sun: Architecture and Public Space in Twentieth-Century European Culture*. London: Reaktion, 2000.

Zapatka, Christian. "In Progress's Own Image: The New York that Robert Moses Built." *Lotus International* 89 (1996), 102–31.

Zeckendorf, William, with Edward McCreary, *The Autobiography of William Zeckendorf*. Chicago, 1987 (reprint); 1st ed. 1970.

CONTRIBUTORS TO THE CATALOG

HILARY BALLON, a professor of architectural and urban history at Columbia University, is the curator of the three concurrent exhibitions on Robert Moses organized in conjunction with this publication.

MARTHA BIONDI is a professor of Afro-American history at Northwestern University.

RAY BROMLEY is a professor in the department of geography and planning, and vice provost for international education at the University at Albany, State University of New York..

PETER EISENSTADT, the editor in chief of the *Encyclopedia of New York State* (Syracuse University Press, 2005), is currently writing a history of Rochdale Village.

ROBERT FISHMAN is a professor of architecture and urban planning at the University of Michigan and a prolific writer on urban topics.

DAVID M. FOXE, a Marshall Scholar and architect, studied the Shore Parkway for a historical inventory and master plan project undertaken by Pressley Associates in Cambridge, Massachusetts.

OWEN D. GUTFREUND is an urban historian at Barnard College, Columbia University, and an expert on highway construction.

MARTA GUTMAN is an architectural historian and architect on the faculty of the City University of New York.

JENNIFER HOCH is a Ph.D. candidate in the history of architecture and urbanism at Harvard University. In 2007, she will defend her dissertation, "Political Designs: Planning, Participation, and Protest in the Urban Renewal Years, 1949–1973."

RACHEL IANNACONE teaches history of modern architecture and landscape architecture at the University of Minnesota, College of Architecture and Landscape Architecture.

KENNETH T. JACKSON is the Jacques Barzun Professor of History and the Social Sciences at Columbia University.

JULIA KITE will graduate from Columbia University in 2007 with a major in urban studies.

JEFFREY A. KROESSLER is an associate professor in the library at John Jay College of Criminal Justice and author of *New York Year by Year: A Chronology of the Great Metropolis* (2002).

MATTHEW GORDON LASNER is a historian of the built environment. His dissertation, "No Lawn to Mow: Cooperatives, Condominiums, and the American Dream, 1881–1973" (Harvard, 2007), is a social and architectural history of middle-class, multifamily housing in the U.S.

KATE LOUIS is a Ph.D. candidate in architectural history at Columbia University.

BENJAMIN LUKE MARCUS received his master of science degree in historic preservation from Columbia University in 2006. His thesis used oral history to examine the architecture and social history of McCarren Pool.

BLAGOVESTA MOMCHEDJIKOVA holds a Ph.D. in performance studies from New York University. Her dissertation focused on the Panorama of the City of New York at the Queens Museum of Art.

LAURA ROSEN oversees a major archive of Moses material as administrator of the Special Archive of the MTA Bridges and Tunnels. She is the author of *Top of the City: New York's Hidden Rooftop World* (Thames and Hudson, 1982) and *Manhattan Shores: An Expedition Around the Island's Edge* (Thames and Hudson, 1998).

JOEL SCHWARTZ was an urban historian on the faculty of Montclair State University; his essay is published posthumously.

PHOTOGRAPH CREDITS

Abbreviations of frequently cited sources:

Avery   Avery Architectural and Fine Arts Library, Columbia University

MTABTSA   Metropolitan Transit Authority Bridges and Tunnels Special Archive

NYCDPR   New York City Department of Parks and Recreation

NYPL   NYPL, Astor, Lenox and Tilden Foundations

Many photographs in this publication are cropped, including all those from the Photoarchive, NYCDPR.

E-1   *Fortune*, June 1938. Wallach Art Gallery

E-2   Library of Congress, Prints and Photographs Division, LC-USZ62-86990

E-3   CSS Photography Archives, courtesy of Community Service Society of New York and Columbia University, Rare Book and Manuscript Library

E-4   *Playground and Recreation*, Aug. 1929. Courtesy Yale University Library

E-5   *Modern Bauformen*, Nov. 1935. Avery

E-6   *Die Gartenkunst*, 2004. Avery

E-   Milstein Division of United States History, Local History and Genealogy, NYPL

E-8   Neg. 12593, Photoarchive, courtesy NYCDPR

E-9   *Architectural Record*, Dec. 1938. Avery

E-10   *Six Years of Progress*, 1940. Parks Library, courtesy NYCDPR

E-11   Milstein Division of United States History, Local History and Genealogy, NYPL

E-12   *Recreation*, Apr. 1939. Courtesy Yale University Library

E-13   *Architectural Record*, Aug. 1931. Avery

E-14   *American Architect and Architecture*, Nov. 1936. Avery

E-15   *Graphic Regional Plan: Atlas and Description*, vol. 1, 1929. Avery

E-16   Courtesy of the Westchester County Archives

E-17   *Graphic Regional Plan: Atlas and Description*, vol. 1, 1929. Avery

E-18   MTABTSA

E-19   Neg. 13275, Photoarchive, courtesy NYCDPR

E-20   Neg. 18793, Photoarchive, courtesy NYCDPR

E-21   Neg. 20774, Photoarchive, courtesy NYCDPR

E-22   *Arterial Progress*, Feb. 1960. Avery

E-23   *Joint Study of Arterial Facilities New York-New Jersey Metropolitan Area*. Jan. 1955. MTABTSA

E-24   *Title I Slum Clearance Progress*, Apr. 16, 1956. Avery

E-25   Courtesy Columbia University, Visual Media Center

E-26   Private collection

E-27   Chicago History Museum

E-28   *Washington Square South: Slum Clearance Plan*, Jan. 1951. Avery

E-29   *Slum Clearance Progress Title I NYC*, July 1957. MTABTSA

E-30   Courtesy the Olnick Organization

E-31   *Horizon*, July 1962. Columbia University, Butler Library

E-32   *Washington Square Southeast: Slum Clearance Plan*, Aug. 1953. Private collection

E-33   Courtesy the Olnick Organization

E-34   MTABTSA

E-35   *West Side Urban Renewal Study*, 1958. Avery

E-36   MTABTSA

E-37   Courtesy the Olnick Organization

E-38   Milstein Division of United States History, Local History and Genealogy, NYPL

E-39   *New York Times*, Mar. 11, 1955

E-40   *New York Times*, May 18, 1957

E-41   New York University Archives, Photographic Collection

E-42   *Cross Manhattan Arterials and Related Improvements*, Nov. 12, 1959. MTABTSA

C-1   *24 Years of Progress*, Jan. 1958. Parks Library, courtesy NYCDPR

C-2   G-PV-4, Map File, courtesy NYCDPR

C-3   Neg. 1299-K, Courtesy New York City Municipal Archives

C-4   Milstein Division of United States History, Local History and Genealogy, NYPL

C-5   Neg. 8432, Photoarchive, courtesy NYCDPR

C-6   Neg. 18259, Photoarchive, courtesy NYCDPR

C-7   Neg. 8439, Photoarchive, courtesy NYCDPR

C-8   Neg. 12646.1, Photoarchive, courtesy NYCDPR

C-9   Neg. 25033, Photoarchive, courtesy NYCDPR

C-10   Neg. 12647, Photoarchive, courtesy NYCDPR

C-11   X-PV-10-251, Map File, courtesy NYCDPR

C-12   Neg. 11490, Photoarchive, courtesy NYCDPR

C-13   Neg. 25045, Photoarchive, courtesy NYCDPR

C-14   Neg. 12151, Photoarchive, courtesy NYCDPR

C-15   Neg. 25749, Photoarchive, courtesy NYCDPR

C-16   Neg. 17582, Photoarchive, courtesy NYCDPR

C-17   Neg. 16945, Photoarchive, courtesy NYCDPR

C-18   Neg. 24502, Photoarchive, courtesy NYCDPR

C-19   Neg. 12645, Photoarchive, courtesy NYCDPR

C-20   M-PV-14-500, Map File, courtesy NYCDPR

C-21   Neg. 12941, Photoarchive, courtesy NYCDPR

C-22   Neg. 12284, Photoarchive, courtesy NYCDPR

C-23   *24 Years of Progress*, Jan. 1958. Parks Library, courtesy NYCDPR

C-24   New York State Parks, Long Island Region

C-25   Neg. 29588, Photoarchive, courtesy NYCDPR

C-26   Neg. 14767, Photoarchive, courtesy NYCDPR

C-27   Neg. 34007.1, Photoarchive, courtesy NYCDPR

C-28   Neg. 5364, Photoarchive, courtesy NYCDPR

C-29   Neg. 17085, Photoarchive, courtesy NYCDPR

C-30 Neg. 7653, Photoarchive, courtesy NYCDPR
C-31 Neg. 12206, Photoarchive, courtesy NYCDPR
C-32 Neg. 17257, Photoarchive, courtesy NYCDPR
C-33 Picture Collection, Branch Libraries, NYPL
C-34 *Future of Jamaica Bay*, Nov. 18, 1938. Avery
C-35 Neg. 14545, Photoarchive, courtesy NYCDPR
C-36 Neg. 12303, Photoarchive, courtesy NYCDPR
C-37 Q-PV-49-1300, Map File, courtesy NYCDPR
C-38 Neg. 13360, Photoarchive, courtesy NYCDPR
C-39 *Rockaway Improvement*, Jun. 1939. Avery
C-40 MTABTSA
C-41 Neg. 17086, Photoarchive, courtesy NYCDPR
C-42 Neg. 21146, Photoarchive, courtesy NYCDPR
C-43 *24 Years of Progress*, Jan. 1958. Parks Library,
     courtesy NYCDPR
C-44 Q-PV-85-100, Map File, courtesy NYCDPR
C-45 Album NYNG, Photoarchive, courtesy NYCDPR
C-46 Neg. 14271, Photoarchive, courtesy NYCDPR
C-47 Milstein Division of United States History, Local
     History and Genealogy, NYPL
C-48 Neg. 12591, Photoarchive, courtesy NYCDPR
C-49 Neg. 25204, Photoarchive, courtesy NYCDPR
C-50 Neg. 12934, Photoarchive, courtesy NYCDPR
C-51 Neg. 22241, Photoarchive, courtesy NYCDPR
C-52 Neg. 12933, Photoarchive, courtesy NYCDPR
C-53 Neg. 21098, Photoarchive, courtesy NYCDPR
C-54 Neg. 13705.1, Photoarchive, courtesy NYCDPR
C-55 Neg. 21033, Photoarchive, courtesy NYCDPR
C-56 Milstein Division of United States History, Local
     History and Genealogy, NYPL
C-57 Neg. 12592, Photoarchive, courtesy NYCDPR
C-58 Neg. 17104, Photoarchive, courtesy NYCDPR
C-59 Neg. 20671.1, Photoarchive, courtesy NYCDPR
C-60 Neg. 14257, Photoarchive, courtesy NYCDPR
C-61 Neg. 7141, Photoarchive, courtesy NYCDPR
C-62 Neg. 12642, Photoarchive, courtesy NYCDPR
C-63 Brochure on Hartford Pavilion, Mar. 1962. MTABTSA
C-64 Neg. 12585, Photoarchive, courtesy NYCDPR
C-65 Neg. 12584.1, Photoarchive, courtesy NYCDPR
C-66 Album Q099, Photoarchive, courtesy NYCDPR
C-67 Neg. SV6623, Photoarchive, courtesy NYCDPR
C-68 Queens Museum of Art
C-69 Associated Press
C-70 MTABTSA
C-71 *Report on the Proposed Development of Ward's Island*,
     Nov. 1937. General Research Division, NYPL
C-72 MTABTSA
C-73 Neg. 53589, Photoarchive, courtesy NYCDPR
C-74 Milstein Division of United States History, Local
     History and Genealogy, NYPL
C-75 Neg. 111587, Photoarchive, courtesy NYCDPR
C-76 Neg. 15407, Photoarchive, courtesy NYCDPR
C-77 Neg. 19562, Photoarchive, courtesy NYCDPR
C-78 Neg. 17840, Photoarchive, courtesy NYCDPR
C-79 Neg. 699C, Federal Writers Collection, courtesy
     New York City Municipal Archives
C-80 MTABTSA
C-81 MTABTSA
C-82 Neg. 12992, Photoarchive, courtesy NYCDPR
C-83 MTABTSA
C-84 MTABTSA

C-85 MTABTSA
C-86 MTABTSA
C-87 MTABTSA
C-88 MTABTSA
C-89 Neg. 53241.3, Photoarchive, courtesy NYCDPR
C-90 *Deegan Expressway, Cross Bronx Expressway,
     Long Island Expressway*, Nov. 1955. MTABTSA
C-91 *Gowanus Improvement*, Nov. 1941. Avery
C-92 Neg. 21863, Photoarchive, courtesy NYCDPR
C-93 *Gowanus Improvement*, Nov. 1941. Avery
C-94 Neg. 25655, Photoarchive, courtesy NYCDPR
C-95 Robert Moses Papers, Manuscripts and Archives
     Division, NYPL
C-96 Neg. 26795, Photoarchive, courtesy NYCDPR
C-97 Neg. 12576, Photoarchive, courtesy NYCDPR
C-98 Neg. SV#84554, Photoarchive, courtesy NYCDPR
C-99 Neg. 20184, Photoarchive, courtesy NYCDPR
C-100 *Arterial Progress*, Nov. 8, 1965. Avery
C-101 MTABTSA
C-102 Milstein Division of United States History,
     Local History and Genealogy, NYPL
C-103 Milstein Division of United States History,
     Local History and Genealogy, NYPL
C-104 MTABTSA
C-105 MTABTSA
C-106 MTABTSA
C-107 *Brooklyn Battery Bridge*, Jan. 23, 1939. MTABTSA
C-108 *Brooklyn Battery Bridge*, Jan. 23, 1939. MTABTSA
C-109 ©Bettmann/CORBIS
C-110 MTABTSA
C-111 MTABTSA
C-112 MTABTSA
C-113 MTABTSA
C-114 *Washington Square South: Slum Clearance Plan*,
     Aug. 1953. Avery
C-115 *Washington Square Southeast: Slum Clearance Plan*,
     Aug. 1953. Avery
C-116 Rendering from rental brochure. New York
     University Archives, Photographic Collection
C-117 New York University Archives, Photographic
     Collection
C-118 New York University Archives, Photographic
     Collection
C-119 New York University Archives, Photographic
     Collection
C-120 *South Village: Slum Clearance Plan*, Jan. 1951. Avery
C-121 MTABTSA
C-122 Neg. 28842, Photoarchive, courtesy NYCDPR
C-123 *Report on ILGWU Cooperative Village, New York:
     East River Housing Corporation*, 1957. Avery
C-124 *Report on ILGWU Cooperative Village, New York:
     East River Housing Corporation*, 1957. Avery
C-125 Photographs and Prints Division, Schomburg Center
     for Research in Black Culture, NYPL
C-126 *North Harlem: Slum Clearance*, Jan. 1951. Avery
C-127 Annual Report (1951), City Planning Commission,
     July 1952. Avery
C-128 *Williamsburg: Slum Clearance Plan*, Jan. 1951.
     Avery
C-129 *Slum Clearance Progress Title I NYC*, July 1957.
     MTABTSA

C-130 MTABTSA
C-131 MTABTSA
C-132 ©Port of New York Authority. MTABTSA
C-133 LIU Brooklyn Archives
C-134 New York University Archives, Photographic
     Collection
C-135 Pei Cobb Freed and Partners
C-136 Pei Cobb Freed and Partners
C-137 Pei Cobb Freed and Partners
C-138 Pei Cobb Freed and Partners
C-139 *Pratt Institute: Slum Clearance Plan*, 1952. Avery
C-140 *Housing and Recreation*, Nov. 22, 1938. Avery
C-141 Neg. 40205-4, Photoarchive, courtesy NYCDPR
C-142 *Seaside Rockaway: Slum Clearance Plan*, Oct. 1954.
     Avery
C-143 *Hammels Rockaway: Slum Clearance Plan*, Nov. 12,
     1956. MTABTSA
C-144 Courtesy Art Green, Inc. Fordham University
     Archives, Bronx, NY
C-145 *Slum Clearance Progress Title I NYC*, July 1957.
     MTABTSA
C-146 Courtesy Rockefeller Archive Center
C-147 Drawings and Archives Collection, Avery
C-148 Drawings and Archives Collection, Avery
C-149 Drawings and Archives Collection, Avery
C-150 Drawings and Archives Collection, Avery
C-151 Drawings and Archives Collection, Avery
C-152 Drawings and Archives Collection, Avery
C-153 *Seward Park: Slum Clearance Plan*, 1956. Avery
C-154 *Seward Park: Slum Clearance Plan*, 1956. Avery
C-155 Matthew Gordon Lasner
C-156 *Story of ILGWU Cooperative Houses, New York:
     United Housing Foundation*, 1962. Courtesy
     Matthew Gordon Lasner
C-157 *Story of ILGWU Cooperative Houses, New York:
     United Housing Foundation*, 1962. Courtesy
     Matthew Gordon Lasner
C-158 *Riverside-Amsterdam: Slum Clearance Plan*,
     Nov. 1958. Avery
C-159 Chicago History Museum
C-160 *Cadman Plaza: Slum Clearance Plan*, Apr. 1959.
     Avery
C-161 *Empire State Architect*, Mar.–Apr. 1965. Avery
C-162 *Empire State Architect*, May–June 1967. Avery
C-163 MTABTSA
C-164 Collection of the Queens Museum of Art
C-165 Drawings and Archives Collection, Avery

INDEX

Page numbers in *italic type* refer to illustrations.